D1440728

THE INSIDERS' GUIDE TO

WILMINGTON
& North Carolina's Southern Coast

By The Sea
Publications
Inc.

THE INSIDERS' GUIDE® TO

WILMINGTON
& North Carolina's Southern Coast

by
Bill DiNome
&
Carol Deakin

Insiders' Publishing Inc.
By The Sea Publications, Inc.

Co-published and marketed by:
By The Sea Publications Inc.
Hanover Center P.O. Box 5386
Wilmington, NC 28403
(910) 763-8464

Co-published and distributed by:
Insiders' Publishing Inc.
The Waterfront • Suite 12
P.O. Box 2057
Manteo, NC 27954
(919) 473-6100

•

FOURTH EDITION
1st printing

•

Publications from The Insiders' Guide® series
are available at special discounts for bulk
purchases for sales promotions, premiums
or fundraisings. Special editions, including
personalized covers, can be created in large
quantities for special needs. For more
information, please write to Insiders'
Publishing Inc., P.O. Box 2057, Manteo, NC
27954 or call (919) 473-6100 x 233.

ISBN 1-57380-028-7

By The Sea Publications Incorporated

President/Publisher
Jay Tervo

Sales and Marketing
Rosemarie Gabriele
Matt Hege
Eugene Clemmer

Administrative Manager
Gerry Tyhacz

Creative Consultant
Ashley Ware

Insiders' Publishing Inc.

Publisher/Editor-in-Chief
Beth P. Storie

President/General Manager
Michael McOwen

Affiliate Sales and Training Director
Rosanne Cheeseman

Partner Services Director
Giles MacMillan

Sales and Marketing Director
Jennifer Risko

Creative Services Director
Mike Lay

Online Services Director
David Haynes

Managing Editor
Theresa Shea Chavez

Fulfillment Director
Gina Twiford

Project Editor
Molly Perkins

Project Artist
Mel Dorsey

Special thanks to N.C. Division of
Travel and Tourism for providing
cover photographs.

Preface

Welcome to the fourth edition of *The Insiders' Guide® to Wilmington and North Carolina's Southern Coast*. Our look has changed — a more streamlined design, a revised geographic order for listings, new sidebars — but we still have the same reliability, comprehensiveness and fully updated facts and tips you've come to expect and which make this *the* guide to the southern North Carolina coast.

As in years past, you'll find recommendations on where to hear a symphony or mosh to rock 'n' roll, charter a dive trip or shop for antiques. You'll find out where to rent a Jet Ski, study yoga, buy original art, avoid traffic snarls, read local news, store your boat, locate emergency medical clinics and repair your bike. Those relocating here will find the chapters on real estate, retirement, medical care, commerce and schools invaluable.

This guide is not merely a checklist of things to do or places to go. Rather, it is designed to give you a sense of the character of the region and its offerings. We've tried to include information that will prove useful not only to short-term visitors but also to newcomers who plan to stay. Even longtime residents and natives may gain new perspectives. We make no attempt to include everything there is to enjoy in the region; however, everything we do include we feel comfortable recommending to our own friends and families. Interspersed throughout the book are vignettes, multiple perspectives, and histories about the places, people and events that have shaped this coastal area.

The guide's usefulness is enhanced by its functional structure. Chapters are arranged according to activities and subjects — restaurants, kidstuff, nightlife, arts, vacation rentals, volunteer opportunities, retirement and senior services, and golf. Within each chap-

ter, the topic is divided by locale, starting with Wilmington, then spinning off toward the outlying beaches and communities. The order in which the locales appear in every chapter is the same as in the Area Overviews chapter: after Wilmington comes Wrightsville Beach, then Pleasure Island (Carolina Beach, Kure Beach, Fort Fisher), Bald Head Island, Southport-Oak Island, the South Brunswick Islands (Holden Beach, Ocean Isle Beach, Sunset Beach), and Topsail Island. Listings within each geographic area are in alphabetical order by business name or activity. A comprehensive index appears in the back of the book.

Every attempt has been made to present accurate, up-to-date information, the result of painstaking research, revision and firsthand experience. Naturally things change, businesses come and go, hotels renovate. Even the shoreline moves — especially after two direct hits by hurricanes Bertha and Fran in July and September of 1996, respectively. Some businesses have been struggling to recover from those storms, especially on Topsail Island, Pleasure Island and Wrightsville Beach. So please let us know about any information you read here that's at odds with what you find in your travels. If you know of an outstanding establishment that deserves to be listed but hasn't been, please drop us a note. Write to us at By The Sea Publications, Hanover Center Box 5386, Wilmington, N.C. 28403; or make comments on our web site: www.insiders.com/explore. Necessary changes will be incorporated into upcoming editions and immediately onto our web site. And when your reading of the guide results in a pleasurable experience, "tell 'em we sent ya."

We hope this book will deepen your appreciation of North Carolina's southern coast as much as it has ours.

Keep in mind that the region's area code is 910. All telephone numbers listed in this book share the 910 area code unless otherwise noted.

Enjoy a quiet beach at the southern tip of New Hanover County at Fort Fisher.

About the Authors

Bill DiNome came to Wilmington, sight unseen, in the summer of 1990 and fell in love with it before his first dolphin sighting. He left behind some (extremely) modest accomplishments as a native New York City musician and award-winning copywriter for the publishing industry. Also left behind were a few unpaid parking tickets and a mother concerned about his eating habits.

In 1991 he spent five months wandering back roads and hiking trails across America. Upon returning, he penned a series of pseudonymous novels published by Berkley/Jove, and his eating habits improved dramatically. Since then, he has worked as a contributing editor for a regional music magazine, community relations director for public radio WHQR 91.3 FM, freelance writer and business copywriter. He continues to write fiction and nonfiction and is an amateur poet who recently added "award-winning" to that credential. Currently he is completing his M.F.A. at the University of North Carolina at Wilmington.

His greatest accomplishment is his marriage to a longtime Wilmington resident who, along with her son, thinks Bill's eating habits are far too improved and has also been an invaluable Insider informant. Bill's many interests include backpacking, travel, cinema, history and mythology, reading and writing, mucking about in caves and occasionally attempting to learn a new piano prelude.

Carol Deakin is a freelance writer and artist who chose Wilmington as her home in the summer of 1986. Eleven years and two hurricanes later, she's glad she did.

A Georgia native who has lived throughout the South for 46 years, she describes Wilmington as the "most Southern city" in which she has lived. Even with an incredible influx of people from up North in recent years, the tone of the city remains essentially the same.

Carol is a 1973 graduate of the University of North Carolina at Greensboro. She has worked as a public relations and marketing director in theater, the public schools and nonprofit organizations. She eventually chose independent work because "it's just more fun."

She is a pen-and-ink illustrator for magazines, books and advertising. She is also writes for local and regional publications, and wrote the editorial section of *Wilmington: Treasure on the Atlantic*, a 1996 coffee-table book published under the auspices of the Greater Wilmington Chamber of Commerce.

Her interests include playing the piano, cooking and staring at her goldfish pond when she has writer's block.

The Wilmington area offers many historic celebrations.

Acknowledgments

Bouquets of Jovian moon blossoms to Deborah Flora, my wife, best friend, comic relief and reality check. She has hung tough throughout the recurring cycles of this project and has proven invaluable to its shaping since she knows every third person in the phone book. Her son, Taj, deserves monster props for putting up with my endless hours at the computer. Special thanks go to our lovely and talented publisher, Jay Tervo.

Kudos to Molly Perkins, an editor of remarkable patience. Heartfelt thanks also go to Michelle Burch, formerly of *Encore* magazine, who didn't have to, but did; the folks at the various chambers of commerce, whose support has been unflagging; Ren Brown at St. Johns Museum of Art; Mimi Cunningham and her staff at UNCW's University Relations office; Betty Parks; the late Betty Polzer; John Taggart of the North Carolina National Estuarine Research Reserve; the inimitable Harry Warren and Tim Bottoms at the Cape Fear Museum; Bubba, who gets me around without a fuss. Sincere thanks to my coauthor, Carol Deakin, for her unwavering support, professionalism and consoling phone calls. Fanfares, knighthood and their favorite chocolates to the many others who fielded my questions, held my hand, set me straight, produced this book and helped me wrestle this beast to the mat — once again. They were great teachers all.

—B.D.

This Insiders' Guide would not have been possible without the generous help, enthusiasm and advice of many people in the Cape Fear area.

Special thanks go to my dear friend Elizabeth Darrow. She provided mental and emotional support, constructive advice, and thoughtful responses to my many questions through all four editions of this book.

I thank Bill DiNome for being a supportive co-author year after year.

My sincere thanks go to JoAnn Fogler who helped me get this job in the first place and is always checking in to make sure I'm meaningfully employed. My piano teacher and friend Joan Gruppe receives my appreciation for bringing music back into my life.

I thank publisher Jay Tervo, Kate Meyer and editor Molly Perkins, not forgetting previous editor Eileen Myers, for their soft-spoken, sensitive and steady guidance throughout the process of writing this guide.

Connie Majure of the Greater Wilmington Chamber of Commerce has been consistently helpful with her knowledge and wonderful sense of humor. Dr. Woody Hall of the Cameron School of Business at UNCW, known as the guru of Wilmington facts, continues to be an extraordinary resource for this book. The staff at the City of Wilmington, and New Hanover, Brunswick and Pender counties and the beach communities consistently were able to cheerfully answer questions and offer suggestions for sources. Thanks year after year to Bob Murphrey, executive director of DARE.

Thanks to cruising guide author Claiborne Young for the benefit of his considerable knowledge about the Cape Fear River and Intracoastal Waterway.

I also thank the artists, layout people, ad folks and everyone else who worked so hard to create this book.

—C. D.

Table of Contents

Getting Around 1
Area Overviews 11
Accommodations 41
Weekly and Long-term Vacation Rentals 65
Camping 77
Restaurants 83
Nightlife 117
Shopping 133
Attractions 163
Annual Events 191
The Arts 203
Kidstuff 221
Daytrips 245
Watersports 255
Sun, Sand and Sea 273
Fishing 281
Marinas and the Intracoastal Waterway 293
Sports, Fitness and Parks 303
Golf 331
Real Estate 343
Retirement 367
Healthcare 375
Schools and Child Care 385
Higher Education and Research 399
Volunteer Opportunities 409
Media 419
Commerce and Industry 425
Worship 433

Directory of Maps

Wilmington and the Southern Coast xii
Topsail Island to Calabash xiii
Downtown Wilmington xiv

Wilmington and the Southern Coast

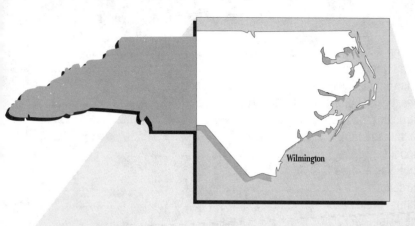

Wilmington

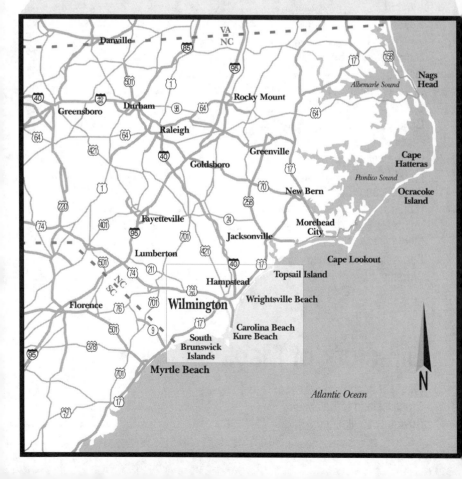

Danville

VA
NC

85

95

501

1

40
85

40

Greensboro

Durham

98

64

Rocky Mount

64

Raleigh

64

421

40

Goldsboro

Greenville

17

17

Albemarle Sound

Nags
Head

158

Cape
Hatteras

Pamlico Sound

70

New Bern

Ocracoke
Island

258

1

220

24

Fayetteville

Jacksonville

Morehead
City

74

95

401

701

Lumberton

421

40

17

Cape Lookout

211

74

Topsail Island

Hampstead

74
76

501

Florence

76

701

Wilmington

Wrightsville Beach

9

17

Carolina Beach
Kure Beach

95

378

501

South
Brunswick
Islands

701

Myrtle Beach

17

Atlantic Ocean

N

Topsail Island to Calabash

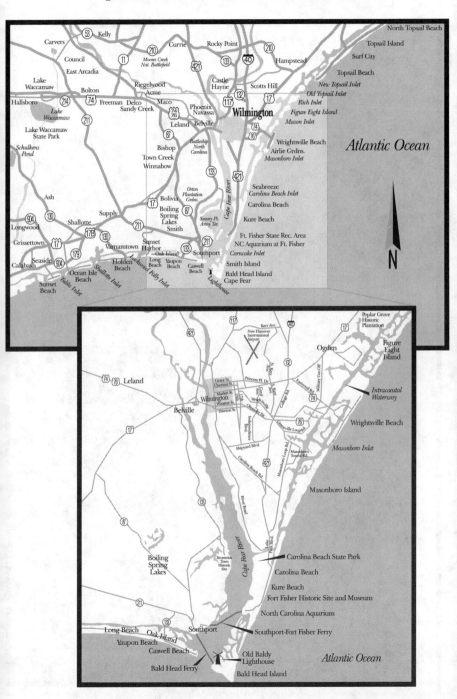

Downtown Wilmington

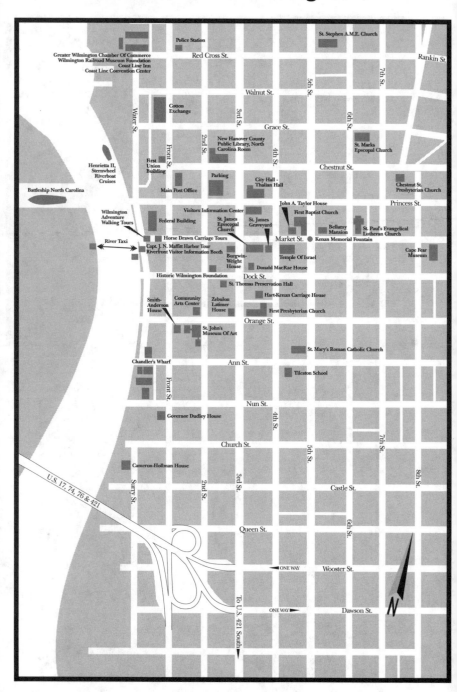

Police Station

St. Stephen A.M.E. Church

Greater Wilmington Chamber Of Commerce
Wilmington Railroad Museum Foundation
Coast Line Inn
Coast Line Convention Center

Red Cross St.

Rankin St.

Walnut St.

5th St.

7th St.

Cotton
Exchange

3rd St.

Grace St.

6th St.

2nd St.

New Hanover County
Public Library, North
Carolina Room

St. Marks
Episcopal Church

4th St.

First
Union
Building

Henrietta II,
Sternwheel
Riverboat
Cruises

Front St.

Parking

Chestnut St.

Battleship North Carolina

Water St.

Main Post Office

City Hall -
Thalian Hall

Chestnut St.
Presbyterian Church

Princess St.

Visitors Information Center

John A. Taylor House

Wilmington
Adventure
Walking Tours

Federal Building

St. James
Episcopal
Church

St. James
Graveyard

First Baptist Church

Bellamy
Mansion

St. Paul's Evangelical
Lutheran Church

Horse Drawn Carriage Tours

Market St.

Kenan Memorial Fountain

River Taxi

Capt. J. N. Maffitt Harbor Tour
Riverfront Visitor Information Booth

Burgwin-
Wright
House

Temple Of Israel

Cape Fear
Museum

Donald MacRae House

Historic Wilmington Foundation

Dock St.

St. Thomas Preservation Hall

Smith-
Anderson
House

Community
Arts Center

Zebulon
Latimer
House

Hart-Kenan Carriage House

First Presbyterian Church

Orange St.

St. John's
Museum Of Art

St. Mary's Roman Catholic Church

Chandler's Wharf

Ann St.

Tileston School

Front St.

Nun St.

Governor Dudley House

4th St.

Church St.

5th St.

Cameron-Hollman House

U.S. 17, 74, 76 & 421

Surry St.

2nd St.

3rd St.

Castle St.

7th St.

6th St.

8th St.

Queen St.

To U.S. 421 South

ONE WAY

Wooster St.

ONE WAY

Dawson St.

N

Getting Around

Getting into the greater Wilmington area by land, sea or air is easier than ever before. Among the most visible signs of this increased accessibility is the far-flung road work — highways and major arteries continue to undergo widening, repaving and other improvements as the area's increased popularity places greater demands upon the infrastructure. Compared to other cities, however, Wilmington's road problems are relatively minor, and folks from larger cities chuckle when they hear locals complaining about the traffic.

To further orient yourself to Wilmington and the immediate area, pick up a copy of the guide map published by the Cape Fear Coast Convention & Visitors Bureau, 341-4030 or (800) 222-4757. It's a great downtown street map and is available free at the Visitors Information Center at the Old Courthouse in Wilmington, 24 N. Third Street, as well as at many hotels and from the Chamber of Commerce, One Estell Lee Place, 762-2611. Realtors' maps are also handy and very detailed.

Roadways

Visitors from anywhere other than our southeastern coast discover what they're missing by way of three primary routes: Interstate 40, U.S. Highway 74, and U.S. Highway 17. But first, some bearings. Situated at the eastern terminus of I-40, Wilmington is about 12 hours from New York City (599 miles) by interstate; 7 hours from Washington, D.C. (374 miles); 4 hours from Charlotte (197 miles); about 3.5 hours from Charleston, South Carolina (169 miles); and about 1.5 hours from Myrtle Beach (72 miles). The interchange between I-40 and Interstate 95 is near Benson, 1.5 hours from Wilmington (about 75 miles). Driving from Raleigh will take almost 2.5 hours (127 miles), while driving from Chapel Hill will take 3 hours.

Interstates and Highways

Interstate 40 is your most likely choice if you're coming long distance from points west (it extends all the way to Barstow, California) or from I-95. Its local stretch is named after one of Wilmington's most famous former residents, basketball star Michael Jordan. It's a fairly dull ride unless counting surfboards on car racks excites you. Services along the stretch between the I-95 interchange and Wilmington are limited, often located well off the highway, and close early — fuel up beforehand if traveling at night. There is only one public rest area along the way, about an hour outside Wilmington. Interstate 40 ends where it enters Wilmington from the north and converges with N.C. Highway 132. It then assumes the name College Road.

From western North Carolina (Whiteville, Rockingham, Charlotte), U.S. Highway 74 is a direct link to downtown Wilmington. It joins U.S. Highway 76 out of Florence, South Carolina, N.C. Highway 211 from Southport, and U.S. Highway 17 from the south.

U.S. Highway 17 is the road to remember from Calabash to Topsail. They don't call it Ocean Highway for nothing. U.S. 17 parallels the coast and intersects every main route to the sea. Entering the region from the south, U.S. 17 intersects N.C. Highway 179, which veers seaward through Calabash. N.C. 179 then hugs the Intracoastal Waterway (ICW), giving access to the picturesque pontoon bridge to Sunset Beach (Sunset Boulevard) and to the Ocean Isle Beach high-span (N.C. Highway 904) before leaning northward into Shallotte, where it rejoins U.S. 17 Business. In Shallotte (pronounced "shu-LOTE"), U.S. 17

Business intersects N.C. Highway 130 (Holden Beach Road), a direct route to that beach community.

Continuing northward, U.S. 17 joins N.C. Highway 211 near the town of Supply. N.C. 211 leads directly into the picturesque village of Southport and is named, appropriately enough, the Southport-Supply Road.

Traveling northward again from Supply, U.S. 17 joins N.C. Highway 87 and U.S. highways 74/76, then crosses the Cape Fear Memorial Bridge into downtown Wilmington. U.S. 17 joins Market Street as it exits the northeast side of town. It then passes through Ogden, Scotts Hill, Hampstead and Holly Ridge. U.S. 17 intersects N.C. 210 and N.C. 50, both of which lead to Topsail Island (that's "TOP-sull"), converging at the drawbridge into Surf City (Roland Avenue). Until 1993 this intersection boasted Topsail Island's only traffic light. Now there's a flashing light in Topsail Beach too. Time marches on.

On Topsail Island, N.C. 50 turns south toward Topsail Beach, while N.C. 210 turns north, passing through North Topsail Beach then back onto the mainland across the New River Inlet Bridge, which affords a superb view of the Intracoastal Waterway. N.C. 210 rejoins U.S. 17 just minutes outside Jacksonville.

Drivers take note: Speed limits at the beaches can be a test of patience and are strictly enforced. Seatbelt checkpoints are common throughout the area. Relax, take it slowly and enjoy.

Streets and Byways

College Road extends north and south through Wilmington about midway between and nearly parallel to both the seashore and the Cape Fear River. As the name suggests, it borders UNC's Wilmington campus. Flanked by strip malls and massive shopping centers, College Road is among the least attractive and most frustrating roadways in the region, so try to avoid it during rush hours and holiday shopping frenzies. To the south, it joins Carolina Beach Road (N.C. Highway 421) at Monkey Junction.

Carolina Beach Road (N.C. 421) is the direct southerly extension of S. Third Street as it exits downtown Wilmington. This road gives access to Pleasure Island (Carolina Beach, Kure Beach, Fort Fisher) all the way to Federal Point.

After crossing the Cape Fear Memorial Bridge as one, N.C. highways 74 and 76 go their separate ways. They both run roughly east and west, N.C. 74 serving the north side of Wilmington and N.C. 76 serving the south side. N.C. 74 consists of Market Street, from downtown past the S. College Road overpass, and the new Smith Creek Parkway. N.C. 76 assumes even more names: from the Cape Fear Memorial Bridge to 17th Street it's Dawson Street (Wooster Street in the opposite direction), then Oleander Drive to just beyond Bradley Creek, then Wrightsville Avenue as it heads toward the beach. Confused? Don't sweat; driving it is easy. These two routes lovingly reunite at the drawbridge onto Harbor Island (Causeway Drive) and Wrightsville Beach.

Wrightsville Avenue, paved with oyster shells once upon a time, was the original beach-bound road from Wilmington. Today its western terminus is at 17th and Dock streets, immediately south of Market Street. It runs diagonally, at a southeasterly glance, until it nearly parallels Oleander Drive all the way to the intersection of Military Cutoff Road (near the stuccoed St. Andrews On-the-Sound Episcopal Church). At this point, Wrightsville Avenue overlaps Highway 76 on its way directly to the drawbridge to Harbor Island and Wrightsville Beach. It is a heavily used road, especially between 17th Street and College Road and over the mile or two nearest the bridge, and warrants entering at intersections with stop lights to save time.

The Intracoastal Waterway

Water, the region's dominant physical feature, makes the southern coast particularly accessible to boaters from Canada to the Keys. Boaters enjoy two options for getting here by water: sailing "outside" through open ocean waters or "inside" via the Intracoastal Waterway (ICW), a.k.a. the Ditch. From New River

> **FYI**
>
> Unless otherwise noted, the area code for all phone numbers in this guide is 910.

Inlet at the northern tip of Topsail Island to the South Carolina border, scores of marinas await you along nearly 90 miles of protected waterway. See our chapter on Marinas for information.

Transportation

City Buses

The Wilmington Transit Authority operates five bus lines that link outlying neighborhoods, the university, shopping centers and downtown. One-way fare is 60¢, 30¢ for senior citizens and the handicapped, and a transfer is 10¢. Discount ticket books are available from any bus driver (11 rides for $6; $3 for senior citizens, the handicapped and students through 12th grade during the school year). There is no bus service on Sunday and major holidays, including Martin Luther King Jr. Day. Routes include East Wilmington-Long Leaf Park (Route 1); Market Street-Marketplace mall-UNCW (Route 2); Brooklyn-Oleander Drive shopping centers (Route 3); New Hanover Regional Medical Center-Brooklyn (Route 5); and Independence and Long Leaf malls-UNCW (Route 6).For information call 343-0106 Monday through Friday from 8 AM to 5 PM and Saturday 8 AM to noon, or 763-9011. The Wilmington Public Transit Guide has a handy map and table of schedules. Ask for one at the Visitors Center, 24 N. Third Street, 341-4030.

There is no direct rail service to Wilmington. The nearest rail station (Amtrak) is in Fayetteville, about 90 minutes from Wilmington.

Car Rentals

You can choose from national chains and independents, and several new-car dealerships also lease cars long-term. Three car-rental companies are based at New Hanover International Airport (see the listing below under Airports.) Other companies offering car rental in the area are:

Enterprise Rentals, 5601 Market Street, Wilmington, 799-4042

Triangle Rental, 3111 Market Street, Wilmington, 251 9812

A & A Rental Inc., 119 Village Road, Shallotte, 754-8200; Sundays and nights, 754-6139.

Long-Distance Bus Lines

Long-distance bus service to Wilmington is provided by **Greyhound**, (800) 231-2222, and **Carolina Trailways**, 762-6625, at the Wilmington bus terminal, 201 Harnett Street between N. Third and N. Front streets.

Taxis and Limousines

The going rate for cabs within Wilmington city limits is $1.10 plus $1.50 per mile. Cab drivers will stop when hailed if between calls, but not if they're on their way to a call. In addition to offering the obvious service, many taxicab companies will also unlock your car if you've locked yourself out. The usual charge is $15.

Limousine service typically runs in the $50 per hour range and may require some hourly minimum (often three hours). If pickup and dropoff locations are outside the company's primary service area (city limits most likely), travel time is usually charged. For service on holidays and weekends in wedding season, most companies require reservations well in advance plus a credit-card deposit.

Wilmington

Lett's Taxi Service, 458-3999
Port City Taxi Inc., 762-1165
Yellow Cab, 762-3322
Affordable Affluence Inc., 251-8999
After Dark Limousine Service, 392-3355
Formal Limousine Service, 395-1191
Prestige Limousine Service, 399-4484

INSIDERS' TIP

Volunteers interested in helping save the endangered loggerhead turtle on Topsail Island are welcome to join the Topsail Island Turtle Project. Call Project Director Jean Beasley, 328-1000.

Photo: Scott Taylor

Pelicans nest on the spoil islands of the Cape Fear River.

Topsail Island
Treasure Coast Taxi, 330-1111

Southport-Oak Island and South Brunswick
A-Plus Taxi Service, 278-6373
Easy Way Transport Service, 579-9926
LC's Taxi Service, 287-3197
Oak Island Cab, 278-6373
Sun & Sea Taxi Cab, 249-6705

Van Service

Van transportation between Wilmington and Raleigh-Durham Airport (RDU) is provided by the **Wilmington Shuttle**, 791-6678 or (800) 273-9206 outside Wilmington, which offers regularly scheduled shuttle service seven days a week. Additional shuttles are added on Sundays in December to accommodate holiday travelers. Pickups and dropoffs in Wilmington are at Shoney's on S. College Road. The Wilmington Shuttle also offers service to Camp Lejeune, making pickups and dropoffs at Shoney's in Jacksonville. Reservations are required.

Airports

New Hanover International Airport is the prime entry point for most people flying into the greater Wilmington area. It and the Myrtle Beach International Airport in nearby South Carolina are nearly equidistant from Shallotte (about 38 miles); so visitors to Calabash and the South Brunswick Islands, especially Ocean Isle Beach and Sunset Beach, might do well to check flight availability at Myrtle Beach. However, those whose destination is Oak Island, Southport, or points north and who are traveling by commercial airline would do better with New Hanover. Others who pilot or charter small aircraft and are destined for Brunswick County should note the Brunswick County Airport, just outside Southport.

Wilmington

New Hanover International Airport
1740 Airport Blvd., Wilmington • 341-4125

It wasn't too long ago that Wilmington's airport was little more than a tiny, non-automated, brick building that served as the air terminal. The sleek new terminal opened in 1990. New Hanover International Airport, which has no direct international flights, is entirely 21st century with its baby-changing areas accessible to dads and baggage carousels. Even the palm trees in the atrium will remain forever green thanks to the wonders of polyurethane. Nonetheless, New Hanover International remains small-town friendly.

New Hanover International is off 23rd Street, 2 miles north of Market Street, within 10 minutes of downtown Wilmington by car and nearly 20 minutes from Wrightsville Beach. Upon exiting the airport, a right turn leads you to U.S. Highway 117 which brings you into downtown Wilmington (a left turn) or north into Castle Hayne (a right turn) and toward Interstate 40.

Airlines: Two companies serve air commuters and travelers.

Atlantic Southeast Airlines (ASA), (800) 282-3424, is the Delta connection with nine flights daily to Atlanta.

USAir, (800) 428-4322, offers six flights daily via Charlotte.

Parking: Short-term parking rates are $1 per half-hour with a maximum 24-hour charge of $5.25. Long-term parking costs $1 per hour, with a maximum charge of $4.50 per day. A limited amount of metered parking (25¢ per 20 minutes) is available just beyond the terminal (on the left when facing the building).

Car Rentals: Three rental companies, offering compact to full-size cars, maintain agents at the airport. Reservations and a confirmation call in advance of your arrival are always recommended.

Budget, 762-8910, (800) 527-0700
Hertz, 762-1010, (800) 654-3131
National, 762-0143, (800) CAR-RENT

The following car rental companies in Wilmington offer free pickup and dropoff service at New Hanover International Airport.

Alamo, 763-6448
Enterprise, 799-4042
Triangle, 251-9812

Southport-Oak Island and South Brunswick

The Brunswick County Airport
4019 Long Beach Rd., Southport • 457-6483

This fast-growing, full-service airport, which has a small terminal, hangars, fuel service and a 4,000-foot paved and lighted runway, can accommodate general aviation aircraft from the smallest ultralights to fairly sizable private jets. The airport is especially convenient to Bald Head Island and the Southport-Oak Island area. The airport supports instrument approaches (GPS, NDB) and offers a variety of services, including flight instruction. Tie-down fees for piston aircraft are $5 per day, $30 per month and $270 per year. The Brunswick County Airport is also the East Coast summer home of Blue Yonder Flying Machines, purveyors of the Quicksilver ultralight aircraft (see the Flying section in our Sports, Fitness and Parks chapter). The airport is on the mainland side of the Oak Island Bridge, on N.C. Highway 133.

Car rental at the Brunswick County Airport is provided by A-Plus, 278-6373, offering older-model "ugly ducklings" at reasonable rates.

Ocean Isle Airstrip
N.C. hwys. 179 and 904, Ocean Isle Beach • 579-6222

This landing strip (4,000 feet, paved) accommodates only small private piston aircraft and air tours, (803) 293-2600. Usage is free to

---

INSIDERS' TIP

Need a ride to the Raleigh-Durham International Airport? Call the Wilmington Shuttle, 791-6678, (800) 273-9206 outside Wilmington, for departure information or to reserve a seat.

the public on a first-come first-served basis. There is no fuel available, and pilots must provide their own tie-downs. The airstrip is operated by Ocean Isle Realty.

Air Charters, Rentals, Leasing

Adventurous souls can charter small aircraft at New Hanover International Airport for a bird's-eye view of the southern coastal region. Most companies offer 24-hour charter service, sales, service and rentals, and all offer flight training. Unless otherwise noted, all are based at New Hanover International.

Aeronautics, 763-4691

Air Wilmington, 763-0146

Iso Aero Service Inc. of Wilmington, 763-8898

Ocean Aire Aviation Inc., Brunswick County Airport, Southport, 457-0710

Ferries

Our local ferries can be (and are) viewed in two ways: as a mode of transportation that saves miles of driving and as one of the least expensive scenic tours.

Southport-Fort Fisher Ferry

The Southport-Fort Fisher ferry, an approximately 30 minute cruise, provides a panoramic view of the mouth of the Cape Fear River above Southport. The passenger lounges of the *Gov. Daniel Russell* and the *Sandy Graham* are comfortable and climate-controlled. The ferry passes dredge-spoil islands where brown pelicans nest and waters are frequented by dolphins. On the Brunswick County side, huge yellow cranes mark the Military Ocean Terminal at Sunny Point, the largest distribution center in the country for military supplies. Other sights include Old Baldy, North Carolina's oldest lighthouse, on Bald Head Island; Price's Creek Lighthouse (1849), which guided Confederate blockade runners through New Inlet during the Civil War; and the Oak Island Lighthouse, the nation's brightest. The ferry can be

part of the far-reaching River Circle Tour that includes Orton Plantation Gardens, Brunswick Town, historic Wilmington, Battleship North Carolina, the North Carolina Aquarium at Fort Fisher, the Fort Fisher Civil War Museum, Carolina and Kure beaches, Southport and the Oak Island beaches. For information on these and other attractions, see our Attractions chapter.

The Southport-Fort Fisher Ferry departs every 50 minutes from each side of the river in the spring, summer and fall. There's a longer wait in the winter. One-way fares are as follows: pedestrians, 50¢; bicycles, $1; vehicles 20 feet or longer, $3; vehicles or combinations measuring up to 32 feet, $6. Call in advance if ferrying larger vehicles. Rates and schedules are subject to change. For information call Southport at 457-6942 or Fort Fisher at 458-3329, or write: P.O. Box 10028, Southport, NC 28461. For statewide ferry information call (800) BY-FERRY.

Summer Schedule (April 1 to October 31)

Departs Southport:	Departs Fort Fisher:
8 AM	8:50 AM
8:50 AM	9:40 AM
9:40 AM	10:30 AM
10:30 AM	11:20 AM
11:20 AM	12:10 PM
12:10 PM	1:00 PM
1:00 PM	1:50 PM
1:50 PM	2:40 PM
2:40 PM	3:30 PM
3:30 PM	4:20 PM
4:20 PM	5:10 PM
5:10 PM	6 PM
6 PM	6:50 PM

Winter Schedule (November 1 to March 31)

Departs Southport::	Departs Fort Fisher:
8 AM	8:50 AM
9:40 AM	10:30 AM
11:20 AM	12:10 PM
1 PM	1:50 PM
2:40 PM	3:30 PM
4:20 PM	5:10 PM
6 PM	6:50 PM

The Days of Ballroom and Beach Cars

Before the days of gas stations and weekend traffic, the only way to get to Wrightsville Beach was the "Beach Car," the electric trolley that ran from Princess and Front streets in downtown Wilmington to what was once the biggest beach attraction south of Atlantic City — Wrightsville Beach's Lumina Pavilion.

The trolley was in place in 1902, replacing an older railway train. The route roughly paralleled the "shell road" (now Wrightsville Avenue) and ran down today's Park Avenue, where a couple of the old station shelters still remain. Operated by the Tidewater Power Company, the beach cars were orange with cream trim, carried 68 passengers each, and made the trip from downtown to the beach in as little as 35 minutes. Five-car trains ran during the height of the season.

In 1903 the Tidewater Power Company purchased an oceanfront lot for $10 at Station 7, the end of the line, where they built the Lumina, named for the thousands of incandescent lights that made the building visible far out at sea. The pavilion, constructed entirely of heart pine, was opened on June 3, 1905, and went through two major expansions in subsequent years. Admission was free before the First World War. It featured a vast promenade, bowling lanes, a ladies' parlor, an upstairs restaurant and downstairs lunch service, dressing rooms, slot machines and other amusements, but the gem of the pavilion was its second-floor dance hall.

The enormous dance floor accommodated hundreds of dancers at once. The high-ceilinged room was festooned with bunting and flags. Some of the era's most famous orchestras and big bands played there, including Kay Kaiser, Guy Lombardo and Cab Calloway. (Wilmington was still the biggest city in North Carolina at the time.) Curiously, a writer in 1910 recalled that opera was favored at the Lumina over so-called popular music of the day. — continued on next page

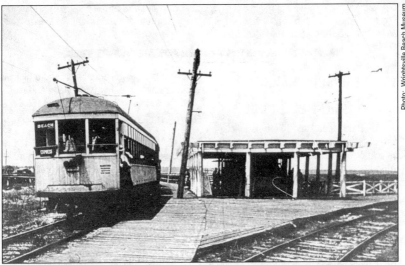

Photo: Wrightsville Beach Museum

The Beach Trolley was a familiar Wrightsville Beach sight in the early 1900s.

— continued from previous page

Other attractions included dance contests, beauty pageants, beach games such as sack races and watersports, and convention dances. Swimmers could rent bathing suits with the word "Lumina" emblazoned on the front. An especially unusual attraction was motion pictures. The owners erected a screen about 50 yards into the surf and projected silent movies that could be viewed from seating on the beach or from the promenade. The screen was moved closer when "talkies" appeared. (This tradition has been revived in the annual "Lumina Daze" celebration, which benefits the Wrightsville Beach Museum of History. See our Annual Events chapter.)

Manners were carefully observed. Jacket and tie were essential. Cheek-to-cheek dancing? Unacceptable! Mrs. Bessie Martin, the Lumina's permanent chaperon, saw to that. No alcoholic beverages or rude behavior were permitted either; Tuck Savage saw to that. Some called Tuck a "supervisor"; today we'd call him a bouncer.

After World War I, the trolley to the beach cost 35¢, which included admission to the Lumina. The trolley line even influenced the birth of Wilmington's early suburbs — Carolina Place, Carolina Heights, Oleander, Audubon, Winter Park — which grew up along the route. In the 1930s, the first automobile route was built to Harbor Island. Billboards sprung up: "In a hurry? Take the Causeway." It wasn't long before the road spanned Banks Channel too. Another road was paved down the length of the island in 1935. The trolley suddenly became a throwback to a more sluggish era and declined in popularity. It made its last run on April 27, 1940. The only Beach Car known to remain today is in Annabelle's Restaurant on Oleander Drive.

The Lumina remained viable a while longer. Hot dogs and surf accessories were sold downstairs. Rock concerts were occasionally held in the 1960s, but by the early '70s the ballroom stood perpetually dark. The pavilion was torn down in 1973. The Lumina lives on in many place names around the beach and, like the old Oceanic Hotel and the Harbor Island Casino, it isn't likely to be forgotten any time soon. It's one of those reminders that perhaps being in a hurry really isn't what the beach is all about.

The photo on the previous page is one of 250 photos soon to be released in Wrightsville Beach, A Pictorial History, *by the nonprofit Wrightsville Beach Preservation Society. For a copy of this book write to the Preservation Society at P.O. Box 584, Wrightsville Beach 28480, or call 256-2569.*

Passenger Ferry to Bald Head Island

The Bald Head Island Ferry is strictly for passengers. Travel on the island is by foot, bicycle or electric cart; cars are not allowed. In Southport, the Bald Head Island Ferry terminal is at Indigo Plantation at the foot of 9th Street, where parking is available. An individual round-trip ferry ticket for is $15 for adults, $8 for children ages 3 to 12. Children 2 and younger ride free. The ferry departs on the hour from 8 AM to 10 PM, seven days a week. There is no ferry at noon or 8 PM. Parking at Southport costs $4 per day.

Special summer ferry packages that include passage, parking, lunch and a historic tour are available. For information and reservations call 457-7390 or (800) 234-1666.

Bike Paths

Level landscape, predominantly well-maintained roads and generally light traffic make touring the coastal plain by bicycle mostly excellent outside Wilmington. The city of Wilmington, however, is behind the times when it comes to regarding bicycles as viable commuter transportation. Busy city roadways have little or no room for cyclists, and roadways that do are frustratingly circuitous. (On that point, be sure to avoid Market Street in Wilmington at all costs.)

Touring is somewhat better. Three state-funded "Bicycling Highways" pass through Wilmington and along the neighboring coast. They are marked by rectangular road signs bearing a green ellipse, a bicycle icon and the route number. One such route is the **River-to-Sea Bike Route** (Route 1), stretching from Riverfront Park at the foot of Market Street in Wilmington to Wrightsville Beach, a ride of just less than 9 miles. You'll have to cross one, recently improved, railroad crossing. Exercise caution on the Bradley Creek bridge: The shoulder is ridged by uneven road seams.

The **Ports of Call** route (Route 3) is a 319-mile seaside excursion from the South Carolina border to the Virginia line. Approximately 110 miles of it lie along the southern coast, giving access to miles of beaches and historic downtown Wilmington.

The **Cape Fear Run** (Route 5) links Raleigh to the mouth of the Cape Fear River at Southport. This 166-mile route crosses the Cape Fear River twice and intersects the Ports of Call. Free maps and information can be obtained from the North Carolina Department of Transportation Bicycle Program, P.O. Box 25201, Raleigh 27611, (919) 733-2804. Although the maps are updated regularly, be ready to improvise when it comes to information on private campgrounds and detours.

The Wilmington Bike Map is a must for local cycling. Free copies can be obtained by contacting the City Transportation Planning Department, P.O. Box 1810, Wilmington 28402, (919) 341-7888.

Carolina Beach...
The Place

Miles of uncrowded coast • Amusements for kids • Great dining •
Entertaiunment for adults • Beach shops to charming boutiques!

Boating/Fishing/Cruising

Dockside Watersports...
Waverunner (PWC) & boat rentals
• 458-0220 •

Cruise Boats
Carolina Beach Docks 458-5626
• 791-3689 •

Nightly Entertainment
Club Tropics.,. Live Entertainment
Ocean Plaza Electric Ballroom, Radio
Flyer live, Janis Joplin Tribute, DJ Stix
Thurs.-Sun. • 458-7883 •

Take The Island With You!
Island Moments...http://island-
moments.wilmington.net

RESTAURANTS
Breakfast Cafe'... Hearty Breakfast
& Bountiful Lunch, daily 6am-2pm
700 N. Lake Park Blvd.
• 458-8897 •

The Cottage...Simply great food. Dine
indoors or out. 1 N. Lake Park Blvd
• 458-4383 •

The Fat Pelican...175 Beers/200 Wines,
Coffee Bar, Patio, Tiki Bar.
27 S. Lake Park Blvd
• 458-4061•

Frank's Pizza...Fabulous Pizza, Subs &
Salads. Free Delivery #8 on the Boardwalk
Dine In or Take Out • 458-7010 •

Harbour Masters...Omlets to Pasta,
Steak & Seafood. Breakfast & Dinner
overlooking Carolina Beach Marina. 315
Canal Drive One of the Islands best kept
secrets! • 458-7013•

J.Councils...Elegant Dining/
French-American Cuisine. Casual Dress
205 Charlotte St. • 458-9411•

Island Pizza...Delicious Italian Pizza.
Authentic Italian Subs & Pastas.
Dine-in, Take Out or Delivery
• 458-0072 •

Red Roof Cafe...Family dining at it's
best. All you can eat buffet, reasonably
priced. 6am-9pm Mon-Fri
6am-10pm Sat&Sun.
102 S. Lake Park Blvd. • 458-3663 •

Ice Cream Parlors
Squigley's...4050 Flavors.
208 S. Lake Park Blvd
• 458-8779 •

Barber Shop
Island Barber, wonderful Old-Fashion
barbering for men & women.
6A N. Lake Park Blvd.• 458-9885 •

Shopping
The Checkered Church
Fine Gifts & Pine Furniture
800 St. Joseph St.
• 458-3140 •

The Gold Rose...UNIQUE Fashions &
Accessories, 6-B N. Lake Park Blvd.
• 458-9770 •

Bank
NationsBank...24-Hour banking, 123
Harper Avenue • 458-8243 •

Accommodations
Ocean Princess Inn... AAA Approved
All ABC Permits. Peaceful. Secluded.
824 Fort Fisher Blvd. (south), Kure Beach
• 458-6712 •

Legal Services
Ned Barnes, Attorney and Counselor At
Law, A-3 Pleasure Island Plaza
• 458-4466 •

ENTERTAINMENT AT THE GAZEBO
Friday & Saturday nights April-September
Courtesy of Pleasure Island Merchants Association

Area Overviews

The story about Wilmington and adjacent barrier islands and river communities begins with the water. The history of this region, at least from the European viewpoint, began with the discovery of a river.

The Cape Fear River

In 1524 when Spanish explorer Giovanni da Verrazano took his French-financed expedition into the river that is now called the Cape Fear, he ushered in a new historical period that eventually would lead to European development of the area. Mysteriously, France had no apparent interest in developing or even claiming the region — something hard to fathom given the explorer's lush description.

Verrazano wrote in his journal: "The open country rising in height above the sandy shore with many faire fields and plaines, full of mightie great woods, some very thicke and some thinne, replenished with divers sorts of trees, as pleasant and delectable to behold, as if possible to imagine."

While the land was deserving of praise, there was something formidable about the river that was eventually reflected in its name. But there was confusion over the name until the late 18th century. Was it Cape Faire or Cape Fear? George Davis, in James Sprunt's *Chronicles of the Cape Fear River*, writes in defense of the Cape Fear name. Davis suggested the river went unnamed for centuries, but the mouth of the river was known from the beginning as Cape Fear. That, he contends, is the reason the cape's name was naturally extended to the river.

Davis wrote in 1879: "Looking to the cape for the idea and reason of its name, we find that it is the southernmost point of Smith's Island — a naked, bleak elbow of sand, jutting far out into the ocean. Immediately in front of it

are the Frying Pan Shoals, pushing out still farther, twenty miles, to sea. Together, they stand for warning and for woe; and together they catch the long majestic roll of the Atlantic as it sweeps through a thousand miles of grandeur and power from the Arctic toward the Gulf. It is the playground of billows and tempests, the kingdom of silence and awe, disturbed by no sound save the sea gull's shriek and the breakers' roar. It's whole aspect is suggestive, not of repose and beauty, but of desolation and terror. Imagination can not adorn it. Romance cannot hallow it. Local pride cannot soften it."

Despite the treacherous passage into the river, settlers from the Massachusetts Bay Colony attempted to create a colony in the mid-17th century but found the area inhospitable. They were followed by a group of English settlers from Barbados who named the settlement Charles Town or Old Town.

This settlement existed until 1667, but failed. Disgruntled Native Americans, pirates, bad weather, weak supply lines, mosquitos and other problems drove the residents south, where they founded the City of Charleston in South Carolina.

Queen Elizabeth opened the area to English colonization as early as 1662, but the going was tough. The Town of Brunswick was founded by English settlers on the west bank of the river in 1725 but withered away as more strategically located Wilmington, on the high east bank, began to prosper. Wilmington was founded in 1732 and incorporated in February 1740 by an act of the North Carolina General Assembly.

Incorporation says something for the tenacity of successful settlers who managed to tame what was apparently a very wild place. But they understood, as do their descendents, that the river posed more opportunities than obstacles. The positioning of the City of Wilmington on a bluff 30 miles north and 5 miles west of the Atlantic, together with the curvature of the shoreline, created a port relatively safe from storms. And what created a challenge for locals would prove to be a protective barrier against outside invaders from England during the Revolutionary War and Union troops during the Civil War.

Wilmington: The Port City

Previously named New Carthage, New Liverpool, Liverpool, New Town and Newton, this east-bank settlement was named Wilmington by Governor Gabriel Johnston to honor his friend Spencer Compton, Earl of Wilmington, in 1739. By 1740 Wilmington was the largest city in North Carolina, with a population of 13,500 city residents and an overall county population of 28,000.

Wilmington prospered as a major port, shipbuilding center and producer of pine forest products. Tar, turpentine and pitch were central to the economy, and lumber from the pine forests was also a lucrative economic resource. At one time, Wilmington was the site of the largest cotton exchange in the world. The waterfront bustled with sailing ships, and steam ships crowded together to pick up or unload precious cargo.

James Sprunt's chronicles, published in 1916, paint a vivid picture in the book's foreword. Sprunt writes: "From early youth, I have loved the Cape Fear River, the ships and the sailors which it bears upon its bosom. As a boy I delighted to wander along the wharves where the sailing ships were moored with their graceful spars and rigging in relief against the sky-line, with men aloft whose uncouth cries and unknown tongues inspired me with a longing for the sea, which I afterwards followed, and for the far-away countries whence they had come."

Downtown Wilmington on the riverfront remains the historical core of the community and is still, in many ways, the neighborhood that defines the region. Suburban neighborhoods may flourish, but there is something fascinating — even compelling

FYI

Unless otherwise noted, the area code for all phone numbers in this guide is 910.

— about the historic homes and buildings downtown. Both visitors and residents are affected by a sense of the ghosts that linger over the scene. Important events happened here, in places that are still standing; places that have not been buried by modern architecture or lost in the trends of a constantly changing American culture.

Home to the county's seat of government throughout more than and two-and-a-half centuries, this urban area has been on the forefront of historic changes. Throughout its history, downtown has been a focal point for virtually everything that has shaped the region's sense of identity and unity. British and Union troops advanced upon it with some difficulty, managing to temporarily occupy the resilient city, but their claims were weak at best. Wilmington was the fall-back position for a weary Lord Cornwallis and his ragged troops at the end of the Revolutionary War, and it was the last Southern port to fall during the Civil War. Despite the temporary setbacks of conquest, Wilmington was never claimed by the outsiders that assailed her.

The 20th Century

Any Wilmingtonian born this century will likely express an awareness of isolation regarding their hometown for most of their lives. Despite several booming eras in its history, Wilmington lagged behind much of North Carolina in many respects through the 20th century.

Obstacles to overland transportation caused by poor roads increasingly separated Wilmington from commerce in the rest of the state. While the Triad and Triangle areas of North Carolina thrived amid a network of interstate highway systems, Wilmington increasingly felt like the distant cousin 100 miles removed. Although U.S. Highway 421 was fine for tourists on their way to area beaches, commerce and industry needed the speed and convenience of an interstate. Having a two-lane blacktop highway as the main artery of access to the city proved to be a profound liability that severely isolated Wilmington.

Wilmington's primary connection to the outside world, before the extension of Interstate 40 from Raleigh in 1991, was the Wilmington and Weldon Railroad. The rail system — the world's longest line at the time at 167 miles — was built in the middle of the 19th century. The railroad promised and delivered prosperity, as goods shipped from all over the world up the Cape Fear to the city could in turn be sent inland at a profit.

Thus, at the end of the 19th century, Wilmington had become the largest city in North Carolina and sported a robust economy. But in 1960 the Wilmington and Weldon Railroad's main office, named the Atlantic Coast Line, was closed and the tracks went largely unused. More than 4,000 families were transferred to Jacksonville, Florida.

Compounding the problems of a slipping local economy, problems with race relations erupted in Wilmington in the 1970s, putting the city on the international map as the home of the Wilmington Ten, a group of black citizens arrested for inciting race riots.

This was a grave time for downtown Wilmington — race riots, white flight from the downtown area, a devastated economy and social despair. Tourists ignored downtown. Beautiful homes fell into disrepair in neighborhoods that were regarded as unsafe. Forlorn, vacant buildings stared blankly over the river, crime was rampant and much of downtown's commerce came to revolve around seedy bars and unsavory dealings.

Fortunately, the story has a happy ending that is actually a new beginning. It was the

omnipresent river that called Wilmingtonians back to reclaim their heritage and their land.

In the early 1970s, a few voices began to question why this beautiful and special city should be lost to neglect. The Wilmington Historic Foundation demanded to know why such valuable architecture should be allowed to rot. City government eyed the situation and determined to do something about it with the creation of the Historic District Commission. Diehard merchants banded together in the establishment of the Downtown Wilmington Association. DARE, the Downtown Area Revitalization Effort, was organized as a public-private successor to the Mayor's Task Force on Revitalization.

It would take volumes to mention each organized group that has contributed to the renewal of downtown Wilmington. Thousands of people are responsible for putting downtown back together. Some of them worked through organizations, but many toiled alone in pursuit of private dreams that would merge with others to form a collective vision. The efforts have resulted in the restoration and maintenance of a national treasure. Wilmington boasts one of the largest districts on the National Historic Register, with homes dating from as early as the middle-1700s. Meticulously restored Victorian, Georgian, Italianate and antebellum homes, from grand mansions to cottages, attest to the previous and current de-

termination of the citizens to maintain the special charm of the neighborhood.

The grassroots movement that drew attention to an area needing renewal is still very much the work of the people who live there. The 200-block downtown historic district is not a mere museum — it is home to real people who do real things to make a living. The neighborhood wasn't merely restored for the sake of remembering the past, it's a place where life goes forward.

Greater Wilmington Today

The $23 million expansion of the New Hanover County International Airport in September 1990 and the linking of Wilmington with Interstate 40 in June 1991 were significant events (see our Getting Around chapter). These advances have brought about dramatic changes in accessibility, population and economic opportunity for the entire Cape Fear region. The impact on downtown Wilmington and its suburbs, as well as area beaches and adjacent counties, is obvious. A 19 percent population increase between 1990 and 1995 suggests people are able to get to Wilmington more easily and, more importantly, are drawn to it and want to stay.

Wilmingtonians are fiercely proud of their city's history and are pleased to share it, al-

though the influx of tourists and newcomers during the last decade has been a bit startling for locals accustomed to isolation. Feelings are, to be honest, a little mixed. It's like inviting a couple of people over for Sunday dinner and, upon opening the door, seeing they've brought a dozen friends with them. All are welcome in a Southern home, of course; it can just give someone a case of the vapors for a moment. One must also, metaphorically speaking, run out into the yard to kill another chicken.

Wilmington graciously welcomes visitors as honored guests in the best Southern tradition. Perhaps the attitude that tourists are, in fact, guests instead of customers is based on a personal awareness that this is our home, and we are allowing people into it.

Hometown pride is good news for the visitor or newcomer. The restaurants, shops and businesses cater to locals, so prices for dining and entertainment are still reasonable (reservations for fine dining are definitely recommended, by the way, and there is only one fine dining establishment downtown that doesn't take personal checks . . . how's that for Southern hospitality!). There are not, in our opinion, too many ventures downtown or even in the surrounding city and county that would be classified as tourist traps. On the contrary, there is much in the way of quality products, services and experiences to be had at reason-

able prices. Community pride is contagious, and locals look to each other to present the area to visitors in a good way.

In the last decade of the 20th century, the Cape Fear River has come to serve as a second focal point of the city's booming tourist industry, vying for tourist attention with the beaches. Hotels and restaurants situated on its banks enjoy brisk business all year long and many have built outdoor dining and bar areas so patrons can enjoy the view of the river, making downtown as appealing to visitors as area beaches.

Wilmingtonians gleefully show off their restored city, and the visitor can expect questions to be answered in enthusiastic detail. Various tours, including walking, car-audio, horse and carriage and boat tours, are available at the foot of Market Street by the river and provide lively narratives of the area's history.

General Statistics

Before describing the varied neighborhoods and specific areas, it seems appropriate to pause and relate some facts about Greater Wilmington.

Wilmington occupies most of New Hanover County. Geographically the second-smallest county in the state with only 185 square miles, New Hanover had a population of approxi-

mately 138,073 as of 1996. Wilmington proper has about 60,000 residents. Projections suggest the population may double by the year 2030. County population density is more than 700 people per square mile, which is in stark contrast to neighboring Pender and Brunswick counties, where there are 33 and 60 people per square mile, respectively. Despite these numbers, these areas are experiencing what some describe as overflow from Wilmington.

The population explosion in the entire Cape Fear area is fueled by many factors, including easier accessibility by land and air, an extremely pleasant four-season climate, scenic beauty, entrepreneurial opportunities and the discovery of the area by the film industry.

Educational opportunities also draw people. The University of North Carolina at Wilmington, long a relatively dormant institution, has taken off in the past decade. Chancellor James Leutze, host of the popular Public Television series "Globe Watch," lends a visionary style of leadership to the university that emphasizes international awareness. The 661-acre campus is among the fastest-growing universities in the 16-campus UNC system. It offers degrees in 60 areas of concentration, including a marine sciences program that was recently ranked fifth-best in the world.

The public school system prides itself on innovation. With a $100.4 million budget, the system devotes 70 percent of its monies to direct instructional costs. There are 30 schools in the New Hanover County Public School System organized as kindergarten to grade 5, grades 6 to 8 and 9 to 12. Educators project there will be more than 21,000 students in the system in 1997.

Employment in the area is concentrated in the services sector and wholesale/retail trade. These two areas account for half the jobs in the county. Unemployment is at approximately 6 percent, although this figure fluctuates regularly and seasonally. Manufacturing accounts for only slightly more than 15 percent of the local jobs. The retail sales business is something of a phenomenon in Greater Wilmington, placing the area sixth in retail sales within the state. The past few years have seen large chains take an interest in Wilmington, which has drawn the likes of Target, Barnes and Noble, Wal-Mart and The Gap (see our Shopping chapter).

Tourism, of course, is a vital industry. Direct tourism and related industries are significant economic factors in the Cape Fear area. At this writing, more than 80,000 people visit the Cape Fear Coast Convention and Visitors Bureau in downtown Wilmington annually. An estimated 1.6 million visitors vacation on the Cape Fear coast and its surrounding islands each year. Despite two damaging hurricanes in 1996, the area's appeal has not been dimin-

ished. Area beaches, with the notable exception of Topsail Island, have been completely restored as of this edition. Be assured Topsail, the island that took the worst of Fran's fury, is getting itself back together.

People who may be considering a move to the area should understand something very important about the local economy: Wages are generally low. The median family income here in 1995 was $34,000. That's slightly higher than the average for the state of North Carolina, but much lower than some of North Carolina's inland cities and certainly lower than wages in other areas of the nation. Some Insiders suspect salaries are going to improve in the near future, with the area becoming more attractive to many people. The film industry, for example, has already brought a different perspective to the area in terms of salaries.

Retirement is beginning to figure significantly in the attraction of the area. People who might have gone to Florida to retire find the southern coast of North Carolina immensely appealing because of the climate and the relatively inexpensive cost of living.

Recreational opportunities are abundant. Some of the finest golf courses and tennis facilities in the country are in New Hanover County (see our Golf and Sports, Fitness and Parks chapters). Boating, sailing and in-the-water recreation are readily accessible. Fishing is both an industry and a serious sport,

with purses as large as $50,000 for the biggest fish landed in the U.S. Open King Mackerel Tournament.

The Wilmington climate is moderate compared with the continental standard. The growing season for plants is long, averaging 244 days. Some types of plants grow all year with temperatures averaging 47 degrees in January and 79.8 degrees in August. Midsummer temperatures average 88 degrees; the average low in the winter is 36.4 degrees. The maritime location makes the climate of Wilmington unusually mild for its latitude.

New Hanover County Areas

Downtown

Downtown pulsates. Aside from being the center of government for Wilmington and New Hanover County, it has become a magnet for retail stores, financial institutions, the cultural arts, entertainment, filmmaking, dining and scenic beauty.

Nightlife is abundant, and it is safe to say that virtually any kind of bar crowd can be found downtown. Dance clubs, jazz bars, karaoke, rock 'n' roll, rhythm and blues venues and more can be found in the 55-block area of the downtown commercial district.

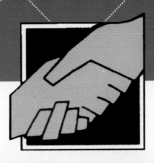

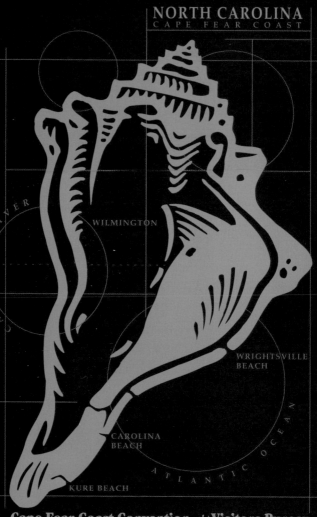

our natural image

NORTH CAROLINA
CAPE FEAR COAST

CAPE FEAR RIVER

WILMINGTON

WRIGHTSVILLE
BEACH

CAROLINA
BEACH

ATLANTIC OCEAN

KURE BEACH

Cape Fear Coast Convention & Visitors Bureau
800.222.4757

pick a color, any color

sofas

supp

fashion shapes

details

chairs

finest natuzzi leathers

sectionals

comfort

250 sensational colors

LeatherEmporium

easy care

loveseats

pick your style, pick your color

recliners

soft

durable

ottomans

wipe it clean

tables

5739 Oleander Drive

the best quality

Wilmington NC

Phone (910) 452-9222

Other arts make their home in the neighborhood too. Thalian Hall, a 19th-century opera house, has been refurbished in a grand manner in recent years. This is the site of traditional and experimental theater presented by national touring companies and more than a dozen local companies, including one of the oldest community theater groups in the country. There are also presentations of music and dance at Thalian Hall.

The Arts Council of the Lower Cape Fear is downtown in the N. Fourth Street revitalization area. St. John's Museum of Art and several commercial galleries are all within a few blocks of the river. Many artists live in the residential area downtown and frequent the cafes, as do film and television stars who are in the area for movie productions.

Perhaps the nicest thing about downtown Wilmington is its pleasant walkability. The Riverwalk, with its view of the Battleship *North Carolina* moored on the western shore, is a pleasant place to stroll, grab a hot dog from a street vendor, listen to free music and gaze at the river.

Because Wilmington is a prominent international port of call, it's likely that a stroller will see an occasional ship being escorted by tugs up the river. Military ships from other nations frequent the city, and there is a service — Dial-A-Sailor — that allows residents to invite sailors into their homes for dinner and cross-cultural exchange. The *Star-News* publishes an announcement when the ships are in town along with the Dial-A-Sailor phone number. The HMS *Bristol*, hailing from England, drops into town now and then, drawing excited locals who throng the docks to greet the crew. As a courtesy, this ship and others offer free tours of their ocean-going quarters.

A walk through the residential area, lush with live oaks draped in Spanish moss, beautiful azaleas and native oleander, is a plant enthusiast's delight. Most of the homes downtown have private gardens that are occasionally opened to the public during special events such as the Azalea Festival in the spring and Riverfest in the fall.

Historic homes marked with informative plaques and friendly neighbors working in their yards provide a delightful and absolutely free experience that appeals to Insiders as much as visitors.

The film industry lends an exciting opportunity for spotting the occasional celebrity or just watching the process of making movies. Filmmaking now accounts for 12 percent of the local economy and promises to grow in the years ahead because of the interest the movie industry has in the region. Stars spotted in recent years include Katherine Hepburn, Alec Baldwin, Kim Basinger, Julie Harris and Anthony Hopkins. Dennis Hopper, of *Easy Rider* fame, owns two downtown buildings and

has plans to open an acting school in Wilmington. Linda Lavin, Broadway star and a woman known affectionately as "Alice," from the '70s TV series, lives on Front Street.

In brief, the city on the river has emerged as a vital and vibrant place in the last decade of the 20th century. Although tourism is crucial, it's also important to note that downtown is the center of government for New Hanover County. The businesses in the downtown Central Business District create a combined economic impact of a half-billion dollars a year on the local economy.

Wilmington often has a seductive effect on its visitors, so be forewarned — even one visit has been known to cause responsible people to go back home and pack up the moving van. Many people are being lured to Wilmington right now, responding to the curious energy of the place.

Wilmington Suburbs

As Wilmington sprawls toward the beaches, so must this guide. With the advent of technology that allowed people to easily move longer distances over the land, the boundaries of Wilmington increasingly pushed toward the sea in two directions: south and east. At the end of the century, there has been dramatic expansion to the north and west. It has become difficult to tell where Wilmington ends and New Hanover County begins.

With the dawn of the 20th century, the automobile and an electric trolley system allowed large numbers of Wilmingtonians to make use of the surrounding land. Wilmington radiates from its urban center through diverse neighborhoods in a crazy quilt of suburban areas. The would-be resident can choose from modest to grand neighborhoods nestled among live oaks or pines. There is a neighborhood for every taste and budget (see our Real Estate chapter).

Market Street is the best indicator of the changes that happen as the city spreads out to meet the beach. There is consensus among locals that a drive from the river on Market Street to the sea, which requires turning onto Eastwood Road near the city limits, reveals a bit of everything that Greater Wilmington has to offer.

Downtown, Market Street is a straight road running past interesting architecture, fountains and monuments as it leaves the river (there is a shocking swerve around the Kenan Memorial Fountain at Fifth Street, so don't gawk too much if you're the driver). Notice what isn't there: The power lines from Fifth to Sixteenth streets were put underground recently, making the intersection at Fifth Street a much more beautiful setting for the venerable Carolina Apartments, the historic Bellamy Mansion Mu-

seum and the First Baptist Church. Beyond the Museum of the Lower Cape Fear (an essential stop if you want a historical overview of the area that includes, but is certainly not limited to, Michael Jordan's uniform and Olympic gold medal as well as the Michael Jordan Discovery Gallery, an interactive, environmental learning center that has nothing to do with basketball), you'll pass New Hanover High School, where football greats Sonny Jurgensen and Roman Gabriel played as teenagers.

Beyond the school, the trees crowd in to create a canopy over the suddenly very narrow road. This is the Mansion District, which was once the affluent suburbs and is still a highly stable and attractive neighborhood. Carolina Place, a historic district neighborhood, is on the right side of the road. As downtown housing prices have skyrocketed with the popularity of the area, the Mansion District and adjacent neighborhoods have enjoyed renewed interest, and the quiet, shady streets off Market Street are a favorite location for families with children.

Next up is venerable Forest Hills, a large, well-manicured cluster of homes built largely in the early 20th century. On the other side of this neighborhood is Independence Mall, with all the modern-day shopping conveniences of Belk, JCPenney and Sears. Past Forest Hills, the signs of commercial enterprise spring up in profusion. Now you can say to yourself, as you see all of the hotels, motels and restaurants along the strip, that you are in Touristland.

Where Market Street meets Kerr (pronounced "car") Avenue, the scene erupts with all the familiar commercial businesses that thrive in every city in America. If you veer off to S. College Road, expect the largest retail-induced traffic snag in all the Lower Cape Fear. The giants of retail are all there, as are restaurants, specialty shops, strip centers and more. It's a shock to locals to see how quickly buildings are going up on previously vacant lots, and city and county governments are struggling to get a handle on some kind of meaningful plan for development.

In the middle of all this commercial activity stands the University of North Carolina at Wilmington. It is surrounded by a broad expanse of grass and the occasional pine tree as well as live oaks and magnolias. If you do not leave Market Street and take the first right under the overpass, you hit Eastwood Road on the approach to Wrightsville Beach. It is approximately a 20-minute drive from the river to the sea on a day with normal traffic, but it can be a half-hour or more if things aren't going well.

The approach to Wrightsville Beach takes you past upscale neighborhoods that are, in several cases, walled from view. Landfall, a private community built around outstanding golf courses designed by Jack Nicklaus and Pete Dye, and a tennis facility presided over by resident expert Cliff Drysdale, is behind a wall and guardhouse on your left. The next sight is the bridge over the Intracoastal Waterway to Harbor Island and Wrightsville Beach.

Wrightsville Beach

Wrightsville Beach is a special place for both the resident and the visitor. It is quite unlike the commercial beaches that often come to mind when one thinks of the coast. This is not a carnival atmosphere; there are no Ferris wheels or gaudy displays of beach merchandise (well, maybe just one), no bumper boats, no arcade. Instead, Wrightsville Beach is primarily an affluent residential community that has its roots in Wilmington. For nearly a century, Wrightsville Beach has been the main retreat from summer heat for residents of Wilmington. Many of the homes are owned by city residents whose families have maintained ownership through the decades, and that is not likely to change during the rest of the century.

Wrightsville Beach was incorporated in 1899 as a resort community. The Tidewater Power Company built a trolley system from downtown to the beach, providing the only land access to the island until 1935. The company, which owned the island, was interested in development and built the Hotel Tarrymore in 1905 to attract visitors and revenue. Later

named The Oceanic, this grand hotel burned down in 1934, along with most structures on the northern half of the island. Lumina, a beach pavilion, was also built by the Tidewater Power Company to attract visitors. On the site of the current Oceanic Restaurant at the south end of the beach, Lumina offered a festive place where locals gathered for swimming, dancing and outdoor movies. The building was demolished in 1973.

Development of the beach continued steadily until 1954 when Hurricane Hazel, a monster of a storm, came ashore and wreaked devastation over the island's homes and buildings. Hazel also shoaled the channel between Wrightsville Beach and adjacent Shell Island. Developers, seeing an opportunity for expansion, filled in the remaining water and joined the islands together. Today, the area is the site of the Shell Island Resort Hotel and numerous condominiums and large homes. In the aftermath of two hurricanes in 1996, the resort hotel finds itself precariously close to an advancing inlet. North Carolina has very strict laws regarding seawalls because of their negative impact on the rest of a beach and the state has denied permission to Shell Island's condominium owners to erect a hard wall. It's a serious example of how important it can be to keep a respectable distance from the sea.

Today's Wrightsville Beach is a very busy and prosperous place. The area is still a stronghold of long-term residents who summer in family homes built to catch the ocean breeze. The permanent residential population is approximately 3,050, but that figure swells considerably in the summer. With a land mass of nearly a square mile, this island manages to maintain its charm despite increasing numbers of visitors. At the peak of the summer season, there are 12,000 overnight visitors and 30,000 daytrippers on the island each day. Surprisingly, brisk commercial development in the form of marinas, restaurants and other services has not seriously changed the residential orientation of the island.

There are a few businesses that stock an assortment of water toys, beach chairs, groceries and beachwear, but most of the island's enterprises center around accommodations, musical entertainment and, of course, dining.

Drawing heavily on local patrons, these establishments offer good service, reasonable prices and some of the freshest seafood on the Atlantic coast.

A visitor to Wrightsville Beach is bound to be impressed by the clean and uncluttered nature of the place. The residential atmosphere encourages a dedication to keeping the beach clean. Lifeguards oversee the safety of swimmers in the summer season, and the beach patrol keeps an eye on the area to make sure laws are obeyed. Alcohol and glass containers are not allowed on the beach. If you have questions, just ask one of the friendly lifeguards.

Boaters, sun worshippers, swimmers, surfers and anglers will find much to appreciate and enjoy about the setting. Public access points, liberally sprinkled across the island, make a day in the sun a free experience for daytrippers — with the notable exception of parking.

Always an issue at Wrightsville Beach, the parking situation was exacerbated by the completion of I-40 in 1991 and the expansion of the airport. In 1996, traffic counts indicated

that 48,000 cars passed over the bridge headed to Wrightsville Beach on the Fourth of July alone. Insiders know the island is extremely crowded during peak summer weekends and are therefore more inclined to leave those times to visitors. On those weekends, visitors are advised to arrive before 9:30 AM and bring plenty of quarters for the parking meters. Parking lots at area restaurants and hotels are vigilantly guarded, and residents are not inclined to allow unknown cars to occupy their driveways. Towing is strictly enforced in no-parking zones.

Opportunities for water-related sports and entertainment are plentiful on Wrightsville Beach. Some of the Cape Fear area's nicest restaurants are on Harbor Island and Wrightsville. Some of the most luxurious marinas along the North Carolina coast are clustered around the bridge at the Intracoastal Waterway and offer a full range of services.

Charter boats, both power and sail, are available in abundance. Jet Ski rental, windsurfing, kayaking and sailing lessons are there for the asking. Bait, tackle, piers and more than enough advice on the best way to fish are all easy to find. Visitors who bring their own boats will appreciate the free boat ramp just north of the first bridge on the Intracoastal Waterway, often called simply the ICW.

Vacation house renters enjoy all the comforts of home. Robert's Market, an astonishingly well-stocked and reasonably priced local grocery store on the island since 1923, caters to local residents. This makes it much more attractive to visitors. There is also a public laundry near the center of the island, although most rental homes have washers and dryers.

The island's very pleasing shoreline, bounded on the east by the Atlantic Ocean and on the west by the equally appealing channel and Intracoastal Waterway, invites visitors to relax. The 5-mile-long beach, regularly renourished to combat erosion, is a smooth stretch of tan sand. The shells that arrive on the shore are not as varied or intact as shell seekers would prefer, but one can stumble upon an occasional treasure.

While the island is losing land on the north end, it's growing on the southern tip. In 1994, land previously deeded to families early in the century resurfaced along Masonboro Inlet in the south. In 1997, the amount of resurfaced land on the south end had increased significantly. The U.S. Army Corps of Engineers intends to reposition the creeping inlet about 200 feet to the north under the auspices of Navigational Servitude — meaning the government has the right, power and obligation to maintain navigable bodies of coastal waters. The question of private property being reclaimed from the sea is one that will puzzle all sides in this situation for some time to come.

A visit to Wrightsville Beach, whether for a day or for a vacation, is bound to be a memorable experience that will be repeated time after time. Since this is a year-round community, it can be experienced and enjoyed almost any time of the year. The island is wonderfully walkable, and you can find everything you need there for a comfortable and memorable vacation. Vacation home renters have the luxury, generally, of reserved parking, so just park the car and forget about it until it's time to leave.

Figure Eight Island

Figure Eight Island is a private, oceanfront resort community. There are no commercial enterprises on the island. It is, in the most extreme sense, a highly restricted residential island of extremely expensive homes. The development includes a yacht club, marina, tennis courts and a boat ramp. The island is connected to the mainland by a causeway bridge, and a guard will only let you onto the island if you've called ahead to someone on the island, such as a friend or a real estate agent, and are on the list at the gate. Unless prior arrangements have been made, you'll be denied access.

You can rent vacation homes here by calling Figure Eight Realty at 686-4400. Some of the larger Wilmington real estate companies may also handle properties on

this exclusive island (see our chapter on Vacation Rentals).

Masonboro Island

Between Wrightsville Beach and Carolina Beach is Masonboro Island. One of the last and largest pristine barrier islands remaining on the southern North Carolina coast, this island is accessible only by boat. While parts of the island belong to private landowners, no development is allowed. Masonboro is a component of the North Carolina National Estuarine Research Reserve. The island is home to gray foxes, cotton rats, a variety of birds, river otters and several species of aquatic life. An especially fun way to visit the island is by small boat, such as a canoe, kayak or Sunfish, so you can float in the shallows away from traffic in the Intracoastal Waterway. Take along a picnic because you won't find a restaurant or any other services on this special island.

Carolina Beach

Just down the road from downtown Wilmington on U.S. 421 is delightful Carolina Beach. Established in 1857 when Joseph Winner planned the streets and lots for the 50 acres of beach property he had purchased, the island's only access was by water. In 1866, a steamship carried vacationers down the Cape Fear River to Snow's Cut, and a small railroad took them the rest of the way into Carolina Beach.

Carolina Beach is the major beach community on the narrow slip of land that is pressed between the Cape Fear River and the Atlantic Ocean. The island, dubbed Pleasure Island a few years ago as part of a marketing plan (a name that is controversial among the residents and may or may not be the name of the place), has several communities, but only three are readily distinguishable: Carolina Beach, Kure Beach and Fort Fisher. All share wide, clean beaches and boast some of the finest fishing along the Cape Fear coast. All are heavily resi-

---

INSIDERS' TIP

Ask your innkeeper for dining suggestions. Most bed and breakfast owners maintain a set of area menus for you to browse.

dential in character, although Carolina Beach has a busy central business district centered around an active yacht basin.

Carolina Beach has undergone a dramatic transformation during the 1990s. Once considered a spot for partiers, the new Carolina Beach is a community dedicated to creating a wholesome family environment. Recent years have seen the cultivation of improved services, pleasant landscaping, attention to zoning and tangible citizen action. The boardwalk is undergoing revitalization with an increase in the number of family-oriented establishments, including a planned arcade with a good atmosphere and restaurants.

A drive through Carolina Beach reveals a pleasant 1950s-style beach of modest cottages, increasingly more upscale single-family dwellings and an abundance of three- and four-story condominiums. Unfortunately, these taller structures were built on the oceanfront and tend to obscure the view of the sea for several congested blocks on the north end. Newer development to the south is much more spread out and lower in height.

In the heart of Carolina Beach is Jubilee Park, one of two amusement parks on the southern coast. Nearby, you'll find waterslides, miniature golf courses and other things that

appeal to the kids. The town also has a movie theater, grocery stores and bait shops.

Anglers will find paradise at Carolina Beach. The surf promises wonderful bounty all year long, and there are plenty of tackle shops and piers as well as the opportunity to experience deep-sea fishing from the sterns of a number of charter boats berthed in the yacht basin. Several annual fishing tournaments are based on the abundance of mackerel, and you can pay a nominal entry fee for a chance to reap as much as $50,000 for the winning fish.

At the extreme northern end of the island as well as on the south at Fort Fisher, the beach is open to four-wheel drive vehicles. While there is a certain allure to driving right off the street onto the sand of this expansive space, don't do it if you are in a car. Getting stuck in the sand is as easy and frustrating as getting stuck in the snow.

Carolina Beach also offers one of the few state parks in the region. For a modest fee, you can camp and enjoy the wonders of nature. Venus's-flytrap, a carnivorous plant, is abundant in the park. This plant, a relic from prehuman existence on the planet, only grows naturally within a 60-mile radius of Wilmington.

Away from the seasonal bustle at the center of town, Carolina Beach is a quiet community of about 5,000 regular residents. That number jumps five times at the peak of the vacation season. The community is growing in appeal to locals from Wilmington for one big reason: It isn't crowded, yet. You have plenty of elbow room on the beach; there is no problem finding parking at the bargain rate of $2 a day in the central business district; and some of the better vacation rental deals are here. Many a Wilmingtonian has given Wrightsville Beach over to visitors for the summer in the past few years and turned to Carolina Beach for a quiet spot on the sand.

Kure Beach and Fort Fisher

Carolina Beach dissolves into the town of Kure Beach to the south. Kure Beach (pronounced "cure-ee") is a younger community where development began in the 1870s when Hans Andersen Kure moved from Denmark and bought large tracts of land in the middle of the island. Apparently, things moved slowly because Kure Beach wasn't incorporated until 1947.

Kure Beach has been described as the quintessential American small town in an oceanside setting. It is overwhelmingly residential, dotted with modest cottages, new houses and several old-style beach motels. Several apartment buildings cluster together in one spot, but there is little else in the way of tall buildings here because condominiums are not allowed. In fact, new structures may not be built taller than 35 feet.

You'll find neither arcade nor amusement park here. There is very little in the way of shopping. A permanent population of only about 700 residents makes for a very close community, but Kure Beach's small size should not lead visitors to think they're out in the boondocks. The town maintains its own municipal services and fire protection, and a local planner describes the community as being "like any big city, only smaller."

Kure Beach will remain small because it is surrounded by buffer zones. The Fort Fisher State Recreation Area and Historic Site is on the south side, and the U.S. Government owns the west side as part of the military terminal at Sunny Point across the Cape Fear River.

If you're looking for peace and quiet in a friendly setting, Kure Beach is the place to go. A word to visitors who bring their dogs: Kure Beach never allows dogs on the beach, not even on a leash. This is the only beach community within the range of this guide that has this policy on a year-round basis.

Farther south, toward the point where the Cape Fear River and the Atlantic Ocean finally converge, the summer homes increase in size and opulence. Twisted live oaks cover the landscape and increase in density until, at last, natural flora overtakes architecture. There are several spots of interest near the end of the island. Fort Fisher, an earthworks fort of significance during the Civil War, appears on the right. The North Carolina Aquarium at Fort Fisher, a fine facility that boasts a touch tank and a close-up encounter with live sharks, comes up on the left. Near the aquarium is a beach where anglers in four-wheel drive vehicles flock to take in the bounty of the waters. At the end of it all is the Fort Fisher-Southport Ferry, possibly the best $3 cruise in the world (see our Getting Around chapter).

All in all, these southernmost beaches of New Hanover County offer 7.5 miles of very pleasant vacationing and living.

Brunswick County Beaches

Southport

Southport is reachable by both ferry and scenic highway. Leaving Wilmington, take the Cape Fear Memorial Bridge and hang a fast left onto N.C. Highway 133 just off U.S. Highways 17, 74 and 76. If you miss it, you can also take N.C. Highway 87, although the N.C. 133 route is very beautiful and offers several attractions, including Orton Plantation, the Carolina Power & Light nuclear plant and Brunswick Town, site of the first successful European colony in the region. For information on the ferry route and schedule, see our chapter on Getting Around.

The city of Southport, in Brunswick County, is steeped in history. This 200-year-old coastal community saw the establishment of North Carolina's first fort in 1754: Fort Johnston. A small community of river pilots, fishermen

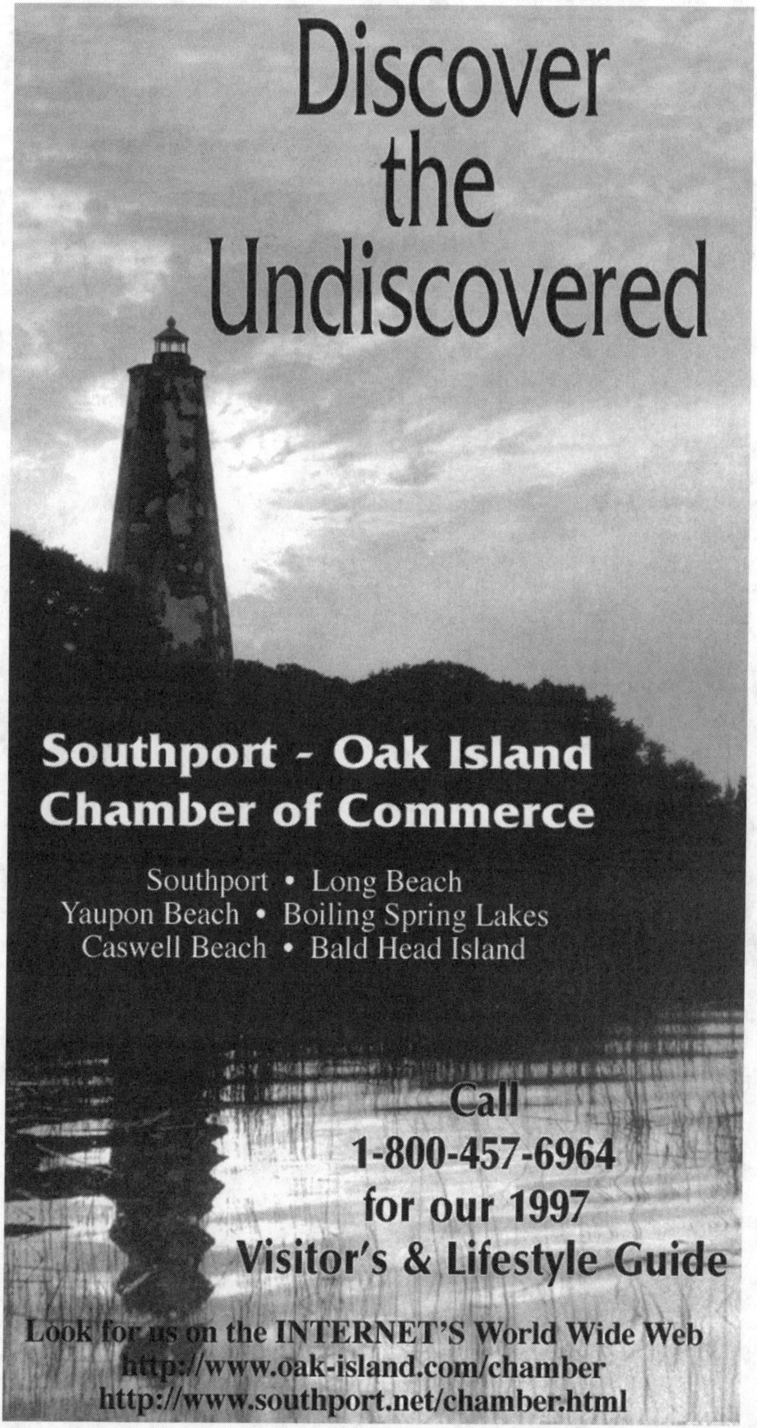

Discover the Undiscovered
Southport - Oak Island Chamber of Commerce
Southport • Long Beach
Yaupon Beach • Boiling Spring Lakes
Caswell Beach • Bald Head Island
Call 1-800-457-6964 for our 1997 Visitor's & Lifestyle Guide
Look for us on the INTERNET'S World Wide Web
http://www.oak-island.com/chamber
http://www.southport.net/chamber.html

Photo: Curtis Krueger

Abundant and exotic plant life is a constant feature
on North Carolina's southern beaches.

and tradespeople grew up around the fort. In 1792, the town of Smithville was created. In 1808, Smithville became the county seat of Brunswick County. For the remainder of the century, the town made plans to link rail service with the existing river traffic to make the community a major southern port, and the city was renamed Southport.

The town is widely regarded as the Fourth of July Capital of North Carolina. Southport celebrated the Fourth of July just after the signing of the Declaration of Independence in 1776. History records that in 1795, citizens gathered at Fort Johnston and observed a 13-gun military salute to the original 13 states. In 1813, a Russian warship was in the harbor and fired a 13-gun salute, and it was on this Fourth of July that fireworks were used for the first time to close the celebration. In 1972, the Fourth of July Festival was chartered and incorporated as the official North Carolina Fourth of July Festival, and it has become a tremendously popular four-day event for residents and visitors.

Southport, listed on the National Register of Historic Places, is ranked by both Rand McNally and Kiplinger as one of the most desirable places in the United States to retire. The live oak-lined streets, charming architecture, quaint shops — most notably an abundance of antiques shops — as well as year-round golf, boating and fishing seasons, create an enormously pleasant environment for the residents of the town. This is the place to go for people who genuinely want to kick back and enjoy beautiful coastal scenery. With a year-round population of 2,400, there's still plenty of elbow room.

Bald Head Island

Just off the coast of Southport and the mainland, at the mouth of the Cape Fear River, is the pristine island of Bald Head. The island is easily identifiable in the distance by the wide-based Bald Head Island lighthouse, a structure built in 1817, retired in 1935 and cataloged as the oldest lighthouse in North Carolina. Once a favorite hiding spot for pirates such as Blackbeard and Stede Bonnet, Bald Head Island is now an affluent residential and resort community of about 80 year-round residents that can only be reached by the island's private ferry or personal boat. The island is graciously open to the public, and the summer population can reach 3,000 with visitors renting vacation homes and playing golf. (See the Golf Chapter for course and rates.)

It is probably safe to say this is one of the most unspoiled beach and maritime forest areas on the North Carolina coast. Despite residential development, as well as a few commercial amenities such as a restaurant, bed and breakfast, general store with deli, marina, golf course, specialty store and electric cart and bike rental business, the island's natural beauty is still protected.

The island has 14 miles of beaches, unspoiled dunes, creeks and forests. The 2,000 acres of land are surrounded by 10,000 acres of salt marshes. The owners have deeded nearby Middle Island and Bluff Island to the state and the Nature Conservancy. The Bald Head Island Conservancy, a non-profit organization, was formed to ensure that the unique natural resources of the island are maintained and preserved.

The Sea Turtle Program, featured on public television, protects and monitors these wonderful creatures. Turtle nesting on Bald Head Island accounts for 50 percent of all turtle eggs laid in North Carolina. There is an Adopt-a-Nest Program that pairs concerned humans with turtles in an effort to protect the nest and encourage the hatchlings toward the sea. Studies in which female turtles were tagged have revealed that pregnant turtles return to the same site every other year. Due to the many species of birds found on the island, the Audubon Society conducts an annual count here as part of its national program.

Something quite special about the island is the absence of cars. Gasoline-powered engines are not allowed. The residents and visitors who rent lovely homes all drive electric carts or ride bicycles. The reduction of noise and pollution during the past decade is one of the finest features of the place. A visitor can come for the day by private ferry service from Indigo Plantation in Southport. The cost is $15

FYI

Unless otherwise noted, the area code for all phone numbers in this guide is 910.

roundtrip. Day parking in Southport is $4, although this is subject to change. For a longer stay, there are many rental units on the island. The cost, compared to rental on much of the mainland, is slightly on the upper end, but so is the experience for the visitor who wants to really get away from it all in quiet style.

Despite Bald Head Island's private status, the welcome mat is always out for visitors. There are several daytripper packages available that include lunch or dinner, historic tours and ferry service. The lighthouse is available for visiting all year, and there is no fee. The well-appointed marina welcomes transients. For information on Bald Head Island's numerous amenities, call (800) 234-1666.

Oak Island

Just across the water from Bald Head Island and Southport is Oak Island, a narrow strip of land that is separated into three beach communities: Caswell Beach, Yaupon Beach and Long Beach.

Caswell Beach is the site of Fort Caswell, a military stronghold that dates from 1826. Fort Caswell is now owned by the North Carolina Baptist Assembly and welcomes visitors of all denominations each year. The community has some summer homes, but the area has mostly permanent residences. The year-round population is 191, but up to 1,200 people can be staying on this part of Oak Island in the summer.

Yaupon Beach is a haven for live oaks and is named for a species of holly that grows in the area. Known as a family beach, Yaupon is populated mainly by permanent residents numbering 780, most of whom are retirees. Recreational areas include a championship golf course, nine beach access points, a picnic area on the Elizabeth River estuary system and fishing piers.

As the name implies, **Long Beach** occupies the longest stretch of beach on Oak Island, but its greater claim to fame is the fact it

is Brunswick County's largest town with a population of more than 4,150. You'll find 52 access points to the absolutely uncrowded beaches, and you'll find a few restaurants and motels. For the most part, a visitor will enjoy renting a house for an extended vacation here. In fact, vacation rental is the liveliest business on the beach with approximately 14 rental companies operating on Oak Island.

South Brunswick Islands

Of the three islands in the group known as the South Brunswick Islands, **Holden Beach** is the longest. Stretching 11 miles along the Atlantic, the island is a jogger's paradise. The village has about 768 permanent residents, and visitors will find a host of opportunities for assimilating themselves into this exceedingly quiet family community. The beach and the sea are the central attractions in this town that prides itself on a serene quality of life.

Ocean Isle Beach is the center island, offering 8 miles of beach with a total resort experience: restaurants, specialty shops, public tennis courts, access to all watersports and a waterslide. This beach has the only high-rise on the South Brunswick Islands. There is an airport that makes getting to Ocean Isle accessible by air, but don't expect to see commercial jets at this relatively small facility. Home to almost 650 full-time residents, Ocean Isle welcomes visitors to a peaceful place.

Sunset Beach, described as a diminutive island gem, is only 3 miles long. Despite its size, this island has experienced a 147 percent population increase between 1990 and 1995, with a current year-round population of 720. Reachable by a one-lane pontoon bridge, making it the only island without a high-rise bridge in Brunswick County, there is sometimes a bit of a wait to access Sunset in the high season. However, the island is well worth the pause in getting there. This bridge will probably be replaced by a high-rise bridge eventually if the Department of Transportation has its

INSIDERS' TIP

Springbrook Farms, the horse-and-carriage tour company in downtown Wilmington, has several horses that look exactly alike. It isn't the same horse making the trips all day.

Area Chambers of Commerce

Chambers of Commerce are great resources for gaining an understanding of the big picture in terms of a community's business, educational, entertainment and institutional flavor. While this organization is not generally in the tourism business, they generally have brochure racks filled with information of interest to the visitor, newcomer and even the longtime resident who just wants to know what's going on.

Greater Wilmington Chamber of Commerce, 1 Estell Lee Place, Wilmington, 762-2611

Carolina Beach Chamber of Commerce, 201 Lumberton Avenue, Carolina Beach, 458-8434

Topsail Area Chamber of Commerce and Tourism, 205 S. Topsail Drive, Topsail Island, 328-4722, (800) 626-2780

Hampstead Chamber of Commerce, U.S. Highway 17, Hampstead, 270-9642, (800) 833-2483

Southport/Oak Island Chamber of Commerce, 4841 Long Beach Road S.E., Southport, 457-6964

South Brunswick Islands Chamber of Commerce, 4948 Main Street, Shallotte, 754-6644, (800) 426-6644

Myrtle Beach Area Chamber of Commerce, 1200 N. Oak Street, Myrtle Beach, S.C., (803) 626-7444

way. Again, this island is residential in character. Some of the best bargains in vacation rental are here, and the visitor who wants a quiet coastal place will do very well to book a house on this beach. As with all of the beaches on the southern coast, quality golfing is available on the mainland. For fishing enthusiasts, there is a full-service pier.

Sunset Beach offers a special delight: a walk to Bird Island at low tide. Bird Island is completely untouched by development at this writing. A walk through the shallow inlet at low tide is easy for children as well as adults. Frequently, there are informal guided tours, announced by posters attached to street markers on the beach, so it's easy to hook up with locals who are pleased to share their knowledge of the island with you. The environment is a purely natural and deeply comforting place where people of the 20th century can experience life as it was before the development of the land.

Calabash

Just a few miles from Sunset Beach is the town of Calabash. This charming seaport is known widely as the "Fried Seafood Capital of the World," with 17 restaurants serving battered-and-fried shrimp, fish and oysters in a style that is indigenous to North Carolina. There are some health-conscious changes in the oil used by many Calabash restaurants these days, but the taste is still authentic Calabash style.

Calabash merged with Carolina Shores in 1993, increasing the number of permanent residents from 221 to 1,200 overnight. Carolina Shores is an affluent, golf course community comprised of mostly retirees. While it wasn't an easy merger, things seem to have settled down considerably, and the town now has 1,398 residents.

INSIDERS' TIP

Grits are made from ground corn and, despite the unfortunate sound of the name, aren't gritty at all. If you've never had them, you're in for a treat.

Shallotte

The town of Shallotte serves as the hub for services for these beach communities. In fact, it is perhaps best-known as the commercial mecca of Brunswick County. Because of its mainland location and island proximity, Shallotte offers residents and visitors the convenience of larger-town living and services. The town has a year-round population of 1,176.

Pender and Onslow Counties

Topsail Island

Topsail Island allegedly got its name from pirates who would hide in the coves awaiting the view of a top of a sail. Once a ship was seen it could be easily ambushed in the channel and relieved of its cargo. Eventually, merchant seamen learned to look for sails over in the coves, and pirating went on the skids.

In 1946 Topsail Island was taken over by the U.S. Navy to begin Project Bumblebee, a missile program that was a predecessor to Florida's rocket program at Cape Canaveral. The first supersonic missiles in the country were tested on this remote island. It was, technically, a secret project, although residents in the mainland area must have noticed the launching of 200 prototype missiles between 1946 and 1948.

Remains of the project can be observed on the island. Seven concrete missile observation towers, including two that have been converted into homes, remain on the island. The launch pad is now the patio for the Jolly Roger Hotel.

Topsail is another fishing community. Topsail Inlet is subject to shoaling, a constant concern. Commercial fishermen with considerable

Photo: Curtis Krueger

The waterfront at Southport is home to many commercial fishing boats.

experience traverse the tricky inlet; pleasure boaters are strongly advised to go south to Masonboro Inlet at Wrightsville Beach for sure passage into the Atlantic. Hurricane Fran also put a new inlet through the island, but it isn't navigable. The island is a haven for sea turtles, and the residents are vigilant in their protection of these creatures. The Topsail Turtle Project dedicates itself each season to preservation and protection of sea turtles.

Topsail Island is largely a residential community. It took a serious whacking with Hurricane Fran, but the community is recovering. Frankly, it lost its marina, several restaurants, quite a few homes and its piers, but the resolve of islanders is bound to return the beautiful island to its former appeal. After all, the view of the ocean is the same.

Surf City is the "big city" of the island, in the center and connected to the mainland by a 40-year-old swing bridge on N.C. Highway 50. Although this is a modest, small town by anyone's standards, it serves the island well with restaurants, a grocery store, gift shops and other commercial enterprises. Surf City was part of what has been described locally as the "miracle mile" in Fran's aftermath, avoiding the destruction that was particularly evident farther north.

Welcome to "Wilmywood"

Believe it or not, more movies are being made each year in Wilmington than in any other American city other than Los Angeles and New York. TV's long-running "Matlock" series, starring Andy Griffith, was made in Wilmington, as were TV's "American Gothic," many commercials, music videos and industrial films. At the heart of this phenomenon is EUE/Screen Gems Studios, a 32-acre complex on N. 23rd Street. Some of the studio's eight sound stages — totaling more than 100,000 square feet — are among the largest in the East. And you've probably seen the backlot several times on screen, although you probably thought you were looking at the streets of New York City, New Orleans, Beirut, Detroit or Bucharest.

The spark that ignited Wilmington's steadily burning film industry came in 1983 when Stephen King's *Firestarter* was filmed at the studios, then owned by Dino DeLaurentis. Carolco Pictures (makers of the *Terminator* films) bought the studio in 1989, then EUE/Screen Gems in 1996. Wilmington's ideal weather, its variety of locations, accessibility to transportation and low labor costs offer the film industry an effective formula for success.

So it's not surprising so many Wilmingtonians have film experience. Local musicians performed in *The Radioland Murders*. Local dancers went *Stomping at the Savoy*. Scores of locals earn their livings as "techies." Hundreds more work as on-screen extras. At least one Wilmington city councilman may be seen in TV commercials. The Cape Fear Filmmakers Accord, 763-3456, is a consortium of crews, staff and screenwriters that publishes its own directory.

— continued on next page

Photo: Carolco Studios

The streets of a bygone New York City came to life on the studio backlot for the filming of *Billy Bathgate*.

— continued from previous page

State-of-the-art recording studios serving the film industry also thrive around town. It's not unusual to see major Hollywood celebrities frequenting local restaurants and clubs while they're in town for a shoot. And fees collected for film permits go toward downtown beautification projects. Just a glance at the following sample of movies and TV shows made in and around Wilmington (the list is always growing) makes it clear why Wilmington has earned the nickname "Wilmywood."

Blue Velvet
Crimes of the Heart
To Gillian on Her 37th Birthday
Virus
Lolita
Against Her Will: The Carrie Buck Story
Fall Time
Bad With Numbers
Justice and a Small Town: The Sandra Prine Story
When We Were Colored
Cannibal Vampire Schoolgirls from Outer Space
Truman Capote's One Christmas
Margaret: A Burning Passion
Empire
Out of Carolina
Firestarter
The Exorcist III
Windmills of the Gods
Tune In Tomorrow
The Lost Capone
Alan and Naomi
Year of the Dragon
The Crow
Everybody Wins
Little Monsters
Loose Cannons
Weekend at Bernie's
Cyborg
A Stoning in Fulham County
Weeds
Too Young the Hero
Noble House
Betsy's Wedding
Dream a Little Dream
Golden Years
29th Street
Sleeping With the Enemy
Super Mario Bros.
Teenage Mutant Ninja Turtles
Teenage Mutant Ninja Turtles II: The Secret of the Ooze
King Kong Lives
The Squeeze
Billy Bathgate
Amos & Andrew

Date with an Angel
The Member of the Wedding
Raw Deal
Simple Justice

Hampton Inn & Suites

Landfall Park

- *Located in the prestigious area of Landfall within walking distance to the Intracoastal waterway and Wilmington's most popular restaurants.*
- *Complimentary Deluxe Style Continental Breakfast.*
- *90 Guest Rooms and 30 Apartment Style Suites.*
- *Suites with full kitchen & fireplace.*
- *Honeymoon Suite with fireplace & whirlpool for two.*
- *Weekly & Monthly rentals available*

- ***Port City Chop House Restaurant is adjacent***
- ***Meeting rooms available with catering services***
- ***Fishing & Golfing packages***
- ***Adjacent nature trail for walking, jogging & biking.***
- ***Rollerblade & Bike rental available*** *(seasonal)*
- ***Kidney shaped pool with Tikki Hut serving beverages & snacks*** *(seasonal)*

1989 Eastwood Road • Wilmington, NC 28403
(910) 256-9600 • 1-800-HAMPTON • Fax (910) 256-1996

Accommodations

A variety of accommodations are available in our region — bed and breakfast inns, resort hotels, efficiency apartments and simple motel lodgings abound.

Travelers are often delighted by the high caliber of bed and breakfast inns in Wilmington, which are comparable to the finest inns anywhere. Most inns here occupy meticulously kept historic homes. Some are as casual as a pajama party while others are steeped in Victorian elegance. Bed and breakfast inns typically do not allow pets, smoking indoors, or very young children unless by prior arrangement. And innkeepers are knowledgeable about the area and will usually assist you in making reservations for shows, meals, charters and golf packages.

Full-service resort and business hotels are strategically located in desirable areas such as Wilmington's riverfront and at Wrightsville Beach. In smaller towns such as Surf City, Carolina Beach, Yaupon Beach and others, lower-priced oceanfront motels are more common. In Wilmington, the motel strip is Market Street west of College Road with some overflow onto College Road itself. You can find motels of every price range there, from the budget Motel 6 to the pricier Ramada Inn. Carolina Beach teems with small, family-run motels concentrated within a small area — no fewer than 15 line Carolina Beach Avenue N. within a half-mile of Harper Avenue. In general, beach motels, especially the older ones, are not known for their stylish decor but rather their great locations.

Daily accommodations on Bald Head Island are limited to one large bed and breakfast inn. There are no hotels or motels. However, some rental homes are available for stays as short as a weekend. See our Weekly and Long-term Cottage Rentals chapter for information about rental accommodations on Bald Head.

We've listed here a cross-section of accommodations — inexpensive and expensive, elegant and downscale, busy and peaceful. Of course, there are many more than what's listed here, but these all share the kind of quality we feel comfortable recommending to our own friends and family.

Price Code

Since prices are subject to change without notice, we provide only price guidelines based on double occupancy per night during the summer ("high" season). Guidelines do not reflect state and local taxes. Most establishments offer lower rates during the off-season, but always confirm rates and necessary amenities before reserving. It may also pay to inquire about corporate, senior citizen or long-term discounts even if such discounts are not mentioned in our descriptions. Most establishments accept major credit cards and personal checks, especially for making payment in advance. Be aware that cancellations, even when made with the required notice, may incur an administrative fee, although you'll find most innkeepers in the region to be reasonable and fair.

$	Less than $75
$$	$75 to $120
$$$	$121 to $150
$$$$	$151 and more

Hurricane Updates

When the eyes of hurricanes Bertha and Fran passed over Wilmington in 1996, the most destructive forces attacked the east-facing beaches and regions in the north of this guide's coverage area, hitting Topsail Island hardest. At press time, owners of many beach accommodations we've recommended in the past, particularly on Topsail, were still unsure of their businesses' futures as they attempted to rebuild and reopen. We've opted to continue listing such businesses when such uncertainty

exists, adding the note, "call ahead for information on availability" where appropriate.

Wilmington

219 South 5th
$$ • 219 S. Fifth St., Wilmington
• 763-5539, (800) 219-7634

In keeping with its slogan, 219 South 5th is indeed "uniquely unpretentious." The Greek Revival Deans-Maffit House (1871) offers three guest rooms of an essentially country French and English style accented with Victorian antiques. Two of the rooms have fireplaces, and the inn includes an efficiency suite. Some rooms have a private bath, some share a bath. The backyard, with its small circular koi pond and attractive loggia, has a nostalgic and relaxing character. Hearty hot breakfasts are a balance of formality and familiarity, blending the use of china, antique glasses and hefty coffee mugs. Off-street parking is accessible from a side street.

Camellia Cottage
$$$ • 118 S. Fourth St., Wilmington
• 763-9171, (800) 763-9171

Standing on a brick-paved street four blocks from the river, Camellia Cottage is a richly appointed, high-peaked Queen Anne Shingle home (built in 1889) that was once the home of prominent Wilmington artist Henry J. MacMillan. Some of his work remains in the home. In fact, artwork abounds throughout the Camellia Cottage, from murals on the wraparound piazza outside to handpainted fireplace tiles. Camellia Cottage offers three spacious guest rooms and one suite, each with its own character. Queen-size, antique-style beds dressed in English linen, private baths and gas-fired hearths are standard. Morning coffee service is provided at your door, and beverages are available in the afternoon. Traditional Southern breakfasts are served with crystal, china and silver. The music room, parlor and sun room are always available to guests. Smoking is not permitted. Guests with allergies, take note of the resident cat, dog and finches.

Catherine's Inn
$$ • 410 S. Front St., Wilmington
• 251-0863, (800) 476-0723

Catherine's occupies the Forshee-Sprunt home (1888), an Italianate structure distinguished by a wraparound front porch and two-story screened-in rear porch, an especially inviting setting for breakfast. It is one of the few bed and breakfast inns directly overlooking the Cape Fear River, a superior sunset vantage point, especially from the two-tiered formal gardens or gazebo. In one of the Victorian double parlors, a piano awaits the musically gifted. The five bedrooms are elegant — one features a sleigh bed, another, antique dolls — and each is adorned with fresh flowers and local artwork. Each room has a king-size or queen bed and private bath. Coffee is delivered to the rooms before breakfast, which is always a hearty affair. Complimentary beer, wine and soda are always available, plus cake and coffee in the evenings and complimentary liqueur at bedtime. You may play horseshoes and croquet on the 300-foot rear lawn, and there's plenty of off-street parking. Bicycles are at your disposal.

FYI

Unless otherwise noted, the area code for all phone numbers in this guide is 910.

Chandler's Wharf Inn
$$-$$$ • 2 Ann St., Wilmington • 815-3510

Few bed and breakfast inns are as distinctive as this, with its superb river view (perfect for sunsets) and the kind of character only a building nearly 150 years old can have. Situated on the cobblestone street of Chandler's Wharf in the Reston-Richardson House (c.1850), across from two of Wilmington's best restaurants and fine shopping, the inn offers two suites featuring antique reproduction furnishings made by local artisans, including a queen-size sleigh bed upstairs. The decor has been described as English country, but is the epitome of quaint, antebellum America. Each suite features a sitting room with fireplace, private shower, coffee maker, cable TV and a personal phone line with an answering machine. Continental breakfasts are included. Among several other guest services, your innkeeper will be pleased to place reservations for you at the inn's affiliated restaurants across the street and at the beach. Chandler's Wharf Inn stands in the midst of everything downtown Wilmington has to offer.

Coast Line Inn
$-$$$ • 503 Nutt St., Wilmington • 763-2800

On the Riverwalk at the historic Coast Line Center, the Inn has 50 rooms, each one with a fine river view. The decor is warmly appointed with artwork, and the rooms are meticulously well-maintained. Computer/modem hookups and coffee makers are available in every room. Complimentary continental breakfasts are placed in baskets outside your room if desired, and laundry service is available. The River's Edge Lounge on the fourth floor is a great place to enjoy sunsets and, on Wednesday and Friday nights, live entertainment. The lounge opens at 5 PM Monday through Saturday. The Coast Line Inn is within easy, safe walking distance of many fine restaurants.

The adjacent Coast Line Convention Center, 501 Nutt Street, 763-6739, occupies a historic building that was once part of Wilmington's railroad depot serving what was then one of the world's most important cotton exchanges. The Convention Center consists of more than 10,000 square feet of space, which can be reconfigured into four rooms of various sizes. It provides a unique setting and ambiance for conferences, seminars, trade and fashion shows, banquets, weddings or practically any other function. There's plenty of parking, and additional hotel accommodations are within easy walking distance.

Comfort Inn Wilmington
$-$$ • 151 S. College Rd., Wilmington • 791-4841

The Comfort Inn, although considered "budget" accommodations, provides excellent amenities for the price. It is a 146-room facility midway between downtown Wilmington and the beach. Laundry and valet services, complimentary beverages in the lobby/ lounge, free local telephone calls, an outdoor pool and a Nautilus center contribute to the Comfort Inn's value. Continental breakfasts and daily newspapers are available each morning in the lobby, and there is no extra charge for children younger than 18 who are staying with their parents. Handicapped-accessible rooms and corporate discounts are available. If you forget any personal toiletries, the staff will provide them free. Reservations may also be made through a central booking service, (800) 221-2222.

Curran House
$$ • 312 S. Third St., Wilmington • 763-6603, (800) 763-6603

This bed and breakfast inn, just three blocks from Wilmington's riverfront, strikes a balance between historic ambiance and kick-up-your-feet comfort. Innkeepers Vickie and Greg Stringer have furnished their downstairs parlor with plush ottomans for just that purpose, and it's an inviting place to browse through one of their many interesting books or play a board game. Full breakfasts, served from 8:30 to 9:30 AM, include homemade breads and muffins with such mainstays as frittatas. Fresh-ground coffee awaits you in the upstairs hallway each morning, and snacks and beverages are available all day. One guest room boasts a king-size four-poster bed. Rattan and some unusual painted furnishings add an island flavor to another room. A third, a European-style room with a massive king-size sleigh bed, offers bath facilities (including a claw-foot tub) behind a tall Venetian screen. All rooms include wing-back easy chairs, private bath, a pair of warm terry robes, hair dryer, telephone, cable TV and VCR and both hypoallergenic and down pillows. Guests are welcome to use the video library of recent films. Curran House occupies the McKay-Green House (1837), which features Queen Anne and Italianate details, decorative fireplaces (nonfunctional) and four porches (one with bench

---

INSIDERS' TIP

Appreciate the value of shoes at the beach: The asphalt and sand get very hot, and there are sand spurs in the grass and dunes. Also, day-sailing in Banks Channel is often over oyster beds.

CAROLINA TEMPLE APARTMENTS
An Island Inn
"Directly on the Ocean"

Phone: 910/256-2773
Fax: 910/256-3878
E-mail: swright168@aol.com
P.O. Box 525
Wrightsville Beach, NC 28480
Late March - November

Completely furnished, air conditioned apartments. All with kitchenettes and private baths. Large, spacious porches. Ocean and sound front beaches. Pier with boat slips. Office: 550 Waynick Blvd.

swing). The second-floor porch in the rear is screened — a great place for morning coffee. Curran House is a nonsmoking home with plenty of off-street parking as well as table tennis and badminton, a fax machine and photocopier. Ask about corporate rates, the Valentine's Day special and other holiday packages.

Front Street Inn
$$-$$$$ • 215 S. Front St., Wilmington • 762-6442

Full of Southwestern ambiance, rooms at the Front Street Inn feature original American art and decor inspired by such namesakes as Monet, Hemingway, Cousteau and O'Keeffe. Full kitchens, wet bars, French doors and exposed brick are typical, and some rooms feature canopied beds, futon sofas and Jacuzzis. The Inn occupies the renovated Salvation Army building (1923), across the street from Chandler's Wharf, and has great views of river sunsets from the second-floor balcony. The Sol y Sombra bar and breakfast room offers continental fare (organic coffee, fruit, yogurt, biscotti), plus beer, wine and champagne, unless room service is preferred. Innkeepers Stefany and Jay Rhodes will cater to any reasonable request (how about supplying chocolates and flowers for an anniversary surprise?). There is plenty of off-street parking. Corpo-

rate and long-term rates are available, and children are welcome.

Graystone Inn
$$$-$$$$ • 100 S. Third St., Wilmington • 763-2000

If Bellamy Mansion stands as the epitome of Civil War-era elegance, Graystone Inn must be its 20th-century successor. This palatial mansion, built in 1906, is the most imposing structure downtown and a historic landmark. The vast ground floor includes a masterpiece of a study paneled in mahogany and focused on a marble fireplace. From the foyer, a grand Renaissance-style staircase made of handcarved oak rises three stories, culminating in the recreation room (a former ballroom) featuring a century-old Brunswick billiard table. The Graystone is frequently used as a set for the movie industry.

Full American breakfasts on weekdays and continental repasts on weekends are provided in the enormous dining room. Beverage service is available throughout the day. At night, wine and sherry are offered. Each of the five guest rooms is as large as a suite in some hotels. All have private full baths. Intercoms between rooms are a special convenience to groups. The Graystone's location is ideal for walking to all downtown Wilmington's attractions.

Landfall Park Hampton Inn & Suites
$$-$$$$• 1989 Eastwood Rd., Wrightsville Beach • 256-9600

This new inn provides high-end amenities, complete with bell staff, just minutes off the beach. From the fountain at the main portico to the island-themed poolside Eagle Bar, the Landfall Park Hampton Inn is geared to the touring visitor and corporate traveler alike. All suites have a kitchen with microwave, stove, dishwasher and refrigerator. The Signature Suite provides true celebrity accommodations, with a double-sided fireplace, elaborate entertainment center and two-person whirlpool bath. Executive one- and two-bedroom suites are perfect for movie-production staff or other business travelers. Desk and data modem are standard. The Landfall Park Hampton Inn serves upscale continental breakfasts and provides valet service on weekdays. A dedicated boardroom and large meeting room (for 30 to 80 people) are suitable for corporate retreats.

Holiday Inn
$$-$$$ • 4903 Market St., Wilmington • 799-1440

With 232 guest rooms, this is Wilmington's largest hotel, providing full-service amenities such as coffee and newspapers each morning. Other conveniences include guest laundry and valet service, room service, a courtesy van, banquet space for up to 100 people, cable TV and On Command Video, and a "For-get Me Not" program providing personal toiletries to guests who forgot their own. The Holiday Inn boasts an outdoor Olympic-size swimming pool and the Glass Garden Restaurant and Lounge next door.

Howard Johnson Plaza Hotel and Conference Center
$$-$$$$ • 5032 Market St., Wilmington • 392-1101, (800) 833-4721

A full-service hotel offering expanded amenities such as in-room coffee makers, the Plaza is 3 miles from downtown and 7 miles from Wrightsville Beach. It is especially well-suited to corporate travelers, having courtesy airport transportation, telephone/computer jacks in all 124 guest rooms, available office equipment and meeting facilities to accommodate up to 500 people. Guests may also avail themselves of the indoor heated pool and whirlpool, sauna, fitness center, laundry and valet service and premium cable TV. The hotel has electronic card lock room keys, three suites and Rigby's Restaurant and Lounge adjoining the main building.

The Inn at St. Thomas Court
$$$-$$$$ • 101 S. Second St., Wilmington • 343-1800, (800) 525-0909

The St. Thomas is a beautifully designed and sophisticated 34-unit accommodation just two blocks from the Cape Fear River. The forthright decor of the rooms ranges from country

French and Southwestern to antebellum and embraces tasteful artwork, replica antique furnishings, handsome rugs over wide-planked floors and modern conveniences. Continental breakfast baskets are delivered to your door at a time you request. Some rooms are fully equipped with kitchenettes, wet bars and washer/dryers and are suitable for long stays. Some rooms have microwave ovens. Second-floor terraces have comfortable chairs for each room. Ample off-street parking is available. The attentive staff will help arrange tee times and assist with planning recreational activities. Office services such as fax and photocopying are available, and rooms are equipped with computer data ports.

Live Oaks Bed & Breakfast
$$ • 318 S. Third St., Wilmington • 762-6733, (888) 762-6732

Live Oaks effectively combines Victorian decor and various relaxing settings with its convenient downtown location. The clapboard Queen Anne structure, the Burris-Poisson House (1883), features beautiful Stick Style (a.k.a. Carpenter Gothic) detailing and numerous places to kick back, including furnished wraparound porches, front and back, and a walled garden with shade trees, pergola, a hammock and benches. Best of all is the water garden with gurgling falls and a pond. The inn's three guest rooms range from intimate to spacious. The Garden Room has a private

entrance off the rear second-story porch. All rooms are furnished with antiques and queen-size beds and feature private baths, central air conditioning and fireplaces. The living room, in addition to its Victorian seating and lace curtains, is graced by bright 11-foot windows, a classic Weaver organ, gramophone and crystal chandelier. The library's handsome 8-foot French doors open upon an enclosed sun porch — ideal for sunsets. Furnishings in the dining room include velvet-upholstered chairs you may recognize from the locally-shot movie, *The Road to Wellville*. Innkeepers Margi and Doug Erickson serve homemade breakfasts over china and unique pressed-glass goblets. Let them know in advance if you have any special dietetic needs. Amenities include laundry service, airport pick-up and drop-off by arrangement, TV in the library, complimentary refreshments and snacks, and a guest refrigerator upstairs. A one-night's deposit is required for reservations. Ask about corporate rates.

Ramada Inn Conference Center
$$-$$$ • 5001 Market St., Wilmington • 799-1730

Full services and affordability make the Ramada an excellent choice for businesspeople and tourists alike. Situated about midway between downtown Wilmington and Wrightsville Beach, the 100-room establishment provides top-notch amenities in keeping with corporate-chain standards. These in-

clude airport transportation, room service, valet and laundry service, cable TV and an outdoor pool. An executive suite features a board room with a refrigerator and wet bar, conference table and adjoining rooms. The Ramada can accommodate banquets for up to 400 people. There is no charge for children younger than 18 staying with parents. The adjoining nightclub is among Wilmington's more popular, featuring Top 40 dance music and shagging. The adjoining restaurant serves breakfast, lunch and dinner. The club and restaurant are open every day. Reservations may be made through a central booking service at (800) 228-2828.

The River Inn
$-$$$ • 314 S. Front St., Wilmington • 763-4891

Among Wilmington's premier bed and breakfast inns, The River Inn is among the few directly overlooking the Cape Fear River. Proprietor Jenny McKinnon Wright has endowed her magnificent turreted Queen Anne home (built 1899) with unvarying elegance without forgoing comfort. Full silver-service breakfasts bring a cosmopolitan flair to Southern-style cooking, with such homemade treats as sweet potato breads, superb frittatas and specially blended coffees. Of particular interest are the inn's convenient downtown location, its back porch with an excellent river view and the exquisite period furnishings, including some art

deco pieces, an 1860s crystal chandelier, a magnificent open staircase, original parquet floors and leaded glass. Each of the inn's three rooms features a private bath, a fireplace and antiques. The room occupying the turret has an antique pencil-post tester bed. Two adjoining rooms with river views may serve as a suite. The River Inn's ambiance is sociable, bright and never too refined for guests to congregate in the kitchen to share conversation and refreshments. Cancellations require a three-day notice.

Rosehill Inn Bed and Breakfast
$$$-$$$$ • 114 S. Third St., Wilmington • 815-0250, (800) 815-0250

The elegant Rosehill Inn takes its place among the most exclusive bed and breakfast inns anywhere. It's a luxurious getaway as appropriate to corporate travelers as to honeymooners. The faithfully restored classic Greek Revival home, the Savage-Bacon House (1848), is tastefully adorned with fine antiques and period wall coverings. It features a wraparound front porch, a magnificent pulpit staircase and large gardens with columned pergola. The inn has six guest rooms, each with its own fireplace (nonfunctioning), a writing desk, bathrobes and a private bath. The Heritage Room boasts a New Orleans gate bed made from antique cast-iron fence parts. The Wedgewood Room echoes the design of the fine china of the same name. Morning coffee

service, use of bicycles, beverage service in the two parlors and nightly turndown service with a cordial and sweets are provided. Breakfasts offer such delights as crab rarebit and morning sherbet. The Rosehill Inn stands three blocks from the Cape Fear River.

Taylor House Inn
Bed and Breakfast
$$ • 14 N. Seventh St., Wilmington
• 763-7581, (800) 382-9982

This home's unassuming exterior conceals an interior of surprising grandeur. The Taylor House (1905) is blessed with vast ceilings, enormous rooms, rich oak woodwork, parquet floors, 10 fireplaces and a magnificent open staircase. Downstairs, a library and separate parlor offer ample room to relax. Formal breakfasts are by candlelight, served on handpainted china and crystal stemware. The five guest rooms are carefully appointed, each with a private bath, period furnishings and phones. One room features a canopied bed. Television is available upon request. Cancellations require 72-hour notice, and children are allowed only by previous arrangement.

Convenient to all of downtown Wilmington, the Taylor House is on a brick-paved street just off Market Street.

The Verandas
$$$-$$$$ • 202 Nun St., Wilmington
• 251-2212

For its sheer grandeur and balance of luxury and comfort, The Verandas is a premier bed and breakfast inn. Its elegance is never off-putting, thanks to proprietors who are affable and laid-back, and the price is a good value for such opulence. The Verandas occupies the Beery mansion (1853), just three blocks from the river in the quiet historic district. It is a massive, white clapboard edifice with four inviting verandas (porches, if you will), an oval garden terrace and screened breakfast patio. Enormous parlors downstairs, with tall pocket windows, 12½-foot ceilings and chandeliers, are meticulously decorated, but not overdone, and full of light. Original artwork abounds. Most of the eight, enormous guest rooms are designed after world-famous hotel suites. Some rooms are as large as 400 square feet. All are corner rooms with

INSIDERS' TIP

New residents of the Topsail-Holly Ridge area can get to know their new hometown by contacting the Topsail Area Newcomers Network (TANN), a year-round group organized by the Topsail Chamber of Commerce, 328-4722.

fireplaces, individual climate control, desk, telephone with modem jack, TV-VCR, sitting area and private bath. The bathrooms are all spacious and have wainscoting, supplemental heat and night lights. Some rooms upstairs have views of nothing but rooftops and tall chimneys or centuries-old treetops. Most beds are new kings and queens of classic design. The nautically designed Boat House Room features twins. A unique attraction is the cupola, high above the city, for an unbroken daytime view or evening toast.

Each morning, fresh coffee is placed in the upstairs hallways. Breakfasts, typically including fruits, baked goods, juices and a hearty main course, may be enjoyed on the patio or terrace in warm weather. Meals are served on tapestry placemats, silverware and crystal. With advance notice, special dietary needs can be accommodated. Stays at the Verandas require two-night minimums on festival weekends and holidays. Corporate discounts apply, and personal checks are welcomed.

Wilmington Hilton
$$$ • 301 N. Water St., Wilmington
• 763-5900, (800) 445-8667

Situated on the Riverwalk, the Hilton is one of downtown Wilmington's premier full-service hotels and corporate meeting centers, with 178 guest rooms, half of which overlook the river. There is no charge for children, regardless of age, who share rooms with their parents. The Hilton's new Poolside & Cabana Bar, complete with ceiling fans and palm trees, is a great place for a sunset cocktail, and on Friday evenings in the summer the pool deck is the scene of the Sunset Celebration, a popular live-music party. On the concierge level, complimentary beverages are served to guests in the evening and continental breakfasts in the morning. Compton's on the Riverwalk is a fine restaurant and lounge serving grilled steaks, seafood and Sunday brunch. The fitness room and poolside Jacuzzi are popular. Eleven meeting rooms, including the Grand Ballroom, can accommodate up to 600 persons with food service. Courtesy vans provide

Photo: Scott Taylor

A flock of pelicans practices takeoffs and landings.

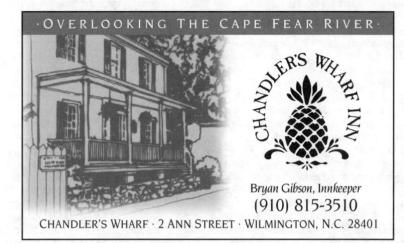

complimentary airport transportation, and if you're arriving by boat, call well in advance to arrange docking out front.

The Wine House
$$ • 311 Cottage Ln., Wilmington
• 763-0511

Perhaps Wilmington's most unusual bed and breakfast inn, the Wine House (the Levi-Hart wine house, to be exact) looks just as you might expect a wine house dating from about 1863 to look. It's a rustic, two-room clapboard building with shuttered windows, standing apart from the owner's residence behind a brick-walled courtyard. Its location on an easy-to-miss lane lends the Wine House an out-of-the-way feeling, right in the heart of downtown Wilmington. Each room is furnished with antiques, a wet bar, a queen-size bed and refrigerator and is blessed with heart-pine floors, a private bath and a fireplace. Breakfasts are continental. Bicycles are available for exploring the city.

The Worth House
$$ • 412 S. Third St., Wilmington
• 762-8562, (800) 340-8559

Francie and John Miller's bed and breakfast inn is a scrupulously restored Queen Anne-style turreted house with a wraparound front porch and a tastefully simple interior that includes a library and parlor. Television is available in the sitting rooms. Special touches include private baths, working fireplaces in most rooms, the accessibility of fax and modem hookups, a laundry room, a large backyard and an ongoing jigsaw puzzle. Breakfasts are hearty and homemade and may be enjoyed in some rooms or on the second-floor porch. Most of the seven guest rooms are large, and beds are classic including four-poster, antique queen-size and king-size plantation beds. Ask about the Azalea Room with its glassed-in veranda or the Hibiscus Room with its sitting room nestled in the corner turret. There is also a two-room upstairs suite with a TV room, perfect for families or groups. Beverages are available to guests all day. The Worth House welcomes children older than 8. Ask about special seasonal and three- to five-night packages.

Wrightsville Beach

Blockade Runner Resort Hotel
$$$$ • 275 Waynick Blvd., Wrightsville Beach • 256-2251, (800) 541-1161

The Blockade Runner is a top-quality oceanfront resort. All 150 rooms have water views, either oceanfront or soundside, some with balconies. Also included are refrigerator, coffee maker, hair dryer, plush bathrobes, an iron and ironing board. Amenities include beach furniture for guests, a health spa and the fine Ocean Terrace Restaurant (see the Restaurants chapter), which has a wide ocean view and hosts the Comedy Zone on Thursday evenings May through September (see the Nightlife chapter). The oceanside deck features a patio bar adjoining the heated indoor/outdoor pool. Room service and bicycles are available, tennis courts are nearby (the hotel provides shuttles) and a sailing center on Banks Channel offers watercraft rentals and lessons for which packages can be arranged. Children's Sand Camper programs and golf packages are also offered, and children younger than 12 stay free when with parents. Conference facilities and banquet services can accommodate up to 400 people. A complementary airport limousine is available, and corporate rates are available all year. For a change of pace, inquire about The Cottage, a 13-room, full-service lodging next door that offers room service, spacious porches and all the amenities of the Blockade Runner.

Carolina Temple Apartments
$-$$, no credit cards • 550 Waynick Blvd., Wrightsville Beach • 256-2773

This is the kind of beach-cottage accommodation our parents remember from their childhood. Carolina Temple Apartments consists of two historic plantation-style cottages built by the Temple family just after the turn of the century. The property runs from the sound side of the island to the ocean, yet the buildings are set back like a well-kept secret. Steve and Mary Wright are third-generation owners of the inn, which was once Station 6 along the Wrightsville Beach trolley line (ask to see the old photos), and the pride with which they run the place is evident everywhere. Steve calls the place a "generational" destination — a family tradition among vacationers who often reserve the same room every visit. Both buildings are classics: central hallways; spacious, breezy, wraparound porches furnished with large rockers and the occasional well-placed hammock; high sun

deck overlooking the ocean; louvered outer doors to each of the sixteen apartments. Rooms are not large but are beautifully maintained, comprising one-, two- and three-room air-conditioned suites with private baths, ceiling fans and fully equipped kitchenettes. Carolina Temple is perfect for couples and families (up to six people). The decor is tropical with luminous beach colors and folksy Caribbean-style artwork. A shaded, dune-front patio, curtained in inclement weather and surrounded by palms and oleander, is a cool place to relax, and there's a communal TV room with a video library the youngsters will enjoy. Rentals from June through August mostly require a one-week minimum (Sunday to Sunday), but split weeks sometimes become available. In spring and autumn, split weeks are always available, and the inn closes during the winter months. Compared to the beach's average nightly rates, Carolina Temple Apartments is an excellent bargain. Extras include a small soundside beach perfect for toddlers, laundry facility, shaded sand box, complimentary morning coffee, soundside docking facilities, library, free parking, cribs and weekend continental breakfasts during spring and fall. Note that, although bed linens are always provided, towels are extra during the summer.

Holiday Inn SunSpree
Resort Wrightsville Beach
$-$$$$ • 1706 N. Lumina Ave., Wrightsville Beach • 256-2231, (800) 532-5362

Key to this resort is a selection of entertainment options for adults and children, including Laff Trax (a live comedy club), karaoke, recreational activities and live outdoor music monthly during the summer. The Guest Activities Center can set you up with bicycles, tennis, waterway cruises and tee times. The KidSpree Vacation Club, for kids ages 4 to 12, offers an oceanfront playground, seasonal supervised activities and a dedi-

Photo: Curtis Krueger

This great white heron is waiting on breakfast.

cated kids' room. Every guest room has at least a partial ocean view, plus microwave, refrigerator, coffee maker, hair dryer and data port phones. The resort's pool (the island's largest) adjoins both the Shades Bar & Grill and the ocean. You may dine at the Beach Club & Cafe, and there's also a convenient market-delicatessen. Children younger than 18 stay free when they share a room with their parents. Children also eat free, with some restrictions. The SunSpree Resort offers discounts and special programs for senior citizens and business travelers, expanded conference and meeting facilities and complimentary airport transportation. Call ahead for information on availability, as the reopening of this resort after Hurricane Fran has been severely delayed.

Summer Sands Motel
$-$$$$ • 104 S. Lumina Ave., Wrightsville Beach • 256-4175, (800) 336-4849

This comfortable 32-suite efficiency motel sits in the heart of "downtown" Wrightsville Beach within a short walk of restaurants, shopping, laundry facilities and the strand, and rooms are ideal for two adults and two kids. Guest rooms have balconies, queen-size beds and queen-size sofabeds, and the rooms facing Banks Channel provide the better view, especially at sunset. The outdoor pool is available during the summer. Monthly stays are available off-season only (November through March).

Surf Suites
$$$$ • 711 S. Lumina Ave., Wrightsville Beach • 256-2275

Calling itself the first and largest "motelminium" on the island and open year round, the Surf offers 46 resort-quality suites with separate bedrooms, a full bath, dining areas, queen-size sleeper sofas, cable TV, telephones and private oceanfront balconies. Amenities include an outdoor pool and sun deck, full maid and linen service. Commercial rates are available, and there is a $10 fee for each additional guest.

Carolina Beach and Kure Beach

Atlantic Towers
$-$$$$ • 1615 S. Lake Park Blvd., Carolina Beach • 458-8313, (800) BEACH-40

This newly refurbished 11-story establishment offers comfortable (if somewhat small) condominium suites with separate bedrooms and full kitchens. Each suite accommodates six to eight guests. All 137 condos are oceanfront, and each has a telephone, cable TV, a private balcony, an exterior terrace entrance, maid service and elevator service. The outdoor pool deck is in view of the ocean and stands beside a gazebo — a perfect place for a picnic.

Beach Harbour Resort
$$$-$$$$ • 302 Canal Dr., Carolina Beach • 458-4185, 458-8667

Consisting of privately owned time-shares, Beach Harbor invites short-term guests to its clean one- and two-bedroom suites. Rooms vary, but each has a balcony, living and dining areas, a full kitchen, cable TV, a sleeper sofa and a washer and dryer. Local calls are free. The resort has an outdoor pool, and most parking is shaded. Beach Harbour is directly across from Harbor Master's Restaurant & Lounge and the Carolina Beach Marina. Call ahead for information on availability.

The Beacon House Inn Bed and Breakfast
$-$$ • 715 Carolina Beach Ave. N., Carolina Beach • 458-6244, 458-7322

Way back when, the builders got this one right: central breezeways on each floor, running from oceanside balcony to soundside balcony, permit the coastal breezes to cool the building all day. The interior has a country-home atmosphere, with a downstairs common room with a fireplace. The nine nonsmoking guest rooms have Queen Anne decor, including cheval mirrors, and are decorated with a lighthouse theme. Rooms are equipped with ceiling fans and paired doors, one of each being louvered to take advantage of that hallway breeze. There is one bath for every two rooms. Full country breakfasts include homemade breads and jams and may be taken on the upstairs balcony overlooking the ocean. A separate cottage with a full kitchen is available by the week and accommodates up to eight people. (Breakfast is not included in cottage rental.) Children are welcome at the cottages. Beacon House is a block from the ocean between Carolina Beach's two fishing piers. The innkeepers also offer dinner, assistance arranging recreational packages and plenty of hospitality. Pets are not permitted.

Cabana De Mar Motel
$$-$$$ • 31 Carolina Ave. N., Carolina Beach • 458-4456, (800) 333-8499

One of the most attractive and well-appointed motel accommodations in Carolina Beach, Cabana De Mar resembles a condominium complex more than a motel. Its 71 condominium suites (one to three bedrooms) are small yet pleasant, with cable TV, elevator access and daily housekeeping service. Some rooms face the ocean and have modest private balconies. Streetside suites are the best value. Laundry rooms are available, but some rooms are equipped with washer/dryers. The motel is within a short walk of central Carolina Beach's attractions and restaurants.

King's Motel
$-$$$ • 318 Carolina Beach Ave. N., Carolina Beach • 458-5594

Highly practical, if not aesthetically sophisticated, King's rooms include basic motel lodgings as well as fully equipped efficiencies (there is no division between the twin double beds and the kitchen area in the efficiencies). All are well-maintained and sanitary and include cable TV, air conditioning and heat, dinettes and a full bath. Many of the 42 rooms (distributed in three buildings) have ocean views and balconies. One building is a duplex cottage suitable for up to seven and eight guests in respective apartments. The oceanside pool is equipped with a slide.

Paradise Inn
$-$$$ • 310 Carolina Beach Ave. N., Carolina Beach • 458-8264

The Paradise is a good bargain with a great location just yards from the surf. Forty-three

Photo: Scott Taylor

North Carolina's southern coast offers magnificent scenery.

units include singles, doubles, efficiencies and three-bedroom cottages complete with a pool, oceanfront breezeway with lounge chairs, outdoor grills and cable TV. The Paradise is within walking distance of downtown Carolina Beach and all the attractions and restaurants to be found there.

Surfside Motor Lodge

$-$$$ • 234 Carolina Beach Ave. N., Carolina Beach • 458-8338

Situated just steps from the beach and one block from the amusements of the Carolina Beach boardwalk, this 80-unit complex offers a variety of accommodations ranging from singles to separate three-bedroom cottages, all with full baths (two baths in the larger units). Two pools are a big plus, as are the outdoor grills, cable TV and oceanfront views. The Surfside offers a good balance among convenience, amenities and price.

Docksider Inn-Oceanfront

$$-$$$ • 202 N. Ft. Fisher Blvd., Kure Beach • 458-4200

This establishment may seem unassuming on the outside, but it's shipshape inside and one of the finest choices for lodging on Pleasure Island. Specially tailored to romantic getaways, the Docksider has 34 clean, mod-

est units, oceanfront and ocean view, almost half of which are efficiencies that include full-size refrigerators. The Captain's Cabins are oceanfront rooms featuring "breakfast in bed" extras (gourmet delights and snacks), VCR, wet bar, coffee maker, toaster and more. The Docksider has a pool with an elevated deck and its own "Sunketch," a high, secluded deck that's perfect for viewing sunsets, all just steps away from the blue Atlantic. The inn offers AARP discounts to seniors 55 and older for midweek stays year-round. Inquire about other midweek discounts as well. On weekends during the high season, two-night minimums apply. Pets are not allowed. The Docksider Inn is just north of K Street in downtown Kure Beach.

Ocean Princess Inn

$$-$$$ • 824 Fort Fisher Blvd., Kure Beach • 458-6712

Ocean Princess Inn is ideally suited to the romantic adult getaway: peaceful, secluded, close by the Fort Fisher State Historic Site and State Recreation Area and graced with every modern amenity, now including a small bar with all ABC permits. Set far back from the road amid windswept live oaks, the inn is a beachy establishment with high decks that offer ocean views. Each guest room features a choice between breakfast basket (a complimentary continental selection) and full breakfast, plus private entrances, TV, coffee maker, refrigerator, microwave and telephone. Six rooms offer Jacuzzis, one of which is on the deck outdoors with an ocean view. A mini-suite is handicapped accessible. Guests can gather in the large, comfortable downstairs den with fireplace. Original local artwork adorns the building. A major attraction is the in-ground heated pool, complete with cabana, Jacuzzi and hot-and-cold showers. The Ocean Princess can accommodate small functions plus conferences of up to 24 people. The inn does not accept pets (the innkeepers have their own) or children, and smoking is restricted to the outdoors.

Seven Seas Inn
$$-$$$ • 130 Ft. Fisher Blvd., Kure Beach • 458-8122

The Seven Seas is a family-oriented establishment still in prime form. Comprised of three buildings — oceanfront, ocean view and pool view — Seven Seas has 32 clean, comfortable rooms in a variety of configurations. Large efficiencies and motel accommodations are roomy and equipped with double beds, telephones, cable TV, individually controlled air conditioning and heat and microwave ovens. The well-kept grounds include fine pool facilities with a shaded cabana, benches and beautiful cactus beds, and a bait and tackle shop. Children will appreciate the game room. When entering Kure Beach by the main road, which is Second Avenue (U.S. 421), look for the enormous agave plant on the ocean side of the road.

Bald Head Island

Theodosia's Bed and Breakfast
$$$-$$$$ • Harbour Village • 457-6563, (800) 656-1812

This, the island's first bed and breakfast inn, is of a quality one expects at Bald Head and occupies an imposing gabled, modern Victorian structure near the marina. The decor and size of the 10 carefully appointed rooms are diverse, variously incorporating floral and Virgin Island motifs, queen-size and double beds, and wrought-iron and wood detailing.

Everywhere there are porches or balconies offering spectacular views of the harbor, river or island marshes. All rooms have private baths (one with Jacuzzi) or showers, cable TV and telephones. The ground-floor guest room is handicapped-accessible. Two rooms occupy the adjoining Carriage House. Innkeepers Lydia and Frank Love formally serve full breakfasts to guests' individual tables. Meals vary in accent among English, Smoky Mountain and Mexican, with local coastal touches as well. Nightly or weekly stays include plenty of little extras such as refreshments, evening desserts and complimentary golf carts and bicycles (Bald Head Island's only permitted mechanized transportation). The inn was named in honor of the daughter of America's most famous duelist, Aaron Burr. She disappeared off the North Carolina coast in 1812 and her ghost is said to fancy Bald Head Island these days. Children may find Theodosia's formality uncomfortable. It is a nonsmoking establishment, and a seven-day cancellation notice is requested.

Southport-Oak Island

Lois Jane's Riverview Inn
$$ • 106 W. Bay St., Southport • 457-6701, (800) 457-1152

Directly overlooking the mouth of the Cape Fear River near the old harbor pilot's tower, this beautifully restored 1892 home has been owned by only one family since its construction. It is a quiet getaway within easy walking distance of Southport's restaurants, river walk, shops and museum. It is currently the only bed and breakfast accommodation in Southport. Porches on the river side of the building are ideal for rocking away the time. Two rooms with private baths and two with a shared bath have queen-size, four-poster beds and period furnishings that have been part of the home for years. The rooms to the front of the building have beautiful river views, and one room has its own entrance to the communal upstairs porch. Full breakfasts, including homemade breads and muffins, are served daily in the dining room, and afternoon hors d'oeuvres and evening sweets are additional touches. Special breakfast arrangements can

Theodosia's
A Bed & Breakfast
Harbour Village
Bald Head Island, North Carolina

A Quality Concept for Bald Head Island

The elegantly appointed, ten room, Theodosia's Bed & Breakfast located in the marina on magical Bald Head Island is your destination by passenger ferry from Southport, North Carolina.

French doors, decks and porches will allow you to enjoy the views of the ocean, rivers, marshes, creeks and the maritime forest. Relax with modern conveniences of private baths, cable TV, and telephones. Attention to details such as varied full breakfasts, complimentary wine and appetizers, golf carts for transportation and bikes are provided with every room to enhance your stay. Golfing, tennis, a swimming pool, croquet court, full dining and bar priviledges are available at our elegant club!

Web Site: http://www.southport.net/theodosia.html

Reservations:
1(800) 656-1812
1(910)-457-6563

be made with advance notice. Coffee is placed in the hallway outside the guest rooms each morning, and a small refrigerator is available there with beverages and snacks. Cancellations require at least 24-hour notice for refunds.

Riverside Motel
$ • 103 W. Bay St., Southport • 457-6986

This small eight-room establishment commands an excellent waterfront view of Southport's harbor with Bald Head Island to the left and Fort Caswell to the right. Situated between the Ships Chandler Restaurant and the Cape Fear Pilot Tower, the Riverside is one of Southport's three multiple-unit accommodations downtown. The cozy double-occupancy rooms are equipped with two double beds, microwave ovens, cable TV, refrigerators, coffee makers, toasters and telephones (local calls are free). The rooms are small and well-kept, and nearly everything in Southport is a short walk away.

Sea Captain Motor Lodge
$ • 608 W. West St., Southport • 457-5263

The Sea Captain, near the Southport Marina, is the largest motel in Southport. Each of the 96 units is modern, well-kept and equipped with a refrigerator, a telephone and a TV. Accommodations include single motel rooms, efficiencies and two-room efficiency apartments with separate sleeping areas. An Olympic-size outdoor pool and shaded gazebo are centrally located among the lodge's four buildings, and there are two adjoining dining facilities: the Sea Captain Restaurant for breakfast and lunch and the Harbourside Lounge for dinner (see our Restaurants chapter.)

Ocean Crest Motel
$-$$ • 1411 E. Beach Dr., Long Beach • 278-3333

Since Wade Goin took ownership of this venerable establishment, it has blossomed to become one of the premier oceanfront

motels in Long Beach. Streetside rooms for up to four guests each offer the best value. All oceanfront rooms feature private balconies, and you can choose between one- and two-bedroom units with kitchenettes or efficiencies. The carpeted rooms are clean and bright and tastefully furnished. All are equipped with individually controlled air conditioning and heat, cable TV and private telephones. The Ocean Crest adjoins the fishing pier of the same name and the Windjammer Restaurant. The complex includes a handsome oceanfront townhouse on the premises with a gas fireplace, two private balconies, a full kitchen, two bedrooms, laundry facilities and two and a half baths.

Driftwood Motel
$ • 604 Ocean Dr., Yaupon Beach • 278-6114

This attractive two-story motel has an oceanfront location, an outdoor pool, laundry facilities, outdoor grills and picnic tables, plus a refrigerator, a telephone and cable TV in every room, all at a reasonable cost. The second-floor verandas provide wonderful views, especially at sunset, and are equipped with deck chairs and tables for relaxing in the ocean breeze. Recently remodeled, the Driftwood offers neat, carpeted rooms, each with its own air conditioning and heat, and a full kitchen is available for all guests to share. Adjoining the kitchen is an outdoor play area for children. The Driftwood is open year round.

Island Resort
$-$$ • 500 Ocean Dr., Yaupon Beach • 278-5644

This motel resort provides at least partial ocean views from most of its neatly kept rooms, plus the option of a freshwater pool and outdoor hot tub. There are 10 motel rooms and 11 efficiency apartments consisting of one or two bedrooms and mini-kitchens. Amenities include laundry facilities, an oceanside gazebo with grills and a private beach access. The Island Resort is open all year.

South Winds Motel
$-$$ • 700 Ocean Dr., Yaupon Beach
• 278-5442

Including singles, doubles and efficiency suites, the accommodations are comfortable at South Winds, an older, well-run operation. It is ideally situated across the street from the beach strand, the Yaupon Beach Fishing Pier and two restaurants. Rooms are quaint and equipped with cable TV, air conditioning and a telephone. The larger accommodations have fully equipped kitchens, sleeper sofas and double beds. Roll-aways are available at a small cost. A cabana adjoins the pool, and an outdoor grill and picnic area are nearby.

South Brunswick Islands

Breakfast Creek Bed & Breakfast
$ • 4361 Ocean Breeze Ave. S.W., Shallotte • 754-3614

With a veranda overlooking the Atlantic at Shallotte Inlet, Breakfast Creek Bed & Breakfast is a contemporary home within minutes of Holden and Ocean Isle beaches. The home sits on 1½ acres of landscaped property filled with live oaks and gardens and bordering a wildlife-filled salt marsh. Marinas on the Intracoastal Waterway are a short walk away, and charter fishing and golf courses are available close by. Two rooms and a suite, all with private baths, are equipped with central air conditioning, ceiling fans and TV. Breakfast Creek is a good, affordable option for those who don't mind not being directly on the beach.

Crescent Moon Inn
$-$$ • 965 Sabbath Home Rd. S.W., Holden Beach • 842-1190

This modern bed and breakfast inn is only 1.5 miles from Holden Beach, and the owners have arranged for guest parking at the beach at no additional cost. Add to this the proximity to the area's dozens of golf courses and easy access to both Wilmington and Myrtle Beach. Crescent Moon Inn is a large white-brick building with a rear deck shaded by tall sycamore, curly-bark birch, apple and pear trees. Guests

are welcome to use the screened-in outdoor Jacuzzi. Flower and herb beds are carefully tended. The decor is attractive and casual, full of earth tones and pastels, fiber rugs, wicker and rattan. Breakfasts range from continental to homemade baked goods, juices and cereals. Beverages and snacks are available all day. The guest rooms have peaked ceilings with beams and skylights and are furnished with king-size, queen-size and twin beds. Two nights minimum are required for stays from June through August and during festival weekends and holidays. Smoking is restricted to the outdoors, and because the proprietors have pets of their own, guest pets are not allowed. Sabbath Home Road runs nearly parallel to the Intracoastal Waterway, about 8 miles south of U.S. Highway 17. Holden Beach Road (N.C .130) from Shallotte, Mt. Pisgah Road or Stone Chimney Road will get you there from Highway 17. Crescent Moon Inn's circular driveway is directly opposite the entrance to the Sea Trace development.

Gray Gull Motel
$ • 3263 Holden Beach Rd. S.W., Holden Beach • 842-6775

Don't be fooled by the low rates. This family-owned motel, the only one at Holden Beach, is very well-maintained and courteously run. Each of the 17 carpeted rooms has cable TV and a telephone as well as easy access to the outdoor pool and picnic tables. The Gray Gull is on the mainland side of the Intracoastal Waterway, just minutes from the beach. The office is in the hardware store next door, where anglers can also buy tackle. Cancellations require 24 hours' notice.

Cooke's Inn Motel
$ • 12 Causeway Dr., Ocean Isle Beach • 579-9001

Cooke's has 35 very clean rooms (three handicapped accessible) with individual air conditioning and heat, twin and double beds, telephones, refrigerators and cable TV. The outdoor pool and sun deck are close to the parking lot, but with the beach only 200 yards away, they aren't the No. 1 attractions anyway. Cooke's, family owned and operated, is also convenient to dining and entertainment, some of which are within walking distance.

Goose Creek Bed & Breakfast

$-$$$ • 1901 Egret St. SW, Ocean Isle Beach • 754-5849, (800) 275-6540

If being eight minutes (a half-mile) from the beach isn't a deterrent, this bed and breakfast inn on the mainland side of the Intracoastal Waterway could be just the lodging you're looking for. Reasonably priced, with family-style breakfast included (homemade baked goods, cereals, juices, coffee), this establishment offers comfortable, large bedrooms, more than 2,000 square feet of outdoor decking and central air in a nonsmoking contemporary beach home within earshot of the ocean surf. There is also a pier from which you can fish. Guests tend to prefer having breakfast on the screened porch overlooking Goose Creek. The four guest rooms are on the third floor, seemingly nestled among the trees, and can be configured as suites with private or shared bathrooms. Goose Creek Bed & Breakfast is within minutes of Brunswick County's numerous golf courses and the many restaurants of Calabash and is nearly equidistant from Wilmington and Myrtle Beach, South Carolina. Note that the proprietors own two well-behaved golden retrievers. Cancellations within 10 days of your stay are subject to a $10 service fee, and no refunds are made for cancellations within 48 hours of your scheduled arrival. Guests without reservations are welcome.

Island Motel

$-$$ • 19 Causeway Dr., Ocean Isle Beach • 579-6019

Above the offices of Island Realty, the Island Motel consists of 10 simple and neat double-occupancy rooms and two two-room suites. Each has air conditioning, a view of the waterway, a TV and telephone. Boat slips out back are also available to guests and give access to the Intracoastal Waterway. An adjoining grocery and supply store (it carries fishing tackle), gas station and the Plaza Marina make the Island Motel about as convenient as anything one could hope for.

Ocean Isle Inn

$$-$$$ • 37 W. First St., Ocean Isle Beach • 579-0750, (800) 352-5988

This 70-room inn features private oceanfront balconies and tranquil soundside views of the marshes and Intracoastal Waterway. The outdoor pool and deck overlook the ocean and have access to the beach; bathers can use the indoor heated pool and hot tub all year long. The carpeted rooms are carefully maintained and handsome. Each is equipped with a refrigerator, cable TV and a telephone, and daily maid service is provided. Some rooms connect. Handicapped facilities and elevators are also available. Guests are entitled to complimentary continental breakfasts and can purchase golf packages offering a choice of play on more than 65 area courses. The Ocean Isle Inn's conference space offers quiet, off-the-beaten-path facilities for business meetings. Be sure to inquire about midweek Supersavers during the off-season, weekly rates, and AAA and AARP discounts.

The Winds Oceanfront Clarion Inn

$$-$$$$ • 310 E. First St., Ocean Isle Beach • 579-6275, (800) 334-3581

This oceanfront resort is an excellent choice for its range of accommodations and prices. Studios, mini-suites, deluxe rooms, one- and two-bedroom suites and separate

houses are all richly appointed and comfortable. Many have indoor whirlpools, and all have kitchen facilities. The grounds are fastidiously landscaped to resemble the tropics with palms, banana trees and flowering plants nestling a series of boardwalks and decks. The heated outdoor pool is enclosed in winter. Choose among a sauna, outdoor Jacuzzi, exercise room, beach bocci, shuffleboard, volleyball and, nearby, tennis to pass the time. In summer, sailboat and bike rentals are available on the premises. Honeymoon and golf packages (available at 90 championship courses) are easily arranged. Some rooms are handicapped accessible, and complimentary continental breakfasts are available.

Topsail Island Area

Bed & Breakfast at Mallard Bay
$$ • 960 Mallard Bay Rd., Hampstead
• 270-3363

This contemporary beach-style home is a single-suite inn directly overlooking the Intracoastal Waterway across from Topsail Island. This is the only bed and breakfast inn in the Hampstead area, and is a short ride from the beach, many golf courses, and downtown Wilmington. The large grounds are extremely quiet, the view excellent, and the Harbour Village Marina is within easy walking distance. The two-room suite is upstairs and features a four-poster bed, antiques, full private bath, TV, VCR and a sitting room with a queen-size sofabed — perfect for couples or small families with children older than 12. A spacious, high deck is ideal for sunbathing, and a canoe is available for exploring the waterway. Innkeeper Phoebe Hood serves full country breakfasts on weekends, continental breakfasts on weekdays and complimentary wine and cheese each afternoon. Laundry facilities are available at no extra cost. A seven-day cancellation policy is in effect, and neither pets nor smoking indoors is allowed.

The Jolly Roger Motel
$-$$ • 803 Ocean Blvd., Topsail Beach
• 328-4616, (800) 633-3196

From rooms with one double bed each to apartment suites, the Jolly Roger has a wide variety of room sizes and amenities, which include daily maid service, cable TV, fully equipped kitchens and baths and room-controlled air conditioning. Fully carpeted efficiency apartments and two-room suites also feature sleeper sofas. Rooms on the second and third floors of the large new annex provide the best ocean views and balconies (not private), but rates for rooms facing inland are substantially cheaper. The hotel office is at the Jolly Roger Fishing Pier next door where you can also arrange deep-sea fishing trips.

The Pink Palace of Topsail
$-$$ • 1222 S. Shore Dr., Surf City
• 328-5114

Casual and comfortable, the Pink Palace is an oceanfront bed and breakfast inn offering private beach access, a choice of three open-air decks (one shaded), a screened-in porch ideal for viewing sunsets and an outdoor hot tub with an ocean view accommodating up to eight people. Innkeeper Micki Tucker hosts guests from September through May, and rooms are available by the week during the summer. Four of its five guest rooms, each with playful murals painted by the innkeeper's daughter, open onto a bright living area with a wet bar. Full American breakfasts are served upstairs, where there is also a loft-like reading nook with books. Two-night minimums are requested for weekend stays. The Pink Palace, the only pink building of its size in the area, is 1.5 miles south of the Surf City light, at the intersection of S. Shore Drive and S. Topsail Drive (N.C. 50).

St. Regis Resort
$$$$ • 2000 New River Inlet Rd., N. Topsail Beach • 328-0778, (800) 682-4882

Each of this resort's 224 privately owned units offers ocean-view balconies, two full baths, fully equipped kitchens and washer/dryer facilities. One-, two- and three-bedroom suites are clean and modern, and even the one-bedroom suites can accommodate four people. Some rooms include a Jacuzzi. The resort comprises three tall buildings fronted by a private beach. Two pools are available, one heated and enclosed by a solarium. Whirlpools, a sun deck, a fitness center, tennis courts, a chipping and putting green and volleyball facilities will satisfy almost every style of vacation. There is also a gift shop, The Pavilion, 328-1487, in Building 1. The Resort requires a 30-day notice for cancellations. You'll find New River Inlet Road branching off New River Drive (N.C. 210) before the high-span bridge. Call for information on availability. Tetterton Management Company is the exclusive on-site management for this hotel.

Sea Vista Motel
$$-$$$ • 1521 Ocean Blvd., Topsail Beach • 328-2171, (800) 732-8478

Much of the Sea Vista's business consists of regular guests. Some of the reasons for that may be its quiet location and its large, bright rooms with full-size appliances, cable TV, balconies and individually controlled air conditioning. Within an easy walk are the Topsail Sound fishing pier and a restaurant. Since individual rooms are privately owned and the decor and furnishings vary, repeat guests often request certain rooms. But all 35 rooms are comfortable and clean and were recently refurbished. They consist of eight efficiencies, five mini-efficiencies and two apartments, which do not enjoy a direct ocean view. The honeymoon suite is an efficiency with a private balcony perched atop the center of the oceanfront building. Discounts apply for senior adults and seven-day stays, and children stay free. Pets are allowed with a $20 surcharge. Call for information on availability.

The Topsail Motel
$-$$$ • 1195 N. Anderson Blvd., Topsail Beach • 328-3381, (800) 726-1795

Consisting of one- and two-bed oceanfront rooms with kitchenettes, two- and three-bed efficiency suites and oceanfront apartments

FYI

Unless otherwise noted, the area code for all phone numbers in this guide is 910.

with full kitchens — 30 units in all — the Topsail Motel offers basic motel amenities and a superb dune-front location. Ground-floor rooms have enclosed patios, and second-floor rooms have a deck balcony. Rooms are equipped with cable TV, telephones and individual air conditioning-heating units. The lawn area is a fine vantage point for an ocean view. Weekly rates offering a one-night discount are available. The motel is 5 miles south of the Surf City stoplight. Call for information on availability.

Villa Capriani Resort
$$$$ • 790 New River Inlet Rd., N. Topsail Beach • 328-1900, (800) 934-2400

Reminiscent of the grand resorts of the Riviera, Villa Capriani is a beautifully landscaped complex that offers on-site dining, tennis and entertainment. The building is constructed of sand-colored stucco with terra cotta roofs and archways. Covered balconies overlook a multilevel courtyard featuring three oceanfront pools (including a baby pool), waterfalls, hot tubs and a cabana bar with a fine ocean view. Choose from oceanfront, ocean view and courtyard view (which overlooks the pools and the ocean). Suites with one, two or three bedrooms are available, fully appointed with full kitchens and washers/dryers. Rooms are well-kept, fully carpeted and furnished in contemporary style. Palliotti's Restaurant is off the courtyard opposite a handsome lounge. An on-site activities director sees to it that no guest can justifiably complain of boredom at Villa Capriani. Entertainment options include live outdoor music, karaoke, line dancing and children's programs in summer. Tetterton Management Company is the on-site management company.

Weekly and Long-term Vacation Rentals

There are seemingly endless opportunities for vacation home rentals on the southern coast; from Topsail Island in the north to Sunset Beach in the south, it's safe to say there is a vacation home for any taste and budget. The number of rental offices on the southern coast — nearly 100 — suggests the tremendous scope of the rental business. Whole houses, duplexes, condominiums and apartments are readily available, although early reservations are increasingly advised.

Renting a vacation home is very different from checking into a hotel. There's no room service — a bed left unmade in the morning will still be unmade when you get back from a romp in the surf, and there's no restaurant downstairs to call for room service. You take care of your own needs, which is actually the best part of this kind of beach vacation. It's your schedule and the opportunity to enjoy your own home away from home; to relish the sense of absolute privacy that simply isn't part of the hotel experience.

In most cases, vacation homes are someone's special investment, second only in importance to their regular homes. The owners may visit their homes several times a year, and it is apparent, in many cases, that the homes bear distinct imprints of the owners. There may be photo albums of the host family and guests. There will likely be a guest book for visitors.

Fitting into someone else's second home can be an intimate experience that often leads to friendships between renter and owner. Along with the money that changes hands in this agreement, there is also an exchange of trust. Some of the more desirable homes develop a list of regulars, and getting into line for these can create a bit of a wait. But once on the list in a favorite spot, you'll be able to count on it for many years to come and will be regarded as a member of an extended family you may never actually meet.

Accommodations and Locations

You can have any kind of place you want in a rental — the only limitation is your budget. Large, contemporary homes on private lots, small cottages, ordinary apartments, comfortable condominiums, fishing trailers, middle-class homes and more are available to the renter.

Generally, the closer a place is to the water, the higher its price. The benefits of an oceanfront house or apartment include an unobstructed view of the ocean, a short walk for a swim in the waves and the ability to keep an eye on the kids from the house as they play on the sand.

Oceanside housing may still have a view, and you may not have to cross a road, but there may be a bit of a walk to reach the sea. Several rows back from the ocean, the prices drop. The walk gets longer, and a view of the water is often just a glimpse. These locations generally have decks built on the rooftops, and there seems to be a competition among homeowners to see who can build the highest on some area beaches.

Soundside housing is on the Intracoastal Waterway or along adjacent channels and sounds. If you have a boat and the house has a pier, or if you simply appreciate quiet coastal views, this can be a very exciting location. Soundside housing is a bit more expensive than housing in the center of each island.

If the effects of the hurricanes of 1996 have you wondering about renting a home this season, be assured all of the affected beaches are gearing up for visitors. Topsail Island and Figure Eight Island took the heaviest hits from the storms, and recovery is going to take at least a full season, but, in the words of locals, "the sun, sand and sea are just as much fun as ever." Many homes have not only been repaired, they've been considerably upgraded. However, returning visitors should expect to notice fewer homes on these islands for now.

A Few Rules

It is important to note that vacation home rental entails rules and regulations that reflect the family orientation of this kind of arrangement. The rental agency's primary allegiance is to the homeowner. The agency maintains the properties for the owners and assumes responsibility for renting the homes to reliable tenants.

There is an age requirement for renting most vacation homes through real estate management companies. Generally, the primary renter must be at least 21 years old, although some companies require the primary renter to be 25. An exception to this may involve marital status. If you're younger than 25 and married, you probably qualify, but companies will differ. Individual inquiry is recommended. Some companies that don't have an actual age requirement take a long, hard look at younger customers and make decisions to rent based on what seems to be intuition.

Most rental agreements forbid house parties on the premises, especially in the quieter beach communities. Rowdiness is very much unappreciated on all area beaches, and a noisy party may cause you to forfeit your rental agreement without a refund. Most homes have a written maximum-occupancy regulation, and you are required to honor it.

Pets

Pets are not allowed. If Fido must come with you, ask your rental agent about services of local kennels. Since your pet is not allowed on most beaches in the summer season, you might want to leave him at home in friendly surroundings. Also, please note this region has a seasonal flea problem, which, more than anything else, dictates this policy. As a local Realtor has written in a brochure, "it only takes two fleas" to cause a flea problem in a house. If you smuggle in a pet and the housekeeping staff that follows you discovers fleas, be assured that your deposit will be used to pay for fumigation.

Furnishings and Amenities

In the majority of rental homes, expect to find most of the comforts of home. Most will have air conditioning, full-service kitchens with coffee makers and microwaves, and cable TV. The grander ones are extremely well-appointed with more comfort features than most permanent homes.

In most cases, you'll need to bring a few housekeeping items. Linens may be your responsibility; if the house has linens, you may be required to do a bit of laundry before your departure. Ask your rental agent for good local sources for linen rentals, beach chairs and anything else you think you'll need.

There is a general expectation that you'll leave the house as clean as you found it. Some rental agencies will provide cleaning service and linens for a fee if you are not particularly inclined toward domestic concerns on your getaway. If you don't clean up and haven't made arrangements for maid service, your deposit will be applied toward this work. The minimum charge is $50.

Cleaning supplies are usually already in the house because a prior vacationer bought them and left them there. It's a nice gesture on your part to do the same, even if current supplies seem ample, and it's essential for

you to provide cleaning supplies if some haven't been left for you. Owners supply vacuum cleaners, mops and brooms. You are responsible for putting out the garbage — just like at home. Some beaches have recycling programs, and you'll be instructed in how to participate in the event that yours does.

Most rental homes have telephones, and you're on your honor not to use them in any way for which the owners would be charged. If your vacation home doesn't have a phone, most rental companies will arrange to get emergency messages to you. Of course, the proliferation of mobile phones makes this issue less important.

You'll bring your own groceries into a rental home, and there is an expectation that you'll leave behind the condiments you haven't used. Items that don't perish easily are usually in the cabinets and refrigerator, left by previous occupants. Enjoy them and contribute your own foods to the larder when you leave for the next guests.

Rates

Prices fall in a wide range from $300 to $3,800 a week, depending upon your choice of beach, luxury factor and season. Bald Head Island, Wrightsville Beach and Figure Eight Island are at the high end. Topsail, Carolina Beach and the Brunswick Beaches offer a broader array of less-pricey accommodations but also have their share of high-end properties. Most agencies will require a deposit, and there are various stipulations in the agreement that you need to be familiar with: A state tax of 6 percent and county room tax of 3 percent are added to the cost.

Rental rates are subject to change without notice, and the following rates are only intended as a general guide. Winter rates may be as much as 30 percent less. A deposit of 50 percent is generally required to confirm reservations. Major credit cards are usually accepted, but other methods of payment are available depending upon the agency's policies.

Photo: Curtis Krueger

Enjoy the late-evening waterfront from a historic Bald Head Island cottage.

The following rental agencies are only some of the fine companies from which you may choose. By no means do we include them all, as it would take an entire book to do so. Select the beach of your choice, and contact the area's convention and visitors bureau or local board of Realtors for the names of other rental companies. Chambers of commerce also carry brochures about rental companies — see the Area Overviews chapter for a list of local chambers of commerce.

Rental Agencies

Wrightsville Beach

Fran Brittain Realty
98 Waynick Blvd., Wrightsville Beach
• 256-2224, (800) 362-9031

This company rents homes and condominiums exclusively on Wrightsville Beach.

Bryant Real Estate
1001 N. Lumina Ave., Wrightsville Beach
• 256-3764, (800) 322-3764

This is the oldest vacation rental agency on Wrightsville Beach, and it handles diverse properties ranging from homes to condominiums or duplexes.

Howard, Perry & Walston Better Homes and Gardens
1322 Airlie Rd., Wrightsville Beach
• 256-2181, (800) 529-7653

This company represents numerous properties on the oceanfront, Intracoastal Waterway and surrounding properties on Wrightsville Beach and in Wilmington. Both Atlantic Rentals and Wrightsville Beach Resort Rentals were merged into this rapidly growing company.

Intracoastal Realty Corporation
605 Causeway Dr., Wrightsville Beach
• 256-3780, (800) 346-2463

This company offers about 200 properties, largely upscale but with a few old-style beach cottages, in a mix of condominiums and single-family homes primarily on Wrightsville Beach.

Figure Eight Island

Figure Eight Realty
15 Bridge Rd., Wilmington • 686-4400, (800) 279-6085

Although many Wrightsville Beach Realtors handle rental properties on Figure Eight Island, this is the only company actually on the private island. It handles luxury properties — all single-family homes, overlooking the ocean, sound or marshes.

Photo: N.C. Travel & Tourism

Enjoy the serenity of a stroll along the beaches of the South Brunswick islands.

Carolina and Kure Beaches

Bullard Realty
1404 S. Lake Park Blvd., Carolina Beach
• 458-4028, (800) 327-5863
Bullard Realty, working since 1985 on the island, offers vacation rental condominiums and cottages on Carolina and Kure beaches.

Carolina Beach Realty
307 Lake Park Blvd., Carolina Beach
• 458-4444, (800) 222-9752
These homes and condominiums for rental are in Carolina Beach, Kure Beach and Fort Fisher.

Coastal Condo-Let
1018 N. Lake Park Blvd., Carolina Beach
• 458-4203, (800) 994-5222
Properties range across the island from Carolina Beach in the north to Fort Fisher in the south for this large company that handles condominiums, cottages, apartments and larger homes.

Davies Realty
1009 N. Lake Park Blvd., Carolina Beach
• 458-0444, (800) 685-4614
This company offers largely oceanfront or oceanview condominium rentals from Carolina Beach to Fort Fisher. Rental units at Ocean Dunes include use of an indoor pool and two outdoor pools, tennis courts, basketball courts, indoor sauna and whirlpool. Another condominium complex, Coral Sands, is on the oceanfront and has a pool for guest use.

Gardner Realty
P.O. Box 2125, Carolina Beach • 458-8503, (800) 697-7924
Gardner Realty offers a large selection of rental properties including apartments, condominiums and single-family homes on Carolina Beach, Kure Beach and Fort Fisher.

Lighthouse Realty
201 Fort Fisher Blvd., Kure Beach
• 458-3300
This small real estate company rents both residential and commercial properties on all of Pleasure Island and throughout New Hanover County.

INSIDERS' TIP

The Brunswick beaches run from east to west, so the sun both rises and sets over the ocean.

United Beach Vacations
1001 N. Lake Park Blvd., Carolina Beach
• 458-9073, (800) 334-5806

This large company manages rental units including condominiums and single-family homes on Carolina Beach, Kure Beach and Fort Fisher.

Walker Realty
501 N. Lake Park Blvd., Carolina Beach
• 458-3388

Carolina Beach, Kure Beach and Fort Fisher are the locations of more than 120 properties handled by this company.

Southport, Bald Head Island, Oak Island

Bald Head Island Information Center
5079 Southport Supply Rd., Southport
• (800) 234-1666

At this writing, this pristine island has 100 rental properties. Each rental includes the use of at least one four-passenger electric golf cart for transportation around the island, where cars are not allowed.

Coldwell Banker Southport-Oak Island Realty
300 Country Club Dr., Yaupon Beach
• 278-6011, (800) 243-8132

Weekly resort rentals are available through this large company that manages 400 cottages, duplexes and condominiums on Oak Island.

Red Carpet, Dorothy Essey & Associates Inc., Realtors
6102 E. Oak Island Dr., Long Beach
• 278-RENT, (800) 849-2322

This company offers properties for rental on Oak Island, in Southport and Boiling Spring Lakes.

Margaret Rudd & Associates Inc., Realtors
210 Country Club Dr., Yaupon Beach
• 278-6523, (800) 733-5213

There are 250 rental properties managed by this company on Oak Island, most of which are single-family homes and condominiums. This office is open seven days a week.

Scruggs & Morrison Realty
4324 E. Beach Dr., Long Beach • 278-5405

This company handles single-family homes and duplexes on Oak Island.

There's plenty of opportunity to explore wide open beaches in the Cape Fear Region.

Shannon's Services Inc.
4902 E. Beach Dr., Long Beach • 278-5251
The oldest rental agency on the beach, this company handles rentals of single-family homes and duplexes on Oak Island.

South Brunswick Islands

Atlantic Vacations
Resorts and Real Estate
131 Ocean Blvd. W., Holden Beach
• 842-8000, (800) 252-7000
This company offers vacation rentals of private homes, condominiums and duplexes ranging from two to 10 bedrooms in all locations on Holden Beach.

Brick Landing Plantation
1900 Goose Creek Rd., Ocean Isle Beach
• 754-4373, (800) 438-3006
This resort/golf community offers golf packages that include accommodations, breakfast and green fees for 18 holes. Tennis can be substituted for one round of golf. Rental of condominiums or townhomes includes maid service at departure.

Brunswickland Realty
123 Ocean Blvd., Holden Beach
• 842-6949, (800) 842-6949
In business since the 1970s, this company manages single-family cottages and larger homes.

Island Realty Vacations
19 Causeway Dr., Ocean Isle Beach
• 579-3599, (800) 589-3599
This company offers cottages and condominiums exclusively on Ocean Isle Beach.

Alan Holden Realty
128 Ocean Blvd. W., Holden Beach
• 842-6061, (800) 720-2200
This busy agency manages more than 400 rental properties, mostly cottages and duplexes as well as a few condos, on Holden Beach.

R.H. McClure Realty Inc.
24 Causeway Dr., Ocean Isle Beach
• 579-3586, (800) 332-5476

Single-family homes and duplexes are handled by this company on Ocean Isle Beach.

McMillan Real Estate
113 Causeway Dr., Ocean Isle Beach
• 579-9100, (800) 353-3533

This company rents a full range of houses and condominiums on Ocean Isle Beach.

Ocean 1 Realty
4310 E. Beach Dr., Long Beach • 278-6677, (800) 231-4882

The oldest rental agency on Oak Island, this company has been serving vacation rental

needs for more than 30 years. It offers single-family homes starting at $350 per week.

Sloane Realty
16 Causeway Dr., Ocean Isle Beach
• 579-6216, (800) 843-6044

The largest and oldest vacation rental business on Ocean Isle Beach has condos and cottages available.

Sunset Properties
419 Sunset Blvd., Sunset Beach
• 579-9900, (800) 446-0218 in N.C., (800) 525-0182 outside N.C.

This large company handles the rental of vacation homes and duplexes exclusively on Sunset Beach.

INSIDERS' TIP

Sea oats are beautiful and decorative, but please leave them in the sand — they're important to preserve the beach from erosion, and it's illegal to pick them whether they're dead or alive.

Sunset Vacations
401 S. Sunset Blvd., Sunset Beach • 579-9000, (800) 331-6428

This company offers a wide assortment of attractive single-family homes for rental on Sunset Beach.

Topsail Island

Jean Brown Real Estate
P.O. Box 2367, Surf City • 328-1640, (800) 745-4480

This large residential sales company has been in the vacation rental business for four seasons and offers properties ranging from large, single-family houses to mobile homes. Inquire into its weekend availability program.

Lewis Realty
412 Roland Ave., Surf City • 328-5211, (800) 233-5211

This small rental agency has rental properties in Surf City and on Topsail Island. The properties are mainly single-family cottages.

Cathy Medlin Real Estate
406 Roland Ave., Surf City • 328-2323, (800) 622-6886

This 19-year veteran of real estate sales also offers the widest range of rental homes and condominiums on Topsail Island.

Topsail Realty
712 S. Anderson Blvd., Topsail Beach • 328-5241, (800) 526-6432

This large company handles a large number of properties that are mostly single-family homes in the quiet oceanfront town of Topsail Beach. It also manages rental for Serenity Point, a development of townhomes on the southern tip of the island.

Ward Realty
P.O. Box 2800, Surf City • 328-3221, (800) 782-6216

"The original developers of Topsail Island," this company handles properties for weekly or weekend vacation rentals.

Stay abreast of
weather reports,
especially during
hurricane season,
and always bring
a radio.

Camping

These ever-changing shores have witnessed an epic succession of campers, from ancient Siouan and Algonquian gatherers whose shell middens littered the coast, to ill-fated European settlers who initially could gain no foothold on the low-lying land, to today's tourists who play the nomad on soil that was once thick with plantation rice and cotton. Despite the fact that most of the finest tracts of coastline have been built upon, campers can live a simpler life still — if only for a few days — here amid the quiet spectacle of the Atlantic.

For the most part there isn't much roughing it when camping here. Campgrounds nearest the beaches are generally RV towns with ample amenities. So, if you'd like to take along the kitchen sink, you may as well take your electric bug-zapper too. But, if you wear your home on your back and have the use of a small boat, leave the parking-lot-style camping behind for the isolation of Masonboro Island. In the off-season, your only neighbors may be pelicans and rabbits. Either way, camping the southern coast is ideal for visitors on a budget, anglers who want to walk to the water each morning and anyone for whom recreation is re-creation.

As the Boy Scouts say, be prepared, especially for blistering sun, sudden electrical storms with heavy downpours, voracious marsh mosquitoes and insidious "no-see-ums" in summer. Temperatures in the region generally are mild, except for the occasional frost in winter. Average summer peak temperature is 88 F; average winter low, 36. April and October average the least rainfall, about three inches each, while July averages the most, nearly eight inches. Be prepared for rain in any season.

Sunscreen is essential. Hats and eye protection are wise, and insect repellent useful. For tent camping, a waterproof tent fly is a must, and a tarp or dining fly is handy when cooking. Pack longer tent stakes or sand stakes for protection against high winds. Stay abreast of weather reports, especially during hurricane season, and always bring a radio.

Bicycle campers will find campgrounds about a day's ride apart, except in the Wilmington vicinity where campgrounds are more numerous. A lightweight camp stove and cook set will come in handy when restaurants aren't convenient and at the many sites where fires are prohibited.

The primary creature hazards are poisonous snakes, which are prevalent in forested areas, and ticks, which have been known to carry disease. Raccoons and other small nocturnal animals are seldom more than a nuisance, although rabid animals are occasionally reported in the rural interior. Normally, the animals posing the greatest threat are human, which is why open fires and alcoholic beverages are restricted in most campgrounds. Beware of poison ivy, poison oak and poison sumac in brushwood and forests.

For hikers or cyclists carrying packs there are two noteworthy local retail outlets for equipment. In business for more than 50 years, **Canady's Sports Center**, 3220 Wrightsville Avenue, 791-6280, is an excellent outdoor outfitter with a varied inventory. Canady's is closed Sunday. Also remarkable is **Cape Fear Outfitters** in the Plaza East Shopping Center, 1934-A Eastwood Road near Wrightsville Beach, 256-1258. They carry a less varied but complete line of equipment for sale and rent. Cape Fear Outfitters is open seven days a week. Your other choices for field gear are discount stores such as **Kmart**, 815 S. College Road, 799-5360, which keeps a decent inventory of fishing and hunting gear in season; and the two area **Wal-Mart** stores, 352 S. College Road, 392-4034, and 5511 Carolina Beach Road at Monkey Junction, 452-0944 — good choices for novices and tailgate campers.

Naturally, the highest rates at private campgrounds apply during the summer and holiday weekends, averaging from about $13 to $22. Some campgrounds charge less, others more. Tent sites are cheaper than RV sites. At most private grounds, weekly rates often discount the seventh day if payment is made in advance. Rentals by the month or longer are extremely limited from April to August. Some campgrounds offer camper storage for a monthly fee. For information on children's summer camps, refer to our Kidstuff chapter.

Wilmington

Camelot Campground
7415 Market St., Wilmington • 686-7705

Twenty minutes from downtown Wilmington, Camelot is better situated for getting to all the local attractions than for getting away from it all. Moreover, the Tomaselli family have endowed their establishment with plenty of its own resort quality. Camelot is Woodall-rated (the most recognized approval among private campgrounds). The tree-shaded grounds include a large swimming pool, a playground, volleyball, horseshoes, a fishing pond, a dump station, 100 campsites (pull-through and tent sites) and full and partial hookups. Independence Day is especially festive at Camelot with musical entertainment. The lodge has clean, tiled restrooms, hot showers, laundry facilities, a grocery and supply store, a game room and mail service. There is even a TV lounge. Near the campground entrance is a convenience store and gas station. Weekly and monthly rates are available, and reservations are accepted.

Carolina Beach Family Campground
9641 River Rd., Wilmington • 392-3322

This wooded, shady, 103-site campground is conveniently situated for cyclists touring the Ports of Call Route and the Cape Fear Run.

The large RV and tent sites are complemented by a swimming pool, hot showers, laundry facilities, a small grocery store and easy access to many area attractions. Partial and full hookups are available as well as air conditioning, electricity and heat. The campground is about a quarter-mile from Carolina Beach Road (U.S. 421) on the Wilmington side of the Snow's Cut bridge.

Masonboro Island

Accessible only by boat, Masonboro Island is the last and largest undisturbed barrier island remaining on the southern North Carolina coast. It is the fourth component of the North Carolina National Estuarine Research Reserve, and deservedly so. This migrating ribbon of sand and uphill terrain about 8 miles in length, immediately south of Wrightsville Beach, offers the camper a secluded, primitive experience in the most pristine environment left on the Cape Fear coast. It is also used by anglers, bird watchers, the occasional hunter, students and surfers (who prefer the north end). Everything you'll need must be packed in, and everything you produce should be packed out — *everything*.

Of the reserve's more than 5,000 acres, about 4,400 acres are tidal marsh and mud flats. So most folks land at the extreme north or south ends, on or near the sandy beaches by the inlets. Pitch camp behind the dunes only and use a cook stove; there is little or no firewood. While the North Carolina Division of Coastal Management hopes to limit its involvement with the island and preserve its traditional uses, they do prohibit polluting the island and camping on and in front of the dune ridge.

Wildlife here is remarkable and fragile. During the warm months, Masonboro Island is one of the most successful nesting areas for loggerhead turtles, a threatened species. Piping plovers, also threatened, feed at the island in winter. Keep your eyes peeled on the marshes for river otters and, at low tides, raccoons. Gray foxes, cotton rats and tiny marsh rabbits all frequent the small maritime forest.

FYI

Unless otherwise noted, the area code for all phone numbers in this guide is 910.

Photo: N.C. Aquarium

You "otter" see how much wildlife there is on the coast of North Carolina.

The marshes, flats and creeks at low tide are excellent places to observe and photograph great blue and little blue herons, tricolor herons, snowy and great egrets, oystercatchers, clapper rails and many other flamboyant birds. Brown pelicans, various terns and gulls, American osprey and shearwaters all live on Masonboro, if not permanently then at least for some part of their lives. Endangered peregrine falcons are rare seasonal visitors.

Be sure to bring mosquito netting and/or insect repellent and plenty of sun protection in the warm months, and trash bags always. Keep in mind that some of the island is still privately owned, especially the north end, and all of it is extremely fragile. The University of North Carolina at Wilmington is in the midst of a three-year visitor-impact study that will attempt to assess the viability of continued camping here. Visitors' behavior and scientific scrutiny together will have some influence on whether Masonboro Island becomes severely restricted. Responsible usage is of paramount importance. For further information about Masonboro Island, see the Islands section in our Attractions chapter.

Carolina Beach

Carolina Beach State Park
Dow Rd., Carolina Beach • 458-8206

Once a campsite for Paleo-Indians, colonial explorers and Confederate troops, Carolina Beach State Park remains a gem among camping destinations. Watersports enthusiasts are minutes from the Cape Fear River, Masonboro Sound and the Atlantic. There is a full-service marina with two launching ramps. Need we mention the great fishing? The park is a bird-watcher's paradise and is home to lizards, snakes (mostly harmless), rare frogs, carnivorous plants (protected) and occasionally alligators, opossums, gray foxes and river otters. Five miles of hiking trails wind through several distinct habitats including maritime forest, pocosin

---

INSIDERS' TIP

Enjoy the nature walk behind the North Carolina Aquarium at Fort Fisher in Kure Beach.

(low, flat, swampy regions) and savanna. Hikers on the Sugar Loaf Trail pass over tidal marsh and dunes and along three lime-sink ponds. Cypress Pond, the most unusual, is dominated by a dwarf cypress swamp forest.

Dense vegetation lends the campsites a fair amount of privacy. Each site has a table and grill, and sites are available on a first-come basis ($9 per site). Drinking water and well-kept restrooms with hot showers are close by. There is a dump station for RVs, but no hookups. Ranger-led interpretive programs deepen visitors' understanding of the region's natural bounty. Unleashed pets and possession of alcoholic beverages are prohibited. The park is 15 miles south of Wilmington, a mile north of Carolina Beach just off U.S. 421 on Dow Road. From Wilmington, make your first right after crossing Snow's Cut bridge. (See also the Sports, Fitness and Parks chapter.)

Southport-Oak Island

Long Beach Family Campground
5011 E. Oak Island Dr., Long Beach
• **278-5737**

Boasting access to the beach and the nightlife of east Oak Island, and located just minutes from historic Southport, this campground is understandably popular all year long. Few of the 157 sites enjoy any shade, but the tent areas are grassy and commonly host foraging sea birds. One tenting area is for groups. Full and partial hookups are available as are flush toilets, hot showers, sewage disposal, tables, a public phone, ice, and seasonal or permanent lease sites.

South Brunswick Islands

Holden Beach Pier
Family Campground
441 Ocean Blvd. W., Holden Beach
• **842-6483**

The reason these 54 sun-baked sites remain jammed all summer with campers living cheek-to-jowl may be explained by their proximity to Holden Beach Pier and the beach. This campground, not the most attractive, is recommended only to die-hard budget vacationers. All sites have water, electric hookups and shaded tables and the grounds essentially comprise an RV village. Pets on leashes are allowed. The adjacent Holden Beach General Store is a full-service grocery and beach-supply store.

Sea Mist Camping Resort
4616 Devane Rd. S.W., Shallotte
• **754-8916**

Sea Mist's panoramic view of Shallotte Inlet and Ocean Isle Beach is enough to entice any camper, but owners Nellie and Baker Harrel don't depend on view alone. Visitors love Sea Mist's pool, reputedly the largest in Brunswick County, with its shaded deck and picnic area. Volleyball, basketball, horseshoes and tetherball are among the activities available. Use of the boat ramp carries no extra charge. This Woodall-rated resort is open year-round and has 245 spacious RV and tent sites with tables. Most have full hookups. The restrooms, bathhouses and coin-operated laundry facilities are clean, and the camp store is open from March 1 through December 1. Perhaps best of all, Sea Mist is only 10 minutes from the attractions of Ocean Isle Beach. Leashed pets are permitted. Daily, monthly and annual rates and storage are available. Reserve early.

Sea Mist is at the Intracoastal Waterway opposite the east end of Ocean Isle Beach. Follow the blue and white camping signs along N.C. Highway 179 to Brick Landing Road and continue to the end of the pavement. Turn left onto Devane Road. (Devane passes through Waterway Campground, 754-8652, a tolerable alternate in case Sea Mist is booked. Waterway is open April 1 through December 1.)

Topsail Island

Rogers Bay Family Campway
4021 Island Dr., North Topsail Beach
• **328-5781**

This colossal camp city (500 sites) is remarkable for its shaded and manicured grounds, its recreational offerings, and its superb location across the road from the sparsely populated beach of northern Topsail Island. Rabbits make frequent visits to

the lawns beneath gnarled live oaks. Open all year, this Woodall-rated facility features a fine in-ground swimming pool, a teen recreation room, a playground, complete hookups, a dump station, three air-conditioned bathhouses, a convenience store, propane refills, camper storage and a laundry room. Nearby attractions are miniature golf and a fine full-length golf course. Weekly, monthly and yearly stays and storage space can be arranged. Permanent sites are available for sale. Weekend reservations require a minimum two-day stay (with $10 deposit); three days are required for holiday weekends. Campfires are prohibited, and pets must be leashed at all times.

Inland

Lake Waccamaw State Park
State Park Rd., Lake Waccamaw
• 669-2928

Lake Waccamaw, named after the region's tribal natives, is the largest Carolina bay (a water-filled depression in Columbus County), 38 miles from Wilmington. It wasn't until the age of aviation that thousands of similar elliptical depressions were noticed dotting the Carolinas' coastal plain. All the depressions are oriented along northwest-southeast axes. Some are lakes. Locals came to call them "bays," referring to the abundance of bay trees — red, sweet and loblolly — that flourish there. About 400,000 Carolina bays exist, ranging in size from a fraction of an acre to more than 5,000 acres. Most are seasonal wetlands filled with fertile peat. Their origin is still a mystery. The hypothesis that an ancient meteor shower or explosion formed them collapsed under scrutiny. A widely accepted theory posits strong winds blowing across a sandy landscape or shallow sea during the last Ice Age. Lake Waccamaw's shallow waters support 52 species of fish. Five species of aquatic animals living here exist nowhere else in the world. A half-mile-long nature trail and the boardwalk are worthwhile.

Visitors to Lake Waccamaw must be willing to rough it slightly. The park is undeveloped, with no more facilities than pit toilets, tables and grills. Three primitive group campsites (no water) are available by reservation and, if not reserved, to individuals and families on a first-come basis. Trailer camping is not allowed.

INSIDERS' TIP

Walk the nature trail at Wilmington's Greenfield Lake, a one-third-mile boardwalk through a luxuriant semitropical cypress swamp.

Permits may be obtained at the ranger station that, in keeping with the bay's mysterious origins, seems to keep no regular routine except an 8 AM opening and 6 PM closing time. If you're lucky, you may reach a ranger by phone at 646-4748; otherwise, call Singletary State Park (another bay lake) at the number listed above. Fees are $5 per site or $1 per person, whichever is higher.

The park is about 7 miles south of U.S. Highway 74/76. Highly visible signs along that route and along N.C. Highway 214 lead the way. Entrance to the park is from Martin Road, which veers off State Road 1947.

You may not land one of these,
but with a PayAnyDay® loan,
you could snag a pretty nice boat

FIRST
CITIZENS
BANK

You're always first.

Atkinson • Burgaw • Carolina Beach • Hampstead
Oak Island • Shallotte • Southport • Wilmington

Member FDIC.

Casual American Dining at its Best

Awesome Salads • Serious Steaks • Very Fresh Fish
Fresh Pastas • Slow Roasted Prime Rib
Rotisserie Chicken • Celery Mashed Potatoes
Fresh Vegetables • Specialty Pizzas

EDDIE ROMANELLI'S RESTAURANT

5400 OLEANDER DRIVE
ACROSS FROM CINEMA SIX • 799-7000

Restaurants

As you might expect from a coastal community, seafood figures prominently practically everywhere you dine on North Carolina's southern coast. These coastal waters are among the most pristine in the east, yielding consistently high-quality seafood, and just about every restaurant worth its salt offers fresh daily catches that may include grouper, mahimahi, shark, swordfish, mackerel, triggerfish, shellfish and a host of other offerings. International cuisines now available in the area include Thai, Indian, Chinese (including Szechuan), Greek, Italian, German, Japanese, Jamaican, French and Australian. The several restaurants serving Mexican food are good places to advance the perpetual quest for the perfect Margarita, but by no means does the search end there. Also represented throughout our coverage area are a number of major restaurant chains (national and regional), such as Subway, Perkins, Fuddruckers, Kenny Rogers Roasters and Outback Steakhouse.

Local Favorites

Naturally, the traditional regional specialties still comprise the heart and soul of Southern coastal dining. The famous Calabash-style seafood is ever-present. It gets its name from the town heralded as the seafood capital of the world for having at least 30 seafood restaurants within a square mile. Calabash-style calls for seasoned cornmeal batter and deep frying and has become synonymous with all-you-can-eat. Calabash restaurants typically serve a huge variety of piping-hot seafood in massive quantities. But that's not all there is to regional cuisine.

Lowcountry steam-offs are buckets filled with a variety of shellfish, potatoes, corn and Old Bay seasoning. When fresh oysters are in season in the fall, oyster roasts abound. While crab is popular, it's crab dip that attracts attention in these parts. Competition is stiff among restaurants boasting the best crab dip. New Year's Eve dinners may include collards and black-eyed peas, symbolic (some say) of paper money and small change, to ensure prosperity in the year to come. These and okra, sweet potatoes, grits, turnip greens, mustard greens and kale are all regional favorites. Hush puppies, those delicious deep-fried dollops of sweet cornmeal dough, take the place of bread on many coastal tables. Hoppin' John, based on black-eyed peas and rice, is a hearty dish seen in many variations. Shrimp and grits is another popular dish appearing in various incarnations from restaurant to restaurant. Boiled peanuts (often pronounced "bawled") are popular snacks, frequently available at roadside stands, and nowhere does pecan pie taste better. Iced tea flows freely, in most places by the pitcher-full, and locals prefer it very sweet.

Wilmington has made its mark in the world of the master brewers of beer. The Wilmington Brewing Company's Dergy Porter and amber ale both won silver medals in the World Beer Championships in 1996. You'll find Dergy's served at many local restaurants. And if fresh, microbrewed beer is your idea of heaven, also look into Wilmington's Front Street Brewery, listed below.

In keeping with the area's resort character and hot summers, dining here is generally very casual. While you might feel out of place wearing shorts at fancier restaurants such as The Pilot House, casual dress is commonplace practically everywhere else. Wearing shorts or polo shirts during the summer, even at the better restaurants, is simply practical and not frowned upon.

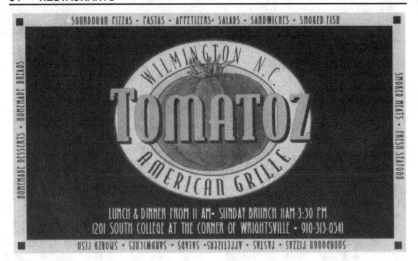

Planning and Pricing

If your favorite restaurant isn't listed here, it may be among the many fine restaurants that are impossible to miss because of reputation or location. We've made an effort to include the more out-of-the-way places that shouldn't be missed, along with some obvious favorites. You can expect to find waiting lists at the most popular restaurants throughout the summer, on holidays and during festivals. Waits are generally not long with few exceptions (Caffe Phoenix during festivals or Outback Steakhouse on S. College Road practically any old night). Wine and beer are available at all restaurants on the southern coast, and most places serve mixed drinks. In winter, hours are frequently curtailed, and some restaurants close entirely during the off-season. Most places also remain open later on Friday and Saturday nights than during the week. Remember to call ahead to verify hours and reservations. You may also want to inquire about early-bird specials and senior citizen discounts. Reservations are generally not required unless your party consists of six persons or more, but most restaurants will accept them.

Price Code

The following price code is based upon a midpriced dinner for two consisting of one appetizer, entrees, desserts and coffee. For restaurants not serving dinner, the code reflects a midpriced lunch for two — individual main courses and beverages. Keep in mind that these codes represent averages; less expensive and more expensive meals are available everywhere, even when ordering the same number of items. In fact, such averages are likely higher than what you'll actually spend. But basing our code on a fixed number of menu items, rather than average dinner checks, avoids inaccuracies introduced when people eat less at more expensive restaurants and makes comparison more precise. Also keep in mind that many restaurants include extras with each entree, yielding a better bargain for the apparent buck; we've tried to indicate where this is the case. The price codes do not reflect the state's 6 percent sales tax or gratuities. The price code used in the descriptions is as follows:

$	Less than $20
$$	$21 to $40
$$$	$41 to $60
$$$$	$61 and up

Most restaurants listed here accept major credit cards. We'll let you know the ones that do not.

Where To Eat

Wilmington

Ari Rang House

$ • 419 S. College Rd., Wilmington
• 392-1292

Among the better places to enjoy sushi in Wilmington, Ari Rang House features a full Ichiban sushi bar and dining room seating. Specializing in Korean and Japanese cuisine for lunch and dinner, Ari Rang also serves dim sum (Chinese stuffed pastries), noodles (try the udon) and imported Asian beers and sake. Main courses include soup and may include such extras as rice and kimchee. Prices are affordable, the staff friendly, and there is plenty of parking. Checks are not accepted. Ari Rang serves lunch Monday through Saturday from 11:30 AM until 3 PM, and dinner Monday through Saturday from 5 to 10 PM (closed Sundays). Gift certificates are available. Be sure to explore the adjoining gift and grocery section.

Bocci

$$$ • 811 Mercer, Wilmington • 763-0067

Touting wood-fired specialties, Bocci is a fine new addition to the local dining scene, featuring an ever-changing menu filled with the flavors of Italy, Asia and Cajun country. Start off with wood-grilled Portobello mushroom with toasted goat cheese, roasted eggplant and olive relish, and you'll have an idea of the richness of Bocci's offerings. Each meal begins with baked garlic and bread. The brochette of lamb is tender, the Bayou crawfish cakes piquant, and the personal pizzas satisfying. We recommend the cannelloni stuffed with sirloin, spinach, herbs and three cheeses or the locally caught fish with tropical fruit chutney. Desserts tend to be excellent. From the enormous, carved double door outside to the classic columned dining area, Bocci is visually appealing with faux marble, trompe l'oeil brick, earth-toned tile, indirect lighting and lustrous wood. Artful photos depicting men playing bocci line the walls. An excellent selection of domestic, Italian and French wines and champagnes is available. Bocci serves dinner from 5 to 10 PM Monday through Saturday (a bit later on weekends) and provides free valet parking.

Breaktime Sports Bar, Billiards & Grill

$ • 127 S. College Rd., Wilmington
• 395-6658

With the addition of its full-service dining area, Breaktime has extended its already wide appeal as Wilmington's largest billiards parlor and popular sports bar. Serving sandwiches, burgers, soups, salads and rotating specials, Breaktime possesses all ABC permits as well as 21 top-quality Brunswick and Diamond playing tables. Three large windows let you view the billiards room from the dining area. A total of 15 televisions in both rooms keep you in touch with the latest sports developments, and there is plenty of arcade-style entertainment. Breaktime is casual — sports shirts and khaki shorts fit right in — but neat attire is required; no tank tops. The grill is open from 11 AM until 10 PM weekdays and until midnight on weekends. The bar stays open until 2 AM.

Caffe Phoenix

$$ • 9 S. Front St., Wilmington • 343-1395

High ceilings, original art, an interior balcony . . . what the Phoenix offers the eyes is more than complemented by a menu of consistent quality that makes it one of the

FYI

Unless otherwise noted, the area code for all phone numbers in this guide is 910.

INSIDERS' TIP

The region's freshest popcorn, available in many varieties (including reduced salt) comes from Vic's Corn Popper, 1616 Shipyard Boulevard (corner of 17th Street), 452-2869.

most appealing dining experiences on Cape Fear. Situated in a historic glass-front building, the Phoenix is also a popular nightspot. The room can become noisy with conversation, but that detracts little from its chic allure.

The regular menu has an Italian accent, along with grilled chicken, shrimp and steaks, and portions tend to be generous. Dressings and sauces are all-natural and made fresh. The special seasonal offerings are always inventive. Recorded music (often classical, jazz, Brazilian) adds to the ambiance. Caffe Phoenix serves lunch, light fare between 3 and 5 PM and dinner; they're closed on Monday. Mixed drinks, a selection of coffees and excellent homemade desserts are served until closing — an excellent choice for a romantic nightcap. Reservations are not accepted.

Chris's Restaurant
$ • 853 S. 17th St., Wilmington • 763-1791
Unassuming and family-run, this is an ex-

cellent choice for authentic, homemade Greek cooking as well as for sandwiches, Italian pastas, burgers and fried seafood. Local politicians and businesspeople have known about Chris's value and quality for years. The pastistsio and moussaka are very good, and you should make it a point to try the dolmathes (stuffed grape leaves) or stuffed cabbage, both local rarities. (Chris's regularly offers vegetarian items.) All main courses come with extras, which may include Grecian bread, vegetables and iced tea. The restaurant, at the corner of Dawson Street, is open from 6 AM until 2 PM. It accommodates take-outs and custom catering.

Crook's By the River
$$$ • 138 S. Front St., Wilmington
• 762-8898
Those who thought grits and hush puppies were the high-water mark of Southern cooking owe it to themselves to visit Crook's. A spin-off of Crook's Corner in Chapel Hill

founded by the late Bill Neal, Crook's By the River sports a similar pink pig above the entrance. Crook's is a fine amalgam of traditional Southern ingredients, cosmopolitan touches and some elusive magic. The shrimp and grits and the vegetarian blackbean cakes are wonderful. Crook's also boasts adventurous local art and an outdoor deck overlooking the river. There's live music in the lounge on weekend nights all year. Menus change frequently, and the Sunday brunch is superb. Crook's serves dinner nightly. Reservations are accepted.

Dragon Garden Chinese Cuisine
$$ • 341-52 S. College Rd., Wilmington
• 452-0708

Dragon Garden is one of Wilmington's better restaurants serving regional Chinese cuisine, and you'll find some quite unusual dishes. Outstanding items include a savory cilantro shrimp and the generously portioned house special pan-fried noodles. The restaurant serves exceedingly affordable lunch combinations, a lunch buffet and á la carte entrees. Unusual appetizers include the crabmeat with cream cheese and the shrimp sizzling rice soup. The restaurant's decor is interesting, with comfortable banquettes in a large, sectioned room with marble detailing and carved woodwork. A circular table with a lazy Susan is available for family-style din-

ing for 10. A separate room accommodates private affairs for up to 60 people. Buffets are also served at dinner Friday through Sunday. Dinner is served every day from 5 PM. Dragon Garden is in the University Commons shopping center, two doors down from Phar-Mor. Take-out orders are welcome.

Eddie Romanelli's
$$ • 5400 Oleander Dr., Wilmington
• 799-7000

Romanelli's offers a high-toned atmosphere suffused with the richness of dark wood, red brick and full carpeting. The menu emphasizes American regional dishes, many with an Italian accent. Among the house specialties are superb crab dip and homemade 10-inch pizzas, some of which are unusual, such as the barbecued chicken pizza and Philly steak pizza. The menu offers a variety of appetizers (try the pesto cheese toast), sandwiches, salads with fresh-made dressings and Italian baked specialties. Lunch and dinner menus are essentially the same, with dinner portions being larger and including soup and salad or a choice of potatoes or pasta. The popular bar adjoining the restaurant has a high, raftered ceiling, skylights and handsome sectional seating. A late-night finger-food menu is served there. Menu and drink specials are offered every day. Romanelli's is open seven days a week.

Elijah's

$$-$$$ • Chandler's Wharf, Water St., Wilmington
• 343-1448

No one can say they've been to Wilmington unless they've tried Elijah's crab dip. Directly on the Cape Fear River, Elijah's offers genuine Low Country fare as well as such delights as oysters Rockefeller and Cajun-spiced New York Strip. Elijah's is two restaurants in one (thus the hyphenated price code): the oyster bar, which includes outdoor deck seating, and the enclosed dining room with its more formal presentation of seafood, poultry, pasta and choice beef. Nautical artwork recalls the building's former incarnation as a maritime museum. The ambiance is casual, and the western exposure makes it a great place for a sundown toast. Elijah's is open seven days a week during the summer but is closed Mondays after Labor Day. It serves lunch, dinner and Sunday brunch. The oyster bar remains open until midnight. Reservations are accepted only for parties of eight or more.

Front Street Brewery

$$ • 9 N. Front St., Wilmington • 251-1935

The Brewery is locally famous for its ales, lagers, stouts and porters, all freshly made on the premises, and for its pub-style food. The restaurant occupies the Foy-Roe Building (1883) with its original, high tin ceiling and heart-pine floors. Wrought-iron railings, historic photos, lush woodwork and a beautiful exterior facade are additional merits. The Brewery specializes in pot pies, fish'n'chips and sandwiches plus nouveau salads, steaks, seafood and poultry, all of which are matched to suit the excellent beers. The desserts, which include homemade ice creams, should not be missed.

Usually on tap are an unfiltered, classic Hefe Weissbier, a hop-bitter Dusseldorf Alt, a popular golden ale and a hearty Irish dry stout. Other beverages are seasonal, such as the very popular raspberry wheat beer (highly recommended), spiced ales in fall and winter, and some unusual drink specials. The Brewery is open for lunch and dinner seven days a week. It closes at midnight Monday through Thursday, a little later Friday and Saturday and at 10 PM on Sunday. Reservations are not accepted.

Goody Goody Omelet House

$ • 3817 Market St., Wilmington • 762-0444

You haven't had a real omelet until you've had a Goody Goody omelet. The hard-working folks at the griddle whip their eggs before slinging omelets that are light, thickly upholstered and humongous. Throw in the grits, biscuits and country ham, and you've got yourself a Southern breakfast you can take with you all day. Goody Goody also serves lunch — burgers, fried chicken and such — but it only stays open until about 2 PM. It's a tiny place with small banquettes and counter seating, so arrive early. Waits are usually brief. The griddle starts to sizzle at 6 AM.

Grouper Nancy's Fine Dining & Spirits

$$$ • 501 Nutt St., Wilmington • 251-8009

Atmospheric and conveniently located in the Coast Line Center downtown, Grouper Nancy's has a personality that suits romantic dining as readily as family and business meals. The brick-walled room, with its high raftered ceiling, is in a historic former railroad terminal. Among the restaurant's more popular entrees, items such as the steak Diane and the New York strip steak au poivre are prepared right at your tableside. Other favorites include the Grouper Nancy (sauteed shrimp over angel hair pasta) and crab meat stuffed filet. Six to eight specials and an 80-item wine list are standard. The colorful, somewhat casual decor includes black-and-white checked table cloths and modest train motifs. Many desserts are prepared on the premises, and the kids will love the Toll House cookie pie. Grouper Nancy's features a full bar and invites an after-dinner cordial, espresso or cappuccino.

Harvest Moon

$$$ • 5704 Oleander Dr., Wilmington
• 772-0172

This attractively designed restaurant blends Old World atmosphere (fluted columns, faux stucco, copper and tile) with contemporary high-tech design. It serves seasonal New Southern innovations that borrow freely from various ethnic styles. The menu is imaginative, ranging from a straightforward fried oyster-and-spinach salad to pecan-crusted venison loin. When you've got

an urge for wild boar barbecue, Harvest Moon is the place to go. The chefs are especially proud of their grilled whisky flank steak and their jambalaya. The restaurant serves lunch Monday through Friday, dinner Monday through Saturday and closes on Sunday. A late-night menu is served 10 to 11 PM Monday through Thursday and 10:30 to midnight on Friday and Saturday. Special requests and dietary requirements are gladly accommodated. You can put your name on the waiting list by telephone (seating, however, cannot be guaranteed for a particular time). Harvest Moon is in the Courtyard Shops On Oleander, nearly equidistant from S. College Road and the Bradley Creek bridge.

Hiro Japanese Steak and Seafood House
$$ • 419 S. College Rd., Wilmington
• 452-3097

Hiro is unique in Wilmington as the only Japanese restaurant in town specializing in teppanyaki. That is, your food is prepared before your eyes at a teppan table. Traditional staples are served, from various tempura dishes and yakitori (skewered chicken) to steaks and seafood hibachi-style. Stand-outs include succulent lobster tail, yakinuki steak (spicy, but not very), teppanyaki shrimp flambé and several combination entrees. Every dinner entree is accompanied by extras, including green tea on request. Portions are generous, a good value. Be prepared to sit

with strangers at the teppan table, which is the nature of this very social style of dining. Hiro offers a children's menu, imported beer and wine (including saki and plum wine), cocktails and a lunch menu, but no sushi. Personal checks are not accepted. The restaurant is in the University Landing Shopping Center.

India Mahal
$ • 4610 Maple St., Wilmington • 799-2089

The only Indian restaurant in Wilmington, India Mahal serves the cuisine of northern India plus a few selections from Bombay and south India. Authentic in every degree, India Mahal will please both neophytes and worldlings. From the wide variety of breads and surprising appetizers to the entrees and chutneys, the selection invites over-ordering. The staff is attentive and happy to adjust the spice of any dish to taste. In keeping with certain traditions, India Mahal does not serve beef. Specialties include sabzian (vegetarian), lamb, sagar (seafood), tandoori dishes (fired clay oven cooking), biryani (rice) and chicken. This is almost certainly the only place in Wilmington to find mango lassi. Luncheons are inexpensive, and take-out orders and catering are available. The restaurant is open seven days a week for lunch and dinner. India Mahal is hidden in a row of storefronts that lies parallel to S. College Road on the northbound side. Enter the parking lot from Wrightsville Avenue (opposite Tomatoz restaurant) or from Maple Street. Look for India Mahal's red sign.

Jimmy's Deli
New York Style Pizzeria
$ • 4418 Shipyard Blvd., Wilmington
• 799-3145

More than a pizzeria, Jimmy's offers casual, delicatessen-style dining featuring Italian specialties, deli sandwiches and subs, and salads. Cold cuts are exclusively Boar's Head brand, and dinner breads are baked fresh daily. As the staff likes to say, it's good food, served fast — and they even deliver. The Sunday buffet (11 AM to 3 PM) is an all-you-can-eat bargain for less than $6. The regular menu features nightly specials, and catering is available. Jimmy's is behind Firestone, next to Long Leaf Mall, and serves meals seven days a week, 7 AM to 10 PM Monday through Saturday, and 11 AM to 8 PM Sunday.

K-38 Baja Grill
$$ • 5410 Oleander Dr., Wilmington
• 395-6040

The name comes from a seaside spot 38 kilometers south of the Baja border where natives prepare foods in roadside shanties for tourists and surfers. Chef Josh Vach brought some of their recipes, inspirations and authentic ingredients home to Wilmington, producing a palette of flavors and textures that stands out among those of other Mexican restaurants. You'll find all the standard offerings, all done well, but K-38's adapted specialties are the most impressive, particularly the chipotlé barbecued shrimp (chipotlé is smoked jalapeño) and pollo de Chimayo. Grilling is the preferred preparation, and all ingredients are fresh. Seekers of the perfect Margarita must visit K-38. The place itself is attractive, decorated with wrought iron, blue glass and other items collected along Josh's travels. A small room on the right is perfect for parties of up to 16 people (reserve in advance), and K-38 now caters off site. K-38 is open for lunch from and dinner.

The bar remains open until your surfing stories are exhausted.

Katy's Great Eats
$ • 1054 S. College Rd., Wilmington
• 395-5289

As popular for its food as for its adjoining sports bar (noted for darts tournies), Katy's is a friendly, laid-back establishment with a homey atmosphere and interesting, odd decorative touches. The restaurant has long been known for its killer burgers (especially the heart-healthy turkey burgers), onion rings and chicken wings (Kluckers, B-52 Bombers). Katy's also offers seafood such as a steamed shrimp boat, seafood-stuffed potatoes and Cajun shrimp dinner salad. Affordable, satisfying cold plates, salads, sauteed and fried seafood and subs and sandwiches are specialties. Seniors are entitled to discounts, and there is a children's menu. The bar features a pool table and foosball. Katy's is on the southbound side of S. College Road (north of Wrightsville Avenue). Doors open for lunch and dinner. Katy's closes on Sunday.

Lox Stock & Bagels
$ • 332 S. College Rd., Wilmington
• 392-0002

Lox Stock & Bagels is definitely not just for Yankees (although "bagel mit a shmear" is understood). LS&B serves real lox (smoked salmon) — great on a toasted bagel with cream cheese and tomato. Their many types of bagels are baked on the premises daily, and there's always a choice of prepared cream cheeses, such as vegetable, olive, blueberry and honey-walnut. LS&B also offers breakfast specials, hot lunch specials, deli sandwiches (try the authentic Reuben) and an array of fresh salads — even creamed herring! You may eat in or take out. LS&B also caters. You'll find LS&B in the Wal-Mart shopping center, facing College Road.

Nuss Strasse Cafe
$$ • 316 Nutt St., Wilmington • 763-5523

The old brick and exposed rafters of

We Specialize In All Forms of Chinese Cuisine, Including Mandarin, Cantonese, Szechuan & Hunan

Beer-Wine
Take-Out & Reservation
452-2607
Party-Birthday-Special Occasions

Regular Menu
Lunch & Dinner Buffet
7 Days A Week
} **Mon. - Sat.** Lunch 11:00-2:30
Dinner 5:00-9:30
Sunday 12:00 - 8:30

326 S. COLLEGE RD. WILMINGTON, NC. (BETWEEN WALMART AND BARNES&NOBLE)

the historic Cotton Exchange befit this cozy establishment, which has been serving authentic German cuisine in a setting reminiscent of a Bavarian country inn since 1985. Seating is divided among three small rooms on different levels. Servers in traditional garb offer national dishes, including bratwurst, wienerwurst and Polish kielbasa as well as hearty sandwiches, hot German potato salad, homemade breads, a host of pastries, imported wines and, of course, excellent German beer (among others). Lunch and dinner are served daily. There is ample parking.

Oriental Palace
$$ • 326 S. College Rd., Wilmington
• 452-2607

Oriental Palace offers a good value for lunch and dinner, especially with its daily buffet. The menu includes Mandarin, Cantonese, Szechuan and Hunan dishes, seven days a week. You'll find the restaurant at the Wal-Mart shopping center between Revco and Omega Sports, facing College Road. Oriental Palace opens at 11 AM everyday (11:30 AM Sunday) and serves dinner until 9:30 PM every day (8:30 Sunday). Large gatherings can be accommodated with 24-hour notice.

Paleo Sun Cafe
$$$ • 35 N. Front St., Wilmington
• 762-7700

As impressive visually as it is culinarily, Paleo Sun has big-city ambiance that is never a put-off. The high-backed wooden chairs are comfortable, the lighting subtle, the service personable, and topping it off are the food and its presentation. A culturally diverse menu offers unusual delights, such as a wild mushroom with cognac cream and herb dumpling appetizer, Indonesian swordfish with mango and caramel ginger sauce, and a variety of salads and soups. Seafood, poultry, meats and pasta are all artfully done. The specials deserve the name, and the wine list will satisfy the most discerning tastes. Paleo Sun offers a variety of coffees and imported beers (including Peru's Cuzco). Among the fine desserts, the Kahlua Cinnamon cheesecake is nirvana. Paleo Sun features live music Wednesday nights and during Sunday brunch. It is open seven days a week, serving lunch, an afternoon menu and dinner. Reservations are not accepted except for large parties, and the wait can often be lengthy. Eat early rather than late to avoid the wait.

The Pilot House
$$$ • 2 Ann St., Wilmington • 343-0200

The Pilot House is among the preemi-

nent dining establishments downtown. Overlooking the Cape Fear River at Chandler's Wharf, the restaurant occupies the historic Craig House (c. 1870) and strives for innovations on high-quality Southern regional cooking. The large menu, featuring sauteed and chargrilled seafood, pasta, heart-healthy selections and a delectable roster of appetizers, changes frequently, so plan repeat visits accordingly. The kitchen staff even grows its own herbs in front of the building. The style of service is semiformal, with linen, Wilton pewter and teamed servers, but the management successfully steers for middle ground. You will see guests dressed in everything from Bermuda shorts to tuxedos. (Lunch is more casual than dinner.) The wine list is carefully chosen and well-rounded. The Pilot House features additional outdoor seating, weather permitting, and serves lunch and dinner Monday through Saturday. Sunday brunch is served seasonally. Reservations are recommended.

P.T.'s Grille
$ • 4544 Fountain Dr., Wilmington
• 392-2293

When you want a freshly grilled burger or chicken sandwich, forget the fast-food mills. P.T.'s can't be beat. Every menu item is a package deal that includes a sandwich (whopping half-pound burgers, tender chicken breast, eight-ounce hot dogs,

fresh roast beef and more), fresh-cut, spiced, skin-on french fries and a soft drink, refill included. Prices are low and quality is high. You place your order by filling in an idiot-proof order form and dropping it through the window if you're eating on the outdoor deck. Your meal is prepared to order and ready in about 10 minutes — fast food that doesn't taste like fast food. P.T.'s Grille is west of S. College Road across from the south end of the UNCW campus. Take-out orders are welcome and may be habit-forming. P.T.'s is open every day.

Rucker John's Restaurant and More
$$ • 5511 Carolina Beach Rd., Wilmington
• 452-1212

Casual, comfortable and providing friendly service, Rucker John's serves salads, beef, poultry, pasta and fish seven days a week for lunch and dinner. Locals frequently recommend the tender barbecued ribs. Salads are made to order, and dressings are made fresh on the premises. Burgers, grilled seafood and croissant sandwiches comprise an ever-popular menu. Lunch and dinner specials and drink specials change daily. A dinner salad and side dish are included with each entree. RJ's serves dinner until 10 PM nightly (a little later on Fridays and Saturdays). Adjoining the oak-trimmed dining area is the lounge, with its horseshoe-shape

Szechuan 132
University Landing
419 S. College Rd.
799-1426
FAX 799-0866

Szechuan 130
(New Location)
Downtown
130 N. Front St.
762-5782

• Szechuan 132 •
Voted Best Oriental Restaurant
Three Years In A Row
Highly Recommended by the
New Times and Chicago Tribune

Take Out Service • Group
Catering
(Both Locations)
Open Lunch and Dinner 7 Days
All ABC Permits

bar, where you can catch the latest sports on TV and order food until midnight. Rucker John's is in the Myrtle Grove Shopping Center at Monkey Junction (where Carolina Beach and S. College roads meet), about 7.3 miles south of downtown Wilmington.

Swensen's
$ • 620 S. College Rd., Wilmington
• 395-6740

Justifiably famous for its ice cream desserts, Swensen's is an inexpensive restaurant that is equally proud of its hearty salads, specialty sandwiches, burgers and lite menu items. All their offerings are generously portioned, and the Reuben, the Blue Max sandwich and two types of veggie sandwiches (hot and cold) are highlights. Swensen's specializes in kids' menus, featuring the popular Cable Car Kids Meal (choice of burger, grilled cheese or PB&J) for children younger than 12. The restaurant's oak interior features "greenhouse" seating amid double-blooming hibiscus. Model trains ply an overhead track suspended by small bridges around the room — always a hit with the kids. Of course, we can't ignore Swensen's amazing desserts, which include ice cream and frozen yogurt ranging from the sinful to heavenly and including low-fat, no-fat, cholesterol-free and no-sugar items. Swensen's opens for lunch and dinner, and during the high season, it

stays open late — 10:30 PM Sunday through Thursday and until midnight Friday and Saturday. (The kitchen closes about an hour before the restaurant.)

Szechuan 132
$$ • 419 S. College Rd., Wilmington
• 799-1426

Szechuan 132 stands out, due in part to the personalities of the proprietor, the engaging Joseph Hou, and his staff. Much of the menu is Cantonese, but Szechuan items such as the hot and sour soup and Szechuan pan-fried noodles live up to their names. The decor is contemporary American. Comfortable banquettes and high-backed chairs invite diners to linger. Mixed drinks are available. Every day, Szechuan 132 offers excellent lunch specials averaging around $7 and accepts take-out orders. Szechuan 132 is in the University Landing Shopping Center, and reservations are recommended for dinner. Lunch and dinner are served daily. Its sister establishment downtown, Szechuan 130, 130 N. Front Street, 762-5782, offers much the same quality and service as well as a daily buffet.

Tomatoz American Grille
$$ • S. College Rd. and Wrightsville Ave., Wilmington • 313-0541

Tomatoz is a great place to satisfy both the heartiest of appetites and the requirements of a health-conscious diet. The menu borrows

freely from various cultures, Italian and Southwestern North American being the most prevalent influences. Ingredients are all-natural and considered for their health value as much as for taste. Sourdough pizzas are made fresh to order with low-fat mozzarella and are available with vegetarian toppings as well as with shrimp or chicken. The pastas, lunch entrees and specialty dishes make delicious use of turkey and seafood, with a smaller representation of beef. Fish and meats are smoked in-house. Portions are generally enormous and come with fresh-baked breads. The nachos appetizer is a meal in itself. Tomatoz carries a good selection of beer, including some made locally. A children's menu, Sunday brunch and (lest we forget) heavenly homemade desserts round out the offerings. The chocolate mousse pie is one of our faves. All this in a unique brick building with spacious seating and attractive decor enlivened by local artwork. Most menu items are available for take out.

Trails End Steak House
**$$$ • Trails End Rd., Wilmington
• 791-2034**

For many locals over many decades, all roads have led to Trails End. Overlooking the Intracoastal Waterway near Whiskey Creek, Trails End is known for three things: steak, beef and red meat. All the steaks here — sirloin, filet of tenderloin, prime rib, Delmonico and more — are broiled over hardwood charcoal. Every entree comes with hors d'oeuvres and salad bar. Trails End is famous for the loyalty of its clientele and staff (a waiter retired in 1993 after 26 years of continuous service). Its colorful history, dating to 1965, is related on the back of the menu and by memorabilia near the entrance (the door handles are horseshoes from the Budweiser Clydesdales). The original building was something of a windowless shack. Rebuilt in 1987 after a fire, the new building is not large (it seats less than 90), but now there are large windows yielding a marvelous waterway vista. The grill is open Monday through Saturday. Reservations are strongly recommended.

Trails End Road is about 7.5 miles south of Wilmington. To find it, take Pine Grove Drive south from Oleander Drive (at Hugh MacRae Park). Turn right onto Masonboro Loop Road. Less than a half-mile after the tiny Whiskey Creek bridge, make the first left onto Trails End Road. Proceed beyond the "End State Road" sign until the scent of charbroiled beef stops you in your tracks.

Water Street Waterfront Restaurant & Sidewalk Cafe
$ • 5 Water St., Wilmington • 343-0042

Housed in the Quince Building (1835), a

former peanut warehouse on the riverfront, the Water Street Restaurant offers moderately priced, offbeat and healthy meals all day, every day, in a softly lit, antique atmosphere that can be quite romantic. Salads (tabouli, shrimp, falafel, fruit, etc.), burgers (including chicken and veggie), burritos and pita pockets (turkey, shrimp, hummus, baba ganouj, etc.) are typical of Water Street's style. Many salad items are available to go. Reservations are recommended for the Sunday Jazz Brunch (10 AM to 2 PM). Sidewalk seating is in full view of the river, and live piano music is frequent. In fact, Water Street Restaurant is an attractive nightspot featuring live jazz every Friday evening beginning at 8 PM and poetry readings on Tuesdays. Lot parking is available at the corner of Dock and Water streets.

Western Sizzlin'
Restaurant Steaks and More
$ • 1602 S. College Rd., Wilmington
• 791-3998

Since 1979 this beef-eaters haven has made serving fresh-cut steaks look easy, as they specialize in preparing sirloin, New York strip, country-fried steak, T-bones, filet mignon, rib eyes and more. Also offered are various chicken items, including a cordon bleu sandwich, and fried catfish — all of it at family-friendly prices. Orders are placed at the service counter and your food comes to your table piping-hot. All meals include salad and dessert; beverages are extra. The County Fair Buffet & Bakery, offering hot and cold items including Southern specialties, is an option to have with your meal or as a meal in itself. All baked goods — brownies, muffins, breads and more — may be packaged to go. Seniors' and children's menus are available. Immediately south of Oleander Drive, Western Sizzlin' opens for lunch and dinner.

Wing Chinese Restaurant
$ • 4002 Oleander Dr., Wilmington
• 799-8178

Wing prepares an expansive menu of Cantonese and Szechuan specialties and perhaps the best-known buffet in Wilmington. All-you-can-eat lunch and dinner buffets typically include shrimp, chicken, fish, pork and beef entrees, plus

INSIDERS' TIP

You can find breakfast-all-day places, which serve meals complete with grits and biscuits, all over the southern coastal area.

occasional surprises such as crab Rangoon (fried wontons stuffed with crab and cream cheese). Buffets are served every day and can be packaged to go. Wing also prepares regular menu items ranging from kung pao chicken and orange beef to mu shu pork, crispy duck and sizzling seafood Wor Bar (sauteed lobster, shrimp and scallops in Szechuan sauce). Special dietary requirements will be honored on request. Free delivery is available within a limited area.

Wrightsville Beach

Beaches

$$$ • 2025 Eastwood Rd., Wrightsville Beach • 256-4622

Decorated with pastel colors and local art, Beaches offers an attractive setting, casual presentation and good quality. The menu is relatively restrained, but what Beaches does, it does well. As you would expect, fresh local seafood comes in a delicious variety of preparations. The coconut shrimp appetizer is a tasty twist on the old Calabash-style, and their seafood chowder is an award-winning recipe. But Beaches' reputation stands most firmly on the excellence of its charbroiled beef. The variety of domestic and imported wines and the full bar offer something for everyone. Most wines cost less than $20 a bottle. Beaches' lounge has become a gathering spot for conversation and televised sports and, on Thursdays, live acoustic music. There is also limited outdoor seating suitable for drinks or light meals. Beaches is open daily for dinner.

The Bridge Tender Restaurant

$$$$ • 1414 Airlie Rd., Wrightsville Beach • 256-3419

The Bridge Tender's tremendous local following is testimony to its consistent high quality and flexibility in pleasing its customers. Situated on the Intracoastal Waterway within view of the Wrightsville Beach drawbridge, this small establishment, founded in 1976, excels in its preparation of fresh seafood and in its nationally recognized, multiple-award-winning domestic wine list. From lamp-lit tables beneath a high raftered ceiling, the view of the waterway marina is romantic. All of the Bridge Tender's offerings are fresh and made from scratch, and it serves only certified Angus beef. Specials change daily, making repeat visits worthwhile. Past specials have included the mixed grill, a Maryland crab cake appetizer and Cajun-spiced shrimp served over rice. The adjoining lounge offers the same excellent scenery along with hot and cold appetizers Monday through Thursday. The Bridge Tender has all ABC permits and serves lunch and dinner Monday through Friday.

Carolina's Food & Drink

$$$ • 1610 Pavilion Pl., Wrightsville Beach • 256-5008

Casual and colorful and just minutes from the beach, Carolina's excels with unusual combinations of flavors borrowing from the Orient, Italy and the American South. Don't be surprised — well, OK, be surprised — when you taste grilled tuna steak with ginger and wasabi, Tuscan-style lamb chops or salads garnished with edible flowers. The changing menu includes homemade soups, colorful salads with and without grilled meat or seafood, grilled free range chicken, steaks and pastas plus such specialties as Carolina's own version of shrimp and grits (topped with prosciutto) and oysters tempura. Open-face pita salads, with or without grilled meat or sharp cheeses, are a treat. For lunch the restaurant serves some Italian-style hot sandwiches as well as specialty sandwiches on 8-inch and 16-inch Italian loaves. Soft lighting and jazz add to an ambiance conducive to conversation. Carolina's has all ABC permits. Lunch and dinner are served every day, and the restaurant stays open a little later on Friday and Saturday. Reservations are accepted, and take-outs and catering are available. Pavilion Place lies a quarter-mile west of the Wrightsville Beach drawbridge and can be entered from either Eastwood Road or Wrightsville Avenue.

Doxey's Market & Cafe

$ • Landfall Shopping Center, Wrightsville Beach • 256-9952

Aside from being one of the area's preeminent outlets for natural groceries and products, Doxey's serves all-natural, high-quality foods at its casual in-store cafe. The salad bar and hot bar feature fresh vegetables (mostly organic), homemade salads, bean cuisine and soups. Sandwiches and daily specials are available. Patrons may dine on the premises or take their meals to go. Landfall Shopping Center is on Eastwood Road at the Military Cutoff Road intersection.

Etrusca Ristorante

$$ • 530 Causeway Dr., Wrightsville Beach • 256-5077

Named for the region of Italy whose history is older than Rome's, Etrusca blends the classic and the modern in both decor and cuisine. Beneath high, angled ceilings, tables are intimate and comfortable, with white linen, Fiesta ware and fresh flowers. Wall sconces add to the warmth of wood and stucco, and works by local artists are always on view. The menu includes traditional dishes ranging from seafood antipasto to saltimbocca and bistecca plus a variety of fresh seafood entrees, and naturally, pasta of a variety to impress any

Florentine. Premium coffees and spirits top it all off nicely. Lunch at Etrusca offers such sandwiches as grilled Portobello mushroom and chargrilled veal burger with provolone. The adjoining Etruscan Bar is the livelier of the restaurant's two lounges and features live entertainment on Friday and Saturday nights. The restaurant serves lunch Sunday through Friday. Dinner is served seven days a week, and a late-night menu is served, as well. Reservations are accepted. Be sure to try the Sunday brunch.

Gardenias

$$$$ • 7105 Wrightsville Ave., Wrightsville Beach • 256-2421

Gardenias is an essential dining experience, an intimate establishment that reasserts the artistry of cuisine and celebrates the passion for great food and wine. Traditional and innovative original dishes comprise an eclectic, evolving menu, and presentation is invariably a visual delight. Chef Tom Mills insists on the highest quality ingredients, including organic vegetables whenever possible, and hand-cut meats. Gardenias' wine list offers more than 20 wines by the glass, and the well-versed staff can assist in matching your courses with complementing wines. The service is exacting, always polished and polite. Gardenias stocks a selection of microbrewery beers, and every house pour for mixed drinks is top-shelf. Breads are freshly baked, coffees custom-blended, and desserts simply incredible. Gardenias offers a wide range of dining experiences, from affordable short courses — soup, composed salad and a great wine, for instance — to multicourse extravaganzas. Attire for Gardenias is what owner Colin Eagles calls "Wrightsville Beach casual" — polo shirts and khakis are fine. Gardenias is open for dinner six days a week beginning in April and Tuesday through Saturday beginning in November. Reservations are requested.

King Neptune

$$ • 11 N. Lumina Ave., Wrightsville Beach • 256-2525

King Neptune has been in business since the '50s, outlasting hurricanes, competition and its original owners but not its appeal. From soups and chowders to steamers, platters and hearty specialties that include steaks and pizza, King Neptune focuses on seafood and does it well. Many menu items have a distinctive island flair, such as the triggerfish with rum-mango sauce, Voodoo Snapper and Jamaican jerk chicken. The Caribbean-colored dining room is large and bright, decorated with local art, beach umbrellas and photographs. After dinner, the adjoining Ol' Nep's Lounge is lively and offers perhaps the widest selection of rums on the cape as well as an international selection of beers (not to mention an endless supply of entertaining sailing and fishing snapshots). King Neptune serves dinner seven days a week and offers senior citizens discounts. The lounge remains open until 1 AM. Free parking is available in the lot across the street.

Manhattan Bagel

$ • 7220 Wrightsville Ave., Wrightsville Beach • 256-1222

This popular franchise makes no bones about celebrating Yankees, displaced and otherwise, right down to its poster-sized historic photos of New York skyscrapers (the Empire State Building under construction!). In any case, the bagels and fixings available here are hard to beat — baked fresh daily and in a sumptuous variety. You'll find various fancy spreads packaged to go, and a selection of bagel sandwiches, breakfast items, lunch salads, and bialys (try 'em, you'll like 'em — especially toasted), all of which you can enjoy on the premises. Party platters are available. The shop is in the Atlantic View Retail Center, immediately west of the drawbridge, and is open every day.

The Oceanic Restaurant

$$$ • 703 S. Lumina Ave., Wrightsville Beach • 256-5551

Few culinary experiences are as delightful as dining on the pier at the Oceanic. As pelicans kite overhead and the surf crashes below, you could be enjoying a chilled drink, fresh blackened swordfish or some of the region's most acclaimed crab dip. Should the weather turn angry, the Oceanic's two floors of indoor seating offer panoramic views. The Oceanic does nothing innovative, but its tried-and-true menu items are satisfying, delicious and a good value. Heart-healthy menu items abound. From entree salads, seafood platters and specialties to chicken, steaks and prime rib, the menu is quite varied, including the kids' menu. Entrees include a variety of extras ranging from salads and she crab soup to hushpuppies, slaw, rice pilaf, vegetables, potatoes and confetti orzo. Juices used in mixed drinks are all squeezed fresh daily. Those seeking the perfect Margarita should dowse here. The maritime decor features historic photographs that are attractions in themselves. Top off your meal with a walk on the pier or beach. Sunday brunch begins at 10 AM, and breakfast is served all day on weekends. Lunch and dinner are served daily. The third-floor banquet room is available for private parties. Free parking is ample.

Ocean Terrace Restaurant

$$$$ • At the Blockade Runner Resort Hotel, 275 Waynick Blvd., Wrightsville Beach • 256-2251

With an unbroken view of the ocean, dining at the Ocean Terrace is everything you'd expect of a premier hotel. To the strains of soft jazz in a comfortable, carpeted room, the

★ Texas Mesquite Steaks ★ Seafood ★
★ Baby Back Barbeque Ribs ★
★ Texas Pheasant ★ Texas Salads ★
★ Children's Menu ★

Landfall Center, Wilmington

All major credit cards accepted.

kitchen serves top-quality Angus beef, poultry, pasta, seafood and salads with distinction and creativity. Recent entrees have included corn bread-stuffed Carolina quail, 20-ounce grilled Porterhouse steak, succulent pork medallions in port wine with dried apples and cranberries, and other sumptuous feasts. Specials are always something to plan for, especially when live lobster is the main course or part of a surf-and-turf combination. The Ocean Terrace serves lunch every day in the restaurant or the adjoining bar. Lunch specialties include hearty sandwiches and salads including a classic Caesar and cold poached salmon. Also available are personal pizzas, appetizers (coconut beer shrimp, house-cured gravlax and more), soups and homemade desserts. Of special interest are the Ocean Terrace's two buffets, the Seafood & Prime Rib Buffet on Saturday nights and the Sunday Jazz Brunch featuring live jazz and a sumptuous spread. Inquire about the seasonal Friday Lobster Nights. Reservations, especially for the buffets, are strongly recommended.

Pusser's Landing at Wally's
$$-$$$ • 4 Marina St., Wrightsville Beach • 256-8500

Famous for its West Indian and nautical ambience, its namesake rum and a menu of vibrantly flavored foods, Pusser's made its area debut in early 1997 at the ever-popular waterside restaurant, Wally's. While Wally's best features remain — boat docks on the Intracoastal Waterway, live outdoor entertainment overlooking the docks on Sunday (3 to 7 PM), and one of the liveliest bar scenes around — Pusser's Landing comprises two restaurants (thus the hyphenated price code), completely redesigned, featuring fine din-

Photo: N.C. Travel & Tourism

What a great way to get back to the basics.

ing and a comfortable cigar lounge upstairs and slightly more casual fare downstairs. (Your attire in both rooms need not differ: neat, beach-casualwear fits right in.) The cozy decor includes a fireplace, gas lights on the canopied porch and roomy wooden tables. Downstairs, Pusser's offers specialty sandwiches (we recomend the West Indian Turkey) and salads, fish 'n' chips, shepherd's pie, chicken roti and more. Try the steam pot of mixed seafood for two. Appetizers served upstairs include fried green tomatoes, onion grass (like thinly sliced onion rings), conch fritters and escargo. From rack of lamb and seafood casserole to prime rib and beyond, the hearty entrees served upstairs come with salad, vegetable and bread. All deserts are made on the premises (the signature desert is rum cake, naturally). Open every day, Pusser's serves lunch, and dinner is served until 11 PM downstairs, until 10:30 PM upstairs. Reservations are accepted for the upstairs only, and the restaurants are completely handicapped accessible.

Vinnie's Steak House & Tavern
$$$$ • Lumina Station, Wrightsville Beach • 256-0995

One of the more eagerly awaited openings in our area was Vinnie's in November of '96, due largely to the reputation of its progenitor in Raleigh, considered among the top places for power meals, dinner deals, schmoozing and being seen. The Wrightsville Beach location promises much the same. Not only are the walls adorned with caricatures of celebrities, à la Sardi's, Vinnie's even has a cigar room for the power smokers among us! Everything here speaks of high quality and high-rollers: dark, elaborate woodwork, comfortable seating and some of the area's most enviable steaks, chops and seafood. All bar drinks are top-shelf. Vinnie's is only open for dinner and drinks, and can get fairly packed in no time. Reservations are only accepted for parties of five or more. The bar opens at 4 PM and dinner is served until everyone has gone home.

Carolina Beach
and Kure Beach

Big Daddy's Seafood Restaurant
$$ • 202 K. Ave., Kure Beach • 458-8622

A Kure Beach institution for three decades, Big Daddy's serves a variety of better-quality seafood and combination platters. Seafood can be broiled, fried, chargrilled, steamed or fixed Calabash-style. These and choice steaks, prime rib and chicken are offered every day in a family-oriented, casual setting. Highlights of Big Daddy's menu include all-you-can-eat, Lowcountry, family-style dining, an inexpensive all-you-can-eat salad bar, special plates for seniors and children and the sizable Surf and Turf Supreme (beef tenderloin with split Alaskan king crab legs). An after-dinner walk along the beach or on the Kure Beach fishing pier (both a block away) further adds to Big Daddy's appeal. Because the restaurant consists of several rooms, its total seating capacity of about 500 people comes as a surprise; it doesn't seem that big. Rare and unusual maritime memorabilia make for entertaining distractions. Entrance to the restaurant is through a colorful gift shop offering novelties and taffy. Patrons frequently make secret wishes and cast coins into the fountain there. Located at the only stop light in Kure Beach, Big Daddy's has all ABC permits and ample parking in front and across the street.

The Cottage
$$ • 1 N. Lake Park Blvd., Carolina Beach • 458-4383

The Cottage occupies a tastefully renovated home, reputedly the oldest in Carolina Beach. The interior is modern, preserving the several ground-level rooms as separate dining areas. In keeping with the owners' motto, "Simple foods well-prepared," the cuisine is a simple, effective combination of Lowcountry and new-American approaches to seafood, chicken and beef with a hint of Italian. The kitchen shows real strength in the appetizers, soups (ask about the tomato-dill and carrot-ginger soups) and desserts. Entrees are served with a small salad and two sides, and the preparations are fresh, natural and heart-healthy. The lunch menu includes affordable sandwiches, salads and quiche, placing the Cottage high on the list of options when coming off the beach hungry. While waiting for your table, enjoy a drink on the front porch. Portions aren't huge, but the Cottage is most worthwhile. A children's menu is available, and kids can pass the wait with a

stack of children's books. The Cottage serves imported and domestic beer and mixed drinks and is open for lunch and dinner Monday through Saturday from March 1 through New Year's Day.

Freddie's Restaurant
$$ • 111 K Ave., Kure Beach • 458-5979

Dining at Freddie's is a curiously pleasant experience. The room is cozy, almost tiny, and the seashore murals, greenery, checkered table coverings and coastal knickknacks will almost certainly make you forget you're in a cinder-block building, but not that you're in Kure Beach, North Carolina. Servers may dress in tuxedo vests, bow ties and sneakers. The owners will come by and chat. The food is hearty, well-prepared and thoroughly homemade. Barbara's Famous Lasagna is just like Mom's (if Mom was Italian). The bread is crusty and fresh, as it should be. Nightly specials are unusual — be sure to try the portabello mushroom Bolognese — and there's always a wide choice if you're a lover of meat (including chops), seafood, poultry or pasta. All entrees come with a large romaine salad with Italian dressing (naturally), bread and a side of pasta. With an appetizer you may not be able to finish dinner, so save room for espresso and dessert. Freddie's is open every day of the year — for dinner only during the week off-season and for lunch and dinner on weekends. It's a few steps from the Kure Beach Pier, under an awning painted red, white and green. Naturally.

J. Council's
$$$$ • 205 Charlotte St., Carolina Beach • 458-9411

Consider J. Council's the gift of opportunity and fine French-American dining. The high-ceilinged main room is spacious and simple, as a former Presbyterian church would be, with bare wood floors and indirect lighting. Linen, white china, silver and crystal lamps grace the tables. This is a place for the adventurous palate to try something new, perhaps escargot,

INSIDERS' TIP

Did you know most local restaurants will package those scrumptious desserts to go?

Photo: Scott Taylor

This rare sighting of a pointy headed, pencil necked, slim shank
has local ornithologists atwitter.

country pâté with a warm basil sauce, wild mushrooms or grouper topped with an herb shrimp mousse and wrapped in puff pastry. The kitchen works wonders with steak, crabmeat, veal and poultry — even breast of pheasant on occasion. Expect all those heavenly French sauces as well. Of the two wine lists, the Captain's Wine Book presents a connoisseur's selection. Tuxedoed servers provide formal service, but you won't feel out of place dressed casually. The main restaurant serves dinner only and closes on Sunday. The Lounge serves a similar menu, in a room reminiscent of a sea captain's home, from 3 PM until midnight every day except Sunday. Reservations for both rooms are strongly recommended. Look for J. Council's steeple off the west side of Lake Park Boulevard as you drive south of Cape Fear Boulevard.

Malley's Restaurant & Pub
$$$ • 103 N. Lake Park Blvd., Carolina Beach • 458-5766

Bred from the success of its Harrisburg, PA, progenitor, this restaurant opened in spring 1997 with a varied menu full of new choices. The long list of appetizers includes tried-and-

true standards and such unusual additions as grilled portabello and brie, and artichoke fritters. Malley's is a casual place specializing in fresh local seafoods used in dinner salads, pasta dishes, bouillabaisse and various meat combinations, such as Chicken Chesapeake (breast of chicken stuffed with crab meat). Dinner entrees, served after 4 PM, also include grilled steaks and barbecue shrimp skewers. Entrees come with salad, bread and vegetable or potato. Rounding out the menu are a variety of burgers and sandwiches. Malley's occupies a high-ceilinged room braced with skylights and floral touches. Balcony seating abounds, and the front porch overlooks the heart of Carolina Beach. Malley's also comprises an adjoining night club, for a complete night's entertainment. Malley's accepts reservations and serves lunch Monday through Friday and dinner every night. Sunday brunch, which includes fresh-cut meats, omelets made to order and homemade desserts, is served from 11 AM to 3 PM.

Marina's Edge
$$ • 300 N. Lake Park Blvd., Carolina Beach • 458-6001

Marina's Edge specializes in steaks, seafood and raw-bar fare, stressing healthful preparation and reasonable prices. It's an interesting reversal that fried foods are more expensive than grilled or sauteed selections. Popular items fill out the menu, from potato skins, shrimp cocktails and shark bites (flash-fried shark meat) to sandwiches, prime rib and crab legs. Chicken Parmigiana, shrimp scampi and shrimp-scallop Alfredo offer appealing Italian twists on the norm. There is also an affordable children's menu. The attractive decor features soothing lavenders, linens of turquoise and white, natural wood and plenty of light. The raw bar and lounge afford comfortable seating for light meals or cocktails. Marina's Edge serves dinner seven days a week and offers lunch on Saturday and Sunday.

Paradise Cafe

$ • 6A N. Lake Park Blvd., Carolina Beach • 458-4020

This intimate little eatery, one block from the Boardwalk, is the place for zesty salads, sandwiches and soups. Sandwiches, such as the Paradise Melt and a classic Reuben, are hefty affairs, and the Carolina Beach Cheese Steak scores highly. The Paradise serves wine and beer, offers daily specials and can package your order to go. From Memorial Day to Labor Day, it's open every day for lunch and dinner. Paradise closes on Sunday in the off season.

Silver Dollar

$, no credit cards • 4 Cape Fear Blvd., Carolina Beach • 458-6811

Locals know the Silver Dollar for more than having the winningest softball team in Carolina Beach (they've whupped every team around for the past six years). This little wood-panelled establishment, just off the Boardwalk, is a local institution, having served shrimp, oysters, crab legs and clams since 1957. Also offered are pizza, wings and fries, and the bar serves wine and pitchers of draft with frosty mugs. It's a casual place filled with the strains of beach music, oldies and classic rock, and it's open every day in summer. Hours are curtailed in spring and fall, and the place closes in winter.

Sweetwater Cafe

$$ • 106 Carl Winner's Ave., Carolina Beach • 458-0500

Sweetwater Cafe offers coastal ambiance, well-prepared fare at a good price and up-close views of the municipal docks, especially from the rooftop deck. Naturally, the menu includes plenty of local seafood, including soft-shell crab in season. Seafood entrees are available fried, Cajun-style or broiled. The restaurant's pride, however, is prime rib, recommended by Insiders. Sweetwater also offers a raw bar menu, steamers, a variety of dinner salads, a good selection of sandwiches and burgers, domestic and imported beer and domestic wine. Indoor seating is intimate, with oil lamps on tables dressed in white linen. Seating on the outdoor decks is more ample, and the lower deck is curtained in the cool weather.

Bald Head Island

The Bald Head Island Club

$$$ • Bald Head Island • 457-7300

Refined yet somewhat relaxed, the Club dining room is a warm atmosphere in which to enjoy a fine selection of seafood, chargrilled steaks, pasta, poultry and fresh desserts. The wine list offers some of the better domestic vintages. The weekly gala buffet, a sumptuous fixed-price feast, is a deservedly popular summer event for which reservations are required. Set in a building reminiscent of coastal New England, the room is modulated by wood, carpeting and floral wallpaper and commands a fine ocean view. The club does not allow T-shirts or cutoffs but does permit dress shorts during the summer.

Entry to the Club requires at least a temporary membership, which is included in accommodation rates for all properties leased through Bald Head Island Management Inc. Temporary memberships may also be arranged for day-visits and group tours through the management office. The Club dining room serves dinner Tuesday through Sunday, Memorial Day to Labor Day. It is closed for the month of January and open on weekends during February.

Call for information on spring and fall schedules. Reservations are always preferred.

Island Chandler Delicatessen
$ • Bald Head Island Marina • 457-7450

This is really no more than the deli counter at the Island Chandler grocery store, but the well-prepared, ready-to-eat foods (cold salads, sandwiches, cheeses, seafood, etc.) can be enjoyed at the tables on the patio overlooking the marina. Be sure to ask for some plastic utensils.

River Pilot Cafe
$$ • Bald Head Island • 457-7390

Boasting the finest ocean view on the island, the River Pilot Cafe and its adjoining lounge serve breakfast, lunch and dinner in a more casual setting than the Club dining room. Nonetheless, the expanded wine list and fine linen provide an upscale tenor to a menu that includes soups, excellent salads and burgers as well as daily meat and seafood specials. In summer, the Cafe serves the island's best breakfasts. It's also a superb vantage from which to view stunning sunsets while enjoying a meal or drink. The River Pilot is open daily during the summer, and reservations are requested for dinner.

Southport-Oak Island

The Chart House
$ • 832 N. Howe St., Southport • 457-4777

Genuine home cooking in an informal, no-frills setting makes The Chart House a popular breakfast and lunch spot for locals. Standard American breakfast items and Belgian waffles are complemented by Southern-style biscuits, country ham and grits. Breakfast is served all day. Daily lunch specials are hearty and inexpensive. Seafood offerings can be fried, grilled or blackened, and grilled meats, home-

made barbecue and fish sandwiches are available.

Del's Restaurant
$$ • 6302 E. Oak Island Dr., Long Beach • 278-3338

Pleasant, small and casual, Del's specializes in Italian-style seafood and regional dishes, pizza, subs and sandwiches. Spaghetti Buckets yielding two to eight servings are something you won't see every day, except at Del's. The friendly staff serves beer, wine and wine coolers as well as a smattering of Cajun-style meat dishes. Call-in orders may be picked up at the drive-through window, and local delivery is available after 5 PM (call 278-1912). Del's is open for lunch and dinner daily.

Harborside Seafood Restaurant and Grille
$$ • 607 W. West St., Southport • 457-0021

The Harborside serves superior regional cuisine with plenty of local atmosphere. Deceptively large for its intimate appearance, the restaurant offers a partial waterfront view across tables set with fresh flowers and lamps, a warm setting in which to enjoy such dishes as a fried goat-cheese salad with sherry-vinaigrette dressing and Chef Phipps' own take on shrimp and grits (made with country ham and brown gravy). The menu emphasizes seafood and soups, but includes various meat dishes, daily specials and a children's menu. Ingredients are all fresh and natural — some herbs are grown right on the premises — and breads are baked fresh daily.

The adjoining oyster/raw bar is a handsome room with nautical motif, high tables and chairs and brass detailing. Steam buckets, appetizers, oysters on the half-shell and other local specialties are served, or you can have cocktails while waiting for your table. The wine list features better domestic pressings and champagnes. Live music is featured on Friday and Saturday nights after dinner in the lounge. The Harborside, near the Southport Marina, is open every day except Sunday and provides plenty of parking.

Jones' Seafood House
$$ • 6404 E. Oak Island Dr., Long Beach
• 278-5231

Jones' Seafood House affords patrons a casual dining experience of high quality. The menu offers all the most popular regional specialties including fresh crabmeat patties, trout filet and grilled shrimp-and-scallop skewers. Meat lovers won't be disappointed by the variety of steaks, chicken and pork and a selection of surf-and-turf combinations. Dinner specials and a children's menu are available, and the restaurant has all ABC permits. All menu items are available for take out. Jones' Seafood House and the lounge are open Monday through Saturday for dinner. Lunch is served on Sundays.

Lucky Fisherman
$ • 4419 Long Beach Rd. S.E. (N.C. 133), Southport • 457-9499

This lively establishment offers a huge all-you-can-eat seafood buffet every night for a mere nine clams per adult. There are usually more than 30 hot items to choose from, made from old Lowcountry recipes modified to accommodate low-cholesterol and reduced-sodium diets. The salad and dessert bars are equally expansive, and nightly specials keep the offerings varied. Entrees are available à la carte and include fresh fried or broiled fish, lobster tails, crab legs and steaks. Early-bird specials and senior citizen discounts are available. A separate children's menu offers popular kid-size meals. Lucky Fisherman is open every day and accepts take-out orders. Reservations and special parties are welcome.

Marge's Restaurant & Waffle House
$ • 5700 E. Oak Island Dr., Long Beach
• 278-3070

Among Long Beach residents Marge's is one of the most popular diner-style eateries for breakfast and lunch. No matter how crowded it gets, the food is served hot, fast and with a smile, and no one will rush you. Table-to-table conversation comes easily as folks dine on large omelets, flaky biscuits, pasta, grilled foods, fried seafood and local specialties such as hush puppies, okra and beans. Marge's is open daily for breakfast (starting at 5:30 AM!) and lunch and serves breakfast all day. Take-out orders are welcome.

Port Charlie's
$$ • 317 W. Bay St., Southport • 457-4395

With a harbor view from practically every seat, Port Charlie's is many Insiders' first choice for quality seafood, steaks, pasta and consistently fine service in Southport. If too much fried fish has jaded your palate, Port Charlie's can revive it with a variety of salads, Cajun-spiced seafood and meat, chargrilled steaks and sauteed veal. Situated next to Southport's old yacht basin, Port Charlie's features limited screened-in porch seating, an attractively rustic dining room and docking facilities for customers (come by boat!). Free snacks are occasionally served in the Marker One Lounge, which also has darts and a juke box. Port Charlie's possesses all ABC permits, serves dinner seven nights a week during the summer and provides ample free parking and senior citizen discounts.

Sandfiddler Seafood Restaurant
$$ • N.C. Hwy. 211, Southport • 457-6588

With its high-pitched roof, plainly set tables and nautical decor, this large establishment offers rustic ambiance and affordable Lowcountry cuisine. Lunch specials, served with hush puppies, slaw and fries, are low-priced, and landlubbers will find plenty of landfood to choose from, including steaks and pit-cooked pork barbecue. Most of the regional seafood staples are available, including deviled crabs, fried fantail shrimp stuffed with crabmeat and a good selection of combination platters. You can get take-out orders too. The Sandfiddler serves lunch Monday through Friday and Sunday. Dinner is served Monday through Friday and Saturday. The restaurant is on the outskirts of Southport near N.C. 87.

Sea Captain Restaurant
$ • 608 W. West St., Southport • 457-5075

The Sea Captain serves affordable, Southern-style breakfasts and lunches in a somewhat cafeteria-style atmosphere. Guests may design their own omelets, and egg substitutes are available. Breakfast is served until 11 AM on weekdays and 2 PM on weekends. Lunch specialties include Cajun-style blackened treats such as beef or shrimp burgers and chicken breast, or you can have the home-style lunch special of meat, two vegetables, rolls or hush puppies. The Sea Captain is next to the Sea Captain Motor Lodge near the Southport Marina.

Thai Peppers
$$ • 115 E. Moore St., Southport • 457-0095

An uncommon dining experience in the Lower Cape Fear, Thai Peppers demands a visit. Thai foods are influenced equally by China and India, so you'll find familiar appetizers, soups and stir-fried entrees from China but also delicious Thai hybrids. Such Thai specialties as satay (skewered meat), ajard (cucumber salad), tom kha gai (chicken coconut milk soup), a wide variety of stir-fries, rice and curries are available. Meals are often served with contemporary Thai music playing in the background. Those who shy away from curry may become true believers once they sample the several varieties offered here. The fried basil leaves with meat (chicken, beef or pork), the stir-fried ginger with meat and the green curry should not be missed. Thai food tends to be spicy, but Thai Peppers will adjust the heat of any dish to taste, avoiding pepper spice entirely if you wish.

Any menu item can be prepared without meat. Founded by Voravit "Tic" Hemawong, a native of Bangkok, Thai Peppers is casual and offers sheltered outdoor seating. Excellent bargains are the lunch specials (appetizer, soup, entree and rice), which change every day. Iced Thai coffee or Thailand's Singha beer are excellent accompaniments. Thai Peppers serves lunch Monday through Friday. Dinner is served nightly. Take-out orders are welcome, and reservations are recommended for parties of more than five. The restaurant closes in winter.

Windjammer Restaurant & Lounge
$$ • 1411 E. Beach Dr., Long Beach • 278-7740

The Windjammer has a solid reputation for fine dining. Through enormous oceanfront windows, the view overlooking the Ocean Crest Pier is superb. The menu emphasizes a variety of seafood served Calabash-style, sauteed or broiled. Freshly cut steaks and chicken make limited appearances. The Windjammer is the only place on the island where you can try the enormous bloomin' onion. The jalapeños stuffed with crabmeat are, as owner Wade Goin puts it, "right famous." In a fairly large, bright room, the Windjammer features occasional live entertainment during the high season and offers breakfast and lunch buffets. It is open every day in the summer and has all ABC permits.

Yacht Basin Provision Company
$$ • 130 Yacht Basin Dr., Southport • 457-0654

This, as one perceptive youngster once put it, is "the secret place," which must be true since it even eluded the Insiders' Guide early on. And what a discovery! A

> **FYI**
> Unless otherwise noted, the area code for all phone numbers in this guide is 910.

casual and entirely outdoor eatery, the Provision Company has the best decor possible, the Southport Yacht Basin and waterfront. It's a place where the honor system is still honored: beverages are self-serve and no guest checks are written. Specialties of the house include great shrimp and crab cakes, conch fritters and grouper salad. Open for lunch and dinner seven days a week from St. Patrick's Day through mid-December, the Provision Company has all ABC permits and is something of a nightspot as well. You may arrive by sea — boat slips are available. You'll find the Provision Company next to the shell shop as you come down Bay Street. Look for the funky green building that once was a provisions house.

South Brunswick Islands

Crabby Oddwaters Restaurant and Bar
$$ • 310 Sunset Blvd., Sunset Beach • 579-6372

If the food weren't so darn good, this upstairs restaurant would still be worth a visit just to read the story of how it got its "damp and crawly name" (a story told in

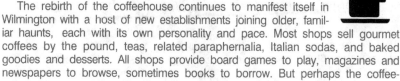

Wilmington Coffeehouses

The rebirth of the coffeehouse continues to manifest itself in Wilmington with a host of new establishments joining older, familiar haunts, each with its own personality and pace. Most shops sell gourmet coffees by the pound, teas, related paraphernalia, Italian sodas, and baked goodies and desserts. All shops provide board games to play, magazines and newspapers to browse, sometimes books to borrow. But perhaps the coffeehouses' greatest value is their contribution to the art of congenial socializing and the act of slowing down, despite the caffeine; to providing forums for sharing news and announcements of cultural events — hallmarks of the highly evolved community.

Cape Fear Coffee & Tea, 24 S. Front Street, 343-1500, was one of the first coffeehouses to open in downtown Wilmington. Its several rocking chairs outdoors are extremely popular. Here you'll find the *New York Times* every day as well as fresh baked goods. It's also a great place to inspect, perhaps buy, local artwork (including some by one of the shop's own servers). The shop is open from 6:30 AM to 10 PM Sunday through Thursday and until midnight Friday and Saturday.

Fontana Caffe, 4555 Fountain Drive, 313-0227, is a European-style coffee bar, specializing only in espressos and specialty concoctions made with Illycaffe brand arabica espresso and featuring drive-through service.

General Assembly, 300 N. Front Street, Wilmington, 343-8890, across the street from the Cotton Exchange, is attractively designed in a Federalist/neo-Georgian style (befitting the London origin of the coffee house tradition), with handsome woodwork and large windows on two sides. This shop boasts one of Wilmington's two scaled-down statues of Liberty.

Java Lane, 4302 Wrightsville Avenue, Wilmington, 313-0704, takes the name "coffeehouse" literally by having turned an entire former residence into a comfortable, attractive place to enjoy your favorite cup o' joe. Choose among easy chairs beside the living room fireplace, office-like desks in the adjoining room or a conference table in the meeting room. Java Lane frequently features live music,

— continued on next page

CAPE FEAR COFFEE & TEA COMPANY™

24 South Front St.
Wilmington, NC

Sun-Thurs 6:30 a.m. to 10:00 p.m.
Fri-Sat 6:30 a.m. to midnight
(910) 343-1500

Fresh Roasted Gourmet Coffee and Bulk Teas

— continued from previous page

including bluegrass and jazz. Schedules tend to be weekly (usually Saturdays from 8 to 10 PM), but be sure to check the chalk board for updates.

Kelly's Coffee Pub, 5751 Oleander Drive in the Philips Azalea Plaza, Wilmington, 392-7693, is as homey as your living room but a little smokier. (After all, this is a pub!) Kelly's is open until 5 PM weekdays and on Saturdays from 9 AM to 5 PM and 7 to 10 PM (closed Sundays). Jazz musicians from the university frequently stop in on Saturdays to play for tips.

Port City Java, 7 N. Front Street, 762-5282, is intimate (OK, that also means small), cozy, artsy, and features comfy chairs and excellent desserts. But what really distinguishes this shop is that they roast their own coffee beans fresh daily, right around the corner. You can smell it for blocks. They also specialize in fruit smoothies and juices, non-java beverages such as Ghirardelli cocoas and the tea blend known as Chai. The shop remains open until 10 PM most nights, later on Fridays and Saturdays. Also visit their Wrightsville Beach location, at Lumina Station on Eastwood Road, 256-0993, where they serve excellent grilled panini (sandwiches) among other delights.

Kona's Coffee Beanery, Plaza East Shopping Center, Wrightsville Beach, 256-5662, offers wide variety of fresh-roasted coffees, plus an assortment of unusual food items, such as avocado toast, in a bright, colorful setting just minutes from the beach.

The Smudged Pot News Bar, 5032 Wrightsville Avenue, Wilmington, 452-3995, has no seating but plenty of magazines and newspapers, bagels, fresh juices, smoothies and shakes. They also deliver bulk coffee and specialize in that other surprise trend of the '90s, cigars. This shop is about midway between College Road and Columbia-Cape Fear Memorial Hospital.

one easy-to-remember sentence of barely more than 400 words). This is a small, handsome restaurant with an enclosed deck overlooking a creek. The tables have holes in the center where you can pitch your shucked shells and, despite the plastic utensils, the ambiance and cuisine are high quality. Local seafood of all types is the focus, featuring the unusual shrimp, scallop or combo "KaBillbobs" and wonderful nightly specials (ask about the spicy Seminole snapper). A limited choice of landfood (and, sometimes, hot jambalaya) is offered. Crabby Oddwaters is above Bill's Seafood — which is owned by a guy named Joe — on the mainland side of the pontoon bridge. It is open for dinner all year.

Duffer's Pub & Deli
$ • Shallotte Plaza, Main St., Shallotte
• 754-7229

Modestly priced and generously portioned subs (cold and hot), uncommon half-pound burgers made with Angus beef (try the bleu cheese), and salads are Duffer's long suit. Subs and sandwiches include a side order, and burgers all come with steak fries. Specialty cold cuts include capocolla (Italian hot ham), prosciutto, and turkey pastrami, and salads are made fresh daily. Sandwiches are made to order, and meals are delivered right to your table. They even serve PB&J for the kids.

FYI

Unless otherwise noted, the area code for all phone numbers in this guide is 910.

J/G's Country Bar-B-Que
$ • Barbecue Rd., Grissettown • 287-3505

If you eat at a Southern-style barbecue joint only once in your life, this is the place to go. For $9 (children younger than 12, $4) you can eat all the smoky chicken, beef and pork barbecue you can handle, along with plenty of other country-style fare, served on cardboard plates. Seating is at long picnic tables that fill half the barn. The other half accommodates the stage and dance floor for the occasional live country music (and sometimes bluegrass) and dancers who come from miles around. Music usually begins about 7 PM. Beverages are extra (pitchers of sweet tea cost a whopping $1.50), and no alcohol is permitted. J/G's is open Wednesday through Saturday from 5 to 10 PM and Sunday from noon to 10 from April through October. Grissettown is north of Sunset and Ocean Isle beaches off U.S. 17. From U.S. 17, take N.C. 904 north for 1.4 miles; turn right onto Russtown Road, go 1.4 miles farther,

turn right down unpaved Barbecue Road and park on the lawn.

Roberto's Pizzeria & Restaurant
$ • Jordan Ave., Holden Beach • 842-4999

Hailing from Philadelphia, the Roberto family brought authentic Italian-American, hand-tossed pizza to Holden Beach. And their Philly cheese steaks are right on the money too. They operate at two locations. The Holden Beach restaurant (the only restaurant on the island) closes from November through March, and the Ocean Isle Beach location, at 6773 Beach Drive (N.C. 179), 579-4999, is open all year. Specialty dinners, hoagies (Philadelphia's name for subs or heroes), burgers, nightly specials, beer and wine are available to eat in, take out or have delivered locally. Both locations are open seven days a week during the summer.

Sharky's Pizza & Deli
$ • Causeway Dr., Ocean Isle Beach
• 579-9177

When owners Al and Ray traded their power suits for bathing suits and opened Sharky's in 1991, their goal was to provide a good place to eat with a great view. They've succeeded. The food at Sharky's isn't fancy but is well-priced and can be enjoyed indoors or on the handicapped-accessible deck overlooking the waterway. You can tie up your boat at Sharky's dock. Thoroughly casual and fun for the whole family, Sharky's offers Lite Bites (wings, chicken tenders, etc.), thin-crust pizza, a nice selection of hot and cold subs, beer, soups and salads. Occasionally, Sharky's hosts family-oriented holiday parties with live music, volleyball and plenty of food. There's even a rooftop band stand. Most days, the stereo pumps lively rock, country and beach music. Ray describes his clientele and staff as "a laid-back, fun-loving, music-loving bunch." Sharky's also provides free local delivery. It is next to the ABC store at the foot of the bridge.

Photo: N.C. Aquarium

This is what snapper looks like before it gets to your plate.

Sugar Shack
$$ • 1609 Hale Beach Rd., Ocean Isle • 579-3844

Don't miss this place. Sugar Shack features authentic Jamaican home cooking (yes, the chef is Jamaican) in a colorful, intimate setting about a mile from the beach. Amid greenery, tropical artwork and floral table coverings, recorded reggae music adds a lively island feel most days, while live music is offered on weekends (don't be surprised if the regulars dance). Sugar Shack specializes in its own recipe for jerk seasoning — a complex blend of scallions, onions, thyme, cinnamon, nutmeg, pepper and magic. The tangy jerk chicken, pork and beef — marinated, barbecued and served with a hot 'n' sweet sauce — anchor a small but delightful menu that also includes Stamp & Go (a traditional spicy cod fritter), Brown Stewed Fish (slowly cooked red snapper) and a curried goat so tender it literally falls off the bone. Most items are marinated, slowly simmered and richly flavored. Nothing is too spicy for the average palate, but imported hot sauce is available if you want to hurt yourself. Some appetizers are enough for a meal, and the Jamaican Sampler is a good introduction. Red Stripe beer and Guinness Stout are served, of course. Other offerings include jerk chicken salads and Cobb salads, fruit dishes, homemade soups as well as burgers and grilled steaks. Sugar Shack is one block south of Ocean Isle Beach Road, a few yards off N.C. 179. (Ocean Isle Beach Road intersects U.S. 17 about 3 miles east of Grissettown.) Take-out orders are welcome. Sugar Shack is open every day in summer, serving lunch until 3 PM and dinner until 9 PM (Sundays until 7 PM).

Twin Lakes Restaurant
$$ • 102 Sunset Blvd., Sunset Beach • 579-6373

Bouncing back from the post-hurricane doldrums better than ever, Twin Lakes' renovations included the addition of a stunning second floor with full bar and a panoramic view of the region's most picturesque watercourse. Twin Lakes stands rooted in the region's long culinary tradition, having family connections linked to the earliest seafood days of nearby Calabash. With its tropical decor enhanced by banana trees outdoors and floral table coverings and local art within, Twin Lakes is an attractive family restaurant that stays busy. The menu has undergone some renovation, too, now including meat and seafood specials nightly. Otherwise, seafood, vegetables and pasta comprise the bulk of the menu. Entrees may be ordered fried, sauteed, grilled, broiled or blackened, and the seafood is never long out of the water. Seafood salads, stir-fry and pasta combinations are all nicely done. As always, irresistible desserts are all homemade by local women (the butterscotch pie is "to die for").

Capt. Willie's Restaurant
$$ • Holden Beach Causeway, Holden Beach • 842-9383

Capt. Willie's, owned and operated by one of the area's grand old families and helmed by a former Norwegian Cruise Lines chef, specializes in fresh country cooking featuring seafood (fried, broiled and blackened), plus a few steak, chicken, pork and barbecue dishes. The buffets for breakfast and lunch and the evening seafood buffet are worthwhile bargains, and the ambiance is casual and friendly. Capt. Willie's is open every day for breakfast, lunch and dinner from 7 AM until 9 PM, and it stands beside the Water Slide Ice Cream shop, a short hop from the beach.

Calabash

Calabash Seafood Hut
$ • 1125 River Rd., Calabash • 579-6723

Don't be surprised to find this tiny place with a line of customers stretching around the corner. It's that popular as much for its low, low prices as for the food, which is as good as anywhere else in Calabash. The seafood platters, offering combinations of Calabash-style fish, shrimp, oysters, crab and scallops, are huge. For only the biggest appetites would the daily specials not suffice (served from 11 AM until 4 PM). Sandwich offerings include soft-shell crab in season. Children will enjoy many items besides the children's menu. All meals are served with a drink (refills included), coleslaw, french fries and hushpuppies. The atmosphere is clean and bright, and everyone there is friendly. The Hut serves lunch and dinner from 11 AM until 9 PM, and they do a brisk take-out business through the street-side window.

Larry's Calabash Seafood Barn
$$ • N.C. 179, Calabash • 579-6976

Unless you insist on having a view of the docks at the foot of River Road, Larry's is one of the better choices for Calabash-style seafood on the other side of town. The all-you-can-eat seafood buffet, which often includes crab legs, and raw bar are frequently cited by Insiders as reasons for repeat visits. Nightly specials include Italian buffets and prime rib. Despite its name, Larry's bears little resemblance to a barn. Rather, it is clean, bright and spacious and features rocking chairs on the front porch. Larry's also serves steaks and mixed drinks and offers golfers' specials (present your scorecard for a discount), a children's menu and discounts to large groups. Larry's is open for dinner every day from mid-March through November.

The Original Calabash Restaurant
$$ • On the waterfront, Calabash • 579-6875

Whether this is actually the first "original" Calabash restaurant is secondary to the fact that it's a decent place to try Calabash-style seafood (Insiders say Beck's "Old Original Calabash Restaurant," established in 1940, was the first). The hamburgers, steaks and chicken seem like distant afterthoughts on a menu outbalanced by seafood — everything from oyster stew and teriyaki shrimp to stuffed flounder in hollandaise and soft-shell crabs. Open every day during the high season, The Original Calabash stands at the foot of River Road in a large parking area rimmed by several competitors, but you can't miss it: it's the one straight ahead with the garish flashing lights. Welcome to Calabash.

Ella's of Calabash
$$ • 1148 River Rd., Calabash • 579-6728

Ella's is among the stalwarts of Calabash that remain open most of the off-season, and they've been doing so since 1950. This is also one of the least flashy establishments; they prefer to draw their patrons with good food, affordable prices and a casual, friendly atmosphere rather than with excessive prefab nautical ambiance. Ella's offers a worth-while lunch special (choice of two seafood, plus slaw, hush puppies and fries) that's a real bargain. Steaks, chicken, oyster roasts (in season), mixed drinks and a children's menu are also available. Ella's is open daily and is almost midway between the water-front and Beach Drive (N.C. 179).

Topsail Island

Betty's Smokehouse Restaurant
$ • NC Hwy. 17 N, Holly Ridge • 329-1708
Real down-home cooking is how Betty's

describes its fare, and the slow-cooked barbecue is locally famous. This is one of the few places around where you'll find the bloomin' onion. Betty's serves breakfast (6:30 to 11 AM), lunch and dinner at family prices, seven days a week. Dinner offer-ings include steaks (seasoned with garlic), chops, crab cakes and local seafood (mostly fried). There are also low-priced seniors' and kids' menus. Betty's is exceed-ingly casual and friendly, and even fea-tures occasional live entertainment. You can't miss it —it's the big place with the wraparound shed roof, one block north of the Holly Ridge traffic light.

Local Pizzerias

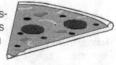

Perhaps due to the influx of Northerners, a pizza renais-sance continues in the Wilmington area. Since the crust is often a pie's most characteristic element, the pizzeria you prefer may depend on crust alone. The following pizze-rias are all highly recommended.

Incredible Pizza, with two locations —1952 Eastwood Road at Plaza East (Wrightsville Beach), 256-0339, and S. College Road at 17th Street Extension,

791-7080, is the pizza most true to its name in the known universe and, in our estimation, ties with Pizza Bistro (below) for the best, most ad-venturous pizza in the greater Wilmington area, hands down. The crust is not too thick, not too doughy.

While we're usually suspicious of anything calling itself "designer," **Pizza Bistro**, 319 N. Front Street, 762-1222, at the Cotton Exchange in Wilmington, bakes up superior, original pizza combinations in a real brick oven and demands a visit, even if the proprietors insist on calling their best-known product "designer pizza." The menu of other Italian specialties is also worthwhile. Sidewalk seating is best on cool evenings when traffic is light (less grime in your wine).

Elizabeth's Pizza, 4304 Market Street, 251-1005, baking thin, crisp-crust pizzas, has long been a Wilmington favorite and also should not be overlooked. (Also try their eggplant manicotti!)

Krazy Pizza & Subs' two locations, 417 S. College Road, 791-0598, and 1616 Shipyard Boulevard at 17th Street, 392-7040, are popular family dining spots, complete with video games for the kids. Pizzas here have soft crusts, and have frequently been voted most popular in local magazine polls.

Numero Uno, 204 Princess Street, 763-1156, is a cozy shop in historic downtown where pizzas feature a light, doughy crust. (Try the calzone, too!)

Vito's Pizzeria, 8 N. Lumina Avenue, Wrightsville Beach, 256-5858, while no longer owned by the original Vito, has been a Wrightsville beach institution for as long as anyone cares to remember, and deservedly so. Crusts here are thin.

Beach's Best Pizzeria, 15 Salisbury Street, Wrightsville Beach, 256-0096, is near Johnny Mercer's Pier and delivers locally. The hand-tossed dough pro-

— continued on next page

— continued from previous page

duces a thin crust that is doughy inside and crispy outside. The pizzeria also serves gyros, subs and beer by the pitcher.

Long Island Pizza, 610 N. River Drive, Surf City, 328-3156, serves up enormous slices of thin-crust pizza within a stone's throw of the ocean.

Roberto's Pizzeria & Restaurant, with two locations — Ocean Boulevard East, Holden Beach, 842-4999, and N.C. Highway 179 at Ocean Isle Beach (on the mainland), 579-4999 — bakes up thick, crispy crusts with some unusual toppings, plus more elaborate Italian fare. They are also known for the area's better Philly cheesesteak sandwiches. The Holden Beach location closes during the off-season.

National franchises such as Domino's and Pizza Hut have several area locations. All these shops except Elizabeth's offer free delivery in limited areas.

Breezeway Restaurant
$$ • Channel and Davis sts., Topsail Beach
• 328-7751

An institution since 1973, the Breezeway is a family restaurant with a great panoramic view of the waterway and a knack for encouraging relaxed dining. Their Lowcountry dinners include the popular crab dip and other crab dishes (crab quesadilla, for instance), surf 'n' turf, grilled and fried chicken and prime rib. Dinner is served every night of the year. Breakfast and lunch are served on weekends in summer. Beer and wine, a children's menu and a daily homemade dessert are also available. The restaurant is adjacent to the Breezeway Motel.

Holland's
Shelter Creek Restaurant
$ • N.C. 53, near Burgaw • 259-5743

Local color is seldom as brilliant as at Holland's. From the moment you step in the door, you know you're in for a country-style treat. Situated over the banks of Holly Shelter Creek, the restaurant adjoins the sport and tackle shop where you may rent canoes, buy hunting supplies or inspect photographs of prize catches. Popular among sportsmen and campers, Holland's serves shrimp, oysters, clam strips, flounder and catfish plus a variety of standard grill fare in a friendly backwoods atmosphere. Holland's is a good 30 miles north of Wilmington (a tad longer from Surf City) on N.C. 53 north of the Holly Shelter Game Land. From I-40, travel about 7.5 miles east, toward Jacksonville. You will find it on the right-hand side next to Holland's Family Campground. The restaurant is open every day for lunch and dinner.

Oceanside Restaurant
$ • Foot of Roland Ave., Surf City
• 328-0619

As in many restaurants along the Carolina coast, the Oceanside is a place where greetings are readily exchanged between strangers. Overlooking the beach, the Oceanside is a popular family eatery (especially on Sundays) that serves breakfast, lunch and dinner seven days a week. The preferred seating is naturally along the oceanfront windows, while larger groups are better accommodated on the inland side. The aptly named Hungry Man Breakfast is a bargain. Burgers, burritos and sandwiches, including soft-shell crab in season, are typical of lunch offerings, while seafood, including combination platters, chicken and a limited choice of steaks round out the evening menu. Beer, wine and desserts are available on request,

INSIDERS' TIP

Joining the WineSeller Wine Club is a great way to learn about wines, meet other wine-lovers, receive news about related events and taste an international selection of pressings. Meetings take place on the first Friday of each month at the WineSeller, 1207 S. Kerr Avenue in Wilmington, 799-5700.

and there is ample parking. The Oceanside is open every day.

Saratoga Restaurant
$$ • N.C. Hwy. 172 at New River Inlet, Sneads Ferry • 327-4031

Since 1979, word of mouth and repeat customers have kept this charming little restaurant a popular destination for quality dinners featuring broiled seafood, steaks and Italian specialties. Only minutes north of Topsail Island, the Saratoga offers casual dining in a refined atmosphere featuring a large working fireplace in winter, soft music, table linen and friendly service. Proprietors Audrey and Orrin Hill (a former ballerina and opera singer, respectively) take pride in such showcase dishes as their shrimp and mushroom bisque, and broiled oysters en brochette (skewered), along with such staples as veal scallopini Marsala and shrimp Creole. The Saratoga opens for dinner every day except Wednesday in summer, Thursday through Sunday off-season. Beer and wine are served, and children's plates are available. Dress casually. Reservations are suggested on weekends and all summer. You'll find Saratoga Restaurant by taking N.C. 172 from U.S. 17 or N.C. 210 toward Sneads Ferry. It's on Old Ferry Road, the last sharp right turn before the New River bridge.

Soundside
$$$ • 209 N. New River Dr., Surf City • 328-0803

Pleasant ambiance, attentive service and quality cuisine make Soundside an above-average dining experience. Established in 1981, Soundside overlooks a tranquil sound perfect for viewing sunsets. Tables are dressed with fresh flowers, handsome tablecloths, lamps and black china. Service is semiformal. Soundside's menu, predominantly seafood, includes unusual dishes such as the smoked salmon with pesto cheesecake. Other highlights include jumbo shrimp Bach (sauteed shrimp baked with tomato salsa and feta) and Parmesan-crusted lemon chicken. Soundside also serves grilled items, prime rib, soups and salads and domestic and imported wines. We suggest reservations for dinner. The excellent Sunday brunch requires no reservations. The restaurant closes during the month of January and is handicapped accessible.

For something more casual, step into The Market next door, a gourmet food and gift shop where you may enjoy all Soundside's non-entree menu items and wine by the glass at candle-lit salon tables on a screened porch overlooking the water. The Market is open seven days a week during the warm season. It's a great place for evening dessert with a loved one.

127 SOUTH COLLEGE
AT MARKET PLACE MALL

BRINGING THE FINEST IN NATIONAL, REGIONAL & LOCAL ENTERTAINMENT.

790 • 5337

WILMINGTONS LARGEST UP SCALE TOP 40 HIGH ENERGY DANCE CLUB.

790 • 5317

Proper Attire Required!

60's, 70's, 80's

Nightlife

The term "nightlife" can mean much different things to locals as opposed to visitors. Plenty of residents spend summer nights searching the beaches for loggerhead turtle nests and helping protect the ones they find. Others prefer the night for offshore fishing. Many youngsters enjoy surprising ghost crabs with their flashlights as the little critters (the crabs) make their nocturnal runs on the beach.

Taken in its usual sense of "going out to be inside someplace else," local nightlife is mostly concentrated in Wilmington, where clubs, bars and theaters are most numerous. Outlying areas, especially the South Brunswick Islands, are famous for their unbroken quiet. But hot spots (a relative term, to be sure) also exist at Wrightsville Beach, Carolina Beach, Surf City and Long Beach, particularly in summer.

Stroll the Riverwalk and Front Street in downtown Wilmington. There are plenty of interesting places along the way in which to pause for a toast or a fresh-brewed cup of coffee. At Wrightsville Beach, Lumina Avenue is often choked with summertime revelers just yards from the quiet beach.

Billiards (see listings in this chapter) and bowling (see our Sports, Fitness and Parks chapter) are fun options for imaginative night owls looking for an alternative to the usual bar scene. Browsing our Attractions chapter will reveal more ideas — a variety of evening cruise opportunities. These include the sternwheeler *Henrietta II* and the *Capt. Maffitt* Sightseeing Cruise on the Cape Fear River, the Winner Cruise Boats at Carolina Beach and the *Hurricane Fleet* out of North Myrtle Beach. Most offer dinner packages.

Those who like to dance may choose among country two-step and line dancing, freeform disco or the area's undisputed monarch of dances, the shag. You can take in an evening of square dancing, contra dancing and clogging to live music (with lessons) at various locations in Wilmington. Call the Cape Fear Contra Dancers, 395-0973, for information.

Fans of classical music should take note of several area presenters that sponsor evening concert programs from October through May. See our chapter on The Arts for complete information on the following classical options.

Since 1930 the **Wilmington Concert Association** has been bringing an amazing roster of world-class musicians and dancers to Wilmington, including such names as Itzhak Perlman, the Beijing Opera, the Canadian Brass and the Alvin Ailey Repertory Dance Ensemble.

UNCW's Kenan Auditorium is the venue for five annual visits by the **North Carolina Symphony**, providing a balance of sturdy classics and classical pops.

The **Chamber Music Society of Wilmington**, launched in 1996, presents highly accomplished professional chamber ensembles performing a variety of programs in the Thalian Hall Ballroom. Founded in 1971, the **Wilmington Symphony Orchestra** is an all-volunteer community orchestra that presents low-priced classical music and pops programs throughout the year with an eye toward the education of young people.

And the **Thalian Hall Center for the Performing Arts** hosts a staggering array of performances. The spectrum has recently embraced stars such as Frank Sinatra, Taj Mahal, Black Umfolosi, the Paul Taylor Dance Company, the Jimmy Dorsey Orchestra, the Shirelles, the Klezmer Conservatory Band and blues singer Koko Taylor, plus unparalleled children's presentations in its Artventure Series.

Thalian Hall is also the focal point for theater in Wilmington (again, see our chapter on The Arts). Also check the newspapers regularly for shows; many companies are itinerant, and shows are often staged in uncommon locations.

Other live entertainment, with the exception of live jazz, is fairly ubiquitous. You will find many nightclubs throughout the region (and the state) that are private. In order for an establishment to serve liquor, it must either earn the bulk of its revenue from the sale of food, or it must be a private club for members and their guests. Alcohol served in clubs that are not private is restricted to beer and wine. Membership to most clubs is inexpensive, usually between $1 and $5 per year. Weekend visitors applying for membership should know that a three-day waiting period must elapse before you can become a full member, but it's easy to be signed in as someone's guest at the door.

What follows is by no means the last word on the area's nightlife. At the end of the chapter is a section on movie theaters, for those whose nightlife tends toward the cinematic.

Nightspots: Bars, Clubs, Live Music Venues and more

Wilmington

Axis
121 Grace St., Wilmington • 763-7332

Like a world on the other side of night, Axis revolves with its own unique cycle. On its busiest nights, it may seem empty near midnight, but night-dwellers fond of industrial, gothic and high-energy dance music begin arriving en masse very late, making Axis one of the more rarefied, hipper night clubs in town. The music is loud, the lighting dim and there's a balcony retreat struck with the artwork of intense, convoluted minds. This private club is open Tuesday through Sunday nights from 10 PM, featuring deejays playing techno music most nights and industrial-gothic Tuesday

Photo: Scott Taylor

Coastal forests are home to another kind of night owl, the great horned owl.

and Sunday. The club rarely features live entertainment. Membership costs $7 per year.

Barbary Coast
116 S. Front St., Wilmington • 762-8996

When you're looking for a nightspot with some atmosphere, check out the Barbary Coast. It's got atmosphere as thick as a pea-soup fog and a crew of die-hard regulars as crusty, salty and fun-loving as the name of the place implies — and those are just the college students. The Coast is old (and looks it), small and serves beer and wine and plenty of it. The decor is classic flotsam and jetsam. The pool tables are popular and the excellent jukebox even more so, but the bathrooms leave much to be desired. If Wilmington were still a pirate-plagued port, Barbary Coast would be the place to find them. It's a good drinkin' bar.

Bessie's
133 N. Front St., Wilmington • 762-0003

Underground lounge lizards flourish in this popular, low-ceilinged basement club, which is actually three bars in one. Bessie's features live rock and blues bands, comedy, small theatrical presentations, dance nights and other occasionally bizarre entertainment, attracting a varied clientele predominantly in their 20s and 30s. Once the site of historic Orton's Billiard Parlor, Bessie's still sports five pool tables, including the one where Willie Mosconi sank a record-breaking 365 balls consecutively in 1953.

The bar sells only beer, wine and soft drinks, and you will find Guinness Stout by the pint.

An adjoining room is a small private club called General Longstreet's Headquarters, so named because it is co-owned by actor Tom Berenger, who portrayed the bearded Confederate in the film *Gettysburg*. It's full of Civil War atmosphere. The jukebox packs a solid cross-section of rock music. Longstreet's is open seven days a week from lunchtime 'til 2 AM. Membership includes membership to Lula's (see later entry).

At the opposite side of Bessie's is the Brick Yard, a sports bar featuring state-of-the-art interactive computer sports programs. The Brick Yard gets its name from its original brick remaining from the old Orton Hotel, which burned in 1949. Bessie's and the Brick Yard are closed Sunday, and you must be 21 or older to enter.

Breaktime Sports Bar,
Billiards & Grill
127 S. College Rd., Wilmington • 395-6658

Wilmington's largest billiards parlor is also a popular sports bar and casual restaurant, serving sandwiches, burgers, soups, salads and more. Breaktime possesses all ABC permits as well as 21 top-quality pool tables, 15 televisions and arcade-style diversions. Neat attire is required; no tank tops. Food is served until 10 PM weekdays and midnight on weekends. The bar serves until 2 AM.

Caffe Phoenix
9 S. Front St., Wilmington • 343-1395

The Phoenix has an appeal that exceeds the high quality of its food. With its soft lighting and regular art exhibits, it exudes both warmth and sophistication. No wonder it has become a favorite rookery for nocturnal birds of many an artistic feather — painters, musicians, models, thespians, plus its share of poseurs and tourists — who gather for a meal or cappuccino, dessert and conversation. Piped-in music typically explores the more interesting niches of classical, jazz and Third World styles. Sidewalk seating is best on quiet evenings. As great a place to begin an evening as it is to end one, the Phoenix is open until 1 AM and keeps a very well-stocked bar (see our Restaurants chapter).

The Comedy Club
The Hilton, 301 N. Water St., Wilmington • 763-5900

The Comedy Club presents nationally headlining comedians in the hotel lounge every Friday and Saturday night from mid-February through autumn. It's a comfortable, attractive nightclub atmosphere where you can enjoy cocktails and some hearty laughs. Admission costs $5, and shows begin at 9 PM.

Crook's By the River
138 S. Front St., Wilmington • 762-8898

Crook's lounge is an essential stopover on the customary weekend pub-crawl along Front Street and therefore a popular gathering base. Trendy perhaps, the lounge is nonetheless attractive and popular among people ranging from college-age to older boomers. The walls are decorated with colorful local artwork, and local musicians, mostly blues players, appear on Thursday and Friday. There is never a cover charge, and Crook's is open to the public. High-quality light food is available late into the night.

The Far Side
119 Grace St., Wilmington • 251-9789

The rock-music scene in Wilmington has been touted in the national press repeatedly. While most agree it has yet to live up to the accolades, one place it is certainly thriving in its ongoing renewals and mutations is the Far Side, a private club featuring the newest, the best, the worst, the loudest, most adventurous, most sincere, local and regional, original rock bands around, playing on a stage one might understatedly call intimate. The Far Side is open to the public every night, serving beer, wine and soft drinks. It's a small joint that's as get-down funky as a good rock club should be.

The Ice House
115 S. Water St., Wilmington • 763-2084

Few Wilmington nightspots enjoy the far-flung renown of the Ice House, thanks largely to its outdoor stage and patio directly overlooking the Cape Fear River, its tugboat deckhouse-turned-bar, the large selection of beer, daily live music at lunch hour and at night (wide-ranging styles, but stressing the blues and local musicians), and absence of a cover charge. During the cold months, the music moves to the stage indoors. The Ice House also serves bar food (burgers, sandwiches, clams, oysters, etc.). Recent improvements included adding a fireplace indoors. The building itself is an old ice house with antiquated ice-making machinery still in operation. The Ice House is a popular singles hangout and always a blast. In many ways, it is to Wilmington what Sloppy Joe's is to Key West. It's open every day.

Jake's Downtown
208 Market St., Wilmington • 251-9220

This live-music rock club has been a long-lived Wilmington institution under several guises and names over the years. It's current name recalls the underground stream called Jacob's Run (which empties into the river at the foot of Dock Street). Jake's specializes in presenting local and regional rock bands and live DJs on Monday nights. Thursday is college night. The building features a good-size stage, high ceiling, wraparound balcony (the building was once a movie theater), and bars upstairs and down. A short menu of munchie foods is also offered.

FYI

Unless otherwise noted, the area code for all phone numbers in this guide is 910.

Katy's Great Eats
1054 S. College Rd., Wilmington
• 395-5289

Wilmington's darts mecca, the bar at Katy's restaurant is a favorite hangout for sports fans. It's almost always buzzing with young locals who come to enjoy the games on big-screen TV and occasional live music.

The Limelight
5001 Market St., Wilmington • 799-1730

More than just a hotel lounge (it adjoins the Ramada Inn), the Limelight is a popular dance club among the mature singles set. Top 40, oldies, classic disco and beach music compose the play list, and shag lessons are offered twice weekly along with a buffet. For shower-stall sopranos and bathroom baritones, karaoke takes place two nights a week when admission is free. Drink specials, occasional contests, ample parking and a full bar with all ABC permits add to the Limelight's amenities.

Lula's
138 S. Front St., Wilmington • 763-0070

Tucked away in the low-ceilinged, stone-walled basement beneath Crook's, Lula's is a cozy, intimate, pub-style private club that seats only about 25 people. Vintage photos of film and music celebrities and a huge American flag overhead adorn the tiny place. The juke-box contains an eclectic selection of rock, funk, blues, Motown and some classic Irish drinking songs. Many of the regular clientele, mostly in their 30s and younger, are familiar friends. Entrance to Lula's is through the rear of the building. Membership at Lula's includes membership at General Longstreet's Headquarters at Bessie's (see earlier entry).

Mickey Ratz
115 S. Front St., Wilmington • 251-1289

This is a cosmopolitan, progressive dance club featuring high-tech lighting, a superior sound system, a large-screen video, occasional live shows and top-notch deejays providing all the energy of a big-city disco. The clientele is largely gay but not exclusively. An outdoor patio provides a pleasant change of ambiance in fair weather.

The Palomino Club
2649 Carolina Beach Rd., Wilmington
• 452-0102

The Palomino is the area's top-name club for country music as well as for Top 40 and occasional spectacles such as kick boxing. The Palomino is a cavernous space — about 25,000 square feet — devoted to dance lessons and dancing on Wednesday, Saturday and Sunday (which is the all-ages family night. Live bands — occasionally national acts — appear most Saturday nights. A private club ($3 per year), the Palomino features a weekly dollar-drink night (Wednesday) and college night (Thursday). The club is available for private parties and receptions.

Port City Java
7 N. Front St., Wilmington • 762-5282

Comfortable seating, artistic decor, plenty of reading material, premium coffees and excellent desserts make this little shop a popular gathering place late into the night (until midnight on weekends, 10 or 11 PM on weeknights). It's within an easy walk of practically everything downtown. If your nightlife ends around sunrise, Port City Java reopens at 6:30 AM.

Rack 'M Pub and Billiards
415 S. College Rd., Wilmington
• 791-5668

This handsome club-style parlor cuts its pool prices in half during the daytime, and ladies play free Monday and Tuesday. Rack 'M is open every day from noon until 2 AM. You'll find it in the rear of the University Landing shopping strip, nearly opposite the Wal-Mart shopping center.

Bertha Then Fran: Two Hurricanes from a Downtowner's Perspective

We had heard from weather forecasters for years that Wilmington was due to have a busy hurricane season in 1996, but no one really believed it. As a community, we were complacent, secure in our collective belief that we were immune to hurricanes. After all, the last serious hurricane for Wilmington and its beaches was in 1954 when Hazel came ashore with 150 mph winds. We had been hit hard once in a century and, forgetting that nature doesn't operate with an understanding of justice, figured we had paid our dues.

So it was with some degree of shock that Wilmington received the punch of Hurricane Bertha in the summer of 1996. Still, this was a relatively mild storm that, in the words of locals, "did some overdue pruning" of the trees. There were astonishing quantities of fallen limbs and trees in the aftermath of Bertha, a storm that had the good manners to pass over the region in the light of day and restrain itself to top winds of 105 mph. It took more than two months for the city and county to pick up the debris and haul it away, but it amounted to no more than an irritation for most residents.

Then, just when the mess was nearly cleared, Wilmington was stunned to see a larger storm pointing toward the area in September.

No one thought Fran, a weak depression that plodded along behind much larger Eduardo, would amount to much. As we waved good-bye to Eduardo when that storm turned out to sea, local weather forecasters gave dire warnings about Fran's possibilities.

We all watched and waited, still skeptical. Justice, you know. Then, Fran was definitely on the way. Weather patterns and the sheer size of the storm meant we would get at least part of it and it would be, at the very least, incredibly wet. All around the area, people got serious about preparation. In the downtown neighborhood, some people put plywood on their windows for the first time and everyone exchanged nervous comments and compared inventories of supplies. As far as we could tell, our block had enough batteries, cans of Sterno, gallons of water and nonperishable foods to survive for a month at least. Only one household evacuated while the rest of us got ready to endure the storm in our homes. We are on some of the highest ground in the region and all of our homes were fifty years old before they had to stand the test of Hazel. We figured they could cope with Fran.

Fran came in the evening as darkness made observation of the wind and rain more difficult than the relatively easy afternoon with Bertha. It was the sound of the wind in the night neighbors would recall as the greatest source of tension. Houses shuddered and roofs groaned with each gust of wind from the east. We lost power early in the evening, so the only news about the storm's course and strength at our house came over a battery-powered television. A national news commentator insisted the storm was coming in at Myrtle Beach about 65 miles to the south, but George Elliott, local meteorologist with WECT-TV 6, followed immediately and said it was approaching the mouth of the Cape Fear River on the same path as Bertha and gave the precise time of landfall.

People who haven't been through a hurricane don't understand the anxiety this kind of weather system produces. It is a very prolonged process that comes in five parts. First, there is anxious anticipation and a run on the stores to get supplies before they're exhausted. Then, the second phase involves observing the wind and rain increase, and

— continued on next page

Photo: Jay Tervo

Hurricane Fran caused considerable damage to many oceanfront cottages.

listening to identify rooftop thuds and watching to see leaks in the ceiling or around windows. Phase three is the eye of the storm, an eerily calm moment when, in the case of Fran, we could see the stars. Phase four is the second half of the storm with wind coming from the opposite direction. The fifth phase is the aftermath when people emerge from their houses — in Fran's case, at dawn — to see what can be seen. There is very little information about the world beyond a few blocks because television and radio reporters are in no better position to assess the damage than anyone else. It is a time of speculation and chainsaws, and a time when the neighbors with the gas range make coffee for everyone else who ordinarily relies on electricity for heating water.

Wilmington's downtown residential and commercial area offered one of the most dramatic visual images as reporters from around the world crowded into town. The steeple of First Baptist Church, a magnificent spire constructed during the Civil War, was ripped from the building and scattered on Market Street. Otherwise, downtown sustained relatively little structural damage compared to the beach communities. Downed power lines dangled, generators droned in the hot night to keep refrigerators running, roads were blocked everywhere by fallen trees and smashed cars.

On this downtown corner, a tin roof was slightly peeled up on one house and another house lost several shutters that slammed into the neighbor's house, and a large oak limb fell on a car around the corner. The street was littered with pieces of tin, asphalt shingles, a commercial stove vent, and tree limbs, but we all looked at each other and could only say, "We were lucky."

The day was spent cutting trees into manageable sections neighbors could carry to the curbside. Bertha was a practice drill and we already discovered it was better to put everyone's debris in one large pile than individual ones because the odds of having it picked up were greater. Although hurricane winds put profound stress on everything in its path, the situation that night in the Cape Fear area was compounded by record rainfall for days prior to the storm. The ground was mush and the trees fell easily. Massive oaks simply gave up a century or more of growth, revealing rootballs up to fifteen feet in diameter. We sipped coffee, revved up the chainsaws, made human chains to carry the debris to the street, and listened to the weird silence that accompanies a loss of electric power in an urban neighborhood.

It was late in the evening when a roar went up for blocks around "The power is on!" There were Rebel yells to be heard in the near and far distance.

— continued from previous page

Our neighbors to the north were generally not as fortunate and in some neighborhoods it took two weeks for power to be restored. On some beaches, we would later learn, it took a month or more.

The next weeks were filled with finding ways to be helpful to friends who had not been so lucky. All of us opened our homes to friends who needed the comforts of a warm bath and a hot meal in an air-conditioned house, and we took gallons of water, grocery supplies and ice to friends up in the Hampstead area who had been particularly hard hit and weren't on a city or community water system.

Only a few months later, there are few signs downtown that two hurricanes made a direct hit. Shattered downtown store windows have been replaced, the blue tarps draped over building and home roofs have almost disappeared, and business is back to normal. Wrightsville and Carolina beaches are making repairs and starting to look forward to a new summer season. Topsail Island and Figure Eight Island took the worst of it, a situation graphically revealed when local newscasters showed aerial footage of the astonishing damage to homes. However, the people of Topsail are already putting their lives and businesses back together. We also learned the Brunswick Beaches and Bald Head Island were almost entirely spared and, in truth, Raleigh, NC — 127 miles inland — saw much more serious damage than even Wilmington.

As an aside, our block's only evacuee drove to Raleigh. Sad to say that's where a tree fell on her car and totalled it. She says she'll stay with us for the next one.

The River Club
15 S. Front St., Wilmington • 762-0001

This large, high-ceilinged private music club specializes in live music (mostly rock, rockabilly-swing and blues) and features a growing roster of national and regional blues headliners plus danceable, well-chosen recorded music. The club is popular across a wide range of age groups and is highly favored, for both its music and its clientele, among people well beyond college. Live bands appear mostly on weekends, when a cover charge may apply, and sometimes on Thursdays. (The club may close on nights when no shows are scheduled.) In lieu of live music, recorded music prevails, typically running a wide gamut of styles, including 1970s disco, and changing from night to night. The River Club is the home of the free Tuesday-night open jam sessions of the Blues Society of the Lower Cape Fear, and the annual Cucalorus festival of independent films in April (you'd be a fool to miss it!). There's also a pool table, two bars, an outdoor patio and refreshingly little attitude. The club is closed Sunday and Monday. Membership costs a measly buck per year.

Rockits Rhythm & Sports Grille
5025 Market St., Wilmington • 791-2001

This is a spacious sports bar featuring live, classic and current rock music on Friday and Saturday nights (no cover Saturday) and shag lessons and beach music (sometimes live) on Wednesday and Friday nights. Unpredictable acts — such as the occasional comic hypnotist-magician — are surprises to watch for. Always popular are the two pool tables, dart boards, Foosball table and free interactive videos. Twenty — count 'em, 20 — TVs, plus two wide-screens, keep everyone up on the most contested games. You'll find Rockits behind the Greentree Inn, where there's plenty of parking, and it's open every night until 2 AM.

INSIDERS' TIP

Join the Cape Fear Contra Dancers, 395-0973, either as a member or a guest, and kick up your heels all around the Wilmington area.

Sunset Celebration at the Hilton
301 N. Water St., Wilmington • 763-5900

Every Friday evening from Memorial Day to just beyond Labor Day, the pool deck at the Hilton springs to life at 5 PM with the weekly Sunset Celebration, Wilmington's answer to "The Love Boat." Featuring local radio deejays, occasional rock bands, free buffets and a variety of contests, Sunset Celebrations are enhanced by spectacular sunsets over the Cape Fear River. They often become extremely crowded with folks in their 20s and 30s, most of them single, who come to meet new friends, dig the music, make silly toasts and imbibe until 10 PM. Cash bars offer mixed drinks and beer. Admission is free.

Water Street Restaurant & Sidewalk Cafe
5 S. Water St., Wilmington • 343-0042

The quiet, cozy atmosphere here invites you to linger with a friend or loved one late into the night, any night of the week. Every Friday from 9 PM to 1 AM, live jazz provides extra incentive to stay (no cover charge). The decor is colorful, somewhat rustic and warm. Sidewalk seating offers a view of the riverfront, and food is always available.

Wave Hog Saloon
12 Dock St., Wilmington • 762-2827

This two-level watering hole is extremely popular among the surf-inspired — lots of "Dude-ish" spoken here. Live rock bands on the ground level keep the place packed and lively most of the summer, though it's open year round.

Wrightsville Beach

Buddy's Crab & Oyster Bar
35 N. Lumina Ave., Wrightsville Beach • 256-8966

Home of the world's smallest dance floor, this little shack stays crammed with summer transients, old-time residents and former yuppies who traded burnout for beachcombing. Festooned with ships' lanterns, pulley blocks, bells, life rings, hundreds of business cards, photos and a 16th-century Seminole dugout, Buddy's also has a jukebox choked with 2,000 attitude-improving songs. Buddy's is open daily and closes at no more specific time than "until."

The Comedy Zone
Blockade Runner Beach Resort, 275 Waynick Blvd., Wrightsville Beach • 256-2251

Every Thursday evening from May through September, visitors to the Ocean Terrace Room at the Blockade Runner enter the Comedy Zone. Featuring two nationally known stand-up comedians doing their thing beginning at 9 PM, these shows are consistently entertaining and well worth the $7 admission fee ($5 with dinner). Drinks are served, and the content of the shows is frequently of an adult nature.

Laff Trax
Holiday Inn Sunspree Resort Wrightsville Beach, 1706 N. Lumina Ave., Wrightsville Beach • 256-2231

Live stand-up comedy reigns at the Holiday Inn's lounge every Saturday night beginning at 9:30. Shows are popular, and seating is limited so arrive early. Admission ($7) is discounted with purchase of dinner before the show. Patrons must be 21 years of age and older. As of this writing, this resort's reopening after last year's hurricanes has been delayed, so call ahead.

Ol' Nep's Lounge
11 N. Lumina Ave., Wrightsville Beach • 256-2525

In the King Neptune Restaurant, Ol' Nep's is as lively as its proprietor, Bernard Carroll who, despite all the photographs of prize catches on the walls, doesn't know the first thing about fishing. He'd much rather be sailing and, as you might expect of a salt, he places some importance upon rum. His "Neptune's Rum Bar" features rums from around the world, including Gosling's and North Carolina's own Outer Banks Rum. Microbrewed and imported beers are always in stock, and an inexpensive Pub Grub menu offers plenty of quality munchies (all are available for take out). Ol' Nep's is open every day and has all ABC permits.

Carolina Beach

Club Astor
110 Harper Ave., Carolina Beach
• 458-7883

Situated at the front of Hotel Astor, a block from the beach, Club Astor is one of Carolina Beach's more popular nightclubs, attracting a diverse crowd that spans generations. Although it's not a huge club (it is among Carolina Beach's largest), it gets fairly slammed on summer weekends. It's open Thursday through Sunday from 7 PM, and during the summer the house band performs practically every Friday and Saturday night, playing beach music, Motown, classic rock, some country and Top 40. A deejay spins the hits between sets. There's never a cover during the winter. You'll find plenty of local atmosphere here.

The Back Alley Lounge
110 Harper Ave., Carolina Beach
• 458-9081

This cozy indoor/outdoor space at the back of the Hotel Astor is open seven days a week, with live entertainment Tuesday through Sunday during the high season (weekends off-season). Wednesday night jam sessions are informal. Enter from the parking lot or through the restaurant.

Cobb's Corner Lounge
217 Carolina Ave. N., Carolina Beach
• 458-8865

Laid-back and friendly, Cobb's Corner is a private sports bar that attracts a mature clientele, many from the nearby motels. You'll find a sunny outdoor deck and darts, and the lounge is open every day during the high season. Schedules of special offerings such as

Photo: Curtis Krueger

Loggerhead turtles make their nests along the coast.

LOOK WHO'S TALKING

Harvard Jennings
3 PM - 5 PM

FM 94.1   AM 980

WAAV

NEWS·TALK·SPORTS

251-9228

cookouts and occasional live bands on the deck, usually tied to current sporting events, are consistently posted. Cobb's Corner stands directly behind Cabana De Mar. Yearly membership costs $10.

Southport-Oak Island

Bogey's
5908 E. Oak Island Dr., Long Beach
• 278-4400

Bogey's is a private club that has been assuming a more sophisticated persona over the years, attracting a more mature clientele and serving food specials on weekends. It is a bright, clean atmosphere filled with beach music and Top 40, mostly spun by deejays. High director's chairs line the bar, banquettes and tables allow for viewing the latest golf and NASCAR events on TV, and there's room left over for dancing. A plus is the open-air patio out back with its own bar.

The Creek
5712 E. Oak Island Dr., Long Beach
• 278-9090

Boasting the largest dance floor on Oak Island, this friendly private club features country and southern rock music, dance lessons, deejays and live bands. Weekly pool tournaments are held using the three tables, and dart leagues are formed off-season. Ping-Pong tourneys are held twice weekly. It's just a darn good place to hang out, and you can tell 'em we said so. The Creek is at the corner of S.E. 58th Street.

Harbor Lite Bar & Grill
1109 N. Howe St., Southport • 457-9021

This tiny neighborhood haunt has little to offer in terms of nightlife, unless you're one of the local barflies who likes to witness harmless practical jokes played on tourists who wander in. The folks are friendly, however, and harmless, and after you've had a beer or two, they'll probably invite you back on Sunday night to hear the occasional visiting bluegrass band. If you're lucky, there may really be a band playing that night.

Harborside Seafood Restaurant and Grille
607 W. West St., Southport • 457-0021

Live music — typically acoustic soloists or duets — is presented in the oyster bar-style lounge after dinner on Friday, Saturday and holidays. It's an attractive, laid-back place where you can converse as well as dance. There is no cover charge, and the restaurant, which is near the Southport Marina, has all ABC permits.

The Oarhouse Lounge
705 Yaupon Dr., Yaupon Beach • 278-5873

You will either love or hate this tiny place on the Yaupon Fishing Pier, but it demands at least a viewing. The low ceiling and walls are hidden beneath ancient strata of business cards, hats, trinkets, undergarments, nautical paraphernalia, photos, signs and gimmicks. The food menu — mainly raw bar and grill fare — is affixed to toilet seats hanging beside the seven crude, lumber tables (some would say "crude" aptly describes the entire place). The place can get fairly crowded in summer, and the only air conditioning is the ocean breeze. Live music is often featured on summer weekends. The Oarhouse is open every day until the wee hours, but never past 2 AM.

Shuckers
6220 E. Oak Island Dr., Long Beach • 278-4944

Home of the Oak Island Shag Club, Shuckers is a great place for dancing into the wee hours to beach music. But according to some, the food is the best thing going (especially the blackened alligator tail). Deejays spin the old hits, and free shag and line-dance lessons are available in the evenings. Shuckers is a private club that serves a full menu, possesses all ABC permits and welcomes new members.

South Brunswick Islands

Steamers Restaurant & Lounge
8 Second St., Ocean Isle Beach • 579-0535

Said to be the hottest nightclub in town, Steamers might live up to the claim even if it weren't on Ocean Isle. A private club, it offers live and recorded music, which leans mostly toward beach, R&B and classic rock with a little country thrown in. Breakfast (from 7 AM), lunch and dinner are served every day, and golfers are especially welcomed. The lounge has an upscale appearance despite the large-screen TV, has all ABC permits and also serves a light bar menu of appetizers.

Topsail Island

The Brass Pelican
2112 N. New River Dr., Surf City • 328-4373

The ads say this is the friendliest bar on the island. The regulars say it's the coolest. The friendliness becomes apparent once they know you; the cool is on the surface. The Brass hosts live rock and beach bands on weekends (some quite loud for a place this size), Thursday through Sunday during the summer. As with many clubs in these parts, a new face turns heads, so get involved in the weekly informal pool or dart tournaments, or the occasional ping-pong match. Check out the outdoor deck. The Brass is a private club and a cut above some others.

The Mermaid
N. New River Dr., Surf City • 328-0781

This restaurant and lounge near the north side of Surf City is known for its live rock bands on weekends and holidays, volleyball and pool tournaments and occasional roughhousing. Night owls can have breakfast here from 11 PM to 3 AM Friday and Saturday. On other nights, karaoke, beach bingo, cards and games help maintain the

Mermaid's disputed claim as Topsail Island's "original" beach bar.

Shenanigans Beach Club Bar & Grill
2107 New River Dr., Surf City • 328-SHAG

The phone number doesn't say it all. More than a shag club, Shenanigans presents several styles of live and jockeyed music, heavy on Top 40 and dance, plus a dense sports atmosphere. You can even do line dancing and karaoke now and then. The summertime entertainment schedule is usually jammed, which goes far toward explaining the sign that reads, "Please keep animals under control."

Sporting two bars (one opens only on summer weekends), an outdoor deck, pool table, darts and big-screen TV, Shenanigans also takes pride in its short menu, served until 10 PM on weekends, 9 PM weekdays. Shenanigans hosts volleyball tourneys and deck parties in summer. The club is in Tilghman's Square, about 3 miles north of the Surf City bridge, "smack dab in the middle of Topsail Island" — that is, 13 miles from either end. As of this writing, Shenanigans had not yet reopened in the wake of last year's hurricanes. Call ahead.

Sir William's Pub
N.C. Hwy. 210, Surf City • 328-3075

A recent addition to Topsail-area nightlife, Sir William's offers a civilized alternative to some of the area's somewhat, shall we say, "less inhibited" establishments. Sir William's features live musical entertainment and, twice each month (alternating Thursdays), the popular Laff Trax series of stand-up comedy. Comics go on at 8:30 PM. Admission to Laff Trax costs $5 in advance, $7 at the door. (Off-season, you even may score the lower advance price up to an hour or so before showtime.) Sir William's is a private club ($1 membership per year) offering frequent pre-show snack buffets, special events, regular line-dance instruction, and they'll even arrange free rides

home for those without designated drivers. Sir William's Pub is on the mainland, about halfway between Food Lion and the Surf City swing bridge.

Movie Theaters

There are plenty of first-run and second-run theaters in the area, but foreign films and art films have frustratingly short runs, and controversial films seldom run at all. It's a paradox, considering the number of films shot in Wilmington and the level of local interest. Luckily, there is **Cinematique of Wilmington**, the series that brings acclaimed foreign and domestic films to town for three-day runs every other week (sometimes more often) to historic Thalian Hall, at Chestnut and Third streets, in Wilmington. Cinematique is a popular bargain at $5 a ticket and benefits St. John's Museum of Art and WHQR 91.3 FM, the local public radio station. Showtimes are usually 1:30 PM on Sunday and 7:30 PM on Monday and Tuesday. You can receive Cinematique mailings by calling 343-1640 or writing: c/o WHQR, 251 N. Front Street, Wilmington, North Carolina 28401.

All movie theaters in the region offer matinee showings every day during the summer, on holidays and most weekends throughout the year at substantial savings over the average $6 ticket price. Since there are so few theaters outside Wilmington, we've listed all theaters together.

Cinema 6, 5335 Oleander Drive, Wilmington, 799-6666, is less than 4 miles from Wrightsville Beach and across the street from a few very good restaurants.

College Road Cinemas, 632 S. College Road, Wilmington, 395-1790, is a six-screen complex that has the most comfortable seats in town. It's behind Swensen's and Taco Bell, across the street from the UNCW campus.

Independence Mall Cinemas, 1843 Independence Boulevard, Wilmington, 392-3333, has three screens right behind Independence Mall, south of Oleander Drive.

North Carolina's southern coast is also a great place to slow down.

Cinema 4, 1020 Carolina Beach Road, Carolina Beach, 458-3444, is a four-screen complex in the Federal Point Plaza shopping center next to Jubilee Amusement Park. This theater charges $3.50 at all times for first-run flicks.

Surf Cinemas, 4836 Long Beach Road SE, Southport, 457-0320, is convenient to the entire Southport-Oak Island area, situated south of the intersection of Long Beach Road and N.C. 211 (Southport-Supply Road).

Carmike 7 Theaters, 1038 Henderson Drive, Jacksonville, 455-3374, provides visitors and residents in the Topsail Island-Holly Ridge area a convenient (and better) alternative to waiting for the video release of the movies they'd like to see.

Cinema 6 Theater, College Plaza, Jacksonville, 346-6626, like the Carmike 7, is a six-screen complex within easy reach of the Topsail Island area.

Poetry Readings

Considering the incomes of poets today, some people say the art is in its dying throes. However, considering the number of public readings and enrollment in college poetry workshops, others say we're experiencing an unprecedented poetry renaissance. The best of times, the worst of times, indeed. You, too, may take part in it, and at no cost — other than laying bare your soul before an audience. Recite your own work, read a classic — bring your bongos! Throughout the year, you can explore the art of spoken music on a weekly and monthly basis in Wilmington, where among younger poets, the Beat generation is being rediscovered and reprocessed in a big way. Poetic styles at local readings range widely, from innocent lyricism to experimental riffing to adult confessional. Performers may be nervous first-timers or theatrical extroverts. The fun is often in the surprise.

Axis
121 Grace St., Wilmington • 763-7332

On the second Sunday of each month at 9 PM, this small night club suspends its loud gothic-industrial rock music long enough to fill the smoky air with some envelope-stretching poetic ravings you're not likely to forget anytime soon. Fortunately, the uninitiated can ease the process with libations from the bar.

Barnes & Noble Booksellers
322 S. College Rd., Wilmington • 395-4825

The cafe at Barnes & Noble assures there's enough caffeine at hand to get you through the mediocre stuff. Readings here are family-friendly and take place on the second Monday of each month beginning at 7:30 PM.

New Hanover County Public Library
201 Chestnut St., Wilmington • 341-4389

OK, so this one doesn't take place at night but at 2:30 PM on the fourth Sunday of the month. (We had to list it somewhere!) This is the longest-running series of poetry readings in the area and comes complete with refreshments, cookies and a well-lit, smoke-free environment. Readings typically conform to a predetermined theme and are suitable for a general audience.

Water Street Restaurant
5 S. Water St., Wilmington • 343-0042

The granddaddy of Wilmington poetry readings in terms of popularity and reputation, these gatherings attract a vast range of readers — some, outright performers — over a vast range of ages and poetic styles. With the added draw of the restaurant's good food and drink, readings here are often standing room only, despite the smoke and the content of the poems, which is frequently adult-themed. Readings begin at 9 PM every Tuesday.

The Area's Finest
Shopping Experience

We invite you
to become a
part of this
enchanting
landmark that
recaptures
the low country
good life —
superlative merchants
of quality goods and services.

Shopping

The Greater Wilmington area is the sixth-largest retail center in North Carolina, and there are abundant opportunities to spend your money here. Since retail is such a big part of the area's economy, it should come as no surprise that quite a number of noteworthy shops won't be listed in this section — it would take an entire book to discuss all the shopping possibilities. A browse around the area's large and small shopping districts promises wonderful opportunities to purchase interesting items.

There were three primary shopping areas within the Wilmington market for a long time, but the lines between them have blurred. The downtown historic neighborhood, Oleander Drive near Independence Mall and the massive shopping corridor along S. College Road from Market Street to Monkey Junction (at the intersection of S. College and Carolina Beach roads) have dominated the retail market for decades. Add to these centers the outrageously fast pace of commercial development of Market Street to the north, the mind-boggling commercial development outside the gates of the Landfall residential neighborhood on Eastwood Road and increased retail centers near the beaches. As more national chains discover Wilmington, stores seem to spring up overnight. Even natives feel a little bewildered when the familiar landscape changes so dramatically.

The good news is that competition has entered the Wilmington marketplace in a big way. The community is large enough now to sustain superstores and price clubs and diverse enough to support many delightful specialty shops. People who live for discounts in shopping will be delighted; those who prefer personalized service at reasonable or even higher prices will find no shortage of shopping possibilities. There is no shortage of an-

tiques stores in this area; be sure to see our Antiques section at the end of this chapter.

Shopping in the southern coast area is an increasingly satisfying and exciting experience. Retailers are becoming more savvy as time passes, taking note of the influx of outsiders from larger cities who expect a higher level of choice, quality and price than has been traditionally offered in this area. There are hundreds of new shopping experiences of all kinds in the works. If the current trend continues, expect Greater Wilmington to continue to rise from its sixth-place retail position in the state to an even higher spot. Be forewarned — the urge to shop is going to be impossible to resist.

General Shopping

Wilmington

Downtown

Historic District shopping options will tug hard at your traveler's checks and credit cards. Downtown has some of the area's most fun shops with low-priced imports as well as some of the region's finer stores that carry upscale merchandise. This is not a shopping district with national names on illuminated signs. There are no big discount chain stores selling the necessities of daily life in giant quantity. Instead, this retail area specializes in unusual items that appeal to shoppers in the mood to pause and ponder their selections. Art, antiques, fine clothing, jewelry, gifts, toys, gourmet items, wine, linens, glass, china, collectibles and more await the discerning downtown shopper.

Part of the charm of this shopping district is its compact size and pleasant walkability.

Park your car in a free space on the street or, if you're shopping at one of the retail/dining centers, park at no cost in their large lots. Downtown is an open-air mall with as astonishing selection of spots in which to pause and take in the beautiful scenes between purchases. Coffee shops, delicatessens, bars, full-service restaurants and even a New York-style hot dog vendor offer constant temptation.

Downtown shopping is separated into three major entities that seem to have merged into one over recent years. Viewed as an extended, outdoor mall, downtown is anchored by two large centers at the northern and southern perimeters of the central shopping district. The Cotton Exchange is a shopping/dining/office complex at the northerly end of the riverfront. Chandler's Wharf occupies the southern end. The area between these shopping meccas is Front Street, a busy corridor lined with restaurants, galleries, banks, services and stores. Streets that cross Front Street offer many shopping possibilities as well. Downtown is also becoming known for its number of antique stores (see our close-up on Antique Shopping in this chapter.)

FYI

Unless otherwise noted, the area code for all phone numbers in this guide is 910.

The Cotton Exchange
321 N. Front St., Wilmington • 343-9896

The site of the largest cotton-exporting company in the world in the 19th century, this collection of eight buildings overlooking the Cape Fear River was converted into a shopping and dining center in the early 1970s. Its renovation marked the beginning of restoration of downtown Wilmington. Shoppers can enjoy a bit of history as they stroll the mall's tri-level space where displays of cotton bales, weighing equipment and photographs tell the story of the center's evolution.

Four restaurants and three dozen interesting stores on three levels in eight buildings make up the Cotton Exchange. Parking is free in the large lot for visitors of the shopping complex. Only a few stores are listed here to suggest the scope of shopping possibilities.

R. Bryan & Company, 763-6860, is probably one of the nicest clothing stores anywhere. Quality and service are impeccable.

The store features fine clothing for men and women in traditional and classic styles. Exclusive brand-name clothing and accessories for both men and women include Burberry, H. Freeman, Robert Talbott, Pringle and Bobby Jones. A second location opened in 1996 at Lumina Station at Wrightsville Beach.

The Beverage Boutique, 762-6760, is a small store with a glorious assortment of domestic and imported wines and beers. The staff takes a keen interest in consumer needs and aims to please by finding and ordering whatever a customer wants. Wines are displayed by country and vintage for ease of selection.

T.S. Brown Jewelers, 762-3467, specializes in gemstones (with more than a thousand loose stones on display) and settings as well as a nice assortment of fine jewelry and costume items. Handcrafted jewelry in original designs by 20 artists makes this a special place to look for unusual items. Owners Tim and Sandy Brown are also designers and will create a custom piece for you.

The Candy Barrel, 762-3727, is a delicious place to browse and settle upon a confectionery decision. Chocolates are homemade and include several varieties of fudge. This store sells all kinds of chocolate-covered nuts, white and dark chocolate-covered pretzels, hard candies, taffies, toffees and fresh popcorn. You'll also find an interesting array of coffees, teas and gourmet foods.

The Kitchen Shoppe, 762-1919, is a dream store for the accomplished and new cook. Calphalon, cookbooks, gadgets, grill items, glassware, cookware and spices make up the dazzling array of items. Owner Liz Kirby usually has a pot of coffee on for customers, and if you're a regular, you just might get a piece of her chocolate cheesecake.

The Write Place, 343-0617, is a card and stationery store that may well qualify for a Guiness record. It is the tiniest store imaginable, crammed with thousands of cards, gift items, buttons, T-shirts and giftwrapping. When you look for merchandise in this store, you should expect to be shoulder to shoulder with other customers who will jockey with you for

space and, certainly, a big laugh because owner Jim Fountain goes to extremes to find really funny stuff for his customers.

The first store in the complex, **The Basket Case**, 763-3956, opened in 1979 when the very notion of a shopping complex on the site (then overlooking a dirt parking lot) was a shocking idea. Owner Jean Hanson has steadily expanded this unusual gift store, stocking it with Department 56, Byer's Choice, Sandicast, Snowbabies and, of course, elaborate plush puppets. Mrs. Hanson delights in animating her puppets for customers.

Two Sisters Bookery, 762-4444, is a wonderful, small bookstore that carries novels, books of local interest, lots of journals for the aspiring writer, greeting cards and angels in all configurations. Service is high-quality, and the staff will locate and order any available books.

Bear Mountain, 762-3575, is a most unusual store filled with stuffed toy bears and even large simulated bear rugs. The store also makes Heirloom Bears, collectible teddybears handcrafted from your unused fur coats, jackets or stoles. It's a great solution to the problem of what to do with old furs hanging in the closet.

A lively store on the upper level, **The City Zoo**, 815-3410, specializes in just about every kind of soft sculpture on a tropical or desert theme imaginable. It has a colorful selection

of cloth cactus plants, fish, exotic wildlife and tropical birds. The store also has outrageous tropical luggage guaranteed not to be confused with anybody else's on the baggage carousel at the airport.

Chandler's Wharf
2 Ann St., Wilmington • No central phone

This center on the river has many appealing shopping opportunities. It evolved over time as a retail/dining complex, but part of it began as a ship's chandler in the 19th century. There was also a maritime museum in the 1970s. There are still some marine artifacts scattered about the grounds — including an old tugboat, an enormous anchor and other reminders of its origins. Cobblestone streets, plank walkways, attractive landscaping and a gorgeous view of the Cape Fear River are some of the features that make shopping at Chandler's Wharf such a pleasant experience. This shopping center was created by Thomas Henry Wright Jr. in the late 1970s and is flourishing today with some of Wilmington's most delightful stores.

This center also boasts two of the most reliable restaurants in Wilmington — The Pilot House and Elijah's — and the pleasure of dining in either one is heightened by having the option of enjoying lunch or dinner on outdoor decks right on the water (see our Restaurants chapter).

The **Quarter of Chandler's Wharf**, 225 S. Water Street, 762-0970, has classic to contemporary dresses, sportswear and accessories for women in sizes 4 to 18 as well as petite clothing for women 5'4" and shorter. This store has been selling fine clothing in this location for nine years. Lots of linens and linen blends — the best fabric to wear in the coastal area most of the year — are available in many appealing styles. The Quarter opened a second location at Lumina Station at Wrightsville Beach in late 1996.

Scentsational, 225 S. Water St., 762-2626, sells scents in every imaginable configuration, but that's only the beginning. It is packed with environmental oils, soaps, shower gels, aromatherapy products and many interesting items owner Paula Dayvault finds at the big city markets. French fragrances and the wonderful scents of Crabtree & Evelyn, Scarborough and others pleasantly fill the room with their aromas. Scentsational also sells French, Egyptian and antique linens. This store offers an unusual design service, MAP, that specializes in recycling your own items to decorate your home.

Salon Deja Vu, 225 S. Water Street, 762-4106, has been serving residents since 1981. Sad to say, its services are not readily available to area visitors who are in town for only a brief vacation. Locals know it takes a bit of a wait to get on Norma Norwood's list of clients, and once people are there they make sure to re-

main on it. Great service, exceptional coloring skills, reasonable prices and stimulating conversation make this tiny salon a big success.

Every candle and accessory you'll ever need for lighting up your home in an aesthetically pleasing way can be found in **Candles Etc.**, 225 S. Water Street, 762-8853. It carries scented candles, hand-dipped tapers, pillars and holders as well as novelty candles. The store moved to a larger space on the same floor in late 1996, so it's now possible to bend over to see something without knocking a display over.

Alligator Pie, 3 Ann Street, 762-1534, offers clothing, toys and furniture for boys and girls ages newborn to the stage right before preteen. Clothing sizes range from newborn to size 14, and the store also sells shoes. The lively and well-stocked store carries Flapdoodles, Sara's Prints, Hot Tot, Cow and Lizard, Viaggi and many more popular brands. There's a great assortment of gifts and lots of knowledgeable help available from the staff.

Adjacent to Elijah's Restaurant in the cobblestoned area, **The Brass Lantern**, 2 Ann Street, 763-2551, is a gift store that specializes in delightful items for the distinctive home. Herend porcelain and pottery, Ceralene Raynaud and Richard Ginori are some of the offerings of this interesting store.

A Proper Garden, 2 Ann Street, 763-7177, has everything for your garden you never knew you needed — until you walk in the door and

find yourself wanting it all. Birdhouses, chimes, gazing globes, fountains, lawn ornaments, swings, hammocks and umbrellas are just some of the items here. This is another downtown store that opened a second location at Lumina Station at Wrightsville Beach.

A exciting new addition to Chandler's Wharf is **Silver Cloud**, 762-5477, a store that sells sterling silver jewelry. Necklaces, bracelets, rings, earrings, pendants, charms and hair ornaments line the cases. Although it is new for Wilmington, this store's owners are longtime retailers with international experience in silver jewelry, most recently in St. Thomas in the Virgin Islands.

The Cape Fear Christmas House
505 Nutt St., Wilmington • 763-1193

Welcome to 8,000 square feet of Christmas that lasts 365 days a year. Both religious and secular items, including a vast array of collectibles, jam this store to the rafters. An hour in this store is enough to get a shopper in the holiday spirit and don't be surprised, even in the heat of August, to find yourself humming a holiday tune as you leave.

Down Island Traders
111 S. Front St., Wilmington • 762-2112

Walk into this store and find yourself transported to Bali. The clothing, decorative accessories, jewelry and other handicrafts are reasonably priced — actually very inexpensive — and there is always something new to peruse. In addition to Indonesian items, this attractive store also has merchandise from all over the world including Southeast Asia, Africa and New Guinea.

Chadsworth Columns
277 N. Front St., Wilmington • 763-7600

A fascinating addition to Wilmington's shopping scene, this store, owned by North Carolinian Jeff Davis, has locations in London and Atlanta. His company, founded in 1987, combines modern materials and technology with classical design and workmanship to create arch columns in the manner of ancient artisans. Greek, Roman and classical columns, both interior and exterior, are created in the company's Georgia location. Some of the materials available include wood, stone and marble. Davis is a member of the Institute for

INSIDERS' TIP

Joining the Book Review Club at Quarter Moon Bookstore in Topsail Beach, 328-4969, is a great way to meet other people who love books — and love talking about them.

the Study of Classical Architecture at the New York Academy of Art. Consultation is by appointment, but browsers are graciously welcome in the storefront columns gallery in downtown Wilmington. For mail order information, call (800) COLUMNS. As an aside, customers of this company include the Virginia Historical Society, David Brinkley, MGM Studios and the Smithsonian.

The Compass Rose Import Company
16 Market St., Wilmington • 763-2302

Compass Rose specializes in old world imports. Exotic Eastern imports include rugs, furnishings, decorative accessories, and things that defy categorization crowd the large space. If you just can't decide, ponder your choice in the rocking chair generally left out front.

Anasazi
16 Market St., Wilmington • 762-8044

This fascinating store on Market Street across from the horse and carriage tour hitching post features Southwestern folk art, Native American crafts, Mexican antiques, hand-blown glassware, wrought iron and home accessories.

CD Alley
8 Market St., Wilmington • 762-4003

At long last, downtown Wilmington has a store that carries CDs, vinyls (which used to be called LPs or records) and tapes. It offers new and used CDs, vinyl and tapes, specializing in blues, jazz, reggae and rock and roll.

Wish You Were Here Greetings and Gifts
17 Market St., Wilmington • 763-9144

Across the street from CD Alley is a very different card and gift shop. You're not going to find cards like these in most shops in Wilmington. And the store also has unusual gifts: Fiesta Ware food bowls for the truly indulged pet, novelty picture frames and excel-

lent quality T-shirts in themes that range from a very tasteful Wilmington shirt to an Elvis collectible.

Island Passage
Jacobi Warehouse, 15 S. Water St., Wilmington • 762-1911

This store moved from 4 Market Street to the Jacobi Warehouse in early 1997. It carries an exciting mix of casual '90s clothing for women. The new, larger space includes a display of some of the most interesting shoes you'll find in the Cape Fear region.

Calhoun's Celtic Imports
Jacobi Warehouse, 15 S. Water St., Wilmington • 763-1990

This is the Cape Fear region's only shop devoted to fine Scottish and Irish imports. Books, posters, art, jewelry, flags, music, genealogical gifts and clothing are all based on the Celtic theme. Owner Laura Lee Calhoun has been pleased with the area's reception to the store and regards docking ships from Great Britain as icing on the cake because the sailors all want to buy gifts from their home ports.

The Old Wilmington City Market
119 S. Water St., Wilmington • 763-9748

This center is a reincarnation of the century-old farmer's market in downtown Wilmington. It's the place to find baked goods, local vegetables, plants, fresh-cut flowers, herbs, local artists' prints, local pottery and baskets, handmade toys, jewelry and crafts at vendor booths and stores built into the space.

Rare Cargo
112 N. Front St., Wilmington • 762-7636

Rare Cargo is a great place for women who love loosely structured linen and flax clothing. Mimi Kessler has a "flax list," and those who crave these clothes need to be on it to take advantage of arrivals because the shipments are snapped up quickly. Prices are in-

INSIDERS' TIP

The Cape Fear area is a busy place for yard sales on almost any weekend of the year, and antiquers are guaranteed to have a good time.

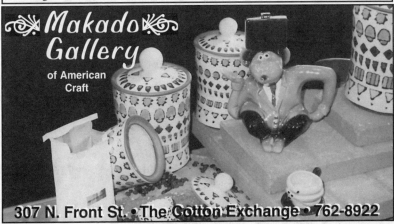

credibly good on the high-quality clothing. The store also has an interesting assortment of art T-shirts, incense, jewelry and unusual gifts. The cheery and laid-back atmosphere enhances the shopping experience.

Teagues
139 N. Front St., Wilmington • 763-8771

Teagues sells a variety of gifts and decorative accessories. Imports from Bali, glassware from Egypt, Poland, Germany and Mexico, candles, jewelry, stuffed animals, cat prints, lots of other cat stuff, cards, pottery by local and regional artists and other items line the shelves.

Eclectic Menage
1600 Market St., Wilmington • 763-6053

Owner Kathryn Ross, an architect who designs area houses, opened this store in an old gas station she tastefully renovated. As the name suggests, the store has everything in terms of home furnishings and accessories that range from contemporary to classical styles. She has an unusual collection of Irish antiques, as well as primitives and classic designs. Decorative arts, new and old pieces, lamps, rugs and porcelains as well as fabric sources are part of the menage.

The Stork's Nest
20 Market St., Wilmington • 251-8008

Since 1985, this has been a great place to find everything for the infant and mother-to-be. European strollers, Madela products, Childcraft furniture, Catamini, Earthlings, Avent, toys, mobiles, Japanese Weekend maternity items and other products makes this store a magnet for discerning parents and parents-to-be. Owner Polly Daniel is an experienced mother herself and brings wisdom and enthusiasm to the shopping experience. New mothers will find her advice invaluable.

Hilda Godwin's
105 Market St., Wilmington • 762-4472

Hilda runs a unique women's clothing shop that features fine sportswear, dresses for all occasions and accessories. While this lovely little store is wonderful for year-round shopping, things really get exciting around the holiday party season.

American Pie
113 Dock St., Wilmington • 251-2131

This is a delightful shop of contemporary American crafts and folk art. You'll discover some of the most unusual arts and crafts in Southeast at this store. If you're seriously into American folk art, ask Elaine Johansen if you can go upstairs to browse around.

Kingoff's Jewelers
10 N. Front St., Wilmington • 762-5219

A downtown jeweler since 1919, Kingoff's offers fine jewelry, watches and repairs and is the exclusive seller of the famed Wilmington Cup. Metalsmith Thomas Brown created the cup to celebrate the city's success in commerce and industry. This pewter cup is a favorite gift for everyone from new babies to civic leaders. There's a second location of Kingoff's in the "burbs" at 1409 Audubon Boulevard, 799-2100.

Toms Drug Store
1 N. Front Street, Wilmington • 762-3391

This is an authentic old-style drugstore that has been a landmark in downtown Wilmington since 1932. Despite a serious face-lift in 1995, the store continues to have an old Wilmington flavor. The complete pharmacy offers free citywide delivery. You can also get lots of opinions on current affairs at Toms. If you want to know, ask Faye or Susan about most anything and they'll have the answer.

Finkelstein's Jewelry and Music Company
6 S. Front Street, Wilmington • 762-5662

This store has been in business since 1906. This combination music store/jewelry store/pawnbroker is a must-stop for the visitor or resident who is drawn to any of these services.

Oleander Drive

Wilmington has a full-service mall, Independence Mall, filled with all of the national and regional stores that shoppers all over America have come to expect in a city. It is the dominant shopping area along Oleander Drive and accounts for a large percentage of the region's shopping experiences.

Independence Mall
3500 Oleander Dr., Wilmington • 392-1776

The mall has nearly a hundred stores in a climate-controlled environment. **Sears**, **JCPenney** and **Belk Beery** anchor this complex of fashion, music, computer, art supplies, food, jewelry, sporting goods and shoe stores.

Naturally, the anchor stores are the main draw for malls. Belk Beery is a first-rate fashion store that has emerged as a department store on par with stores in much larger metropolitan areas. For Wilmingtonians, the Belk store is a special shopping experience. Belk opened a second, smaller store at the Landfall Center in late 1996, offering convenience to a rapidly growing population in the area north of Wilmington. Sears and JCPenney at Independence Mall are exactly the same stores customers have come to rely upon across America. Sears has a full service auto department.

There are one-hour photo developing stores, sporting goods shops, nine jewelry stores, software stores, video stores, a half-dozen shoe stores, a cinema, music stores, apparel dealers in large quantity, restaurants, a store where everything is a dollar, beauty salons, a tobacco shop, import shops, banking services, and a **B. Dalton Bookseller**. **Perry's Emporium** with its handsome wood and leaded-glass facade, is a visually exciting store that specializes in estate jewelry, loose diamonds and antique watches, and has two gemologists and two appraisers on staff.

The area around the mall bustles with shopping possibilities too. Several smaller centers and stores offer exciting shopping opportunities.

Hanover Center
3501 Oleander Dr., Wilmington

This lively strip center has grown increasingly stronger in recent years and is a nice complement to Independence Mall. It houses **Rose's** (a discount department store), **Eckerd Drugs** and **Harris Teeter**, the area's upscale supermarket chain, as well as a post office for added convenience.

Looking for a food gift? Also in the Hanover Center is **Temptations**, 763-6662, established in 1987. It offers an expansive selection of gourmet treats including candies, cookies, cheese straws, nuts, sauces, pastas, coffees, teas, wines, micro-brewed beers and North Carolina specialty foods. Two refrigerated chocolate cases hold luxury chocolate. This gourmet foods and wine store also boasts a cafe where you can pick up a croissant and coffee in the morning and shop at the same time.

A & G Sportswear, 762-0194, is a fine clothing store for men and women that carries sought-after linen, the area's favorite apparel fabric in summer, available in Elliott Lauren linen and Richard Malcolm Irish linen. It also

has a Jams World section with several styles of affordable dresses in 100 percent washable rayon from Honolulu. Hawaiian shirts for men in this line are available in button-up rayon. Other men's lines are Greg Norman golf apparel, Ruff Hewn and Brighton Shoes and leather belts.

Azalea Plaza
3700 Oleander Dr., Wilmington

The next strip to the east of Hanover Center is Azalea Plaza. The two centers seem to merge into one and their proximity makes this side of Oleander Drive across from Independence Mall a great place to shop for a variety of needs.

This center is home to superstores. At **Office Depot**, 392-9013, you'll find enormous selection, low prices and good customer service at the Office Depot. This store has a large selection of computers, software, computer accessories, paper supplies, calendars, planners, office furniture, files, copier services and more. If you can't find your need for your of-

fice here, it probably doesn't exist. **Books-A-Million**, 452-1519, has at least a million books are in its huge store beside Office Depot. Nicely sectioned into categories that range the spectrum of hardbacks and paperbacks, it's a place a book lover could easily spend hours roaming from section to section. There are large areas devoted to deeply discounted books and also racks and racks of the newest in fiction and nonfiction. It also has a large card and gift section. **Pier 1 Imports**, 392-3151, is one of the largest chains offering home furnishings, accessories, candles, glassware, serving pieces, placemats, eucalyptus, rugs, clothing and more. This is the place to go for rattan or furniture at good prices, and it also has a vast selection of cushions, pillows, window treatments, knickknacks and more.

Space Savers
1411 Floral Pky., Wilmington • 791-4949

Across the street from Pier 1 is a really fun store for people who want to figure ways to store their household items. Do-it-yourself closet shelving, plastic storage containers, kitchen storage systems and endless opportunities to just put stuff away inspire the most serious packrat to spend hours here.

Martha's Vineyard
1205 Floral Pky., Wilmington • 799-1782

This place is just down the street from Pier 1 in an eggplant-colored house between Oleander Drive and Wrightsville Avenue. This store is packed with a broad range of gifts for everyone from infants to grandparents. Home accessories, garden gifts, kitchen items, pillows, kitchen and bath linens, jewelry and a large selection of golf-theme gifts lines the walls and shelves of this store. If you need jam spoons topped with little bagels or croissants, this should be your first stop!

Audubon Village
1400 Audubon Blvd., Wilmington

A special strip mall that needs to be mentioned is Audubon Village just a bit east of Independence Mall on the other side of Oleander Drive. This small center has some very nice stores, including Kingoff's Jewelers mentioned in the Downtown Wilmington shopping section. **Rebecca's Lingerie Ltd.**, 313-6620, opened in 1986, offers everyday undergarment items as well as lounging attire and special-occasion lingerie. Rebecca's also specializes in mastectomy needs. Discreet and sensitive service is a hallmark of Rebecca's, where state-of-the-art fitting is matched with a genuine desire to help women during and after the post-surgical transition. For other lingerie needs, Rebecca's is simply a great place to shop for oneself or for someone special.

Country Vogue, 791-3082, is an upscale, ready-to-wear ladies' store that has been a Wilmington fixture for more than a half-century. It sells top-of-the-line brands including David Brooks and Robert Scott. Clothing runs the gamut from sportswear to dressy dresses, including evening and mother-of-the-bride wear.

Another Wilmington veteran retailer in Audubon Village, **The Wonder Shop**, 799-4511, has been selling ladies clothing since 1932. Its inventory ranges from sportswear to cocktail dresses to Panache and Mycra Pac rainwear. It is the exclusive area retailer of Bleyle and also carries Canvasbacks, Austin Reed, Ann May, Teri Jon, Chetta B, UMI, Henry Lee, Kenar and Jackie Benard.

S. College Road

This part of Wilmington is home to the mega-stores. **Sam's**, **Wal-Mart**, **Kmart**, **Lowe's**, and **Phar-mor** are some of the destinations if you need home-improvement materials, auto parts, industrial-size bags of party chips and — well, you know what you need. Sam's is Wilmington's only price club and there are membership restrictions that apply. All over America these stores are just the same. Discount prices, high volume and national brands

are hallmarks of the stores that dominate S. College Road. These are the places where, in many cases, your neck starts to hurt from looking up.

There are also some smaller, interesting stores interspersed among these retail giants. Furniture is a big business in town, and many of the large stores — as well as small ones — are on or near this road.

Sutton-Council Furniture
421 S. College Rd., Wilmington • 799-9000

This store is an established and reliable place to buy quality furniture in Wilmington. This store has more than 40,000 square feet of showroom space where you'll see such brands of furniture as Pennsylvania House, Statton, Hickory-White, Council Craftsman, the Bob Timberlake Collection, Hickory Chair, Thayer Coggin and more. Sutton-Council is a Karastan Gallery dealer.

INSIDERS' TIP

Go camera-crazy! Join the Cape Fear Camera Club, 251-1273.

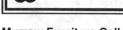
Murrow Furniture Galleries
3514 S. College Rd., Wilmington
• 799-4010

At the other end of the street from Sutton Furniture, beyond the intersection of Shipyard Boulevard, is Murrow Furniture Galleries. It has 45,000 square feet in its showroom and sells such brands as Council Craftsmen, Century, Bernhardt, Hickory Chair, Statton, Southwood, Tropitone, Woodard, Kincaid, Maitland Smith, Baker, Bradington Young, LaBarge, and all major medium to high-end accessory lines such as Howard Miller clocks. Murrow Furniture is also discounted and has a full staff of designers in-house.

Ecko Furniture
424 S. College Rd., Wilmington • 452-5442

This is a really fun place for people seeking contemporary, quality furniture on a budget. Materials and workmanship are excellent on Ecko pieces. Those undaunted by minor assembly of some of the furniture will find their efforts well rewarded in terms of aesthetics and value.

Barnes & Noble Booksellers
322 S. College Rd., Wilmington • 395-4825

It's a given that this huge bookstore is going to carry every book you could ever want or need, but what is special is its extremely comfortable, inviting atmosphere. Big puffy chairs liberally sprinkled around the store invite browsers to grab a Starbuck's cup of coffee and a pastry at the store's cafe, then settle down for a read. Extremely involved in the community, Barnes & Noble has something going on every night ranging from meeting of community groups to mini-productions by local theater companies to book clubs. The children's department is larger than most bookstores and has a stage for story time three days a week. There's also a massive gift section with a display of unusual greeting cards, writing journals from the cheapest to the most luxurious, book accessories and calligraphy pens.

McAllister & Solomon Books
4402 Wrightsville Ave., Wilmington
• 350-0189

People who love vintage, rare or just plain hard-to-find books will really enjoy a browse through McAllister & Solomon Books, just a block off S. College Road. This store stocks used and rare books, maps, photographs, manuscripts and postcards. Books are bought, sold and traded. With 15,000 titles in store at any given time, McAllister & Solomon now has access to a database of 1.4 million books daily through a computerized out-of-print search network. The staff can also do quick searches online.

Other Wilmington Areas

While it is impossible to name all of the great stores throughout the area, there are

Everything
You Need....

Fashion,
Selection,
Quality,
and Value...

Find it all at Independence Mall,
Wilmington's Best Shopping Destination!

Come see why Independence Mall
is where Wilmington shops —
over 85 great stores plus Belk Beery,
Sears and JCPenney, showcasing
everything you need....from footwear
to fashion, sporting goods to gadgets,
books to stereo equipment and
the latest fads to special gifts!

Welcome to the Cape Fear Coast,
and Independence Mall!

INDEPENDENCE MALL
Wilmington's Best Shopping Destination.

3500 Oleander Drive - Belk Beery, Sears, JCPenney and over 85 other fine stores.
Open Monday-Saturday 10 am-9 pm. Sunday 12:30 pm-6 pm. Department store hours may vary.

some that don't fall into highlighted shopping areas but deserve special mention here.

The Great Harvest Bread Company
4302 Market St., North 17 Shopping Center, Wilmington • 763-0003

This bakery specializes in breads, mainly whole wheat. They meal their own wheat, use the highest protein wheat available and never use oils, fats or preservatives. Everything is truly from scratch. The bakery offers Breads of the Month, some of which are destined to become regular items, including spinach-feta bread, sundried tomato-pesto bread, cheddar-garlic bread and lots of fruit breads. Muffins, scones and cookies are regular items. Citing a philosophy of awareness of their role as a "village baker," Great Harvest donates its space, ingredients, staff and advertising to a local nonprofit organization one day each year and lets that agency have all of the day's profits.

Paula's Health Hut
3405 Wrightsville Ave., Wilmington • 791-0200

If you're into vitamins, health foods, diet, homeopathic products and all-natural items

for your body, Paula's Health Hut is a must. It has Wilmington's largest selection of vitamins, health foods, diet and all-natural products. The courteous staff is glad to share their knowledge and latest information.

The Red Dinette
2325 Market Street, Wilmington • 343-8920

The Red Dinette has contemporary furnishings and home accessories with a decidedly unusual twist. Handpainted furniture, eclectic items and what owner Greg Taylor describes as "refimitive" (Greg's own word for refined primitive) are the features that place this little store in a category all by itself. Services here include custom handpainting and finishing.

Canady's Sport Center
3220 Wrightsville Ave., Wilmington • 791-6280

They say they sell "Everything for the Sportsman," and it appears to be true. Marine items, Schwinn bikes, guns, decoys, sport knives, ski outfits, boots, canoes, tents, camping supplies and hiking items are just some of the goods in this extremely reasonable and

INSIDERS' TIP

Since some stores and restaurants don't take out-of-town checks, be sure to bring your credit cards or traveler's checks along.

well-stocked store. The cool and cold weather jackets are so densely packed throughout half of the store in the winter that it's a little bit of a struggle to get through the racks, but the January sale is well-worth it. When hurricanes strike, head to Canady's because they sell Sterno — canned heat — an item surprisingly hard to find in Wilmington. Its great for heating soup when the power is out.

The Learning Express
The Courtyard, 5704 Oleander Dr., Wilmington • 397-0301

This store's slogan is "Toys that Capture Imaginations." It's a great shopping experience for kids and their parents because everything in it offers educational opportunities. There's an extensive dress-up section, ranging from glittery flappers to a create-a-cape kit to cowgirl and cowboy duds. Puzzles range the complexity spectrum and there are science kits for all age levels. The store also carries books, games, Brio, Playmobile, Manhattan Baby and Beanie Babies. The size of the store doubled in 1997 to create 3,300 square feet of fun.

Windrose Furniture Company
5629 Oleander Dr., Wilmington • 799-5793

Located in Bradley Square across the street from the Learning Express and Harvest Moon Restaurant, Windrose carries some of the most unusual handcrafted furniture and home accessories in the region. American-made, handcrafted needlepoint rugs, rice paper batik shades, items crafted in Israel, handmade fountains, pottery and interesting clocks are just some of the offerings. It sells pencil-post beds, entertainment centers, armoires and limited edition prints. An exciting line of upholstered and slip-covered furniture by J.M. Paquet, a company owned by women, is not only beautiful and comfortable (down stuffing!), but the slipcovers are also machine washable.

Townhouse Art & Frame Center Inc.
737 St. James Dr., Wilmington • 791-2113

This store is somewhat hidden in St. James Village between the main part of the village and the back road to College Road Cinemas. There is an excellent selection of art supplies for everyone from students to professionals. Brushes, stretched canvas, canvas strips, colored pencils, markers, a wide range of papers, presentation portfolios and more are on display. Half of the large building is occupied by a comprehensive frame shop that offers everything from do-it-yourself to museum-standard mounting and framing.

Adjacent to Wrightsville Beach

Truth be told, there is not a lot of shopping on this primarily residential beach but there's an explosion of retail growth over the bridge on the mainland side.

Landfall Shopping Center
Eastwood Dr. and Military Cutoff Rd., Wilmington • 256-9473

Located just minutes from Wrightsville Beach, this robust center has entered the retail arena in a brisk way in the past few years. This retail, dining and service center lies just outside the gates of the Landfall residential subdivision. It offers a smaller version of **Belk-Beery Department Store** and may other stores.

If you're looking for health foods, natural beauty aids, organic vegetables (something hard to find in quantity in the area) and an extensive line of Japanese cooking products, **Doxey's Market and Cafe**, 256-9952, is a one-of-a-kind store in the Cape Fear region. The healthful cafe inside makes it a favorite dining or take-out spot for the discerning vegetarian.

An exciting store for cooks and people who enjoy entertaining, **The Seasoned Gourmet**, 256-9488, is a real comer in the culinary arts stores beginning to pepper Wilmington. There's high emphasis on cookware, including handpainted ceramics in one-of-a-kind designs by Pennsylvania artist Anita Ambrose. The store sells KitchenAid mixers, cookbooks, linens, Wustoff knives, Cuisinart, gift baskets, gourmet foods, handpainted trays and cheeseboxes, lazy Susans and some unusual

furniture. Each Tuesday on a seasonal basis, the store offers cooking classes that range from French to Asian to Southwestern and beyond. A new addition for 1997 is an impressive offering of imported cheeses.

Something Special Florist and Gifts, 256-0020, bills itself as having the "most beautiful flowers in Wilmington," and, indeed, no one could disagree with that self-assessment. Designer Jerry Rivenbark creates exquisite floral arrangements, and the store offers a nice selection of gifts. The store expanded in 1996 when it moved to a new location "under the tower." It carries custom gourmet baskets, live plants, planters, pottery, cards, home accessories and gardening gifts.

Also in Landfall Center is **Tavernay's Jewelers**, 256-1122, the second location of this Wilmington business. A beautiful store, it's a fitting setting for a place where you can buy the work of Henry Dumay, exclusively offered by Tavernay's in both Carolinas. Dumay's works have been bought by Diana Ross, Princess Di, Hillary Clinton and Elizabeth Taylor.

The Julia, 256-1175, moved from downtown Wilmington to the Landfall Center in 1995. Offering better women's apparel since 1916, this veteran retailer sells evening wear, daytime wear and "a bit of casual". Some of its clothing makers include Tom and Linda Platt, Mondi, Votre Nom and Tamotsu.

HobbyTown USA, 256-0902, describes itself as "toys for the big kids." Remote-controlled helicopters, planes and boats, train sets, racing sets and thousands of model kits are enough to bring out the kid in anyone. Sure, the real children in the family will find a lot to entertain themselves, but the grown-ups in the house are going to have a good time here.

If you're into outdoor sports, **Aussie Island Surf Shop**, 256-5454, has a mind-boggling array of clothing and equipment for surfers on sea, street and snow as well as casual sport clothing and beachwear. There are lots of surfboards on display. Wave surfers can get a surf report for the area beaches by calling Aussie Island at 256-5757.

J.S. Anderson, 256-8893, a younger sister store to A & G Sportwear, offers a full line of Jams complete with a Caribbean cabana modeled after a house that store owner Steve Anderson stays in on Grand Caymans every Christmas. The store carries trendy items including resort wear for ladies and men, Brighton shoes and leather belts and gifts.

The Fisherman's Wife
1425 Airlie Rd., Wilmington • 256-5505

This store specializes in decorative accessories and gifts with a fishy theme, including home accent pieces. "Playful prints, perky pottery, funky folk art" made by hand, are a regular feature of this store's offerings. It has a wide array of tableware, ceramic lamps, candlesticks, books, toys, T-shirts, pewter tub and sink stoppers, drawer pulls and starfish hooks, cookbooks and a year-round Christmas room.

Whiting & Company
The Galleria, 6800 Wrightsville Ave., Wilmington • 256-3993

Casualwear for women and men in brands such as Nautica and Kenar are hallmarks of this store near Wrightsville Beach. Look to this store for hard-to-find linen clothing and sportswear.

Outer Banks Hammocks
7228 Wrightsville Ave., Wilmington • 256-4001

Outer Banks Hammocks sells its own high-quality hammocks, rope and wood-related items, such as porch swings, deck chairs and hanging chairs. Owner Clark Helton has established a reputation for products that are durable and comfortable. Generous sizing is a plus, and oak and ash hardwoods and soft-spun polyester rope make these hammocks hold up to the weather. Hammock pillows and cushions are all made of Sunbrella. Drive by most any day and watch Helton's employees handweaving hammocks right in front of the store. It's an attraction in itself.

Plaza East Shopping Center
1946 Eastwood Rd., Wilmington • 256-4782

Plaza East Shopping Center has several unique specialty stores. **Trends Home Furnishings**, 256-3003, carries transitional to contemporary furnishings and accessories. A walk-through reveals couches, chairs, dining furniture, rugs, lamps, occasional furniture, wall art and more.

Airlie Moon, 256-0655, has an eclectic assortment of pottery, candles, handmade blank books, sculpture, glass, body lotions and jewelry. There's a metaphysical theme to the place, too, so check out the counter for information on area meetings and groups.

At **Easy Living**, 256-5370, you'll find cookware, a wide assortment of serving pieces, glassware, table linens and grill accessories all perfectly suited to coastal living and entertaining. The store carries All-Clad, Nancy Calhoun dishes, rugs, wall art and doormats. A bridal registry service is available.

If you want to head into the outdoors, **Cape Fear Outfitters**, 256-1258, is the store to visit first. It is stocked with everything you'll need to enjoy an adventure in nature: tents, sleeping bags, backpacks, outdoor clothing, kayaks and touring canoes. The store also arranges guided trips into the wilds of the Cape Fear region and rents kayaks and canoes to adventurers.

A member of a huge chain that carries boating supplies, hardware and accessories, **West Marine**, 256-7878, is a welcome addition to the Wilmington shopping scene for boaters. As a personal service, West Marine will also be happy to pick up cruising boaters at the docks on the Intracoastal Waterway who want or need to shop in their store. It's open seven days a week.

Embellishments, 256-5263, carries a wide selection of gifts suitable for weddings, birthdays or special holidays. It has a Bridal Registry, stationery and gifts particularly suited for bridal attendants, and features handblown glass by Simon Pearce.

Clockwise Clocks
7040 Wrightsville Ave., Wilmington
• 256-2576

Located near the Galleria between Airlie Road and Eastwood Road, this store is in a hard-to-spot space in a new, small commercial/retail center: Twelve Oaks. Clockwise Clocks carries mostly mechanical-wind clocks including new pieces by Howard Miller and exquisite handmade pieces by Foster Campos — such as his mahogany Banjo Clock. The store carries mantle clocks, grandfather clocks and a full line of Chelsea marine clocks. It offers complete repair services and rumor has it the owner has become "clocksmith to the stars."

Lumina Station
1900 Eastwood Rd., Wilmington
• 256-0900

A center that has caused a considerable stir near Wrightsville Beach is Lumina Station, opened in late 1996. Thoughtfully constructed with tremendous respect for the natural setting, locals generally agree this upscale center, with attractive Lowcountry architecture and forested setting, is a plus for the community. The following is a partial listing of the stores there, and the visitor is going to discover many other shopping opportunities.

The Quarter, 256-6011, has classic to contemporary and casual to cocktail clothing for women in upscale lines such as Lady Boudin and Robert Scott. Just like the downtown shop, this store carries quality clothing and prides itself on personal service.

At **A Proper Garden**, 256-0377, owner Peg Beam has "furnishings" for the garden as well as great gifts for your gardening friends and home accessories. Garden stepping stones, delicate, bubbling fountains, tasteful yard art, topiaries and sculpture for home or garden jam the store.

At **R. Bryan Collections**, 256-9943, a contemporary boutique for women, Sheri Bryan has assembled a collection of the latest upscale, traditional trends and wardrobe essentials for women.

Another downtown shop with a second spot in this center, **Alligator Pie**, 509-1600, is a complete children's boutique specializing in international designs in sizes newborn to 16. It also has gifts, toys, accessories and clothing.

Bristol Books, 256-4490, is a small independent bookstore offering a wide range of books, magazines, newspapers, cards and fine stationery in a cozy bookstore setting. Personal service and community involvement are

hallmarks of Bristol that keep it highly competitive in a market with several much larger bookstores.

Wrightsville Beach

Redix
120 Causeway Dr., Wrightsville Beach
• 256-2201

This is simply a gratifying store for shoppers looking for a variety of items. Redix is a beach goods store that has everything from rafts to sandchairs to groceries to boogie boards, but it also has one of the best selections of excellent quality clothing for men and women in the whole Cape Fear region. Swimsuits, sweaters, shorts, slacks, dresses and more jam half of the large building. When Redix has sales, such as after Christmas, you can get great bargains on Liz Claiborne, Jones of New York, Robert Scott and other quality name brands.

Sweetwater Surf Shop
10 N. Lumina Ave., Wrightsville Beach
• 256-3821

Sweetwater has everything the surfer will ever need — and then some. Spyder, Xanadu and Bessell are some of the quality brands of boards it carries. It also has a repair service for the occasional unhappy landing. You'll also find swimsuits, women's fashions, shoes, sunglasses and accessories.

Island Passage
1 Lumina Ave., Wrightsville Beach
• 256-6990

Just like the downtown and Bald Head Island stores, Island Passage has fun, casual clothing and accessories for women. Lots of linens, loosely structured clothing, swimsuits, funky shoes and other interesting and fun apparel are in this store.

Carolina Beach

There are several places to shop in Carolina Beach. Something important to know is that most of the smaller retail stores — as well as restaurants — have limited hours in the winter season. Many of them close up altogether until the tourist seasons kicks off anew in March or April. However, several specialty-shop merchants are parting ways with this tradition and staying open all year. This is good news for the off-season visitor.

Wings
807 N. Lake Park Blvd., Carolina Beach
• 458-4488

Welcome to the ultimate beach goods store that is large enough to stay open all year in a town that is largely seasonal. Whether you

Photo: Curtis Krueger

Insiders take the opportunity to participate in festivals that
celebrate the rich history of the area.

want Boogie Boards, beach clothing for the family, windsocks, beach toys or T-shirts made your way, Wings is the place to find whatever you need.

Island Tackle & Hardware
15 Federal Point Shopping Center, Carolina Beach • 458-3049

This is your first stop for fishing supplies. This combination hardware and tackle store sells bait, offshore lures, rods and reels, line, coolers — everything an angler needs and then some. For damage done to reels by the big fish off the Carolina Beach shores, Island Tackle & Hardware also repairs reels. It is open all year because, after all, the fish never stop biting.

Linda's
201 N. Lake Park Boulevard, Carolina Beach • 458-7116

This fairly large year-round store has a wide assortment of ladies sportswear, dresses for special evenings on the town, swimwear, costume jewelry, scarves and other accessories. Linda's offers resortwear made of comfortable, machine-washable, low maintenance material in stylish cuts and colors.

The Gold Rose Apparel
6-B N. Lake Park Blvd., Carolina Beach • 458-9770

The Gold Rose is a quality women's clothing store that offers outfits suitable for daywear or parties. Owner Barbara Brant is also a seamstress who will create scarves to coordinate with any outfit in the shop. The clothing is all American-made, all washable and very reasonably priced. The Gold Rose also carries a full range of accessories with the exception of shoes. Although the store is open all year, hours are reduced in January and February.

Island Appliance
716 N. Lake Park Blvd., Carolina Beach • 458-3070

This store sells and services all major brands of appliances including window air conditioners, refrigerators and freezers, washers and dryers, dishwashers, microwaves and ranges. Some of its brand-name items include KitchenAid, Jenn-Air, Whirlpool, Roper and RCA. Low prices and free local delivery are appealing features of this appliance/service store.

The Sea Horse Gallery
112 Cape Fear Blvd., Carolina Beach • 458-7284

The Sea Horse Gallery is open year-round with limited winter hours. It stocks all kinds of gifts, including a good selection of jewelry, greeting cards, stuffed animals, Spencer Collin lighthouses and an assortment of handcrafted items.

PK's
10 S. Lake Park Blvd., Carolina Beach • 458-3090

PK's is a gift boutique owned by the Kure Beach postmaster. Patty Compton's store is in its sixth year and recently underwent extensive remodelling. Clothing for women is described by the owner as "fun and glitzy" casual and resortwear. PK's sells Lefton Lighthouses, crystal, salt-and-pepper sets, brass, 14K gold charms, lots of jewelry, pewter miniatures, frames by Fiji, clay art, ceramics and music boxes. Check out the assortment of unique cookie jars. The store prides itself on a high level of service, including good prices, shipping and gift wrapping.

Southport-Oak Island

Northrop Mall
111 E. Moore St., Southport • 457-9569

Antique shoppers will be delighted to discover 25 antique and collectibles dealers under one roof just a few feet down the street from the Antique Mall.

Swayne's Crafts & Things
817 N. Howe St., Southport • 457-6589

This store carries a selection of garden supplies, craft supplies for the hobbyist, fabrics, floral products, shells, gifts and souvenirs.

The Driftwood Shell Shop
122 Yacht Basin St., Southport • 457-5466

With souvenirs, jewelry, T-shirts and Sure Catch Tackle, The Driftwood, on the Southport boar harbor, 457-4545, is touted as one of the area's most complete fishing tackle centers. It's also an official weigh station to verify your tall tales of the future.

Little Professor Book Center
4930 Long Beach Rd., S.E. , Southport
• 457-9653, (800) 722-2323

Located in River Run Shopping Center is this family book store open seven days a week. This store is big on personal customer service. It's motto is: "We'll help you find the books you love." Before heading out to relax on the beach, drop by for books and magazines and pick up some cards to send the folks back home.

Miss Patti's Porch
122 E. Moore St., Southport • 457-5052

This store sells handcrafted and handpainted tin pins. (Its forerunner was Tin Pan Alley.) Miss Patti specializes in the themes of cats and angels done in tinwork and carries a wide array of country collectibles.

Oak Island Senior Center Craft Shop
5918 E. Oak Island Dr., Long Beach
• 278-5224

This unusual shop, operated as a nonprofit organization, has gifts made by its members for sale as well as classes in crafts ranging from decoupage to pottery to paintings. It also sells art and craft supplies.

Boat House Gifts
5606 E. Oak Island Dr., Long Beach
• 278-9856

Boat House Gifts carries Tom Clark's sculptural creations, collectible sand dollars, Swarovski Silver Crystal Miniatures, lighthouses, prints, jewelry and cards.

Lynne's Hallmark Shop & Treasure Room
103 Yaupon Dr., Yaupon Beach • 278-9352

This store has Hallmark greeting cards, fashion jewelry, saltwater taffy, shells, beach bags and souvenirs of your visit to the beach.

Philomena Moultries Boutique
5813 E. Oak Island Dr., Long Beach
• 278-9352

This small boutique offers an array of fine

and fun gifts, children's clothing, books, tapes, costume and fine jewelry and angels.

South Brunswick Islands

The Cockle Shell
Holden Beach Cswy., Holden Beach
• 842-6030

Need some sand dollar hardener? Maybe you never thought you would need this particular item, but maybe you've never had an opportunity to find whole sand dollars like you will on the Brunswick Beaches. This store not only has this mystical ingredient but also sells live hermit crabs, coral, a wide variety of seashells, books, jewelry and lamps.

Carson Cards and Gifts
Twin Creek Plaza, Shallotte • 754-9968

Carson has shelves of collectibles including Tom Clark Gnomes, Hummel figurines, Porcelain Birds by Andrea and more as well as a full inventory of greeting cards.

Pelican Square Books & Ball Cards
1647 Seaside Rd., Sunset Beach
• 579-8770

This store carries top-10 hardback and paperback books as well as a general line of books, newspapers and magazines. It has ball cards too.

Calabash Nautical Gifts
9973 Beach Dr., Calabash • 579-2611

Drop by here when you're feeling particularly nautical and want to accessorize your home with sailorly stuff. This store also carries collectibles such as Department 56 and Tom Clark Gnomes and boasts over 3 million ornaments. You'll also find golf equipment and clothing.

The Furniture Patch of Calabash
10283 Beach Dr. S.W., N.C. Hwy. 179, Calabash • 579-2001

This company is owned by the same family that owns Murrow Furniture Galleries in Wilmington. It carries more than 350 major lines, including Lexington, Stanley, Hickory White, Hickory Chair, Kincaid, Broyhill and National Mt. Airy. As is the case with sister

urrow
furniture galleries
...for styles that are naturally you

3514 So. College Rd. • P.O. Box 4337, Wilmington, NC 28406 • (910) 799-4010
Hours: Monday-Friday 8:30-5:30, Saturday, 9:00-5:30

store Murrow, the Furniture Patch of Calabash sells top-quality furnishings at discounted prices and ships all over the world. There is a designer on staff who will help customers with interior statements that range from casual to formal. The Furniture Patch of Calabash is the last company in North Carolina before crossing the South Carolina line.

Topsail Island

Topsail Island has seen tremendous growth in retail business during the past few years. Despite the primarily residential orientation of this island, there are some fun places to shop. Some businesses ceased operation after the hurricanes, but it is already apparent to the observer that the island is going to see a lot of new stores and services soon.

Spinnaker Surf & Sport
111 N. Shore Dr., Surf City • 328-2311

Spinnaker has kites and windsocks, surfing apparel, new and used surfboards, resort wear, Rollerblades and Jimmy Buffett/Caribbean Soul T-shirts and souvenirs.

The Topsail Island Trading Company
201 New River Dr., Surf City • 328-1905

Despite a couple of hurricanes, this store is celebrating its 11th year in business. The store, patterned after a Maryland lighthouse, has fun resort wear, T-shirts, quality toys and unusual gifts. Delicious fudge, freshly made in the store, is shipped across the country. The store is also the home of Topsail Scenic Boat Tours and Turtle Island Ventures, a guided kayak nature tour.

The Market Gourmet Gift Shop
209 N. New River Dr., Surf City • 328-0803

This store stocks a variety of gourmet foods, wines, candies and specialty gift items. If you get tired of shopping, just sit down in the cozy bar and sip a piña colada while you watch the sun set over the sound. Or wander over to the Soundside restaurant for a great meal (See our Restaurants chapter.)

Island Super Store
N.C. Hwy. 210, North Topsail • 328-5351

Three miles north of the Surf City bridge, this beach and party supplier also has a butcher shop, groceries, fresh produce, hurricane supplies, garden supplies, hardware, stuff for your boat, camping equipment, books, newspapers and virtually everything you forgot to bring on your beach vacation. Best of all, it's open seven days a week all year long.

Docksider Gifts & Shells
14061 Ocean Hwy. 50, Surf City • 328-1421

Docksider is filled with souvenirs, fresh saltwater taffy, clothing and accessories, costume and fine jewelry, post cards, puzzles, back scratchers, stuffed animals, lighthouses, crystals, shell-filled lamps, flags, nautical items, soaps, Christmas ornaments and more. As an added service, you can have the shark teeth you found on the beach wired while you wait so you can wear your treasure home and amaze your inland friends.

Antiques Shopping

Downtown

On and adjacent to Front Street, the Downtown Wilmington shopping corridor has many stores that will attract both visitors and residents to a potential shopping frenzy. Antiques stores rapidly are becoming primary retail operations downtown, and the area has approximately 20 stores specializing in valuable antiques and interesting old things. You can find most of these stores along Front Street, and a knot of them are on nearby Castle Street.

There is a Historic Downtown Wilmington Antique Dealers Association, and most of the stores will provide you with a map that pinpoints the other shops. Needless to say, it is easy to plan a whole day around antiquing in downtown Wilmington. Park the car anywhere along Front Street or adjacent streets and set off on foot to discover these stores. There are so many of them that they can't all be included here, so pick up the map and go on an adventure.

About Time Antiques
30 N. Front St., Wilmington • 762-9902

If you're into pottery, glassware, French and Victorian furniture and linens, this is a good stop on your tour of antique shops.

Angel's Antiques and Auctions
545 Castle St., Wilmington • 763-1210

Another of the new group of antique shops on Castle Street, you can find furniture, glassware and collectibles in this shop that's connected in location and work to Antique Emporium.

Antique Emporium
539 Castle St., Wilmington • 762-0609

What isn't in this store? Lamps, weathervanes, furniture, glass, duck decoys, jewelry, china, dolls, vintage appliances and more jam the space.

Antiques of Old Wilmington
25 S. Front St., Wilmington • 763-6011

Walnut and mahogany furniture, glassware and accessories can all be found at this longtime store.

Butterflies Castle Antiques
606 ½ Castle St., Wilmington • 251-0405

This antique store specializes in Chinese exports, a wide variety of antique furniture and an assortment of glassware.

Butte's Antiques
302 N. Front St., Wilmington • 343-0059

A relatively new addition to Wilmington's antiques scene, this is an extremely appealing one. Rather than collectibles, Butte's Antiques concentrates on 18th- and 19th-century American and English furniture and appropriate accessories. This period furniture store buys estates and specializes in Chippendale, Queen Anne and Federal furniture. It also has Chinese export porcelain, chandeliers and estate silver.

Cameron's Antiques & Collectibles
15 S. Water St., Wilmington • 343-6950

Located in the Jacobi Warehouse, Cameron's concentrates on collectibles from the 1800s to the 1970s. An unusual feature of Cameron's is that it sells old-style candies: Kit-Kats, Atomic Fireballs and B.B. Batts.

Michael Moore Antiques
20 S. Front St., Wilmington • 763-0300

This store occupies a building with Hollingsworth American Country. These businesses complement each other with Moore's collection of collectibles, toys and furniture and Hollingsworth's reproductions.

Provenance Antiques & Interiors
306 N. Front St., Wilmington • 343-1590

Provenance is an upscale antiques and interiors store that carries imported English and Continental antique furniture as well as porcelain, silver, prints and clocks.

Other Areas

While the bulk of the area's antiques stores are clustered downtown, there are also endless opportunities to shop around the region. Listed below are a few stores in Wilmington and Southport.

Auld Stokley Antiques
7250 Market St., Wilmington • 686-9620

This store specializes in fine antique furniture of mahogany, walnut, oak and pine as well as primitives.

Cape Fear Antiques Center
1606 Market St., Wilmington • 763-1837

With more than 8,000 square feet of quality antiques, collectibles and glassware, this place could take the better part of a day to examine.

The Antique Mall
108 E. Moore St., Southport • 457-4982

Antique lovers will appreciate that this store has 15 dealers in three buildings. Here you'll find an abundance of furniture and collectibles. The mall is open Monday through Saturday from 10 AM to 5 PM.

WILMINGTON
Morning Star
Sunday Star-News

Courtesy New Hanover County Public Library, Louis T. Moore collection.

What is now one of the most respected newspapers in North Carolina began life above a grocery store at 3 S. Water Street, Wilmington.

The *Morning Star* was owned by William H. Bernard, a Confederate veteran. In the aftermath of war, he saw the need for courageous leadership in the South.

The first issue of the *Star*, a four page evening newspaper, appeared on September, 23 1867. The following month The Wilmington *Morning Star* made its first appearance, replacing the evening paper.

In the 1920's the *Star* began publication of the afternoon *Evening News*. The corporation then published the *Star*, the *News* and the *Sunday Star-News*.

The company was bought in 1975 by the New York Times Company. Publication of the *News* ceased that same year, leaving the *Morning Star* and the *Sunday Star-News* as the surviving papers and explains the split personality in the names.

The *Morning Star* is today the oldest daily newspaper in continuous publication in North Carolina.

Attractions

Two things have shaped the types of attractions that flourish on the southern coast: history and geography. The area's rich historical legacy manifests itself in museums, monuments, churches and living structures that speak eloquently of our inherited past. And the proximity to the sea of a culturally vibrant city and its satellite settlements lends a distinct resort quality to the entire region.

Downtown Wilmington's historic attractions might even be called organic because they are so integral to the identity of Cape Fear. Sites such as Brunswick Town, Fort Fisher and Topsail Island's Assembly Building convey specific eras and events as no textbook or commemoration can.

The historic district of downtown Wilmington practically groans under the weight of its history, and it is the most varied single attraction in the area, easily explored by foot, by boat or by horse-drawn carriage. By 1850 Wilmington was the largest city in North Carolina. As a port city, it was on a par with other great southern ports such as Galveston and New Orleans. But when the Atlantic Coast Line Railroad company pulled out of Wilmington in the 1960s, the city went into such a rapid decline that even its skyline was flattened by the demolition of several buildings and railroad facilities on the north side of town.

Downtown was all but deserted until a core of local entrepreneurs revitalized and restored their hometown. In 1974, downtown Wilmington became the state's largest urban district listed in the National Register of Historic Places. Many of the images of Wilmington's bustling past are preserved in the North Carolina Room at the public library's main branch at 201 Chestnut Street in downtown Wilmington. Likewise, the Cape Fear Museum and the Wilmington Railroad Museum interpret the region's history in far-reaching exhibits. Together these places, all listed below, are excellent resources for interpreting what you see today or exploring the history further.

The region is so rich in history, it would be impossible to list every historic attraction in a book this size. So, as you travel to such places as Southport's Old Smithville Burial Ground, stay alert for other sites with similar stories to tell, such as Southport's old Morse Cemetery on W. West Street and the John N. Smith Cemetery on Leonard Street off Herring Drive. Memorials are so abundant you may miss the one at Bonnet's Creek (Moore Street north of downtown Southport), at the mouth of which the Gentleman Pirate Stede Bonnet used to hide his corsair. (This and many other sites are on the Southport Trail, listed below.) Other memorials also bear silent testimony to the past, such as the shipwrecks that are awash at low tide and may be spied from the beaches (for example, the blockade runner *Vesta*, run aground February 4, 1864, south of Tubbs Inlet in about 10 feet of water; and the blockade runner *Bendigo*, run aground January 11, 1864, a mile southwest of Lockwood Folly Inlet in about 15 feet of water).

Many attractions are typical of the seashore: excellent fishing, fine seafood dining, the many cruise opportunities. No beach resort would be complete without water slides, go-cart tracks or batting cages, so take note of these places listed in the Kidstuff chapter; they are definitely not for kids only. These amusements, as well as miniature golf, movies and bowling, are concentrated along our most heavily traveled routes. In Wilmington, Oleander Drive east of 41st Street is the predominant amusement strip, having several more attractions than listed here. North of Ocean Isle Beach, Beach Drive (N.C. Highway 179/904) is another strip, with its share of go-carts, miniature golf and curiosities. Near the foot of Yaupon Pier on Oak Island stands an arcade and seaside miniature-golf course. Topsail Beach and Surf City share the limelight as Topsail Island's two centers of attractions. It would be redundant to list every enterprise; you're bound to stumble across them as you gravitate toward each community's entertainment center.

Not all local attractions are summertime flings. The world's largest living Christmas tree is decorated and lit nightly during the Christmas season in Wilmington. Not your average Christmas tree, it is a 400-year-old live oak in Hilton Park, a few minutes north of downtown on N.C. Highway 133/U.S. Highway 117. Another great holiday display is Calder Court, a cul-de-sac in the King's Grant subdivision. To get there, drive north on N.C. Highway 132 (College Road) about 1.25 miles beyond the Market Street overpass. Turn right onto Kings Drive and take the next two lefts, then douse the headlights to witness one of the most flamboyant demonstrations of Christmas illumination anywhere. Cars often line up all the way down the street, not one with its lights on. In recent years, the show has been catching on elsewhere in the King's Grant neighborhood.

It would be difficult to overstate the importance of the region's gardens, for which North Carolina is rightfully famous. The fact that the North Carolina Azalea Festival, to which garden tours are focal, is based in Wilmington makes a strong case for the southern coast's horticultural significance. Annual and perennial plantings are well-supported public works. Two privately owned gardens open to the public — Airlie Gardens and Orton Plantation — are simply spectacular in springtime.

What follows, then, are descriptions of the area's prime general attractions followed by a brief section on the southern coast's islands. Wilmington's attractions have been grouped into three subsections: Downtown Wilmington, Around Wilmington and Outside Wilmington. Within each section, all attractions are listed alphabetically. Information to supplement this guide can be obtained at several locations: the Cape Fear Coast Convention & Visitors Bureau, 24 N. Third Street, 341-4030, in the 1892 courthouse building; the visitors information booth at the foot of Market Street in

Wilmington; public libraries, especially New Hanover County's main branch at Third and Chestnut streets in Wilmington; in Southport, the Southport 2000 Visitors' Center, 107 E. Nash Street, 457-7927; the Greater Topsail Area Chamber of Commerce, 203 Roland Drive in Surf City, 328-4722 or (800) 626-2780. Of course, all the area's chambers of commerce are helpful; see our Area Overviews for a list.

General Attractions

Downtown Wilmington

Battleship North Carolina
Cape Fear River, Wilmington • 251-5797

The Battleship *North Carolina*, enshrined in a berth on Eagle Island across the river from downtown Wilmington, is dedicated to the 10,000 North Carolinians who gave their lives during World War II. Commissioned in 1941, the 44,800-ton warship wielded nine 16-inch turreted guns and carries nickel-steel hull armor 16 to 18 inches thick. It was this plating that undoubtedly helped her survive at least one direct torpedo hit in 1942. In fact, the "Immortal Showboat" is renowned for its relatively small number of casualties.

The battleship came to its present home in 1961. It took a swarm of tugboats to maneuver the 728-foot vessel into its berth, where the river is only 500 feet wide. Predictably, the bow became stuck in the mud. When the tugs succeeded in freeing the ship, they failed to prevent it from slamming into Fergus's Ark, a floating restaurant moored at the foot of Princess Street. Wilmington gained a battleship and lost a restaurant.

Battleship *North Carolina* is open for tours every day of the year from 8 AM to sunset. You can drive to it easily enough, but the Battleship River Taxi is more fun (see the *Capt. Maffitt* Sightseeing Cruise below). Choose between two self-guided tours, both of which begin with a 10-minute orientation film. The full two-hour tour takes you above and below decks and includes the pilot house, turrets, a rare Kingfisher float plane, crew's quarters and the galley. The hour-long tour takes in fewer decks and eliminates much of the climbing. Only the main deck is handicapped-accessible. Tours cost $8 for those 12 and older and $4 for children ages 6 to 11. Discounts ($1 off) apply for senior citizens age 65 and older and for active-duty military personnel. Picnic grounds and ample RV parking adjoin the berth. There is no extra charge for unscheduled appearances by old Charlie, the alligator who makes his home near the ship at the river's edge.

Bellamy Mansion
Museum of Design Arts
503 Market St., Wilmington • 251-3700

The assertion that Bellamy Mansion is Wilmington's premiere statement of prewar opulence and wealth is impossible to contest. ("Prewar" here refers to the War Between the States, a.k.a. the Civil War, the War of Northern Aggression, the Great Unpleasantness.) This four-story, 22-room wooden palace, completed in 1861, is a classic example of Greek Revival and Italianate architecture. Its majesty is immediately evident in 14 fluted exterior Corinthian columns. Most of the craftwork is the product of African-American slave artisans, some of whom were granted their freedom on the steps of this very building. Before plans were set to renovate and restore the mansion in 1972, it hadn't been lived in since 1946. Volunteer guides are sure to point out the glassed-in portion of a wall left unrestored to illustrate the extent of a 1972 arson. That event was linked to the disfavor in which the Bellamy Mansion has been held by some locals who see it as a symbol of slavery, which further legitimizes the mansion's value as a historic and cultural landmark.

As a museum, the mansion's exhibits embrace regional architecture, landscape architecture, preservation and decorative arts, and hosts multimedia traveling exhibits, workshops, films, lectures, slide shows and other activities. Ongoing and painstaking restoration qualifies Bellamy Mansion as an important work in progress. Outside, the gardens have recently been restored. Forthcoming restorations will include the slave quarters (a rare example of urban slave housing) and the carriage house.

FYI
Unless otherwise noted, the area code for all phone numbers in this guide is 910.

Bellamy Mansion is open to the public Wednesday to Saturday from 10 AM to 5 PM and Sunday 1 to 5 PM. Fees are $5 for adults, $3 for children ages 6 through 12. Members of Preservation North Carolina are admitted free.

Burgwin-Wright House
224 Market St., Wilmington • 762-0570

When Lord Charles Cornwallis fled his slim victory near Guilford Courthouse in central North Carolina in 1781, still in danger of a rebel pursuit, he repaired to Wilmington, then a town of 200 houses. He lodged at the gracious Georgian home of John Burgwin (pronounced "bur-GWIN"), a wealthy planter and politician, and made it his headquarters. The home, completed in 1770, is distinguished by two-story porches on two sides and six levels of tiered gardens. The massive ballast-stone foundation remains from the previously abandoned town jail, beneath which was a dungeon where Cornwallis held his prisoners. Volunteers for the National Society of the Colonial Dames, the building's present owners, can point out the trap door leading to it. Underground, an old brick tunnel communicates to the river. Rumored to have concealed pirate treasure or slaves on the Underground Railroad, it is only a sluice for a stream called Jacob's Run.

The Burgwin-Wright House is one of the great restoration/reconstruction achievements in the state, and visitors may peruse the carefully appointed rooms and period furnishings for $3 (students, $1). The museum is open Tuesday through Saturday 10 AM to 4 PM.

Cape Fear Museum
814 Market St., Wilmington • 341-4350

For an overview of the cultural and natural histories of the Cape Fear region from prehistory to the present, the Cape Fear Museum, established in 1898, stands unsurpassed. A miniature re-creation of the second battle of Fort Fisher and a remarkable scale model of the Wilmington waterfront, c. 1863, are of special interest. The Michael Jordan Discovery Gallery, including a popular display case housing many of the basketball star's personal items, is a long-term interactive natural history exhibit for the entire family. The Discovery Gallery includes a crawl-through beaver lodge, Pleistocene-era fossils and an entertaining Venus's-flytrap model you can feed with stuffed "bugs." Children's activities, videos, special events and acclaimed touring exhibits contribute to making the Cape Fear Museum not only one of the primary repositories of local history but also a place where learning is fun.

The museum is open Tuesday through Saturday 9 AM to 5 PM, Sunday 2 to 5 PM and is handicapped-accessible. Admission is $2 for adults 18 to 65; $1 for children 5 to 17, college students with valid ID and seniors older than 65. Children younger than 5 and Museum Associates are admitted free. Admission is free to all on the first and third Sundays each month and the first day of each month.

Capt. Maffitt Sightseeing Cruise
Riverfront Park, Wilmington • 343-1611, (800) 676-0162

Named for Capt. John Newland Maffitt, one of the Confederacy's most successful blockade runners, this is a converted World War II Navy launch affording 45-minute sightseeing cruises along the Cape Fear River with live historical narration. Cruises set out at 11 AM and 3 PM daily from Memorial Day to Labor Day. The *Maffitt* is available for charter throughout the year, and it doubles as the Battleship River Taxi during the summer. No reservations are necessary, and it runs on the quarter-hour from 10 AM to 5 PM outside of cruise times. Also see our listing for Battleship *North Carolina*, above.

Chandler's Wharf
Water and Ann sts., Wilmington • 815-3510

In the late 1970s, Chandler's Wharf was an Old Wilmington riverfront reconstruction complete with a museum and seven historic ships moored at the adjoining docks. More than 100 years ago, the area was choked with mercantile warehouses, its sheds filled with naval stores, tools, cotton and guano, its wharves lined with merchantmen. A disastrous (and suspicious) fire in August 1874 changed the site forever. Today much of the flavor —

and none of the odor — of that era remains, and Chandler's Wharf is again a business district; more accurately, a shopping and dining district. Two historic homes transformed into shops stand along the cobblestone street, wooden sidewalks and the rails of the former waterfront railway. You'll find a jeweler/gemologist shop, two restaurants (Elijah's and The Pilot House) and boutiques set amid flowers, a small herb garden, benches and nautical artifacts. On the corner immediately north, a renovated warehouse contains more shops. The tugboat *John Taxis*, reputedly the oldest in America, sits above the water's edge. For more on wharf businesses, see our Restaurants and Shopping chapters.

Chestnut Street United Presbyterian Church
710 N. Sixth St., Wilmington • 762-1074

This tiny church (1858), originally a mission chapel of First Presbyterian Church (see below), is a remarkable example of Stick Style, or Carpenter Gothic, architecture. Set well back from the road, its exterior details include decorative bargeboards with repeating acorn pendants, board-and-batten construction, a louvered bell tower (with carillon) and paired Gothic windows. When the congregation formed in 1858, the chapel was surrendered by the mother church to the new, black congregation, which purchased the building in 1867. The congregation's many distinguished members have included the first Negro president of Biddle University (now Johnson C. Smith University), publisher of Wilmington's first Negro newspaper, a member of the original Fisk University Jubilee Singers, the first African-American graduate of MIT, and North Carolina's first black physician.

First Baptist Church
529 N. Fifth St., Wilmington • 763-2647

Having lost its stunning 197-foot, copper-sheathed steeple to Hurricane Fran in 1996, this is still Wilmington's tallest church, if only in the hearts of the townspeople, many of whom are rallying to rebuild it. For years this tower, the taller of two, had been known to visibly sway even in an "average" wind. The congregation dates to 1808, and construction of the red brick building began in 1859. The

church was not completed until 1870 because of the Civil War, when Confederate and Union forces in turn used the higher steeple as a lookout. Its architecture is Early English Gothic Revival with hints of Richardson Romanesque, as in its varicolored materials and its horizontal mass relieved by the verticality of the spires, with their narrow, gabled vents. Inside, the pews, galleries and ceiling vents are of native heart pine. Being the first Baptist church in the region, this is the mother church of many other Baptist churches in Wilmington. The church offices occupy an equally interesting building next door, the Conoley House (1859), which exhibits such classic Italianate elements as frieze vents and brackets, and fluted wooden columns.

First Presbyterian Church
125 S. Third St., Wilmington • 762-6688

Organized as early as 1760, this congregation continues to have among its members some of the most influential Wilmingtonians. The Rev. Joseph R. Wilson was pastor from

1874 until 1885; his son, Thomas Woodrow Wilson, grew up to become slightly more famous. The church itself, with its finials and soaring stone spire topped with a metal rooster (a symbol of the Protestant Reformation), blends Late Gothic and Renaissance styles, and is the congregation's fourth home, the previous three having succumbed to fire. During the Union occupation, the lectern Bible was stolen from the third church, which burned on New Year's Eve, 1925. The stolen Bible was returned years later to become all that remains of the previous sanctuary. Today, intricate tracery distinguishes fine stained-glass windows along the nave, as well as the vast West window and the chancel rose. The original 1928 E. M. Skinner organ, with its original pneumatic console, is used regularly. Handsomely stenciled beams, arches and trusses support a steep gabled roof. Downstairs is the Kenan Chapel, with its transverse Romanesque arches. The education building behind the sanctuary is quintessential Tudor, complete with exterior beams set in stucco, wide squared arches, casement windows with diamond panes, interior ceiling beams and eccentric compound chimneys. Having undergone major renovation in the early 1990s, First Presbyterian is an impressive sight. Its carillon can be heard daily throughout the historic district.

Horse-drawn Carriage Tour
Market St. between Water and Front sts., Wilmington • 251-8889

See historic downtown Wilmington the old-fashioned way — by horse-drawn carriage. This half-hour ride in a French-top surrey is narrated by a knowledgeable driver in 19th-century garb, who offers interesting anecdotes about the historic mansions and waterfront along the way. At busy times such as Azalea Festival and Riverfest, horse-drawn trolleys are used. Tours operate Tuesday through Sunday from 10 AM to 10 PM, April through October. In November, December and March, the carriages roll Friday 7 to 10 PM, Saturday 11 AM to 10 PM and Sunday 11 AM to 4 PM. Ride by appointment during January and February. The individual fee is $8; $4 for children younger than 12.

Henrietta II
London Wharf, Wilmington • 343-1611, (800) 676-0162

This 149-passenger sternwheel riverboat offers an ideal vantage point for viewing the riverside sights, or dancing and dining in a dining salon complete with bar. From April through December, the *Henrietta II* keeps a varied cruise schedule that includes 90-minute sightseeing and moonlight cruises ($9 per adult; $4 for children younger than 12; 2½-hour entertainment dinner cruises Thursday through Saturday during the summer ($29 to $32.50); and 2-hour sunset dinner cruises on Wednesday ($22 per adult, $15 per child. Special events cruises include the Sweetheart Cruise in February, the Azalea Festival Cruise in April, the Fireworks Cruise on July 4, the

Riverfest Cruise in October, the Holiday Flotilla in November, Christmas Lights cruises and the New Year's Eve party in December. Private parties are accommodated year round, and six-hour nature cruises run in the summer. The *Henrietta II* docks along the Riverwalk near the Hilton Hotel. Call for schedules.

Oakdale Cemetery
520 N. 15th St., Wilmington

When Nance Martin died at sea in 1857, her body was preserved, seated in a chair, in a large cask of rum. Six months later she was interred at Oakdale Cemetery, cask and all. Her monument and many other curious, beautiful and historic markers are to be found within the labyrinth of Oakdale Cemetery, Wilmington's first municipal burial ground, opened in 1855. At the cemetery office, you can pick up a free map detailing some of the more interesting interments, such as the volunteer firefighter buried with the faithful dog that gave its life trying to save his master, and Mrs. Rose O'Neal Greenhow, a Confederate courier who drowned while running the blockade at Fort Fisher in 1864. Amid the profusion of monuments lies a field oddly lacking in markers—the mass grave of hundreds of victims of the 1862 yellow fever epidemic. The architecture of Oakdale's monuments, its Victorian landscaping and the abundance of dogwood trees, make Oakdale beautiful in every season. The cemetery is open until 5 PM every day. Bicycles are not permitted.

The Riverwalk
Riverfront Park, along Water St., Wilmington

The heart and soul of downtown Wilmington is its riverfront. At one time a bustling, gritty confusion of warehouses, docks and sheds, all suffused with the odor of turpentine, the wharf was the state's most important commercial port. Experience Wilmington's charm and historical continuity by strolling the Riverwalk. Dining, shopping and lodging establishments now line the red-brick road, and live entertainment takes place at the small Riverfront Stage on Saturday and Sunday evenings from June to early August. Check with the visitors information booth at the foot of Market Street for schedules. Immediately north, schooners, pleasure boats and replicas of historic ships frequently visit the municipal dock. Coast Guard cutters and the occasional British naval vessel dock beyond the Federal Court House; some allow touring, especially during festivals. Benches, picnic tables, a fountain and snack vendors complete the scene, one of Wilmington's most popular.

St. James Episcopal Church and Burial Ground
25 S. Third St., Wilmington • 763-1628

St. James is the oldest church in continuous use in Wilmington, and it wears its age well. The parish was established in 1729 in Brunswick Town across the river (also see St. Philip's Parish, below). The congregation's original Wilmington church wasn't completed until 1770. It was seized in 1781 by Tarleton's Dragoons under Cornwallis. Tarleton had the pews removed, and the church became a stable. The original church was taken down in 1839 and some of its materials used to construct the present church, an Early Gothic Revival building with pinnacled square towers, battlements and lancet windows. The architect, Thomas U. Walter, is best known for his 1865 cast-iron dome on the U.S. Capitol. A repeat performance of pew-tossing was enacted during the Civil War when occupying Federal forces used the church as a hospital. A letter written by the pastor asking President Lincoln for reparation still exists. It was never delivered, having been completed the day news arrived of Lincoln's assassination. Within the church hangs a celebrated painting of Christ (*ECCE HOMO*) captured from one of the Spanish pirate ships that attacked Brunswick Town in 1748. The sanctuary also boasts a handsome wood-slat ceiling and beam-and-truss construction. The graveyard at the corner of Fourth and Market streets was in use from 1745 to 1855 and bears considerable historic importance. Here lies the patriot Cornelius Harnett, remembered for antagoniz-

ing the British by reading the Declaration of Independence aloud at the Halifax Courthouse in 1776. He died in a British prison during the war. America's first playwright, Thomas Godfrey, is also memorialized here. The cemetery once occupied grounds over which Market Street now stretches, which explains why utility workers periodically (and inadvertently) unearth human remains outside the present burial ground. Visitors are welcome to take self-guided tours of the church between 9 AM and early afternoon when services are not underway. Informative brochures are available in the vestibule.

St. John's Museum of Art
114 Orange St., Wilmington • 763-0281

Even if St. John's didn't possess one of the world's major collections of Mary Cassatt color prints, it would still be a potent force in the Southeast's art culture. Housed in three distinctive restored buildings (one a former church), the museum boasts a fine sculpture garden, an outstanding collection of Jugtown pottery, touring exhibits, a working studio for art classes, lectures, workshops and an extensive survey of regional and national artists, all of them world-class. Educational programs for children, films, concerts and a gift shop are among the museum's offerings. Admission is $2 per adult, $5 per family and $1 for children younger than 18. Children younger than 5 and museum members may enter free. Admission on the first Sunday of every month is free to all.

St. Marks Episcopal Church
600 Grace St., Wilmington • 763-3210

Established in 1875, this was the first Episcopal church for blacks in North Carolina, and it has enjoyed uninterrupted services since that time. The building (completed in 1875) is a simple Gothic Revival structure with a buttressed nave and octagonal bell tower.

St. Mary's Roman Catholic Church
412 Ann St., Wilmington • 762-5491

Numerous historical writers have referred to this Spanish Baroque edifice (built 1908-1911) as a major architectural creation, often pointing out the elaborate tiling, especially inside the dome which embraces most of this church's cross-vaulted interior space. The plan of the brick building is based on the Greek cross, with enormous semicircular stained-glass windows in the transept vaults, arcade windows in the apse and symmetrical square towers in front. Over the main entrance, in stained glass, is an imitation of DaVinci's *Last Supper*. A coin given by Maria Anna Jones, the first black Catholic in North Carolina, is placed inside the cornerstone. Rose Greenhow, a Confederate spy who drowned off Fort Fisher, was a member of the congregation.

St. Paul's Evangelical Lutheran Church
603 Market St., Wilmington • 762-4882

Responding to the growing number of German Lutherans in Wilmington, North Carolina's Lutheran Synod organized St. Paul's in 1858. Services began in 1861, as the Civil War broke. Construction came to a halt when the German artisans working on the building volunteered for the 18th North Carolina Regiment and became the first local unit in active duty. The building was occupied, and badly damaged, by Union troops after the fall of Fort Fisher in early 1865. Horses were stabled in the building and its wooden furnishings used as firewood. The completed church was dedicated in 1869, only to burn in 1894. It was promptly rebuilt. There have been several additions and renovations since. Today the building is remarkable for its blend of austere Greek Revival elements outside (such as the entablature, pediments and pilasters) and Gothic Revival (such as the slender spire, clustered interior piers, and large lancet windows). Also notable is its color-patterned slate roof and copper finials, and the gently arcing pew arrangement. Paneling removed during renovations in 1995-96 uncovered beautiful stenciling on the ceiling panels and ribs in the vestibule, nave and chancel.

Temple of Israel
1 S. Fourth St., Wilmington • 762-0000

The first Jewish temple in North Carolina, this unique Moorish Revival building was erected in 1875 and '76 for a Reform congregation formed in 1867. Its two square towers are topped by small onion domes, and the paired, diamond-paned windows exhibit a mix of architrave shapes including Romanesque, trefoil and Anglo-Saxon arches. The temple was once shared for two years with neighboring Methodists when the Methodist church was destroyed in 1886.

Thalian Hall/City Hall
310 Chestnut St., Wilmington • 343-3664

Since its renovation and expansion in the late 1980s, the name has been, more accurately, Thalian Hall Center for the Performing Arts. And yes, it does share the same roof with City Hall. Conceived as a combined political and cultural center, Thalian was built between 1855 and 1858. During its first 75 years, the hall brought every great national performer, and some surprising celebrities, to its stage: Lillian Russell, Buffalo Bill Cody, John Philip Sousa, Oscar Wilde and Tom Thumb, to name a few. That tradition continues today. Full-scale musicals, light opera and internationally renowned dance companies are only a portion of Thalian's consistent, high-quality programming. Today the center consists of two theaters — the Main Stage and the Studio Theater — plus a ballroom (which doubles as the city council chambers).

With its Corinthian columns and ornate proscenium, it's no wonder Thalian Hall is on the National Register of Historic Places. Historic tours are offered at 11 AM and 3 PM Monday through Friday and at 2 PM Saturday. The cost is $5 for adults, $3 for children. Group rates are available.

Wilmington Adventure Walking Tour
The foot of Market St., Wilmington • 763-1785

Lifelong Wilmington resident Bob Jenkins, the man with the straw hat and walking cane, walks fast but talks slowly, passionately and knowledgeably about his hometown. Expounding upon architectural details, family lineage and historic events, Bob whisks you through 250 years of history in about an hour. You'll see residences, churches and public buildings. Tours begin from the foot of Market Street at 10 AM and 2 PM daily, weather permitting. A $10 fee is charged. Although no reservations are required, it's best to call

Photo: Bill DiNome

Southport's Old Smithville Burial Ground is a leap into the past.

ahead, especially in summer. Tours begin at the flagpole at the foot of Market Street.

Wilmington Railroad Museum
501 Nutt St., Wilmington • 763-2634

The dramatic transformation that Wilmington underwent when the Atlantic Coast Line Railroad closed its Wilmington operations in the late 1950s are clearly borne out by the museum's fine photographs and artifacts. Beyond history, the Railroad Museum is a kind of funhouse for people fascinated by trains and train culture. And who isn't?

For $2 ($1 for children ages 6 to 11), you can climb into a real steam locomotive and clang its bell for as long as your kids will let you. Inside, volunteers (some of whom are walking histories themselves) will guide you to exhibits explaining why the 19th-century Wilmington & Weldon Railroad was called the "Well Done," and that the ghost of beheaded flagman Joe Baldwin is behind the Maco Light — at least one volunteer claims to have seen it. Ask about the museum's Memories book in

which visitors are encouraged to share their favorite train memories; it includes entries by famous people who have visited Wilmington.

The museum building was the railroad's freight traffic office and is listed on the National Register of Historic Places. Visitors can run the model trains in the enormous railroad diorama upstairs, maintained by the Cape Fear Model Railroad Club (for membership information contact the museum). Children will also enjoy the railroad theaterette. Adult programming, children's workshops and group discounts are available. The museum also invites you to "conduct" your birthday parties on their caboose. The rental fee includes souvenirs and a tour of the museum, and train-theme refreshments can be arranged. Museum hours are 10 AM to 5 PM Tuesday through Saturday and 1 to 5 PM Sunday.

Zebulon Latimer House
126 S. Third St., Wilmington • 762-0492

This magnificent Italianate building, built by a prosperous merchant from Connecticut,

dates from 1852 and is remarkable for its original furnishings and art work. The house boasts
fine architectural details such as window cor-
nices and wreaths in the frieze openings, all
made of cast iron, and a piazza with intricate,
wrought-iron tracery. Behind the building
stands a rare (and possibly Wilmington's oldest) example of urban slave quarters, now a
private residence. What sets the Latimer House
apart from most other museums is the fact
that it was continuously lived in for more than
a century, until it became home to the Lower
Cape Fear Historical Society in 1963. It has
the look of a home where the family has just
stepped out.

The Historical Society is one of the primary local sources for genealogical and historical research. For information on membership write to: P.O. Box 813, Wilmington, North
Carolina 28402. Guided house tours are offered Tuesday through Saturday from 10 AM
to 4 PM (adults $3, youths younger than 12,
$1), and Walk & Talk Tours, which encom-
pass about 12 blocks of the historic district
and last 90 minutes, are given for $5 every
Wednesday at 10 AM. The museum is open
Tuesday from 10 AM to 4 PM, Wednesday
and Thursday 10 AM to 1 PM and by appointment by calling 763-5869.

Around Wilmington

Airlie Gardens
Airlie Rd., Wrightsville Beach • 763-4646
These spectacular private gardens along
Wrightsville Sound can be viewed by car and
on foot. With only one formal garden on the
grounds, Airlie gives the impression of a
dreamland forest. Majestic trees draped with
moss; multicolored azaleas and camellias bordering pools plied by swans; arbors, bridges
and a jasmine-covered stone pergola add to
the grandeur of these 20 acres. You may view
the picturesque Lebanon Chapel (1835) and
one of the county's oldest cemeteries from a
distance. The gardens are open to the public
from the last week in March until the first week
in May (peak azalea season), from 8 AM until
6 PM, and the fee is $8 per person. Group
rates and senior discounts are available, and
children younger than 12 are admitted free.

Airlie Gardens is 7 miles east of downtown
Wilmington.

Air Tours
New Hanover International Airport
From the air, tours in this area may offer
some surprises such as pods of dolphin offshore and the mysterious inland ellipses
known as Carolina bays. All you need to do to
go aloft is pick up the phone and reserve a
flight with one of the fixed-based operators at
New Hanover International Airport. Very often
they'll have a plane available that afternoon or
the next day. Tours are available by the half-
hour and by the hour and usually require a
minimum of three passengers. Don't forget
the camera.

ISO Aero, 763-8898, is a good first choice
because it flies high-wing Cessna 172s, which
yield greater downward visibility than low-wing
planes. Tours begin at $12 per half-hour per
person (three person minimum). ISO is on the
airport's East Ramp access on N. Kerr Avenue.

Aeronautics, 763-4691, and its affiliate, Air
Wilmington, 763-0146, will fly three passengers in a Piper Warrior for $85 per hour or in a
Piper Arrow for $100 per hour (both Pipers are
low-wing models). Also available is a two-pas-
senger Beechcraft Skipper. One good flight
follows the Intracoastal Waterway to Figure
Eight Island and back, a half-hour flight, for
$59. You may choose your own destinations
as well, based on the same half-hour fare. Both
operators are at the airport's General Aviation
facility. From the airport's main entrance on
23rd Street, make the first left onto Gardner
Avenue, then bear right to General Aviation.

Ever land a plane on water? Kitty Hawk Air
Services Inc., 791-3034, offers seaplane flights
and thrilling water landings beginning at $20
per person for half-hour flights (minimum party
of two). Call for reservations and boarding information.

Greenfield Lake and Gardens
U.S. 421 S., Wilmington
In springtime the colors here are simply
eye-popping. In summer the algae-covered
waters and Spanish moss recall the days when
this was an unpopulated cypress swamp. In
winter the bare tree trunks rise from the lake

with stark verticality. Herons, egrets and ducks are regular visitors as are hawks and cardinals. The 5-mile lakeview drive is a pleasure in any season, and there's a paved path, suitable for walking or cycling, surrounding the entire lake. Greenfield Lake is 2 miles south of downtown Wilmington along S. Third Street. (See our chapter on Sports, Fitness and Parks.)

Jungle Rapids Family Fun Park
5320 Oleander Dr., Wilmington • 791-0666

This self-contained amusement mecca underwent a dramatic renovation early this year, the most obvious change being a new, larger Grand Prix go-cart track with bridge overpasses, banked turns, timing devices and new cars. Riders must be at least 16 years old to drive. A spin in the go-carts costs $4 per session, three drives are $10, or you can pay by the hour. Now add the water slides, bumper boats, miniature golf, laser-tag arena, high-tech arcade, indoor playground with ball pits and snack bar, and you've got plenty to keep you and the kids busy all year. The indoor attractions are a good rainy-day choice. The four water slides are excellent and include Crocodile Aisle (the fastest on the hill) and a baby slide. Lifeguards are on duty, and there are ample lockers, picnic tables, chairs and umbrellas. All-day admission to the slides is less than $10, which includes one bumper-boat ride. The arcade sponsors tournaments in air hockey, video road racing and other high-profile teenage pursuits. Jungle Rapids also caters colorful kids' parties on site.

The park is open from 10 AM to 11 PM every day. Water slides close at 8 PM. Inquire about the All-Day Water Park Pass that allows admittance to every attraction. Peak hours can be crowded. Everything except the water attractions is open all year (also see our Kidstuff chapter).

New Hanover County Extension Service Arboretum
6206 Oleander Dr., Wilmington • 452-6393

This 6-acre teaching and learning facility is the only arboretum in southeastern North Carolina. An extension of the University of North Carolina, the arboretum was formally opened in 1989 and is still in the midst of development. These gardens rank among the finer theme gardens in the area. Boardwalks and paths wind through a profusion of plants, grasses, flowers, trees, shrubs, herbs and vegetables, and there is plenty of shaded seating. Several sections, such as the Herb Garden, with its variety of medicinal, culinary, fragrance and tea species, are sponsored by local garden clubs. The arboretum assists commercial and private horticultural enterprises and helps residents create attractive home landscapes. This last mission is served by the Garden Hotline, 452-6396, wherein volunteer master gardeners field questions about horticulture from 9 AM to 5 PM.

The arboretum sponsors and hosts seminars, classes (including hunting safety) and workshops. Some of the programs offer certificates upon completion. Admission to the arboretum is free, and it's open daily from 8 AM to dusk. Volunteer docents lead tours on request. Donations are welcome and much-needed. Enter the grounds from Oleander Drive (U.S. Highway 76) immediately east of Greenville Loop Road and west of the Bradley Creek bridge. And, yes, the arboretum is available for weddings.

Showtyme Skating Center
5216 Oleander Dr., Wilmington • 791-6000

Showtyme offers genuine family fun in the context of indoor roller skating. Skaters roll to music, the styles of which change from night to night and range from current pop to oldies to Christian. The rink has a well-stocked pro shop providing sales, rentals and repairs; an arcade and a snack lounge. The rink is open seven days a week year round. The center keeps daytime hours Saturday and Sunday and evening hours Monday through Saturday. Extended summer hours are in effect during school recess and include weekday afternoons. Rates are an affordable $3 to $4.50. In keeping with the management's wish to foster good moral fiber, house rules prohibit profanity, intoxicants and anything but appropriate clothing. The facilities are also available for private rental. The rink sponsors a competing speed-skating team and hosts its own roller-hockey league (see our Sports, Fitness and Parks chapter). Showtyme is near the intersection of Oleander Drive and Forest Park Road, 5 miles from downtown.

Photo: N.C. Travel & Tourism

The USS *North Carolina* participated in every major engagement
in the Pacific during World War II.

Sunset Skating Center
341 Shipyard Blvd., Wilmington
• 791-8550

The Sunset Skating Center, founded in 1959, may fool you. On a typical Friday evening, the empty parking lot gives no indication that there may be hundreds of happy skaters inside, "talking in circles," "figuring things out," rolling to rock music. That's because children and adolescents make up the bulk of Sunset's clientele, and the Carter family, operator of the

center since 1964, are so well trusted that parents often leave their children at Sunset to enjoy the evening themselves. Among Sunset's offerings are what's known in coded parlance as "72747" sessions, i.e., overnight skating sessions, usually on holidays, that run from 7 PM to 7 AM for $7 ($8 without coupon) — "no sleeping bags, no in-and-out privileges, everyone must skate, everyone must have fun."

Skating at Sunset is affordable: admission ranges from $2 on Wednesday and Thursday evenings to $3.50 on Friday and Saturday evenings. Skate rentals run $1 to $2, there's a pro shop on premises, and the center offers day-care groups, private skating parties, fund-raiser sessions, video games and special men's and ladies' sessions. As Sunset's brochure says, "Where else can you find so much to do for half the price of a haircut?"

Stadium Batting Cages
5570 Oleander Dr., Wilmington • 791-9660
Hallmarks of resort towns are the batting cages, and these are the only ones for miles around. The throwing machines are the armature type, not the kind with spinning wheels that throw wild every third pitch. There are baseball and softball cages pitching at a variety of speeds, and the fastballs are mighty fast. Helmets and bats are included. One $1 token gets you 12 pitches, and you can save on 72 for $5. It's a great way to practice your swing, vent some steam or spend an otherwise routine lunch hour. Hours are 2 to 10 PM on weekdays, 10 AM to 10 PM Saturdays and 12 to 9 PM Sundays.

Outside Wilmington

Poplar Grove Plantation
10200 U.S. Hwy. 17, Scotts Hill • 686-9518
The 1850 Greek Revival house was the focus of this 628-acre plantation that was supported by as many as 64 slaves prior to the Civil War. Today costumed guides lead visitors and recount its history. Skills important to daily 19th-century life, such as weaving, smithery and basketry, are frequently demonstrated. A restaurant and country store add to Poplar Grove's attraction as do the many events held here throughout the year, including Halloween hayrides and the Medieval Festival in June. Listed on the National Register of Historic Places, Poplar Grove Plantation is 8 miles outside Wilmington on U.S. 17 at the Pender

County line. It is open to the public Monday through Saturday 9 AM to 5 PM and Sunday noon to 5 PM. Fees are $6 for adults, $5 for senior citizens and military personnel with active IDs and $3 for students ages 6 to 15.

Wrightsville Beach

Blockade Runner Resort
Waynick Blvd., Wrightsville Beach • 350-2628
In the warm season, a cruise aboard the 40-foot pontoon vessel along the calm Intracoastal Waterway affords a fine way to view the landscape and wildlife of the tidal environment. The Blockade Runner Resort sponsors nature excursions and shuttles to Masonboro Island from 10 AM to 1:15 PM daily during the summer. Excursions, guided by a marine biologist, cost $25 per adult, $15 for children. Shuttles cost $10 per person. One-hour harbor cruises set out at 11 AM and noon and cost $10 per person. Sunset cruises ($18 per adult, $10 per child) sail from 6:30 to 8:30 PM, and coolers are welcome. Walk-ins are accepted, but reservations are recommended in the high season.

Water Ways Sailing School
Wrightsville Beach • 256-4282, (800) 562-SAIL
Owner Jerry Outlaw and his staff offer captained and bare-boat charters for local excursions on a variety of sailboats accommodating up to six passengers each. Participate in actually sailing the vessel as much or as little as you wish. Destinations are flexible, and responsible consumption of alcohol is permitted. Water Ways' staff consists of all USCG-licensed captains and American Sailing Association-certified instructors. Captained charters range in price from $260 for half-day or sunset trips (3 hours) to $375 for full-day (6 hours). Reservations are required. (Also see the Sailing section of our Watersports chapter.)

INSIDERS' TIP
UNCW's Ev-Henwood Nature Preserve at 6150 Rock Creek Road, 962-3197 or 253-6066, in the Town Creek community along the Cape Fear River, offers walking trails, interpretive displays and a picnic area. Admission is free!

Wrightsville Beach Museum of History
303 W. Salisbury St., Wrightsville Beach • 256-2569

The newest attraction on Wrightsville Beach, this museum is housed in the Myers cottage, one of the oldest cottages on the beach (built in 1907). The museum presents beach history and lifeways through permanent exhibits featuring a scale model of the oldest built-up section of the beach, photos, furniture, artifacts, a slide show and recorded oral histories, plus rotating exhibits on loggerhead turtles, surfing, the Civil War, shipwrecks, hurricanes and beach nightlife at such bygone attractions as the Lumina Pavilion. Admission is by donation. Upon crossing the drawbridge, bear left at the "Welcome to Wrightsville Beach" sign; the museum is on the right near the volleyball courts beyond the fire station.

Carolina Beach/ Kure Beach

Carolina Beach Boardwalk

Spanning the oceanfront in the middle of town, the boardwalk is the heart and soul of Carolina Beach. It includes the actual beachside boardwalk plus paved walks bordering a multitude of arcades, nightclubs, miniature golf courses, pubs, billiard parlors and novelty shops. Colorful and crowded in summertime, the entire area has the aura of an amusement park, complete with a bumper car pavilion and cotton candy. Several restaurants are a short walk from the beach, and parking is nearby. The strand along the boardwalk is the site of Carolina Beach's annual Beach Music Festival, which draws thousands of shagging music-lovers each July (see our Annual Events chapter).

Jubilee Amusement Park
1000 N. Lake Park Blvd., Carolina Beach • 458-9017

With 20 rides, three water slides, kiddie pool, three go-cart tracks, an arcade, gift shop, picnic area and live entertainment, newly refurbished Jubilee Park is a mecca for families. New additions include the Rain Room (walk through a cooling mist without drenching), the Human Slingshot (an open, "reverse bunjee" capsule that shoots you safely 150 feet straight up!). Most of the rides are kiddie-size, and there is no admission fee. Individual rides range in price from a little over a dollar for kiddie rides to $12.95 for money-saving all-day passes ($8.95 for kids younger than 5), which permit unlimited use (rides only). Season passes are the best bargain ($44.95). Waterslides and go-carts are priced separately. Height requirements apply for go-carts other than the junior racetrack ($2.95 per session), and the NASCAR track ($4 per session) also requires a driver's license. An all-day waterslide pass costs $7.95, and the price comes down after 5 PM.

Fort Fisher-Southport Ferry
U.S. Hwy. 421, south of Kure Beach • 457-6942

More than transportation, this half-hour crossing is a journey into the natural and social history of the Cape Fear River. You'll have excellent views of Federal Point, Zeke's Island and The Rocks from the upper deck. On the Southport side, you'll spot the historic Price's Creek Lighthouse at the mouth of the inlet. The crew are knowledgeable, and the cabin is air-conditioned. When traveling between Southport and New Hanover County, timing your trip to the ferry schedule makes getting there half the fun. (See our Getting Around chapter for schedules.) One-way fees are 50¢ for pedestrians, $1 for cyclists, $3 for vehicles less than 20 feet in length and $6 for vehicles or combinations up to 32 feet long.

Fort Fisher State Historic Site
U.S. 421, south of Kure Beach • 458-5538

Fort Fisher was the last Confederate stronghold to fall to Union forces during the War Between the States. It was the linchpin of the Confederate Army's Cape Fear Defense System, which included forts Caswell, Anderson and Johnson and a series of batteries. Largely due to the tenacity of its defenders, the port of Wilmington was never entirely sealed by the Union blockade until January 1865. The Union bombardment of Fort Fisher was the heaviest naval demonstration in history up to that time.

Today all that remains are the earthworks, the largest in the South. The remainder of the fort has been claimed by the ocean. However, a fine museum, uniformed demonstrations and re-enactments make Fort Fisher well worth a visit. Don't miss the underwater archaeology exhibit, Hidden Beneath the Waves, housed in a small outbuilding beside the parking lot. Thirty-minute guided walking tours allow you to walk the earthworks, and slide programs take place every half-hour. The Cove, a tree-shaded picnic area across the road, overlooks the ocean and makes an excellent place to relax or walk. However, swimming here is discouraged due to dangerous currents and underwater hazards.

Since Fort Fisher is an archaeological site, metal detectors are prohibited. Museum hours are 9 AM to 5 PM Monday through Saturday and 1 to 5 PM Sunday. It is open all year, and admission is free (donations are requested). The site, about 19 miles south of Wilmington, was once commonly known as Federal Point. The ferry from Southport is an excellent and timesaving way to get there from Brunswick County. Also close by are the North Carolina Aquarium (see next entry) and the Fort Fisher State Recreation Area (see our Sports, Fitness and Parks chapter).

North Carolina Aquarium at Fort Fisher
Ft. Fisher Blvd., Kure Beach • 458-8257

Housing the largest shark tank in the state, the Aquarium at Fort Fisher also boasts an intriguing ray and skate tank. But its touch tank seems to elicit the greatest reaction from visitors — especially those who squeamishly pick up a horseshoe crab or get squirted by a startled conch. The outdoor pond is filled with fish and turtles, and the barn swallows that nest beneath the building zoom in and out just above visitors' heads. Field trips, films and live animal exhibits are offered, and nature trails loop through the grounds. The self-guided Marsh Nature Trail leads visitors to the World War II-era pillbox in which Robert Harrell, the Fort Fisher Hermit, lived from about 1955 until his death in 1972. Shark feedings take place at 3:30 PM on Tuesday, Thursday and Sunday. Daily fish feedings are at 3:30 PM. There is an outdoor picnic deck and beach access

nearby. The Aquarium, 20 miles south of Wilmington, is open 9 AM to 5 PM Monday through Saturday and 1 to 5 PM Sunday. Admission fees are $3 for adults, $2 for senior citizens and military personnel and $1 for children ages 6 to 18.

Winner Cruise Boats
Carl Winner Ave., Carolina Beach
• 458-5356

The Winner family is as integral to Carolina Beach as Fort Fisher (and goes back about as far), and their fishing and cruise boats are rightly famous. You may choose from among four cruise ships practically any night of the week during the summer and on weekends in the off-season: the *Winner Queen*, the *Winner Speed Queen*, the *Winner Cruise Queen* (all 150-passenger vessels) and the 400-passenger *Royal Queen*. Suitable for people of all ages and launching from the Carolina Beach municipal docks, the Winner cruises make regularly scheduled 90-minute excursions of the Intracoastal Waterway (at 8 and 9:30 PM)

for as little as $5 per person. During spring and summer you may purchase cruises with or without dinner. All vessels have three public decks with dance floors, bars and full restaurants. The vessels are also available for private charter.

Bald Head Island

Bald Head Island Historic Tour and Lunch including Old Baldy Lighthouse
Departure from W. Ninth St., Southport
• 457-5003

This guided-tour package may be the most convenient way for a daytripper to get to know Bald Head past and present. The journey begins with a 10 AM ferry departure from Indigo Plantation (W. Ninth Street, Southport). The 90-minute tour includes Old Baldy and Captain Charlie's Station. Put into service in 1817, Old Baldy is the state's oldest standing lighthouse, the second of three lighthouses built on the island to guide ships across the Cape Fear Bar and into the river channel. The fee ($32 per adult, $27 per child younger than 12) includes parking at the ferry terminal, roundtrip ferry and lunch at the River Pilot Cafe. Diners may choose a specially prepared entree and a beverage from the chef's menu (gratuities included). You may choose a return ferry between 1:30 and 4:30 PM. Reservations are required.

Southport-Oak Island

The Deck
Family Entertainment Center
5524 E. Beach Dr. at S.E. 58th St., Long Beach • 278-4111

Open whenever school is out (primarily only weekends and holidays in the off-season), the Deck is a focal point for youngsters on Oak Island and features a swimming pool, an arcade, a dance floor with disco lighting and a jukebox, snack bar and pool tables. The Deck rents beach items (including surfboards and body boards) and sells gifts. Its location across the road from Lighthouse Miniature Golf, water bumper rides and the Go-Dog go-cart track keeps this end of Oak Island pretty lively. For information on the Deck's swimming pool, see the Swimming section in the Watersports chapter.

Fort Caswell
Caswell Beach Rd., Caswell Beach • 278-9501

Considered one of the strongest forts of its time, Fort Caswell originally encompassed some 2,800 acres at the east end of Oak Island. Completed in 1838, the compound consisted of earthen ramparts enclosing a roughly pentagonal brick-and-masonry fort and the citadel. Caswell proved to be so effective a deterrent during the Civil War that it saw little action. Supply lines were cut after Fort Fisher fell to Union forces in January 1865, so before abandoning the fort, the Caswell garrison detonated the powder magazine, heavily damaging the citadel and surrounding earthworks. What remains of the citadel is essentially unaltered and is maintained by the Baptist Assembly of North Carolina, which owns the prop-

erty. A more expansive system of batteries and a sea wall were constructed during the war-wary years from 1885 to 1902. Fort Caswell is open for self-guided visits Monday through Friday 8 AM to 5 PM and Saturday 8 AM to 4 PM. Admission is $2.

Ocean Aire Aviation Inc.
Brunswick County Airport, 380 Long Beach Rd., Southport • 457-0710

Aviators Larry Ryan and John Martin own two certified aircraft — a high-wing and a low-wing — used for air tours. They can accommodate up to three passengers at a time for a base rate of $15 per person for 15 minutes. A variety of tours lasting up to an hour are available within the range from Wrightsville Beach to Little River (north of Myrtle Beach). Flights are available seven days a week during the summer and by appointment off-season. Brunswick County Airport is on the mainland side of the Oak Island high span.

Summer Fun Beach Days
Long Beach Cabana, foot of 40th St. E., Long Beach • 253-4357

One afternoon each month from May through September, Brunswick County Parks and Recreation sponsors live musical performances, volleyball, fun and games at the Cabana, a public beach-access facility overlooking the ocean. Admission is free, and things start kicking around 1 PM. Featured musical styles tend toward island sounds as well as parrot-head (Jimmy Buffett-style) and beach music. Times and dates vary, so check with Parks and Rec for up-to-the-minute schedules.

Old Brunswick Town State Historic Site
Off N.C. Hwy. 133, Southport • 371-6613

At this site stood the first successful permanent European settlement between Charleston and New Bern. It was founded in 1726 by Roger and Maurice Moore (who recognized an unprecedented real estate opportunity in the wake of the Tuscarora War, 1711-1713), and the site served as port and political center. Russelborough, home of two royal governors, once stood nearby. In 1748 the settlement was attacked by Spanish privateers, who were soundly defeated in a surprise counterattack by the Brunswick settlers. A painting of Christ (*Ecce Homo*), reputedly 400 years old, was among the Spanish ship's plunder and now hangs in St. James Episcopal Church in Wilmington. At Brunswick Town in 1765, one of the first instances of armed resistance to the British crown occurred in response to the Stamp Act. In time, the upstart upriver port of Wilmington superseded Brunswick. In 1776 the British burned Brunswick, and in 1862 Fort Anderson was built there to help defend Port Wilmington.

Until recently, occasional church services were still held in the ruins of St. Philip's Church. The other low-lying ruins and Fort Anderson's earthworks may not be visually impressive, but the stories told about them by volunteers dressed in period garb are interesting as is the museum.

Admission to the historic site is free. Hours from April 1 through October 31 are 9 AM to 5 PM Monday through Saturday and 1 to 5 PM Sunday. From November 1 through March 31, visit between 10 AM and 4 PM Tuesday through Saturday and 1 and 4 PM Sunday. The site is closed Monday during winter. From Wilmington, take N.C. 133 about 18 miles to Plantation Road. Signs will direct you to the site (exit left) that lies close to Orton Plantation Gardens.

Orton Plantation Gardens
Off N.C. Hwy. 133, Southport • 371-6851

This property represents one of the region's oldest historically significant residences in continuous use. The family names associated with it make up the very root and fiber of Cape Fear's history. Built in 1725 by the imperious "King" Roger Moore, founder of Brunswick Town, the main residence at Orton Plantation underwent several expansions to become the archetype of Old Southern elegance. It survived the ravages of the Civil War despite being used as a Union hospital after the fall of Fort Fisher. Thereafter it stood abandoned for 19 years until it was purchased

and refurbished by Col. Kenneth McKenzie Murchison, CSA. In 1904 the property passed to the Sprunt family, related to the Murchisons by marriage, and the plantation gardens began taking shape. In 1915 the family built Luola's Chapel, a Doric structure of modest grandeur available today for meetings and private weddings.

The gardens, both formal and natural, are among the most beautiful in the east, comprising ponds, fountains, statuary, footbridges and stands of cypress. The elaborately sculpted Scroll Garden overlooks former rice fields. Elsewhere are the tombs of Roger Moore and his family.

The best times to visit Orton Plantation span from late winter to early summer. Camellias, azaleas, pansies, flowering trees and other ornamentals bloom in early spring; later, oleander, hydrangea, crepe myrtle, magnolia and annuals burst with color. Bring insect repellent in the summer. If you're lucky, you may catch a glimpse of Buster, the 10-foot gator who has lived in the lagoon near the house for many years. He's been known to sun himself in front of the gardens.

Touring the gardens takes an easily paced hour or more. They are open every day from March through August 8 AM to 6 PM; September through November 10 AM to 5 PM. Admission is $8 ($7 for seniors; $3 for children ages 6 to 12). Orton Plantation is off N.C. 133, 18 miles south of Wilmington and 10 miles north of Southport. Nearby are the historic sites of Brunswick Town and Fort Anderson.

Fort Johnson
Davis and Bay sts., Southport • 457-7927

The first working military installation in the state and reputedly the world's smallest, Fort Johnson was commissioned in 1754 to command the mouth of the Cape Fear River. A bevy of tradespeople, fishermen and river pilots soon followed, and so the town of Smithville was born (renamed Southport in 1887). During the Civil War, Confederate forces added Fort Johnson to their Cape Fear Defense System, which included forts Caswell, Anderson and Fisher. Fort Johnson's fortifications no longer stand, but the site is redolent with memories of those times and is one of the attractions listed on the Southport Trail (below). The remaining original structures house personnel assigned to the Sunny Point Military Ocean Terminal, an ordnance depot a few miles north.

The Grove
Franklin Square Park, E. West and Howe sts., Southport

Shaded by centuries-old live oaks and aflame with color in spring, this is a park to savor — a place in which to drink in the spirit of old Smithville. The walls and entrances that embrace the Grove were constructed of ballast stones used in ships more than 100 years ago. Set back among the oaks, stately Franklin Square Gallery, 457-5450, now displaying art in several media, was once a schoolhouse then City Hall. The park is a place to indulge in local legend by taking a drink of well water from the old pump — a draught that is sure to bring you back again.

Keziah Memorial Park
W. Moore and S. Lord sts, Southport

A shady little park with a gazebo, benches and a partial view of the waterfront, Keziah Park is notable for its uncannily bent live oak. Estimated to be 800 years old, the tree is called the "Indian Trail Tree" after the legend that it was curved while a sapling by ancient natives who used it to blaze the approach to their preferred fishing grounds beyond. It later rooted itself a second time, completing an arch.

Maritime Museum
166 N. Howe St., Southport • 456-0003

Read "Gentleman Pirate" Stede Bonnet's plea for clemency, delivered just before he was hanged; view treasures rescued from local shipwrecks; see a 2,000-year-old Indian canoe fragment; learn about hurricanes, sharks' teeth, shrimping nets and much more, in one of the region's newest and most ambitious museums. Many of the exhibits are hands-on, and a Jeopardy-styled trivia board is a favorite of history buffs of all ages. The

museum is within walking distance of restaurants and shopping. Hours are 10 AM to 4 PM Tuesday through Saturday. Admission is $2 for adults ages 16 and older; $1 for seniors and children.

Old Smithville Burial Ground
E. Moore and S. Rhett sts., Southport

"'The Winds and the Sea sing their requiem and shall forever more. . . .'" Profoundly evocative of the harsh realities endured by Southport's long-gone seafarers, the Old Smithville Burial Ground (1804) is a must-see. Obelisks to lost river pilots, monuments to entire crews and families who lived and died by the sea and stoic elegies memorialize Southport's past as no other historic site can. Many of the names immortalized on these stones live on among descendants still living in the area.

Southport Trail
Southport • 457-7927

This mile-long walking tour links 24 historic landmarks, among them the tiny Old Brunswick County Jail, Fort Johnson and the Stede Bonnet Memorial. Architectural beauty abounds along the route, revealing Queen Anne gables, Southport arch and bow and porches trimmed in gingerbread. The free brochure describing this informal, self-guided chain of discoveries can be obtained at the Southport 2000 Visitor Information Center, 107 E. Nash Street, Monday through Saturday from 10 AM to 5 PM in summer. The tour begins at this location. Off-season, call for information.

St. Philip's Episcopal Church
E. Moore and Dry sts., Southport • 457-5643

Southport's oldest church in continuous use, St. Philip's is a beautiful clapboard church erected in 1843, partly through the efforts of Colonel Thomas Childs, then commander of Fort Johnson, one block east. It stands beside Southport City Hall. The first vestry (elected 1850) ushered the church into the diocese as "Old St. Philips" in memory of the original church of St. Philip in colonial Brunswick Town (below). Within the present church flies every flag that has flown over the parish's two incarnations since 1741, includ-

ing the Spanish, English and Confederate. The building exhibits Carpenter-style Greek Revival elements, particularly evident in the pediments and exterior wooden pilasters, as well as English Gothic details. Entrance is made through the small, square tower, with its louvered belfry, simple exterior arcading, and colored-glass lancet windows. The church's side windows of diamond-paned clear glass flood the sanctuary with light, illuminating the handsome tongue-and-groove woodwork on the walls and ceiling. It's a beautiful, quiet place that remains open 24 hours a day for meditation, prayer or rest.

St. Philip's Parish
Old Brunswick Town State Historic Site, Off N.C. 133, north of Southport • 371-6613

After St. James Episcopal Church left Brunswick Town in favor of the rival port of Wilmington, the Anglican parish of St. Philip formed in 1741 and in 1754 began building a stone church at Brunswick, the seat of royal government in the colony. Having struggled with finances and a destructive hurricane, the church was finally completed in 1768, only to be burned by the British in 1776 (the colony's first armed resistance to the Stamp Act had occurred nearby at the royal governor's residence). Today, all that remains of St. Philip's church, the only colonial church in southeastern North Carolina, is a rectangular shell — 25-foot-high walls, three feet thick — plus several Colonial-era graves (some of which are resurfacing with time). The ruin's round-arched window ports are intact and possibly suggest Georgian detailing, but little solid evidence exists about the building's original appearance beyond some glazing on the brick. Three entrances exist, in the west, north and south walls, and three, triptych-style windows open the east wall. Until recently, several local congregations held periodic services within the ruins. The body of North Carolina's first royal governor (Arthur Dobbs) is reputed to have been interred at St. Philip's, as he requested, but has never been identified. St. Philip's Episcopal Church in Southport (above) was named after the colonial parish to perpetuate its memory. (Also see the listing for Old Brunswick Town State Historic Site above.)

Trinity United Methodist Church
209 E. Nash St., Southport • 457-6633

Built c. 1890 for a total of $3,300, this church is the third to occupy its site. Today the building features two of the area's best stained-glass windows (at either side of the sanctuary); handsome, diagonally paneled walls; and "beaded" ceiling (i.e., finished with narrow, half-round moldings), finished by a 15-year-old carpenter. Emblazoned across the original front-transom window is the abbreviation "M.E.C.S." — Methodist Episcopal Church, South — a remnant of the days when the church was still split from its northerly brethren due to the Civil War. The clapboard exterior includes Shingle-style detailing, cedar-shingled roof and gabled bell tower. Trinity Church stands at the corner of N. Atlantic Avenue, up the street from the Southport 2000 Visitors Center and the Fire Department.

Waterfront Park
Bay St., foot of Howe St., Southport

This is possibly the most relaxing vantage point in Southport. From the swings overlooking the waterfront one can see Old Baldy Lighthouse and Oak Island Lighthouse (the brightest in the nation). Take a seat on Whittlers' Bench beneath the shade tree at the foot of Howe Street, a great place to whittle and swap fish tales. Sitting here, Old Smithville is not difficult to imagine. Gone are the pirate ships and menhaden boats, but the procession of ferries, freighters, barges and sailboats keeps Southport's maritime tradition alive.

Stroll or cycle the Historic Riverwalk trail, an easy 0.7-mile scenic route that meanders from the City Pier, past the fisheries and the small boat harbor and culminates at a 750-foot boardwalk, with benches and handrails, over the tidal marsh near Southport Marina. Leave your bike in the rack and walk on for an

unbroken view of the Intracoastal Waterway and the ship channel. It's a restful place on a breezy day, where the only sounds you're likely to hear are the croaking of crows and the clank of halyards.

South Brunswick Islands

Museum of Coastal Carolina
Second St., Ocean Isle Beach • 579-1016

Standing on the ocean floor would be a wonderful way to experience the marine environment up close. Visitors to this museum can do the next best thing — visit the Reef Room, believed to be the largest natural history diorama in the Southeast. Above you, sharks, dolphins, game fish and locally common smaller fish "swim in place" while all types of crustaceans creep below. The remains of a shipwreck, dating from about 1800, rest on the "sea" bottom. Elsewhere, Civil War artifacts, tidal exhibits, a display of shark jaws and many other exhibits bring the natural history of the southern coast vividly to life. Don't miss the Native American cypress canoes, pottery and other artifacts, and the antique fishing equipment.

Admission is $3 for adults and $1 for kids 12 and younger. Summer hours (Memorial Day through Labor Day) are 9 AM to 5 PM Monday through Saturday (until 9 PM Thursday) and 1 to 5 PM Sunday. In autumn, winter and spring, the museum is open only on weekends from 9 AM to 5 PM Saturday and 1 to 5 PM Sunday. From the bridge onto the island, turn left on Second Street at the water slide. The museum entrance will be on the left.

Hurricane Fleet
and Capt. Jim's Marina
Little River Marina, Little River
• (803) 249-7775

Little River is a stone's throw from Calabash, so when you're down that way and want a cruise, the Hurricane Fleet has an array of

INSIDERS' TIP

When walking the beaches on late-summer nights, be careful not to disturb loggerhead turtle nests and the smooth "runways" people build to assist the newborns' run to the sea.

cruise options aboard the *Hurricane*. Most popular is the Adventure Cruise ($15 adult; $12 children younger than 12), which brings passengers practically stem-to-stern with working shrimpers, who often give away interesting sea shells and souvenirs. Ocean Cruises are inshore coasting jaunts (same price). Open-boat breakfasts (buffet or à la carte) are served on the aptly named Breakfast Cruises ($16, including tax and tip). Dinner Cruises depart four times a week year round, and dancing is added on Thursdays in season ($29.75 plus tax and tip). On Wednesdays in season, families will enjoy the well-priced Country Barbecue Cruises, which feature dinners with all the trimmings ($20 per adult; $15 per child.)

Ocean Isle Beach Water Slide
3 Second St., Ocean Isle Beach
• 579-9678

You can't miss the water slides as you cruise across the causeway onto Ocean Isle Beach. From the tops of the slides you get a stunning view of the ocean and beach. The slides are open only during the summer, and hourly or daily tickets are available for less than $10 all day. Refreshments and snacks are available at shops nearby.

Topsail Island

The Patio Playground
807 S. Anderson Blvd., Topsail Beach
• 328-6491

"What is that thing?" is the common refrain of folks new to the Patio when they first lay eyes on the Gyrogym. A printed handout explains that the Gyrogym is a "no-impact workout and a thrill to ride." Looking like an oversized gyroscope, the multiple steel hoops lock the rider into a whirling, 360-degree environment said to yield sensations of weightlessness without the side effects of motion sickness. There are some restrictions as to who may ride — no pregnant women, for example — and the ride doesn't come cheap: $5 for up to 5 minutes. The Patio, with its arcade, pool tables and miniature golf course, is a popular hangout for youth, and it rents various recreational items such as bicycles, surf boards and umbrellas. You'll find it in bustling downtown Topsail Beach, 6.4 miles south of the bridge into Surf City.

The Topsail Island Museum: Missiles and More
720 Channel Blvd., Topsail Beach
• 328-4722, (800) 626-2780

After World War II, the U.S. Navy transformed the sleepy island of Topsail into a test site for its missile-development program, code-named Operation Bumblebee. America's first ramjet-driven guided missiles were the project's legacy as well as the many concrete towers remaining along the length of the island. The Assembly Building, where the missiles were put together, is now a National Historic Treasure and a museum, housing exhibits about Operation Bumblebee, nearby Camp Davis, local history and prehistory and area nature. Showing continuously is "An Oral History of Topsail Island," featuring several longtime residents sharing their memories of the island's development. The museum is open from 2 to 4 PM on Wednesday, Saturday and Sunday, April through October; other times by appointment. Admission is free. Guided tours can be arranged through the Greater Topsail Chamber of Commerce in Surf City (phone numbers above). The Historical Society of Topsail Island, P.O. Box 2645, Surf City, North Carolina 28445, can also provide tours by appointment.

Topsail Skating Rink
714 S. Anderson Blvd., Topsail Beach
• 328-2381

An institution for more than 40 years, this quaint, unpretentious, upstairs roller rink is in a lime-green house above the town's tiny post office. It is open 7 to 10 PM seven nights a week between Easter weekend and Labor Day. Sessions are inexpensive, $3.50 to $4.50, as are the available skate rentals. The building is near Flake Avenue, an easy walk from the Patio Playground.

Topsail Scenic Boat Tours at Topsail Island Trading Company
201 New River Dr., Surf City • 328-1905

Utmost relaxation is found touring the Intracoastal Waterway and adjoining inshore waters in the 33-foot pontoon boat *Kristy's*

Kruiser II. It's an excellent way to view local wildlife while enjoying conversation and cool breezes beneath a shady canopy. The tours leave the soundside dock behind the trading post every summer day at 1, 3, 5 and 7 PM. Tours last about 90 minutes and cost $13 per person; kids younger than 6 ride for half-price and kids under 2 ride free. Ice is furnished, and you may bring your favorite beverages or coolers. The vessel is handicapped-accessible and is equipped with a private toilet. Reservations are recommended. Private charters for up to 20 people are available. For recorded information, call 328-FUNN or 328-TOUR.

Topsail Scenic Flights Inc.
Holly Ridge Airport, Holly Ridge
• 329-0684

The airplane tour service most convenient to the Topsail Island-Holly Ridge area (about 10 minutes from Surf City), TSF flies high-wing Cessna 172s, accommodating up to three adults at a time (or an equivalent payload of young'uns). Flights 20 to 45 minutes in duration start at $10 per person, based on a party of three. You may fly the shoreline or have TSF tailor the flight to your wishes. All planes and pilots are FAA-certified. Appointments are recommended, but walk-ins are welcome. To get there from the Surf City drawbridge (N.C. 50), simply turn right (north) on U.S. 17, then

right again at Nations Bank on Main Street. You'll see signs for the airport a short way along. From the N.C. 210 high-span bridge at North Topsail Beach, head south on U.S. 17 (a left turn) and turn left again at the bank. Due to last year's storms, call ahead to verify availability; also try 328-FUNN or 328-TOUR.

Treasure Island Family Fun Park
N.C. Hwy. 210, Sneads Ferry • 327-2700

Grand Prix go-cart racing, water slides, bumper boats, kiddie rides and an 18-hole miniature golf course are the main attractions at this park about 10 minutes north of Topsail Island. Ice cream, snacks and an arcade may make it difficult for parents to get away cheaply, so look for discount coupons (good before 6 PM) at visitors centers and wherever tourist information is distributed. All-day passes are available for as low as $12.95. Treasure Island Park is open every day until 10 PM in the warm season and is just a few minutes from the North Topsail bridge.

Other Islands

Masonboro Island

Evidence suggests that the first stretch of continental American coastline described by a European explorer may have been the beach

Orton Plantation, a former rice plantation, opens its gardens each spring to visitors.

Photo: N.C. Travel & Tourism

now called Masonboro Island. The explorer was Giovanni Verrazzano; the year, 1524. During the Civil War, Masonboro's beaches were visited by the destruction of three blockade runners and one Union blockader.

Before 1952 Masonboro was not an island, but was attached to the mainland. In that year Carolina Beach Inlet was cut, giving Carolina Beach its boom in the tourist fishing trade and creating the last and largest undisturbed barrier island remaining on the southern North Carolina coast, 8-mile long Masonboro Island. Masonboro is now the fourth component of the North Carolina National Estuarine Research Reserve, the other three being Zeke's Island, which lies south of Federal Point in the Cape Fear River (see below), Currituck Banks and Rachel Carson Island, these last lying farther north.

Masonboro is unique for a number of reasons. Its proximity to a large population center and its undeveloped condition make it a "distant" getaway only 5 miles from Wilmington. It receives fresh water from upland runoff, not from a tidal river as most other estuarine systems do. The island is little more than a shifting ribbon of vegetated sand backed by 4,400 acres of salt marsh, tidal flats and creeks. The oceanfront dune is capped in places by shrub thicket and a small maritime forest of live oak, loblolly pine and red cedar. But what impresses most is the profusion of wildlife, some abundant and some endangered, in an essentially natural state.

Endangered loggerhead turtles successfully nest here, as do terns, gulls, ghost crabs and brown pelicans. Their neighbors include gray foxes, marsh rabbits, opossums, raccoons and river otters. Several types of heron, snowy egrets, willets, black skimmers and clapper rails all forage in the creeks and mud flats at low tide. The estuarine waters teem with 44 species of fish and a multitude of shellfish, snails, sponges and worms. Its accessi-

FYI

Unless otherwise noted, the area code for all phone numbers in this guide is 910.

bility to UNCW's marine biology program, among the world's best, makes Masonboro an ideal classroom for the study of human impact on natural habitat.

The island is a peaceful place where generations of locals have fished, hunted, sunbathed, swum, surfed, camped and sat back to witness nature. Small wonder Masonboro Island has always been close to locals' hearts. Accordingly, the Coastal Management Division of the North Carolina Department of Environment, Health and Natural Resources administers the island with as little intrusion as possible. Camping, hunting and other traditional activities pursued here are allowed to continue, albeit under monitoring intended to determine whether the island can withstand such impact. So far, so good.

If you don't own a boat and can't rent one for getting to Masonboro, refer to the listing for Turtle Island Ventures in the Rowing and Canoeing section of our Watersports and Rentals chapter, or see the listing for Scenic & Sunset Cruises at the Blockade Runner Resort, above.

The efforts to preserve Masonboro Island are spearheaded by the Society for Masonboro Island Inc., 256-5777, a nonprofit membership corporation. Much of the island, especially at the north end, remains with private landowners who could at any time alter the natural habitat or prohibit use by the public. The society's goal is to see the island acquired for public purposes and maintained in its undeveloped state. This is accomplished by facilitating negotiations between the state and landowners for the purchase of island tracts, among other means. The society sponsors public education through a newsletter, nature walks, volunteer island cleanups and a speakers bureau. Membership in the society is inexpensive, ranging from $5 for students and $10 for individuals to $100 for donors and $250 for

INSIDERS' TIP

Blues lovers have an excellent resource in the Blues Society of the Lower Cape Fear, which sponsors open jam sessions every Tuesday at the River Club, 762-0001, in Wilmington.

lifetime members. For more information write: P.O. Box 855, Wrightsville Beach, North Carolina 28480. Information on Masonboro Island and barrier island habitats may also be obtained through UNCW's Center for Marine Science Research, 7205 Wrightsville Avenue, Wilmington, North Carolina 28403, 256-3721.

Zeke's Island

You can walk to this island reserve in the Cape Fear River, and you need not walk on water. Simply drive down by the boat ramp at Federal Point (beyond the ferry terminal) and at low tide, walk the Rocks, a breakwater first erected in 1873, that extends beyond Zeke's Island for just more than 3 miles. You can go by boat if keeping your feet on the tricky rocks isn't your idea of fun.

This component of the North Carolina National Estuarine Research Reserve, totaling 1,160 acres, comprises Zeke's Island, North Island, No-Name Island and the Basin, the body of water enclosed by the breakwater. The varied habitats include salt marshes, beaches, tidal flats and estuarine waters. Bottle-nosed dolphins, red-tailed hawks, ospreys and colonies of fiddler crabs will keep you looking in every direction. Fishing, sunbathing and boating are the primary pursuits here, and hunting within regulations is allowed. Bring everything you need, pack out everything you bring, and don't forget drinking water!

Go Wild All Night — Join a Turtle Watch!

Summertime nightlife at our beaches also means wildlife. North Carolina's beaches are the northernmost nesting area for loggerhead turtles, fascinating creatures threatened with extinction. All along our shores, people concerned for the survival of these ancient denizens turn out on summer nights to help protect their nests and hatchlings.

The loggerhead (*Caretta caretta*) is among the largest of the sea turtles. Adults average more than 3 feet in length and weigh about 300 pounds. Between early May and late October, the mother turtle creeps ashore at the very spot where she herself was hatched, to lay her eggs along the dunes above the high-water line. She covers them over to incubate them in the warm sand. A single female may lay 120 spherical eggs at once and repeat the process up to six times a season. The hatchlings begin to appear in July, with the peak hatching period being September. Hatching usually occurs at night, an entire nest erupting all at once into scores of cute, three-inch-long hatchlings.

Getting across the beach strand and into the water is a perilous journey for the little critters. The baby turtles make a great meal for ravenous crabs, gulls and raccoons, which is why loggerhead moms lay eggs in such great numbers. The hatchlings can even get stranded in a human footprint. This is where humans can help.

Under the auspices of the North Carolina Wildlife Commission, turtle conservation programs along our coast provide much-needed protection to turtles and education to humans. Certain volunteers are trained to render emergency medical services. It is otherwise illegal even to touch such federally protected species unless they're injured or in serious distress. Volunteers are always needed to assist with locating and marking nests. When nests are due to hatch, volunteers smooth out turtle runways to help the newborns in their run to the sea. The primary roles of the turtle project are to protect all marine turtles, to educate the public, to report turtle activity and to stay out of turtles' way. As turtle-watchers are fond of saying, the right of a turtle to be is more important than our right to see.

The Topsail Turtle Project (TTP), organized in 1986, sponsors weekly talks for the public at the Surf City Town Hall, 328-4131, on Thursday at 4 PM during the summer.

— continued on next page

A loggerhead mom lays her eggs in a nest high above the waterline.

They also provide free volunteer training in late April and maintain a small turtle exhibit at Town Hall. TTP is now in the process of establishing the Karen Beasley Sea Turtle Rescue and Rehabilitation Center, the first of its kind in the state, at Topsail Beach. Topsail Island gets an average of 100 turtle nests each year.

It's easy to help, mainly by observing a few simple guidelines:

• Avoid disturbing a turtle crawling to or from the ocean.

• Avoid leaving outdoor lights on all night, particularly at the oceanfront. Lights can disorient turtles and cause them to lose their direction.

• Keep a respectful distance from nesting turtles and don't shine lights in their eyes or harass them in any way. (Besides, it's illegal.) Sit quietly and watch nature take its marvelous course.

• Report turtle sightings and turtle tracks (they may indicate the location of a nest). Adult turtle tracks look like single bulldozer tracks heading straight into the water.

• Never disturb a nest. This also means avoiding the dune line in nesting season when driving off-road vehicles on the beach. Known nests are clearly marked with brightly colored ribbon.

• Pick up trash. That's right! Keeping beaches clean will help reduce the need for sanitation machinery which can crush turtle eggs.

You can help. Volunteering requires commitment and hard work (and some loss of sleep). Or you can simply notify qualified turtle watchers at the numbers below when you see turtles or signs of nests.

Wrightsville Beach, 256-4913
Carolina Beach, Kure Beach, 458-0015
Southport, Yaupon Beach, Long Beach, 278-5518
Caswell Beach, 278-4507
Holden Beach, 842-7242; pager 754-0766
Ocean Isle Beach, 579-9513; pager 754-1272
Sunset Beach, 579-2994 or 579-5862
Topsail Island, 328-1000

To report dead turtles and violations anywhere in North Carolina call (800) 662-7137. For more information call the North Carolina Sea Turtle Project at (919) 729-1359.

Carolina & Kure Beaches
Calendar of Events

1997

June 21	Beach Music Festival
July 11,12	East Coast King Mackerel Tournament
Oct 11, 12	Seafood, Blues, & Jazz Festival
Oct 18,19	Fall Surf Fishing Tournament
Nov 28	Light Up At The Lake
Dec 5	Island of Lights Parade
Dec 6	Flotilla
Dec 13	Tour of Homes
Dec 31	New Years Eve Countdown

1998

March 28	Seafood Chowder Cook-Off
May 2-3	25th Annual Spring Festival
May 16,17	6th Annual Spring Classic Surf Fishing Tournament
June 20	Beach Music Festival

For More Information: email: ckbeach@wilmington.net
http://caro-kure.wilmington.net

Pleasure Island
Chamber of
Commerce
(910) 458-8434

Pleasure Island
Merchant
Association
(910)458-3354

Annual Events

Don't walk out the door or book a flight without checking this chapter first! There may well be a special event happening you wouldn't want to miss. And we don't want you smacking your forehead if you do miss something unnecessarily. So we've listed all the region's most popular annual events in one goof-proof, month-by-month list. Each listing provides the event's street location, an information phone number and admission fees. (Naturally, call ahead for events listed with unspecified fees.) Should you require further information, call the appropriate chamber of commerce for the location. For events in the greater Wilmington area, you may also contact the Cape Fear Coast Convention & Visitors Bureau, 341-4030 or (800) 222-4757. Annual fishing and golf tournaments, sailing regattas and athletic events are listed in their respective chapters.

January

Greater Wilmington Antique Show and Sale
Coast Line Convention Center, 501 Nutt St., Wilmington • 452-0680

Wilmington's largest show of its kind draws antique dealers from near and far to display and sell their wares. Admission is $4.

Metaphysic Expo
Coast Line Convention Center, 501 Nutt St., Wilmington • 392-2909

Astrology, astral projection, cyrstal therapy, aural photography, parapsychology, psychic counseling, channeling, past-life exploration, herbology, health food — all this and more becomes mainstream, not marginal, at this annual exposition of the metaphysical and spiritual arts and practices. The expo runs for two weekend days in mid-January from 10 AM to 8:30 PM, and admission is $3.

Martin Luther King Day March and Commemoration
Martin Luther King Center, 410 S. Eighth St., Wilmington • 341-7866

Martin Luther King Day has special resonance to Wilmingtonians because (among other reasons) Dr. King was scheduled to speak here the day he was assassinated. Wilmington honors his memory on the third Monday of January with a short commemorative, multiracial march from Williston Middle School, 401 S. 10th Street, to the Martin Luther King Center, where celebrations include music, speeches, theatrical presentations and more. Admission is free.

February

The "How Does Your Garden Grow? Show!"
Coast Line Convention Center, 501 Nutt St., Wilmington • 452-6393 or 763-6739

Get an early jump on the long North Carolina growing season by viewing what's new in landscape design and know-how. Exhibits, lectures and demonstrations present innovative products, designs and techniques for improving the surroundings of your home or business. Door prizes are awarded, and the show offers plenty of gift items that gardeners and landscapers would enjoy. The two-day show takes place in early February and is sponsored by the New Hanover County Extension Service Arboretum, which is itself a wonderful place to visit any time of year (see the Attractions chapter). Admission to the show costs $3.50.

The Connoisseurs' Wine & Art Auction
Graystone Inn, 100 S. Third St., Wilmington • 343-1640, 763-0281

This elegant fund-raising soiree, hosted in one of Wilmington's stateliest mansions, is as prestigious as it is exciting. Rare specialty wines donated by private collectors and art objects supplied by St. John's Museum of Art and by individuals go under the gavel while a silent auction proceeds throughout the evening. Wine-tasting, gourmet hors d'oeuvres and musical accompaniment round out the event that benefits public radio WHQR 91.3 FM and St. John's Museum. Seating is limited to 100. Admission is $40.

The North Carolina Jazz Festival
The Wilmington Hilton, 301 N. Water St., Wilmington • 763-8585

The performers' roster of the North Carolina Jazz Festival over the years reads like a Who's Who in Dixieland and mainstream jazz. Players have included Milt Hinton, Ken Peplowski, Art Hodes, Frank Tate, Bob Wilber, Kenny Davern and Bob Rosengarden, performing in a variety of arrangements in which every player is a headliner. The Friday and Saturday night performances, for which tickets may sell out a year in advance, enjoy a cabaret setting at the Wilmington Hilton's ballroom. A preview performance takes place on Thursday night at Thalian Hall, 310 Chestnut Street, 343-3664. Ticket for the Hilton performances cost $25 per evening.

March

The Quilters By the Sea Quilt Show
Coast Line Convention Center, 501 Nutt St., Wilmington • 763-6739

The Quilt Show is Wilmington's major quilting extravaganza, sponsored by the area's guild of note, Quilters By the Sea. The show features an open competition with several categories, demonstrations, raffles, and sales. Finished quilts from around the state are displayed, and competitive "challenges" are posed in which quilters must create quilt elements that meet predetermined criteria. A $5 admission fee is charged.

Long Beach Horse-A-Thon
Long Beach • 278-1000

The only time horses are permitted on the beaches of Oak Island is for this early-March event sponsored by and benefiting the Long Beach Volunteer Fire Department. An admission fee is charged.

A Day at the Docks
Jordan Blvd., Holden Beach • 754-6644

Ever hear of a Bopple Race? Care to take a free boat ride with a charter fishing fleet? Combine all that with food, entertainment, a blessing of the boats and a sunset boat parade, and you've got one of Holden Beach's most popular hometown get-togethers. Admission is free. (P.S.: A Bobble Race consists of throwing numbered apples off the bridge into the Intracoastal Waterway and betting which ones will float past a certain point first. All proceeds benefit a good cause, and the apples are biodegradable. Fish like 'em too!)

FYI

Unless otherwise noted, the area code for all phone numbers in this guide is 910.

Southern Lights Festival
Various locations • (800) 222-4757 U.S., (800) 457-8912 Canada

Southern Lights is a week-long series of events for which the greater Wilmington area plays host to our snowbound northern neighbors (particularly Canadians) in celebration of our shared heritage. The feast is an amalgam of performing arts, entertainment, recreation, golf packages and tours, and it embraces primarily the coast from Wilmington south to Kure Beach. Admission fees vary. Discounted air travel is provided through USAir, (800) 334-8644. Admission fees vary.

Robert Ruark Chili Cookoff
Franklin Square Park, Southport • 457-5494

The Robert Ruark Chili Cookoff in late-March is a competition featuring more varieties of the dish than the famous hunter and author ever dreamed of cooking in his

Photo: N.C. Travel & Tourism

The world's largest living Christmas tree, a 75-foot-tall water oak in Wilmington, is estimated to be more than 300 years old and is decorated each Christmas season.

Southport home. Arts, crafts and entertainment offer diversions to salivating spectators as they taste samples. (The phone number above is for Leggett's Store.) Admission is free, but food costs extra.

April

Poplar Grove Herb Fair
Poplar Grove Historic Plantation, 10200 Hwy. 17 N. • 686-9518

The Poplar Grove Herb Fair offers displays, workshops and class instruction in the many aspects of herb growing and use, plus a plant and garden sale. Choose from single classes and whole-day classes, with or without lunch included (food is also available at vendors outside). Class registration costs about $35 per day. Admission to the fair is free.

The North Carolina Azalea Festival
Various locations • 763-0905

Azalea Fest, the semiofficial opening of "The Season" in Wilmington, features scores of musical and theatrical performances, garden tours and house tours throughout the city and Wrightsville Beach. A grand parade downtown kicks off a weekend of free outdoor en-

tertainment on several stages and a street fair filled with foods, crafts and throngs of people along the riverfront. You may tour public and private gardens throughout the area over a period of days. (Admission is $10, and children younger than 12 go along free with a paying adult.) Musical performances typically feature several top-name performers in a variety of styles each year. Recent headliners have included Aretha Franklin, Frank Sinatra, Liza Minelli, Alan Jackson, Lou Rawls, Gladys Knight, Kitty Wells and Reba McEntire. Tickets for festival performances are available by mail from The North Carolina Azalea Festival at Wilmington, P.O. Box 51, Wilmington, NC 28402. Concert ticket prices range approximately from $25 to $45.

Azalea Sale
New Hanover County Extension Service Arboretum, 6206 Oleander Dr., Wilmington • 452-6393

For two weeks coinciding with the North Carolina Azalea Festival, the arboretum hosts the Master Gardeners' Association's spectacular azalea sale, offering a profusion of colorful plants in a variety that's sure to astound. On the Friday of Azalea Festival weekend, the Arboretum also serves locally made southern barbecue at a nominal additional cost. All proceeds benefit the arboretum, a non-profit organization. Admission costs $6 in advance, $7 at the door.

Topsail Area Spring Fling
Surf City • (800) 626-2780

The annual Topsail Area Spring Fling celebrates the rites of spring on the last weekend in April with the Surf & Turf Triathlon (bike/swim/5K run, $20 preregistration), miniature golf and hole-in-one tourneys, arts and crafts, music and more. The events are free.

Cucalorus Film Festival
Downtown Wilmington • 343-3664, 762-4003

Presenting three days of "native North Carolina" feature films, shorts, videos and live music that are so good you'll be amazed you haven't heard of them before, this festival is the brain child of Twinkle Doon, a collective of independent Wilmington filmmakers. Works by international filmmakers are sometimes featured also. This is the event that draws every local artist, actor, musician and poseur out of the woodwork. (By the way, a cucalorus is a piece of equipment used on sets to create the effect of dappled light.) Shows take place at the River Club, 15 S. Front Street, 762-0001, and at Thalian Hall, 310 Chestnut Street, 343-3664. Admission varies from $6 for an entire night of shorts to $7 per feature film. Screening passes with and without brunch are also available.

Medieval Festival
Poplar Grove Historic Plantation, 10200 Hwy. 17 N. • 686-9518

The Society for Creative Anachronism offers a merry old time of jousting and other tournament events, dancing, demonstrations, crafts (medieval and modern) and costumes plus plenty of fresh foods. Admission is free.

May

Pleasure Island Spring Festival
Cape Fear Blvd., Carolina Beach
• 458-8434

This weekend festival is filled with live entertainment and arts and crafts. It is the spring "bookend" event to the Fall Festival in October. It's free.

Art in the Park
Franklin Square Park, Southport
• 457-5450

Local and regional artists working in many media present their work for sale beneath Southport's venerable live oaks on the second Saturday of May from 10 AM to 3 PM. The event is sponsored by the Associated Artists of Southport and is free.

Battleship North Carolina Memorial Day Observance
Battleship North Carolina, U.S. Hwy. 421 N., Wilmington • 251-5797

Memorial Day is observed aboard the Battleship North Carolina with free music, guest speakers and other special events. Tours of the ship are available for a fee ($6; $3 children ages 6 to 11). The site of the Battleship North Carolina Memorial is near the junction of highways 17, 74, 76 and 421 and is easily accessible from any bridge serving Wilmington.

Memorial Day Observance
Fort Fisher State Historic Site, U.S. 421, Fort Fisher • 458-5538

Fort Fisher State Historic Site is a fitting place for Memorial Day observances, being the location not only of the Confederacy's last fort to fall to the Union, but also a militarily important site from Colonial days right to the present. It is a site redolent with suffering and sacrifice. The Civil War Museum and the Underwater Archaeology exhibit are also open to

INSIDERS' TIP

Watch news listings in October for the Cape Fear Filmmakers' Accord's annual Haunted House. It's one of the region's best, put together by movie-industry pros, and it benefits a good cause too. Information: 763-8811.

the public. The event is free but a donation is requested for the museum.

Memorial Day Observance
Topsail Beach Assembly Building, 720 Channel Blvd., Topsail Beach • 328-0666

Topsail Island hosts Memorial Day celebrations featuring picnics, entertainment and a memorial service. It's free.

June

Beach Music Festival
Beach strand, Carolina Beach • 458-8434

The Carolina Beach Beach Music Festival is one of the largest music events of its kind, featuring live big-name bands and shagging right on the beach at the heart of Carolina Beach. Admission is $10.

Poplar Grove Summer Fair
Poplar Grove Historic Plantation, 10200 Hwy. 17 N., Wilmington • 686-9518

A vestige of the ancient Midsummer's Day festival, Poplar Grove's fair celebrates summer with offerings of food, refreshments, entertainment and pony rides.

July

North Carolina Fourth of July Festival
Downtown Southport and Oak Island • 457-6964

Southport's Independence Day celebration is among the biggest and most spectacular in the state. It all begins on Friday of the holiday weekend on Long Beach with surfing, volleyball, sand castle building, watermelon eating, horseshoe tossing and tug o' war contests. Three more days of festivities follow, including live music, foot races, children's field events, a street dance, a firefighters competition, arts

and crafts, antiques, a parade and more. The celebration culminates in one of the grandest fireworks displays on the coast, at the mouth of the Cape Fear River over the Southport waterfront.

Fourth of July Fireworks
Wilmington Waterfront • 341-7855

Tens of thousands of people turn out for Wilmington's best fireworks of the year, viewing the rockets' red glare over the Battleship North Carolina Memorial from every vantage point imaginable. Find a rooftop (legally), if you can. It's free.

Wacky Golf Cart Parade
Bald Head Island • 457-7500

At such a stylish location as Bald Head Island, it's refreshing to see golf carts decorated according to such sober themes as "Tacky Tourist," in celebration of the Fourth of July. Other categories are "Patriotic," "Bald Head Island," and "Environmental." It's an accurately named event, and great fun. More than 100 carts took part in 1996. The parade leaves Old Baldy lighthouse at 11 AM led by Uncle Sam — sometimes Auntie Sam — atop a fire truck. The parade ends at the Bald Head Island Club, where festivities continue until 4 PM, offering food, beverages, wacky activities and live music. Registration is required to parade your wacky cart (preregistration encouraged), and "off-islanders" are welcome. The event is free. Be aware that ferry costs can be substantial for families (see our Getting Around chapter).

Surf, Sun & Sand Celebration
Wrightsville Beach • 256-7925

If you're up to playing a grueling tournament of beach volleyball in the sun, here's your chance to shine. If you'd rather watch, you'll have plenty of company while enjoying the live music and food. Tournaments require a registration fee per team, but spectating is free.

INSIDERS' TIP

When your Christmas tree has lost its needles, the New Hanover County Recycling Program can tell you where to take it — call 341-4373. Trees left in the parking lot at the N.C. Aquarium at Fort Fisher, 458-8257, will be used to help protect beach dunes from erosion.

Lumina Daze

Blockade Runner Beach Resort, 275 Waynick Blvd., Wrightsville Beach • 256-2569, 256-2251

Recalling the days when the Lumina Pavilion was the focus of beach-goers' entertainment and imaginations, Lumina Daze offers movies right on the beach, 1930s-style swing music, a slide show of old Wrightsville Beach, a kayak "surf rodeo" and a full-moon ocean swim. The particular full moon providing the romantic lighting is in July. The daze descends at 7:30 PM. Proceeds benefit the Wrightsville Beach Preservation Society, administrators of the Wrightsville Beach Museum of History. Admission is $8.

August

Sneads Ferry Shrimp Festival

Sneads Ferry Waterfront • 327-3343

This event, one of the bigger celebrations of one of earth's smaller critters, kicks off with a parade that launches a weekend of crafts, live music, dancing, boiled and fried shrimp, carnival rides and more. Sneads Ferry is about 15 minutes north of Topsail Island. Admission is $2 for adults and free for children younger than 12.

September

Labor Day Arts & Crafts Beach Fest

Middleton Park, Long Beach • 278-3708

This one-day affair, from 10 AM until 5 PM on day one of the Labor Day weekend, features local and regional artists and craftsmakers displaying and selling their goods, plus food concessions, all within sight of the ocean (or nearly so). The event is free.

Piney Woods Festival

Hugh MacRae Park, Oleander Dr. at Greenville Loop Rd., Wilmington • 762-4223

The Piney Woods Festival is a multi-ethnic celebration featuring international foods, music, dance, crafts and demonstrations, held every Labor Day weekend and sponsored by the Arts Council of the Lower Cape Fear. It's free.

Greek Festival

St. Nicholas Greek Orthodox Church, 608 S. College Rd., Wilmington • 392-4484

The Greek Festival is a wonderful opportunity (for some people, the only opportunity) to sample homemade moussaka, baklava and other Greek delicacies. Live Greek music, cultural presentations, demonstrations, cooking classes, travel videos and souvenirs, and even a Greek-style taverna, round out this gala weekend-long celebration, which usually occurs the weekend following Labor Day. The event is free, but food costs extra.

Autumn with Topsail Beach Arts & Entertainment Festival

Downtown Topsail Beach • (800) 626-2780

Topsail Beach may be at the south end of Topsail Island, but the entire region takes part in this celebration of hometown pride. The weekend features artwork and music; a pancake breakfast and fish dinner; the "Outdoor Taste of Topsail," a collection of fresh food concessions selling tasty fare from more than a dozen restaurants within a 30-mile radius; and live Saturday-night entertainment at the historic Assembly Building (fee charged). It all gets underway on the third weekend of September.

National Beach Sweep

Area beaches • 762-0965

This is a day for locals to clean up the area's beaches and put another tourist season behind them. Volunteers are asked to join in preserving the area's pure water and habitats for birds and fishes, an especially important task in lieu of the last hurricane season. The cleanup is held every year on the third Saturday in September. For Topsail Island call (800) 626-2780.

North Carolina Spot Festival

Topsail High School, U.S. Hwy. 17 N., Hampstead • 270-4715

Here's a fabulous feast of fish (fried for this event), with arts and crafts, games, variety shows, all kinds of food, the North Carolina Spot Festival Pageant, and a bake sale as well as carnival rides (fee required). The event is sponsored by the Hampstead Volunteer Fire Department and is the area's only annual fund-raising event, benefiting senior citizen programs and fire and EMS providers.

David Walker Day Festival and Concert
Martin Luther King Jr. Center, 401 S. 8th St., Wilmington • 763-3935

This two-day fair memorializes the great African-American abolitionist, thinker and native of Wilmington by spotlighting regional entertainers and artists and promoting cultural awareness for all, with emphasis on African-American culture. The diversity of offerings is impressive and features live music, guest speakers, crafts and novelties, children's rides (fee required) and food concessions. It takes place during the last weekend of September at the Martin Luther King Jr. Center and adjoining Robert Strange Park. Events are free.

Bark in the Park
Wrightsville Beach Park, Wrightsville Beach • 256-7925

The annual Bark in the Park is an opportunity to show off how well-behaved, how well-groomed and how smart your pooch is — and even how much it looks like you! Events include the Come 'n' Get It Frisbee Disc Competition, the dog/owner Look-Alike contest and demonstrations by local canine law enforcement divisions, grooming experts and obedience trainers. Prizes are awarded for some events. Admission is free.

October

Riverfest
Wilmington • 452-6862 or 799-4867

Riverfest is Wilmington's citywide celebration of the river, something like autumn's answer to Azalea Festival. It features regattas, water races (including homemade rafts), an enormous street fair with food and crafts, stage shows, a beer garden, live arts performances and music, an ever-popular waiter's

wine race (runners carry bottles and wineglasses on trays) and a cast of thousands. The events are free, and shuttle service is provided to downtown from Independence Mall.

Fall Festival
Cape Fear Blvd., Carolina Beach • 458-8434

A great way to celebrate the turn of season, Fall Festival offers free live entertainment, pony rides and hay rides, plus plenty of food, crafts, and activities.

Family Fest
Middleton Park, Long Beach • 278-5518

As this event takes place after the busy summer season, kids can have all the food concessions and activities to themselves. Well, almost. They'll have to take turns with their parents dunking city officials in the dunking booth — all in good fun, of course. The events are free.

Celebrate Wilmington!
Various locations • 962-3547 or 762-4223

Celebrate Wilmington! brings together a vast array of arts and entertainment from mid-October through late-November. A colorful Beaux-Arts Parade kicks off five weeks of art exhibitions, concerts, stage plays, gala feats, craft shows and sales and dance performances held throughout the city. Accommodations information is also available at the number above. Admission costs vary.

New Hanover County Fair
County Fair Grounds, Carolina Beach Rd., Wilmington • 763-4439

The New Hanover County Fair is about the area's biggest to-do when it comes to kids' rides, a petting zoo, games, agricultural contests, exhibits, stage shows and food. The $8 ticket price includes it all and parking. The fair is open from 5 to 11 PM for two weeks in late October. The Fair Grounds are opposite the Echo Farms subdivision.

INSIDERS' TIP

Riverfest features a Raft Regatta that's always good for a few laughs.

Bud Light Chili Cookoff
**Hugh MacRae Park, Wilmington
• 763-6216**

Now here's a competitive feast that truly does amount to a hill o' beans. You'll be able to sample the winning recipes beginning at 1 PM. Live musical entertainment begins at noon and proceeds benefit the Domestic Violence Shelter and Services. Admission is $3.

Festival By the Sea
Holden Beach • 842-7380

Tens of thousands of people are discovering this down-home romp, which takes place over the last full weekend of October. It begins with a kids' Halloween carnival at the fire house on Friday. On Saturday there's a parade on the causeway and a huge outdoor festival beneath the bridge (head of Jordan Boulevard), with live music, food and more than 160 craft booths. Contests on the beach (no fee) include kite-flying, sand sculpture and horseshoe-toss. The fleet of foot may participate in 5K, 10K, or 1-mile races for a nominal fee. Saturday night features a street dance with live music. Plan to arrive early and carpool. (Parking laws are relaxed for the duration.) Admission to the festival is free.

North Carolina Oyster Festival
West Brunswick High School, U.S. Hwy. 130, Shallotte • 754-6644

If you can find a better oyster-shucking competition go there, because the N.C. Oyster Shucking Championship at the N.C. Oyster Festival is hard to beat. It's so popular, an amateur division has been added to the competition. Featuring mountains of the South Brunswick Islands' favorite food, in season at this time, the festival also offers continuous live music featuring a headline performance by The Embers, more than one hundred arts and crafts vendors and more. It's a three-day party on the third weekend of October. Admission is $1. The high school is just north of U.S. Highway 17 Bypass, off Whiteville Road (N.C. 130).

Halloween History-Mystery Tour
Bellamy Mansion Museum, 503 Market St., Wilmington • 251-3700

This otherwise gorgeous mansion takes on an eerie aspect just for Halloween, and you can tour it from 4:30 to 8:30 PM the weekend prior to trick-or-treating. Proceeds benefit the museum. Tickets are $10 in advance, $12 at the door.

Photo: Cape Fear Coast Convention and Visitors Bureau

Downtown Wilmington hosts many festivals throughout the year.

Halloween Festival
Poplar Grove Historic Plantation, 10200 U.S. Hwy. 17, Wilmington • 686-9518

Kids love Poplar Grove's haunted barn and playground, spooky hay rides (by moonlight or sunlight), costume party, carnival rides, the palm reader, costume contest and games at the Halloween Festival. Admission is free, but some activities require a fee. Events take place the weekend prior to Halloween. A parking donation benefiting a local nonprofit organization may be requested.

Harley-Davidson Charity Halloween Run
Start at 6615 Market St., Wilmington • 791-9997

Beginning at Carolina Coast Harley-Davidson, which sponsors the event, big-hearted bikers in full Halloween costume (hey, there's a stretch), ride their rigs to a chosen watering hole on Front Street, where tattoos are momentarily forgotten and the five best costumes are elected for cash prizes. The event benefits a local charity and begins at noon the weekend prior to Halloween. Admission is $10.

November

Fall Native American Pow-Wow
Poplar Grove Historic Plantation, 10200 U.S. Hwy. 17, Wilmington • 686-9518

Celebrate the traditions and innovations on tradition of American's native peoples at this intertribal pow wow in early November. Featured are colorful dance contests, native drumming and singing, storytelling, authentic tepee lodges, demonstrations, arts and crafts, and food and refreshments. Admission is $5 for adults, $2 for seniors and $3 for children younger than 12.

Holly Festival
Fire and Rescue Dept., U.S. Hwy. 17 N., Holly Ridge • 329-7081

This affair, held outside the Fire Department in downtown Holly Ridge, fetes this small town with arts and crafts, entertainment, dances, clowns, food and a parade. The events are free, and concession proceeds benefit the Onslow County Parks and Recreation Department.

Robert Ruark Festival
Various locations, Southport • 457-5494

Of the two Ruark celebrations each year in Southport, this one, in early November, emphasizes the area's literary and artistic legacies. The centerpieces of the festival are its writing competitions (poetry and short fiction) and a juried art show, for which prizes are awarded. Literary symposiums and receptions (at which winners are recognized) round out the festival. Locations include area art galleries such as the Blue Dolphin on Long Beach Road and Southport City Hall. The festival is free, but competitions require a fee to enter.

Marine Expo
Coast Line Convention Center, 501 Nutt St., Wilmington • 962-3351

This annual exposition, on the third weekend of November, touts all the latest and greatest in vessels, equipment and accessories, from floating docks to global positioning systems. If it has to do with boats and boating, you're bound to find it here. Admission is free.

Festival of Trees
Wilmington Hilton, 301 N. Water St., Wilmington • 763-4700

Festival of Trees, a benefit for Cape Fear Hospice, is a dazzling display of scores of dressed Christmas trees at the Wilmington Hilton. Accompanying this is Children's Festival Land, featuring Mr. and Mrs. Claus, holiday crafts and hands-on activities and entertainment. One week-long pass entitles you to enter both events repeatedly. Tickets are $8 for adults and $6 for children.

Wrightsville Beach Holiday Flotilla
Banks Channel • 256-0722, 256-0411

This floating parade of brightly lit and wildly decorated watercraft of all shapes and sizes is one of the true highlights of the holiday season. It's free and typically takes place on the last weekend of November and includes a holiday fair, an arts and crafts show, children's art show, rides, food and performing artists. Fireworks brighten the party, after which everyone hits the town. For information, write Flotilla, P.O. Box 713, Wrightsville Beach, N.C. 28480.

Christmas By-The-Sea Parade
Yaupon and Long beaches • 457-6964

This colorful holiday parade, on the first Friday of December, begins in Yaupon Beach and proceeds down Oak Island Drive. The event is accompanied by a merchant open house along the route.

Oak Island Tour of Homes
Long Beach • 278-5518

Visit Oak Island's historic and lavish modern homes dressed in holiday regalia and partake of holiday spirit, Southern style. Homes are open for touring during the first weekend in December. Tickets are $5.

December

Old Wilmington by Candlelight
Various locations, Wilmington • 762-0492

This is one of the most popular and atmospheric of the holiday home tours. Each year, nearly a score of Wilmington's most historic homes, churches and businesses are opened to guests for two days on the first weekend in December, from 4 to 8 PM. Stroll into Christmases past and see how yesterday's lifestyles have been adapted to our time. You're invited to enjoy cider and cookies at the Latimer House as well. The tour is self-guided. Proceeds benefit Latimer House and the Lower Cape Fear Historical Society. Tickets are $15.

Toy Jam
Location TBA, Wilmington • 343-1640

Toy Jam is a night of live music of many styles and has become a very popular Christmas tradition. Admission requires a new, unwrapped toy, to be distributed to needy children by the Salvation Army. The event is sponsored by Public Radio WHQR and is held in a

downtown restaurant. Santa and Mrs. Claus typically make an early appearance. Volunteers to assist with the event are always needed.

Island of Lights Festival
Various locations, Carolina and Kure beaches • 458-8434

The Island of Lights Festival at Pleasure Island features several events, most of them free, beginning with a holiday parade on the first Friday in December. On Saturday there follows an evening holiday flotilla in full seasonal regalia, running from Snow's Cut to Town Marina (Carolina Beach) and back. The Island of Lights Tour of Homes, held the following Saturday, features refreshments and Southern hospitality on a self-guided tour of some of Carolina Beach's most elegant homes. The Tour of Homes costs $15 per person.

Southport Christmas Home Tour and Flotilla
Various locations, Southport • 457-7927

Southport's Christmas Homes Tour and Flotilla in mid-December combines a candlelight walking tour of Southport's historic riverfront homes from 5 to 9 PM ($8 admission) and a lively regatta of seasonally decorated vessels that sail the lower Cape Fear River by Waterfront Park that same evening (inquire about registration to participate; viewing is free!). The events usually take place the second Saturday in December.

Wilmington Boys Choir
St. Paul's Episcopal Church, 16 N. 16th St., • 799-5073

Since 1895, the Wilmington Boys Choir has distinguished itself with fine performances throughout the state, in Washington, D.C., and overseas. Its annual Christmas concert is always well-attended and features carols, hymns and popular holiday songs. Admission is by donation.

INSIDERS' TIP

If you're surf fishing and catch a bluefish — which is most likely — be sure to cook it right away. This fish doesn't hold up well under refrigeration.

Winter Holiday Fest
Sneads Ferry Community Building, Sneads Ferry • 327-3343

Sneads Ferry, the small seaside village known for its Shrimp Festival in August, officially kicks off its holiday observances with a tree-lighting ceremony and a community music program at 7 PM on the second Friday of December. Next day features a pancake breakfast with Santa from 7 to 11 AM and a community lunch from noon to 4 PM (there is a charge for these activities). Also on Saturday is a holiday craft show beginning at 10 AM and a children's music program beginning at 7 PM. The music and art continues on Sunday at noon. All programs are free. The Community Building is located on Park Lane, which is off Sneads Ferry Road (N.C. Highway 172) a few minutes north of Topsail Island.

Poplar Grove Christmas Celebration
Poplar Grove Historic Plantation, 10200 Hwy. 17 N. • 686-9518

There are few places that evoke bygone days as well as Poplar Grove Plantation, especially at holiday time. The Christmas Celebration here features seasonal arts and crafts, a beautifully decorated historic open house ($4 fee required to tour) and appearances by Victorian-style Mr. and Mrs. Santa Claus. Admission is free.

Walk-In Messiah
Kenan Auditorium, UNCW, 601 S. College Rd., Wilmington • 962-3500

The Walk-In *Messiah* is a concert sing-along with the Wilmington Symphony Orchestra, featuring carols and Handel's classic cantata. If you'd like to join in with the chorus for *Messiah*, you may attend a matinee rehearsal. Scores are available for the singing public in advance. Be sure to buy tickets early; the event typically sells out by late October. Tickets are $20 and $16. If you miss out on tickets for the evening performance, inquire about matinee rehearsal ($4).

Largest Living Christmas Tree
Hilton Park, Castle Hayne Rd., Wilmington • 341-4030

The lighting of the world's "largest living Christmas tree," an enormous decorated live oak, has been a Wilmington tradition since 1928. On a Friday evening in mid-December, the town turns out with the mayor, a brass band and a chorus, and the festivities begin at 6 PM. At 6:30, the tree is lit to the sounds of music and voices raised in song, and everyone joins in. The tree remains lit nightly from 5:30 to 10 PM until the end of December.

Carolina Beach New Year's Eve Countdown Party
Carolina Beach Boardwalk • 458-8434

Ring in the new year with food, refreshments and a street dance accompanied by live music (beach music, naturally!), culminating in the descent of an enormous beach ball at midnight. Top it off with fireworks and you've got yourself a beach-style New Year to remember. The fun begins at 10 PM on December 31 at the public gazebo.

UNCW Activities & Leadership Center

presents

1997~98

Arts & Lecture Series

Jessica Care Moore
SATURDAY • SEPTEMBER 20, 1997

Edward James Olmos
TUESDAY • SEPTEMBER 30, 1997

Squonk Opera
FRIDAY • NOVEMBER 14, 1997

Brosseau Danceworks
SATURDAY • JANUARY 31, 1998

Plus weekly coffeehouses, exhibits, comedy & concerts!

Call 910/962-3827 for more information
UNCW Activities and Leadership Center
Division of Student Affairs
Events subject to change.

The Arts

Although Wilmington and the Cape Fear region are geographically far flung from the world's acknowledged cultural centers, the area boasts a lively arts scene that is largely homegrown. While a significant sampling of cultural arts opportunities comes to town by way of touring shows, an incredible portion of it is local talent that can take its place among the world's best arts offerings.

While there are many formal settings for the arts in the forms of theater, live music, visual art, writing and art education in the region, what is truly exciting about Wilmington's artistic environment is the awareness art is not just something to be observed — it is something to be lived.

Downtown Wilmington is a magnet for artists, and a visitor is likely to stumble upon people practicing their various arts on street corners. On almost any nice day, there are artists on corners sketching the scene or a saxophone player sounding the blues. Step into downtown restaurants and encounter magnificent musical talent performing for free. Or eavesdrop on a group of creatively dressed people having wine or caffe latte during off-hours at local restaurants discussing their writing, plays, canvasses, scores. Theater is literally everywhere from basement bars to movie crews filming on the street.

Compound the excitement of a thriving local arts community with touring artists and shows and the air is nearly electric with creativity. The art that comes to town from other places is, to say the least, not too shabby. Roll the clock back and visit Wilmington in 1858 to witness the building of Thalian Hall Center for the Performing Arts. This performance theater, a cornerstone of Wilmington culture, saw stars the magnitude of Lillian Russell, Maurice Barrymore, Oscar Wilde and John Philip Sousa in the early days. Come closer in time and consider these performances: Al Hirt, Peter Nero, the Paul Taylor Dance Company, Chet Atkins, Frank Sinatra, Judy Collins and Koko Taylor.

Across town at the University of North Carolina at Wilmington, audiences have enjoyed the performances of Itzak Perleman, Livia Sohn, the Alvin Ailey Repertory Company and James Galway. Too highbrow? How about Frank Sinatra, Roberta Flack, Reba McEntire, Kenny Rogers, the Beach Boys, The Embers and Ray Charles?

The visual arts occupy an important position in the region's cultural experiences. In addition to dozens of commercial art galleries, the region has St. John's Museum of Art in downtown Wilmington, regarded as one of the finest art museums in the southeast. However, St. John's is probably best cherished by the community for the attention it lavishes on important local artists. Touring shows of national and international importance are regularly paired with exhibitions of the work of local and regional artists.

The Community Arts Center is a small building but a potent force for the encouragement of the arts across all disciplines in the area. Music, pottery, ceramics, dance, painting, drawing, theater and more are offered to the masses by professionals at extremely low cost, allowing Cape Fear people of all ages to try their hand at being artistically creative.

The Arts Council of the Lower Cape Fear is a central facilitator and coordinator for the arts in the area. This organization works diligently to create opportunities for the arts to flourish, documenting the activities of various arts organizations, providing local artists with vital information and funding to further their professional development and sponsoring innovative arts programs in area schools.

The Cape Fear region is a rich environment for the arts, offering a variety of opportunities for both creating and enjoying the cultural arts. Listed below is just a sampling of the arts scene in the region.

Museums, Performance Halls and Organizations

Acme Art
711 N. Fifth Ave., Wilmington • 763-8010

This is an artists' warehouse of working studios for rent at reasonable cost. Now and then, the warehouse opens to the public to show the works in progress.

Arts Council of the Lower Cape Fear
807 N. Fourth St., Wilmington • 763-2787

The Arts Council of the Lower Cape Fear has direct and indirect impact on the growth of the arts. It stands as an advocate for regional creativity, searches for ways to locate funding through grants for exceptional artists and seeks to focus community attention on this resource. It sponsors the A+ Program in the public schools. It also administers the Emerging Artists Program annually, a project grant program that provides financial support to developing professionals. The program began in 1987 and has offered grants of approximately $1,000 each to more than 80 local artists in a full range of disciplines. The Arts Council also co-sponsors Celebrate Wilmington, an effort to promote all arts in the area in October and November. The Piney Woods Cultural Heritage Festival, a two-day outdoor arts fair held in Hugh MacRae Park, is the major annual fund raiser for this community organization. The organization publishes a monthly arts calendar for the entire area in the Sunday *Star-News*.

Cape Fear Filmmakers' Accord
21 Market St., Wilmington • 763-3456

A nonprofit organization of film industry professionals, this group promotes TV and film production in southeastern North Carolina. It publishes a directory of locations and contacts, serves as a liaison with business and government and provides help with initial scouting locations.

The Community Arts Center
120 S. Second St., Wilmington • 341-7860

Managed by the Thalian Association, this Parks and Recreation center is primarily a learning facility where anyone may go to take low-cost lessons in any of a full range of disciplines. Music, pottery, ceramics, dance, painting, drawing and more are offered at the center. For nominal fees, students of all ages can experience hands-on work under the direction of highly-skilled local artists and craftspeople. There is something for every age and level of ability.

Odell Williamson Auditorium
Brunswick Community College, 150 College Rd., Bolivia • 343-0203 ext. 406

Built in 1993 on the campus of Brunswick Community College, this 1,500-seat proscenium auditorium offers entertainment opportunities in the heart of Brunswick County only 22 minutes from the bridge at Wilmington. In its short history, the auditorium has presented the talents of the North Carolina Symphony, the U.S. Marine Band, the Kingston Trio, the North Carolina Shakespeare Festival, the Tommy Dorsey Orchestra, the Lettermen, Lee Greenwood, Pebo Bryson and, in 1997, a presentation of "The Odd Couple" starring Jamie Farr and William Christopher (Klinger and Father Mulcahey from the TV show "M.A.S.H.") and various national touring companies. The auditorium has a subscription season each year as well as national dance competitions. In 1997 it is initiating a Christian Contemporary Artists series. For tickets call 754-3133.

St. John's Museum of Art
114 Orange St., Wilmington • 763-0281

This exceptional museum houses a collection of 18th-, 19th- and 20th-century North Carolina and American art and presents temporary exhibitions. In addition to a stunning permanent collection of 18th-, 19th- and 20th-century visual art, the museum owns an extensive collection of the works of such artists as Mary Cassatt, Minnie Evans, Claude Howell, Elisabeth Augusta Chant, Jacob Marling, Will-

Wilmington Symphony Orchestra

For concert information call 910.791.9262

iam Frerichs, Elliot Daingerfield, Hobson Pittman, Francis Speight and Will Henry Stevens. There is particular emphasis on three centuries of North Carolina art. Decorative arts from North Carolina include a major collection of Jugtown Pottery. The Sales Gallery represents more than 80 artists in the Southeast. The nonprofit museum offers ongoing classes for children and adults in its Cowan House studio as well as lectures, concerts, symposia and more on the visual arts and related cultural topics. A docent program provides guided tours and art appreciation talks to school and civic groups. (See our Attractions chapter.)

Thalian Hall
Center for the Performing Arts
310 Chestnut St., Wilmington • 343-3664

Built in 1858, this majestic performance center has gone through several restorations and, at this time, offers three performance spaces. There is a 752-seat main theater, the 250-seat Council Chamber and a 136-seat studio theater. With a lively local performing arts community and the addition of touring companies, at least one of the spaces is in use each evening or afternoon. More than 35 area arts and civic organizations use the facility, and more than 250 performances in music, theater and dance are presented each year. (See our Attractions chapter.)

Wilmington Art Association
P.O. Box 3033, Azalea Sta., Wilmington
• 392-3835

This association is composed of local visual artists. The group holds juried exhibitions in the spring and fall; it also holds meetings on topics of interest and sponsors frequent workshops and critiques. Membership at $20 annually entitles members to monthly meetings, participation in shows and a monthly newsletter. The Azalea Festival Show, held at St. Thomas Preservation Hall on Dock Street, is generally juried by a national arts figure. Recent jurors have been Alex Powers and Tom Lynch. The association has 160 members.

Galleries

American Pie
113 Dock St., Wilmington • 251-2131

Contemporary American crafts and folk art are just some of the niches filled by this lively gallery. There is a special section of one-of-a-kind small press, handmade books, unusual jewelry, handblown glass, paintings, papier-mâché sculpture and ceramics. Upstairs are the works of self-taught Southern artists and folk art.

Art Accents
3502-B Wrightsville Ave., Wilmington • 799-2256

This gallery features lithographs and serigraphs by world-renowned artists including Howard Behrens, Kerry Hallam, Don Hatfield, Itzchak Tarkay, Alice Riordan, Aldo Luongo, John Powell, Sally Caldwell Fisher, Fanny Brennan, John Asaro, Charles Fazzino, Henri Plisson and Eyvind Earle. The gallery has a unique focus in the area with its international emphasis. It is also an official Walt Disney animation gallery, selling sericels of cartoons.

Christie's Gallery
3308 Wrightsville Ave., Wilmington • 397-0094

Fine art, prints, posters, pottery, jewelry and restoration services are available at this relatively new and extremely interesting gallery that carries the work of Ruth Franklin, Russell Yerkes, J. Baughman, Dan Goad, Gorge, Aldo Luongo and others. Originals by Picasso and Miro are occasionally available.

Deborah Jamieson and Associates Showroom/Gallery/ Interior Design Services
Bradley Oaks Professional Park, 6317 Oleander Dr., Wilmington • 395-1818

Fine artwork by local, regional and national artists working in oil, watercolor and mixed media as well as in sculptures, vases and other functional accessories are on display with periodic changes. The gallery features the works of local artists including Elizabeth Darrow, Fritzi Huber, Sandra Brett, Jodie Rippy, Michael Costello and Hiroshi Sueyoshi.

Fidler's Gallery and Framing
The Cotton Exchange, Wilmington • 762-2001

Fidler's specializes in limited-edition reproductions by Bob Timberlake, Sallie Middleton, Bev Doolittle, Neil Watson, Robert Bateman, Charles Wysocki, James Gurney, John Stobart and others. This gallery also carries original work.

Franklin Square Gallery
Howe and West sts., behind Franklin Square, Southport • 457-5450

Operated by the nonprofit Associated Artists of Southport, this gallery is housed in an impressive historic building in the heart of Southport. The use of the building, and a building next door utilized as a pottery studio, was made possible by the farsighted City of Southport in a decision to rent it to the artists for next to nothing. The expectation was that the artists would create and maintain an important cultural center and, indeed, they have. The building is filled with work by exclusively local artists and ranges from paintings to pottery to dollhouse miniatures.

Golden Gallery
The Cotton Exchange, Wilmington • 762-4651

Mary Ellen Golden's original watercolors of the area scenery, son John W. Golden's exceptional photography and husband John C. Golden Jr.'s music cassettes are featured in this family gallery. Mary Ellen has been painting in watercolor since 1974 and has been in the Cotton Exchange since 1977. Her techniques and tips are on a video, "Watercolor Can Be Easy," available for sale in the gallery.

Griffith Gallery
120-B, S. Front St., Wilmington • 815-0044

This gallery features the scenery of the North Carolina coast in a realistic style of paintings with heavy emphasis on maritime themes.

FYI

Unless otherwise noted, the area code for all phone numbers in this guide is 910.

WILMINGTON
CONCERT
ASSOCIATION
1997-1998

❧

presents its 68th Season

Saturday • November 15, 1997
San Francisco Western Opera Theater
"Carmen"

Sung in French, English Supertitles

Thursday • January 15, 1998
Arcadi Volodos
Piano

Wednesday • February 25, 1998
Ballet du Capitole de Toulouse

Thursday • April 16, 1998
New Israel Woodwind Quintet

*Bringing concert artists of
international reputation to Southeastern
North Carolina*

Subscriptions may be ordered by telephone and charged to
VISA or Mastercard by calling the Kenan Auditorium
Box Office at 962-3500 or 1-800-732-3643.

Artist Ed Griffith paints area scenes of downtown Wilmington, the beaches, North Carolina lighthouses and ships in acrylics with a sharp eye and a highly skilled hand. Both originals and limited-edition prints as well as select smaller prints are available.

Makado Gallery
The Cotton Exchange, Wilmington
• 762-8922

The Makado Gallery specializes in contemporary fine arts, handblown glass, whimsical clocks, kaleidoscopes, fine woods, work by local wood-turners and handmade jewelry. It offers contemporary crafts by more than 300 American artists including Tom Torrens, Josh Simpson, Corki Weeks, Tom Thresher and Henry Bergeson. Featured local artists include Floy Dawson, Mike Overton, Ed Jacobsen and Marshall Milton. Makado also features Fire Island Hotglass by Matthew Labarbera.

New Elements Gallery
216 N. Front St., Wilmington • 343-8997

New Elements offers changing exhibitions of fine art by regional artists and nationally recognized artists. Works in oil, watercolor, collage, mixed media and original arts are displayed. Decorative and functional pieces in glass, ceramics, jewelry, fiber and wood are also offered. Exhibiting artists include Virginia Wright-Frierson, Dorothy Gillespie, Claude Howell, Kyle Highsmith, Nancy Tuttle May, Hiroshi Sueyoshi, Michael Van Hout, Brian Andreas (creator of StoryPeople), Richard Garrison, Jodie Rippy, Dina Wilde-Ramsing, Gladys Faris, Betty Brown and Mary Shreves Crow. Jewelry by Patricia Locke is also featured.

New Elements Motifs
The Galleria, 6766 Wrightsville Ave., Wilmington • 256-4707

New Elements Gallery downtown opened a second location, New Elements Motifs, near Wrightsville Beach in early 1997. Offering a different focus from the downtown gallery, it features fine art, furniture and home furnishings, including lighting, that fall under the category of functional art. It includes work by many of the same artists as the downtown location, but also offers the work of Anthony Ulinski, Charles Spreitzer, Chaty/Tysver, Barrett Debusk, Tom Kennedy, Susan Shepherd, Jana Ugone, George Kovacs and Kathleen Gibbs.

The Wrightsville Gallery
Lumina Station, 1900 Eastwood Rd. Ste. 7, Wilmington • 256-5278

Opened in late 1996 at an upscale shopping center near Wrightsville, this gallery is a relative newcomer to the scene but has made a dramatic presentation. Originals and limited edition work by local, regional, national and international artists are presented in what owner Lee Avant describes as "an ever-changing gallery" where artists display on short-term contracts. Artists who had shown include, but are not limited to, Caroline Landis, Susan Baehmann, Greg Ford, Sara Schweitzer Keane, Bob Graham, Maryanne K. Jenkins, Judy Crane, Babak Emanuel and Wyland.

Music

Azalea Coast
Chorus of Sweet Adelines
7209 Anaca Pt., Wilmington • 270-3313

This organization exists to promote and preserve the art of singing four-part harmony, the barbershop style that's one of the oldest American art forms for women.

Blues Society
of the Lower Cape Fear
P.O. Box 1487, Wilmington • 341-7350

Amateur and professional musicians devoted to the preservation and encouragement of the blues make up this lively group. There are free jam sessions locally, and the organization sponsors a major annual blues festival.

Cape Fear Chordsmen
1341 John's Creek Rd., Wilmington • 799-5850

This is Wilmington's chapter of the Society for the Preservation and Encouragement of Barber Shop Quartet singing in America. Members practice male four-part harmony singing weekly at the Unitarian-Universalist Fellowship, 4313 Lake Avenue, Wilmington.

Chamber Music Society of Wilmington

1997/98 Season

SEPTEMBER 21, 1997
Voice of the Whale
Music of George Crumb and J.N. Hummel

OCTOBER 26, 1997
EAST WINDS
Music for winds and piano featuring Mozart, Hindemith and Rimsky-Korsakov

JANUARY 25, 1998
Soirée Française
Music of Ravel and Debussy for harp, winds & strings

FEBRUARY 22, 1998
THE CASSATT QUARTET
"...the Cassatt are an extraordinary quartet. These four women throw out a voluptuous wall of sound and present a luminous program"
-Fanfare Magazine

All Concerts are on Sundays at 7:30 pm in the Thalian Hall Ballroom.

◆

**Subscriptions are $48 for all four concerts. To order call 962-3500.
For Single Tickets at $16 call 343-3664.**

*The Chamber Music Society's traditional **Children's Concerts** & "**Instrumental Petting Zoo**" will be offered on the afternoons of Sept. 21, Oct. 26 and Jan. 25.*

**FOR FURTHER INFORMATION CALL 791-7331
THE CHAMBER MUSIC SOCIETY OF WILMINGTON
2307 MIMOSA PL. • WILMINGTON, NC 28403**

Chamber Music Society of Wilmington

Petrea Warneck, Exec. Dir., 233 Seagull Ln., Wilmington • 791-7331

A new and long-awaited addition to the Wilmington music scene, the Chamber Music Society of Wilmington is a nonprofit organization that brings world-class chamber music concerts to the Thalian Hall Ballroom. Past performances have included the Ciompi Quartet, the American Chamber Ensemble and "Scapati" Piano Quartet as well as a series of Children's Concerts including an Instrumental Petting Zoo.

Cape Fear Symphony Orchestra

8355 Vintage Club Cir., Wilmington • 686-1836

This orchestra, formed in June of 1996, is similar to the Wilmington Symphony Orchestra. In fact, about a third of the musicians play in both orchestras. The Cape Fear Symphony Orchestra performs four concerts a year at Thalian Hall. Professional musicians from New Hanover, Brunswick and Pender counties are invited to audition. The orchestra emphasizes familiar orchestral pieces that range from classical to popular.

Harmony Belles

1341 John's Creek Rd., Wilmington • 799-5850

A local women's group formed in 1986, this group sings four-part harmony a cappella. Rehearsals are on Tuesday evenings at the New Hanover County Senior Center.

North Carolina Jazz Festival

Wilmington • 763-8585

This weekend festival takes place in February and features mainstream jazz performances by national and international stars. The main event is held at the Wilmington Hilton, and a preview program is given at Thalian Hall the day before. (See our Annual Events chapter.)

North Carolina Symphony

805 N. Third St., Wilmington • 763-0141

This New Hanover County chapter of the

fine art gallery

Featuring Lithographs & serigraphs
by world renowned artists

3502-B Wrightsville Avenue
Wilmington, NC
Tuesday - Friday 10 to 5
Saturday 10 - 3

(910)799-2256

state symphony sponsors five public concerts a year at UNCW's Kenan Auditorium. For tickets, call Kenan auditorium at 791-9695.

Suzuki Talent Education of Wilmington
4428 Mockingbird Ln., Wilmington • 395-0510

Independent piano and violin teachers in the Suzuki method of early childhood music education organize children's recitals and schedule workshops.

Wilmington Academy of Music
1635 Wellington Ave., Wilmington • 392-1590

This private school, founded in 1987, offers a full range of music instruction in voice, piano, guitar, harp, violin, viola, cello, percussion, horns, tuba, oboe, bagpipe and more for students of all ages. Theory, orchestration, arranging, Yamaha and Suzuki music education, jazz studies and other classes are available. Weekly private lessons and monthly group lessons, recitals and master classes are offered. The school has a community orchestra.

Wilmington Boys Choir
205 Dover Rd., Wilmington • 799-5073

This is a choral group for boys ages 8 to 15 with a repertoire of classical and traditional music. They perform in the area throughout the year and give special holiday concerts. Annual tours have taken the group to Washington, D.C., in performance at the Kennedy Center. Admission is by audition.

INSIDERS' TIP

The Community Arts Center in downtown Wilmington has outstanding pottery classes taught by Hiroshi Sueyoshi and Dina Wilde-Ramsing.

Wilmington Choral Society
P.O. Box 4642, Wilmington • 458-5164

A large chorus for mostly classical vocal works, the society presents up to four major concerts each season. Members rehearse weekly. This organization was founded in 1929.

Wilmington Concert Association
1203 Windsor Dr., Wilmington • 343-1344, 395-3294

A public subscription series, this group is responsible for bringing four or five classical music and dance concerts to Wilmington each year at UNCW's Kenan Auditorium. The association, established in 1929, regularly enjoys subscriptions of more than 800 each season in a house that seats 960. Performers in recent years have included the San Francisco Western Opera Theatre, Alvin Ailey Repertory Ensemble and the Canadian Brass. The association's mission is to "bring internationally acclaimed musical artists to Wilmington."

Wilmington Concert Band
517 Bedford Forest Ave., Wilmington • 799-5543

A volunteer community performing organization, this organization seeks musicians with a nearly-professional skill level. Auditions are not required but a minimum of two years instrumental experience is expected.

Wilmington Symphony Orchestra
4701 Wrightsville Ave., Bldg. 3 Ste. 208, Wilmington • 791-9262

University of North Carolina at Wilmington students and faculty members as well as musicians from the community comprise this all-volunteer symphony orchestra. There are five classical concerts per season. The 1996-1997 season marks the 25th anniversary of this orchestra.

Women of Wilmington Chorale
205 Dover Rd., Wilmington • 799-5073

Classical and folk repertoire are the focus of this group, known by their initials, WOW. The group is most active in the summer, and no auditions are required.

Theater

Wilmington has a rich theatrical tradition that is continually expanding. Wilmington's Thalian Hall Center for the Performing Arts is home to the Thalian Association, the oldest continuous community theater in the country

Photo: N.C. Travel & Tourism

Thalian Hall is a classic 19th-century American community theater in Wilmington.

dating from 1788. The theater hosts professional and amateur productions on an almost nightly basis. There are several local theatrical companies that present original and popular productions at such area locations as Kenan Auditorium at the University of North Carolina at Wilmington, the Scottish Rite Temple on 17th Street, schools and churches. Additionally Wilmington is on the circuit for touring dance companies, symphonies and musicals.

Ad Hoc Theatre Company
1630 41st St., Wilmington • 791-2035

This company offers experimental theater with plays by local writers.

Big Dawg Productions
1910 Wolcott Ave., Wilmington • 762-7182

Dedicated to producing experimental theater, this company stands outside of the mainstream in an effort to reach a more diverse audience than traditional theater.

INSIDERS' TIP

Be mindful of not parking in a large section of the Historic District residential neighborhood between midnight and 3 AM because those hours are reserved for residents only.

Thalian Hall is one of the focal points for theater in Wilmington.

PROFESSIONAL PROFILE
Private Piano Instruction

Barbara McKenzie, internationally acclaimed pianist and teacher, offers distinctive private piano instruction whether you are beginning piano or wanting to advance your keyboard skills and musical training. Child or adult, she is dedicated to helping each of her students realize their own potential and enjoy their musical creativity. For the advanced student, she offers rigorous training, a step by step approach to mastering keyboard technique through relaxation. Her own international performance experience and imagination helps each student strengthen their sense of stylistic interpretation.

Barbara McKenzie has given piano and chamber music master-classes at the Tschaikowsky Conservatory in Moscow, the Franz Liszt Hochschule in Welmar, as well as the national conservatories in Cairo, Ankara and Belgrade. She was faculty for piano and chamber music at the Onsabruck Conservatory, West Germany before returning to her native North Carolina. She is a N.C. Arts Council "artsist in residence" and makes her home in Wilmington.

For more information call 343-1049

Cape Fear Shakespeare
516 Dock St., Wilmington • 251-9457

This summer Shakespeare festival offers free outdoor performances of the Bard's most familiar plays along with a "street fair." Performers of all ages are encouraged to audition.

Friends of David Walker
P.O. Box 1153, Wilmington • 763-3935

Multicultural performances are sponsored by this nonprofit group named for a 19th-century Wilmington abolitionist. An annual festival to celebrate David Walker's birthday is held the last Saturday in September at the Martin Luther King Center in Robert Strange Park. (See our Annual Events chapter.)

Opera House Theatre
2011 Carolina Beach Rd., Wilmington • 762-4234

A professional theater company presided over by artistic director Lou Criscuolo, this group stages seven major productions and two to three experimental works each season in Thalian Hall. Guest artists and directors are frequent. Auditions are open.

INSIDERS' TIP

After a night out downtown, stop into any of the great coffeehouses along Front Street for a cappuccino or espresso. Pastries too!

Playwrights Producing Company
Wilmington • 763-7922

A nonprofit company supporting emerging North Carolina playwrights, this organization looks for scripts-in-progress, which are read by actors and critiqued by the audience. Selected productions or original plays are presented. Membership is open to all with a $10 membership fee.

Pride! Productions
Wilmington • 343-8661

This producing organization finances a variety of plays offering multicultural impact and reflecting alternative appeal. Interested directors with projects that need underwriting are invited to inquire.

Tapestry Theatre Company
228 N. Front St., No. 308, Wilmington • 763-8830

A nonprofit professional theater company, this group is dedicated to producing small, important works of contemporary and classical theater.

Thalian Association
120 S. Second St., Wilmington • 251-1788

The oldest theatrical group in the area, the Thalian Association stages five productions annually, including three musicals. The Second Stage Series of small plays in Thalian Hall's Studio Theatre are performed during summer. An allied group, the Thalian Association Children's Theatre, stages performances by young casts and holds workshops for children. In 1994 this company took up residence in the Community Arts Center to manage the Parks and Recreation facility.

University Theatre
University of North Carolina at Wilmington, 601 S. College Rd., Wilmington • 395-3446

The University Theatre, produced by the school's Department of Fine Arts, is an educational theater devoted to the creative advancement of theater arts. Four major plays are produced during the academic year with experimental work produced on demand. University Theatre provides an environment for students to participate in and learn about all aspects of theater.

Willis Richardson Players
508 Barclay Hills Dr., Wilmington • 791-1584, ext. 209

A community theater specializing in dramas by minority playwrights, the Willis Richardson Players perform works of particular interest to minority audiences.

Dance

Cape Fear Theatre Ballet
Wilmington • 799-0900, 395-3798

Founded in 1991, this company's mission is to bring dance theater to southeastern North Carolina. It offers public performances, educational workshops, master dance classes and community outreach special events. Approximately 35 dancers ages 10 to 17 are selected yearly through auditions.

Writing

North Carolina Writers' Network
Wilmington • 350-3908; Carrboro • (919) 929-0535

This state organization helps writers sharpen their skills in poetry, fiction, nonfiction, playwriting and technical writing. Writer workshops and conferences are often held in the Wilmington area. This organization is an important resource for local writers.

North Carolina Poetry Society
838 Everetts Creek Dr., Wilmington • 686-1751

The objectives of the society are to foster the writing of poetry; to bring together in meetings of mutual interest and fellowship the poets of North Carolina; to encourage the study, writing and publication of poetry; and to develop a public taste for the reading and appreciation of poetry. Annual meetings are held in Southern Pines.

Playwrights Producing Company
Wilmington • 763-7922

A nonprofit company supporting emerging North Carolina playwrights, this organization looks for scripts-in-progress, which are

read by actors and critiqued by the audience. Selected productions or original plays are presented. Membership is open to all for a $10 membership fee.

Crafts

Azalea Coast Smockers Guild
228 Forest Rd., Wilmington • 395-5201

This group teaches smocking and heirloom sewing and publishes a newsletter for its members.

Quilters by the Sea
314 Grovedere Ln., Hampstead • 270-9960

This group encourages the highest standards of design and technique in all forms of quilting. Activities include quilt shows and exhibits as well as seminars and workshops on all levels. (See our Annual Events chapter.)

Port City Basketmakers
Poplar Grove Plantation, 10200 U.S Hwy. 17 N., Wilmington • 686-4868

This group's mission is to stimulate interest in the art of basketry. It meets the fourth Sunday of every month at 2:30 at Poplar Grove Plantation. Special workshops are available for novice and advanced weavers.

Seashore Weavers and Spinners
418 Windemere Rd., Wilmington • 763-4804

This organization exists for those who are

Wilmington's Artistic Journey

Claude Howell sits in his fourth-story apartment in downtown Wilmington overlooking the city that has been his home since his birth in 1915. Founder of the Art Department at the University of North Carolina at Wilmington and recipient of numerous accolades

for a superior career as an artist, Howell also is regarded widely for his scholarly writings and journalistic musings. His personal journal includes 140 volumes and is available at the New Hanover County Public Library. Mr. Howell was honored at St. John's Museum of Art in 1995 on the occasion of his 80th birthday, and he greeted more than 600 admirers at the blacktie event. In 1996, the City of Wilmington dedicated the Claude Howell Park, located at the foot of Orange Street on the river.

Howell is a keen observer of the life around him and graciously has shared his observations of the development of the visual arts in Wilmington.

When I was growing up, there was very little culture in Wilmington. It was sort of a dead period. There had been culture in Wilmington in the 1700s and also around the time of the Civil War, but, when I was growing up, there were no galleries; there was no museum.

I was 21 years old before I saw my first exhibition of original oil paintings. That was not in Wilmington; that was In Washington, D.C. I went on a trip. And that was the only way that you could see anything that was at all contemporary in those days.

Miss Elisabeth Chant arrived in Wilmington in 1922 and opened her studio and began to teach. A lot of people were interested in the arts like me: young and very naive and unknowledgeable. But she also organized, or got the nice women in Wilmington to organize, around 1923, the Wilmington Artists' League. And they had meetings; and they put on exhibitions — not just of their work, because women of Wilmington had frequently done that — they brought in exhibitions.

One of the first ones that I remember was in the parish house of St. James Church. It had just been built and that was in 1923. Well, this really sort of opened the eyes of a lot of people in Wilmington — mainly women — to the value of the arts.

There also was this to be considered — we pooh-pooh it today, but I think it's one of the greatest influences on culture in Wilmington — the women's clubs. The North Carolina Sorosis, which was organized in Wilmington, had an annual exhibition. And several times — it was always statewide — the state show was in Wilmington. Judges would come down. It was a juried show. And this was very exciting to local people who were studying art.

Wilmington was terribly isolated, which, of course, was and still is its greatest virtue. Very few people knew about Wilmington in those days. The people of the state were doing their own thing. They paid no attention to Wilmington; Wilmington paid no attention to the state. So, we always felt that we lived in the state of New Hanover, rather than the state of North Carolina. When you crossed the river, you came into the then-known world, but Wilmington was an unknown place. — continued on next page

Photo: The Wilmington Star-News Inc.

Claude Howell

— continued on next page

[When I was young,] I always would have to exhibit in other places; I couldn't exhibit in Wilmington. There was a movement by people here, all this time, to try to get a gallery or museum started. The first step was when Hester Donnelly and Virginia McQueen opened the artists gallery on Post Office Alley. This lasted a number of years and had changing monthly exhibitions, primarily of local people. Occasionally they would import someone, and there were several historical shows that were very exciting. One was portraits before the Civil War from Wilmington homes. That was a good show.

Now, the gallery foundered at the end, and it was just at this time that Gar Faulkner and Jimmy McCoy were running the St. John's Tavern in the old St. John's Lodge on Orange Street. Well, Jimmy died. His brother, Henry, who didn't live in Wilmington, offered to give the building to an organization here with a 99-year lease if they would open a gallery. So, Hester Donnelly and a great many other people got together and formed an organization called St. John's Organization so that they could accept this gift. Later on, Henry gave the building outright to Wilmington in memory of his brother.

That's how St. John's Museum of Art got started, but it took a long time to get it going. It opened in 1953. That, at last, gave Wilmington artists a place to exhibit. But it wasn't all sweetness and light because, in the beginning, they had only amateurs running the gallery, and that made a lot of professionals mad, including me. And then, they got a professional, and they decided that they needed to import shows. This made a lot of the would-be artists in Wilmington furious because they only wanted a place to exhibit their own work.

So, we had that fight to overcome; but it has weathered all these storms. And now the art of painting seems to be flourishing in this community.

Claude Howell passed away in February of 1997. His memorial service was held on March 15th, two days before his 82nd birthday. Services were held at First Presbyterian Church on S. Third Street where Ren Brown, Director of St. John's Museum of Art, delivered a eulogy. In a stirring moment, Ren Brown recounted Claude Howell's final words before his death. The artist was lying in the same bed where he was born in the Carolina Apartments. He pointed a finger at a work at the foot of the bed on the wall and said simply, "I did that."

After the service, Howell's ashes were buried in the garden of St. John's Museum of Art as hundreds of people lifted glasses of champagne to celebrate his life and his profound impact on the cultural arts in Wilmington.

interested in weaving, spinning, natural dyeing and other fiber-related crafts.

Photography and Film

Cape Fear Camera Club
301 Honeycutt Dr., Wilmington • 392-5692

Founded in 1987, this organization is a forum for photographic interests within the community. More than 50 members partici-pate in education, travel, outings, workshops and friendly competition.

Cape Fear Filmmakers' Accord
21 Market St., Wilmington • 763-3456

A nonprofit organization of film industry professionals, this group promotes TV and film production in southeastern North Carolina. It publishes a directory of locations and contacts, serves as a liaison with business and government and provides help with initial scouting locations.

To be truly among animals, especially those of the petting variety, check out Ashton Farm in Burgaw.

Kidstuff

Among a parent's greatest resources for entertaining kids (besides the area's beaches and waterways) are the various museums, which offer classes and workshops in arts and crafts, and the North Carolina Aquarium at Fort Fisher, which also offers classes and workshops as well as outdoor activities. Also, opportunities for adolescents to learn boating skills, to participate in gymnasium and team sports and to take part in many other activities, both physical and cerebral, exist with the various parks and recreation departments throughout the area. To contact these resources, see the listings in our chapters on Watersports and Rentals, and Sports, Fitness and Parks.

For this chapter, we've tried to ferret out some of the participatory activities that are easily overlooked as well as the bare necessities of kidstuff to balance the ubiquitous consumer-oriented offerings. Keep in mind that many of the activities listed here are not strictly for kids; conversely, many attractions and activities listed in other chapters are not exclusively for adults. Be sure to comb other chapters — especially Attractions; Sports, Fitness and Parks; and Watersports and Rentals —for great kidstuff ideas.

Each section in this chapter deals with a type of activity or interest: Animals, Arts, Amusements (including hobbies and toys), Exploring Nature, Farms, Holidays (including birthday ideas), Getting Physical, Getting Wet, Going Mental (for inquisitive minds), Summer Camps, Eats and Sweets. Information on child care can be found in our Education and Child Care chapter.

Animals

Locals cherish the fact that our region is still not so urbanized as to have removed all wildlife from among us. In fact, it is not uncommon to witness hawks, ospreys and turkey vultures taking lunch breaks on roadsides within Wilmington city limits. Deer are frequently sighted in outlying areas at dusk. And watching dolphins cavort mere yards offshore can be endlessly entertaining. To be truly among animals, especially of the petting variety, also check Ashton Farm, listed in the "Summer Camps" section below, and Greenfield Lake, listed later under "Exploring Nature" in this chapter and in the Attractions chapter.

North Carolina Aquarium at Fort Fisher
Ft. Fisher Blvd., Fort Fisher • 458-8257

The touching tank is not the aquarium's only eye-popping attraction for children of all ages. The outdoor carp and turtle pond is also a riot of activity, especially with the many barn swallows that nest beneath the building's overhang swooping just inches above spectators' heads all day. A walk along trails through the salt marshes is also likely to offer sudden, delightful sightings of small marsh animals and birds. The aquarium is 20 miles south of

Wilmington, and is open 9 AM to 5 PM Monday through Saturday and 1 to 5 PM Sunday. Admission fees are $3 for adults, $2 for senior citizens and military personnel and $1 for children 6 to 18 years old. For more information about the aquarium, see the "Exploring Nature" section below and our Attractions chapter.

Tote-Em-In Zoo
5811 Carolina Beach Rd., Wilmington
• 791-0472
With its lion's mouth entrance, this place is hard to miss. Tote-Em-In has been a Wilmington fixture since 1951. Within its small parcel of land (too small by today's zoo standards) live more than 100 species of animals including a camel, a zebra, baboons, many types of monkeys, antelope, peacocks, parrots and wallabies, not to mention various waterfowl. There are also two museums, one featuring mounted specimens and the other a collection of artifacts of various pedigrees. The zoo is open from March through late November, 9 AM to about 5 PM every day. Admission is $4 for visitors 12 and older and $2 for children younger than 12.

FYI
Unless otherwise noted, the area code for all phone numbers in this guide is 910.

Arts
Once again, checking into the various parks and recreation departments in your area can be rewarding since many of them offer art classes. Two facilities hosting such activities are the **Community Arts Center** (see later entry) and the **Martin Luther King Jr. Center**, 410 S. Eighth Street, 341-7866. The **Davis Center** in Maides Park on Manly Avenue (north of Princess Place Drive), 341-7867, and administered by Wilmington Parks and Recreation, offers free after-school activities that include arts and crafts, language arts and creative writing. For art supplies, see **Hungate's Arts-Crafts & Hobbies** in the "Amusements" section below.

Wilmington has an abundance of dance schools catering to young children. We have listed only a few that come well recommended and offer a variety of styles.

Baldwin-Copeland Studio of Dance
4711-1/2 Oleander Dr., Wilmington
• 791-0602, 791-5834
Since 1960 this studio has been teaching children as young as 2 (as well as adults) the fundamentals of dance. The emphasis here leans toward modern, jazz and folk styles.

The Ballet School of Wilmington
2250 Shipyard Blvd., Wilmington
• 799-0900
Anne Goodrum, whose background includes dancing with the Atlanta Ballet and working as artistic director of the Wilmington Civic Ballet, directs Wilmington's only school dedicated exclusively to classical ballet. This school emphasizes the style's fundamental basics, and Ms. Goodrum is known for setting pieces on the dancers, allowing them to witness and share in the evolution of the dance.

Danceworks Studio for the Performing Arts
4209 Oleander Dr., Wilmington • 392-0375
In addition to teaching all the styles of dance commonly taught in our region — jazz, tap, ballet and pointe — founders Brad and Jenny Moranz specialize in the practical approach to teaching musical theater. This includes film work, which is their professional background (they are active performers on stage and film). Thus, Danceworks accepts dance students no younger than 4 and students of musical theater age 9 and older, including adults. Their studio features one-way viewing windows so parents can observe the classes unseen.

Community Arts Center
120 S. Second St., Wilmington • 341-7860
This city-owned facility (a former USO building of World War II-vintage) is the focal year-round arts facilitator for children. Its annual Arts Camp offers school-age children six weeks of hands-on creative fun in practically every medium imaginable, including painting, pottery, music, dance, acting and photography. Offerings change, so call for current in-

formation and register early. Some adult classes are open to young adults ages 13 to 17, with permission of the instructor.

The Center is managed by the Thalian Association, 251-1788, the nation's oldest continuous theatrical organization. The Thalian Association Children's Theater stages performances by young casts during the school year. Thalian Association Forte, a youth singing group, is open to vocalists ages 15 to 18. Auditions are held in January.

Finklestein's Music
6 Front St., Wilmington • 762-5662

Finklestein's music store (not to mention its adjoining pawn shop) has stood in the same location longer than most trees in the area. Offering a wide array of new and used instruments, Finklestein's also offers lessons, catering primarily to students of popular and rock music.

Kindermusik
(800) 628-5687

Kindermusik is a program of music learning and movement for children ages 18 months to 7 years, designed to facilitate children's creative expression, listening, communication and group skills. It incorporates singing, movement, musical play and a practical approach to writing and reading the language of music. This program is a four-semester, sequential curriculum structured in three age tiers. The

program is published by Music Resources International, P.O. Box 13765, Greensboro, NC 27415. In the greater Wilmington area, there are three licensed Kindermusik teachers who offer a variety of schedules. Call the toll-free number above to find the program nearest you.

The Music Loft
413 S. College Rd., Wilmington • 799-9310

The Music Loft is among the better music shops in town, especially when it comes to repair of acoustic string instruments such as guitars, dulcimers and banjos by master luthier Steve Gillham. Electronic instruments and equipment are also offered, including recording equipment, and lessons are available.

St. John's Art Academy
St. John's Museum of Art, 114 Orange St., Wilmington • 762-0281

Designed as a supplement to basic art instruction for children from elementary through high-school age, St. John's Art Academy offers several excellent opportunities, including the Exploring Visual Arts classes for 4th and 5th graders, Beginning Drawing and Design for 6th through 8th graders and Portfolio Preparation for 9th through 12th graders. Studio classes, multiple series and workshops for children ages 5 through high-school age are ongoing. Costs average $75 per semester plus materials.

Suzuki Method Music Education
Lorraine Westermark, Suzuki Talent Education of Wilmington • 395-0510
University of North Carolina at Wilmington, Fine Arts Department, 601 S. College Road • 395-3415
Wilmington Academy of Music, 1635 Wellington Avenue • 392-1590

This tried-and-true method of early-childhood music education accepts students as young as 3 (for violin) and older students as well. The method relies heavily upon parental involvement during young students' lessons and is well-represented in the area by independent teachers affiliated with several groups.

Wilmington Boys Choir
16 N. 16th St., Wilmington • 799-5073

Formed in 1985, the Wilmington Boys Choir regularly performs classical and traditional vocal music throughout the area and elsewhere in the state. A nonprofit organization, the choir stresses education and musical appreciation as well as performance technique and is directed by Ms. Sandy Errante. The Choir is actually two choruses in one: a soprano-alto group for boys ages 8 to 13 and a tenor-bass group for ages 14 to 17. Auditions are required, and candidates are expected to fulfill a 10-month commitment involving two rehearsals per week plus performances and a $125 tuition per year. Rehearsals are held at St. Paul's Episcopal Church, at the address above, but the choir is nondenominational.

Wilmington Dance Academy
3333 Wrightsville Ave., Wilmington • 791-7660

This academy accepts children as young as 3, who participate in creative movement classes, something of a pre-dance class. With four teachers on staff, Wilmington Dance has been operating since 1986 and teaches a variety of styles, including ballet, tap, jazz and modern group acrobatics. Classes are taught Monday through Thursday.

Oak Island School of Dance & Art
210 Yaupon Dr., Yaupon Beach • 278-6110

The only dance school on Oak Island, this one teaches a spectrum of styles, including ballet, tap, jazz, creative movement and "danceplay."

Brunswick School of Dance
920 Ocean Hwy. W., Supply • 754-8281, 754-6106

Housed in a remodeled country store since 1982, Brunswick School of Dance specializes in teaching children from age 3 the basics of movement and strives to build self-esteem and confidence. Class size averages nine students. Most classes take place in the afternoon Monday through Thursday, and there are morning classes for preschoolers. Round-trip van pickup service is available. Styles taught to older students include ballet, tap, jazz, pointe and acrobatics. Adult classes include aerobics, ballroom dancing and shagging. The school is convenient to most of the South Brunswick Islands.

Amusements

Here we go slightly farther afield than you may expect in defining what constitutes "amusements." When the kids are in a funk that can only be shaken by gut-scrambling rides, go-carts, batting cages and the like, check our Attractions chapter to locate such opportunities. But for kids in need of a certain baseball card to complete the collection, a tube of cobalt blue to finish the painting or the newest interactive video game on CD, you've come to the right place.

In the realm of sports cards and comics, the Wilmington Elks Lodge, 5102 Oleander

Don't want to eat that catch? Turn it into art at the aquarium.

Drive in Wilmington, 799-2365, is noteworthy for its periodic card-and-comics shows, which attract collectors and vendors from miles around.

Wilmington

Cool World Family Fun Center
5725 Oleander Drive, Wilmington
• **791-8700**

While tooling down Oleander Drive, your kids will undoubtedly notice this place. The arcade is only as cool as any amusement park arcade and equally pricey. Offered are all the popular (and violent) video games and pinball machines, simulated racing games, Skee-Ball and air hockey. It's open every day from noon until 11 PM except Saturdays, when it's stays open until midnight.

Fanboy Comics & Cards
419 S. College Rd., Wilmington • 452-7828

Offering a dazzling array of comic books for children and adults, Fanboy also carries collections, posters, role-playing games, collectors' cards (other than sports) and accessories. New releases are always stocked, and subscriptions can be arranged. Fanboy is in the University Landing strip mall (across the

road from the Rock-ola Cafe) and is open seven days a week.

The Game Giant
1537 S. College Rd., Wilmington
• **792-0626**

Specializing in new and used video games and game systems, The Game Giant accepts trade-ins for store credit, the amount of which varies according to the condition of, and demand for, the individual game. The store also rents games and carries every major brand. The Game Giant is beside Honey Baked Ham on the northbound side of S. College Road (south of Oleander Drive) and is open Monday through Saturday.

The Game Plan
Video Game Exchange
4405 Wrightsville Ave., Wilmington
• **799-4386**

Here, too, kids can exchange their old or unwanted video games and equipment for credits redeemable on a choice of secondhand but yet-unbeaten games in good playing condition. Credit for specific games fluctuates depending on supply and demand, and additional credits are earned for games in their original boxes or with instructions in good condition. The Game Plan trades all types of popular games and accessories, new and used, including Nintendo, Super Nintendo, Sega, Sega CD, Game Boy and others. New games and systems may be ordered. Games may be trial-run in the store.

Goldings Hobbies
4410 Market St., Wilmington • 763-9395, 343-9406

Goldings truthfully advertises itself as offering "one of Wilmington's largest and most complete lines of hobbies." The vast inventory goes well beyond plastic model kits, train supplies, radio-controlled models, dolls, art supplies and role-playing adventure games to include all manner of raw materials for the artist and craftsperson, from plaster molds to googly-eyes and aisles stuffed with every odd piece of whaddya-callits a creative mind could imagine. Don't miss it. Goldings is behind the Shell station at the intersection of Market Street and Kerr Avenue.

Hungate's Arts-Crafts & Hobbies
Independence Mall, 3500 Oleander Dr., Wilmington • 799-2738

Hungate's stocks an impressive inventory of art supplies, including stretched canvas, model trains, rockets, toys, puzzles, novelties, miniature collectibles and a huge array of role-playing games and books. In the mall's JCPenney wing, this is a store for kids of all ages.

J & C Sportscards & Collectibles
3517 Wrightsville Ave., Wilmington • 392-8550

J & C is among the premier card shops in the area with its broad spectrum of collectibles, including sports plaques, commemorative bottles and cans, NASCAR die-casts and toys, college-team cards, puzzles, cards derived from movies, TV shows and video games and figurines. The store's appeal, therefore, draws as many adults as kids. For the completist, J

& C stocks tens of thousands of common cards back to 1981 as well as prized singles that are far older. A must-see for the serious collector, J & C is open Monday through Saturday, 10 AM to 6:30 PM.

Memory Lane Comics
5751 Oleander Dr., Wilmington • 392-6647

Stocking one of the area's largest inventories of comic books (new and old), collections, non-sport and gaming cards and supplies, Memory Lane is an essential stopover for comic fans. Also stocked are animations, old toys and other oddities. You'll find the shop in the Philips' Azalea Plaza a short distance west of the Greenville Loop Road intersection. Memory Lane is open every day.

The Olde Wilmington Toy Company
309 N. Front Street, Wilmington • 251-1404

This is a unique toy shop in the Danhardt Building at the Cotton Exchange. Proprietor Stephanie Carr, a former educator, specializes in hard-to-find games and toys, both classic and educational. Hers is a place where children are welcome to try out certain toys, provided they use the magic words, "Please" and "May I?" You'll find few nationally advertised products and none that inspire aggression. From classic windups to doll houses to unusual kites, the Olde Wilmington Toy Company has something to inspire everyone.

Sears
Independence Mall, 3500 Oleander Dr., Wilmington • 452-6200

Don't overlook Sears when looking for toys, particularly video game systems.

Toys R Us
4510 Oleander Drive, Wilmington • 791-9067

The inevitable hunt for a child's toy may well lead you to this gargantuan toy store near the intersection of S. College Road, not far

---

INSIDERS' TIP

Fans of model trains can get on the right track with the Cape Fear Model Railroad Club, 763-2634, which meets at the Wilmington Railroad Museum, 501 Nutt Street and welcomes novices as well as experts.

from Independence Mall. Toys R Us probably offers the largest selection of interactive video games in Wilmington.

U.S. Trolls
2305 Market St., Wilmington • 251-2270

Young children will enjoy stories performed with troll dolls handmade by their Finnish creators, Helena, Minna and Johannes Kuuskoski, at U.S. Trolls. Story time takes place every Saturday at 2 PM in a home just east of 23rd Street. Parents will appreciate the free admission. The trolls are cute, some are furry and all are for sale. There's parking in the rear of the building with easy exit to 23rd Street. U.S. Trolls is open Monday through Saturday 10 AM to 6 PM.

Wes' Card Shop
1930 Carolina Beach Rd., Wilmington • 343-8830

This shop in the Summer Hill Square shopping center immediately north of Legion Stadium has a reputation for bargaining and for carrying more singles than many other card shops, despite its more limited inventory. Wes specializes in baseball, basketball, football and some hockey cards, plus accessories.

Outside Wilmington

Coastal Sports Cards & Apparel
4830-B Main St., Shallotte • 755-6100

This well-stocked shop, in the Vision Square shopping strip, excels with its wide range of sports cards (including racing and hockey), magazines, autographed collectibles, official team shirts and hats and other curiosities. Coastal Sports Cards is open Monday through Saturday from 10 AM to 6 PM.

Exploring Nature

The Beaches

The most accessible, most affordable and most attractive source of fun for kids on the southern coast is naturally the same that draws adults in droves: the beaches and nearby waterways. So no matter what your kids' ages, get 'em down to the water, from Topsail to Calabash. Try a different beach now and then

to pique their interest; there's a great difference in character from beach to beach.

Combining activities with beach visits may also be worthwhile. Driving a four-wheel-drive vehicle on the beach at the Fort Fisher State Recreation Area is a bouncy jaunt most kids love. The area offers pristine surf, calm tidal waters on the inland side suitable for toddlers, great fishing and, just minutes away, a fine Civil War museum and historic site. See the "Off-Roading" section in the Sports, Fitness and Parks chapter.

Greenfield Lake and Gardens
U.S. 421 S., Wilmington • 341-7855

Greenfield Lake and Gardens, a short drive down Third Street from downtown Wilmington, is another ideal outdoor entertainment for children. Toddlers will certainly enjoy feeding the many ducks and geese that gather at the lake shore. In fact, Greenfield Lake attracts many types of wildlife that will challenge a child's imagination and naming skills. Most youngsters love taking excursions in the paddle boats or canoes that can be rented at the dock on the north side of the lake off Third Street. Rates are reasonable: Paddle boats cost $2 per half-hour; canoes cost $3 for the first hour and $1.50 each additional hour. Life jackets are included. Playgrounds and picnic areas abound near the dock. Older children may cherish a day's fishing from any of the lake's several small piers and bridges or from your own johnboat, which can be launched from the ramp on W. Lake Shore Drive, just off Third Street. The park is open from dawn until dusk.

North Carolina Aquarium at Fort Fisher
Fort Fisher Blvd., south of Kure Beach • 458-7468

Besides everything the aquarium is famous for (see the chapter on Attractions), it also specializes in excursions and learning programs designed with kids in mind. Typical programs here may address topics such as Animals Without Backbones, Shark Bites and Nature Crafts. The aquarium's Ocean Odyssey series allows children ages 7 to 10 to learn about ecology, marine animals and coastal wildlife (children should be prepared to get wet on certain excursions).

Children's Discovery are sessions that offer storytelling and "critter creating" for preschoolers. Outings are ongoing, vary widely and are led by qualified personnel. Programs on the water have recently included hunting for shells, the Japanese art of fish-printing, surf fishing, cleaning and cooking coastal cuisine, salt-marsh hikes and canoeing the marshes, explorations of local plant life and sand casting.

Admissions range from free to $7. Special events often mark holidays and seasons with appropriate crafts. Contact the aquarium for seasonal brochures. For weekly listings, also check the community calendar in the "Neighbors" section of the Wednesday *Wilmington Star-News*. Regular hours are 9 AM to 5 PM Monday through Saturday and 1 to 5 PM Sunday.

Carolina Beach State Park
Dow Rd., Carolina Beach • 458-8206

In addition to all there is to do and see in this park (see our chapter on Sports, Fitness and Parks), the Sugar Loaf sand dune is one place that kids love. Running up and tumbling down is a simple pleasure, to be sure, perhaps the best kind. Elsewhere in the park, kids are challenged to locate the several carnivorous plants indigenous to the area: sun dews, pitcher plants and the famous Venus's flytrap. Be sure to instruct the children about the plants' rarity and delicacy, and leave them as you found them. You can visit the park from dawn to dusk.

Farms

Lewis Strawberry Nursery
Castle Hayne Rd., Wilmington • No phone

Picking strawberries can be almost as much fun as eating them. In late spring, peaking in May, the berries at Lewis' Nursery ripen into succulent concentrations of juicy, deep-red sweetness that almost defy belief. Whether you and the kids pick 'em yourselves or buy them by the quart, strawberries are a treat.

Lewis' Nursery is less than 3 miles north of the 23rd Street intersection on Castle Hayne Road (Highway 117), and it's open for picking (depending on the supply of berries!) every day from 8 AM to 6 PM.

Holden Brothers Farm Market
5600 U.S. Hwy. 17 W, Shallotte • 579-4500

Bring the kids to pick strawberries, sweet corn, cantaloupes, watermelons, pumpkins and other vegetables in season. The fields and market are open only from April 1 through Christmas and are located 3 miles south of Shallotte.

Holidays

Several holiday events geared for kids are listed in the chapter on Annual Events. What we offer here, then, is a cross-section of lesser-known offerings grouped by holiday, plus some ideas about special venues offering birthday party services. Be sure to stop by the Cape Fear Coast Convention & Visitors Bureau at 24 N. Third Street in Wilmington, to request the latest publications for holiday events, particularly the Christmas season brochure that includes information on festivities in Carolina and Kure beaches. They can be reached by phone at 341-4030, (800) 222-4757 or (800) 457-8912 in Canada.

New Hanover County Public Library
201 Chestnut Street, Wilmington
• 341-4392

The public library hosts programs for several holidays. Offerings include ghostly tales at Halloween, teachings about Thanksgivings past and present, and a look at the many ways Christmas is celebrated around the world. Children also help make decorations and trim the library tree. Story sessions are geared for particular age groups ranging from ages 6 to 10 and last from 30 minutes to just under an hour. Call the library for schedules and events at locations other than the main branch. Admission is free.

INSIDERS' TIP

Stories and music suitable for children of all ages are broadcast Saturday morning at 7:30 by public radio WHQR 91.3 FM.

Halloween

Cape Fear Filmmakers Accord Haunted House
21 Market St., Wilmington • 763-3456

The Accord sponsors perhaps the most flamboyant Halloween haunted house in the region as a fund-raiser and publicity vehicle, putting all their talent for movie magic to work for a truly impressive and often convincing abode of ghouls and ghosts. Locations change from year to year; admission is $4.

Christmas

Santa Claus at Independence Mall
3500 Oleander Dr., Wilmington • 392-1776

Santa Claus arrives at the mall every year in mid-November and remains ensconced in winter glory in the mall's central plaza until his midnight ride on Christmas Eve. Also featured is a month-long program of live, seasonal music.

Christmas Lights at Calder Court
Wilmington • No phone

Calder Court, a cul de sac in the Kings Grant subdivision off N.C. Highway 132 (College Road), is a must-see for kids and adults during the weeks prior to Christmas. Each year, residents of Calder Court (and, increasingly, the entire subdivision) adorn their homes with an incredible array of lights and decorations, attracting caravans of people who turn off their headlights to view the spectacle in all its glory. To get there from S. College Road, turn right onto Kings Drive, which is about 1.25 miles north of the Market Street overpass. Then make two left turns. Just follow the line of cars ahead; you can't miss it.

Christmas for Kids & Others Concert
Thalian Hall Center for the Performing Arts, 310 Chestnut St., Wilmington • 343-3664 or (800) 523-2820

The Wilmington Choral Society presents this seasonal concert program in early De-

Photo: N.C. Aquarium

Locals take the future of the endangered loggerhead turtle very seriously.

cember. Tickets cost $8 for adults and $6 for children, students and senior citizens.

The Enchanted Toy Shop
Thalian Hall Center for the Performing Arts, 310 Chestnut St., Wilmington
• 343-3664

The Enchanted Toy Shop is a ballet staged annually by the Cape Fear Theatre Ballet in mid-December. Performed by local dancers, some of them quite young, it makes a festive

bookend to Thalian's other great holiday production, *The Nutcracker*. Call for tickets early on — October's not too soon — for ticket information and schedules. Ticket prices range from about $12 to $18.

Kwanzaa

This eight-day African-American cultural celebration is observed yearly in the Wilmington area during the week between Christmas and New Year's Day. The word re-

Did You Say (gulp!) G-G-Ghosts?

Mysterious footsteps . . . misty apparitions . . . playful pranks . . . empty rockers rocking . . . . Some say the true soul of a place is its ghosts, and the southern coast region has more specters than golfers. (We're not complaining.) Sleep in a historic house long enough — a night or two might do it — and you're likely to make an acquaintance! Insiders take their ectoplasms seriously because, as the following oft-told tidbits suggest, wraiths have been a coastal way of life (and death) for a long, long time.

Capt. Harper's Ghostly Rescue

Back in 1897 Captain John M. Harper, a renowned Cape Fear River skipper, found he didn't need a dark and stormy night for a convincing ghost story — but it sure didn't hurt. He used to tell this story himself.

While making the passage from Wilmington to Smithville (now Southport) through a terrible winter storm, Harper was regaled by his sole passenger, a Scot, within the

— continued on next page

Photo: Courtesy of Thalian Hall

Many Insiders believe that a ghost called the Gossamer Lady is a frequent visitor at Thalian Hall.

ferry's pilot house. The Scot told a tale about an ancestor of his, one of three Highlanders captured by the British during the American Revolution and imprisoned nearby at colonial Brunswick Town. The three captives were condemned to die, but one of them, the passenger's ancestor, made his escape. The other two were not so lucky.

Soon after the tale was told, Capt. Harper's steamer ran hard aground on a shoal opposite the site of old Brunswick Town. There was nothing to do but wait for the tide to change and keep warm below decks. While they were there, a deck hand burst in, terrified. On deck moments before, he said, he had seen an unkempt man, dripping wet, his face contorted as if in pain. The apparition held the rail with one hand and pointed into the darkness with the other, and when the deck hand went to touch his arm, the man vanished.

Harper doubted the crewman's sobriety. But when the tide had shifted and the ship was again under way, Harper, too, witnessed the impossible. After distinctly hearing a human cry, he and his entire crew spied an old rowing barge with two emaciated men on deck, their injured legs and arms manacled and chained. Harper ordered a rope cast to them, but the barge disappeared into the darkness.

Harper continued on his course and very soon came upon a capsized ship to which two men clung for their lives in the icy, black waters. They were found in the direction in which the first apparition on deck had pointed. With the Scotsman's tale fresh in their minds, Harper's crew rescued the two survivors, the last of a riverboat's crew of seven. Evidently some ghosts, despite their own former suffering, believe in doing good deeds.

The Maco Light

Until the Atlantic Coast Railroad tore up the tracks running west through Maco, many locals living today had witnessed the strange swaying light at the old Maco crossing. President Grover Cleveland spoke about it publicly during his 1888 re-election campaign. *Life* magazine even reported it to the nation in 1957. The story is that of Joe Baldwin, a flagman who, one pitch-dark night in 1867, was riding a caboose that lost its coupling pin. Separated from the train, the caboose had slowed nearly to a halt when Joe spied the light of a speeding passenger train coming right at him. He stood at the back of the caboose waving a lantern in warning, but the oncoming train couldn't stop. In the collision Joe was killed instantly, decapitated. His head was never found, but ever since then, a single swaying light could be seen over the tracks at that very spot. It was seen so frequently that trainmen routinely mounted two lights on their trains, one red and one green, so as not to be confused with the Maco Light, which hasn't been seen since the tracks were lifted. It seems Old Joe Baldwin's warnings are no longer needed.

The House on Gallows Hill

It is said that back when Wilmington barely stretched beyond what is now Third Street, the high ground just off the main road, past the old St. James burial ground, was a hanging ground. Criminals, we're told, who went to their Maker on the hill were buried nearby. But when the town outgrew its former bounds, the old gallows were dismantled and houses constructed, among them the Price-Gause House, built in 1843. Fortunately for its residents, the home's invisible guest is a playful one, occasionally mischievous but never baleful. The ghost, who is lately called George, seems to favor phantom pipe tobacco and spectral sweet potatoes — judging by the smells that occasionally greet the living occupants, employees of an architectural firm. Other incidents? A rocker that rocks itself no matter where it's placed; clearly audible footsteps when no one's there; mysteriously clouding mirrors; and perhaps best of all,

— continued on next page

— continued from previous page

quilts yanked from beds while people lay sleeping. It's a wonder no one hears hearty laughter too.

There are many other ghostly yarns to spin about North Carolina's southern coast — the Edwardian thespians of Thalian Hall; the visitations of Samuel Jocelyn to prove he was buried alive; the phantom Confederate General William Whiting, still leading the defense of Fort Fisher. You can read the stories in books available at regional public libraries and stores: *Tar Heel Ghosts* by John Harden (Chapel Hill: University of North Carolina Press, 1954); *Haunted Wilmington . . . and the Cape Fear Coast* by Brooks Newton Preik (Wilmington, N.C.: Banks Channel Books, 1995); and *Ghosts of the Carolinas* by Nancy Roberts (Columbia: University of South Carolina Press, 1962).

fers to the harvest's "first fruit." For information on events, call the Cape Fear Coast Convention & Visitors Bureau, 341-4030. Public radio WHQR 91.3 FM, 343-1640, broadcasts its own Kwanzaa production, "Season's Griot," created and performed by local storyteller and musician Madafo Lloyd Wilson each year. Tune in or call for details.

Easter

Easter Egg Hunt
Poplar Grove Historic Plantation, 10200 U.S. Hwy. 17 N., Scotts Hill • 686-9518
Young children always get a big thrill out of the annual Easter Egg Hunt. The setting is attractive, and Poplar Grove offers other diversions for the entire family.

Fourth of July

Refer to the chapter on Annual Events for a complete rundown of Independence Day feasts and fireworks.

Birthday Parties

If you're looking for an extra-special place to give your child a memorable birthday party, look into these venues, all of which offer colorful party rooms and services, including the use of the arcades, games and more. Also don't overlook your local bowling center; per-

game prices for children younger than 12 are often discounted. See the "Bowling" section in our chapter on Sports, Fitness and Parks for listings.

Jungle Rapids Family Fun Park
5320 Oleander Drive, Wilmington • 791-0666
Jungle Rapids offers several different birthday packages that vary according to age and price. Choose from packages that include go-carts, laser-tag (for older children), video games or minigolf. Two-hour packages can feature play time, a party in a private party room with a hostess, lunch, cake, a T-shirt for the birthday child, all paper products and balloons.

Putt-Putt Golf & Games
4117 Oleander Drive, Wilmington • 392-6660
Putt-Putt offers special deals for two-hour birthday parties that feature all the golf kids can play in that time. In addition each partygoer receives 16 tokens for video games (20 tokens for the kid of honor). Ice cream, soft drinks, a group photo, use of the party room and a special pizza deal are also included.

Cape Fear Museum
814 Market St., Wilmington • 341-4350
The Cape Fear Museum designs educational theme parties for children.

INSIDERS' TIP

Azalea Festival in April always brings a world-renowned circus to Wilmington — in a real big top!

Photo: Scott Taylor

Crabs can pack a nasty pinch. Watch your toes!

Athletic Zone
4405 Northchase Pkwy., Wilmington • 452-5020

You can combine a game of soccer, basketball, volleyball or roller hockey with your child's birthday party at this indoor sports facility. You supply the party goods and protective sport gear.

Getting Physical

Check the chapter on Sports, Fitness and Parks for information on field and team sports for children of school age. What's included here are physical activities that either apply specifically to young children or would otherwise fall through the cracks of the sports categories. Also, don't overlook the dance opportunities noted above in the "Arts" section.

The Boxing & Fitness Center
602 N. Fourth St., Wilmington • 341-7872

Administered by Wilmington Parks and Recreation Department, the Boxing Center welcomes grade school-age children to participate in fitness training and professionally supervised boxing. Six-week sessions in fitness for overweight youths ages 10 to 15 take place throughout the year after school hours Monday through Friday. Fitness equipment here includes treadmills, Lifecycles, free weights, a universal gym, jump ropes, heavy bags, boxing gloves and scheduled exercise classes — all this for the bargain-basement annual membership price of $10 for city residents, $13 for others.

Fit For Fun
UNCW campus, Wilmington • 341-7855

This is a program sponsored by the Wilmington Recreation Department that affords children ages 18 months to 5 years exercise two days a week, with parental accompaniment. Two sessions, divided by age, take place each week on the UNCW campus on Monday and Wednesday mornings. Soft-soled shoes (sneakers) are required, and class size is limited to 30 children and 30 parents. Cost is low — $1 for Wilmington residents, $1.50 for non-residents — and preregistration is required.

The Kid's Gym
5710 Oleander Dr., Ste. 211, Wilmington • 799-2553

The Kids' Gym offers a variety of noncompetitive, educational gymnastics classes for ages 4 months and up into the teens. Classes also feature numbers, colors and music through the use of obstacles and games — what the staff of certified teachers and gymnasts calls "a physical Sesame Street" — all in a clean, positive atmosphere. A full-day preschool program is also available. Kids' Night Out gives kids and parents an evening to themselves each weekend. The Kids' Gym also facilitates birthday parties hosted by Teddy Tumblebear; half- and full-day summer camps for children ages 3 to 12 (open to nonmembers on a weekly basis and useful to visitors); karate; a nursery; morning preschool (9 AM to noon); postnatal exercise classes for moms; an after-school program; and a gymnastics demonstration team that emphasizes performance rather than competition. Nursery service is also available. Memberships cost $25 per month for one child, $30 a month for two children or more. The Kids' Gym is a member business of U.S. Gymnastics.

The Martin Luther King Jr. Center
410 S. Eighth St., Wilmington • 341-7866

On the third Thursday of each month, Wilmington Parks and Recreation sponsors a sports night, essentially an evening of basketball, from 6 to 8 PM. Other activities include karate, field trips and table tennis (perhaps not everyone's idea of "getting physical").

Getting Wet

As if the ocean weren't enough, Cape Fear offers plenty of other opportunities for kids to douse themselves, and some of them are downright thrilling. We're referring to water slides. One of the best is at the **Jungle Rapids Family Fun Park**, 5320 Oleander Drive, 791-0888, in Wilmington, described at the top of this chapter and in the chapter on Attractions. **Jubilee Park**, 1000 N. Lake Park Boulevard in Carolina Beach, 458-6067, features a popular slide. Also check out their "Rain Room," a place to get nicely misted with drenching on a hot day. In South Brunswick, the **Magic Mountain Water Slide** in Holden Beach, 842-2727, has five killer flumes, and **Ocean Isle Beach** hosts its own water slide on Causeway Drive. Most of these attractions are open seven days a week between Memorial and Labor days, from about 10 AM until 9

PM. Prices hover around $3 and $4 per half-hour, with discounts for longer sessions, ranging from about $8 to $12 for the whole day. Prices usually drop after 5 PM.

Beyond these, kids can find places to get wet in our Watersports and Rentals chapter or our Sports, Fitness and Parks chapter, where local swimming pools are listed.

Going Mental

Babbage's Software
Independence Mall, 3500 Oleander Dr., Wilmington • 791-8168

Babbage's carries a fine selection of video games, CD-ROMs and computer accessories — much of it educational — in addition to its wide range of other computer software for a variety of needs.

Books-A-Million
3737 Oleander Dr., Wilmington • 452-1519

This book superstore adjacent to Office Depot hosts story hours for young children every Saturday at 3 PM. When the children's section is otherwise quiet, kids enjoy playing on the "train-car" benches. The locomotive houses a TV that shows ongoing children's videos to keep kids entertained while mom and dad browse nearby.

Brunswick County Library
Monday: Southport Library, 109 W. Moore St., Southport • 457-6237
Tuesday: Leland Library, 487 Village Rd., Leland • 371-9442
Wednesday: G. V. Barbee Branch Library, 818 Yaupon Dr., Yaupon Beach • 278-4283
Thursday: Rourk Branch, 5068 Main St., Shallotte • 754-6578

Storytimes for children ages 2 through 5 are offered at these Brunswick County public libraries at 10 AM one day each week, according to the schedule above. The Brunswick County Library also hosts a summer reading program for school-aged children. The six-week program involves weekly meetings and activities at the branch libraries and awards incentive prizes. Be sure also to inquire about the library's weekly Preschool Music Hour, offering children the opportunity to sing, move creatively, play instruments, and in doing so, (believe it or not) very possibly improve their spatial abilities and math skills. (Music really does make you smarter!) Participation in all library programs is free.

Sneads Ferry Public Library
242 Sneads Ferry Rd., Sneads Ferry • 327-6471

This branch of the Onslow County Public Library, convenient to northern Topsail Island, invites children ages 3 and older to participate in stories, cartoons, crafts and short movies every Wednesday at 10:30 AM throughout the year, except for six weeks in the summer when the summer reading program kicks in. Reading for the summer program adheres to predetermined themes appropriate for a range of reading levels. All programs are free.

Cape Fear Astronomical Club
Wilmington • 762-1033

Kids old enough to understand that those bright objects in the night sky are incredibly distant will appreciate the occasional sky observations, using members' telescopes,

sponsored by the Astronomical Society to raise interest in membership. Viewing sessions are announced in the calendar of the *Wilmington Star-News*. The public is also invited to the society's monthly meetings that feature interesting films and presentations. Meetings take place on the first Sunday each month (or the second, if delayed by a holiday) and are also announced in the newspaper. The society is open to everyone of any age, regardless of any astronomical knowledge, and young teenagers are among its current members.

In addition to the popular public viewing sessions, the society also undertakes periodic school talks and trips to planetariums. Membership has one prerequisite, if one could call it that: a sincere interest in astronomy and in learning more about it. Memberships cost $20 per year ($25 for families) and include the society's monthly newsletter, *Cape Fear Skies*. Members also participate in picnics and an exhibition booth at Riverfest. The society's mailing address is 305 N. 21st Street, Wilmington 28405.

Carolina Kite Club
Wrightsville Beach • No phone

Is kite-flying an amusement, a physical activity, an art or a nature exploration? We decided it was all of these and therefore deserving of our "Going Mental" section.

There are no better places to fly kites than at the beach, with its steady winds. The Carolina Kite Club is an informal clutch of devotees who gather at the south end of Wrightsville Beach on Sunday mornings in the warmer seasons. Meetings are often announced in the calendar sections of the *Star-News*. For additional information on local kite flying, see the section by that name in the Sports, Fitness and Parks chapter.

Learning Express
5704 Oleander Dr., Wilmington • 397-0301

Learning Express is among those rare places that capture kids' imaginations with high-quality alternatives to the run-of-the-mill products for kids. Interactive and entertaining, the store succeeds in making learning fun for kids from infancy to early adolescence. The staff includes education and child-development professionals with broad knowledge of the products, which translates into excellent service.

Learning Express is organized in sections geared to particular interests, such as Whiz Kids (computer books and software), Science & Nature (including electronics and nature projects), Let's Pretend (fantasy dress-up), Great Beginnings (for infants and toddlers), Transit (including wind-up race cars), etc. This is the place to find that volcano your child needs for the diorama. Ask about professional discounts and gift services. Learning Express, at the Courtyard on Oleander, is open from 9:30 AM to early evening Monday through Saturday. It opens Sunday only during the summer, from 1 to 5 PM.

New Hanover County Public Library Children's Room
Main branch, 201 Chestnut St. • 341-4392
Carolina Beach branch, 300 Cape Fear Blvd. • 458-5016
Myrtle Grove branch, 5155 S. College Rd. • 452-6414
Plaza East Library, Plaza East Shopping Center, Wrightsville Beach • 256-2173

The library is an excellent resource for stimulating entertainment that isn't limited to story times. Activities are designed for children in three age groups. Toddler Time offers stories, songs and interactive finger plays just for babies ages 18 months to 3 years and their parents. Preschooler Storytime may include films and is geared for ages 3 to 5. Book Break is intended for children 6 to 10 years old and presents longer stories, read-alouds, activities and films. All events are offered weekly on different days at different branches of the library, giving you a choice of schedules. The main branch is the only one offering activities all year long. All programs are free and open to the public.

Other library programs are cut from a wide and colorful cloth. Recurring programs include a Babysitter's Workshop, designed to teach young people ages 12 to 15 about babysitting, safety, child development, simple snacks and activities. Family programs may present history as related in song, African dance or readings by children's authors. Call the library's Youth Services office at the number above to inquire about schedules and registration, which may be limited for some workshops.

Seahawk Chess Club
University Union 105, UNCW, 601 S. College Rd., Wilmington • 395-3841

This club, based on the UNCW campus and facilitated by advanced competitors, is a great place for players to sharpen their skills and learn new tactics. Novices and nonstudents are welcome.

Wilmington Table Tennis Association
Tileston School, Fifth and Ann sts., Wilmington • 395-5644

Table tennis players of all ages and skill levels are welcome to join the association on Monday and Wednesday nights from 7 to 9 PM. There is no initial fee to join, and if you don't have your own paddle, the association can usually provide one.

L Bookworm
3004 Holden Beach Rd. S.W., Holden Beach • 842-7380

Barbara and Jim Lowell's bookstore, housed in a converted former church building, is a community gathering place that offers storytimes for children ages 4 through 8 on Wednesdays at 11 AM in the summer. The store also features a good children's section that includes used books at low prices.

School Room

Shallotte Plaza, #7 Main St., Shallotte
• 754-2345

Sure, the professional teacher will find plenty of educational supplies and materials here, but School Room is also a real bonanza for the inquisitive child. School Room stocks a stimulating variety of games ranging from traditional board games to state-of-the-art computer games, science projects, puzzles, educational posters and foreign-language workbooks. There's also a children's section complete with small desk and black board (which we're told the kids love to erase). This small shop is jammed with interesting stuff catering to children from pre-K to junior high. It's next door to Dairy Queen (a potential bargaining chip for parents).

Summer Camps

Day camps and sports camps, rather than overnight camps, are the norm in the southern coastal region. For sports camps, children must own basic personal equipment, including protective gear. Team items such as bats and balls are provided. Be sure to review our chapter on Sports, Fitness and Parks as well. Day campers generally need only swim suits, towels and sneakers to get the most out of their camp experiences.

An extremely useful publication, *Summer Alternatives*, lists dozens of summer activities for school-aged children in our area. It is published in late April by the New Hanover County School board and may be obtained free at any middle and elementary school office and at the Board of Education offices, 1802 S. 15th Street in Wilmington.

Ashton Farm Summer Day Camp

5645 U.S. 117 S., Burgaw • 259-2431

Ashton Farm is 72 acres of historic plantation about 18 miles north of Wilmington. Owners Sally and Jim Martin provide children ages 5 to 13 with down-to-earth fun. Kids participate in farm life, sports with minimized competition and nature. Among the activities are swimming, canoeing, riding, softball, hiking, crafts, animal care, rodeos, archery and ice cream-making. One-week sessions ($75 per week) from June to August are available (daily with permission). Discounts apply for additional weeks and/or additional children registered. A special "Mini Camp" ($40) is available for three days in June for preschoolers. The camp provides round-trip transportation to Wilmington, camper health insurance and drinks. Single-day camps have been added to coincide with school holidays and weekends.

Brigade Boys and Girls Club

2759 Vance St., Wilmington • 791-4282

Between the last day of school and the first day back in the fall, children may share in games, computer activities, arts and crafts and library activities, Monday through Friday from 10 AM to 6 PM. An early program is also available from 6:30 to 10 AM. Cost is about $150 for the summer plus a $25 annual membership.

Cape Fear Museum

814 Market St., Wilmington • 341-4350

A variety of activities involving dinosaurs, local history and nature are available to children ages 5 to 12 in full- and half-day camps at the museum, five days a week from June 10 through August 16. Fees range from $50 to $85 (discounted for museum members).

Girls Incorporated Day Camp

1502 Castle St., Wilmington • 763-6674

Girls Inc. offers half-day and full-day camps in Wilmington and Burgaw. Activities include sports, crafts, swimming, computer classes, sewing, field trips, career exploration, science projects, cooking and guest speakers. The Wilmington camp accepts girls only from kindergarten to age 18. The Burgaw camp accepts boys and girls from kindergarten to age 15. Fees are approximately $40 per week for full-day camp, $25 per week for half-days plus a $10 registration fee. Half-day camps are also available to students year round.

The Kids' Gym

5710 Oleander Dr., Ste. 211, Wilmington
• 799-2553

The Kids' Gym offers summer camp for children ages 3 to 12. Programs include gymnastics, exercise, arts and crafts and field trips and run in two-week sessions or longer. Check with them in early spring for schedules and program information.

National Youth Sport Program at UNCW
601 S. College Rd., Wilmington • 395-3262

Eligibility for this free camp, for children ages 10 through 16, is determined by application (available from school counselors and physical education instructors). Offerings include golf, soccer, swimming, tennis, drug and alcohol awareness, nutrition and career choices. Medical exams are given prior to attendance, and transportation and lunch are provided. The camp runs five days a week from mid-June through mid-July.

University of North Carolina at Wilmington
Athletic Dept., 601 S. College Rd., Wilmington • 395-3232

UNCW sponsors one-week summer sports camps in baseball, basketball, tennis, swimming, volleyball and soccer. Attendees may be as young as 3 years old or as old as seniors in high school. These sessions give younger players a good foundation for the games and emphasize fundamentals. Camps are also available for men's and women's basketball. Camps can be arranged for full or half days and for team or individual instruction. Deposits are required, and prices range from about $75 for a half-day junior session to $250 for full-week adult camps. Call for information early in the season, as these camps tend to be quite popular.

UNCW Summer Science by the Sea Day Camp
601 S. College Rd., Wilmington • 395-3193

Children ages 7 through 12 who are interested in the marine environment and the outdoors may enjoy this university-sponsored day camp. Choose from among nine weekly sessions beginning in early June. Weekly fees begin at $65 for early registration (a bit higher later). In-depth studies of marine life, college-level field and laboratory science, tropical ecosystems, dolphin behavior and even Australia's Great Barrier Reef are also open to more motivated students, ages 11 to 15, through UNCW's various camp offerings. Fees range from $450 to $3,625. Airfare, lodging, meals and amenities may be included, depending on the program. Call for details.

UNCW's University Children's Academy Camps
601 S. College Rd., Wilmington • 395-3195

For children in kindergarten through grade 6, UNCW offers a variety of music camps and arts-and-crafts camps, the latter including basic drawing and investigating cultural art through stories and crafts. Also available are environmental camps that explore the rain forest and endangered, extinct and existing animals for ages 9 through 12. A camp about fairy tales and folk tales is offered for ages 9 through 12 in which participants write and publish their own stories. Fees range from $65 to $85. Most camps last one week, some longer, and meetings range from 90 minutes to four or more hours in the morning.

Wilmington Family YMCA
2710 Market St., Wilmington • 251-9622

Camp Tuscarora is a day camp for children ages 5 to 11 and offers daily trips to nearby Poplar Grove Plantation. Archery, swimming, music and overnight trips are among the many offerings. Camp Seaweed meets at the North Chase subdivision (north of Wilmington) and offers similar activities, except no field trips. Inquire about their "Campership" scholarships and counselor-in-training program (ages to 15). Five two-week sessions begin in mid-June. Costs begin at $60 per week for members, plus a onetime registration fee of $25. Discounts apply when registering more than one child per family.

Kiddy Korner Kinder Kamp is a half-day preschool day camp offering age-appropriate activities to a maximum of 25 participants. Fees are $15 for members, $20 for nonmembers. Weekly and three-day sessions are offered. Scholarships are available.

The Wilmington Hammerheads Professional Soccer Club Clinic and Camp Programs
1630 Military Cutoff Rd., Ste. 200 G-H, Wilmington • 341-5102

In cooperation with the Cape Fear Youth Soccer Association, Wilmington's new professional soccer team, the Hammerheads, offers camps and clinics led by Hammerhead players and staff with coaches from around the country. Sessions are open to boys and girls

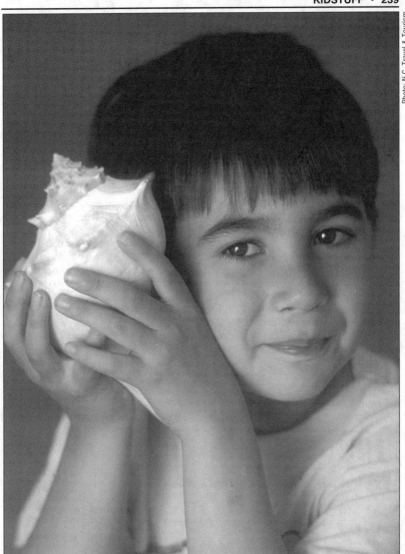

If you listen closely, you can hear the ocean.

of all ages, and some begin in January. Offerings include coach's clinics, training sessions, individual technical training, specialized sessions for strikers and goalkeepers, small-sided and 11-vs.-11 play and scholarship opportunities. Full-week camps (9 AM until 1 PM) cost $75 per player, T-shirt included. Call for schedule information and register early.

**City of Wilmington
Summer Traditions Camp**
302 Willard St., Wilmington • 341-7855
    Arts and crafts, swimming, sports, drama, field trips and other activities for children ages 5 and older are available through Wilmington's Recreation Department at Johnson Elementary School (1100 McRae Street) from mid-

June through early August for less than $70 per week for full days, $40 per week for half days. Children with mental and physical handicaps are welcome.

YWCA of Wilmington
2815 S. College Rd., Wilmington
• 799-6820

Summer day camps for tots and juniors, from kindergarten to age 12, are open weekdays from June through August. Activities include swimming, skating and field trips. Fees begin at $15 per day ($57 per week) plus a parent or guardian membership of $20 and a nonrefundable annual registration fee. Membership is $15 for children 12 and older.

Wrightsville Beach
Parks & Recreation
1 Bob Sawyer Dr., Wrightsville Beach
• 256-7925

Summer Day Camp orchestrates a variety of activities for children ages 6 to 11, including organized games, arts and crafts, field trips and beach fun. Two-week sessions run June through August and require fees beginning at less than $100 for residents.

Brunswick County
Parks & Recreation
Planning Bldg., Brunswick Co. Gov. Complex, 20 Referendum Dr., Bolivia
• 253-4357, (800) 222-4790

Summer sports camps in baseball, soccer and wrestling are offered at various parks in Brunswick County from June through August. Register early.

Eats

The vast majority of restaurants in our region caters to young people by offering well-priced children's menus. Several among them are notable.

Katy's Great Eats
1054 S. College Rd., Wilmington
• 395-5289

Katy's is well-liked by locals and provides families the opportunity to dine together with few diversions beyond some interesting memorabilia, TV and a Foosball table nearby.

If your child is lucky, the one kid-sized booth may be available when you visit.

Causeway Cafe
114 Causeway Dr., Wrightsville Beach
• 256-3730

This is an extremely popular breakfast spot on Wrightsville Beach, just east of the drawbridge. The specialty pancakes and waffles are delectable and can be made in a variety of amusing shapes for children. Arrive early and be sure to ask about the fresh fruit toppings of the day.

Rock-ola Cafe
418 S. College Rd., Wilmington
• 791-4288

Rock-ola takes a tack similar to that of the famous Hard Rock Cafe, with classic rock 'n' roll and decorations but less noise. Its menu includes several selections for children.

Chuck E Cheese's Pizza
4389 Oleander Dr., Wilmington • 392-1234

The ubiquitous Chuck E Cheese's has plenty of diversions to make eating a kid's least concern.

Elizabeth's Pizza
4304 Market St., Wilmington • 251-1005

Kids like the pizza and other Italian dishes, but are fascinated by the several fish tanks that divide the room.

El Vaquero
4238 Market St., Wilmington • 815-0706

The quesadilla and the other items on the children's menu offer a nice change-up from other run-of-the-mill choices, and the virgin daiquiri makes for a colorful, cold dessert.

Sweets

No discussion of kidstuff would be complete without something for the sweet tooth. By sweets we mean not only candy but also baked goods and ice cream. As you travel the coast, you'll be tempted by all manner of strategically placed retailers who will dulcify your day; what follows here are some of the kings and queens of confectionery, the barons of bonbon. Read on at the risk of your waistline. Your kids will love you for it.

Apple Annie's Bake Shop
Outlet Mall, S. College Rd., Wilmington • 799-9023
Landfall Shopping Center, Wrightsville Beach • 256-6585

Two locations mean the satisfaction of a sugar craving will seldom take you too far out of your way. Baking everything fresh daily, Apple Annie's offers a sumptuous array of specialty cakes and cupcakes, cookies and plenty more. Don't pass up their hazelnut-cream-filled Paris brest! This is one of those shops in which the air itself is intoxicating. (Outlet Mall is opposite the south perimeter of the UNCW campus.)

Baskin-Robbins 31 Flavors
Ice Cream and Yogurt Store
3809 Oleander Dr., Wilmington • 791-7192

Baskin-Robbins offers the typical wide variety of flavors, plus frozen yogurt, fat-free desserts and low-fat yogurt cakes.

The Candy Barrel
309 N. Front St., Wilmington • 762-3727

Situated in the Cotton Exchange downtown, The Candy Barrel specializes in taffy, fudge and candy by the pound, including scrumptious homemade chocolate clusters of many kinds. The treats don't come cheap here, but the quality and selection are such that a little goes a long way.

Candy Express
Independence Mall, 3500 Oleander Dr., Wilmington • 791-5089

A dieter's nightmare and a kid's dream come true, Candy Express is a good place to shop for that gumball machine you've always wanted as well as dessert sauces, gift tins and coffee mugs.

The Scoop
Ice Cream & Sandwich Shoppe
The Cotton Exchange, Wilmington • 763-3566

For frozen confections as well as snacks and sandwiches a short walk from

Photo: N.C. Travel & Tourism

Aquariums, touch tanks with living sea creatures, films, field trips and exhibits of the coastal area are featured at the North Carolina Aquarium at Fort Fisher.

Wilmington's riverfront, there's The Scoop. Seating just outside the tiny shop offers an extremely pleasant shaded place in which to enjoy dessert in practically any season. It's a fine stopover for the weary shopper.

Swensen's
620 S. College Rd., Wilmington • 395-6740

San Francisco's contribution to calorie-collecting, Swensen's ranks high (some say highest) among local ice cream parlors. The Outrageous Sundaes are often too much for all but the most voracious. The kids' treat called Mr. San Francisco is an ice cream creation shaped like a clown, with bubble-gum eyes and nose and a chocolate-dipped cone hat. Swensen's is a full-service restaurant and serves a children's menu. A miniature train circles the ceiling of the dining room.

Toms Drug Company
1 N. Front St., Wilmington • 762-3391

We often wonder how many children and their parents walk away from Riverfront Park craving sweets and leaving empty-handed because they didn't know that Toms stocks plenty of candies. Buying sweets in a drugstore makes sense, particularly if chocolate is your drug of choice. Toms offers a good selection.

Vic's Corn Popper
1616 Shipyard Blvd., Wilmington • 452-2869

Popcorn in a sweets listing? You bet, especially if it's Vic's freshly made caramel corn. Vic's is an award-winning popcorn franchise, and you'll find more different kinds of popcorn than you may have seen before.

Wolber's Ice Cream
3 N. Lumina Ave., Wrightsville Beach • 256-3770

In a former trolley car in the center of "downtown" Wrightsville Beach, Wolber's serves all manner of ice cream treats, snow cones and soft drinks during the warm season from mid-April through early October. Off-season, check into Wolber's Garden Deli, 256-3770, right across the street.

Ms. Muffet's Yogurt Shop
7110 Wrightsville Ave., Wrightsville Beach • 256-6031

One of the few yogurt shops around with a drive-up window, Ms. Muffet's offers a great selection of rich frozen yogurts, a smorgasbord of toppings and fat-free and cholesterol-free indulgences. Ms. Muffet's, in the Cross Point Plaza shopping center, is convenient to Wrightsville Beach and has indoor seating and plenty of parking.

Dairy Queen
201 N. Fort Fisher Blvd., Kure Beach • 458-9788

This "full treat" establishment, one block from the ocean, features a spacious, shady porch with plenty of bench seating, handicap access and ample parking. Did we mention great ice cream?

Seven Seas Ice Cream
126 N. Fort Fisher Blvd., Kure Beach • 458-8122

Seven Seas offers locally made hand-scooped ice cream and ice-cream desserts. Treats can be enjoyed at tables out front. Seven Seas is part of the Seven Seas Inn, and it's open seven days a week in summer.

Fudge Company
201 New River Dr., Surf City • 328-1905

The Fudge Company at Topsail Trading Company makes a variety of fresh, cream-and-butter fudge to die for — more than 30 flavors, in fact, including sucrose-free.

Yogurt Plus
208 N. New River Dr., Surf City • 328-1224

The yogurt here tastes so good, the kids may not care that it's good for them. Fat-free, sugar-free and cholesterol-free desserts are the specialty here, and it all tastes wonderfully sinful.

Back Porch Ice Cream Shoppe
1572 Thomasboro Rd., Calabash • 579-1533

Back Porch, across from Callahan's Gift Shop, serves 21 hand-dipped ice cream and yogurt flavors, homemade waffle cones and plenty of other delights. Try the Hawaiian Ice.

Back Deck Grill
311 S. Topsail Dr., Surf City • 328-0500

Thick shakes and large fresh-baked brownies that stand up well to ice cream are just some of the delights your kids will enjoy at the Back Deck. You can also get egg creams (a Yankee concoction having no egg), 24 flavors of soft and hand-dipped ice cream as well as full lunches and dinners with a can't-miss kids' menu ranging from peanut butter-and-jelly sandwiches to fish 'n' chips and steaks. The Back Deck Grill has an excellent soundside view and is open seven days a week in summer. (There's even live music in the evenings on Friday and Saturday. Don't tell the kids!) The Grill is a quarter-mile south of the Surf City traffic light.

Shopping is probably tied for first place with sunshine when it comes to the Grand Strand's most popular attractions.

Daytrips

It is beyond our ken why anyone would want to go beyond North Carolina's southern coast when there's so much to do and see right here. Yet an urge comes now and then to explore and, luckily, interesting destinations are close enough for a daytrip. The following are teasingly brief overviews of two coastal destinations — Myrtle Beach, South Carolina, and North Carolina's Central Coast. Use them as pointers for planning your daytrip. For complete information on these areas, pick up copies of *The Insiders' Guide® to Myrtle Beach and The Grand Strand* and *The Insiders' Guide® to North Carolina's Central Coast and New Bern*, or call (800) 955-1860 to order either book.

Myrtle Beach

For decades the Grand Strand, stretching nearly unbroken for 60 sun-drenched miles from the Little River south to historic Georgetown, has been the standard by which all other beach resorts are measured. As a tourist destination, it rivals Orlando and Las Vegas. Myrtle Beach's permanent, year-round population of only 28,000 hosted an estimated 13 million visitors in 1996. On a single summer's day that year, a cool 572,000 visitors were counted. Such magnetism is undoubtedly due to the town's abundance of lodging, dining and shopping opportunities, its world-class golf courses, a profusion of amusements, and its ideal weather and magnificent beaches.

For the daytripper, the Strand's entertainment nerve center is Myrtle Beach. For a mile on either side of the Pavilion, the focus of downtown Myrtle Beach is Ocean Boulevard, a hotbed of activity. It's understandable that Wilmingtonians look upon Myrtle Beach with equal amounts of interest and relief that their hometown is so different. Interestingly more North Carolinians visit Myrtle Beach than visitors from any other state, including South Carolina.

Myrtle Beach is approximately 72 miles from downtown Wilmington, a drive of little more than 90 minutes. U.S. Highway 17 is the artery that gets you there.

Before entering Myrtle Beach proper, the length of U.S. 17 (here called Kings Highway) is known as Restaurant Row, where dining establishments stand shoulder to shoulder. There are more than 1,500 restaurants along the Grand Strand. Along with all the usual regional specialties, you'll find other samples of Southern fare such as chicken bog (chicken, seasoned rice and sausage), she-crab soup, alligator stew and crawfish. All-you-can-eat buffets are ubiquitous, so bring your appetite.

The Myrtle Beach Area Chamber of Commerce operates four information centers where you can pick up, or order, scads of information about the area:

Myrtle Beach Office, 1200 N. Oak Street, Myrtle Beach, (803) 626-7444

North Myrtle Beach Office, 213 U.S. Highway 17 N., North Myrtle Beach, (803) 249-3519

South Strand Office, 3401 S. Highway 17 Business, Murrells Inlet, (803) 651-1010

Official Grand Strand Welcome Center, 2090 U.S. Highway 501 E. at Horry-Georgetown Technical College, Conway, (803) 626-6619

To request brochures only from the Chamber, call (800) 356-3016.

The South Carolina Welcome Center on U.S. 17 near Little River is a convenient place for daytrippers from the Cape Fear area to gather brochures about the Grand Strand or about South Carolina in general. Many of the publications contain discount coupons that are good at dozens of Grand Strand locations.

Shopping

Shopping is probably tied for first place with sunshine when it comes to the Grand Strand's most popular attractions. The area is replete with shops and boutiques of every description and specialty, but it's the discount shops and factory outlet stores that garner the most renown.

More than at any other single location, shoppers wear their plastic thin at the mammoth **Outlet Park at Waccamaw**, a three-mall complex equal in size to five football fields. The park houses 125 factory stores, movie theaters and an enormous food court. It's the home of Waccamaw Pottery (a home decor superstore) and Waccamaw Linen. Outlet Park is on Highway 501 immediately west of the Intracoastal Waterway. There's even an on-site hotel for those who live — and vacation — to shop.

Another popular shopping mecca, consisting of 120 shops, factory-direct stores and restaurants, is the attractive **Barefoot Landing**, on U.S. 17 in North Myrtle Beach. The complex also houses children's rides; the **Alabama Theatre**, (803) 272-1111, home of the musical group by the same name; the **Barefoot Princess Riverboat**, (803) 272-7743; and **Alligator Adventure**, (803) 361-0789, a zoo of regional and exotic reptiles, amphibians and birds. All of it surrounds a lake and borders the Intracoastal Waterway.

Forty-seven discount outlets await you at the **Myrtle Beach Factory Stores**, on Highway 501 N., (803) 236-5100, about 3 miles west of the Intracoastal Waterway. Among the newer outlet complexes, this includes the "Off Fifth" Saks Fifth Avenue and Lenox China.

Attractions

More than a mere attraction, the **Myrtle Beach Pavilion Amusement Park**, on the oceanfront at Ninth Avenue N., (803) 448-6456, is the symbolic heart of Myrtle Beach. Just a few blocks south, the **Family Kingdom Amusement Park**, 300 Fourth Avenue S., (803) 626-3447, is another classic. Along the oceanfront the Boardwalk offers an array of shops, food stands and nightlife. Myrtle Beach is also home to some of the more outrageous

miniature golf courses you'll see anywhere — more than 40 in all. Simply cruising the Boulevard is so popular among the swimsuit-clad that at peak hours, traffic seldom approaches the 25 mph speed limit. Visitors are drawn by the thousands to the batting cages, go-cart tracks, arcades, water parks, amusement rides, wacky museums, souvenir shops and attractions.

Myrtle Waves Water Park, 3000 10th Avenue N. Extension, (803) 448-1026, open from mid-April to mid-September, is among the larger and more popular water parks. The **Myrtle Beach Grand Prix**, 3201 S. Kings Highway, (803) 238-4783, features go-carts, speed boats and the exhilarating Hydro Racer. A single fee to Myrtle Waves also grants admission to **Wild Water and Wheels**, 910 U.S. 17 S., (803) 238-9453, in Surfside Beach, about 6 miles south of Myrtle Beach. Don't overlook the boating, kayaking and sightseeing opportunities available on the nearby waterways. There are also some worthwhile historic attractions.

The city of Myrtle Beach provides 10 beach wheelchairs and maintains dune crossovers to the beach at 15 locations between 28th Avenue S. and 81st Avenue N. Beach wheelchairs are kept at lifeguard stations during the summer. During the off-season, inquire at the Police Department. Their use is free for the asking. Time restrictions may apply in summer.

Brookgreen Gardens, 1931 Brookgreen Gardens Drive, Murrells Inlet, (803) 237-4218, listed on the National Register of Historic Places, is the first and largest permanent outdoor installation of American figurative sculpture and demands a visit. Brookgreen is a 9,000-acre arboretum, wildlife preserve, aviary and museum rolled into one, so pack a picnic lunch. Brookgreen boasts more than 500 works by hundreds of top-name sculptors and continues to expand in scope. Guided tours, lectures and occasional workshops and concerts are offered. Brookgreen Gardens is 18 miles south of Myrtle Beach, off U.S. 17. The gardens are open daily, except Christmas, from 9:30 AM to 4:45 PM, and there is an admission charge.

Myrtle Beach Speedway, 4300 U.S. 501, (803) 236-0500, is, for auto-racing fans, the

Photo: Scott Taylor

While in Beaufort, take a look across Taylor's Creek on the downtown waterfront for a glimpse of the wild horses.

real thing: a nationally ranked track that hosts weekly races from March through September, including the NASCAR Winston Racing series, the NASCAR Dash, the Busch Grand National in mid-June and the 400-lap All Pro in late November.

The **Hurricane Fleet**, (803) 249-3571, offers a variety of cruise opportunities originating from the Little River Marina, (803) 249-7775, in Little River, South Carolina (a short drive from Calabash). Their Adventure Cruises take to inshore waters where passengers get a close-up glimpse of fishing vessels and shrimpers at work. Breakfast cruises offer an open-boat buffet or à la carte morning meals for $16, which includes tax and tip. Dance cruises sail Tuesday, Thursday, Friday and Saturday evenings and cost $29.75 per person. Country Barbecue cruises take place weekly in season and include dinner with all the trimmings for $20 per adult and $15 per child. Inquire about other cruises.

Head boats are also available at **Captain Dick's Marina**, 4123 U.S. 17 Business in Murrells Inlet, (803) 651-3676. Captain Dick's also offers sightseeing cruises, ocean speedboat rides, watercraft rentals and parasailing.

Entertainment

Nightlife and Myrtle Beach are practically synonymous. Live music, dancing, dinner attractions and stage shows form the core of one of the most active seaside scenes anywhere, and there are plenty of open-air bars along the boardwalk in which to relax over a drink with the sound of the surf as the backdrop.

All the fun is not reserved for adults. Non-alcoholic nightspots such as **The Attic**, (803) 448-6456, a club at the Pavilion, cater to kids younger than 21 who enjoy dancing, music and socializing.

The preeminent dinner attractions and live theaters in the area are quite touristy, and ticket prices pack a wallop, but the shows are consistently well-done and family-friendly. Reservations are recommended for all of them. The first of its kind in the area, the **Carolina Opry**, at the north junction of U.S. 17 Bypass and

U.S. 17 Business, (803) 238-8888, is one of the state's top tourist attractions. Shows offer a mix of comedy and music — standard country hits, bluegrass, gospel and medleys drawn from popular oldies — plus special Christmas shows.

A new attraction is the **Eddie Miles Theater**, 701 Main Street in North Myrtle Beach, (803) 280-6999, featuring impressions of Elvis and a different musical program each night.

Legends in Concert, 301 U.S. 17 Business S. in Surfside Beach, (803) 238-7827, is a Vegas-style musical extravaganza featuring impersonations of famous performers of yesterday and today. For reservations call (800) 960-7469.

In the 1970s a then-unknown group named Alabama played for tips at the Bowery in downtown Myrtle Beach, earning a loyal following. Having since become national superstars, Alabama has made their home base the 2,200-seat **Alabama Theatre**, 4750 U.S. 17 S., (803) 272-1111 or (800) 342-2262, at Barefoot Landing in North Myrtle Beach. The American Pride Show, performed there six nights a week, features music (country and rock), comedy and dancing.

One of the area's two dinner attractions, the **Dixie Stampede**, 8901-B U.S. 17 Business, (803) 497-9700, owned by Dolly Parton, is a theatrical icon of Southern culture, complete with music, horsemanship and a colorful depiction of the conflict between the North and South. The 90-minute show is complemented by dinner. Shows are staged from February through December at 5 PM (7 PM during the summer).

Fantasy Harbour-Waccamaw, on U.S. 501, is one of Myrtle Beach's largest entertainment complexes including the **Gatlin Brothers Theatre**, (803) 236-8800, showcasing the Grammy Award-winning country music trio; the **Ronnie Milsap Theatre**, (803) 236-1303; **Snoopy's Magic On Ice**, (803) 236-4400, a glitzy, professional ice-skating and illusions show; and the **Cercle Theatre**, (803) 236-1740, with

world-famous impressionist Rich Little presiding. One booking service can handle ticket orders for these attractions: call (803) 236-8500 or (800) 681-5209. Also at Fantasy Harbour is **Medieval Times Dinner & Tournament**, (803) 236-8080 or (800) 436-4386, a medieval version of the dinner attraction.

One of the grandest entertainment complexes anywhere is **Broadway At The Beach**, on U.S. 17 Bypass at 21st Avenue N. This 350-acre attraction includes no fewer than nine nightclubs, the 2,700-seat Carolina Palace Theater, the Ripley's Sea Aquarium, the IMAX Discovery Theater, twelve restaurants (including a Planet Hollywood and a pyramidal Hard Rock Cafe), a 23-acre lake featuring water taxi tours and pedal boats, the Carolinas' largest movie complex (the sixteen-screen Carmike Cineplex), a Hampton Inn and oodles of shopping. For information call (800) FUN-IN-MB. Call (803) 444-3200 for a free visitors guide.

The shag was named the Official State Dance in 1984. It is so closely identified with beach music (a derivative of old rhythm and blues) that locals contend the dance came first. The dance did engender the **Society of Stranders** (S.O.S.), (803) 782-7582, an organization of the Association of Carolina Shag Clubs. The society's annual Spring Safari in April and the Autumn Migration in October attract thousands of shaggers doing their thing on Main Street in North Myrtle Beach, a reputed birthplace of the shag. In January shaggers compete in the National Shag Dance Championships, part of the S.O.S. Mid-Winter Classic.

Studebaker's, 21st Avenue N., (803) 448-9747, is a popular place to shag and attracts a relatively mature crowd. Studebaker's features a large dance floor, and DJs spin 30 years of "nonstop bop." Studebaker's is open every day until the wee hours.

2001, 920 Lake Arrowhead Road off U.S. 17 at the north end of Myrtle Beach, (803) 449-9434, is a private club for members and their guests. 2001 boasts three different clubs

INSIDERS' TIP

Residents of Harkers Island on the Central Coast are descendents of a whaling community that existed on Shackleford Banks before a hurricane swept over their community in the late 19th century.

under one roof, including a high-tech dance club, an oldies and beach music club and a very lively piano bar. 2001 offers valet parking, plus an on-site deli for those late-night munchies. Guests may move freely from club to club.

Golf

With nearly one hundred courses, some designed by the top names in the game, the area's self-proclaimed title as the Golf Capital of the World is well-justified (3.9 million paid rounds were played in 1995!). And although the courses' popularity sometimes translates into crowds and waiting time, their prices are too competitive to be ignored. There are also plenty of driving ranges, par 3 courses and pro shops scattered up and down the Strand. Greens fees are lowest from November through February, and golf packages are accordingly most affordable during that time. The Chamber of Commerce, (803) 626-7444, can provide details on packages, or you can call (800) 845-4653 for Myrtle Beach Golf Holiday's free 152-page Golf Vacation Planner. You may also want to pick up a copy of The Insiders' Guide® to Golf in the Carolinas to find detailed information about some of the area's best courses.

Among the annual golf highlights is the four-day, 72-hole **DuPont World Amateur Handicap Championship**. Played on 50 area courses, it is the largest tournament of its kind. Call (800) 833-8798 for information.

Other local annual tournaments include the **Mark A. Sloan Memorial Cancer Benefit Golf Tournament**, (803) 449-0015, played in August. The **Energizer Senior Tour Championship**, (803) 444-4782, is played in November. The **Charles Tilghman Junior Tournament**, (803) 249-1524, is played in early December.

A useful publication for planning a visit to Myrtle Beach around one of the many events held there annually is Grand Strand Festivals, Events, and Tournaments: The Myrtle Beach Area, published by the Myrtle Beach Area Chamber of Commerce, (803) 626-7444. The booklet includes information on fishing and golf tournaments as well as sport, art, and cultural festivals.

North Carolina's Central Coast

Within two hours, north by northeast up the Ocean Highway (U.S. Highway 17) from Wilmington, are a multitude of daytripper possibilities that promise fascinating maritime themes. The area known as the Crystal Coast (Bogue Banks, Morehead City and quaint Beaufort) and historic New Bern with the sprawling banks of the Neuse River as it spills into the Pamlico Sound, offer endless opportunities to enjoy this special part of the North Carolina coastline and adjacent waters.

The Crystal Coast shares much in common with the Cape Fear Coast. Both areas boast beautiful, significant rivers; both have miles of oceanside communities; both have great opportunities for dining; and, of course, both have deep historical roots. However, they are different enough to make visiting each of them a unique experience.

If you have access to a boat — large or small, power or sail — the trip to the Crystal Coast from Wilmington will take longer than two hours. But if you enjoy beautiful coastal scenery, you will find this a very relaxing trip. A fast powerboat can transport you to Morehead City in a matter of four to five hours on the Intracoastal Waterway. A sailboat will take the better part of the day from sunrise to sunset before you are safely berthed for the night. If the weather turns foul, you should plan two days to reach Morehead City, and three to get into the Neuse River near New Bern up a section of the ICW. With the exception of this passage that connects the ocean with the Neuse River, there are many marinas along the way that welcome transient boaters.

By car simply head up U.S. 17. Veer off U.S. 17 onto N.C. Highway 172 and cut through the Marine base, Camp Lejeune, near Jacksonville. People who have never been on a military base will find this an unusual environment, with tank-crossing signs and trucks filled with Marines training in artillery practice. The sentries at the gate used to issue passes but they seem to have decided to do away with paperwork and just give a continual salute.

After crossing the base, go east on N.C. Highway 24 toward Beaufort. It is a trip of less than 100 miles from Wilmington, and there are many views of North Carolina's waters and charming coastal communities along the way.

Swansboro

Swansboro, an historic coastal town that dates back to the early 18th century, is a pleasant stopover after about an hour of travel from Wilmington. Situated on the White Oak River and the Intracoastal Waterway, this lovely little town is surrounded by water. It becomes quickly obvious that the town is in love with boating. The public access boat ramp is jammed with trucks and trailers, and the waters teem with commercial and pleasure craft.

Swansboro has a particularly attractive downtown historic area lined with antiques shops, art galleries and restaurants. Look for signs leading to the district just off N.C. 24, and enter the area that is concentrated within three blocks on the shores of the White Oak River. Parking is free, the merchants are friendly, there are lots of interesting things to buy, and this is an altogether delightful spot to visit.

Bogue Banks

Back on N.C. 24, travel another 20 minutes until N.C. Highway 58 appears on the right. This is the southern entrance to Bogue Banks. You'll cross a dramatic fixed bridge that gives nearly a bird's-eye view of the Intracoastal Waterway. The communities along approximately 20 miles of the island are widely varied. **Emerald Isle** is heavily residential with attractive homes. **Indian Beach** is largely trailer parks. **Salter Path** is a jumble of commercial and residential land uses.

Pine Knoll Shores is an exclusive residential area of windswept live oaks and kudzu with attractive single-family homes and condominiums as well as hotels and the occasional restaurant. This beach also offers the

North Carolina Aquarium at Pine Knoll Shores, (919) 247-4003, a lively facility that includes a "Living Shipwreck," a touch tank, salt-marsh explorations and workshops on surf fishing. At the northern end of the island is **Atlantic Beach**, a smorgasbord of beach amenities that includes an amusement park with a Ferris wheel, a civil war fort, a fishing pier, shopping opportunities, fast food places, restaurants and motels.

Morehead City

Cross over the bridge at the northern end of Bogue Banks and enter Morehead City, home to the North Carolina State Port Authority — another thing Wilmington and the Crystal Coast have in common — and a multitude of restaurants specializing in fresh seafood. The undisputed traditional leader of dining in Morehead City is the **Sanitary Fish Market**, 501 Evans Street, (919) 247-3111. The restaurant seats 600 diners and serves fresh broiled or fried seafoods, homemade chowders and Tar Heel hush puppies that truly melt in your mouth. **The Charter Restaurant**, (919) 726-9036, also on the waterfront, serves delicious crab cakes, stuffed shrimp and flounder, prime rib and a salad bar seven days a week.

Beaufort

Just a few miles from Morehead City is the magical town of Beaufort. Beaufort is so gorgeous that it seems more like a postcard than a real place. This little laid-back coastal community nestles up to international waters and is a gateway from the Atlantic Ocean to American waterways. Taylor's Creek, the body of water in front of the town's quaint commercial district, is filled with sailcraft and powerboats from all over the world. Just up Taylor's Creek, you can catch sight of a menhaden fishing fleet. Beyond it is the Core Sound and a view of Harker's Island, home to some of this country's earliest shipbuilders.

INSIDERS' TIP

The Hammocks Beach State Park ferry carries passengers only to a pristine barrier island just off N.C. Highway 24 west of Swansboro. This 25-minute crossing is just $2 for adults.

Photo: Scott Taylor

The coastal environment is a feast for the observant eye.

This daytripper's favorite pursuit is sitting at the **Dock House** in downtown Beaufort overlooking Taylor's Creek, ordering a scrumptious shrimp burger or taco salad, listening to local music, usually live, and watching the boats at anchor or the ones that come and go in this busy maritime environment. As you munch on delicious, inexpensive food, there is excitement at suddenly noticing the wild horses that wander around on Carrot Island across Taylor's Creek. The horses are stocky, furry steeds that pretty much care for themselves on their little windswept island. In a world where horses are rarely seen running free, this is a stirring sight. If you want a closer vantage point, the **Shackleford Banks and Carrot Island Ferry Service**, departing from Harpoon Willie's Dock at the foot of Orange Street, 728-6888, will be happy to take you over for a fee. There are also boat tours, all readily apparent at the Beaufort Docks.

The island chain across from the Beaufort Waterfront is part of the **Rachel Carson Estaurine Research Reserve**. Free guided tours are offered each month from April to August. Inquire at the **North Carolina Maritime Museum**, 315 Front Street, (919) 728-7317, about tour times. One catch: You have

to provide your own water transportation to get to the island. If you use the ferry service, expect to pay up to $12 for a round-trip journey, but remember the island tour is free.

The sheer beauty of the scenery at the Beaufort waterfront is enough to lull a visitor into sitting in a pleasant trance for a long time, but there is also the allure of nearby shops and attractions. Within an easy walk are stores, many appealing restaurants, the **North Carolina Maritime Museum**, the **Beaufort Restoration Grounds** and a delightful neighborhood of historic homes. The visitor who wants to stay overnight — and who wouldn't? — can find gracious bed and breakfast accommodations right in the heart of this area.

Shoppers will enjoy a variety of stores along the waterfront. **Handscapes Gallery**, Somerset Square, 400 Front Street, sells an attractive assortment of North Carolina pottery, jewelry, wood, glass and paintings. Next door in the same building, the **Rocking Chair Bookstore** has a fine selection of books for children and adults. **Scuttlebutt**, 433 Front Street, sells a large selection of books about the sea and boating. NOAA charts, cruising guides and chartbooks make this a must-stop for passing boaters. **Chadwick House**, 119 Turner Street, has delightful gifts for the home

Photo: Scott Taylor

Waters off North Carolina's coast beckon visitors from all over the world.

and garden including lamps, prints, paintings, linens and garden ornaments.

Diners will be overwhelmed with restaurant possibilities on just one daytrip. The **Beaufort Grocery Co.**, 117 Queen Street, (919) 728-3899, a lunch and dinner restaurant, offers fine dining and a full delicatessen. Breads and desserts are baked daily. The **Front Street Grill** on the Beaufort waterfront at 419 Front Street, (919) 728-3118, has a reputation as an interesting restaurant that uses unusual spices in fresh presentations of seafood, chicken, pasta and homemade soups. The **Spouter Inn**, 218 Front Street, (919) 728-5190, is a charming spot where diners enjoy a memorable clam chowder, creative seafood specialties and a great view thanks to its waterfront location. **Clawson's 1905 Restaurant**, 429 Front Street, 728-2133, long a dining fixture on the Beaufort waterfront, expanded dramatically in 1996 and serves wonderful all-American fare.

New Bern

The small city of New Bern lies along the Neuse River, a gorgeous, deep body of water that is quite different from the Cape Fear River. The Neuse River, 3 miles wide at points, is the largest river in North Carolina. As any sailor will tell you, this is absolute sailing paradise. From New Bern down to the Pamlico Sound, sailors of virtually any level of competency enjoy the experience with little worry about running aground or bumping into the shore. The vast expanse of the river, coupled with some of the finest shoreline amenities on the East Coast, creates a perfect environment for all boaters.

Car travelers will appreciate the lovely view of the river and will certainly enjoy the many opportunities to shop, dine and stay overnight in historic New Bern, which was settled by the Swiss in 1710. Reach it by car from Beaufort by taking U.S. 70 North and slipping off immediately onto U.S. 17 into New Bern. You may be interested to know that New Bern is the place where Pepsi Cola was invented. This rather sleepy little town was the site of the first public schools, the first meeting of the North Carolina Legislature and the state's first bank.

The biggest tourist attraction in New Bern is **Tryon Palace**. Built in 1770 for the Colonial governor William Tryon, the palace burned in 1798 but was reconstructed in the 1950s according to the original architectural plans. The palace is furnished with objects dating from the third quarter of the 18th century. These rare English and American antiques were selected to approximate an inventory of Gov. Tryon's possessions made two years after he left New Bern to become governor of the colony of New York.

Tryon Palace and its many historic sites are open year round, with the exception of major holidays, and include tours, historical dramas and crafts demonstrations. For information, call (919) 514-4900 or (800) 767-1560, or write Tryon Palace Historic Sites and Gardens, P.O. Box 1007, New Bern 28563.

Watersports

It is said that once you get salt water in your veins, you'll never leave, and no wonder. The waters of this part of the Atlantic are warmed by the Gulf Stream, which not only makes for long seasons for watersports, but also brings a surprising array of tropical sea life. North Carolina's beaches are arguably the finest on the Eastern seaboard, given the combination of mild weather, warm water temperatures, good water quality, clean, uncrowded beaches and availability of services. With the breadth of watersports available in our region, sports enthusiasts can splurge. Even whitewater rafting in North Carolina's mountains is available to locals at reasonable prices through Wilmington Parks and Recreation Department, 343-3685. The opportunities are limited only by your desire and stamina. But you need to be aware of local ordinances.

For example, swimming and surfing within 100 feet of most fishing piers are forbidden (less of a problem this season, thanks to last year's two hurricanes), and walking on protected dunes carries a minimum $50 fine. Some beaches do not allow any dogs on the beach during the summer season, while others are more accommodating, usually off-season, if the animals are leashed. The sections that follow tell you more about local variations (also see the Fishing chapter).

The Boating section of this chapter includes details on safety, rentals and boaters' maps and charts. Be sure to check the Fishing chapter for information on the locations of boat ramps. The point is, every section relating to water activities will complement your primary interest.

Personal Watercraft

If you've got your own water buggy, there are beach access points on Wrightsville Beach suitable for beach trailers. One of the easiest is at the foot of Causeway Drive (straight ahead from the fixed bridge). Another is the paved access to the left of the Oceanic Restaurant on S. Lumina Avenue, provided there are no volleyball tournaments that day. On Topsail Island access points are fewer, largely due to dune erosion. Your best bet would be the crossover near the center of Surf City.

All the rental craft available in our area launch into the Intracoastal Waterway. Be sure to respect the limitations set by the individual rental services. They must operate within the parameters of their permits.

If you own your own jet scooter, be aware that North Carolina requires it be registered. See the Boat Registration section below. Also, stay out of shallow waters, especially at low tides. Not doing so contributes to the destruction of oyster beds and other marsh wildlife.

Rentals

Performance Watercraft
Wilmington • 799-WAVE

Performance delivers jet craft (sit-down models) to Wilmington-area waterways year round; so at least a day's notice is your best bet. It also organizes jet-craft tours of the Cape Fear River and the Northeast Cape Fear, and an experienced guide will accompany you if you desire. Crafts include Sea-Doos, Polaris and Yamaha Wave models. Hourly and daily rates begin at $45, and a credit card and a driver's license are required to place a deposit. Patrons must be 25 years old to rent and 16 years old to operate the craft. Travelers' checks are welcomed, and group rates are available.

Dockside Watersports
100 Spencer Farlow Dr., Carolina Beach • 458-0220

Dockside rents Polaris and Yamaha craft, beginning at less than $50 per hour, and offers special three-hour packages. Board right at the dock at Snow's Cut Marina. Reserve in advance to ride any day of the week, April through October, from 9 or 10 AM until dusk. (Off-season, ask about availability.) A credit card is required. (Dockside also rents boats, canoes and windsurfers; check the appropriate sections in this chapter.) Spencer Farlow Drive is beneath the Snow's Cut bridge; when driving south, make a 180-degree turn at the first exit.

Ocean Isle Marina
43 Causeway Dr., Ocean Isle Beach • 579-0848

You can rent Waverunners from the marina office/tackle shop starting at around $40 for the first hour. Most major credit cards are accepted but not required.

Sunset Watersports
301 Sunset Blvd., Sunset Beach • 579-7365

This shop has a limited supply of Waverunners, which calls for early reservations.

Topsail Water Sports
1184 N. Anderson Blvd., Topsail Beach • 328-1141

This service has been popular since the mid-1980s. It rents late-model Waverunners and Jet Skis starting at around $30 per half-hour and $50 per hour. Reservations are suggested, and most major credit cards are accepted. It's open seven days a week from April

to October. You'll find them opposite the Topsail Motel.

S & S Water Sports Inc.
Davis St. and Channel Blvd., Topsail Beach • 328-7751

S & S Water Sports is at the Breezeway Motel and rents Waverunners for $30 per half-hour and $50 per hour. It is open seven days a week during the warm season starting at about 9:30 AM. Grab one of their rack cards at visitors centers and restaurants and receive a $5 discount on the hourly rate.

Boating

At times boating in the lower Cape Fear involves competition with oceangoing vessels, thin water or the treacherous shoals that won the Carolina coast the moniker "Graveyard of the Atlantic." In contrast, the upper Cape Fear River, its northeast branch and the winding creeks of the coastal plain offer a genuine taste of the old Southeast to those with small boats or canoes. Tannins leached from the cypresses keep these waters the color of coffee. Many creeks are overhung by trees, moss and, in summer, the occasional snake. Early spring and late autumn are particularly good times to go, since they are bug-free. See the chapter on Fishing for boat ramp locations.

The U.S. Coast Guard Auxiliary conducts free Courtesy Motorboat Examinations (CME). The exams are not required for boat registration. For information, call 395-1865, or the Marine Safety Office at 343-4882. You will be referred to the examining flotilla officer nearest you. Local chapters of the nonprofit U.S. Power Squadrons (USPS), America's largest private boating association, also offer the USPS Boating Course on a regular basis in Wilmington, Wrightsville Beach, Hampstead, Southport and Shallotte. The $20 fee includes materials, and you need not be a USPS member to participate. For information on the USPS classes closest to you, call (800) 336-BOAT.

For ship-to-shore calling along the Cape Fear Coast, contact the Wilmington Marine

Operator on channel 26. For shore-to-ship calls dial 726-1070.

To report emergencies to the Coast Guard, all initial radio calls should be made on channel 16/158.8 mhz. The Wrightsville Beach Coast Guard station's telephone number is 256-3469.

An excellent resource for boaters of all kinds is the *North Carolina Coastal Boating Guide*, compiled by the N.C. Department of Transportation. Obtain a free copy by calling (919) 733-2520; ask for the Map Department.

Among the several marine communications servicers in Wilmington, Ship and Shore Communications Inc., 6337 Oleander Drive, 350-0014 or 350-0015, is one to note. Dealing in complete two-way electronics, Ship and Shore sells and services navigation and positioning devices (including GPS), depth finders and fish finders. It carries a complete line of CB and VHF radios, radar, LORAN and auto pilot. The store, across from Bradley Creek Marina, is open every day except Sunday in the high season.

Boat Registration

North Carolina requires that motorized craft of any size (including water-jet craft) and sailboats 14 feet and longer be registered. The cost is $8 per year, $20 for three years. Renewal forms are mailed about two months prior to expiration. Titles are optional ($20). Further information on boating regulations may be obtained from the N.C. Wildlife Resources Commission Boat Registration Section, 512 N. Salisbury Street, Raleigh, N.C. 27604-1188, (800) 628-3773. The following businesses and offices can provide the necessary forms and information:

Canady's Sports Center, 3220 Wrightsville Avenue, Wilmington, 791-6280

Johnson Marine Services, 2029 Turner Nursery Road, Wilmington, 686-7565

N.C. Department of Motor Vehicles License Plates Office, 14689 U.S. Highway 17 S., Hampstead, 270-9010

Stewart Hardware, 1635 Howe Street, Southport, 457-5544

Shallotte Marine Supplies, Main Street, Shallotte, 754-6962

Motorboat Rentals

If you would like to rent a power boat, note that advance reservations are essential in summer. Most proprietors require a deposit, a valid drivers' license or major credit card, plus a signed waiver of liability.

Dockside Watersports
100 Spencer Farlow Dr., Carolina Beach
• 458-0220

Dockside Watersports rents 14-foot john boats and 19-foot center-console outboards. Rentals are available any day of the week, April to October 1, from 9 or 10 AM until dusk, and off-season by appointment. Four-hour rentals begin at around $70 for the smaller craft and about $170 for the larger. Dockside is at the Snow's Cut Marina. Reserve in advance. Major credit cards are accepted.

Entropy Rentals & Charters
Wrightsville Beach • 395-2401

On the Intracoastal Waterway at Wrightsville Beach and at Johnson Marine in Hampstead, Entropy rents its own line of Sea Mark power boats, manufactured in Rocky Point, N.C. Fully equipped center-console vessels are available by the day or week. For a nominal fee, Entropy also rents water skis and equipment. The twelve-hour day rate is about $240. Most major credit cards are accepted. Call ahead for reservations and location information.

Ocean Isle Marina
43 Causeway Dr., Ocean Isle Beach
• 579-0848

This shop rents fishing boats, pontoon boats, ski boats as well as sailboats starting at around $125 per half-day.

Topsail Water Sports
1184 N. Anderson Blvd., Topsail Beach
• 328-1141

When in Topsail Beach you may rent 14-foot power boats for $50 per hour; 22-foot cabin cruisers starting at $135 per hour; and pontoon boats for $125 per hour. Day rates offer savings. All craft come with regulation safety equipment, and the folks at Topsail

Water Sports will provide basic instruction if needed. You'll find them across the road from the Topsail Motel every day from April to October. Reservations are recommended.

Canoeing

Touring the lower Cape Fear River in a canoe isn't recommended for beginners because the river is a commercial shipping channel. But for the experienced canoeist, the lower Cape Fear holds some nice surprises. Some who frequent these waters have been known to gather wild rice bequeathed by the vanished rice plantations of the past. The Black River, a protected tributary of the Cape Fear River noted for its old-growth stands of bald cypress, is an excellent, scenic canoeing choice, as are several of those rivers' tributaries. And a canoe makes excellent transportation for exploring the tidal marshes and barrier islands all along our coast.

Cape Fear Outfitters
Plaza East Shopping Center, Wrightsville Beach • 256-1258

Cape Fear Outfitters rents canoes starting at $25 per hour. It is convenient to the protected waters on the soundside of Wrightsville Beach. Safety equipment is included.

Dockside Watersports
100 Spencer Farlow Dr., Carolina Beach • 458-0220

Dockside rents canoes and all safety equipment beginning at $10 for the first hour and about $5 per hour thereafter. Major credit cards accepted. It's at the Snow's Cut Marina.

Island Passage
Bald Head Island Marina • 457-4944

An interesting area to explore by canoe is Bald Head Creek and salt marsh, the state's largest single expanse of salt marsh, on Bald Head Island. The creek is a tidal waterway, so excursions should be planned accordingly.

"Full Creek Safaris" can be arranged at the marina through Island Passage, who will also ferry your golf cart to your take-out point. The unguided safari lasts two hours and costs $30 per canoe, each of which is suitable for up to three adults.

Holland's Shelter Creek Fish Camp
N.C. 53, Burgaw • 259-5743

For paddling on the winding, blackwater Holly Shelter Creek, Holland's rents canoes for a flat $15 fee per day. You launch right behind the restaurant. The building at Holland's is a colorful restaurant and sporting supply store adjoining a camp ground. You'll find it a few miles east of I-40.

Rowing and Kayaking

The popularity of kayaking continues to grow and offers unprecedented opportunities for enjoying the local coastal wetlands and scenic rivers. Some enterprises, such as Wilmington's Turtle Island Ventures (below), emphasize ecological responsibility and education, and bring paddlers into intimate contact with wildlife and a silence that, for some, may be unfamiliar.

Cape Fear River Rowing Club
Wilmington • 762-2878

Team rowing, a favorite pastime on the Cape Fear River for ages, was revived locally in 1989 with the formation of the Cape Fear River Rowing Club. Members cruise past shipwrecks, historic downtown Wilmington and old rice fields upriver — all the while enjoying plenty of exercise and friendly company. By becoming a CFRRC member you are entitled to use the club's boats, share in activities such as group rows and annual "tip drill" exercises and compete in regattas. For insurance purposes, members are required to join the U.S. Rowing Association, which costs $40 annually for individuals, $75 families and $25 students. This is the only nonrefundable fee in-

INSIDERS' TIP

Glass containers are not welcomed on any beach strand. At Wrightsville Beach, having one can earn you an $85 fine!

Photo: N.C. Travel & Tourism

A rare restored World War II Kingfisher float plane is a significant feature of the Battleship *North Carolina*.

volved. After an initial dry lesson, you must sign a waiver of liability and pay the dues ($150 annually for singles, $225 families, $100 students). If you change your mind, your dues will be refunded. A series of free lessons will get the uninitiated started. The club's quarterly newsletter contains the latest news on club events, regattas and related items.

Turtle Island Ventures
P.O. Box 10563, Wilmington 28405
• 392-4243, (800) 64-KAYAK

Ecologically focused tours of salt marshes, barrier islands and the Cape Fear River are TIV's specialty, the dual goal being the enjoyment of the sport and the broadening of stewardship of our natural resources. Guides are registered and have backgrounds in environmental education and the sciences. Novice kayakers are as welcome as experts, and the craft are lightweight and stable. Tours lasting 2.5 hours cost $30; half-day excursions including lunch, $50. Longer trips afford opportunities for swimming, snorkeling, photography and more. Special tours, such as overnights with gourmet vegetarian meals, can be de-

signed for you, and persons with disabilities or special needs can be accommodated. Depart from sites throughout the greater Wilmington area, including Hampstead, Topsail Island, Carolina Beach and Oak Island, seven days a week year round. Visa and MasterCard are accepted. Remember to bring your own water shoes or sandals, sun protection and water bottle.

Cape Fear Outfitters
Plaza East Shopping Ctr., Wrightsville Beach • 256-1258

This business sells and rents a variety of sit-on-top and cockpit kayaks (and canoes), including Mad River, Dagger, Ocean Kayak and North Carolina's own Wilderness Systems touring boats, made in High Point. Kayak rentals cost $35 per day, $20 per half-day. Visa or MasterCard is accepted, all accessories and basic instruction are included, and kayaks put into Banks Channel. Reservations are preferred, and rentals are available every day in the summer. Plaza East Shopping Center is between Eastwood Road and Wrightsville Avenue near Wrightsville Beach.

Ship's Store
Windsurfing & Sailing Center
275 Waynick Blvd., Wrightsville Beach
• 256-9463

Ship's Store rents sea kayaks (SeaYaks), tandems and sit-on-tops) from $15 per hour from its dock on Banks Channel, opposite the Blockade Runner Hotel. The company offers tours (two or three hours and half-day) on Tuesdays, Thursdays and Sundays and by appointment. Lessons are offered on Mondays, Wednesdays and Saturdays in the summer at 9 AM, 1 PM, 5 PM and by appointment. The Center is open seven days a week. Reservations are recommended.

Beach Fun Rentals
Holden Beach Rd. S.W., Holden Beach
• 842-9600

Beach Fun Rentals recently added kayaks to its wide inventory of beach-related paraphernalia. Rates are competitive, and the shop is open every day in the summer.

Ocean Isle Beach Rentals
at The Winds Clarion Inn
310 E. First St., Ocean Isle Beach
• 579-7575, 754-4538

Ocean Kayak rentals here are competitively priced. A credit card is required for deposit. Ocean Isle Beach Rentals is open seven days a week, May through September, from 9 AM

to 5 PM and by appointment in spring and autumn.

Julie's Rentals
2 Main St., Sunset Beach • 579-1211

Julie's is a complete beach-rental shop that rents kayaks (singles and doubles) as well as many other recreational items. Rates begin around $30 for four hours for singles, $45 for doubles.

Herring's Tackle & Beach Shop
701 New River Dr., Surf City • 328-3291

On Topsail Island, Herring's rents and sells canoes and tandem kayaks (as well as many other beach items). Rentals cost $35 for a full day (sunup to sundown), and $25 for a half-day (sunup to 1 PM or 1 PM to sundown).

Topsail Water Sports
1184 N. Anderson Blvd., Topsail Beach
• 328-1141

Topsail Water Sports rents kayaks for $20 per half-hour, $30 per hour. It is opposite the Topsail Motel and operates every day from April to October.

Sailing

An event eagerly awaited by salts and lubbers alike is the Holiday Flotilla at Wrightsville Beach, held just after Thanksgiving, in which

Photo: N.C. Travel & Tourism

Area sailing organizations hold local regattas throughout the year.

boaters (power and sail) adorn their craft in the most flamboyant seasonal decoration possible for an evening cruise through Motts and Banks channels. Prizes are awarded for the best-decorated craft at the Post Flotilla Awards Dance, and fireworks are an added attraction. Check local listings for information, or call the Cape Fear Coast Convention & Visitors Bureau, 341-4030.

It would be useful to note that anchorage in Banks Channel, Wrightsville Beach, is free. Thirty days seems to be the average limit before the authorities pay a visit or post a nastygram, but boaters have been known to stay longer. Find complete information on anchorage and marina services in our chapter on Marinas and the Intracoastal Waterway.

Wrightsville Beach Ocean Racing Association
P.O. Box 113, Wrightsville Beach 28480

For serious competition sailors and those who just love to cruise, WBORA (spoken as "WoBORa") is the local organization of note. Founded in 1967, it is an active nonprofit corporation that promotes and sponsors sailboat cruising and racing in the Cape Fear region and elsewhere along the North Carolina coast. Its members are a decidedly fun-loving bunch. WBORA provides race and cruise schedule management and development, hosts sailing seminars, participates in community programs, assists in youth sailing and organizes social activities around sailing events. Sailing events span the season from spring to fall, with social events sprinkled throughout the year. Among the highlights are the Coca-Cola Regatta, the Governor's Cup, The Bald Head Island Cruise and Race (which is followed by the year's landmark party), a year-end awards banquet, and the Mid-Summer Cruise from Masonboro Island to the Cape Lookout Light. Boats of various types may compete, and a performance handicap racing factor is figured into the standings. There is one specialty-class race in which only J-24s compete.

WBORA is a member organization of the U.S. Sailing Association, the South Atlantic Yacht Racing Union and a charter member of the North Carolina Yacht Racing Association. Membership is open to all, and dues depend on the extent of your participation. An annual

handbook and frequent newsletter are published for members. WBORA does not maintain permanent offices. Information may be obtained from the association's officers. For 1997 they are Commodore Bob Cowen, 791-5616, Vice Commodore Rona Garm, 452-1817, and Race Committee Chair Sam Barfield, 251-2133.

Hobie Fleet 101
Wrightsville Beach • 256-6468 or 256-6624

Hobie Fleet 101 is a local sailing club open to anyone interested in sailing Hobie Cats. It is part of Division 9 (including both Carolinas plus Virginia and Georgia) of the North American Hobie Cat Association. Ownership of a Hobie is not required, since qualified members can obtain use of the fleet boat for the summer for a mere $40. Family membership costs $25 annually, and meetings are held monthly. Among their events are the Mid-Summer Offshore Regatta in July, open to Hobies of all classes, and the Frostbite Series, which runs from October through Christmas.

Sailing Instruction and Rentals

Water Ways Sailing School
7110 Wrightsville Ave., Wrightsville Beach • 256-4282, (800) 562-SAIL

Jerry Outlaw's Water Ways Sailing School is the only sailing school in the Carolinas certified by the American Sailing Association (ASA). The ASA awarded Water Ways the association's highest honor two years in a row by naming it the 1995 and '96 School of the Year. Capt. Outlaw has also received the ASA's Outstanding Instructor award three years consecutively, 1993-95. Water Ways offers a battery of sailing courses taught entirely by USCG-licensed captains. Courses include: Basic Sailing (2 days), Basic Coastal Cruising, Intermediate Coastal Cruising (Bareboat Charter), Coastal Navigation and Advanced Coastal Cruising. The Water Ways fleet boasts a variety of craft ranging from a Catalina 22 to a Hunter 335. The boats are available for rent. Captained and bareboat charters are also available for local excursions.

Carolina Yacht Club
401 S. Lumina Ave., Wrightsville Beach
• 256-3396

This is the oldest private sailing club on Cape Fear. The club sponsors regional competitions and events and offers training to members.

Ship's Store
Windsurfing & Sailing Center
275 Waynick Blvd., Wrightsville Beach
• 256-9463

Among the most complete enterprises of its kind, the Sailing Center rents Hobie Cats, 14-foot DaySailors, Sunfish and more. Prices range from $20 per hour to $100 for 4 hours. The center also offers lessons and group discounts. The minimum age to rent is 18; the minimum age to ride is 6. Boats launch from the center's dock opposite the Blockade Runner Resort Hotel.

Dockside Watersports
100 Spencer Farlow Dr., Carolina Beach
• 458-0220

Small sailboats (14-foot Hobie Cats and Sunfish) may be rented at the Snows Cut Marina for about $70 per half day, $125 per full day. Ask about off-season specials, and reserve in advance. Major credit cards are accepted. Dockside Watersports is at the Snow's Cut Marina.

Cape Fear Boat Rentals
Long Beach • 278-1880

Oak Island residents and visitors may rent a variety of small sailboats, including Sunfish and Butterfly craft (great for kids), and have them delivered, too, seven days a week from May through August. Life preservers are included. Rentals are by the day ($50) or by the week only, and credit cards are not accepted.

Ocean Isle Beach Rentals
at The Winds Clarion Inn
310 E. First St., Ocean Isle Beach
• 579-7575, 754-4538

This shop rents a 14-foot Aquacat for $30 per hour or $110 per day with a credit card deposit. Lessons are included, if needed. (It also rents beach items such as umbrellas and chairs.) Ocean Isle Beach Rentals is open

seven days a week, May through September, from 9 AM to 5 PM, and by appointment in spring and autumn.

Topsail Water Sports
1184 N. Anderson Blvd., Topsail Beach
• 328-1141

John and Gay Maxwell's shop is a local favorite. You can rent Hobie Cats (14-foot and 16-foot) and other small craft at fees ranging from $30 per hour to $90 per day. Half-day and full-day sailboat charters with a certified captain and lessons are also available. Reservations are necessary, and most major credit cards are accepted. It's open seven days a week April to October.

Supplies,
Accessories and Repair

There are many more businesses in the area that provide good service for marine supplies and repair than are listed here, but we've listed those that come recommended.

Boater's World
Discount Marine Center
University Commons Shopping Ctr.,
S. College Rd., Wilmington • 452-3000

When it comes to marine supplies, accessories, gear and clothing, there's very little that Boater's World doesn't carry. And as if an inventory that's well-displayed, comprehensive and well-priced weren't enough, the staff is expert and polite. It's are open seven days a week.

Overton's Discount
Boating Supplies
5912 Oleander Dr., Wilmington • 313-0022

Overton's is among the more trusted suppliers of boating equipment and accessories, including electronics, hardware and cleaning supplies. It even carries water skis and swim wear and has recently moved to more spacious digs. It's closed on Sunday.

Pennington's Marine
97 Heathcliff Rd., Wilmington • 392-7488

Pennington's has a reputation for honesty and competence when it comes to marine repair, including that of outboards. Pickup service is available.

Scuba Diving and Snorkeling

Diving the southern coastal waters offers rewarding experiences to collectors, nature-watchers and wreck divers, despite there being no true coral reefs in these latitudes. A surprising variety of tropical fish species inhabit these waters, including blue angel fish, damsel fish and moray eels as well as several varieties of sea fans, some as large as three feet in height. Spiny oysters, deer cowries, helmet shells, trumpet tritons and queen conchs can be found here.

Among the places where it is easiest to find tropical aquatic life is 23 Mile Rock, a 12-mile-long ledge running roughly perpendicular to the coast. Another 15 miles out, the Lobster Ledge, a low-lying formation 120 feet deep, is a collectors' target. There are several smaller ledges close to shore in shallower water better suited for less-experienced divers. Visibility at offshore sites averages 40 feet, but inshore visibility is seldom better than 20 feet. The coastal waters can be dived all year long, having temperatures ranging between the upper 50s in winter and low 80s in summer. However, many local charters typically end their diving season in early fall. Some charters organize destination trips thereafter.

Good snorkeling in the region is a matter of knowing when and where to go. Near-shore bottoms are mostly packed sand devoid of the rugged features that make for good viewing and collecting, but a good guide can lead you to rewarding areas. When the wind is right and the tide is rising, places such as the Wrightsville Beach jetty offer good viewing and visibility. The many creeks and estuaries support an abundance of life, and the shorter visibility, averaging 15 to 20 feet, is no obstacle in water so shallow. The waters around piers in Banks Channel at Wrightsville Beach are fair but often murky, and currents are strong. Only experienced snorkelers should attempt these waters or those in local inlets, which are treacherous, and then only at stopped tides. It is neither safe nor legal to swim beneath oceanside fishing piers. When in doubt, contact a local dive shop for information.

This region of the Graveyard of the Atlantic offers unparalleled opportunities for wreck divers. From Tubbs Inlet (near Sunset Beach) to New River Inlet (North Topsail Beach) 20 of the dozens of known shipwrecks resting here are accessible and safe. Most are Confederate blockade runners, one is a tanker torpedoed by the Nazi sub U-158, and several were sunk as part of North Carolina's artificial reef program (see the Fishing chapter for more on artificial reefs). These and higher-risk wrecks can be located with the assistance of dive shops.

Wreck diving is an advanced skill. Research prior to a dive is essential in terms of the target, techniques and potential dangers, which in this region include live ammunition and explosives that may be found on World War II wrecks. Contact the proper authorities if you observe anything suspicious, and leave it alone! Under state law all wrecks and underwater artifacts that have remained unclaimed for more than 10 years are declared state property. Anyone interested in searching for artifacts should file for a permit with the North Carolina Department of Cultural Resources, 109 E. Jones Street, Raleigh 27611.

Charter boats can be arranged for dive trips through all the dive shops listed here, but there are others. Also check the marinas for fishing charters that accommodate dive trips. Hanover Fishing Charters, 256-3636, and Sea Lady Charters, 452-9955 or (800) 242-2493, both out of Wrightsville Beach, and the *Flo-Jo* out of Carolina Beach, 458-5454 or (800) 356-5669, are good resources for charters run by experienced crew. Many charter boats are primarily fishing boats, so if you need custom diving craft, be sure to inquire.

INSIDERS' TIP

When kayaking or canoeing the tidal marshes, be sure to wear protective footwear. Oyster beds abound in these shallow waters.

Photo: Mark Courtney

Crosstown traffic got you down?

Most dive shops can lead you to a certification class if they don't offer one themselves. Also, proof of diver's certification is required by shops or dive masters when renting equipment, booking charters or purchasing air fills.

Dive Shops

Aquatic Safaris & Divers Emporium
5751-4 Oleander Dr., Wilmington • 392-4386

This PADI training facility is one of Wilmington's largest full-service charter services and dive shops, offering daily dive charters and air fills, including Nitrox. It carries a full range of equipment for sale and rent. Snorkeling equipment is for sale only. The shop is certified by major manufacturers to perform repairs on all life-support equipment and most other equipment as well. It's open seven days a week during the summer and six days a week off-season.

Entropy Rentals & Charters
Wrightsville Beach • 395-2401

PADI-certified Capt. Pete Klingenberger guides wreck- and reef-diving trips for up to six persons at a time. His Sea Mark vessels, equipped with full electronics, dock on the Intracoastal Waterway at Wrightsville Beach and at Johnson Marine in Hampstead.

Offshore Adventures
301 Wood Dale Dr., Wilmington • 799-2895

Offshore Adventures offers dive charters with professional crew aboard its custom 31-foot Bertram and scuba instruction during the warm season. It also provides equipment rentals. In winter, destination dives are organized for those willing to travel.

Bottom Time
6014 Wrightsville Ave., Wilmington • 397-0181, (800) NITROX1

This is a PADI five-star facility and among the largest sport diving and snorkeling facilities in the region. Services include rentals, repair, sales, air (standard and Nitrox), guided snorkeling tours and instruction in diving and snorkeling. Local charters and customized dive travels to warmer climes during the winter are available. The staff is fully certified, and the business is a National Association of Underwater Instructors (NAUI) facility. In summer Bottom Time is open Monday through Saturday. Their Cape Fear season closes by early November.

Ocean Ray
1315 S. College Rd., Wilmington
• 392-9989, (800) 645-5554

Not a dive shop, Ocean Ray is a manufacturer of quality custom-fit wet and dry suits. Wet suits are made in 3 mm and 6 mm thicknesses. Dry suits are 6 mm-thick G231 nitrogen-blown Rubatex. All suits carry a three-year warranty. Ocean Ray ships throughout North America and Europe and does alterations and repairs on all name-brand suits. Direct sales to the public are available at the retail outlet at the address above.

Scuba South Diving Company
222 S. River Dr., Southport • 457-5201

Among the most respected diving experts in the Southport area is Wayne Strickland, who specializes in dive charters to some of the less-frequented targets off the Cape, plus such well-known sites as the *City of Houston*, a passenger freighter that sank in 1878 and which Strickland salvaged for the Southport Maritime Museum. (Artifacts are on display.) Strickland will arrange dives to any site along the southern coast. Trips are aboard his custom 52-foot *Scuba South II*. Scuba South sells and rents a full store of equipment, including wet and dry suits, and provides air fills.

Southport Scuba and Water Sport
610 W. West St., Southport • 457-1944

Southport Scuba specializes in sales and rentals of equipment, instruction, charters and commercial diving. It also provides local information to divers. It shares retail space with Ocean Outfitters, a purveyor of nautical apparel and accessories, in a shop at the foot of W. West Street near the Southport Marina.

Holden Beach Surf & Scuba
3172-4 Holden Beach Rd. S.W., Holden Beach • 842-6899

Bob Huey's dive and surf shop, on N.C. 130 in the Palmetto Plaza shopping strip on the mainland side of the waterway, carries practically everything needed for diving including air fills and computers. Bob is a USCG-certified boat captain and diver, and his wife is a PADI-certified dive master. They conduct lessons at a nearby pool during the summer. Their shop is open seven days a week March

through December and on weekends in January and February.

East Coast Discount Dive Center
Causeway Dr., Surf City • 328-1887

Doug Medlin's East Coast Discount Dive Center is part of his East Coast Discount Bait & Tackle Shop. The Center provides complete dive services including sales, rentals, certification classes and air. The shop is staffed by certified divers and is open seven days a week during the high season. Charter excursions include dives on various World War II wrecks, 23 Mile Rock, 18 Mile Rock and many other sites on request. Trips to common dive sites are well-priced.

Water-Skiing

The protected waters of the lower Cape Fear River, from Carolina Beach south, are the most popular for water-skiing the greater Wilmington area. These waters are convenient to public boat ramps in Carolina Beach, including those at the marina at Carolina Beach State Park and at Federal Point. Throughout most of the region, the wider channels of the Intracoastal Waterway and adjoining sounds offer skiing opportunities, boat traffic allowing. The wide mouths of the Shallotte River and Lockwood Folly near Varnumtown are just adequate. The relatively hushed surf along the Brunswick Islands is well-suited to skiing, yielding about 22 miles of shoreline from Ocean Isle Beach to Sunset Beach. Big Lake, in the community of Boiling Springs Lakes 8 miles northwest of Southport on N.C. 87, is a long, narrow body of water that's excellent for water-skiing. There is a free public boat ramp off Alton Lennon Drive.

Check with the rental services listed in Motorboat Rentals, above, if you need to rent a towing craft. Many, if not most, services and some boating supply shops also rent skis and equipment.

Surfing

California surfers who come to the southern coast of North Carolina agree: The surf may be less spectacular than on the West Coast, but the water is warmer, the season longer and the surfers less obnoxious. Conditions were considered good enough for the U.S. Amateur Surfing Championships's Mid-Atlantic Regionals to be held at Wrightsville Beach in 1996. And surfers here are making their mark worldwide. Wrightsville Beach's own Ben Bourgeois became the 1996 Junior Men's Amateur World Champion, having won the Quicksilver Grommet World Championship in Bali the year before. Former Men's World Champion Bill Curry is a local resident and one of six local members of the Eastern Surf Association's All-Star team (which includes his son, Chris). And now that surfing has joined the pantheon of Olympic events (beginning in the year 2000), local surfing has naturally gained further status. (Surf shops throughout the region can provide information on surfing competitions.)

The beaches running north and south — Topsail Island down to Fort Fisher — experience consistently better surf, especially when a nor'easter blows, than the Brunswick beaches with their east-west orientation. (The Brunswick beaches are fine for bodyboarding.) A favored surfing spot is Masonboro Island's north end near the jetty; however, it's not an easy place to reach since Masonboro Inlet is an active boat channel with dangerous currents. Crossing over from the soundside (the Intracoastal Waterway) and hiking to the beach is a good idea.

Wrightsville Beach has the most stringent rules governing surfing. Between 11 AM and 4 PM during the summer (Memorial to Labor Day), surfing is restricted to surf zones (also called sounds), which are two-block segments of the beach that move south, two streets at a time, each day. Any lifeguard can tell you where the zone currently is. Zones do not apply during the off-season. Leash laws, however, are in effect year round. Surfing within 150 feet of fishing piers is prohibited. On northern Topsail Island, surfing is prohibited near Onslow County's Public Beach Access pavilions.

Surfers on the Brunswick Islands say the surfing near the piers is best, but on Ocean Isle Beach (where there are no rotating zones), ordinances require surfers to remain a full 1,000 feet away from the pier (though it's not always enforced). Staying clear just makes good sense, given the amount of lost fishing tackle and barnacle-encrusted pilings that lie in wait for reckless surfers. The occasional feat of shooting the pier is like a train wreck: fascinating yet terrifying.

Wrightsville Beach Parks and Recreation
1 Bob Sawyer Dr., Wrightsville Beach • 256-7925

June through August, weekly beginner surfing lessons for advanced ocean swimmers 10 and older are available. The course covers surfing etiquette, paddling, wave-catching, maneuvers and basic surfing principles.

The Eastern Surfing Association
256-8604, 395-5865

The ESA, the largest surfing association in the world, is well-represented in the Wilmington area, having more members in the southern North Carolina district than anywhere else on the Eastern Seaboard. The ESA promotes amateur competitive surfing and fair play worldwide and environmental interests locally (the latter often in cooperation with the Surfrider Foundation, below). The local chapter sponsors five to six contests yearly, provides a framework for ranking amateur surfers and is your best source of information about non-ESA surfing events. The ESA's first all-women's surfing competition, the Wahines Championship, launches in August 1997. Annual ESA membership costs $20, which includes a newsletter and subscription to *Surfing* magazine. Write: ESA/SNC, P.O. Box 542, Wrightsville Beach 28480.

The Surfrider Foundation
Cape Fear Chapter • 350-8282, 256-0233 (infoline)

Headquartered in California, the Surfrider Foundation is a nonprofit international environmental organization working to preserve the world's beaches through direct action (primarily clean-ups), conservation and education. The Cape Fear Chapter sponsors beach sweeps, the Adopt-A-Beach-Access program and Storm Drain Stenciling in association with Wrightsville Beach Parks and Recreation. Open meetings are held regularly.

Surf Reports

Daily surf reports for Wrightsville Beach are broadcast by the radio station Surf 107-FM at 7:25 AM and 3:30 PM. Aussie Island Surf Shop, 256-5454, maintains a 24-hour surf-report phone line, 256-5757, for conditions at Wrightsville Beach. Reports by phone are also provided by Surf City Surf Shop, 256-4353; Sweetwater Surf Shop, 256-8184; and Star-Line, 762-1996 ext. 2213, all for conditions at Wrightsville Beach. For Topsail Island, call Spinnaker Surf & Sport, 328-2311. Also check into local surf shops, listed below.

Surfboard Rentals

There is no shortage of places to rent a stick if you don't have one of your own. Check with the surf shops below or these specialty watersports shops.

S & S Water Sports, Davis Street and Channel Boulevard, Topsail Beach • 328-7751

Beach Fun Rentals, 3324 Holden Beach Road S.W., Holden Beach • 842-9600

Ocean Isle Beach Rentals at The Winds Clarion Inn, 310 E. First Street, Ocean Isle Beach • 579-7575 or 754-4538

Topsail Water Sports, 1184 N. Anderson Boulevard, Topsail Beach • 328-1141

Surf Shops

The many surf shops in the area offer a complete selection of surf gear, apparel and accessories, including wet suits and videos. You can buy a new or used stick, rent one by the day, and get yours repaired. Shops can lead you to local people who customize boards too. Most surf shops also are the best places to find everything you'll need for skateboarding and in-line skating, including parts and accessories, as well as surfwear and skatewear, designer eyewear, shoes and sandals, jewelry and boogie boards. Most area shops are open seven days a week in season.

Aussie Island Surf Shop, 1319 Military Cutoff Road, Wilmington, 256-5454

Bert's Surf Shop, 5740 Oleander Drive, Wilmington, 392-4501; U.S. Highway 421, Carolina Beach, 458-9047; Norton Street and Yaupon Beach Drive, Yaupon Beach, 278-6679; N. New River Drive, Surf City, 328-1010

Hot Wax Surf Shop, 4510 Hoggard Drive, Wilmington, 791-9283

Surf City Surf Shop, 530 Causeway Drive, Wrightsville Beach, 256-2265

Sweetwater Surf Shop, 10 N. Lumina Avenue, Wrightsville Beach, 256-3821

The Cove Surf Shop, 107 Cape Fear Boulevard, Carolina Beach, 458-4671

Local Call Surf Shop, 609 Yaupon Beach Drive, Yaupon Beach, 278-3306

Holden Beach Surf & Scuba, 3172-4 Holden Beach Road S.W., Holden Beach, 842-6899

Salty's Surf Shop, First Street, Ocean Isle Beach, 579-6223

Spinnaker Surf & Sport, 111 N. Shore Drive, Surf City, 328-2311

Swimming

The southern coast is blessed with clean, relatively clear, refreshing waters and a long outdoor season. Water temperatures become comfortable usually no later than the middle of spring, generally hovering in the 75 to 80 degree range by summer. Only at the end of the season do temperatures approach those of the waters farther south. Most beaches consist of fine, clean sand. Together with the shores of the Outer Banks and farther north, the southern coast gives evidence that North Carolina does indeed have the finest beaches in the east.

Except during storm surges, the surf is generally moderate. Most beach communities employ lifeguards during the summer, but the beaches are unstaffed otherwise. Swimming in a few areas is hazardous, such as at the extreme east end of Ocean Isle Beach and along the Fort Fisher Historic Site because of either strong currents or underwater debris. All hazardous areas are well-marked (see the chapter on Sun, Sand and Sea for more on beach-going).

Check the facilities listed below if pool-swimming is more to your liking.

YMCA
2710 Market St., Wilmington • 251-9622

The Y boasts two pools to accommodate its many members, and it has extensive hours. Classes in water aerobics are among their many offerings.

YWCA
2815 S. College Rd., Wilmington
• 799-6820

The YWCA boasts excellent facilities, water aerobics and swimming instruction by highly qualified staff. Instruction in lifesaving is also one of the YWCA's specialties.

The Deck
Family Entertainment Center
5524 E. Beach Dr., Long Beach • 278-4111

The Deck operates a pool that is open to the public. All-day passes are $3.50 for kids, $4.50 for adults and are good 10 AM to 5 PM — come and go as you please. Weekly passes ($15 any age) are good seven days from the day of purchase and include admission to night swims, 7 to 11:30 PM (see also the Attractions chapter). The Deck is open every day from Memorial to Labor Day.

City of Wilmington
Public Swimming Pools
General Information 341-7855

The Wilmington recreation department maintains three public pools, open only during the summer: Shipp Pool at Southside Park (beside Legion Stadium), Carolina Beach Road, 341-7863; Jackson Pool at Northside Park, 750 Bess Street, 341-7866; and Murphy

Pool at Robert Strange Park, 410 S. 8th Street, 341-7866. Admission fees are nominal.

Wrightsville Beach
Parks and Recreation
1 Bob Sawyer Dr., Wrightsville Beach
• 256-7925

Wrightsville Beach Parks and Recreation offers beginner and advanced-beginner swimming lessons for youth ages 4 to 11. Lessons are conducted June through August in two-week sessions.

Marine Corps Base Camp Lejeune
MWR Recreation Division's
Athletics Branch
Jacksonville • 451-5430

The MWR Recreation Division of the local Marine Corps base sponsors stiff swimming competitions as part of their annual Grand Prix Series of sporting events. These include the Masters Swim I held in January, the Masters Swim II in June and the Davy Jones Open Ocean Swim in July. These events (and others listed in the Sports, Fitness and Parks chapter) take place within the confines of Camp Lejeune in Jacksonville, about 20 minutes from North Topsail Beach. All events are open to military personnel and the general public of all ages, and they typically draw a nationwide field of competitors. Entry forms and information can be obtained by contacting the division's Fitness Director, 451-5430 (fax: 451-2093), between 8 AM and 4 PM, Monday through Friday.

Windsurfing

One of the best and most popular windsurfing areas is The Basin, the partially protected body of water off Federal Point at the southern end of Pleasure Island. Accessible from a public boat ramp down the road from the ferry terminal, the Basin is enclosed by the Rocks, a 3.3-mile breakwater that ex-

---

INSIDERS' TIP

When at Sunset Beach, check into Julie's Rentals, 2 Main Street, 579-1211, for a wide range of recreational equipment (including body boards) and household items for rent.

tends to Zeke's Island and beyond. Mott's Channel and Banks Channel on the soundside of Wrightsville Beach are popular spots, but you'll have to contend with the boat traffic. Advanced windsurfers prefer the oceanside of the jetty at the south end of Wrightsville Beach where action is fairly guaranteed.

Around Topsail Island, the choices are the Intracoastal Waterway and the ocean. The inlets north and south of the island are not well-suited to uninterrupted runs. Along Oak Island and the South Brunswick Islands, the ocean is your best bet, although limited stretches of the ICW are OK for beginners (near the Ocean Isle Beach bridge when it's not busy, for example). Shallotte Inlet and River are narrow but worth a shot. Up-to-date information on windsurfing competitions, usually held in the fall, may be available at the outlets listed here.

Ship's Store
Windsurfing & Sailing Center
275 Waynick Blvd., Wrightsville Beach
• 256-9463

Ship's Store rents sailboards at reasonable rates by the hour ($15 first hour) and in blocks of hours. Surfers put in at Banks Channel opposite the Blockade Runner Hotel. Instructors are available on Thursdays and Fridays during the summer to teach four-hour windsurfing classes ($60). The store in the Atlantic View Retail Center on Wrightsville Avenue is open for sales all year.

Ocean Isle Beach Rentals
at The Winds Clarion Inn
310 E. First St., Ocean Isle Beach
• 579-7575, 754-4538

Windsurfers are available for rent at $20 per day. A credit card deposit is required.

Dockside Watersports
100 Spencer Farlow Dr., Carolina Beach
• 458-0220

Dockside Watersports rents sailboards beginning at $15 for the first hour from Snows Cut Marina. The craft are already in the water, ready to go. Reserve in advance when possible. Major credit cards are accepted.

Topsail Water Sports
1184 N. Anderson Blvd., Topsail Beach
• 328-1141

You can rent windboards for $15 per half-hour or $40 per hour, and this shop also offers lessons. Reservations are recommended.

Beach Access

Public beach access is a system of pedestrian right-of-ways, dune crossovers, parking lots and, at some locations, restroom and shower facilities. A few have food concessions. Except in public lots on Wrightsville Beach, where parking meters must be fed during the summer only, parking everywhere is free. At Wrightsville Beach, signs indicating beach access paths are readily visible, marked with a large orange sun over blue water. Note that most communities prohibit glass containers and vehicles on the strand. Kure Beach also prohibits dogs and alcohol. Keep in mind that in most beach communities crossing dunes at places other than approved crossovers can earn you a minimum $50 fine.

On Wrightsville Beach, public access with restrooms, metered parking and a shower are across S. Lumina Avenue from the Oceanic Restaurant and Crystal Pier near Nathan Avenue. Restrooms and a shower are at the foot of Salisbury Street near Johnny Mercer's Pier. Parking is also available adjacent to the Holiday Inn to the north and on either side of the Duneridge Resort, about 1 mile north of Salisbury Street. One of the Duneridge lots has restrooms. At the north end of Wrightsville Beach, there is parking on both sides of Shell Island Resort. On summer weekends, unless you're parking a bicycle, arrive before 10 AM or after 2 PM to find a parking place.

At Carolina and Kure Beaches, public beach access points and parking generally are situated at the foot of every second street. Public restrooms and showers are also available along the boardwalk, the most popular being at the foot of Cape Fear Boulevard.

On Caswell Beach Road along eastern Oak Island, about a half-mile east of the Fort Caswell Lighthouse at Caswell Beach, the public beach access consists of a large gravel parking lot with no facilities. The area is open from 5 AM to 11 PM, and prohibitions include camping, the use of alcohol, firearms, fires and cars on the strand.

In Yaupon Beach, there are nine beach access points with parking. The less crowded ones are naturally the ones farther from the pier, especially to the west.

There are 52 public beach accesses along the 8 miles of Long Beach oceanfront. The Cabana at the foot of 40th Street E. is one of the liveliest access points, being the site of Brunswick County Parks & Recreation's Summer Fun Beach Days (see the Attractions chapter). There's plenty of parking, a concession stand and showers. Most other access points have no services except the one at the foot of S. Middletown Avenue where retail and food stores are an easy walk from the beach. Most of the public accesses in Long Beach have limited parking, especially close to S. Middletown Avenue.

The majority of beach accesses on 11-mile-long Holden Beach are private, but public access points abound at the east end (Avenues A through E), near Jordan Boulevard and at Ferry Road. Several others are west of the bridge. Parking along Ocean Boulevard is prohibited. A Regional Beach Access facility with showers, restrooms and parking, open 6 AM to 11 PM, is nearly under the bridge off Jordan Boulevard, where limited parking and covered tables are available.

On Ocean Isle Beach, access is concentrated around the center of town, near the foot of the causeway.

Beach access on Sunset Beach is indicated by small white posts about 100 yards apart. There are no sidewalks and little parking. The paved parking lot adjacent to Sunset Fishing Pier is convenient to the beach and pier facilities.

Note that all the access facilities listed below for Topsail Island were damaged by the hurricanes of '96. Their present conditions may differ from the descriptions that follow.

In North Topsail Beach, in addition to various access points without services, Onslow County maintains a large Public Beach Ac-

Photo: N.C. Travel & Tourism

The sound behind Wrightsville Beach offers smooth sailing for windsurfers.

cess (No. 2) about 2 miles north of Tilghman's Square in Surf City. This facility has ample parking, a handicap ramp to the building only, showers, restrooms and phones. Snack vendors are usually on hand nearby. This facility is open April 1 to September 30 from 9 AM to 8 PM daily. Off-season it closes at 5 PM. A little more than 4 miles north, Onslow County Public Beach Access No. 1 is a bigger facility with similar amenities. It features handicap access to the beach and a concession on the premises.

In Surf City, access with parking and restrooms is at the foot of New Bern Avenue. Handicap access is only to the dune-top deck. Along Topsail Beach, access with limited parking is available at the foot of nearly every cross street. South of Florida Avenue, a series of stairways provides crossovers with street parking along Ocean Boulevard.

Stay off the
sand dunes.
They're a vital
part of the
beach
environment
and provide
homes for a
variety of beach
animals.

Sun, Sand and Sea

There's nothing like lazing around on a sunny beach under a Carolina blue sky, taking an occasional dip in the beautiful waters off North Carolina's southern coast or cruising down the Intracoastal Waterway on a powerboat, sailboat or kayak.

Vacationing by the water is the most popular way for people to relax, which probably explains why many visitors end up being residents on the coast by retirement age, if not before. It's the lure of island living; it's the simplicity of bare feet and casual clothing; it's the worry-free life of paradise. But everyone, including Insiders, needs to be reminded that even in such a paradise, there are some good tips to follow for a safe, enjoyable vacation.

The Sun

No matter what your age or complexion, it's very important to wear sunscreen on the beach. In recent years, the sun has had more of a searing effect on even relatively insensitive skin. A sunburn, sad to say, is just going to fall off and make you look like you're molting in a week or so.

You can burn even on a cloudy day because up to 90 percent of the sun's rays penetrate clouds and can still damage your skin. Surfaces such as sand, concrete and water can reflect up to 85 percent of the sun's rays.

Sunscreen with an appropriate SPF (sun protection factor) should be a daily habit. No matter how immune you think you are to sunburn, you should slather yourself in the best protection you can find, especially when on the open beach. After swimming, put more on. Children need special skin protection. More than half of the skin damage done by the sun happens in the first 18 years of life. Using waterproof sunblock will save you from having to constantly reapply it on your kids as they dart back and forth between the sand and the water many times during an hour.

Dermatologists recommend an SPF of at least 15 for children. Infants need sunblock, a hat, lightweight clothing and a beach umbrella. Even under an umbrella, the reflective rays are still present.

Wide-brimmed straw hats are very popular in the area, so you can enjoy their protection and look cool at the same time. In the heat of summer, wear light-colored clothing for maximum comfort. Look for linen and cotton clothing because these fabrics breathe better than synthetics. Synthetics feel much like Saran wrap after only a few minutes in the summer sun. Stay out of the sun in the hottest part of the day in the summer, generally between 11 AM and 3 PM. You can have a long morning on the beach and hours in the afternoon without exposing yourself to the depleting effects of excessive summer heat.

Alcohol, which isn't allowed on area beaches anyway, is debilitating in the heat. Take a cooler of Gatorade or lemonade, and you'll enjoy yourself much more on the beach or on the water. Also, the Coast Guard doesn't take kindly to drunk boaters, so if you must drink, be moderate. If the long arm of the law doesn't worry you, think of this: beer will just make you thirstier under the hot sun.

The Sand

Beaches in the Wilmington area vary in width and shell diversity, but they all have one thing in common. Even after two hurricanes in 1996, there are mostly beautiful expanses of sand. Sand, though, slips inside your swimsuit when you swim, makes your hair sticky, cakes between your toes and is unpleasant if it blows into your sandwich. Take a blanket or old quilt along with you to put under your beach chair. The sand will eventually creep over the edges, especially on a windy day, but this gives you a relatively clean base of operations for your beach visit.

Take a gallon container of fresh water to the beach because it's wonderful for rinsing sand and salt out of your hair after a swim in the ocean. You can rinse your whole body if you're frugal with the stream. Many area beaches also offer shower facilities at access points.

Sand is one of the greatest natural pumices available. City feet calloused by work shoes get sanded down to smoothness in a week of walking barefoot on the beach. So, kick your shoes off and go for a walk.

You can see all kinds of amazing things on a long stroll along the beach. Sharks' teeth are found at Topsail Beach. Keen observers will spot these teeth, ebony in color and varied in shape, by their characteristic glint in the sand or at the water's edge.The Brunswick beaches yield other interesting treasures — whole sand dollars are frequent finds. Look for the all-white skeletal sand dollars, and return the brown, furry ones to the water — they may be still alive. They also smell terrible if you put them in your car to take them home. Arrowheads from ancient Native American tribes can be found on these beaches if you are observant.

The sand dunes bear some mention: Please stay off them. The dunes are a vital part of the beach environment and provide homes for a variety of beach animals. Particularly as the area makes its recovery from the summer storms of 1996, these dunes are important to retard erosion and protect the homes on the islands. Also, on the purely practical side, there is a stiff fine if you climb in the dunes or disturb any of the vegetation. Fines are as high as $500, and it could put a dent in your vacation allowance if you go on a wild romp through the dunes. So, be forewarned and stay off them.

There are some other laws worth noting: Don't take glass containers on the beach; don't let your dog run loose until you check local ordinances, and if you take it for a walk, pick up its "business" so other people don't step in it; don't let your parking meter expire (bring plenty of quarters to Wrightsville Beach); don't take alcohol to the beach; and don't litter. The beach patrol is a nice bunch of people, but they take their job seriously.

Area beaches welcome visitors, and there are plenty of marked public access points for travel over the dunes to the beach. Without exception, beaches in this part of North Carolina are primarily residential neighborhoods with fairly limited commercial development. Most of the homes are private property, and residents don't take kindly to people tramping through their yards. Getting from the asphalt to the beach also requires footwear. The road can get painfully hot, and there are vicious sandspurs waiting for your delicate feet. The sand on the beach above the high-water mark can sizzle in the summer, so protect your feet.

There is an interesting phenomenon that occurs on the beaches in the fall. At times, on a night walk, you can kick up a phosphorescent light show with your bare feet in the sand. It sort of makes you feel like you're walking through stars. Night on the sand is a special time. Many a person has been inspired to take a moonlight stroll and a dip in the ocean. However, a word of warning about taking a swim in the buff. For one thing, you can be arrested. For another, it's easy to lose your bearings. The currents move curiously, and you can end up at another spot on the beach in the dark without so much as a clue to your whereabouts (and with little more than the night air to clothe you).

The Sea

Ah, the beautiful sea. You can stare quietly at it, splash around in it, boat on it, surf on it and use it in many other fun and relaxing ways. Since Wilmington is a major port, international freighters and other travelers can be seen coming or going, so a pair of binoculars is a valuable asset for watching boats and ships. Windsurfers, sailboats and ocean-going kayaks are readily available for rent when you're ready to get on the water yourself. Swimming is tremendously popular on area beaches because the water is a comfortable temperature and clean. While floating around on an air mattress just beyond the breakers, you can often see 10 feet down to the sandy bottom.

Photo: Bill DiNome

Storms can crop up quickly, so be prepared.

Lifeguards are posted at many of the beaches in the area during the summer vacation season, and there is a good reason for this: Riptides and undertows are unseen dangers lurking beneath the waves — dangers that Insiders respect. If you are swimming and are suddenly pulled in a frightening way by the currents, the most important thing to remember is to stay calm. Panic leads to exertion, which leads to fatigue. If you find yourself in a riptide, relax and let it carry you on its natural course toward the sea. Within a few minutes, it will dissipate. Then, you can swim parallel to the shoreline to get out of the riptide area and back to shore. Do not try to swim straight back into shore against the riptide; you'll only tire yourself out.

Swim in areas with lifeguards, and if there aren't any keep close to shore. Pay attention to your location. Many people don't realize that inlets are not places to swim. They look incredibly inviting and seem safe, yet they are the most dangerous places for swimming. As

any boater knows, inlets are daunting places for navigation because the currents are swift. If the prospect of being swept out to sea isn't scary enough for you, then consider this: Sharks love to lie in the bottoms of inlets to aerate their gills.

The Cape Fear River isn't really suitable for swimming. It is 38 feet deep on average and known for deep, racing currents, and alligators and big eels! The Battleship North Carolina, moored on the west bank of the river across from downtown Wilmington, is the regular hangout of Charlie the Alligator. While alligators aren't generally known for their aggression toward people, they have been known to snatch domestic animals, waterfowl and other small creatures.

Wrightsville Beach is a popular place for surfing, but there are some regulations regarding it, and you should ask the lifeguard about designated surfing zones, which shift each day. (See our Watersports chapter for more information on surf zones.) You must wear a leash

INSIDERS' TIP

When combing the beaches for sharks' teeth, scrutinize the coarse sand most carefully. The teeth show up best when they are wet.

and will be immediately chastised if you are not attached to your board. Lifeguards are fastidious about enforcing this rule.

The tides are such an important factor in coastal communities that they're a part of the daily weather forecast. Be aware of them if you splash out to sandbars or islands at low tide. Changing tides could make the trip back to shore a daunting swim.

Regarding weather, take thunderstorms seriously. Get out of the water and off the beach when these often spectacular weather events take place. Lightning on the beach means business, and you should seek immediate shelter inside a building or in your car. Also, a hurricane watch is a good reason to leave an area and the worst reason to arrive to watch nature in upheaval. Area beaches are often evacuated when hurricanes threaten. Some of the area's worst storms involve tidal surges and high winds on sunny days. If you're going boating pay attention to weather warnings because you may not be able to predict a storm if you look at the sky.

There are many opportunities for boating along the southern coast. If you trailer your own boat, there are ample public boat ramps throughout the entire area. If you choose to leave your boat at the water, there are more than 70 marinas that offer a variety of services including dry-dockage, wetslips and storage. Boating possibilities include the Cape Fear River and its adjacent branches, the Atlantic Ocean, the Intracoastal Waterway and lakes. Fuel and other amenities are available on the southern coastline, generally on the Intracoastal Waterway. If you don't have a boat of your own, you can take advantage of one of the charter services for sailing craft and, of course, tour and deep-sea fishing boats that cater to all cruising needs.

Boaters should understand the rules of the road when operating their own boats or when chartering someone else's. Boat traffic can border on congestion in some areas such as Banks Channel in Wrightsville Beach, and it's

important to have some understanding of the basics.

Perhaps the most important thing about boating is preparation. Supplies are a good place to start. File a float plan. This can be as official or informal as your circumstances require. The point is that you should tell someone where you're going and when you expect to return. Motors don't always work, and tides never stop. Don't make your loved ones on shore worry about your whereabouts if you're late returning. You are required to have one life jacket for each person on your boat, and the Coast Guard is within its rights to stop you and see that you have proper equipment. Adults may use their own judgment about wearing a life jacket; children should automatically be strapped into one. It isn't comfortable, but these things save people's lives.

Carry sufficient liquids, not only for the humans aboard but for your dog if you choose to take Rover along. Discourage your pet from drinking sea water, and have fresh water available. And, obviously, don't drive drunk on the water. Carry an emergency kit that contains flares, a fire extinguisher and various repair items. If you're going to be out after dark, attend to your running lights. The Intracoastal Waterway is also a highway for commerce, and you want to be sure that barges know you're out there in the dark. Educate yourself on basic navigation. Especially in congested areas, which abound on the Intracoastal Waterway at Wrightsville Beach and Carolina Beach, understand markers and their meanings. A Power Squadron course, probably available in your city or town, is an invaluable experience before boating.

Boats under sail always have the right of way over powercraft. If power is your chosen method of boating, be considerate of the instability your wake can create for sailboats. Remember that Wilmington is a major port, and some whopping vessels travel the shipping lanes into the Cape Fear River. Give these vessels wide berth. Large ships have a suck-

The best way to cook firm-fleshed fish such as snapper or grouper is on the grill, wrapped in bacon and basted with melted butter, lemon juice and pressed garlic.

The Troublesome Whale at Wrightsville Beach

The story begins, according to Mary Ann Brittain in her book, *A Whale Called Trouble*, with these words: "In the spring of 1928 an enormous dead whale washed ashore at Wrightsville Beach, North Carolina. The animal weighed 100,000 pounds —

as much as 10 elephants. It measured 54 feet, 2 inches long — as long as two school buses — and 33 feet around the middle. Its tail was 14 feet wide. This whale, a sperm whale, meant lots of trouble for the people who had to decide what to do with it. In fact, 'Trouble' became its name."

Coastal residents expect to be surprised by what the tide brings in now and then, and beached whales or other large aquatic animals account for the most surprising — and saddest — tidal offerings. But the arrival of an animal of this size surely had an element of shock that has been unmatched by any other grounding this century on area beaches.

It was such an awesome sight that the *Wilmington Star-News* estimated it attracted more than 50,000 visitors from six states, probably making it the largest single tourist attraction in the history of Wrightsville Beach.

After the number of gawkers started to dwindle, no doubt driven off by the smell of 50 tons of rotting flesh and bone, Mayor Kidder of Wilmington said something had to be done with the whale. Fortunately that old axiom about one man's trash being another's treasure came into play. As Brittain writes: "Although the dead whale was becoming a bigger problem for many people, it provided a rare opportunity for the North Carolina State Museum of Natural History. This was the museum's first chance to get an entire sperm whale skeleton for display in Raleigh."

The logistics of moving the whale seemed insurmountable on two fronts: funding and technology. The creative director of the museum, Herbert Brimley, and assistant Harry T. Davis came up with a plan to haul the animal back into the water, tow it to

— continued on next page

Photo: Scott Taylor

Whales are frequent visitors to the waters of coastal North Carolina,
but you usually have to watch carefully.

— continued from previous page

nearby, uninhabited Topsail Inlet and beach it anew. At that site the whale could be stripped of its flesh, the bones could be buried for a time, and a truck from the museum could eventually dig it up, take it to Raleigh and put the whole skeleton back together.

Stone Towing Company tugboats had a tremendous struggle pulling the whale off the beach and even snapped a cable during the process. Undaunted, they dug a trench and wrapped the body with cable eight times. After an hour of strenuous workout on the part of the tug engines, Trouble was on his way out to sea where a museum boat was waiting to receive him.

Unfortunately, the cables wrapped around the whale made it difficult for the museum boat to tie their lines to the now adrift animal. Brittain describes the scene: "Boat and whale began to drift dangerously near the breakers. Both the whale and the boat were in danger of being lost. However, the crew of a nearby Coast Guard cutter sighted the museum's boat. Its strange movements made them suspect that the boat was involved in something illegal, like "whiskey running." But when the Coast Guardsmen saw Trouble, they understood the boat's odd movements. The cutter helped tow the creature into an inlet where it was beached."

A happy ending? Not quite. In the night, the body washed across the channel and landed on a shoal yards from the beach. The museum director and assistant decided just to have the body chopped right there and transported the bones by boat to the beach. It took eight workers to cut away 20 tons of stinking whale flesh. The bones were buried in the sand so the clinging flesh could decompose for more than six months.

After the bones were transported to Raleigh, they were buried again. Director Brimley noticed the bones still had a terrible smell. Brittain writes, "They smelled, he said, like a fertilizer factory that had been turned into a home for unexpurgated skunks." Ten months later, the skeleton was moved to the North Carolina Museum of Natural History where it was kept on the roof until an early winter freeze forced the staff to bring it inside.

It took Brimley and Davis six weeks to put the bony puzzle together and hang it in the museum. Today visitors can marvel at the sight and imagine the view on Wrightsville Beach the morning Trouble came ashore.

A postscript: Trouble may have been a problem for the beach, but his name also applied to the circumstances that brought him to land. Workers slicing away at the flesh took note of a wound in the whale's back that was most likely the cause of his death. It is speculated the wound was caused by an explosive projectile from a whaling ship off the coast of Charleston. Thanks to the considerable trouble this great beast caused after he had been so mercilessly troubled by people, his painstakingly preserved skeleton will help serve as an important reminder of the majesty of these mammals and the importance of extending global protection to them.

---

ing action on the water around them, and barges require several miles in which to stop. If you sail in the way of commercial vessels, you should know that your right-of-way won't amount to much if impact occurs.

Emergencies happen on the water. The Coast Guard is particular about what constitutes an emergency, and they will not immediately come to your rescue in all situations. Generally only life or environment-threatening situations will receive the attention of the Coast Guard. Running aground in the waterway is rarely considered an emergency because if you get stuck, there is local understanding you can walk to shore. Commercial towing companies will arrive if you get stuck on a sandbar and call for help on your radio; and, believe this Insider who has been stuck hard aground a few times, their service is worthwhile. A sailboat with a fixed keel is virtually guaranteed to go aground at some point, and it isn't always possible to get loose without a sturdy towboat.

The area's waters are full of shoals, so keep an eye on your depth-sounder. If you don't have one, and charts suggest shallow waters, steer clear of questionable areas. The Intracoastal Waterway is susceptible to shoaling near inlets, and you can't rely on charts for accuracy since changes occur frequently.

Being out on a boat often inspires hunger, and it seems very romantic to poke about the channels in search of fresh oysters. This isn't recommended. Leave the oysters to the professionals who know the uncontaminated areas.

This region is rich in seafood, and visitors, especially those who rent beach houses where they can cook, will find wonderful variety in fresh fish and shellfish in area seafood stores. You can certainly catch your own fish and guarantee its freshness; but you don't have to do that if you aren't inclined to do so.

The most important tips in purchasing the fruits of the sea involve your most basic senses. Start with your nose. Seafood shouldn't smell overly fishy. Continue with your eyes. A fresh fish with its head intact will have clear eyes that guarantee it just came from the water. A fillet will look moist and will not be discolored or faded. Feel the fish. It should be firm.

Insiders know that the area is abundant in delicious shrimp. A traditional shrimperoo includes sheets of newspaper spread on a big table heaped with steamed shrimp. Guests peel their own. It's a messy bit of heaven.

The southern coast boasts the best that sun, sand and sea have to offer. Come prepared to enjoy a safe and fun visit. For more information contact the Cape Fear Coast Visitor Information Bureau at 341-4030.

- **Fastest Head Boats at Carolina Beach**
- **Private Charters**
- **Individual Tickets**
- **Group Rates Available**

Real Gulf Stream Fishing

Departing from Carolina Beach Docks.
Tickets may be purchased in advance at the
Pirate Ticket Office
All Day and Half Day Trips
Dolphin - Watching Trips
Two Supersize Boats
Famous Moonlight Cruises
Live DJ
Food and Beverages Available
ABC Permit

910-458-5626 or 910-791-3689

Pirate Fishing & Cruising Boats
Carolina Beach Docks
Captain Tom Rothrock

Fishing

For anglers, the southern coast is very nearly paradise. Blue-green inshore waters tempered and cleansed by the Gulf Stream, the deep-blue offshore waters of the Gulf Stream itself, saltwater estuaries where many saltwater species breed, and dozens of winding freshwater creeks teeming with life await eager anglers. Whether you're interested in lazing alongside a shady creek in slow pursuit of catfish, surf-casting for blues, or pitting yourself against mighty deep-sea game fish, it's all here. Even at Wilmington's Greenfield Lake, where one lucky guy hauled in a 40-pound carp in 1995, opportunities abound. Strict catch limits and catch-and-tag programs have helped several saltwater fish populations thrive and keep the fishing prospects looking good.

Since the early 1970s, the Division of Marine Fisheries has been involved in the creation of artificial reefs that provide habitats for a plethora of undersea life. These reefs consist of old ships, railroad cars, bridge rubble, concrete and FADs (Fish Attracting Devices, whatever they are). Using the motto "We sink 'em—you fish 'em," the reef-builders have created 20 such reefs along the coast to date. Judging by the numbers of sheepshead, mackerel and billfish landed on an average day, the program seems to be paying off. (Surely, the men who landed the 937-pound tiger shark in the Poor Boy Shark Tournament in August 1993 think so.) A chart will lead you to these sites as well as to the scores of fish-filled wrecks littering this area.

Small-boat owners have many fishing opportunities — around the pilings of Pfizer Pharmaceutical Company's pier in the Cape Fear River north of Price's Creek, for example. The mouths of most creeks and some inlets are good spots, especially during incoming tides when you and your bait can drift in with the bait fish. Use caution at ocean inlets during outgoing tides.

As a result of direct hits upon North Carolina's southern coast by hurricanes Bertha and Fran in 1996, most of the fish in the Northeast Cape Fear River are gone. Fishing there probably won't pay off until late 1997. And ocean anglers who prefer pier fishing should embrace surf casting this year since so many piers along the east-facing beaches were destroyed, with the greatest losses occurring on Topsail Island (where piers are most numerous). Some piers are already being rebuilt, others may be rebuilt and still others are gone forever. In the section on Fishing Piers, we've attempted to indicate the status of each one. If you don't see your favorite pier listed, cherish your photographs. Brunswick County piers, all the way from Southport to Sunset, were essentially untouched and remain in good condition. In response to readers' requests, we've also noted which piers are handicapped-accessible.

Fishing Licenses

While licenses are not currently required for hook-and-line saltwater fishing, authorities are currently considering them. A decision could be made within the shelf life of this edition of the *Insiders' Guide*, so check with the businesses below that handle licenses for updates. (Individual recreational saltwater licenses are expected to cost about $15 annually, if authorized.) In any case, you must observe size and bag limits. Familiarize yourself with regulations, which are posted at most piers and marinas. Freshwater licenses are issued by the North Carolina Wildlife Resources Commission, (919) 662-4370. Licenses range greatly in price and privileges and may be combined with a hunting license. Licenses may be purchased locally at selected retailers.

In Wilmington

Tackle Express Tackle Mart, 4100 Oleander Drive, 392-3472

Kmart, 815 S. College Road, 799-5360

Wal-Mart, 352 S. College Road, 392-4034

In Pender County

Holland's Shelter Creek Fish Camp, N.C. Highway 53, 259-5743

Hampstead Village Pharmacy, in the Hampstead Village Shopping Center, U.S. Highway 17 (about 2 miles north of town center), 270-3411

In South Brunswick

Stewart Hardware, Highway 211 near the Sandfiddler Restaurant in Southport, 457-5544

Wal-Mart, 4540 Main Street in Shallotte, 754-2880

Pawn-USA, 5001-4 Main Street in Shallotte, 754-7918

Holden Beach True Value Hardware, 3008 Holden Beach Road, 842-5440

Island Tackle and Gifts, N.C. Highway 179 between Ocean Isle Beach and Sunset Beach, 579-6116

Note that fishing from most bridges in the area is restricted since bridges often transverse boat channels. Be certain to check the signs on particular bridges before casting. For a wide range of information on boating access, inland fishing, species information (especially trout), lake and stream stock and maps, call the North Carolina Wildlife Resources Commission at (919) 733-3634 or write: 512 N. Salisbury Street, Raleigh, N.C. 27604-1188.

If you're traveling without tackle, rental gear is fairly abundant. Among the places to check are these shops in addition to the fishing piers listed below: Herring's Tackle in Surf City (Topsail Island), 328-3291; and Beach Fun Rentals on Holden Beach Road S.W. (on the mainland side of the bridge), 842-9600. Tackle shops are abundant along the coast. Be sure to inquire whether particular shops rent equipment.

FYI

Unless otherwise noted, the area code for all phone numbers in this guide is 910.

So much for knowing what to do. What follows is information on where and when to do it: annual fishing tournaments, where to get up-to-date fishing reports, fishing piers and boat ramps, a cross-section of head boats and charters and surf fishing. Of course, we've included recommendations for some special places to cast your lure or net.

Southern Coast Saltwater Fishing Tournaments

Lately tournament fishing has been luring larger schools of anglers with tens of thousands of dollars in prize bait. Many contests recognize tag and release as part of the Governor's Cup Billfishing Conservation series. Check current listings at tackle shops, marinas and visitors centers.

May

Bald Head Island Fishing Rodeo, Bald Head Island Marina, (800) 234-1666

July

East Coast Got-Em-On King Mackerel Classic, Carolina Beach Yacht Basin, Carolina Beach, 458-9576

Hampstead King Mackerel Tournament, Harbor Village Marina, Hampstead, 270-4017

August

Poor Boy Shark Tournament, Hugh's Marina, Shallotte Point, 754-6233

Long Bay Lady Anglers King Mackerel Tournament, Sure Catch Tackle Shop, Southport, 457-4545

Sneads Ferry King Mackerel Tournament, New River Marina, Sneads Ferry, 327-2106 or 327-9691

Topsail Offshore Fishing Club King Mackerel Tournament, Topsail Marina, Topsail Beach, 328-5681

September

South Brunswick Isles King Mackerel Tournament, call for location, 754-6644

Wrightsville Beach King Mackerel Tournament, Bridge Tender Marina, Wrightsville Beach, 392-3666

U.S. Open King Mackerel Tournament, Southport Marina, Southport, 457-6964

October
Pleasure Island Surf Fishing Tournament, Carolina Beach, 458-8434

Boat Ramps

The North Carolina Wildlife Resources Commission maintains free ramps for pleasure boaters and anglers. Parking is generally scarce in the summer months in the busier locations such as Wrightsville Beach. The ramps are identified by black-and-white, diamond-shaped "Wildlife" signs. For information on public boat access, call (919) 733-3633. Included here are some private ramps as well.

Wilmington
Dram Tree Park on the corner of Castle and Surry streets off Front Street in downtown Wilmington is almost beneath the Cape Fear Memorial Bridge and gives access to the Cape Fear River.

Castle Hayne
In Castle Hayne access to the Northeast Cape Fear River is by a ramp next to the N.C. Highway 117 bridge.

Pender County
The Northeast Cape Fear River and its tributary creeks are accessible by three public ramps:

A ramp that allows access to the west bank of the river from I-40 can be reached by taking N.C. Highway 53 east about 1.7 miles, then County Road 1512 to its end.

A public ramp on the east bank is off County Road 1520 about 7.7 miles north of N.C. Highway 210. The intersection of Highway 210 and Secondary Road 1520 lies about 3 miles east of I-40 (Exit 408).

Holland's Shelter Creek Campground and Restaurant, 259-5743, is 7.5 miles east of I-40 down Highway 53. Canoes are for rent ($15

flat fee), and the restaurant offers a memorable glimpse of local style. The private ramp gives access to Holly Shelter Creek (see the chapters on Camping and Restaurants).

The Beaches
At Wrightsville Beach next to the U.S. Highway 74/76 drawbridge is a public ramp accessible from either side of the main road. This access to the Intracoastal is very busy in summer months, especially on weekends.

On Pleasure Island, there are four ramps east of Highway 421 at Snow's Cut. Coming south, make a hairpin right turn at the south end of Snow's Cut bridge, onto Bridge Barrier Road. Turn right at Spencer Farlow Road and follow it less than a half-mile to the Wildlife sign. The lot is down a short road on your left. If you're coming north from Carolina Beach, exit Highway 421 at Lewis Road just before the bridge and take an immediate left onto Access Road. Spencer Farlow Road is less than a half-mile ahead. Another ramp is at the end of Highway 421, south of the Fort Fisher ferry terminal and gives access to the Basin off Federal Point.

Also on Pleasure Island, Carolina Beach State Park, 458-8206, Dow Road has four ramps ($3 per day), a marina and ample parking. Access is to the Cape Fear River.

The ramp directly beneath the Highway 210 high span in North Topsail Beach is generally uncrowded. It is accessible from the last turnout from the northbound side of Highway 210 before the bridge. Access is to New River Inlet.

Across the Intracoastal from North Topsail Beach is a ramp at the foot of County Road 1529. From Highway 17, drive east from Folkstone on Old Folkstone Road (County Road 1518), which intersects 1529 about 2 miles on.

For freshwater fishing in north Brunswick, a public ramp gives access to historic Towne Creek and its tributaries at the eastern end of County Road 1521, about 1.5 miles east of Winnabow, off Highway 17.

Brunswick Islands

At the foot of County Route 1101, accessible from Highway 133 on the mainland side of Oak Island, the public ramp gives direct access to the Intracoastal Waterway.

At Sunset Harbor, east of Lockwood Folly River, a public boat ramp gives access to Lockwood Folly River and Inlet and the Intracoastal Waterway. From Highway 211, take County Route 1112 about 6 miles south and turn right at Lockwood Folly Road. Follow to its end.

At Holden Beach, public boat ramps are under the Highway 130 bridge on the island side.

Freshwater anglers may launch into the east bank of the Waccamaw River at the Highway 904 bridge at Pineway, about 5 miles north of the South Carolina border.

Fishing Reports

The most up-to-date sources of fishing information are charter captains, fishing piers and tackle shops. The radio station Beach 106.3-FM (WCCA) airs fishing reports twice a day on weekdays at 7 AM and 5 PM. Star-Line, a telephone service of the *Wilmington Star-News*, provides daily fishing and weather reports for the price of a local call, 762-1996 extension 2212.

Fishing Piers

Each of the piers in the area has its own personality. Some have been made crooked — those that survive — by years of battering by the ocean and gales. Some are festooned with odd novelties and memorabilia. Most of them proudly display photographs of trophies reeled up from the sea. Almost all charge a fee for fishing permits, good for a 24-hour period beginning at 6 AM. Bottom fishing generally costs $3 to $5 per day and king fishing about twice as much. Most piers offer season fishing permits, tackle shops, snack bars, wet cleaning tables and restrooms.

Keep in mind that, due to hurricane damage, some telephone numbers may be temporarily disconnected or may change without notice. We've listed the piers' most recently published numbers.

Wilmington

River Road Park
6300 River Rd., Wilmington • 341-7198

This county park, south of the State Port about 8 miles from downtown Wilmington and opposite Sugar Pine Drive, features a 240-foot, handicapped-accessible fishing pier on the Cape Fear River. The park is handicapped-accessible and is open from 8 AM to dusk.

Wrightsville Beach

Crystal Pier
703 S. Lumina Ave., Wrightsville Beach • 256-5551

Crystal Pier, sometimes called Oceanic Pier, is at the Oceanic Restaurant. It survived hurricane Fran in a somewhat truncated condition, and as of this writing had not reopened for fishing. The pier has no tackle shop and prohibits vulgarity. Assuming its reopening, permits are sold at the restaurant's front desk. It has no handicap access.

Johnnie Mercer's Pier
Foot of E. Salisbury St., Wrightsville Beach • 256-2743

This popular pier lost about half its length during hurricane Fran. There are plans to rebuild the pier in concrete, complete with a new, handicap-accessible pier house. Call ahead for more information, as this will take time. As things now stand, fishing has resumed, but because of the pier's shortened length the water is quite thin at low tide. Mercer's Pier features a tackle shop that sells bait and an arcade that is a favorite hangout for teens.

Carolina/Kure Beaches

Carolina Beach Pier
Salt Marsh Ln. and Canal St., Carolina Beach • 458-5518

Another pier shortened by Fran's fury, Caroline Beach Pier is currently open to fishing, and plans are in place to rebuild the lost length. Free parking at this northernmost pier on Carolina Beach is for customers only.

Beach parking costs $3 per day. Handicap access is difficult.

Kure Beach Pier
Ave. K , Kure Beach • 458-5524

Fully rebuilt and operational, Kure Beach Pier issues permits that are good from midnight to midnight. The new facilities include a grill, an arcade with four pool tables, complete tackle shop and souvenir store, and handicap accessibility. No alcoholic beverages (including beer) are permitted.

Southport-Oak Island

City Pier
Waterfront Park, Bay St., Southport

This small, handicapped-accessible pier near the mouth of the Cape Fear River is a municipal facility, and usage is free.

Southport/Oak Island

Long Beach Pier
**2729 W. Beach Dr., Long Beach
• 278-5962**

Located near the far west end of Oak Island, Long Beach Pier is the longest pier in the state, measuring 1,012 feet. Some folks use shopping carts to move their gear the distance. Three things are not welcomed here: shark fishing, net casting and profanity. The owners perform rod-and-reel repairs on the premises, and there is good handicapped access.

Ocean Crest Pier
1411 E. Beach Dr., Long Beach • 278-6674, 278-3333

This 1,000-foot pier, near 14th Place E., has a tackle shop and allows handicapped anglers to fish for free. The owners do not allow shark fishing but do provide a shelter of sorts at the T-shaped far end that is reserved for king fishers. Daily permits cost $5 for bottom fishing and $9 for king mackerel. Season permits cost $75 for bottom fishing and $125 for kings. The Windjammer restaurant adjoins the pier.

Yaupon Pier
**Foot of Womblie Ave., Yaupon Beach
• 278-9400**

This is the highest pier in the state, yet it's handicapped accessible. The owners were convinced by the persuasive March storm of '93 — not the hurricanes of '96 — that some remodeling was in order and added 130 feet of pier. The Pirate's Cove Restaurant adjoins the pier, as does the unique Oar House Lounge, a must-see that won't appeal to everyone.

South Brunswick Islands

Holden Beach Pier
**441 Ocean Blvd. W., Holden Beach
• 842-6483**

Holden Beach Pier prohibits the use of nets and the consumption of alcoholic beverages. It sells three-day and seven-day fishing permits and live bait. A grill and snack counter adjoin a game room that's fairly busy in summer. The restrooms are often poorly kept. This is one of only three area piers (including Ocean Isle and Sunset Beach, below) that charge spectators a fee (25¢) for walking the pier. Handicap access is good.

Ocean Isle Pier
**Foot of Causeway Dr., Ocean Isle Beach
• 579-6873**

The steep ramp to the pier gets slippery when wet and is not handicapped friendly. The large game room and small grill are popular in summer.

Sunset Pier
**Foot of Sunset Blvd., Sunset Beach
• 579-6630**

There is no running water at the cleaning

INSIDERS' TIP

After treating the pain and swelling of a jellyfish sting, remove the stingers (nematocysts) by applying shaving cream and gently shaving the area.

table, but amenities include a snack bar, game room, bait for sale and handicapped accessibility. Handicapped persons may find the rest rooms a little difficult.

Topsail Island

Barnacle Bill's Fishing Pier
Shore Dr., Surf City • 328-3661

The owners of Barnacle Bill's planned to reopen the pier as of this writing but had not yet begun rebuilding. The pier had been a colorful attraction — a busy, cluttered place with a pool room, a salty clientele and often loud country music playing.

Jolly Roger Pier
Foot of Flake Ave., Surf City • 328-4616

Rebuilding of the Jolly Roger had begun when we went to press. It is the only ocean pier on the southern half of Topsail Island, standing 6 miles south of Surf City, and its patio is what remains of a launch pad built for Project Bumblebee, the Navy's historic missile-development program. Plans for rebuilding included a new handicapped-accessible side ramp.

Ocean City Fishing Pier
New River Dr., Surf City • 328-5701, (800) 358-2318

No plans to rebuild this pier were in place as we went to press, but it's possible there will be. The white observation tower at the foot of the pier is another remnant of Operation Bumblebee, a top-secret Navy missile project conducted on the island in the late 1940s. The pier stood opposite Herring's Bait & Tackle Shop, actually 3 miles north of Surf City.

Salty's Pier
1798 New River Inlet Rd., N. Topsail Beach • 328-0221

Plans to rebuild Salty's Pier were unre-

solved at press time. In the past, the pier shop offered a good selection of rods, reels and accessories for sale and rent as well as fresh bait and a small variety of beverages and microwavable foods. Anglers could kick back and relax on bench seats with backs. Salty's is just north of the Villa Capriani Resort.

Surf City Pier
N. Shore Dr., Surf City • 328-3521

Surf City Pier was in the process of rebuilding as we went to press and should be fully operational by summer of 1997. One block south of Roland Avenue in the heart of Surf City, this handicapped-accessible pier is a busy, family-oriented establishment that prohibits alcohol and drunks. The busy snack bar rents chairs and other beach supplies. Indoors, a large game room will keep the kids twitching their joy sticks. Special bottom-fishing rates apply to children: $2 daily, $15 per season (April 1 to November 30).

Fly Fishing

The fastest-growing niche in fishing these days seems to be saltwater fly fishing, possessing all the artistry and finesse of freshwater fly fishing with the adrenaline rush of ocean game fishing thrown in. Neophytes and aficionados of saltwater fly fishing should take note of the following invaluable resources in the Wilmington area, in addition to many tackle shops throughout the region.

Digh's Country Sports Gallery
1988 Eastwood Rd., Wrightsville Beach • 256-2060

Wilmington's exclusive Orvis dealer, Digh's (rhymes with "dyes") offers the services of full-time, expert fly-fishing guides for any type of local fly-fishing action. Gulf Stream trips are aboard a Bertram sportfisherman, and inshore trips are aboard Boston Whalers and custom flat boats. Digh's is also the local sponsor of

INSIDERS' TIP

When boating the Intracoastal Waterway around Surf City on weekends, tie up to Greg Gilmore's Float Mart, a convenience store on pontoons that stocks everything from sodas and sandwiches to spark plugs, bug spray and bait.

the Orvis saltwater fly-fishing school. Arranging worldwide hunting, fishing (salt and fresh-water) and travel packages is among Digh's specialties. The handsomely designed store stocks casual and sport clothing and original sporting art in various media. You'll find Orvis rods and reels, fly-tying materials, books and luggage. You can even call for the day's fishing report. In summer Digh's is open 10 AM to 7 PM Monday through Friday, 9 AM to 5 PM Saturday and 11 AM to 4 PM Sunday.

Intracoastal Angler
6303 Oleander Dr., #102, Wilmington
• 395-6255

Intracoastal Angler has attracted the attention of national fishing publications and for good reason. Boasting perhaps the most elaborate fly-tying department in the state, this full-service fly shop and outfitter provides expert guide service, boat charter, clinics, lessons, a full line of apparel, equipment and tackle for both salt and fresh water. The staff is friendly and professional. From mid-April through the warm season, owner Tyler Stone captains his own 20-foot center-console vessel, *Misguided*, for inshore and offshore charters geared for everything from Atlantic bonita and Spanish mackerel to barracuda, amberjack and tarpon. Intracoastal Angler stocks top-name rods and reels as well as books and videos in a visually appealing shop at the Saltworks Station, immediately south of the Bradley Creek bridge (on the westbound side) and across from the Arboretum. The shop is open Monday through Saturday from 9 AM to 6 PM and noon to 5 PM Sunday during the warm season.

Head Boats and Charters

From Topsail's Treasure Coast to Calabash, there are fishing vessels aplenty. Choose among head boats (a.k.a. party boats) accommodating dozens of people and six-pack charters accommodating up to six passengers. Head boats average $50 to $75 per person for full-day excursions; charters range anywhere from $300 for half-day excursions to $1,200 for an entire day of Gulf Stream fishing. From our shores, the Gulf Stream can be 40 to 70 miles off shore, depending on currents and the marina from which you embark.

Certain provisions are common to all charters: first mate, onboard coolers and ice, all the bait and tackle you'll need for kings, tuna, dolphin, wahoo, billfish and more. They'll offer a variety of trips, typically half-day and full-day, inshore and offshore, and sometimes overnight, and most are available for tournaments and diving trips (reserve early). If you can't find enough friends to chip in to cover the cost, ask about split charters; many captains book them. Most charter captains prefer reservations but will accept walk-ons when possible. With advance notice, many will arrange food packages, and some may even arrange hotel packages. Optional electric reels may be available, usually costing about 10 bucks. While most six-pack charters are unable to bring wheelchairs aboard, crews are often very accommodating of handicapped passengers, sometimes leaving the wheelchair ashore and providing secure seating on deck, right where the action is. Call the vessel of your choice in advance for details.

Walk-ons are always welcome on head boats. Handicapped accessibility to most large head boats tends to be good, but varies from ship to ship and with weather conditions. Head boats are also equipped with full galleys and air-conditioned lounges.

Remember that no one can guarantee sea conditions. If your captain decides to turn back before you've landed a smoker, rest assured he knows what he's doing. Captains reserve the right to cancel trips if conditions are unsafe for the vessel or passengers.

So many fishing vessels are available all along our coast, we've listed below only those locations (marinas mostly) booking several charters from one office. Also check our Marinas chapter for more options.

There are no charters running directly out of Wilmington. Look instead for charters and head boats running from Wrightsville Beach and Carolina Beach.

Carolina Beach is the Gulf Stream fishing hub between Bald Head and Topsail islands. A large number of vessels run out of the Carolina Beach Municipal Docks at Carl Winner Street and Canal Drive. Parking ($3 per day in summer) is available on the marina's west side. Sea captains being the rugged individualists they are, there is no central booking office for

Surf fishing is a relaxing way to spend an afternoon.

Photo: Scott Taylor

these vessels. But since you should know something about what you're chartering in advance, your best bet is to simply walk the docks and eye each one. Signs and brochures there will give you all the booking information you'll need in lieu of the Old Man himself.

Charters in southern Brunswick County are concentrated at the Southport Marina, Blue Point Marina at the western tip of Oak Island, at Holden Beach and Ocean Isle Beach. Head Boats dock only in Calabash and at nearby Little River, South Carolina. Here we've listed a few central sources where you'll find a number of vessels. The types of vessels — six-packs or head boats — available at each location are indicated.

Carolina Sport Fishing Charters (six-packs), Wrightsville Beach, 799-8144

Hanover Fishing Charters (six-packs), Wrightsville Beach, 256-3636

Outer Limits Fishing Adventures (six packs), Carolina Beach, 395-4943.

Pirate Fishing & Cruise Charters (head boats), Carolina Beach, 458-5626

Winner Gulf Stream Fishing & Cruise Boats (head boats), Carolina Beach, 458-FISH

Southport Marina (six-packs), Southport, 457-9900, 457-5261

Blue Water Point Marina (both), Long Beach, 278-1230

Holden Beach Marina (both), Holden Beach, 842-5447

Capt'n Pete's Seafood Market (both), Holden Beach, 842-6675

Ocean Isle Marina (six-packs), Ocean Isle Beach, 579-0848

Capt. Jim's Marina (head boats), Calabash, 579-3660

Hurricane Fleet (head boats), Little River Marina, Little River, South Carolina, (803) 249-4575, (803) 249-7775

Osprey Charters (six-packs), Topsail Beach, 328-3641

Swan Point Marina, Sneads Ferry (north of Topsail Island), 327-1081

Surf Fishing

We've all heard this type of exchange between anglers: "Where'd you catch it?" asks the hopeful one. "In the mouth," replies the successful one. Well, we can't reveal every secret fishing hole in the region (we're still learning them ourselves), but we can recommend a few to get you started.

On Wrightsville Beach, an exceptional surf-fishing spot is behind the jetty at Masonboro Inlet, on the south end of the island. Do not fish from the jetty itself; it's dangerous and illegal.

The Fort Fisher State Recreation Area is an undeveloped 4-mile stretch of beach and tidal marsh, approximately 6 miles south of Carolina Beach, accessible by four-wheel-drive

North Carolina Fishing: What's Hot and When!

January Trout, sea bass, some grouper, some snapper, bluefish, oysters, clams

February Trout, sea bass, some grouper, some snapper, bluefish, oysters, clams

March Grouper, sea trout, sea bass, bluefish, croaker, oysters, some snapper, some clams

April Bluefish, channel bass, grouper, snapper, croaker, sea trout, sea mullet, some king mackerel, some oysters, some clams

May King mackerel, bluefish, grouper, some flounder, cobia, tuna, some sharks, crabs, soft crabs, some sea mullet

June Blue marlin, white marlin, dolphin, wahoo, cobia, king mackerel, bluefish, tuna, summer flounder, snapper, grouper, some Spanish mackerel, crabs, soft crabs, sharks

July Dolphin, wahoo, tuna, blue marlin, white marlin, snapper, grouper, summer flounder, bluefish, Spanish mackerel, crab, some soft crabs, some sea mullet, sharks

August Dolphin, wahoo, tuna, grouper, snapper, Spanish mackerel, bluefish, some speckled trout, some spots, some sea mullet, sharks, crabs

September Grouper, snapper, Spanish mackerel, king mackerel, spots, sharks, bluefish, some speckled trout, sea mullet, some channel bass

October King mackerel, bluefish, snapper grouper, channel bass, spots, speckled trout, some flounder, sharks, some oysters

November King mackerel, bluefish, speckled trout, flounder, snapper, grouper, clams, some sharks, some sea mullet

December Bluefish, flounder, speckled trout, oysters, clams, sea trout, some snapper, some sea bass, some grouper

Courtesy of N.C. Department of Environment, Health & Natural Resources, Division of Marine Fisheries

---

vehicle. At the entrance to the area, off U.S. 421 before the North Carolina Aquarium (bear left at the fork), there is a public beach access with restrooms, a shower and snack bar. Otherwise, there are no services, so bring everything you'll need (also see "Off-Roading" in the Sports and Fitness chapter).

Another good spot, Carolina Beach Inlet at the north end of Pleasure Island, is also accessible by four-wheel-drive. A less-known and more restricted fishing spot on Pleasure Island lies off Dow Road. For 3 miles south of Spartanburg Avenue, foot paths enter the woods from the roadside (you may notice vehicles parked there). Foot traffic only is permitted since this is an environmentally sensitive area owned by the federal government (the No

Trespassing warnings are never enforced). The trails lead to the Cape Fear River, but the northernmost trails open upon a secluded inlet where bait fish are often stirred into a frenzy by the unseen feeders. It's also a good place to picnic and relax, but observe posted restrictions, which may change from time to time.

Fishing The Rocks is a unique outing. The Rocks is a 3.3-mile breakwater extending from Federal Point, south of the Fort Fisher Ferry terminal. The water enclosed by it around Zeke's Island is called the Basin, and fishing on both sides of the barrier can be excellent. Walking the Rocks can be hazardous; enter upon them only at low tide.

The Point, at the west end of Oak Island bordering Lockwood Folly Inlet, is a produc-

Photo: Bill DiNome

The character of each pier is a reflection of the storms it survives.

tive spot for surf fishing. It's a fairly long walk to the water, but you can drive there if you've got an off-road vehicle and a permit ($50 from the town of Long Beach). Beach driving there is permitted only off-season, from September 15 to April 15.

Access to New River Inlet, at the north end of Topsail Island, can be gained from the boat ramp parking lot directly beneath the N.C. Highway 210 high span. It's usually a very quiet place. You'll find it at the last turnout from the northbound side of N.C. 210 before the bridge. Unmarked footpaths wind through the brush to the water.

When fishing the beaches, observe local dune ordinances and keep off the dunes except at established crossovers. Most beach communities levy fines for trespassing upon dunes. In North Topsail Beach, for example, you may be tagged with a hefty $500 fine for ignoring the warning signs, which apply equally to private property.

The Middle Atlantic
Intracoastal
Waterway runs
from Norfolk,
Virginia, to Miami,
Florida, and
is maintained by
the U.S. Army
Corps of Engineers.

Marinas and the Intracoastal Waterway

Part of the pleasure of life along the southern coast involves getting on the water, and there is no more immediately accessible or friendlier passageway than the Intracoastal Waterway. Built during the Roosevelt years, the ICW was created as a commercial waterway to move goods up and down the coast. Secondarily, but more importantly now, the water trail known affectionately as "the ditch" is a busy place for pleasure craft.

The Middle Atlantic Intracoastal Waterway runs from Norfolk, Virginia, to Miami, Florida, and is maintained by the U.S. Army Corps of Engineers. It links sounds and rivers into the most extensive system of inland waters in the country and provides carefully charted cruising waters for every kind of boater. North Carolina's portion of the Intracoastal Waterway generally lies between the mainland and barrier islands, stretching across sounds, down rivers and through man-made ditches. It is largely undeveloped throughout the southern North Carolina coast. Egrets abound in this wilderness, dolphins speed alongside boats, and people from many points of origin convene to travel together and share stories.

The area's mild temperatures make pleasure-boating on the Intracoastal Waterway comfortable from March until the latter part of December, so there is a very long season to enjoy this special part of North Carolina's southern coast.

Marinas

After a long cruise or even a short daytrip into the Atlantic and back into the ICW, marinas are probably one of the most beautiful sights a boater can see. Fuel, beverages, restaurants, overnight berths, ship's stores, repairs and nearby services make a boater's experience much more pleasant. While there are more than 90 marinas along North Carolina's southern coast, what follows is a condensed listing. For detailed and candid information on all of these marinas, pick up a copy of native North Carolinian Claiborne Young's *Cruising Guide to Coastal North Carolina*.

As of this edition, Topsail Island no longer has a marina. Hurricane Fran wreaked havoc on the marina business there and, although one may return in the future, it's obvious to locals that there won't be one in the next two or more years. So, marina coverage begins just north of Wilmington.

Pender County

Harbour Village Marina
101 Harbour Village Dr., Hampstead
• 270-4017

Just off U.S. Highway 17 north of Wilmington at Belvedere Plantation, turn into Harbour Village and follow the road and signs to the marina. From the water, this marina is located to the north of flashing daybeacon 96. There's a golf course, a large country club and tennis courts. The marina portion of the development has all of the amenities a boater could want, including a boater's lounge, transportation to restaurants, showers and a laundry. Boating guests can also enjoy swimming, tennis and golf for a fee.

New Hanover County

Canady's Marina
7624 Mason's Landing Rd., Wilmington
• 686-9116

Johnson Marina
2029 Turner Nursery Rd., Wilmington
• 686-7565

Scott's Hill Marina
2570 Scott's Hill Loop Rd., Wilmington
• 686-0896

Oak Winds Marina
2127 Middle Sound Loop Rd., Wilmington • 686-0445

Carolina Yacht Yard
2107 Middle Sound Rd., Wilmington • 686-0004

Mason's Marina
7421 Mt. Pleasant Dr., Wilmington • 686-7661

Pages Creek is home to a cluster of marinas and marine services. You can reach all of them by taking Middle Sound Loop Road off U.S. 17 at the light at Ogden. On the water, it is north of flashing daybeacon 122. This creek is just south of Figure Eight Island, which has a private marina just for the use of the island's residents. Pages Creek is more hospitable to transients and, while these marinas shouldn't be regarded as regular transient stops, they're very accommodating.

The marinas at Page's Creek mostly cater to locals whose boats are permanently berthed there. You won't generally find overnight dockage at these marinas with the exception of Scotts Hill Marina. You will find extensive repair services as well as fuel at Carolina Yacht Yard, Johnson Marina and Scotts Hill Marina. The others mostly provide slips or dry-dockage to regulars. Johnson Marina also has a ramp.

Wrightsville Beach

This beach took a whacking during Hurricane Fran's visit, but things recovered within a matter of months. Floating docks and boats went flying onto the mainland during the storm but the affluence of this beach community allowed for relatively quick repair. This is one of the best places along the coastline not only for services but also for a tremendous amount of fun. The area is rich in marinas that welcome, in most cases, transient boaters.

To get to these marinas, take Eastwood Road from U.S. 17 or, if coming from downtown Wilmington, take Oleander Drive or Market Street, both of which intersect with Eastwood. Several marinas are just before the first bridge leading to Wrightsville Beach on Airlie Road to the right. Others are across the bridge on Harbour Island, also to the right. For those with trailered craft, there's a free Wildlife Access Ramp just to the north of the first bridge over to Harbour Island. A note of caution: this ramp is not in good shape at this writing and the storms had nothing to do with the situation. Hopefully, governmental promises for funding to get it in good repair soon will be honored.

FYI
Unless otherwise noted, the area code for all phone numbers in this guide is 910.

Wrightsville Marina
1 Marina St., Wrightsville Beach
• 256-6666

Located on the eastern shore of the ICW just south of the bridge, this is a luxurious place to dock for the night since the marina offers power, water, telephone, cable TV connections, fuel and mechanical repairs. There is even a swimming pool available for transients. Pusser's, a large restaurant overlooking the marina, has just taken over the building formerly occupied by Wally's Restaurant.

Atlantic Marine
130 Short St., Wrightsville Beach
• 256-9911

Just past Wrightsville Marina, Motts Channel opens in the direction of the Atlantic Ocean. This marina offers repair services and is oriented to serving locals with its dry-docked small-craft facilities. Gasoline is the only service for transients. There are no overnight berths available to transients.

Seapath Yacht Club
330 Causeway Dr., Wrightsville Beach
• 256-6681

Next up on Motts Channel and just down the road from Wrightsville Marina, this well-appointed marina has some transient dockage with power, water, fuel and cable TV con-

Photo: Sherry White, N. C. Aquarium at Pine Knoll Shores

Catch a triggerfish and you've got one of the best seafood dinners around.

nections. A store provides many essential supplies, and George, the manager, is a heck of a nice guy. Seapath is very close to Banks Channel and is the nearest approach to the Atlantic Ocean, although Bradley Creek Marina farther south is just about as close to Masonboro Inlet.

Bridge Tender Marina and Restaurant
Airlie Rd., Wrightsville Beach • 256-6550

On the western shore, directly across from Wrightsville Marina on Airlie Road, is a marina with a bonus: a great local seafood and steak restaurant. The marina offers all amenities, including gas and diesel fuel. One word of caution: The current is very swift here, so mind your slippage on entering and be ready with a boathook to fend off some very expensive craft docked nearby.

Dockside Marina
1306 Airlie Rd., Wrightsville Beach • 256-3579

Overnight space and amenities for boaters are also available at this small marina that also boasts the Dockside Restaurant, a great place to get a shrimpburger in a basket.

Bradley Creek Boatominium
6338 Oleander Dr., Wilmington • 350-0029

As you travel south on the Intracoastal Waterway or take Airlie Road from Wrightsville Beach and take a left onto Oleander Drive, you'll come upon this large marina just south of the bridge on Bradley Creek. Located on the western shore of the ICW, this is a large, modern facility that, sadly for the transient, is not a place to stop for the night. This is a large dry-dock and wetslip facility that serves the local community. Fuel is available.

Boathouse Marina
6334 Oleander Dr., Wilmington • 350-0023

This is a dry-dock facility with haul-outs and repair service just past Bradley Creek's facility. It offers gasoline and has a ship's store.

Masonboro Boatyard and Marina
609 Trails End Rd., Wilmington • 791-1893

Masonboro took a severe hit with Fran but, in the resilient way of coastal people after a storm, this marina is getting it back together. No doubt the docks will be rebuilt by the time this book comes to print, and in early 1997 the channel was dredged. Masonboro is a delightful place to spend the night. Some boaters dock and end up staying for years. The scenery is absolutely lovely from the front row of floating docks. This facility specializes in repairs and has haul-out services as well as below-the-water repairs and other maintenance services. It has one of the largest inventories of diesel engine parts in the region. If you want to do your own out-of-the-water repairs, this facility allows it. You'll find a ship's store and friendly staff at this special marina, and you are guaranteed to find some interesting conversation among the residents. Masonboro Boatyard Marina has been operated by the same people since 1968.

On land, travel down Oleander Drive toward Wilmington until you come to Piner Road at Hugh McRae park on the left. Take the left and, when you come to a fork in the road, take the right fork onto Masonboro Loop Road. In a couple of miles, take note of a small bridge and a road to the left with a sign that points out Masonboro Marina and the Trails End Steak House.

Carolina Beach

Below Masonboro Sound, there is a stretch with no marinas. The shoreline becomes residential in character, and there is not another port until you get close to Carolina Beach.

Carolina Inlet Marina
801 Paoli Ct., Wilmington • 392-0580

Just north of Snow's Cut, this marina has fuel, a ship's store, parts and a full assortment of repair services. There is limited transient dockage at this marina; call the Inlet Watch Yacht Club at 392-7106 for transient reservations. To get there by land, go down Oleander Drive and take a left on S. College Road. Drive through Monkey Junction where U.S. Highway 421 converges, and pick up this highway heading south. Carolina Inlet Marina is on the left just before crossing the bridge over Snow's Cut into Carolina Beach.

Harbour Point and Pleasure Island Marina & Resort
Spencer Farlow Dr., Carolina Beach • 458-7368, (800) 989-2589

Approved by CAMA permit in early 1997, this is the newest marina along the southern North Carolina coast. It will offer 92 slips for sale or long-term lease as well as space for transient dockage. The floating piers will be fitted with power and freshwater lines. At this point, look to the nearby Carolina Beach Park marina for fuel. The marina will offer a ship's store, casual restaurant, showers and an outdoor eating area. Yacht club memberships are open to residents and nonresidents. It is located south of Snow's Cut Marina to starboard.

Snow's Cut Landing Marina
100 Spencer Farlow Dr., Carolina Beach • 458-7400

This marina is on the channel's western shore just south of Snow's Cut as it makes its way into Carolina Beach's harbor. This is a friendly marina that welcomes transients, but there are some big changes happening here in 1997. Townhomes are being built, and it is becoming more of a residential marina community. Fuel and boatyard services will no longer be offered.

Carolina Beach Municipal Marina
207 Canal Dr., Carolina Beach • 458-2985

This city marina is at the southern end of the channel in Carolina Beach. Fuel is available, but mooring is tight. The marina seems mostly dedicated to fishing charter and party boats, and the southern side of it is packed with ticket booths. You can sometimes find an overnight berth but not always. It's a good spot for a brief visit, particularly if you want to disembark in the heart of Carolina Beach and avail yourself of the fare at several restaurants and fastfood places.

INSIDERS' TIP

Most of the navigational markers on the Cape Fear River have been renumbered, and the changes won't show up until new NOAA charts are printed in a couple of years.

Carolina Beach State Park Marina
Carolina Beach State Park, Carolina Beach • 458-7770

Leaving Carolina Beach and heading toward the Cape Fear River, Snow's cut is the passage. On land, just go over the Snow's Cut Bridge on U.S. 421 S. and take the first right into the campgrounds. This marina offers a ramp, fuel and ample overnight dockage. If you're weary of being on a boat, you can pitch a tent and roast marshmallows over a campfire in the park.

Wilmington

It can be a very bumpy 15-mile ride from Snow's Cut across the Cape Fear River into Southport and the more protected Intracoastal Waterway. This is a major shipping lane to the State Port at Wilmington as well as the route for the Southport-Fort Fisher Ferry. Before crossing over, take a northerly route up the Cape Fear River where you will find increasingly improved opportunities to dock and take advantage of visiting Wilmington's historic center.

Something of great importance to boaters entering the Cape Fear River from Snow's Cut or the ocean is that all of the navigational markers have been redone. It's a confusing situation at best because NOAA charts won't show these corrections for at least two years. When in doubt, just fall back on the boater's rule: Keep red markers to your right going toward Wilmington and keep them to you left when returning to the sea.

Wilmington Marine Center
3410 River Rd., Wilmington • 395-5055

This excellent marina comes into view to starboard several miles up the Cape Fear River from Snow's Cut. It can also be reached by leaving U.S. 421 just north of the Snow's Cut Bridge or veering off onto River Road at the N.C. State Ports on Burnett Boulevard. This facility, the sole marina on the Cape Fear (until Bennett Brothers Yachts build their new marina north of downtown Wilmington on the river in 1997), specializes in service and storage of larger yachts and offers repairs and lift-out services as well as fuel. Dockage, power, water, showers and fuel are available to transients and regulars.

Downtown Wilmington Waterfront

While downtown isn't a marina and there is no fuel available, it bears mention to boaters looking for a very interesting stopover.

The Hilton
301 N. Water St. • 763-5900

The Hilton offers water and power to overnight boating guests on docks in front of the hotel. At 50¢ a foot, it's a wonderful bargain to be in immediate proximity to historic downtown Wilmington. If you're docked here, please look through the Restaurants, Shopping and entertainment chapters in this guide. Happy news for previous visitors who had to climb the ladder at low tide: This section of the Riverwalk now has floating docks.

City of Wilmington Municipal Docks
302 Willard St., Wilmington • 341-7855

The municipal docks to the south of the Hilton are available for brief visits but are not set up for extended stays. The general rule seems to be a limit of 72 hours of free dockage all along the downtown waterfront. Longer stays may be arranged through the City of Wilmington by special permit but, frankly, nobody official seems to take much notice unless a yacht is docked for months and the tax people take a look. The situation on the downtown Wilmington waterfront for transients is very much improved this year with new floating docks, and more plans are in the works to continue to make downtown a boating destination.

Bald Head Island

Bald Head Island Marina
Bald Head Island • 457-7380

This marina offers slips, fuel, restaurants and lift-out service as well as a gracious welcome to this lovely island. Bald Head Island Marina is not reachable by a road and the only way you're going to get there is by boat. Odds are you're not going to take the ferry if the marina is your destination for boating. You'll just boat right in and be delighted you did. This marina primarily serves a private, residential community where many of the homes are also vacation rentals, but it has the welcome mat out for visitors. Stop by for a rest in a beautiful setting, provisions, fuel and the opportunity for a walking adventure on this historic island. Be sure to visit the Bald Head Island lighthouse for a brisk climb and a panoramic view of the area.

Southport-Oak Island

The Brunswick Marinas took absolutely no hit at all from hurricanes in 1996. Mother Nature was kind to Brunswick as both hurricanes went to the north into Wilmington.

Southport Marina Inc.
W. West Place, Southport • 457-5261

This immaculate marina is on the Southport waterfront just south of downtown. By land, take U.S. 17 from Wilmington and a left onto N.C. Highway 132 to Southport. At the intersection of N.C. Highway 211, take a left and go as far as you can without going into the water. Then take a right and drive a few blocks until the marina comes into view on the left. This marina's extensive docks welcome the cruising boater with fuel, power, transient slips, restaurants, repair service, a clubhouse and supplies. It is one of only about a dozen North Carolina marinas with pump-outs. Something interesting is that this marina is owned by the government and leased to operators.

Blue Water Point Marina Resort
W. Beach Dr. to 57th Pl., Long Beach • 278-1230

Blue Water offers slip rentals, boat rentals, gas and diesel, bait, tackle and ice. It also has deep sea fishing charters and party boats. As if that isn't enough, it also offers airboat rides. The marina is located at ICW Marker #33. The new owners seem particularly accommodating to boating visitors.

South Brunswick Islands

Hughes Marina
1800 Village Point Rd., Shallotte • 754-6233

Hughes Marina is available for overnight accommodations with transient slips, fuel and shore power. However, the current is particularly swift here so boaters will need to pay careful attention while docking. If you'd like a night ashore, the marina has a motel and restaurant on the property.

Holden Beach Marina
3238 Pompano St., Holden Beach • 842-5447

This marina at the tip of Oak Island is regarded as one of the friendliest marinas on the North Carolina coast. It is a full-service marina with fuel, transient slips and complete services. It is on the waterway's northern banks in Supply.

Ocean Isle Marina
43 Causeway Dr., Ocean Isle Beach • 579-0848

This marina has gas and diesel fuel, bait and tackle, boat equipment and ice. Launch your own boat from it or charter a half-day or all-day fishing boat from the marina. In addition to fishing boat rentals, the marina also rents pontoon boats, wave runners, and rods and reels.

Pelican Pointe Marina
2000 Sommersett Rd., Ocean Isle Beach • 579-6440

This a full-service marina at marker 98 on the ICW offers gas and diesel fuel, extensive dry indoor boat storage for boats up to 32 feet, a staff of certified mechanics and a 9-ton boat forklift standing by. Pelican Pointe has a ships store complete with boat parts and supplies, beer, ice and fishing tackle. It also offers boat rentals.

INSIDERS' TIP

Always insist that children on your boat wear their lifejackets no matter how much they protest. Keep adult jackets within immediate reach.

Photo: Scott Taylor

A wooden boat is a terrible thing to waste.

Marsh Harbour Marina
10155 Beach Dr. S.W., Calabash
• 579-3500

Prepare to be impressed. This large marina has 221 slips, gas and diesel fuel, complete repair service, supplies and even a pump-out station. There are shoreside showers and a small ship's store just behind the fuel dock. The marina has shore power and water. It welcomes transients to berth in a spot from which boaters can stroll mere minutes to choose from one of three dozen Calabash restaurants — and there's even a laundry facility along the way. The marina is particularly well-sheltered for overnight dockage.

The River Keeper

Bouton Baldridge works in a small, even cramped, office in downtown Wilmington and ponders the future of the Cape Fear River that flows less than 50 yards from his desk. Two volunteers pore intently over documents nearby. There are no windows and very little in the way of office furniture, so the visitor is immediately struck by the fact this must be a struggling venture.

Close-up

The walls are covered with maps of the river as it makes its way from Greensboro to the ocean, a journey of hundreds of miles. There are a few newspaper articles tacked up, proudly displayed to demonstrate media attention paid to the work of this organization. Inexpensively produced newsletters and brochures are stacked on old tables.

This is the office of Cape Fear River Watch, the workplace of one paid staff member — courtesy of a recent grant by the Z. Smith Reynolds Foundation — and 600 volunteers who all share one thing in common: a determination to protect the Cape Fear River. Although the office is modest, the organization's goals are ambitious.

Cape Fear River Watch came into being in 1995 when Baldridge was struck with a notion that Wilmington's river needed protection as much as the highly publicized

— continued on next page

Neuse River to the north. Baldridge, a one-time graduate student in environmental science, read an article about the environmental problems in the Neuse River — unexplained fish kills, high algae levels, agricultural pollution, industrial pollution — and was heartened to note a river keeper had been hired by a grassroots organization in Raleigh (also funded with seed money from Z. Smith Reynolds) to search for the source of these and other problems there.

"I read this article by *Star-News* reporter Kirsten Mitchell," says Baldridge, "and I found myself thinking the Cape Fear, although very different from the Neuse, also needed a river keeper. So several of us started talking, and we got to work on it. After two years, we were able to get a grant that would allow me to do this work full-time as the Cape Fear River keeper.

"The Neuse is important, but so is the Cape Fear. More people in Raleigh were familiar with the Neuse because it flows from Raleigh (the seat of the government)

Photo: Wilmington Star News

Bouty Baldridge keeps a close eye on the waters from this canoe.

to New Bern. We weren't getting as much attention as the Neuse, and I felt it was important to make the needs of our river known."

The importance of the Cape Fear to Wilmington, as well as North Carolina, is profound. "Fayetteville upstream relies on this river for 60 percent of its municipal water. Wilmington draws on it 100 percent. Many smaller communities on the way look to this river for their needs," says Baldridge. "This is a great natural resource that is in danger from overdevelopment, hog farm overspill, industrial pollutants, chemical spills and overuse, and the problem is nobody really knows what kind of shape it's in now compared to the past."

The grant money for Baldridge's river keeper job came with a requirement he embraced: regular testing of the waters along 80 miles of the Cape Fear over time to determine a baseline. No one knows what shape the river is in because there is nothing upon which to base comparisons. "We really don't know what our readings should be for it to be for a healthy river," says Baldridge, "So our work involves trying to determine where we are now. We don't have the obvious problems of the Neuse but now is when we should start making sure we never do."

The Cape Fear River is very different from the Neuse River because the Wilmington river is connected directly to the ocean and the Neuse isn't. The Neuse is relatively slow-moving, even stagnant in areas, so fish kills tend to stay in place and algae isn't flushed out with a rapidly moving tide. The Cape Fear's fast currents tend to disperse pollution rapidly. Additionally, the extensive wetlands that lie alongside the Cape Fear have excellent filtration powers.

"Unfortunately, rapid residential development, hog farms and confusion over jurisdiction are causing real problems," says Baldridge. "We have a concern with the fact that hog farms, a major contributor to increased nitrates in the water supply, are allowed to operate under relaxed legislative conditions. Then there's the concern that water quality isn't overseen by one agency. There are different rules, for example, for the Forestry Department and the Department of Water Quality Control. The people in charge of water quality don't have jurisdiction over what's happening on the land. The people in charge of the land issues don't have control over what's happening in the water."

There are more questions than answers about the river's health, and Baldridge notes that without serious commitment from government it's going to be a long process to gather information, analyze it and take steps to protect the Cape Fear as well as the other rivers and streams of the state.

For now, Baldridge and the volunteers operate with a fleet of five boats — one canoe and four small powercraft — as well as 100 individual small craft on call from volunteers to keep an eye on the Cape Fear. The group relies on people who use the water recreationally to report unusual sightings such as fish kills, water discoloration, oil spills, fishing violations and dredging or filling in wetlands. Some volunteers in Cape Fear River Watch are assigned creeks and streams to monitor.

Raising public awareness is high on the list of goals for Cape Fear River Watch because, unfortunately, it's like that line in Joni Mitchell's song "Big Yellow Taxi" — "You don't know what you've got 'til it's gone." That's one reason the group has labeled storm drains downtown with stenciled lettering that announces the fact the drains empty into the river. If people can be made to understand that the pollutants they flush back into the water supply can cause environmental problems, that awareness will go a long way toward stopping abuses of the river.

"People take the Cape Fear River for granted," says Baldridge. "We're so used to having it that we can't imagine not having it. People need to remember that Wilmington wouldn't even be here if it were not for that river."

To join the effort to protect the river, observers of spills and kills are encouraged to call the river keeper at 762-5606. People who want to join in support of the effort may become members of the Cape Fear River Watch by calling the same number or writing to the organization at 119 S. Water Street, Wilmington, North Carolina 28401.

THE WILMINGTON FAMILY YMCA
HAS EVERYTHING YOU NEED
TO GET STARTED:

Gym, 2 Indoor Pools, Jacuzzi, 4 Racquetball Courts, 1/4 Mile Outdoor Track, Locker Rooms, Aerobics, and Water Aerobic Classes, Whirlpool, Steam Room, Sauna, Towels, Nautilus, Nordic Track, Lifecycles, Step Climbers, Rowing Machines and Much, Much More!

Ask about our special rates for Senior Citizens

*The Wilmington Family YMCA is New Hanover County's largest child care provider, providing several summer day camps, and school-age child care at 14 local elementary schools.

The Wilmington Family YMCA is a non-profit association committed to a mission of putting Judeo-Christian principles into practice through programs that build healthy body, mind and spirit for all.

We Strengthen More Than Muscles

2710 Market Street   •   251-9622

Sports, Fitness and Parks

Except for snow skiing, rappelling and rock climbing, just about every kind of sport you could ask for is offered in the southern coast region. (Actually, there is a club, the Cape Fear Ski & Outing Club, 799-8035, that organizes snow ski trips.)

In this chapter, we've included listings of where to find or join the sport of your choice. Useful businesses and services are described along the way and at chapter's end. The daily "Lifestyles" pages of the *Wilmington Star-News* also provide a handy guide to recreation throughout the region so check them periodically.

Parents should note that registration fees for youth league sports are often discounted when registering more than one child in the same league. Be sure to inquire.

This guide has separate chapters for golf and watersports, the latter including boating and canoeing. We've included a description of area parks and their facilities at the end of this chapter.

Recreation Departments

Local and county parks-and-recreation departments organize a staggering selection of activities, including team sports for all ages. Be sure to check with them when looking into your sport. They specialize in offering seniors a plethora of activities that includes archery, croquet, tae-kwon-do and water aerobics. Here are the recreation departments' main addresses and office numbers:

Wilmington, 302 Willard Street, Wilmington, 341-7855

Wilmington Athletics, Empie Park, 3405 Park Avenue, Wilmington, 343-3680

Wrightsville Beach, 1 Bob Sawyer Drive, Wrightsville Beach, 256-7925

Carolina Beach, 1121 N. Lake Park Boulevard, Carolina Beach, 458-7416

Long Beach, 4601 E. Oak Island Drive, Long Beach, 278-5518

Southport, Stevens Park, 107 E. Nash Street, Southport, 457-7945

New Hanover County, 414 Chestnut Street, Room 103, Wilmington, 341-7198

Brunswick County, Planning Building, Government Complex, Bolivia, 253-2670

Onslow County, 1250 Onslow Pines Road, Jacksonville, 347-5332

Recreation

Baseball and Little League

The region has several leagues for youth baseball, but there are no public leagues for adults. Among the youth leagues are those sponsored by the area's several Optimist Clubs, organizations committed to service to youth. The youth leagues offer divisions from T-ball for toddlers to baseball for teens up to age 18, and some offer softball too. Registration generally takes place from early February through mid-March and carries a modest fee (about $25 to $45). Registrants will need to present their birth certificates. The playing season begins in April.

New Hanover Youth Baseball, Wilmington, 791-5578

Cape Fear Optimist Club, Wilmington, 762-0434

Winter Park Optimist Club, Wilmington, 256-9994

Myrtle Grove Optimist Club, Wilmington, 343-0111

YMCA, Wilmington, 251-9622

Brunswick County Parks and Recreation, 253-4357, (800) 222-4790

Onslow County Parks and Recreation, 347-5332

Wilmington Sharks

P.O. Box 15233, Wilmington 28412
• 343-5621

Debuting in 1997, the Wilmington Sharks is one of 16 teams in the new Coastal Plain League (CPL), a summer league featuring undergraduate college players competing in six North Carolina cities. The level of play is said to be between that of A and AA minor league teams, and the entertainment is ideal for the entire family. A number of Sharks players are also known as players for UNCW, N.C. State, and Old Dominion University. The league's 50-game regular season is capped by a best-of-three championship playoff, played in mid-August. The Sharks play their 25 home games, beginning around Memorial Day, at Legion Stadium on Carolina Beach Road, 2.3 miles south of Market Street. Single-ticket prices range from $3 to $5. Season tickets go on sale in early March and cost $75 for box seats, $65 for reserved.

Basketball

Winter Park Optimist, 799-3788, offers a seasonal basketball league for boys and girls ages 13-15.

Launched in 1996, Wilmington's annual **3 On 3 Memorial Basketball Tournament** pits three-person teams against one another in a double-elimination competition sponsored by Hoggard High School DECA and area businesses. The tournament is played outdoors one morning in mid-May at UNCW's front courts. Trophies and gift certificates are awarded to first, second and third place teams. Players must be older than 15 and must not play on a college or professional team. Pre-registration costs $45 per team. For more in-

formation and a registration form, write Hoggard DECA c/o R. Krulac, 4305 Shipyard Blvd., Wilmington, NC 28403, or call 392-6400.

The **Wilmington Family YMCA**, 2710 Market Street, 251-9622, hosts leagues for boys and girls ages 6 to 12 during the winter and offers inexpensive court passes to teenagers who wish to join informal games. It also offers men's leagues throughout the year.

For adults and seniors, weekly and Saturday games are organized from December through March by **Wilmington Parks and Recreation**, 343-3680.

Athletic Zone, 4405 Northchase Pkwy. N.E., in Wilmington, 452-5020, is an indoor facility that organizes and hosts basketball games and leagues. Playing schedules may vary according to participation.

Wrightsville Beach Parks and Recreation, 256-7925, offers four-on-four league games for adults on weeknights from June through August.

Brunswick County Parks and Recreation, 253-4357, (800) 222-4790, conducts one-week youth basketball camps in summer for ages 6 to 15. Referee clinics are also offered to persons of any age. There is also an adult men's basketball league with separate spring and fall divisions. Registration is open to teams only. A youth basketball league for children ages 5 to 13 runs from December through March.

For those to the north of Wilmington, **Onslow County Parks and Recreation**, 347-5332, offers youth basketball for children ages 7 to 18.

Bicycling

Touring most of North Carolina's southern coastal plain by bicycle can be as ideal as touring gets. Roads tend to be lightly trafficked, and most motorists have a fairly high awareness of cyclists. It's a different story within Wilmington city limits unfortunately, where a large convoy local commuter cyclists took to the roads in protest in February 1997 to raise awareness of the lack of safe roadways, the most glaring example being Market Street. But

Photo: Scott Taylor

Splash around in swimming pools to beat the summer heat.

that shouldn't scare you off from visiting Wilmington by bicycle or from touring the rest of our coastal region. State-funded touring routes are well planned and marked by rectangular road signs bearing a green ellipse, a bicycle icon and the route number. One such route is the River-to-Sea Bike Route (Route 1), stretching from Riverfront Park at the foot of Market Street in Wilmington to Wrightsville Beach, a ride of just less than 9 miles. Exercise caution on the Bradley Creek bridge: The shoulder is ridged by uneven road seams.

The state-funded Bicycling Highways are worth trying. The **Ports of Call** (Route 3) is a 319-mile seaside excursion from the South Carolina border to the Virginia line. Approximately 110 miles of it lie within the southern coast region, giving access to miles of beaches and historic downtown Wilmington. The **Cape Fear Run** (Route 5) links Raleigh to the mouth of the Cape Fear River at Southport. This 166-mile route crosses the Cape Fear River twice and intersects the Ports of Call. Free maps and information can be obtained from the North Carolina Department of Transportation Bicycle Program, (919) 733-2804, P.O. Box 25201, Raleigh 27611. Although the maps are updated regularly, be ready to improvise when it comes to information on private campgrounds and detours.

The **Wilmington Bike Map** is a must for local cycling. Free copies can be obtained by contacting the City Transportation Planning Department, P.O. Box 1810, Wilmington 28402, (919) 341-7888.

A curiosity about Wilmington: According to city code, it is technically unlawful to ride unregistered bicycles on public streets and alleys within the city (yes, we're totally surprised by this, too). And while that's a law we've never, ever, heard of being enforced — or even obeyed — it's worthy of note because registration with the city police may actually help you recover your ride in the event of theft. Reports suggest that some 700 bikes were ripped off in 1995 — about $174,000 worth. (They used to hang horse-thieves, didn't they?) Most bikes recovered by the police are never claimed and are auctioned off at year's end. You can register your wheels at police headquarters downtown, 115 Redcross Street, 343-3600, or at any of four neighborhood stations. It's free to Wilmington residents, one buck for New Hanover County residents.

The **Coastal Carolina Bike Trek**, sponsored by the American Lung Association of North Carolina, is a fund-raising event that allows participants a unique opportunity to ride 70 or 100 miles of the area's most beautiful roadways over a two-day period in April. The

Photo: Scott Taylor

There's nothing like a lazy fall afternoon for some intense fishing.

route begins and ends in Kure Beach, looping through Southport and Wilmington. Riders can choose their own pace. Meals, technical support and the ferry to Southport are provided. Participants may take time to visit historic sites along the way, relax on the beach or by the pool and spend Saturday evening dancing on an Intracoastal Waterway cruise. What you are asked to do in return is raise funds to fight lung disease. Prizes are awarded. Organizers require all riders to wear helmets. For complete information and registration forms, contact **Trek Headquarters Wilmington**, P.O. Box 3577, Wilmington 28406, 395-5864 or (800) 821-6205.

The **Cape Fear Cyclists Club**, 799-6444, is a good social and information network, and it's an active sponsor of a number of tours, training rides and races as well as a racing team. It provides opportunities to join the U.S. Cycling Federation and discounts on equipment at local shops. The Club also sponsors the annual **By-The-River Biathlon** series of three races taking place January through March. Each race consists of a 3.1-

mile run and a 15-mile bike ride. The entry fee of $20 includes a sweatshirt and T-shirt. It's a good idea to register early; the races are limited to 150 entrants each. More information may be obtained by calling Two Wheeler Dealer at the number above, or by writing to Cape Fear Cyclists, Box 3466, Wilmington 28406.

Sales, Service and Rentals

There are several excellent bicycle specialty shops in our area that sell new and used bicycles and provide repair services. Many businesses also offer rentals; competitive rates are typically around $15 per day.

Aussie Island Surf Shop
1319 Military Cutoff Rd., Wilmington • 256-5454

Aussie Island, in the Landfall Shopping Center at the intersection of Eastwood Road, rents Earth Cruisers by the hour, day or week. Rentals begin at $5 per day and $50 per week.

Bicycle Works
4547 Fountain Dr., Wilmington
• 313-1415

Bicycle Works is near the university and is open seven days a week. In addition to renting mountain bikes and beach cruisers, the shop sells new and used bicycles and provides repair services.

Bill Curry's Cycling and Fitness
2509 S. College Rd., Wilmington
• 392-4433

Bill Curry's is among the finer bike shops in the region and carries a varied inventory of bicycles and accessories. The shop also offers professional repair service. They also specialize in Schwinn cardiovascular-fitness equipment sales and service. However, they do not rent bicycles.

Chain Reaction Bicycling Center
7220 Wrightsville Ave., Wilmington
• 256-3304

Chain Reaction, in the Atlantic View Shopping Center immediately west of the drawbridge to Wrightsville Beach, carries mid-line and low-end mountain bikes and beach cruisers. It also sells new and used bikes and does repairs.

Two Wheeler Dealer
4406 Wrightsville Ave., Wilmington
• 799-6444

One of the largest bicycle shops around, Two Wheeler stocks a vast array of bicycles, including some vintage models and second-hand bikes, plus touring equipment, tricycles, bike trailers, infant seats — practically anything that rolls on spoked wheels — and accessories. Professional repairwork and fitting are done on premises. Two Wheeler is also a place to find racing information and equipment and to connect with the Cape Fear Cyclists Club.

Rainbow Bike Rentals
215 Atlanta Ave. #3C, Carolina Beach
• 458-9113

Rainbow delivers rental bikes, all one-speed Earth-Cruisers, anywhere from Kure Beach to Figure Eight Island. Bicycles with baskets and child carriers are available. A deposit is required.

Ocean Rentals
4014 E. Beach Dr., Long Beach • 278-4460

Ocean Rentals is more than just a place to rent beach-cruising bikes on Oak Island. You may rent four bikes for less than $100 for an entire week. (The shop also rents practically anything you could possibly need for the beach.) Delivery and pickup are free with $10 minimum orders.

Boomer's Bikes & More
111 Jordan Blvd., Holden Beach
• 842-7840, 579-1211

Boomer's rents bicycles and tandems and other models by the hour, day and week (as well as many other beach items). They're at Tarheel Video next to the Post Office. Boomers also sells bikes and does repairs.

Julie's Bike Rentals
2 Main St., Sunset Beach • 579-1211

Affiliated with Boomer's (above), Julie's is a bicycle-cum-beach-rental shop that offers beach cruisers, tandems, adult trikes (which are excellent for some handicapped persons), and the Suncycle recumbent bikes. Julie's is open year-round, although you may need to call ahead in the off-season.

The Patio Playground
807 S. Anderson Blvd., (N.C. 50), Topsail Beach • 328-6491

You can rent bicycles for the measly price of $2 per hour and up to $45 per week, tax included. There is no deposit, but identification is required.

INSIDERS' TIP

Of the two bridges leading into Wilmington, cyclists prefer the U.S. Highway 421 N. bridge, which is wider and safer than the Cape Fear Memorial Bridge.

Bowling

Most bowling centers in our area not only host leagues but also host private parties. Some have even added live music and dancing to their lounge entertainment, and all are family-oriented. Competitive prices average about $2.65 per game for adults on weekends. Prices on weekdays and for children younger than 12 may be lower. Try **Bowler's Choice**, 5115 Oleander Dr., Wilmington, 791-2528; **Cardinal Lanes**, 3907 Shipyard Boulevard, Wilmington, 799-3023 or 7026 Market Street, Scotts Hill, 686-4223; or **Brunswick County Bowling Center**, 630 Village Road, Shallotte, 754-2695

Boxing

For more than 20 years, the **Boxing & Fitness Center** at 602 N. Fourth Street, Wilmington, 341-7872, has been teaching children and adults the techniques and sportsmanship of boxing and physical fitness. Equipped with a regulation-size ring, free weights and a basic fitness center, it offers memberships that are among the best bargains in town.

Fitness Centers

The many fine fitness centers along the coast generally offer state-of-the-art apparatus and certified instructors. Aerobics classes have become standard, as have the use of Lifecycles, treadmills, free weights and StairMasters. Membership costs usually include a onetime registration fee plus a monthly fee for a required term, but many local centers cater to the short-term visitor by offering daily, weekly and monthly rates.

Gold's Gym Fitness & Aerobics
4310 Shipyard Blvd., Wilmington
• 350-8289

Meticulously equipped and maintained, and deservedly popular, Gold's is a full-service fitness center known for its attentive staff, good location with ample parking (Long Leaf Mall) and its array of equipment. It was voted Wilmington's most popular fitness center two years in a row (1995 and '96) in a local poll.

Offerings include personally designed exercise programs and one-to-one training; cardiovascular equipment, including StairMaster and the Reebok SkyWalker; a variety of aerobics classes; resistance and free-weight training; tanning (at extra cost); dry sauna; child care (free to full members and staffed by CPR-certified personnel); and a pro shop. Circuit equipment is sequentially arranged for a complete body workout. An Aerobics Hotline, 350-6778, makes daily class schedules readily available. Gold's also offers the "FAST Track" food and exercise management system. Members of Gold's Gym are entitled to use any other Gold's Gym anywhere (500 nationally). Memberships are available by the day, week, month and year.

Pro-Fit
23 N. Front St., Wilmington • 763-7224

Wilmington's downtown professional crowd enjoys Pro-Fit as much for its chic location and ground-floor view of Front Street as for its excellent facilities and services, which include free weights, cardiac equipment and personal trainers.

Walden's Gym
North 17 Shopping Center, Market St., Wilmington • 763-7444
6400 Carolina Beach Rd., Wilmington • 395-7002

Can't sleep at night? Can't seem to fit your hours to any fitness center's? One of Walden's two locations could be for you. Walden's is the area's only health club with doors open around the clock, seven days a week. Somewhat less glitzy than some other clubs around (and proportionally priced), Walden's offers all the free weights and cardiovascular training you'd expect, plus personal training, circuit training and tanning. You'll find the North 17 Shopping Center just west of Kerr Avenue.

Wilmington Athletic Club
2026 S. 16th St., Wilmington • 763-9655

"The Wac" is an attractive, family-oriented establishment hosting sports, including basketball, racquetball and coed volleyball. It offers a steam room, sauna, an outdoor pool, a nursery with CPR-trained staff and swimming lessons. Fitness consultations and nutritional lectures are frequently offered. Short-term contracts are available.

Wilmington Family YMCA
2710 Market St., Wilmington • 251-9622

Offering a wide variety of fitness and educational activities, the Family Y features ample facilities, such as a large gym, two indoor pools, a Jacuzzi, four racquetball courts, Nautilus equipment and even sunbathing decks. Athletic fields with a track and playground are also available. Aerobics (including water classes), t'ai chi ch'uan, arthritis aquatics classes and massage therapy are just a few of the Y's vast offerings. League sports for adults and youth are organized seasonally, and youth are eligible for limited, reduced-rate gym passes in summer.

YWCA of Wilmington
2815 S. College Rd., Wilmington
• 799-6820

Its elaborate swimming programs include full-scale ocean lifesaving, and the facility trains and certifies more lifeguards that any other in eastern North Carolina. Indoor activities include low-impact, step and water aerobics; toning classes; dance in many styles for kids ages 2 and older; karate for kids and adults; kids' gymnastics; water basketball for teens; and t'ai chi ch'uan. Child care is also available.

Wilmington Parks and Recreation
Wilmington • 341-7855

Wilmington Parks and Recreation offers special exercise classes for youth who are overweight, physically impaired and inner-city bound. Senior adults will find fitness classes tailored to their needs, plus low-impact aerobics, water aerobics and floor Slimnastics for adults 55 and older.

PT Connection
5710 Oleander Dr., Wilmington • 792-1200, (800) 750-7384

For the utmost in personal attention, PT Connection specializes exclusively in high-end personal training tailored to the individual. State-of-the-art equipment and staff expertise come together in a positive, upbeat atmosphere where the work is hard, the quality high, and the clientele predominantly affluent. Fees are set on a per-session basis. Massage therapy is also available. PT Connection is open from 5:30 AM until 9 PM every day. You'll find it in the Oleander Business Center, suite 210, next to the Kids' Gym.

The Crest Fitness Center
38 N. Lumina Ave., Wrightsville Beach
• 256-5758

This long-lived establishment, now under new management, is the only fitness center on Wrightsville Beach. Despite that, The Crest's prices are more than reasonable, and day passes are available for those fitness-conscious travelers just passing through. A complete Nautilus program is available, as well as aerobics classes, free weights, personal training, tanning beds and a nursery. Because of its location The Crest boasts that it's the fitness center with the "largest outdoor swimming area" (you guessed it, saltwater fans). A variety of memberships are offered, including corporate, student, weekly, monthly, daily — even passes for motel lodgers. The Crest is open seven days a week from 6:30 AM to 9 PM, and parking is available.

Body Dimensions
5241 Main St., Shallotte • 754-3808

Emphasizing the natural approach to lifelong fitness, the folks at Body Dimensions offer a full line of free weights, aerobics classes, treadmills, stair climbers and Badger/Magnum strength systems. Short-term visitors to the area benefit from daily, weekly, monthly and other short-term rates. The center is open every day except Sunday and is in the South Park Plaza, the first shopping plaza when traveling north into Shallotte along U.S. Highway 17 Business (Main Street).

Brunswick County Parks and Recreation
Bolivia • 253-2670, (800) 222-4790

For $15 per month or $4 per drop-in, you may participate in step aerobics classes (provide your own step) twice each week at two Brunswick County locations — at the Town

Creek and Leland community buildings. Low-impact aerobics is also offered twice weekly at the Lockwood Folly Community Building. Registration is available on location, and the one-hour classes usually get underway at around 6:30 PM.

Coastal Fitness
5140 Sellers Rd., Shallotte • 754-2772

Coastal Fitness, not far from the South Brunswick Islands, has separate rooms for free weights and exercise machinery such as treadmills, Lifecycles, and Climbmax steppers. There is also a massage therapist on the premises. Daily and weekly memberships are available — great for visitors. A staffed nursery, tanning beds, tae-kwon-do and sauna are offered, as are CPR classes and health supplies. Coastal Fitness is open seven days a week. Sellers Road, on the south side of Shallotte, is the first right-hand fork from U.S. Highway 17 Business when traveling north into Shallotte (just beyond South Park Plaza).

Aerobics with Freddie J. King
Surf City Baptist Church, 304 Wilmington Ave., Surf City • 328-1532

Personal trainer and certified fitness counselor Freddie King leads weekly aerobics classes (nonsectarian) on Friday mornings. Participants are welcomed to register at the door, and there is no minimum number of classes required to enroll. A small donation is requested.

Forever Fit Fitness Center
214 Sneads Ferry Rd., Sneads Ferry • 327-2293

Stressing a balanced regimen for fitness, Forever Fit offers strength training, a full line of cardio-equipment, step and aerobic classes, circuit training, tae-kwon-do, dance (line, ballet, tap, jazz), tanning, a personal trainer on staff and AFAA-certified instructors. Water aerobics are offered in June, July and August only. Short-term visitors can benefit from daily and weekly visitor rates, and individual memberships begin as low as $40 per month. Forever Fit is convenient to the northern Topsail Island area.

Flying

The local dearth of sizable hills and, therefore, reliable updrafts, limits local aviation to powered flight. Among the surprises of a bird's-eye view is sighting the so-called Carolina bays, the enormous elliptical depressions in the earth first "discovered" from the air (see

Photo: Mark Courtney

An astounding variety of birds visits Greenfield Lake in Wilmington.

Lake Waccamaw State Park in our chapter on Camping).

Blue Yonder Flying Machines
Brunswick County Airport, 380 Long Beach Rd. (N.C. Hwy. 133), Southport
• 278-8277

Some say that unless you feel the wind in your face, you're not really flying. Among that faction you might find Adam Parsons, who promotes the flying of Quicksilver ultralights. They look like a cross between a hang glider and a Wright brothers' original. The Quicksilver aircraft meet all aviation requirements, even though the pilot (and passenger, in some models) is suspended in an open cockpit. Adam offers introductory flights and training with a certified instructor and sells a variety of Quicksilver aircraft.

Rentals and Instruction

Flyers can rent conventional aircraft at New Hanover International and Brunswick County airports. Most companies offer 24-hour charter service and flight training.

Aeronautics
New Hanover International Airport, 1740 Airport Blvd., Wilmington • 763-4691
Air Wilmington
New Hanover International Airport, 1740 Airport Blvd., Wilmington • 763-4691

Aeronautics and its affiliate, Air Wilmington, offer flight instruction, aircraft rentals and sightseeing tours.

ISO Aero Service Inc. of Wilmington
1410 N. Kerr Ave., Wilmington • 763-8898, 762-1024

Offering rentals, instruction and sightseeing, ISO is also located at New Hanover County Airport.

Ocean Aire Aviation
Brunswick County Airport, 380 Long Beach Rd. (N.C. Hwy. 133), Southport
• 457-0710

Larry Ryan and John Martin offer flight instruction and other flight services and can also arrange aircraft rentals.

Football

League football beyond the scholastic realm is focused upon two organizing bodies, the Pop Warner league and Brunswick County Parks and Recreation. Look into registration during June; most teams commence practicing in August.

Pop Warner Football
Wilmington • 799-7950

Pop Warner organizes tackle football teams for boys and girls age 7 to 14 in Pee Wee, Midget and Mighty Mights divisions.

Brunswick County Parks and Recreation
Bolivia • 253-4357, (800) 222-4790

Brunswick County's league is open to kids ages 10 to 13. If you're interested in becoming a referee, inquire about Brunswick County's referee clinics.

Horseback Riding

Although English (hunt seat) style is favored in this region, Western is available. Most stables and riding academies offer boarding, instruction, rentals and trail rides. Some stables do their own shoeing. Tack shops are scarce. Most stables and academies will assist you in locating the equipment you need.

Canterbury Stable
6021 Wrightsville Ave., Wilmington
• 791-6502

Canterbury specializes in private and group riding instruction, boarding, training and showing but no rentals.

Castle Stables
5513 Sidbury Rd., Castle Hayne
• 675-1113

English-style instruction is offered on a plush 120-acre spread a few minutes north of Wilmington. A lighted training ring and a jumping ring are available.

Fox Fire Farm
7724 Sidbury Rd., Castle Hayne
• 686-4495

The folks at Fox Fire train riders and their

horses in English riding and help find horses for purchase and lease.

Hanover Stables
5901 Bizzel Ave., Castle Hayne • 675-8923

Offering 19 acres of pasture and lighted ring trails, Hanover Stables teaches English and Western styles of riding. Also available are sales, boarding and professional training.

The Castle Hayne Saddle Shop
11975 U.S. Hwy 117., Castle Hayne
• 675-1805

This friendly full-service shop is a few minutes north of Wilmington. It carries everything necessary for riding (English and Western), including feed and instructional videos. Expert leather repair can be arranged.

Tuscarora Tack Shop
5128 Wrightsville Ave., Wilmington
• 791-0900

Tuscarora specializes in English riding apparel and equipment, including saddlery, boots and grooming supplies. The shop, convenient from S. College Road, is closed on Thursdays and Sundays.

Lo-Di Farms
610 Old Folkstone Rd., Sneads Ferry
• 327-2040

Convenient to Topsail Island, Lo-Di boards, leases and rents horses and ponies. Horses for special occasions can be reserved, and the owners will haul if needed.

Cottonpatch Farms
Cottonpatch Rd., Shallotte • 754-9288

Judy Hilburn's farm is a high-quality training facility that sells horses and teaches owners to ride and show. Judy occasionally breeds horses. Youth riders are welcome.

Sea Horse Riding Stables
Boonesneck Rd., Holden Beach
• 842-8002

Sea Horse provides English and Western lessons, shoeing and training. Their 18 acres, 3 miles off Holden Beach Road, are laced with shady trails, and the kids will love the pony rides.

Peachtree Stables
810 Hickman Rd., Calabash • 287-4790

With 120 acres nearly adjacent to the South Carolina state line, Peachtree Stables is convenient to the entire southeastern corner of Brunswick County and northeastern South Carolina. The trails traverse 70 acres, much of it shady. Peachtree offers hourly trail rides, full boarding facilities, a tack shop, two outdoor riding rings and an indoor riding arena. Group and private instruction is given in English and Western styles. Horses are available for lease and for sale, and moonlight rides along the beach can be arranged.

Hunting

There are several game lands in the region where hunters may pursue big and small game, including dove, deer, rabbit, wild turkey and black bear. Game lands are typically leased from individual landowners and companies by North Carolina Wildlife Resources Commission, Division of Wildlife Management, 412 N. Salisbury Street, Raleigh 27604, (919) 733-7291. Some lands are owned outright by the commission. Most game lands are accessible from public roads, while some have only water access.

The 48,795-acre **Holly Shelter Game Land** in Pender County is the largest local game land. It is a varied wetland of pocosins (peat-bottomed lowlands) and pine savannas, threaded by winding creeks and existing in some noncontiguous parcels. The Holly Shelter Game Land is north of Wilmington, roughly between Highway 17 west to the northeast Cape Fear River and between highways 210 and 53.

The **Green Swamp Game Land**, a 14,851-acre expanse lying in nearly one contiguous block bordered by Highway 211 in Brunswick County, is among the most isolated areas remaining in southeastern North Carolina, an easy place in which to get turned around for a couple of days. Foot travel only is permitted here. Much of the land, as the name suggests, is low-lying wetland and pocosin, and it is owned by the Nature Conservancy.

Lying in New Hanover County, the **Sutton**

Lake Game Land is a 3,322-acre land leased from CP&L. It is bordered by Highway 421 and the Cape Fear River.

Hunting, mainly for fowl, is allowed on **Zeke's Island Coastal Preserve**, which lies across the Basin from Fort Fisher. Access to it is only by boat or by foot across the Rocks, a tricky 3-mile breakwater that is awash at high tide.

Canady's Sports Center, 3220 Wrightsville Avenue, 791-6280, in Wilmington, is among the best one-stop retail shops for hunters, whether rifle or bow; staffers are practiced and knowledgeable in each. Clothing, field gear and a good selection of binoculars are stocked. Canady's is open Monday through Saturday.

Hunting Licenses

Hunting licenses are issued by the North Carolina Wildlife Resources Commission, License Section. They can be purchased specifically for small game ($15), big game ($25) and combined with fishing licenses ($20; small game only). The sportsman's license ($40) permits the holder to pursue all types of hunting, including bowhunting and game land use, and saves money in the long run. Call the License Section of the North Carolina Wildlife Resources Commission at 662-4370 for more information. Licenses may be purchased at several local sports shops and hardware stores. Inquire about licenses at the places listed below.

Kmart, 815 S. College Road, Wilmington, 799-5360

Pawn USA, three Wilmington locations: 3922 Market Street, 763-7682; 2392 Carolina Beach Road, 251-1200; 4127 Oleander Drive, 392-1177

Tackle Express Tacklemart, 4100 Oleander Drive, Wilmington, 392-3472

Wal-Mart, Wal-Mart Shopping Center, 352 S. College Road, Wilmington, 392-4034

Mobile Home Store & Hardware, 5601 Castle Hayne Road, Castle Hayne, 675-9205

Hampstead Village Pharmacy, U.S. Highway 17, Hampstead, 270-3411, 270-3414

Holland's Shelter Creek Fish Camp, N.C. Highway 53 east of Burgaw, 259-5743

Roses, 1505 N. Howe Street, Southport, 457-9573

Stewart Hardware, 1635 Howe Street, Southport, 457-5544

Holden Beach True Value, 3008 Holden Beach Road, Holden Beach, 842-5440

Island Tackle & Gifts, 6855-3 Beach Drive SW, Ocean Isle Beach, 579-6116

Pawn USA, 5001-4 Main Street, Shallotte, 754-7918

Wal-Mart, 4540 Main Street, Shallotte, 754-2880

Photo: Scott Taylor

Surf's up!

In-line and Roller Skating

The popularity of in-line skating in the region continues to grow with the population, despite the fact that skating conditions within towns such as Wilmington, Southport and Shallotte are relatively poor. In 1996 the city of Wilmington completely banned in-line skating (and skateboarding) in the downtown historic district. Recreational and commuter skaters on city streets and sidewalks can be fined, so consider practicing elsewhere and drive to work like everybody else. Skating and skateboarding potentially face a similar situation in Southport where, as we go to press, prohibitive ordinances were being considered.

So where do you go to skate?

The 'burbs, of course! where the pavement is new and traffic is light. But the 'burbs aren't all there is. The UNCW campus offers long stretches of wide, paved walks, including smooth, curvy stretches surrounding the newly built lake at the university commons. The nearly 5-mile-long bike path around Greenfield Lake in Wilmington is as picturesque as any place else in the state, particularly in early spring; just be watchful of nasty bumps and breaks in the asphalt due to tree roots. The pavement in the few Wilmington parks that have any was mostly damaged by the hurricanes of '96, so parks are out — except for basketball courts. They're small, but not bad for beginners.

One of the best places to skate is the "Loop" at Wrightsville Beach. Consisting of paved walks totaling approximately 2.5 miles, the Loop runs along Wrightsville Beach Park, Causeway Drive, Lumina Avenue and Salisbury Street. There are plenty of places to stop for a cool refreshment or a dip in the ocean along the way. The No. 1 place to skate on Oak Island consists of the nearly 7 miles of municipal sidewalks along Oak Island Drive in Long Beach. Ramps, rather than curbs, meet every intersection. Recently paved Yacht Drive, which stretches the length of Long Beach on the north side of the island, is also an excellent choice. On the south side, Dolphin Drive, just one block from the ocean, is an OK choice,

FYI

Unless otherwise noted, the area code for all phone numbers in this guide is 910.

but you'll have to deal with some motor traffic. Avoid Beach Drive altogether, with its heavy traffic and gravel. A true skate-haven is Bald Head Island where the only other traffic on the smoothly paved byways is golf carts and bicycles.

It seems as if anyone who's not interested in skating for its own sake or for commuting is playing roller hockey. Enter, the **Cape Fear Roller Hockey League**, 791-1572, the area's first organized in-line skating venture. A participating member of the new North Carolina Inline Hockey League, the Cape Fear league is open to youth and adults in two divisions: ages 7 to 14 and 15 and older. The 11-game season is played at locations throughout five states from Virginia to Georgia. The first state championships and regional championships are scheduled for 1997. Participation costs $95 for youth, $80 for adults, and does not include equipment. Registration and information may be obtained at Play It Again Sports, 3530 S. College Road, 791-1572, and at the Athletic Zone (below).

Showtyme Skating Center
5216 Oleander Dr., Wilmington • 791-6000

Showtyme sponsors and hosts the Showtyme Roller Hockey League, offering instruction, practice and game time to players in four age groups: 6 to 9, 10 to 12, 13 to 16 and adult. There is no age limit. The fee for each 10-week session is $45 per player, which includes helmet, shin guards, gloves and stick. The league's traveling team competes at nearby rinks.

Athletic Zone
4405 Northchase Pkwy N.E., Wilmington • 452-5020

New to the area in 1996, Athletic Zone has two indoor rinks offering open skating nights, in-line roller hockey and in-line skating lessons (as well as several other indoor sports). The hockey rink is regulation size, and players of all ages are welcome. The Zone is the nerve center of the Cape Fear Roller Hockey League (see above). Registering entire teams offers vast per-person savings. The Zone has some skates available for rent and a small pro shop operated by Play It Again Sports, but players must expect to supply all their own equipment. Pick-up games cost $5 per hour.

Instructor Certification Program of the International In-Line Skating Association
201 N. Front St., #306, Wilmington
• **762-7004**

Now headquartered in Wilmington, the ICP promotes the health and longevity of the sport by offering skating lessons for groups and individuals, producing certified instructors, and advocating safe skating, public skate paths and nonaggressive skating practices. The ICP is the service-oriented educational wing of the International In-Line Skating Association, the trade organization representing the interests of in-line skate manufacturers. Fees for lessons vary widely according to locale and number of pupils.

Julie's Rentals
2 Main St., Sunset Beach • 579-1211

Julie's is a complete beach-rental shop that rents in-line skates as well as many other recreational items, all year long.

Lacrosse

Call it bagataway, lax, or just plain cool, this rugged and almost legendary game, like soccer, has been making great strides recently in the greater Wilmington area, spearheaded by a strong program at Cape Fear Academy and recently aided by the fledgling Hoggard Lacrosse Club. Ten regional middle schools and four high schools now field lacrosse teams. The University of North Carolina at Wilmington fields two teams, a men's team and the only all-female team currently in our area. The listings below describe playing opportunities that exist beyond school teams.

Hoggard Lacrosse Club
4308 Peachtree Ave., Wilmington
• **313-6740**

Not yet a varsity club (they hope to be), this rapidly growing coed club is at present open to all players of middle-school and high-school age. The club is a true grassroots project with an enormous amount of dedication at every level (two players earned lacrosse scholarships in 1996). It is directed by head coach Pat Kavanagh, who has 25 years of experience coaching and playing a variety of sports. The club competes locally and around the state and is currently expanding its reach to other mid-Atlantic states. There are two squads, and an all-female team is being formed. The club keeps a fairly stiff practice schedule during the season, and home games are played at Hoggard High School in Wilmington, mostly on Saturday afternoons. Some practices are indoors. Players supply their own equipment, and no fee is required (although donations are welcomed). The club is always in need of additional hands-on support, especially in terms of fund-raising, transportation and referees.

Cape Fear Academy Lacrosse Camp
3900 S. College Rd., Wilmington
• **791-0287**

This summer day camp for boys, ages 11 to 18 in two age divisions, runs for about one month beginning in mid-June. Four-hour sessions begin at 4:30 PM and are directed by the Academy's head lacrosse coach with assistance from members of the UNCW Lacrosse Club, the Cape Fear Lacrosse Club, and coaches from the New Hanover County Schools. Instruction emphasizes fundamentals, rules and team play, and the camp culminates in a round-robin tournament. The cost is exceedingly reasonable (about $80 per camper), and equipment is available (campers should supply their own cleats).

INSIDERS' TIP

The Breakfast Club, 815-5006, is an outdoor walking club for people 55 years and older in Wilmington. It meets every Tuesday and Thursday at 8:30 AM in the New Hanover Regional Medical Center lobby.

Athletic Zone
4405 Northchase Pkwy. N.E., Wilmington
• 452-5020

Indoor lacrosse is hosted at this facility on the north side of town. The playing "field" doubles as a regulation-size roller-hockey rink. Players must supply their own equipment. As of this writing, a new league is currently in formation.

Kite Flying

Steady beach winds are ideal for kite flying. Of course, it pays to use common sense; beware of power lines, piers, boat masts and homes. Stunt kites, which can fly close to the ground, may annoy some beachgoers. Fort Fisher, the north ends of Topsail Island and Carolina Beach, and the south end of

Grace Under Pressure: Michael Jordan

"You gotta love the NBA: where else could you see the greatest athletes in the world under one roof . . . and Michael Jordan above it."
— Frank Layden, former NBA coach

It would be difficult to find a person today who hasn't seen or heard of basketball great Michael Jordan. But among the more surprising discoveries made by newcomers to Wilmington is that Michael Jeffrey Jordan, born in Brooklyn, N.Y., spent most of his early years — 1963 through 1981 — right here, polishing his game and wearing number 23 on the courts of Laney High School. Jordan also played football, baseball and track before being recruited by the University of North Carolina at Chapel Hill.

Michael Jordan first made his mark upon the national sports scene when, as a freshman at UNC in 1982, he scored both the first and the last deciding points against Georgetown, finishing with a 17-foot two-pointer that clinched the National Collegiate Athletic Association (NCAA) championship for UNC. From then on, the 6'6" guard demonstrated a steady refinement typified by tenacity, competitiveness and a complete focus that only sharpened under pressure. His determination led UNC Coach Dean Smith to remark, "I had never seen a player listen so closely to what the coaches said and then go and do it."

The emerging list of Michael's achievements confirmed his greatness, beginning with being named College Player of the Year in 1983 and 1984. He earned his first Olympic gold medal playing for the 1984 U.S. team. Upon turning professional after his junior year in college, Jordan was drafted by the Chicago Bulls, immediately winning Rookie of the Year honors in 1985. A foot injury hobbled his second professional season, but he went on to become the NBA's leading scorer for seven

A teenaged Michael Jordan, then playing football for Laney High School, Wilmington

Photo: Cape Fear Museum

— continued on next page

— continued on next page

consecutive years thereafter, 1987-1993, with a career average of 32.3 points per game. He was named Most Valuable Player in 1988, 1991 and 1992 and led the Bulls to three consecutive NBA championships (1991-93). He played on the U.S. "Dream Team" in the 1992 Olympic Games, where he earned his second Olympic gold medal.

Besides having a section of Interstate 40 dedicated in his name in 1991, a long-term natural history exhibit at the Cape Fear Museum was dedicated to Wilmington's most famous athlete in June 1995, with Michael in attendance. The 1385-square-foot Michael Jordan Discovery Gallery consists of interactive exhibits highlighting three coastal North Carolina ecosystems (upland forest, bottomland and maritime forest) and is ideal for the entire family (see the museum's listing in the Attractions chapter). But for "Air Jordan" fans, perhaps the most intriguing part of the exhibit is the display case at the gallery entrance. Here you can see Michael's very first paycheck stub (for $119.75) from his first after-school job at Whitey's El-Berta Restaurant on Market Street as well as a perfect-attendance certificate from Noble Middle School, his 1984 Olympic gold medal and various other items from his youth in North Carolina.

Personable, outgoing and thoroughly telegenic, Michael Jordan became known the world over as a spokesman for a variety of consumer products, the first African-American to become effective in such a role. Following the tragic death of his father in 1993, Michael announced his retirement from basketball. He returned to the other game closest to his heart, baseball, playing in the professional minor league for 18 months before retiring in March 1995 to return to basketball's Chicago Bulls where great promise still lies ahead.

If you want to read more about Michael Jordan, check out *Hang Time: Days and Dreams with Michael Jordan* by Bob Greene (Doubleday, 1992).

Wrightsville Beach are fitting places to tie your hopes and dreams to a colorful swath and send them aloft.

The **Carolina Kite Club** (no phone) is an informal club that meets Sunday mornings from 9 AM to noon at the south end of Wrightsville Beach. In summer get there early: The small, metered parking area fills quickly. Gatherings are usually listed in the *Wilmington Star-News*' Sunday calendar.

Marksmanship and Riflery

Shooting enthusiasts may like to note the periodic gun shows held at the **National Guard Armory** at 2221 Carolina Beach Road

in Wilmington, 762-0214. Vendors carry everything from antique and replica black-powder firearms to state-of-the-art rifles and pistols, plus ammunition. Also, practically every pawn shop in the region carries an inventory of guns. Check local directories.

Water & Woods Hunting & Fishing
4405 Wrightsville Ave., Wilmington
• 791-4855

This small shop offers new and used guns, hunting and reloading supplies as well as fishing tackle.

Digh's Country Sports Gallery
1988 Eastwood Rd., Wrightsville Beach
• 256-2060

In the autumn, owner Bobby Digh, a pro-

Photo: Scott Taylor

Life quickly becomes elemental at the seashore.

fessional gun fitter and certified shooting instructor, provides laser-assisted custom tailoring of high-quality Orvis shotguns, which are then manufactured to your body's specifications. Digh's is in the Plaza East Shopping Center, west of the drawbridge, and is open 10 AM to 7 PM Monday through Friday, 9 AM to 5 PM Saturday and 11 AM to 4 PM Sunday in the summer.

Rocky Point Shooters World
14565 Ashton Rd., Rocky Point • 259-7333
This small (50-foot) indoor pistol range offers automatically retrievable targets in a comfortable, safe, air-conditioned setting. Rifles no larger than .22 caliber are allowed. Safety training and marksmanship can be arranged by the staff. Daily rates start at $4.50 per half-hour, and long-term memberships are avail-

able. Rocky Point is about 25-minutes north of Wilmington.

Martial Arts
Whether it's the sword technique of iaido, the open-hand style of karate, or the throws and take-downs of jujitsu that interest you; whether it's self-defense, physical fitness, mental focus or competition you desire; all that and more, is available in our region. Martial arts schools generally offer classes on a term basis, usually monthly or yearly.

Bushin-Kai Karate
2875 Carolina Beach Rd., Wilmington • 395-2170
Del C. Russ, an instructor for 31 years, teaches traditional martial arts, including Japa-

nese sword art (iaido), aiki-kai aikido, toyama and ko-dachi. Inquire about family rates.

Champion Karate Center
4231 Princess Place Dr., Wilmington
• 343-9398

Owner/instructor John Maynard welcomes physically-challenged students, including the sightless. Maynard was personally trained by Chuck Norris, and his studio is part of Norris's United Fighting Arts Organization. Champion offers a weight room and guidance for those interested in competition. Maynard also operates a location in Hampstead.

Martial Arts Center
2595 S. 17th St., Wilmington • 799-1188

Jim Irwin, a sixth-degree black belt, includes study in Okinawa, kempo and kobudo at his studio. He also offers private instruction, schedules permitting.

Jung's Tae Kwon Do Academy
4623 Market St., Wilmington • 392-6980

Jung's teaches traditional karate, kung fu and hapkido. Instructor Yong Jung is a ninth dan-degree black belt with more than 40 years of teaching experience. He is assisted by a fifth dan black belt instructor. The Academy also sells supplies and equipment.

Stover's Martial Arts
2505 S. College Rd., Wilmington
• 791-3656

Stover's is Wilmington's oldest school of martial arts. Mr. Stover, a seventh-degree black belt, stresses fundamentals in a variety of styles, including karate, kempo, jujitsu, kung fu and traditional weapons. Classes meet evenings, Monday through Thursday.

Wilmington Family YMCA
2710 Market St., Wilmington • 251-9622

The Family Y offers karate, t'ai chi and judo classes, with U.S. Judo Association membership included. Costs range from $25 to $40 per month, excluding memberships and gear.

YWCA of Wilmington
2815 S. College Rd., Wilmington
• 799-6820

Evening karate classes for adults are offered twice weekly for a $30 per month fee ($20 for members). A small registration fee is extra. T'ai chi ch'uan is offered periodically.

Coastal Fitness
5140 Sellers Rd., Shallotte • 754-2772

Tae-kwon-do is offered at this fitness center on the south side of town. Participation involves membership, available in short terms. Coastal Fitness is open seven days a week. Sellers Road is the first right-hand fork from U.S. Highway 17 Business when traveling north into Shallotte (just beyond South Park Plaza).

Forever Fit Fitness Center
214 Sneads Ferry Rd., Sneads Ferry
• 327-2293

Forever Fit offers tae-kwon-do within convenient reach of northern Topsail Island. Short-term visitors can benefit from daily and weekly visitor rates, and individual memberships begin as low as $40 per month.

Off-Roading

While most beaches prohibit vehicles, there are a couple of relatively unspoiled areas where off-road enthusiasts (especially those who fish) can indulge themselves. But driving off-road is a two-edged sword: The vehicles that make these beautiful areas accessible also erode them. Observe regulations closely and use common sense when off-roading. This is your living room.

The best off-roading around is at the **Fort Fisher State Recreation Area**, an undeveloped 4-mile reach of strand and tidal marsh 5 miles south of Carolina Beach, off U.S. Highway 421. The earth within the marsh area is firm at low tide, and fiddler crabs, egrets, ibis and herons are common. The deeper tidal pools are suitable for bathing, especially for toddlers. Passage onto the beach is through marked crossovers only. The sand here is loose and deep. At high tide, the strand becomes very narrow and may even prevent you from turning around. Also, the marsh floods at high tide. Plan accordingly.

The **north end of Carolina Beach** at the end of Canal Drive is also open to off-roading. This area becomes quite busy in the warmer months.

Fishermen and beachgoers can drive the beach at the **west end of Long Beach** (Oak Island) at Lockwood Folly Inlet. This gives access to the **Point**, a popular surf-fishing area. The "catch" is this: A permit is required from the town of Long Beach, 4601 E. Oak Island Drive, 278-5011, and it costs a whopping $50. Beach driving is only permitted between September 15 and April 15.

Racquetball

Check listings for Fitness Centers to locate those that have racquetball courts. Each year racquetball and handball tournaments are sponsored by the **Wilmington Family YMCA**, 251-9622, which has four courts available to members by reservation.

Rugby

Cape Fear Rugby Club
Laney Football Stadium, N.C. Hwy. 132, Wilmington • 395-2331

This club has more than 100 members and is the three-time defending Division II state champion. They play and practice Tuesday evenings at Laney Football Stadium on Highway 132 N. in Wilmington. The club produces the Cape Fear Sevens Rugby Tournament each July. Considered one of the finest showcases of Sevens rugby in the East, the event attracts 70-odd teams from Europe, Canada, Japan and South Africa — well more than 700 players. Games are held at UNCW on College Road and are free. Ranked second in the state in 1993, the club is always interested in recruiting new members. Other numbers to call are 762-8324 and 763-0902.

Running and Walking

Among the most beautiful places in Wilmington to jog or walk is the 4.5-mile loop around **Greenfield Lake**, south of downtown. The scenic paved path bears mile markers and follows the undulating lake shore across two wooden foot bridges (slippery when wet).

On Wrightsville Beach, the sidewalk **Loop** is an approximately 2.5-mile circuit popular among locals. The Loop encompasses a portion of the perimeter of Wrightsville Beach Park, Causeway Drive, Lumina Avenue and Salisbury Street. The park also features an outdoor fitness trail in the field off Causeway Drive.

Wilmington Parks and Recreation invites youth ages 6 to 14 to join the **National Track Program**. Call 341-7855 to register.

The **Wilmington Roadrunners Club**, based at the YMCA, 2710 Market Street, 251-9622, sponsors races, picnics, fun runs and evening runs; provides information on technique and safety; and welcomes entire families. Also sponsored by the club is the **Cape Fear Flyers** youth track organization. Membership in the Roadrunners Club includes newsletter and magazine subscriptions, discounts on gear, the opportunity to take a discounted corporate membership in the YMCA, plus other perks. Yearly individual membership costs $20; families $25.

The Roadrunners, the Wilmington Family Y and several area businesses sponsor the **Wilmington Tri-Span Run** each July, an 8K run that crosses all three bridge spans along the Wilmington waterfront and that's sure to test your mettle. It also features a 1-mile fun run/walk. Early registration costs $12, and there are 13 age divisions for the 8K run.

The American Lung Association sponsors the **Reindeer Romp**, a 1-mile and 5K walk or run held each December along Greenfield Lake. Prizes are awarded for performance as well as for costumes. Registration fees begin at $8 for children and $12 for adults. For information, call the ALA: 395-5864 or (800) 821-6205.

The annual **Leprechaun Run**, sponsored by the New Hanover-Pender Medical Society Alliance, consists of two events held at Wrightsville Beach each March. The 1-mile walk is an out-and-back course entirely on the beach strand. Half of the 5K run is on paved road and half is on the beach. Cash prizes go to the top men and women overall winners in the 5K run, and other prizes go to top three men and women in 12 narrow age groups ranging from 12 to older than 60. Special awards are given to kids age 12 and younger for the best St. Patrick's Day costume, and there is a post-race awards party. Early entry fees range from $8 for individual children to $35 for families. Proceeds benefit local healthcare projects. For information, call 452-7486 or 251-1198 or write: Leprechaun Run, Medical Society Alliance, 2259 S. 17th Street, Wilmington 28401.

The National Multiple Sclerosis Society sponsors the annual **MS Walk** in early April, a fund-raising event in which participants raise and collect pledges and walk the loop around Greenfield Lake. Incentives and prizes are awarded. For information or to register, call (800) 477-2955 or write: The MS Walk, National Multiple Sclerosis Society, Greater Carolinas Chapter, 1515 Mockingbird Lane, Suite 1000, Charlotte 28209.

The **Halloween Moonlight 5K Run** takes place on the UNCW campus beginning at 8 PM on Halloween night. Late registration is accepted beginning at 6:30 PM, and food and beverages are served following the race. Registration costs $10 in advance, $12 after October 21. To register, call the UNCW Athletics Department, 962-3889

The annual **North Carolina Oyster Festival Road Race** in October is Sunset Beach's contribution to footrace frenzy. Open to runners of all ages, the event comprises three races — a 10K, 5K and a 1-mile Fun Run (this last has no age divisions). For information or registration, call (800) 426-6644, fax (910) 754-6539 or write the South Brunswick Islands Chamber of Commerce, P.O. Box 130, Shallotte, NC 28459. Preregistration deadline is mid-October.

The **Bald Head Island Annual Maritime Classic Road Race** is an annual event held in November that features a 10K and 5K foot race. Call 457-5003.

The **Surf & Turf Triathlon** is an annual race associated with the Greater Topsail Area Spring Fling, a festival held on Topsail Island

on the last weekend of April. Preregistration for the biking-swimming-5K running competition costs $20. For information, call (800) 626-2780.

The **LeJeune Grand Prix Series**, hosted by the Marine Corps Base at Camp Lejeune (near Jacksonville), 451-5430, offers several foot races and other challenges. These highly-competitive events draw nationally-ranked challengers. Camp Lejeune's **Oktoberfest Family 5K Fun Run**, in late September, is not part of the Grand Prix Series, but is one of three runs designed to promote family wellness. It is open to anyone who can walk, run, jog, stroll or be carried the 5K distance. The course is suitable for strollers and carriages.

The **Island Walking Club**, sponsored by Carolina Beach Parks and Recreation, 458-7416, organizes daily invigorating beach strolls. Meet at 7 AM weekdays at the Carolina Beach Community Building at Third and Raleigh streets.

Walking classes that incorporate stretching techniques are led by personal trainer and fitness counselor **Freddie J. King** (a woman) every Tuesday morning at 9 AM at the Assembly Building in Topsail Beach. Everyone is welcome and a small donation is requested. Call 328-1532 for more information.

Skateboarding

The city of Wilmington dealt a controversial blow to skateboarders and in-line skaters in 1996 by banning those activities downtown where, it so happens, there are paved hills best suited to these sports. Skateboarding in the town of Southport had already been banned for some time. There is still a strong skateboarding presence on the UNCW campus, where responsible boarders who respect property may ride freely.

The Skate Barn
Pansy Ln., Hampstead • 270-3497

This is the area's indoor skateboarding facility of note. Formerly known as the Middle School Indoor Skate Park, the Skate Barn features a 6-foot ramp, a 3-foot-deep bowl and a full street course, as well as a full accessories shop, snack machines, video games and a foosball table. "Cheapie" nights are Mondays and Thursdays: Skaters with helmets ride for $3; without helmets for $5. Other days it's $5 with helmet; $8 without. Release forms must be signed to use the facility (parents or guardians must sign for children younger than 18). To get there, take Highway 17 to Hampstead, turn west onto Peanut Road, then right onto unpaved Pansy Lane. The Skate Barn is open every day — Monday through Friday from 4 to 10 PM; Saturday from 1 to 10 PM; and Sunday from 1 to 6 PM.

Soccer

Soccer fever continues to sweep this area. Youth and adult leagues continue to grow in popularity, and the fields are constantly busy on weekends. Wilmington is home to the U.S. Independent Soccer League professional team, the **Wilmington Hammerheads**, who use Laney High School as their home field until the team's own complex is completed. The Hammerheads also conduct affordable, specialized clinics, camps and individual instruction for players and coaches — as low as $5 per day for clinics and $10 per hour for individual lessons. Clinics run year round and include spring break and summer sessions. They also contribute some coaching for the Cape Fear Youth Soccer Association's "classic" games. For information about programs and matches, call the Hammerheads office at 256-0975 or write: Wilmington Hammerheads, 1630 Military Cutoff Road, Suite 200 G-H, Wilmington 28403.

Perhaps the best news for parents and players is that the investment necessary to play soccer is fairly low, generally limited to a onetime registration fee averaging $25 and shin guards that cost less than $20.

Cape Fear
Youth Soccer Association
P.O. Box 5454, Station #1, Wilmington 28403 • 675-2713

Boasting 134 teams and roughly 1,800 players in the recreational division alone, the CFYSA, a member of the U.S. Soccer Federation, is the area's soccer authority. Their programs include adults, and plans are afoot to expand further, so don't be surprised when

they drop the word "youth" from their name. League play proceeds in two yearly cycles, fall and spring, with the year-end Hanover Cup tournament beginning in late April. The CFYSA invites players of nearly all ages to play on any of a variety of teams. Classic (a.k.a. "select") teams are formed through trials and may travel around and outside the state, as tournaments determine. Recreational teams are open to all players without tryouts. Challenge teams, a level between recreational and classic and formed by tryout and draft, are a new endeavor. Licensed coaches lead all teams, and all matches are supervised by officials and referees. CFYSA games are held at the Hugh MacRae athletic fields (behind Hoggard High School off Shipyard Boulevard) on weekends during fall and spring. Register in July and in January. In addition, the association sponsors an indoor league that plays at Athletic Zone, 4405 Northchase Pkwy NE, 452-5020, on the north side of Wilmington. The CFYSA also offers coaching clinics, uniforms, access to supplementary insurance, newsletters, summer camps and more.

Wilmington Parks and Recreation
Athletic Office • 343-3680

An adult soccer league plays from May through July. The league's growing popularity often makes it difficult for new teams to enter, especially late in the preseason. Games are held at Legion Stadium on Carolina Beach Road, 2.5 miles south of downtown Wilmington.

Wilmington Family YMCA
2710 Market St. • 251-9622

The Y also sponsors league games for boys and girls ages 3 to 11 during the spring and fall.

Brunswick County
Parks and Recreation
Bolivia • 253-4357, (800) 222-4790

From September through November, Brunswick County Parks and Recreation organizes youth soccer for players ages 5 to 14 (the oldest players must still be in middle school). Soccer camps are popular from June through August. Early registration is recommended.

Onslow County
Parks and Recreation
Jacksonville • 347-5332

Onslow Parks and Rec hosts a coed league for adults 30 years and older. Teams with up to 20 players can register for $170. Play starts in February and continues through mid-May. Games are played at Hubert Bypass Park in the town of Hubert, convenient to the northern reaches of this guide's coverage.

Softball

Refer also to the section on baseball in this chapter for information on the optimist clubs, Wrightsville Beach Parks and Recreation and Onslow County Parks and Recreation, which also sponsor softball leagues.

Wilmington Parks and Recreation
Wilmington • 341-7855

Parks and Recreation hosts adult men's, women's and coed leagues and a league for seniors during spring and fall. The adult leagues run in two seasons. Team registration for the fall season is in August. Registration for the spring season is in March. Fees range from $200 to $400 per team.

Wilmington's
Cape Fear Optimist Club
Wilmington • 762-8957

This group sponsors The Cape Fear Belles softball league for girls in two age groups: 13 to 15 and 12 and younger. The Belles' 13- to 15-year-olds All Star Team won the 1993 state championship.

Carolina Beach
Parks and Recreation
Carolina Beach • 458-7416

Carolina Beach hosts a two-day, open softball tournament in August. If you can scrape up a team, your own softballs and the $100 entry fee, you're in.

Brunswick County
Parks and Recreation
Bolivia • (800) 222-4790

The county sponsors separate softball leagues for adult men and for girls in the spring and an adult coed league in the fall. People of all ages are welcome to participate in their umpire clinics. Call for schedules and fees.

Tennis

Practically every larger public park in the region has at least two courts (see Parks at the end of this chapter). The University of North Carolina at Wilmington also hosts summer tennis camps for youth (see Summer Camps, above). **Wilmington Parks and Recreation** offers tennis for youth and seniors from March through November. Mr. PeeWee tennis for ages 4 to 7 takes place September through November and March through May.

The Wilmington Seagulls Tennis Association sponsors the annual **Sickle Cell Open Tennis Tournament**, which takes place at a Wilmington park in mid-September and is governed by USTA rules. Singles and doubles matches are the best of three sets. Evening play could be under lights. Entry fee is $12, and awards are presented. For registration information, write WSTA Tennis Tournament, 226 Normandy Drive, Wilmington, NC 28412, or call 392-0568, 341-7841 (days) or 251-5676 (days).

If your racket needs repair or you need a new pair of shorts, stop by **Tennis With Love Ltd.** at 4303 Oleander Drive in Wilmington, 791-3128, in the easy-to-miss Landmark Plaza near Oh!Brian's restaurant. This shop specializes in restringing tennis and racquetball frames and carries clothing, shoes and accessories. It's a shop that lives up to its name.

Greater Wilmington
Tennis Association
Wilmington • 392-5807

The GWTA organizes tournaments for serious players. The tournaments are open to all

---

INSIDERS' TIP

Brunswick County beaches are some of the nicest family-oriented beaches anywhere.

in singles, doubles and mixed doubles divisions. Registration fees vary, beginning around $10. You can also call Wilmington Parks and Recreation for information, 343-3680.

USTA Team Tennis Association
Wilmington • 392-5807

The Association organizes adult-league team tennis from March through May. Match-winners may go on to compete at the district, sectional and national levels.

The Wilmington Tennis Ladder
Wilmington • 791-7764

The Wilmington Tennis Ladder is a monthly newsletter as well as a service that matches players in open challenges in every category. The season (August 1 through January 31) is designed to prepare players for the USTA Team Tennis tournaments that begin in March. The newsletter lists category captains and current standings. The cost is $15 for six months.

Wrightsville Beach Parks and Recreation
Wrightsville Beach • 256-7925

This department sponsors all levels of group instruction for adults and children age 5 and older from March through October and a Women's Tennis Day every Thursday 9 AM to noon year round, weather permitting.

Brierwood Golf Club
10 Brierwood Rd. near Shallotte city limits • 754-4660

This private club offers its four outdoor courts for public play for a nominal fee (about $3).

Ocean Isle Beach Golf Course
Ocean Isle Beach Dr. (on the mainland), • 579-2610

Two outdoor courts available to the public for a very small fee.

Brunswick County Parks and Recreation
Bolivia • 254-4357

All six Brunswick County District Parks maintain tennis courts for public use. See the section on Parks below.

Track and Field

Track and field is mostly school-related in this region, but **Brunswick County Parks and Recreation** has a program for youth in the Leland area (northern Brunswick County). The program operates in summer and emphasizes fun and technique more than winning.

Superheroes can tackle the annual **Wilmington Triathlon**, sponsored by the Wilmington Family YMCA, 251-9622, in mid-September. The combination 2K saltwater swim, 45K bike race and 10K run may be entered by individuals and three-member teams, ages 14 and older. Entry forms are available from the YMCA, 2710 Market Street, Wilmington, NC 28403. You may also call 762-3357.

The Marine Corps Base, Camp Lejeune, hosts the annual **Lejeune Grand Prix Series** from January through October. The series consists of 11 challenges, each one more grueling than the next. Among them are the Tour d'Pain (February), the European Cross Country (March), the Armed Forces Day 5K (May), the Mud, Sweat & Gears Duathlon (June), the Wet & Wild Biathlon (August) and the Lejeune Triathlon (September). Events take place within the confines of Camp Lejeune (near Jacksonville). Events are open to civilians of all ages. Entry forms and information can be obtained by contacting the fitness director, 451-5430.

Ultimate

Like any beach community worth its salt, we take Frisbee seriously. Two teams in the 1993 World Championships came from Wilmington: UNCW's men's team (1993 national champs) and the Port City Slickers, 791-8623, an unaffiliated men's team, half of which is made up of UNCW grads. UNCW's women's team was also 1991-92 national collegiate champs and remain a top-ranked force. All three of these powerhouses participate in a sport that is undergoing a surge in popularity, even to the point that talk is focusing on whether to introduce referees.

Volleyball

If you're not accustomed to playing in sand, you're in for a workout. Some say it will either whip you into shape or kill you. But not all volleyball in the area is outdoors. If you survive the summer playing in sand, your improved agility and jumping may manifest themselves dramatically on a hard court in winter. As you might expect, competition is fairly stiff, and local players generally take their games seriously.

Athletic Zone
4405 Northchase Pkwy. N.E., Wilmington • 452-5020

This indoor facility on the north side of town offers a good place to play during the winter. Team registration is the most economical way to play, but pickup games may be available at nominal cost.

Wilmington Family YMCA
2710 Market St., Wilmington • 251-922

In conjunction with the Federal Outdoor Volleyball Association (FOVA), the Y sponsors one tournament each month from March to October at Wrightsville Beach. There are three doubles divisions — novice, intermediate and advanced — and sign-up is at 8:30 AM on weekends. Games begin at 9 AM.

Capt'n Bill's Backyard Grill
4240 Market St., Wilmington • 762-0111

These are the only sand courts within city limits. They are behind the North 17 shopping center. Join a pickup game for a buck per player, or register your team in one of Capt'n Bill's leagues. Hot food and cold drinks are served by the courtside grill.

Wilmington Parks and Recreation
Wilmington • 343-3680

Wilmington Parks and Recreation has fall and spring coed volleyball for adults. Teams must register early to participate in this crowded league, usually by the end of July for the fall season and by early January for the spring.

Wrightsville Beach Parks and Recreation
Wrightsville Beach • 256-7925

Wrightsville Beach Parks and Recreation sponsors doubles tournaments with round-robin play in men's, women's and mixed categories. Games are held March through October on the beach strand.

If you'd like to put up your own net on Wrightsville Beach, you'll have to get permission from the folks at Parks and Recreation. It's easy. On Carolina Beach, check with the lifeguard on duty in the zone where you'd like to play before staking your net.

Brunswick County Parks and Recreation
Bolivia • (800) 222-4790

Adult team volleyball in Brunswick County is sponsored by Brunswick County Parks and Recreation. Players must be 18 or older and out of high school. The season runs from late October through March. Inquire about registration early.

Onslow County Parks and Recreation
Jacksonville • 347-5332

Folks 16 and older from Onslow and northern Pender counties may enter teams in Onslow County Parks and Recreation's volleyball league. Contact them in July for registration information. The indoor matches commence during the third week of September.

Sharky's Pizza & Deli
Ocean Isle Beach Cswy. Ocean Isle Beach • 579-9177

Sharky's now has a sand court, and you can even arrive by boat (docking facilities are available). Food and refreshments are within easy "serving" distance.

INSIDERS' TIP

Use the outdoor shower if your beach house has one. It will really help keep sand from being tracked inside and make clean-up easier.

Wrestling

Brunswick County Parks and Recreation, 253-4357 or (800) 222-4790, is about the only agency sponsoring wrestling teams outside the schools. The league boasts two national champs among its alumni. The county has a scholastic league (ages 5 to 14) and a freestyle league (any age). Inquire early about the availability of summer wrestling camp.

Yoga

In addition to the listings below, fitness centers occasionally offer classes. For individual instructors, information and contacts, check the bulletin boards at the Tidal Creek Food Co-op, 4406 Wrightsville Avenue, 799-2667, and Doxey's Market & Cafe, Landfall Shopping Center (Eastwood and Military Cutoff roads), 256-9952, both in Wilmington.

Wilmington Family YMCA
2710 Market St. • 251-9622

The Y offers regular classes for members and is a good resource for locating private instructors.

Haren (Ed Pickett)
c/o Unitarian Universalist Fellowship
4313 Lake Ave., Wilmington • 395-4431

A proponent of Kripalu yoga, or "posture-flow" yoga, Haren instructs informal weekly classes in Wilmington. Kripalu yoga emphasizes spontaneous movement rather than static form and is thought to be a rediscovery of yoga's most ancient traditions. Classes are open to anyone for a voluntary donation.

Wrightsville Beach Parks and Recreation
Wrightsville Beach • 256-7925

Wrightsville Beach Parks and Recreation offers year-round morning and evening classes emphasizing flexibility, alignment, conditioning and stress-reduction techniques.

Parks

We've grouped state, county and city parks by location since all three types can be found within Wilmington or Carolina Beach city limits. Refer to the Index if you're unsure of a park's location.

Wilmington

The 32 public parks maintained by the city of Wilmington differ widely. From the historic Riverwalk of downtown's Riverfront Park and the athletic fields of Empie Park to the sculpted benches of Carolina Courtyard and sunken cypress stands of Greenfield Lake, there is always a park nearby with the kind of recreation or quiet you desire. Here is a cross-section of the larger city parks and their facilities. Inquiries about particular facilities at Wilmington parks can be directed to the Wilmington Parks and Recreation Department's athletic office, 343-3680.

Empie Park
Park Ave. at Independence Blvd., Wilmington

Empie has lighted baseball fields, picnic shelters, a playground, bike racks and a concession stand. Due to popular demand, tennis courts here must be reserved in advance ($3 for city residents; $4 nonresidents) by calling the Wilmington Athletics office (located at the park) at 343-3860.

Greenfield Park
U.S. Hwy. 421 (Carolina Beach Rd.), Wilmington

Greenfield Lake and its surrounding gardens are the centerpiece of Wilmington's park system and a scenic wonder that changes character from season to season. Among the city's oldest parks, it was a working plantation and, later, a carnival grounds. The lake attracts a wide variety of birds and is rumored to contain alligators. When the azaleas bloom in early spring, the area explodes in a dazzling profusion of color. Stands of flowering magnolia, dogwood, long leaf pine and live oak — many hung with Spanish moss — line the shady 5-mile Lake Shore Drive.

On the north side of the 158-acre park are lighted tennis courts, playgrounds, picnic areas, a concession stand and docks where canoes and paddleboats are available for rent. A free public boat ramp is on W. Lake Shore Drive immediately east of Highway 421. The benches at mid-span on Lions Bridge are a wonderful spot to relax on a breezy day. Open-air performances are presented in summer at the amphitheater off W. Lake Shore Drive, adjacent to the Municipal Rose Garden. An excellent place to observe wildlife is from the Rupert Bryan Memorial Nature Trail, an easy one-third-mile looped boardwalk through dense cypress swamp. The trail head is through the parking lot off E. Lake Shore Drive between Yaupon and Cypress drives.

Legion Stadium
Carolina Beach Rd. (U.S. 421), Wilmington

Beside Greenfield Lake, approximately 1.75 miles south of the Cape Fear Memorial Bridge, Legion Stadium is home to several local high school sports teams. The site also has lighted athletic fields, tennis courts and a swimming pool as well as plenty of parking. The pool fee is $1 for adults and 50¢ for children.

Hugh MacRae Park
Oleander Dr., east of S. College Rd., Wilmington

This county park of tall pines is, appropriately, the site of the Piney Woods Festival in early September. Playgrounds, lighted tennis courts, athletic fields, sheltered picnic areas, a scenic pond and a concession stand explain this park's popularity.

Northside Park
Between Sixth and MacRae sts., north of Taylor St.

The pool is the main attraction here, and sheltered picnic areas are available too. The pool fee is $1 for adults and 50¢ for children.

Riverfront Park
Water St., Wilmington

For many locals, this park epitomizes Wilmington life. Once congested with the wharves of the state's busiest port, the Riverwalk is now a place for quiet strolls, sightseeing, shopping, live outdoor music and dining. The sternwheeler *Henrietta II* and the tour boat *Capt. Maffitt* dock here. You'll also find a visitors' information booth. Historic sailing ships visiting town often dock here and usually offer tours.

Robert Strange Park
Eighth and Nun sts., Wilmington

The heart of this park is its swimming pool (fee: $1 adults, 50¢ children). Other facilities include a recreation center, restrooms, playground, picnic shelters, softball fields and lighted tennis and basketball courts.

Snow's Cut Park
River Rd., near Snow's Cut bridge, Wilmington

Divided into two sections along River Road, one directly beneath the bridge and the other some 100 yards west, this county park offers shady picnic grounds, sheltered tables, a gazebo and pedestrian access to Snow's Cut. It is very near Carolina Beach Family Campground. For shelter reservations call 341-7198.

Wrightsville Beach Park
Causeway Dr., Wrightsville Beach

This sprawling recreation and athletic facility is impossible to miss when traveling Causeway Drive. Thirteen acres in breadth, it includes tennis courts, basketball courts, a softball field, a football/soccer field, sand volleyball courts, playground equipment and a fitness trail. The 2.5-mile sidewalk "Loop" bordering much of the park and traversing both of the island's bridges is popular among walkers and joggers.

Carolina Beach and Kure Beach

Carolina Beach State Park
Dow Rd., Carolina Beach • 458-8206

This is one of the most biologically diverse parks in North Carolina and a contender for the most beautiful park in the area. Maritime forest, sandhill terrain, waterfront and sand ridges support carnivorous plants and centuries-old live oaks. Five miles of easy trails wind throughout the park. The marina offers boat ramps ($3) and 42 boat slips off the Cape Fear River. Excellent overnight camping facilities are available. The park is on Pleasure Island, 1 mile north of Carolina Beach and less than a half-mile from Highway 421, off Dow Road. Day use is free.

Carolina Lake Park
Atlanta Ave. and U.S. Hwy. 421, Carolina Beach

Primarily a picnic site, this 11-acre park has four gazebos, sheltered picnic tables and a playground.

The Cove at
Fort Fisher State Historic Site
U.S. Hwy. 421 S., Kure Beach • 458-5538

This is a beautiful getaway, about 6 miles south of Carolina Beach. Bordering the beach and a rocky sea wall, a grove of windswept live oaks provides shade for the picnic tables and grills. Come to fish and sunbathe — but don't swim: dangerous currents and underwater hazards make it risky. Parking is available south of the museum, near the Ft. Fisher Memorial and at the museum itself, across the road. The nearest restrooms are at the Fort Fisher Recreation Area Public Access, 1 mile south. Otherwise, there are no facilities.

Mike Chappell Park
Dow Rd., Carolina Beach

Two lighted ball fields and a football/soccer field make up the greatest area of this 10-acre park, which also offers picnic tables, two tennis courts, two lighted sand volleyball courts and a playground. The park is bounded by Sumter Avenue and Clarendon Boulevard.

Joe Eakes Park
K Ave. at Seventh St., Kure Beach

This small park, not a long walk from the beach, offers a playground, two tennis courts and volleyball and basketball courts.

Brunswick County

The following six District Parks are maintained by the Brunswick County Parks and Recreation Department. All have excellent facilities, including tennis courts, ball fields, football/soccer fields, basketball courts, playgrounds and picnic shelters. Most of them also feature shuffleboard courts and

horseshoe pits, plus community buildings for use by groups for such occasions as reunions, exercise classes and other events. For specific information about any of the district parks, or to reserve picnic shelters and community buildings, call 253-4357. Tennis players at Ocean Isle Beach also may note the town's public courts on Third Street across from the Museum of Coastal Carolina.

Leland District Park
Village Rd., Leland

This is a 13-acre community park, situated behind the Leland Post Office. Facilities include a community building, playground and sand volleyball courts.

Lockwood District Park
N.C. Hwy. 211, a mile north of U.S. Hwy. 17

The park is a mile north of the town of Supply. Its community building, however, is at Holden Beach. The park offers shuffleboard and horseshoes.

Northwest District Park
U.S. Hwy.74/76, 2 miles west of the Leland overpass.

This park lies 15 minutes west of Wilmington, on the south side of the highway.

Smithville District Park
N.C. Hwy. 133 near Southport

Smithville District Park includes beach-style volleyball courts.

Shallotte District Park
Old Hwy. 17, 1 mile south of Shallotte

To find this park from Highway 17, follow signs for Highway 17 Business.

Town Creek District Park
U.S. Hwy. 17, near Winnabow

You can't miss this park on the east side of the road, about 15 or 20 minutes south of Wilmington.

E. F. Middleton Park
E. Oak Island Dr. at S.E. 47th St., Long Beach

The primary city park in Long Beach, Middleton Park offers a large playground with sand pits, swings and climbing bars, plus two tennis courts, basketball courts, a baseball field and picnic tables with some shade. The park is across the street from Town Hall and the emergency medical station.

Ev-Henwood Preserve
6150 Rock Creek Rd., Town Creek
• 253-6066, 962-3197

This recently opened nature preserve, owned and administered by the University of North Carolina at Wilmington, comprises 174 acres of lush woodland threaded with marked trails and educational displays. Among the many natural points of interest is an old tar kiln of the type once ubiquitous throughout the region. (At present, only about 74 acres are open to the public.) Suitable for families, the preserve is open during daylight hours seven days a week. Picnic tables and a restroom are available, and there's an on-site caretaker. Don't forget the camera and lunch! Admission is free.

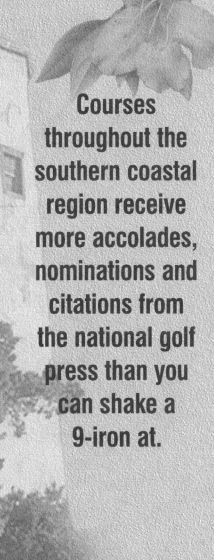

Courses throughout the southern coastal region receive more accolades, nominations and citations from the national golf press than you can shake a 9-iron at.

Golf

More new golf courses sprout up along our southern coast than anywhere else in North Carolina. Brunswick County already boasts nearly 30 facilities, many part of residential golf communities or concentrated in the Sunset Beach-Calabash area near the South Carolina border. Courses throughout the southern coastal region receive more accolades, nominations and citations from the national golf press than you can shake a 9-iron at. The area features several world-class course designs bearing the signatures of Tom Fazio, P.B. Dye, Dan Maples, Hale Irwin, George Cobb and Willard Byrd. Players familiar with the Myrtle Beach area are discovering that our courses offer far less crowded and less hurried playing at prices that encourage multiple rounds per day, all year long. Professional Golfers Association and fund-raising tournaments are increasingly finding host clubs locally. And if there's one other essential factor you should know about golf in this region, it's wind, particularly on Bald Head Island, which makes play along this coast an especially formidable treat.

Most local courses are semiprivate, which means they're open to the public while club memberships are also available. Memberships, of course, offer various benefits and privileges, such as lower fees or preferred tee times.

Greens fees vary according to season and location. At semiprivate courses, they range widely from about $20 to $100 and more, but average between $30 and $40. Fees are highest during the peak months (late March to early May and mid-September to early November) and at the more exclusive clubs. All the better courses offer practice ranges. Overall, the region's courses offer an excellent balance between price and playing conditions. Summer rates, and discounts for seniors, corporations and groups are commonplace. Many pro shops at the courses rent clubs to travelers unable to pack their own.

Below we describe some of the better courses, judged by overall beauty, location and variety of challenges. We've also included a few independent driving ranges throughout the area, retail shops that offer equipment and repairs and come highly recommended by Insiders, information on golf package and services, and local annual tournaments. Complete listings of courses can be found at the various chambers of commerce throughout the region.

Courses

Wilmington

The Cape Golf & Racquet Club
535 The Cape Blvd., Wilmington
• 799-3110

A mile north of Carolina Beach, this semiprivate par 72 championship course is meticulously landscaped amid 24 lakes, ponds and marshland. The bermudagrass fairways comprise a championship yardage of 6800 yards with a 73.5 rating from the blue tees and a slope of 135. Signature double greens grace the 15th and 17th holes. The grounds include a fully-stocked pro shop, driving range, putting and chipping greens as well as locker rooms with showers, a cocktail lounge, the full-service Mulligans Pub, banquet facilities and a snack bar. Club members also have access to the Cape's swimming pool and tennis courts. Greens fees vary from inexpensive to moderate.

Echo Farms
Golf & Country Club
4114 Echo Farms Blvd., Wilmington
• 791-9318

This semiprivate course is distinguished by lakes that come into play on nine holes, stands of moss-draped hardwood and some of the finest bentgrass greens in Wilmington. Designed by Gene Hamm, this former dairy farm (the original farmhouse near the 17th hole is still occupied) is now a par 72 challenge rated between 69.6 and 72.7 with slopes from 121 to 131. Echo Farms recently completed improvements, fully returning the course to its original glory (it was built in 1974). A driving range, practice greens, full restaurant, bar and snack lounge are open to all. The pro shop does regripping. Echo Farms has developed a fine teaching facility offering clinics and private lessons. The course is 5 miles south of downtown Wilmington on Carolina Beach Road (Highway 421).

FYI

Unless otherwise noted, the area code for all phone numbers in this guide is 910.

Inland Greens
5945 Inland Greens Dr., Wilmington
• 452-9900

This less-known public par 3 course is a good place to sharpen your short game. Holes average just over 100 yards, and the greens are in good condition. Almost midway between Wrightsville Beach and downtown Wilmington, the course is hidden off Cardinal Drive between Eastwood Road and Market Street.

Landfall
1550 Landfall Dr. • 256-8411

Play on Landfall's two superlative courses, designed by Jack Nicklaus and Pete Dye, is restricted to members (and members' guests) of the exclusive Landfall Club. Memberships are available to Landfall property owners and nonowners, and the rewards for golfing members include challenges unparalleled in the majority of area courses. Both courses are tastefully situated along the Intracoastal Waterway in a perfectly manicured setting.

The par 72 Nicklaus course is perhaps the more forgiving of the two. With a rating of 72.6 and slopes ranging from 120 to 137, it looks easier on paper than it really is, thanks largely to the many carries over marshes and water. The 6th hole, for instance, is a tough par 3 playing 190 yards from the back (85 from the front), with little more than marsh all the way to the green. Hole 17's island green is backed with a bunker that's a poor bailout given its 5-foot forward lip.

Another island green is the signature hole on the Dye course. Completely waterbound, the kidney-shaped 11th green (135-yard, par 3) slopes away from the sand trap that collars half its perimeter. The Dye course is probably the tougher of the two. It is a par 72 rated at 73.9 from the back (slope: 116-135). Plenty of uneven lies, marshes and pot bunkers demand that the players push the envelope of their games to the utmost. Both courses feature bentgrass greens. Fairways and roughs stay green all year.

Members also have access to Landfall's elaborate sports center, which has 14 tennis courts (hard, composition and grass), a croquet course, an NCAA short-course pool and many indoor facilities.

Porters Neck Plantation
and Country Club
1202 Porters Neck Rd., Wilmington
• 686-1177

Porters Neck is an aficionado's course, a combination of picture-perfect aesthetics and strategic challenges designed by Tom Fazio, *Golf Digest's* top-ranked golf architect in America. This is a championship course (par 72, slope 130) that emphasizes careful club selection and pin placement. Impeccably maintained fairways undulate in sometimes deceptive fashion. Enormous waste bunkers and lakes abound, some of which span the entire distance from tee to green (Holes 11, 13, 14). Distinctive waste mounds, planted with native grasses, add to the course's unique look. Each hole presents conditions to make the most accurate golfer uncomfortable, yet leave no player unfulfilled.

About 6 miles from Wilmington, this course winds through a private residential development on the Intracoastal Waterway. Greens fees are at the high end of the local scale. Public play is invited but limited. The pro shop offers a few services such as regripping. The entrance gate is a little over a mile in from the property limit on Porters Neck Road.

Wilmington Golf Course
311 Wallace Ave., Wilmington • 791-0558

Relatively flat and among the more populated courses, the "Muni" is Wilmington's only municipal course. It features a practice fairway left of the 9th hole. Entrance to the par 71 facility is either from Oleander Drive or from Pine Grove Drive, a seven-minute drive from downtown. Compared to other local courses, the Muni has a relative dearth of water hazards, but the stream crossing the fairways of holes 2 (495-yard par 5) and 12 (519-yard par 5) is in just the wrong place for many golfers. There is only one serious dogleg. The clubhouse and pro shop are open everyday from 7 AM until sundown. The clubhouse has showers and lockers in the men's room only. Greens fees are $6 weekdays (higher on weekends) for city residents, and nine-hole rounds are available. Groups are limited to fours, and no onesomes or twosomes are permitted before 1:30 PM.

Carolina Beach

Beau Rivage Plantation Golf & Country Club
6230 Carolina Beach Rd., Wilmington • 392-9022, (800) 628-7080

Elevations as much as 72 feet and scads of bunkers (including two waste bunkers) place this course among the more dramatically landscaped ones in New Hanover County. It is a semiprivate par 72 course (slope: 114-136) in which water hazards come into play on eight holes. Hole 4 (206-yard par 3) is notable for its island tee-box for women and a carry that is entirely over water. Its well-watered bentgrass green is protected on three sides. The pro shop does some repairs, and its inventory emphasizes soft goods. Lessons are available. A bar and grill and restaurant provide attractive settings for post-round analysis. Beau Rivage is a residential development, and club memberships are available to nonresidents. A 32-suite hotel adjoins the clubhouse.

Bald Head Island

Bald Head Island Club
Bald Head Island • 457-7310

Extremely demanding, due as much to the ocean wind as to George Cobb's brilliant design, this par 72 course is among the scenic gems on the east coast. Exposed greens on its ocean side contrast sharply with interior holes lined with palms and pines. Four sets of tees yield course lengths from 5150 to 7040 yards. The links-style finishing holes run alongside the ocean. The Club currently hosts its own pro-am tournament, to which spectators are welcome. Bald Head Island is accessible only by ferry, and tee times are required. A driving range and snack bar are available, and other elegant amenities are nearby. Golf Getaway packages ($99 per person per night, everything included) can be arranged year round by calling (800) 432-RENT. A Day Golf Package includes parking, ferry, transfers, cart and greens fee for 18 holes.

Southport-Oak Island

The Gauntlet Golf Club
N.C. Hwy. 211, Southport • 253-3008, (800) 247-4806

With a championship slope of 142, it's no wonder that designer P.B. Dye called this, "My most challenging course yet." Its carries over many water hazards have been described as heroic, while its multilevel fairways, bulkheads and variety of grasses are stamped with the Dye hallmark. Each hole bears a name indicative of its character, such as The Moats, Loch Ness, Quest and The Moor. The final three holes, which include the No. 1 handicap (the 9th hole, 449 yards from the pro tee), play into and over a series of marshes and lakes for a spectacular finish. Five sets of tees present a variety of plays. Most tee boxes are elevated. The Gauntlet and its new companion course, the Members Club (below), are 4 miles outside Southport and offer fine views of the Intracoastal Waterway. Caddies, a complete practice facility and lessons are available. A restaurant and lounge are close by.

The Members Club
at St. James Plantation
N.C. Hwy. 211, Southport • 253-9500, (800) 474-9277

New in 1996, this Hale Irwin-designed par-72 course utilizes the natural lay of the land to good effect, forgoing moguls and flashy, amusement-park landscaping. The course has been called user-friendly (73.5 slope from the back) although, being so close to the Intracoastal Waterway, wind can prove deeply trying. Watch out for the 15th hole, a par-5 with lateral water hazards squeezing the fairway into a bottleneck about 200 yards down, and more water in front of the green — potentially an express ticket to bogeyland. Video instruction programs are available at the pro shop, and the entire facility has all the amenities of the most exclusive clubs, such as practice greens and sand traps, a driving range, and on-site professionals. The Members Club invites nonmembers to be "members for a day."

Oak Island
Golf & Country Club
928 Caswell Beach Rd., Caswell Beach • 278-5275, (800) 278-5275

One of Brunswick County's older courses, this George Cobb creation is home to the Southport-Oak Island Masters Putting Tournament. It is a forgiving course, par 72, that will be enjoyed by players of varying skills. Its wide bermudagrass fairways are relatively short, lined with live oak and tall pines and not too fortified with water hazards. But that ocean wind! The clubhouse is less than 200 yards from the Atlantic, and sea breezes can frustrate the best players. Hole 9 (handicap 18) may send you to the Duffers Restaurant and Lounge early. This course, with its bermudagrass greens, driving range, putting green and swimming pool, underwent improvements recently and remains quite popular. Buffet breakfasts are also available in season.

South Brunswick Islands

Lockwood Golf Links
19 Clubhouse Dr., Holden Beach • 842-5666, (800) 537-9043

This is a classic Willard Byrd-designed par 72 course. Beautifully set at the confluence of Lockwood Folly River and the Intracoastal Waterway, it has no parallel fairways. Tricky, sloping bentgrass greens are protected by ample clear ponds, particularly at the 11th hole (which is best approached from below, putting uphill). The unique touch of lining some water hazards with "beaches" of oyster shells makes for handsome landscaping but difficult sighting of white balls and potentially frustrat-

Photo: N. C. Travel & Tourism

Wind is almost always a factor on Bald Head Island.

ing wedge work. Lockwood's amenities include a restaurant and lounge, driving range, putting green and pro shop. Lockwood Golf Links plays host to the annual Carolina's PGA Seniors Pro-Am Golf Tournament each November and the Cheerwine College Tournament in June.

Brierwood Golf Club
10 Brierwood Rd., Shallotte • 754-4660, 754-7076

Brierwood was the first golf community built along the South Brunswick Islands. About 7 miles north of Ocean Isle Beach, it is a player-friendly, par 72, championship course (slope 129) distinguished by plenty of freshwater obstacles and surrounded by residential properties. Fourteen holes present water hazards, such as part of a 3-acre lake that traverses the 10th fairway. The clubhouse includes a pro shop and the Blue Heron Bar & Grill, with its superb outdoor balcony-seating above a lake. Calls for tee times can be received 24 hours a day. The entrance to this semiprivate course is just off Highway 179 at the Shallotte town limit.

Brick Landing Plantation
N.C. Hwy. 179, Ocean Isle Beach
• 754-5545, (800) 438-3006

With 41 sand traps and 12 water holes, this handsome waterfront course was rated by *Florida Golf Week* magazine as among the top-

50 distinctive golf courses in the Southeast. Its bermudagrass fairways wind among freshwater lakes and through salt marshes, offering striking visual contrasts and championship challenges. The 17th hole finishes dramatically along the Intracoastal Waterway. Total course length is 6943 yards, a par 72 rated at 72.1. Amenities include a 19th-hole snack bar, a lunch and cocktail lounge, and practice facilities. Golf schools, clinics and full-time instructors are available as well as tennis and family vacation packages and memberships.

Oyster Bay
N.C. Hwy. 179, Sunset Beach • 579-3528, (800) 697-8372

The signature hole (the par 3 17th) is one of two island greens that are sure to push you to excel. This is an exceedingly challenging and imaginative public course (par 70, slope 134, rating 71.6) featuring stark elevations; beautiful, deadly lakes; and even a few trees smack in the middle of some fairways. Oyster Bay is one of the area's two Legends courses. It was voted Resort Course of the Year (1983) and among the top 50 public courses in the country (1990) by *Golf Digest*. The notorious 3rd hole (460 yards, par 4) presents the course's toughest two greens — one is designated daily. As with other Legends courses, Oyster Bay features computerized golf carts that tell you precise distances to greens from where the cart stands. Each cart is also equipped with club-and-ball cleaner, a cooler and ice, and beverage carts roam the course. The management enforces a dress code, and fees tend toward the medium-to-high.

Sea Trail
Golf Resort & Conference Center
211 Clubhouse Rd., Sunset Beach
• **287-1100, (800) 624-6601**

With its three par-72 courses and overnight accommodations, Sea Trail is an all-out golf resort known locally for its attractive balance of price, friendliness and outstanding playing conditions. About a mile from the beach, Sea Trail has its share of wind and water. Three sets of tees on each course — the Dan Maples (slope: 129), Rees Jones (132) and Willard Byrd (128) — present a variety of challenges that make these bermudagrass fairways and bentgrass greens memorable. Maples' 17th hole (190-yard, par 3) is the signature hole with its scenic appeal, a large oak tree blocking the right-hand approach and deep bunkers. A restaurant (Tavern on the Tee, at the Maples clubhouse), two lounges and many meeting facilities add to Sea Trail's appeal. Two clubs, one for members and one for resort guests, offer tennis and swimming. Golf packages, including bookings at neighboring courses, may be arranged on site.

Calabash Golf Links
820 Thomasboro Rd., Calabash
• **575-5000, (800) 841-5971**

New in 1996, this par 72 course features large greens, soft doglegs, and some lateral water hazards, but no over-water carries. Fairways are lined mostly with saplings. Greens fees are on the low end of average. Designed by Willard Byrd, the course offers four tee positions, few substantial elevations and an overall slope of 128.

Carolina Shores Golf
& Country Club
99 Carolina Shores Dr., Calabash
• **579-2181, (800) 762-8813**

This par-72 Tom Jackson creation, built in 1974, will reward even moderately careful golfers with better-than-usual games without killing themselves, so it tends to be popular. With

a slope of 128 from the back, it's an attractive, traditional, well-bunkered course set within a residential community. There are four par 5 holes (1, 7, 13, 18), and the 570-yard 18th, crowded with traps, is appropriately named The Last Mile. You'll find the clubhouse off Country Club Road.

Marsh Harbor Golf Links
N.C. Hwy. 179, Calabash • **579-3161, (800) 552-2660**

It wouldn't be enough to describe Marsh Harbor as the course with the toughest hole on the southern coast (according to a formal survey of area pros and amateurs). While the par 5 17th certainly is redoubtable, this championship par 71 Dan Maples creation is better known as one of the most lavishly beautiful courses on the Brunswick coast and among Golf Digest's top 25 public courses in America. Don't be misled by the blue-tee yardage (6690). The design emphasizes shot-making and trickiness, yielding a blue-tee rating of 73.3 (slope 134). Holes tend to be short and tight off the tees with generally small bermudagrass greens. All are well-bunkered, perhaps to compensate for the relative lack of water hazards. Five fairways are marsh-bound. There are some excellent par 3s, and players with single-digit handicaps will be formidably challenged. The much-touted 17th hole (570 yards from the back) demands two virtuoso carries over marshes before reaching the well-protected green. Marsh Harbor, a Legends course, straddles the state line. Greens fees lie at the medium-to-high end of the local average. Its upscale character is also evident in the handsome, well-stocked pro shop, roving beverage carts and computerized golf carts complete with club-and-ball cleaners, coolers and ice. A restaurant-style snack bar, driving range and putting greens are available, and the management enforces a dress code.

The Pearl Golf Links
N.C. Hwy. 179, Calabash • **579-8132**

These two par 72 courses, east and west, will have you wanting to play 36 straight, so start early. Architect Dan Maples endowed these links with theatrical bentgrass island greens, washboard fairways and solid challenges that yield ratings of 73.1 (east) and 73.2 (west). Course lengths are on the long side (7011 west; 6895 east), so break out the lumber and let 'er rip. A pro shop, snack bar, cocktail lounge and driving range are open year round.

Topsail Island

Belvedere Plantation Golf & Country Club
2368 Country Club Dr., Hampstead • 270-2703

Developed in 1975, Belvedere Plantation's course, designed by Russell Burney, is a narrow par 71 with plenty of water and small bermudagrass greens. Hole three (180-yard par 3) stands out for its carry over water to an elevated green. The blue tees are rated slightly higher than the course's overall par 71 and have a slope of 131. Belvedere is a busy course with affordable greens fees and discounts for residents of local counties. The clubhouse has a limited pro shop. Although part of a golf community, Belvedere offers club memberships to nonresidents as well. Golf schools lasting three to four days are available with overnight accommodations. Belvedere is less than a mile from Topsail Greens Country Club, about 18 miles north of Wilmington off U.S. Highway 17 N.

Olde Point
U.S. 17 N., Hampstead • 270-2403

The 11th hole has been called Jezebel for its wickedly frustrating ways. Considered one of the two toughest holes on all the southern coast by many area pros and amateurs (the other being the 17th at Marsh Harbor in Calabash), this long, narrow 589-yard par 5 is a gradual dogleg right that slopes laterally downward to the right into the woods and consistently defies players' depth perception. The course is buffeted by winds almost all year round, especially the second hole (372-yard par 3), where the wind is usually in your face and the well-bunkered green is surrounded on three sides by water. With four tee positions and slopes of 115 to 136, Olde Point is among the finer challenges in the area.

Topsail Greens Golf and Country Club
19774 U.S. Hwy. 17 N., Hampstead • 270-2883

This semiprivate par 71 course has a slope range of 113 to 121. While its overall length is not particularly daunting, it presents respectable challenges and several birdie opportunities to blue-tee players and a sense of satisfaction to those playing the shorter tees. Five holes require sizable carries over water, and two others have water beside the fairways. Greens of bermudagrass are mostly elevated. The 8th is the signature hole, a 159-yard par 3 played to an island green protected on both forward flanks by sand traps. The course is laid out on a roughly east-west axis, and hole 14 is about 200 yards from the Intracoastal Waterway. Winds are capricious. Greens fees are on the low end of the average, making Topsail Greens popular yet not overrun. This course is near two other excellent courses (Belvedere Plantation and Olde Point), about 18 miles outside Wilmington. Lessons, practice facilities and a full-service restaurant are among the extras. Topsail Greens hosts the annual benefit Kool Aid Golf Tournament in mid-December.

North Shore Country Club
N.C. Hwy. 210, Sneads Ferry • 327-2410, (800) 828-5035

Notorious for its long carries over water, North Shore is among the best-conditioned courses in the Topsail Island area. With a championship slope of 137 (seniors 115), it is also among the most challenging. In fact, not very long ago it was rated among the top 20 new courses of the decade by *Golf Reporter Magazine* and called "one of the best new courses in 1989" by *Golf Digest*. It is also quite affordable. North Shore's bermudagrass fairways are fraught with extensive mounding, tall pines and menacing blue waters to keep you from the bentgrass greens. Occasionally strong sea breezes will greet you as you step up to the elevated tee boxes. The 9th hole (412-yard par 4) is memorable for its necessary 250-yard tee shot; anything less is in the drink.

Designed by Bob Moore, North Shore is on the mainland side of the North Topsail Beach bridge, a crossing that offers a fine view of the course, the surrounding waterways and the ocean. Extras at North Shore include a pro shop, bar and grill, driving range, practice green and lockers. Late-day discounts are available. North Shore hosts two annual tournaments: the Stump Sound Rotary Golf Tournament in May and the Kiwanis Loggerhead Golf Tournament in October. Preregistration

opens about one month prior to each. Call the club for further information.

Driving Ranges

Wilmington

Coastal Golf Center and Carolina Custom Discount Golf
6987 Market St., Wilmington • 791-9010

More than a driving range, Coastal is a superior one-stop facility for practicing, instruction, equipment and repairs. Stations on the lighted 257-yard driving range feature well-kept grass mats and tees. Three PGA instructors are on staff, and the pro shop offers all repair services including regripping, shafting, refinishing and other customizing. The pro shop carries a varied inventory of apparel, accessories and books and also rents sets. Coastal Golf Center, 4 miles outside Wilmington on Highway 17 (Market Street) near the intersection with Military Cutoff Road, is one of five affiliated stores based in Raleigh. The center is open Monday through Saturday during the summer; hours are somewhat curtailed throughout the rest of the year.

Perfect Golf Practice Facility
5026 Oleander Dr., Wilmington • 791-7155

This facility offers an undulating grassy field with raised greens, complete with flags, to imitate course conditions. Stations are grass only (no fixed tees) and include club stands. The facility is lighted and open year round. Club repair and PGA lessons can be arranged on site. Perfect Golf is open seven days in summer.

Valley Golf Center & Driving Range
4416 S. College Rd., Wilmington • 395-2750

Convenient to Carolina Beach and Wilmington, this large, lighted facility has 40 lighted tee stations plus mats and a grass hitting area as well as sand trap areas. A covered hitting area allows practice during inclement weather. The fully-stocked pro shop offers repairs, accessories and instruction with PGA staff professionals. Valley Golf Center, just north of Monkey Junction, is open every day year round, 9 AM to 10 PM.

Southport-Oak Island and South Brunswick Islands

Holden Beach Driving Range
N.C. Hwy. 130, Holden Beach • 842-3717
This lighted practice facility offers lessons by Class-A PGA professionals, and, as any good resort-area attraction should, it has batting cages next door.

Pro Tee Practice Range
N.C. Hwy. 179, Ocean Isle Beach • 754-4700
This attractive, lighted facility is designed for players who appreciate quality. Two 18-station bermudagrass tee boxes flank a mat area with rubber tees. The pro shop stocks basic accessories, refreshments and snacks, and the management performs minor equipment repairs. Pro Tee is a half-mile west of the Brick Landing Plantation Golf Course and is open daily during the summer.

Equipment and Repairs

Nevada Bob's
5629 Oleander Dr., Wilmington • 799-4212
Nevada Bob's is a chain store that boasts an extraordinarily broad selection of new equipment and accessories, a flair for handsome presentation and a knowledgeable, attentive staff. It has the air of a connoisseur's shop, right down to the indoor netted tee station on which to test prospective clubs. There is also an artificial indoor putting green. Nevada Bob's is in the Bradley Square shopping center on the westbound side of Oleander. The store is open seven days a week.

Pro Golf Discount
914 S. Kerr Ave., Wilmington • 392-9405
Affiliated with the nationwide Pro Golf chain, this shop stocks a complete line of major brand equipment and accessories, including "experienced" golf balls and rental clubs. They maintain a full club-repair department, and regripping and customizing of metal clubs are done on premises (woods are sent out). The store is attractively designed and includes a carpeted putting area for fitting putters. You will find Pro Golf a few doors south of the Wilshire Boulevard intersection. Pro Golf Discount is open Monday through Saturday.

Tee Smith Custom Golf Clubs
1047 S. Kerr Ave., Wilmington • 395-4008
Tee Smith has been customizing and repairing clubs commercially since 1975 and carries the approval of pro shops throughout the Wilmington area. Simple repairs such as regripping often have a one-day turnaround. It carries a full line of top-name brands and is open all year Monday through Saturday.

Golf Tech
6408 Beach Dr. (N.C. Hwy. 179), Ocean Isle Beach • 579-3446
Keith Steagall's method of custom club design, by which he promises "lower scores through advanced club technology," is coming into increasing demand in several states. Keith builds and custom fits clubs and performs all kinds of repair, including refinishing. His full-line pro shop carries major brands, including Harvey Penick and Golfsmith equipment. Golf Tech also stocks used balls and rental clubs. The shop is open from 8 AM to 6 PM Monday through Saturday most of the year.

INSIDERS' TIP

Watch the clock when traveling to and from Wrightsville Beach. The drawbridge rises on the hour and can substantially delay summertime traffic.

The Golf Bag
16525 U.S. 17 S., Hampstead • 270-2980

Few pro shops boast the breadth of services and supplies offered by Tom Tirey at The Golf Bag. As affable as he is knowledgeable about the game, Tom customizes and repairs clubs and maintains a full line of golf equipment, accessories and all the little things, including gift items and instructional videos. He emphasizes his stock of ladies golf apparel and equipment for lefties. The Golf Bag is a half-mile from Olde Point golf course, less than 14 miles from Wilmington.

Photo: N. C. Travel & Tourism

There are magnificent golf opportunities in the area.

Packages and Services

Most travel agencies and local hotels arrange golf packages directly. Some people prefer central reservations services for the convenience and discounted rates.

3D Golf Vacations, (800) 377-2985, offers two all-inclusive packages, premiere and regular, as part of either a "fly-drive" or "drive-in" program. Packages include play at the more exclusive courses in southeastern North Carolina and representatives who escort you to your destination upon arrival in the area. Golf vacations to Ireland, Scotland and France are also available. The mailing address is P.O. Box 4874, Calabash, NC 28467.

The **American Lung Association Golf Privilege Card** offers discounts for one year on more than 135 rounds of golf played at 123 courses throughout North Carolina — with unlimited play on four courses within the range of this guide plus hundreds more rounds in Virginia and South Carolina — nearly 300 courses in all, including nine in nearby Myrtle Beach. The card costs $40. Buy three and get one free. Some restrictions apply. Contact the American Lung Association of North Carolina, Southeast Area, P.O. Box 40236, Fayetteville, NC 28309, or call 486-5864 or (800) 821-6205.

Brunswick County Parks and Recreation, 253-4357 or (800) 222-4790, sponsors a youth golf program affiliated with the national Hook a Kid On Golf program. Registration is limited, so inquire in April about the upcoming season that runs from June through August.

Coastal Golfaway, 791-8494 or (800) 791-8497, books customized packages of all price ranges and amenities, from Wilmington to Hilton Head, South Carolina.

Tee-Times Inc., 256-8043 or (800) 447-0450, is a Wilmington-based service that can arrange everything for your golf vacation — tee times, accommodations, airline tickets and rental cars.

Twin Travel & Cruises, 799- 5225 locally or (800) 365-8003, offers complete golf packages serving more than 80 courses from the greater Wilmington area south to Pawley's Island, South Carolina. It can handle everything from air fare and accommodations to tee times, restaurants, group outings, golf clinics, meetings and conventions. Offices open at 9 AM Monday through Saturday ('til 3 PM) and stay open late on Tuesday and Thursday ('til 9 PM).

The **Wilmington Golf Association**, 256-2251 or (800) 545-5494, disseminates information on, and accepts reservations for, packages provided by the area's leading courses and hotels.

For more information on golfing in North and South Carolina, pick up a copy of *The Insiders' Guide® to Golf in the Carolinas*.

Annual Tournaments

The annual **American Cancer Society Tournament**, played in August, pits four men or women per team in a scramble. Winners are eligible to compete in the state championship tournament in early autumn. The tournament is played each year at one of three courses in the Topsail-Hampstead area (north of Wilmington): Topsail Greens, Belvedere and Olde Point. Call one of those courses (listed above) for information.

The **Kool Aid Golf Tournament** in mid-December is a team event that brings together golfers, veterans and lovers of "golden oldie" rock 'n' roll. It is played at Topsail Greens Golf Club in Hampstead, 18 miles north of Wilmington. Prizes for the three top-placing teams may include free golf packages and concert tickets. The tournament is handicapped to level the field. Teams of four may register for $180, and individuals for $45. Registration includes lunch and beverages. For information, call 488-1133 or contact the Topsail Area Chamber of Commerce, 205 S. Topsail Drive, Surf City, N.C. 28445, 328-4722 or (800) 626-2780.

North Shore Country Club, N.C. Hwy. 210, Sneads Ferry, 327-2410 or (800) 828-5035, hosts two annual tournaments: the **Stump Sound Rotary Golf Tournament** in May and the **Kiwanis Loggerhead Golf Tournament** in early October. Preregistration opens about one month prior.

Carolina Beach is a very pleasant beach town with clean, wide beaches, an abundance of fishing opportunities, several nice restaurants and a growing sense of community pride that makes living here a charming prospect.

PROTECTING OUR AREA'S GREATEST RESOURCE

Our region is special for many reasons—from its beautiful beaches and scenic countryside to the friendly neighborhoods and tree-lined streets. And, it's our job to help maintain the health of people living in those neighborhoods and towns. Through health screenings that can detect disease in the early stages to treatment of the most severe injuries and illnesses, we're here with the expertise you need—when you need it most. After all, we have an important resource to protect—you.

VitaLine: Local 815-5188 or Toll Free 1-888-815-5188
Health Information. All Day. All Night.

CELEBRATING
30 years
1967 – 1997
OF COMMUNITY HEALTH

New Hanover Regional
Medical Center Proudly
Celebrates 30 Years Of
Serving The Community

New Hanover Regional Medical Center

2131 S. 17th Street
Wilmington, NC 28401

Tee Time ~ Anytime

Cypress
Island
GOLF AND RAQUET CLUB

Developed by
Cypress Green, Inc.
Marketed by
Gulf Stream Realty Group
392-6200 or 1-800-360-3020

Real Estate

There's an inside joke that says newcomers are required to get their real estate licenses when they move into the area. Real estate is one of the biggest businesses in the southern coastal region. Although there are already more than 200 real estate offices and thousands of people with their active licenses in the Greater Wilmington area (and this doesn't take into account Topsail Island to the north or the long string of Brunswick beaches to the south), people in this business can stay busy night and day.

The coastal area is limited to an approximately 180-degree radius of land. Unlike inland cities where real estate sales are possible in all directions, one can't go very far east in this coastal community without landing in the Atlantic Ocean. This creates a scarcity of land. Consequently, land has a disproportionately high value in some areas, especially if it is in view of the river, Intracoastal Waterway or the ocean. Local real estate company representatives report that as of 1996 it is very hard to find a desirable half-acre piece of land in any location for less than $50,000. Prime lots can go for as little as $150,000 and as high as $2 million in some sites on or near the water.

These prices are likely to continue to climb if the current trend holds. From 1996 to 1997, local Realtors estimated that housing costs jumped as much as 10 percent on average with an increase of as much as 20 to even 30 percent in upscale beach communities. There has been a tremendous amount of positive publicity about the region in national and state publications during the past few years, so many people are acquainted with the area and are interested in moving here. As demand continues to increase, prices continue to rise.

Prospective home or land buyers who thought the problems caused by two hurricanes in 1996 would drive down prices will discover this is not the case at all. While there was heavy storm damage in some beach communities to the north of Wilmington, making recovery a lengthy process for some areas, it has already become apparent to locals that beach dwellers are intent on rebuilding their homes and communities. And most beaches in the region fared reasonably well through both storms. Consequently, real estate bargains at the beach as a result of hurricanes are a matter of wishful thinking on the part of potential buyers.

The good news is that housing is still remarkably affordable throughout the Cape Fear region compared to some more affluent parts of the country. There is also tremendous diversity in terms of neighborhoods, housing styles, scenery and price. There are smaller, new homes for as low as $70,000; there are truly vintage homes in need of repair for even less. At the top end, one may spend well into the millions for a fine new home in an upscale neighborhood, but $150,000 will buy a very nice home in a number of fine neighborhoods.

It would be impossible in this guide to write about every neighborhood because, even as this book goes to press, new neighborhoods are sprouting in the area. What follows is information about established neighborhoods, average prices and other general facts. For specific information, contact an area Realtor.

Neighborhoods

Downtown Wilmington

It has been said by many a native that downtown Wilmington is a separate place from the rest of the city and New Hanover County. The tone is absolutely different from any other neighborhood in the region.

Two To Six Acre Private Estates

WhiteBridge offers the best of everything in its recreation facilities, surroundings and its distinguished quality homes. And just as important, it has an atmosphere that appeals to those rare people who expect a level of personal privacy within a protected community and have the ability to obtain it.

Discover uncommon choices in residential living at WhiteBridge. Expertly developed estate sites, from two to six acres, provide a lush backdrop for distinguished homes. At WhitBridge, lifestyle choices are diverse. Homesites overlook elegant ponds, pristine meadows or are tucked into hardwood forests.

- Only 75 lots on 300 acres of land, with finished homes also available.
- A neighborhood protected by architectural controls and restrictions without confining your lifestyle. Privacy with social amenities including swimming pool with outdoor pavilion, tennis courts, miles of natural trails and a 20-acre bird sanctuary
- Custom homes by WhiteBridge Construction available.
- Homes on estate-sized lots from the 300's.

WHITEBRIDGE

The Alternative To Heavily Restricted Half-Acre Living

Located on Hwy. 17, just 11 minutes North of Wilmington

For more information, stop by or write: P.O. Box 963, Hampstead, NC 28443

(919) 270-2000 • (800) 480-2007

WILCOX & WILCOX BUILDERS/DEVELOPERS
BROKERS PROTECTED

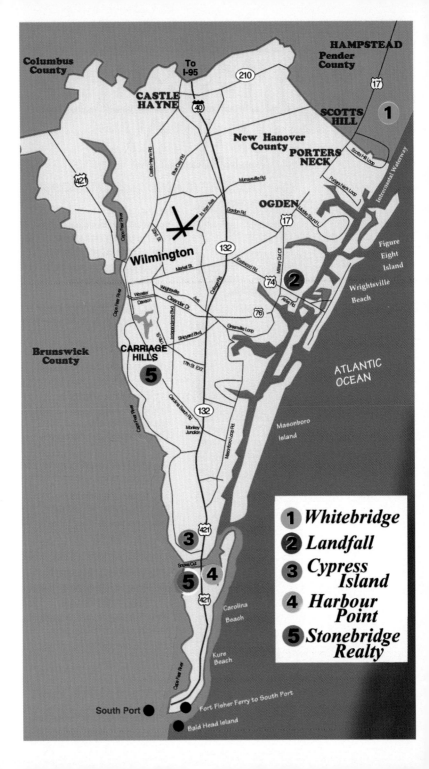

Many of the homes date from the mid to late 1800s as well as into the first quarter of the 20th century. There are stunning examples of Victorian, Italianate, Renaissance, Neoclassical and Revivalist architecture. Homes in the area — small cottages and large mansions alike — feature high ceilings, hardwood floors, fascinating detail, front porches and all of the interesting characteristics one would expect of vintage homes.

The neighborhood is home to an eclectic population. Downtown is a very interesting melting pot of races, professions and family configurations. What the entire neighborhood seems to have in common is a mutual appreciation for the particular amenities of downtown: great architecture, easily accessible cultural arts opportunities, fine dining, friendly shopping, the center of city and county government, walks along a beautiful riverfront, and a strong sense of community identity.

If you are looking for history and charm as well as an energetic and culturally inspirational atmosphere, downtown is definitely the place to be. Relatively few homes come on the market in the more established center of the neighborhood, and the ones that do aren't available for very long unless they are very large and, therefore, quite expensive. For the most part, this is an extremely stable neighborhood where investment in property continues to be advantageous.

People thinking about moving into the district should know that National Historic Registry status entails quite a few unusual rules that apply to homes within the district. The exterior paint color comes under the auspices of the Historic District Commission. Changing the existing color of a home requires obtaining a Certificate of Appropriateness. The removal of established trees is a matter that also requires seeking permission. And don't even think about vinyl siding unless you plan to incur the wrath of both the authorities and neighbors. Sometimes these rules are an annoyance, but everyone downtown will agree they have helped create a special place.

Within the district proper most homes have been restored, but there are still handyman

FYI

Unless otherwise noted, the area code for all phone numbers in this guide is 910.

bargains to be had in the areas outside of the district in the Historic Overlay. It takes a person with vision and to redo some of the deteriorated architectural gems in these neighborhoods. The level of downtown neighborhood restoration is the most stable at the river and diminishes as you head east toward the ocean at about Eighth Street.

The residential neighborhoods to the north of Market Street are generating high interest at this time and are seeing quality restoration efforts. The N. Fourth Street Business District Project, a renewal effort supported in part by the City of Wilmington, business owners and residents along this corridor, promises to open new options to people who want to live downtown. To the south, the natural boundary of the neighborhood is the Cape Fear Memorial Bridge. Quality restorative development has happened on S. Second, Queen and Castle streets.

Houses average $180,000 to $250,000 in the district proper, but one may spend considerably more or slightly less. The general market consists of single family homes. There are also a few condominium or duplex developments and some opportunities to have a rental apartment within one's own home.

Some solidly rediscovered neighborhoods beyond downtown are the Mansion District and nearby Carolina Heights and Carolina Place. Both flank Market Street beyond 15th Street. These neighborhoods date from the 1920s, and architectural style varies. In the Mansion District you can certainly purchase a mansion-style home, but there are also appealing cottages. In Carolina Heights you'll find bungalows priced as low as the $60s. Yes, homes at this price need some fix-up, but this neighborhood has become the new magnet for urban pioneers in search of an investment payoff. Carolina Heights begins roughly at 17th Street and continues to 23rd Street. It is widely regarded as the new frontier for not only residential investors but also homeowners, largely thanks to its relatively new status as an Historic Registry District. It also is comfortably close to venerable Forest Hills.

Wilmington and New Hanover County Suburbs

Forest Hills is, without dispute, a fine address. This large and very stable neighborhood was once a suburb of downtown. Today it is a conveniently located neighborhood of older homes that date from as early as the 1920s. Well-maintained lawns, large setbacks, quietness and gorgeous live oaks are the hallmarks of this neighborhood. After Hurricanes Fran and Bertha, there was some worry about the number of oaks that fell, but a drive through the neighborhood only a few months later revealed that the neighborhood is still well-named. There are canopied lanes and lots of Southern shade.

You'll find relatively few resales in this neighborhood. There is diversity in square footage and architectural style, so there is diversity in price. You can find a home for as low as $120,000 or you could spend a half-million or more here. An attractive feature of this neighborhood is its proximity to shopping and services. It is minutes from the largest mall in the region.

Pine Valley, near S. College Road around Longleaf Mall, is about three decades old as a development. It has attracted many Wilmingtonians to its quiet, pine tree-dotted blocks. A nearby golf course and clubhouse are easily accessible to people who want to live in a stable neighborhood that isn't necessarily exclusive in terms of price. Homes, largely brick ranches, range from $110,000 to more than $300,000.

The building boom that has come to New Hanover County and Wilmington during the past few years makes it nearly impossible to mention all of the new and established neighborhoods that offer attractive housing in the area. Pick a location that fits your budget and aesthetics, and discover a neighborhood that will perfectly suit your needs. Luxury homes, patio homes, villas, townhomes, cluster homes, condominiums and more await the new buyer.

Wilmington and New Hanover County Mainland Waterway Communities

On the mainland side of the Intracoastal Waterway from Wrightsville Beach is the planned community of Landfall, 2015 Pembroke Jones Drive, 256-6111. This neighborhood, walled and protected by guards at security gates, offers a pristine environment of immaculate lawns, beautiful homes, three clubhouses, private golf courses designed by the likes of Jack Nicklaus and Pete Dye, a tennis facility overseen in person by Landfall resident Cliff Drysdale, an eight-lane Olympic-size swimming pool and more. Single-family homes range from $372,000 to $3 million; homesites range from $60,000 to $1 million. Landfall currently has 800 homes. The Landfall Club, a large recreational/dining, special occasions complex of 31,000 square feet, opened in 1997.

Greenville Loop and Masonboro Sound are to the south of Wrightsville Beach on the mainland. This land along the sound is home to many attractive neighborhoods, many of which have direct access to the water and, in some cases, their own boatslips for the use of community residents. At this writing, these county neighborhoods have the economic advantage of being outside of the city of Wilmington, which means there are no city property taxes, but annexation plans are afoot for many outlying neighborhoods in the immediate future.

A word about services in the county (water, sewer and waste disposal come as a package for city residents): Depending on where you live outside the city, sewer service is provided either by the county sewer service or individual septic tanks; some water supply is handled by entire communities and some people have private wells; waste-disposal service is hired by county residents either individually or collectively as a neighborhood.

INSIDERS' TIP

Good insulation is important in area homes to keep power bills low during the summer months.

Waterway Communities North of Wilmington

Porters Neck Plantation, 1202 Porters Neck Road, 686-7400 or (800) 423-5695, is north of Wilmington and Wrightsville Beach just off U.S. Highway 17. The Tom Fazio-designed golf course is a key feature of this very attractive neighborhood of homes that appeals to active people. There is a sports complex, complete with heated lap pool, clay tennis courts and a fitness center. The new clubhouse was completed in 1996. Traditional single-family homes are available in sizes ranging from 1,600 to 2,000 square feet with prices beginning at $190,000. A 2,000-square-foot home on the golf course begins at $250,000. Homes away from the course with 3,000 square feet start at $240,000. Homesites begin at $50,000.

Figure Eight Island is a private neighborhood of very expensive homes and homesites. Lots range from $125,000 to $400,000; home prices run from an average of $700,000. There is a yacht club and private harbor for residents of this lovely island where there is no commercial development. Shopping is available in nearby Ogden and Hampstead.

WhiteBridge at Hampstead is one of the area's newest developments of larger homes on larger lots. With an average home size of 3,600 square feet and lots ranging from two to

six acres, WhiteBridge is located on 300 acres of land near the Intracoastal Waterway. The neighborhood offers a swimming pool with outdoor pavilion, lighted tennis courts, miles of bridle and nature trails and a 20-acre bird sanctuary. This is the site of two annual matches held by the Wilmington Polo Club. Lot prices range from $85,000 to $130,000.

South of Wilmington

Travel south of Wilmington on U.S. Highway 421 toward Carolina Beach and notice all of the different neighborhoods along the way. Notice, too, that two themes dominate this area: golf and water. Where the Cape Fear River rushes to meet the Atlantic Ocean, this increasingly narrow strip of land is home to heavy residential use with recreation a constant consideration. There are retirement and general lifestyle communities situated around golf courses, including the sprawling developments of single-family homes at Echo Farms and, a few miles down Highway 421, The Cape. Paralleling U.S. 421 closer to the river is River Road, a previously remote area that has been discovered and is now home to several major residential developments.

Just north of the Snow's Cut Bridge on River Road is the new development of Cypress Island. It consists of 1,400- to 1,700-square-foot single-family homes and 1,200- to

1,800-square-foot townhomes. Homes and lots are offered as a package deal starting at $138,900 for single-family homes and $114,900 for townhomes. The community has a 14-acre nature preserve with nature trail that meanders beside Telfare Creek, three stocked fishing lakes, a clubhouse, pool and tennis courts. The nine-hole, par-three golf course is scheduled to open in the spring of 1998.

Wrightsville Beach

Wrightsville Beach is highly residentially developed. For the most part, houses are close together, and a person who craves the mythical remote island life is not going to find it here. Happily, development has been largely controlled, thanks to vigilance on the part of local residents, and the relative density of development is quite palatable.

This is a pretty beach town. It's clean, there is little in the way of garishness, and the local constable does a fine job keeping order in the face of masses of visitors. A person who appreciates small-town living in a beach atmosphere with the convenience of a nearby city will adore this place. There are 5 miles of clean beach on which to jog or simply stroll. On just about any day of the year, you'll see surfers waiting for the big one, although the biggest waves are usually reserved for the hours preceding big storms.

There is very little for sale on this popular beach these days as far as single family homes are concerned. Many of the existing homes stay in families generation after generation. Quite a few of them are used only as summer homes since many of them are not heated. When homes do go on the market, the price tag is large. Expect to pay an average of at least $500,000 for any single-family home and don't be surprised by much higher prices.

Since the available land is all but exhausted in terms of development on the island — and since locals are not appreciative of high-rises — most of the opportunities for purchase are either replacement of older houses with new ones or, more likely, in condominiums. One may easily spend $200,000 to $350,000 for a two-bedroom condominium on Wrightsville Beach. Something to note is that the northern end of the beach, an area called Shell Island, is in danger from erosion unless continual expenditures are made to keep the ocean at bay. Since there has been considerable development at this end of the beach, presumably the erosion problems will continue to be addressed by dredging of the channel and renourishment of the sand.

Carolina Beach, Kure Beach and Fort Fisher

Cross over the bridge on U.S. 421 at Snow's Cut, a U.S. Army Corps of Engineers project that connects the ICW with the Cape Fear River and waters to the south, and you fall right into Carolina Beach.

This island represents some interesting prospects for home ownership in the Cape Fear region. Prices are considerably lower than the rest of New Hanover County because the island is somewhat outside the immediate Wilmington area in terms of perception. The truth is it only takes 20 minutes of easy highway driving to get to Carolina Beach from downtown and suburban Wilmington.

Carolina Beach is a very pleasant beach town with clean, wide beaches, an abundance of fishing opportunities, several nice restaurants and a growing sense of community pride that makes living here a charming prospect. Carolina Beach is one of the new-growth areas for New Hanover County's coastal dwellers and offers excellent value to the first or second-home owner. There is an assortment of ownership opportunities on Carolina Beach that range from condominiums to cottages. There are several high-rises, many multistory buildings on the northern end, an abundance of small homes and, particularly toward the south end at Fort Fisher, quite a few larger homes.

Homes can be purchased for prices as low as $80,000 and can rise to a half-million dollars along Carolina Beach, Wilmington Beach, Kure Beach and Fort Fisher.

The farther south you go on this island, the more fascinating the scenery becomes. Down at Fort Fisher, beautiful live oak foliage seems to have been sculpted over the centuries by the sea breezes. At the most southerly tip of this strip of land, the watery panorama of the Cape Fear River converges with the Atlantic Ocean near Bald Head Island.

Bald Head Island

It takes 20 minutes to cross from the ferry landing at Indigo Plantation to Bald Head Island, a beautiful bit of land where there are no high-rises, no shopping malls and no crowds. There are also no cars. Everyone travels by electric golf cart or bicycle. You'll find a clubhouse with a pool, a George Cobb-designed golf course, tennis courts, a marina, limited shopping and opportunities for fine and casual dining. This is a resort atmosphere and, to be sure, the year-round residential population count is quite low at about 150. It is largely a vacation spot where most of the homes are available for weekly rental. Homesites range from $50,000 to several hundreds of thousands of dollars. New cottages start as low as $260,000 but can rapidly rise toward the $500,000 range and more than a million. Single-family homes, townhouses and villas dot the island and are connected by a meandering golf-cart path. There are now 600 homes on the island. Inquiries about real estate sales should be directed to Bald Head Island, (800) 888-3707.

Southport-Oak Island

The charming fishing village of Southport attracts not only retirees but also families and folks who have decided to get out of the rat race. Southport's geographical location on the

Cape Fear River near the Atlantic Ocean provides some lovely coastal scenery. Bald Head Island lies between Southport and the ocean. Oak Island serves as a barrier to the ocean on the south side.

Southport's quaint historic neighborhood of homes dates from the late 1800s and offers mostly restored, single-family residences. The handyperson can find a smaller dwelling for around $50,000 but, as a local Realtor says, you can also expect to put another $50,000 into it before you move in. Houses on the waterfront are larger, and a 2,500-square-foot home may run from $250,000 to $300,000. Newer homes may cost more. Along River Drive, one can spend up to $500,000. Naturally, the farther back from the water, the lower the price. A nice finished house in Southport will average around $150,000 for 1,500 square feet.

Subdivision areas are growing rapidly in and near Southport. These include Indigo Plantation, Arbor Creek, St. James Plantation and Marsh Creek. These neighborhoods offer a broad range of surprisingly affordable new homes in attractive settings with some very pleasant amenities. New homes are nestled in lovely settings that can cost as little as $120,000 for a home/site package or as much as $500,000 for a 2,500 square-foot home in a prime location.

Across the ICW from Southport is Oak Island. This island has three beach communities: **Caswell Beach**, **Yaupon Beach** and **Long Beach**. All these communities have resort rentals, but they are overwhelmingly occupied by permanent residents. There is very little in the way of commercial development, and activity on the island is generally families getting together at the church or the firehouse for social occasions. Prices for single-family homes range from $60,000 to $600,000. At the center of the island, one can expect to pay from $80,000 to $130,000 for a small home. Long Beach, the biggest geographical area on Oak Island, has oceanside properties for less than $150,000.

South Brunswick Islands

Holden Beach

The next island down the coast is Holden Beach. A remarkable bridge connects the mainland with Holden and some say it's a surprise attraction in itself. You get a breathtaking view of the whole island, the marshes, the Intracoastal Waterway and the Atlantic Ocean from the top of this fixed bridge as it rises 65 feet above the mainland (at high water) and careens dizzily to the island. Holden Beach is another family beach. In fact, every beach we'll tell you about in the rest of the chapter, which will geographically take us to the South Carolina line, fits into the family-beach category.

Prices for real estate are climbing rapidly. An oceanfront cottage of 1,800 square feet may cost $190,000 and more. An oceanfront lot with wide beach strand ranges from $140,000 to $300,000. Second row lots, depending upon view and water access by way of a canal, begin at $40,000 and may be as high as $70,000. Duplexes, condominiums and other multifamily dwellings on the oceanfront begin at $150,000.

Ocean Isle

Ocean Isle is an 8-mile-long island approximately ¼-mile wide that lies at the center of South Brunswick's three barrier islands. The sandy beaches face directly south, providing sunshine all day. Beach residents are accustomed to seeing the sun rise and set over the ocean, but it's a little disorienting for newcomers at first. The island has a stable year-round population of 500 residents, ensuring a sense of community.

The island, identifiable from a distance by virtue of a solitary high-rise, is an appealing residential environment of largely single-family homes. They range in price from several hundred thousands on the oceanfront to $100,000 in the middle of the island. Naturally, properties on the Intracoastal Waterway side facing the mainland also fetch larger prices.

Sunset Beach

This beach may have thousands of visitors in the summer, but it is home to only about 80 year-round residents. It is overwhelmingly occupied by single-family dwellings, but there is a trend toward large duplexes on the oceanfront. This is because the island homes are on septic systems, and the oceanfront lots are the only ones that can accommodate two systems on one lot. Lots may range from $50,000 to $300,000 depending upon location. Four finger canals, regularly dredged, escalate the cost of interior lots. Duplexes of 2,000 square feet can cost $300,000. Single homes may range as high as $400,000. In general, homes average between $135,000 and $160,000.

Calabash

Carolina Shores is a golf-oriented neighborhood that attracts a high proportion of retired folks to its appealing setting. Homes, mostly one-story plans, average between $100,000 and $165,000. Calabash and Carolina Shores have had some disputes in the past that essentially amounted to the development trying to secede from the town. Things have settled down considerably and they seem to be happily merged. The town of Calabash is a fishing village with its share of famous restaurants that specialize in Calabash-style seafood. Calabash homes range from $75,000 to $170,000 and attract a wide range of families and individuals who appreciate the easy pace of the area.

Topsail Island

Topsail Island is rumored to have some of the best opportunities for beach real estate. Located 45 minutes north up U.S. 17 from

Wilmington (take N.C. Highway 210 past Hampstead, then a right on N.C. Highway 50 into Surf City), this community has surprising diversity in housing. Unlike the pricier beaches to the immediate south, Topsail Island offers homes for $100,000 or less in some cases. New 2,000-square-foot homes can cost as much as $250,000 to $350,000 on the ocean, although there are not yet many homes this large on the island. The norm is more 1,500 to 1,800 square feet, and prices average $175,000 to $200,000. Lots across the waterway on the mainland can still be purchased for as low as $10,000 for a half-acre site.

Topsail is still mostly a second-home market. There are only about 2,000 year-round residents on this quiet island. Recent development has put all of the necessities of life close to residents with ample grocery stores, convenience marts and other services either available on the island or the mainland.

Real Estate Companies

Any one of an abundance of area real estate companies will be happy to assist you in your search for a new home. The companies included here represent a fraction of the reputable companies working along the Cape Fear Coast.

Wilmington

Adam and Hilliard Realty
3912 Shipyard Blvd., Wilmington
• 799-7500, (800) 628-7089

This company, established in 1979, specializes in sales in Wilmington and New Hanover County. It represents the Birch Creek development on Wrightsville Avenue and represents Howell Builders in Snug Harbour, Wessex in Covil Estates, Crosswinds and Windward Oaks. Adam and Hilliard Realty is a member of Genesis Relocation Services. Wilmington Regional Association of Realtors

in 1996 named this company their Most Cooperative Firm for the eighth time since 1980.

Bachman Realty
2411 Middle Sound Loop Rd., Wilmington
• 686-4099, (800) 470-4099

The broker-in-charge is a long-term permanent resident of Figure Eight Island and is intimately familiar with properties on this attractive island. The company also offers properties along the waterfront throughout New Hanover and Pender counties as well as emphasis on Historic Downtown Wilmington. It is a member of RELO relocation service.

Century 21-Brock Mills
802 S. College Rd., Wilmington
• 395-8266, (800) 521-4746
Bypass 117, Burgaw • 259-7717

Gardner and Associates Realty merged with Brock Mills in early 1996 to create a larger company. It offers properties throughout New Hanover and Brunswick counties. Established in 1977 as Brock Mills, this company sells more than 500 properties a year and is an International Centurion company. This is an Inrelco company that specializes in relocation. It received the Quality Service Award by Century 21 International, special recognition given to the top 5 percent of all Century 21 firms in the country.

Century 21, Sweyer & Associates
1630 Military Cut-off Rd., Ste. 110, Wilmington • 256-0021, (800) 352-0021

This company has been in business since 1987, meeting residential housing needs in New Hanover, Pender and Brunswick counties with 50 agents. Designated as the top Century 21 producer in both Carolinas in 1996, it is projected to sell up to 1,000 homes in 1997. In addition to general representation, it also represents Courtney Pines and new homes in Kure Beach. The company has a full-time, in-house relocation service and a prelicensing school for aspiring Realtors. A mortgage bank is conveniently located within the office.

INSIDERS' TIP

If fixing up an historic home suits your interests, contact the Historic Wilmington Foundation at 762-2511 for information about low-interest loans that may be available in certain neighborhoods.

Clark-Teachey Realtors
1430 Commonwealth Dr., Landfall Ctr., Wilmington • 256-1155, (800) 497-7325

Established in 1991 as a residential company, this partnership of native Wilmingtonians traces its roots to 1970. It represents Northchase's Lakemoor, Berkleigh and Regency Manor, Hidden Forest, Tidalholm, Tidalholm Village, Summers Glen, the Commons, Silva Terra, Emerald Forest, Willloughby Park, and Kensington Place. It has 45 agents and offers in-house relocation.

Coldwell Banker Baker Properties
6336 Oleander Dr., Ste. 1, Wilmington • 395-5566, (800) 776-6110
25 Market St., Wilmington • 251-2234, (800) 232-7719

This company focuses on residential sales and is heavily involved in sales of new construction. Greenway Village, Alamosa Place, Dominion Place, Maxwell Place, Regency Manor, Danbury Forest, Courtney Pines, Williamsburg Place, Pine Hollow, Shinn Creek Estates and Newbury Woods are some of the developments they represent. This company is a member of four separate relocation services.

Coldwell Banker Sea Coast Realty
5710 Oleander Dr. Suite 200, Wilmington • 799-3435, (800) 522-9624

This company has about 50 agents. It handles properties in Wilmington and New Hanover County in diverse locations including Whitehurst, Harvest Grove, Arrondale, River Hills, Autumn Brook, Southeast Harbor, Stonegate, Brooks Landing, Mason Bend, Upper Reach and Evergreen Park. Sea Coast Realty was awarded the Premier Office Designation by Coldwell Banker in 1997.

Dallas Harris
Real Estate Construction
7208 Wrightsville Ave., Wilmington • 256-4475, (800) 277-5003

Dallas Harris, both a builder and a Realtor, specializes in patio homes and single-family homes near Wrightsville Beach. Properties handled include Planters Walk, English Moor at West Bay Estates, Eastport and Pepper Tree at Covil Estates, and the company sells lots to builders in Wessex, Vantage Point and Snug Harbour. Two new neighborhoods are opening at West Bay Estates in 1996. Homes range from 1,400 to 1,800 square feet and cost between $100,000 and $175,000.

Dunlea Realty
2005 Eastwood Rd., Ste. 100, Wilmington • 256-3063, (800) 438-6532

In business since 1956, this is one of the area's longest established real estate companies. Dunlea Realty has 15 full-time agents who handle both commercial and residential properties in New Hanover, Brunswick and Pender counties. Its focus is on properties that range from $150,000 and up. It is a member of the HMS Relocation Service.

Figure Eight Realty
15 Bridge Rd., Wilmington • 686-4400, (800) 279-6085

While other companies may sell Figure Eight houses, this is the only real estate company located on this exclusively residential island. It places its focus on island housing, a neighborhood comprised of luxury, single-family homes without commercial enterprises on the island. Figure Eight Realty is a small company housed in a space in the private marina's yacht club. This company also offers vacation rentals on the island.

G. Flowers Realty
411 Chestnut St., Wilmington • 762-7146, (800) 421-6063

Properties represented by this small company range all over New Hanover County but are concentrated heavily on downtown/urban residential and commercial properties in developing neighborhoods. G. Flowers Realty also offers investment counseling services.

Gulfstream Realty
5653 Carolina Beach Rd., Wilmington • 458-4747, (800) 360-3020

This company handles general real estate sales in New Hanover, Brunswick and Pender counties. It is currently marketing Tiara Park at The Cape, a townhouse community, and Cypress Island, a new development on River Road consisting of single-family homes and townhouses as well as a clubhouse, a 9-hole,

par 3 golf course, swimming pool and nature trail. Gulfstream Realty sells mainland and beach properties.

Harbour Town Associates Real Estate
7040 Wrightsville Ave., Ste. 1, Wilmington
• 256-0032, (800) 521-8132

In business since 1985, this relatively young company has 30 agents and high visibility. A full-service brokerage, Harbour Town Associates ranges the territory both geographically and in terms of price. It is the exclusive listing agent for Demarest Landing, Breezewood, Saponas Pointe, and has many new projects underway. It is a member of RELO/The International Relocation Network, the oldest and largest network of independent real estate brokers.

Howard, Perry and Walston Realty Inc./ Better Homes and Gardens
803 S. College Rd., Wilmington
• 799-1194, (800) 768-1194,
new home sales 791-8874
222 Causeway Dr., Wrightsville Beach
• property management 256-2181,
general brokerage 256-5771

This company is part of a network of more than 600 real estate associates from the coast to the Raleigh area. This Wilmington office is the fourth-largest real estate company within the Better Homes and Gardens national network and 37th-largest brokerage in America. After purchasing Landmark Real Estate in 1996, this company now has more than 70 agents. Exclusively representing more than nine communities in Wilmington, it also lists and sells properties in New Hanover, Pender and Brunswick counties. The company sold more than 1.4 billion in real estate between the Raleigh area and the coast in 1996.

Intracoastal Realty Corporation
534 Causeway Dr., Wrightsville Beach
• 256-4503
1900 Eastwood Rd., Ste. 38, Lumina Station, Wilmington • 256-4503,
(800) 533-1840

This market leader has been in business in the area since 1974. An exclusive affiliate of Sotheby's International Realty, it is a resort and residential property specialist. This company has listings throughout the region. It is a member of the Relo relocation service. Neighborhoods exclusively represented include Porters Neck Plantation, a golf course community north of Wilmington, and Masonboro Forest, a new 260-lot subdivision near Masonboro Sound. It also represents Bayshore Estates, Carelton and many others.

Jeanette Golder Realty
7208 Wrightsville Ave., Wilmington
• 256-6659, (800) 642-6443
This small company of five agents specializes in residential sales and development in New Hanover, Brunswick and Pender counties, selling homes that range from $35,000 to nearly $2 million. In addition to general properties, it also represents the Deerfield community at Hampstead.

K-O Realty
P.O. Box 1147, Wilmington 28402
• 458-7632
This one-broker/agent business has been representing buyers only in Wilmington, New Hanover, Brunswick and Pender counties since 1979. Christian Kjaer-Olsen doesn't accept listings.

Laney Real Estate
4918 Randall Pky., Wilmington • 799-9660, (800) 628-3021
The Galleria, 6800 Wrightsville Ave., Wilmington • 256-0056, (800) 733-1428
Lake Park Blvd., Carolina Beach • 458-3739, (800) 235-9068
201 Yaupon Dr., Oak Island • 278-9800, (888) 708-9800
Topsail Island • 329-0920, (800) 846-0472
This company, founded in 1978, has residential, commercial and property management divisions that range New Hanover, Brunswick and Pender counties from its five offices. It has 75 full-time agents. Laney Real Estate is a member of RELO, an international relocation network.

Landfall Associates
1985 Eastwood Rd., Ste. 100, Wilmington
• 256-6111, (800) 227-8208
This company deals exclusively with the fine properties in Landfall, a private neighborhood of single homes, villas, patio homes, condominiums and homesites. The community boasts numerous amenities including Jack Nicklaus and Pete Dye golf courses and the Cliff Drysdale tennis/sports center. The new 31,000-square-foot Landfall Club opened in early 1997.

New Home Marketplace
3501 Market St., Wilmington • 251-2288, (800) 200-2466
New Home Marketplace is the only full-service real estate company in the area that specializes in selling new, newer and newly renovated homes. The company offers full general brokerage services for the entire Wilmington area including Pender and Brunswick counties. Developments represented include Timber Creek, Avenshire, Carnoustie at Porters Neck Country Club, Sawgrass , Merestone, Cassimir Commons,

Orton Plantation is a fine example of Greek Revival architecture.

Tifton Park, The Lakes, Woods Edge, Vineyard Green and Chapman Ridge.

Port City Properties
1209 Market St., Wilmington • 251-0615

Established in 1995, Port City Properties represents residential and commercial properties in New Hanover, Brunswick and Pender counties through 18 agents, half of whom have been directly involved in historic property renovation of their own homes. The company ranges the full geographical and price spectrum, and specializes in downtown properties as well as beach properties. Port City Properties renovated its own turn-of-the-century building in the downtown area, the former Yopp funeral home.

Prudential Carolinas Realty
4130 Oleander Dr., Ste. 100, Wilmington
• 395-2000, (800) 336-5654
530 Causeway Dr., Wrightsville Beach
• 256-9299, (800) 562-9299

This large company covers the Greater Wilmington area. It specializes in corporate relocation services provided by certified relocation experts. It handles new residential developments such as Sycamore Landing, Wedgefield, Crosswinds, Stonegate and Stonington.

Nancy Rassier Real Estate
217 S. Second St., Wilmington • 762-4272

This small company specializes in historic residential properties as well as waterfront resi-

dential. The broker spent 18 years as a broker in Bucks County, Pennsylvania prior to moving to downtown Wilmington in 1993. She received the Pennsylvania Association of Realtors Lifetime Excellence Award. Nancy Rassier Real Estate focuses on New Hanover County and coastal Pender County properties that range from $150,000 to $1 million.

RE/MAX
Extraordinary Properties
1986 Eastwood Rd., Wilmington
• 256-8171, (800) 299-9909

This firm represents extraordinary properties at Landfall, Porters Neck, Wrightsville Beach and Figure Eight Island. It specializes in upscale properties along or near the waterfront. RE/MAX has its own international relocation network and is a full-service residential agency.

Select-Internet Realty
14710 Hwy. 17 N., Hampstead • 270-2017, (800) 535-6538
712 Country Club Rd., Hampstead
• 270-3312, (800) 867-8941

This company is primarily involved in relocation sales and services in the Pender County area, although it also has a number of projects in Wilmington and New Hanover County.

Carolina Beach, Kure Beach and Fort Fisher

Bullard Realty
1404 S. Lake Park Blvd., Carolina Beach
• 458- 4028, (800) 327-5863

Bullard Realty has 12 years of experience

INSIDERS' TIP

If your new home isn't on city or community water systems, you may want to investigate installing a water treatment system.

in the business of listing and selling homes, condominiums and beach and commercial properties. Broker Beth Bullard has 17 years of experience in real estate. Her company handles rentals on Carolina and Kure beaches.

Century 21 Castle Realty
1006 S. Lake Park Blvd., Carolina Beach
• 458-8224, (800) 360-8225

This company specializes in beach properties, both residential and commercial, on Carolina Beach, Kure Beach and Fort Fisher as well as on the mainland in New Hanover County. The owners are Carolina Beach natives who have been in the real estate business since 1979. The company offers referral and relocation services through an international network.

Coldwell Banker
United Realty Group
1001 N. Lake Park Blvd., Carolina Beach
• 458-4401

This company, on the island since 1984, specializes in sales not only on the island from Carolina Beach to Fort Fisher but also on the beach and mainland communities in New Hanover, Brunswick and Pender counties. Formerly United Resorts, this company joined Coldwell Banker in late 1996 and now offers the services of the extensive Coldwell Banker Referral Network.

Davies Realty
1009 N. Lake Park Blvd., Unit 1-C, Carolina Beach • 458-0444, (800) 685-4614

This relatively new firm has been focusing its residential and commercial real estate sales on Pleasure Island from Carolina Beach in the north to Fort Fisher in the south since 1992. It is also branching out into the greater Wilmington area. It currently is one of the listing agents for Carolina Beach Village, a community of new townhomes, patio homes and lots.

Gardner Realty
C-4 Pleasure Island Plz., Carolina Beach
• 458-8503, (800) 697-7924

Gardner Realty sells homes, duplexes and condominiums throughout the Wilmington

area including properties on Carolina Beach, Wilmington Beach, Kure Beach and Fort Fisher. It also offers property management services.

Harbour Point Town Homes and Pleasure Island Marina & Resort
Spencer Farlow Dr., Carolina Beach
• 458-4534, (800) 989-2589

This new 15-acre condominium/boating community on the waterfront at Snow's Cut offers 66 end-unit townhomes under construction beginning in the spring of 1997. Each unit is 2,300 square feet, and price range averages $225,000. Amenities for this new neighborhood include a 92-slip marina (see our Marinas Chapter), clubhouse and swimming pool. The resort will have a raised walkway with gazebo for strolls along the waterfront as well as a picnic area. The neighborhood is easily accessible by taking an immediate right off the Snow's Cut Bridge (U.S. 421 South) and loops under the bridge to Spencer Farlow Drive.

Lighthouse Realty
201 Fort Fisher Blvd., North Kure Beach
• 458-3300

This small real estate company sells both residential and commercial properties on all of Pleasure Island and throughout New Hanover County. It is centrally located in Kure Beach, the community that lies between Carolina Beach to the north and Fort Fisher to the south.

Tucker Bros. Realty
201 Harper Ave, Carolina Beach
• 458-8211

Tucker Bros. Realty has been in real estate on the island since 1973, selling homes from Federal Point just south of Monkey Junction to Fort Fisher at the southern tip of Pleasure Island. The owners are Carolina Beach natives with family roots on the island.

Walker Realty
501 N. Lake Park Blvd., Carolina Beach
• 458-3388

This company sells houses and condo-

FYI

Unless otherwise noted, the area code for all phone numbers in this guide is 910.

miniums on the 7-mile-long island. Many vacation renters who contract with this firm for rentals eventually return as home purchasers. Self-described as "one of the new kids on the block," Walker Realty has established a reputation for quality service since it began in 1984.

Bald Head Island

Bald Head Island Real Estate
P.O. Box 3069, Bald Head Island
• 457-7400, (800) 888-3707

This company sells single-family homes, cottages, condominiums and homesites exclusively on Bald Head Island. Available areas include property along the Cape Fear River, the Atlantic Ocean, the creek side, a maritime forest and an 18-hole golf course. Condominiums begin at $170,000, and the median range for single-family homes is around $450,000. The island is well-suited to the needs of homeowners seeking a stree-free lifestyle where the only road traffic is electric golf carts. The island is only reachable by passenger ferry or private boat.

Southport-Oak Island

Coldwell Banker Southport-Oak Island Realty
607 N. Howe St., Southport • 457-6713, (800) 346-7671
300 Country Club Dr., Yaupon Beach
• 278-3311, (800) 841-4950

This company covers Southport, Oak Island and Boiling Spring Lakes and Brunswick County selling single-family homes, condominiums, duplexes and land. This is the largest franchise firm in Brunswick County. A member of the International Resort Property Network, it specializes in finding temporary accommodations for corporations in need of this service for their employees.

Century 21 Dorothy Essey and Associates Inc.
6102 E. Oak Island Dr., Long Beach
• 278-3361, (800) 849-2322
105 E. Moore St., Southport • 457-4577, (800) 469-4577

This real estate company covers Southport and Oak Island as well as Boiling Spring Lakes.

Source: Jay Tervo

Walk the nature trail behind the North Carolina Aquarium at Fort Fisher.

It offers general brokerage and services for single-family homes, condominiums, duplexes, lots and commercial properties. The company has a new-home specialist on staff.

Margaret Rudd & Associates Inc., Realtors
210 Country Club Dr., Yaupon Beach
• 278-5213, (800) 733-5213
1023 N. Howe St., Southport • 457-5258, (800) 733-5258

This large and firmly established real estate company covers Southport, Long Beach and Brunswick County. It offers diverse properties that range from Southport's historic district to properties on the beachfront, Intracoastal Waterway, marshfront and wooded areas of Oak Island.

Scruggs & Morrison Realty
6101 E. Oak Island Dr., Long Beach
• 278-5405

Scruggs & Morrison Realty, a long-established company, serves Southport, Oak Island's three beach communities and Brunswick County through the sale of residential and commercial properties near the water and on the mainland. The company also specializes in property management.

South Brunswick Islands

Alan Holden Realty
128 Ocean Blvd. W., Holden Beach
• 842-6061, (800) 720-2200

This is the largest and oldest real estate company handling sales and rentals on Holden Beach. The Holden family bought the island from King George of England in 1756. Mr. Holden, broker-in-charge, was the first baby born to a Holden Beach resident in 1949. This company built a large percentage of homes on the island.

Coastal Development and Realty
131 Ocean Blvd. W., Holden Beach
• 842-4939, (800) 262-7820

Coastal Development & Realty has been on the island since about 1985. It build its large oceanfront office in 1992. In addition to general real estate services, the owner is

a builder/developer/designer who has brought new architecture to Holden Beach with his Summerville Collection. These homes have a Charleston flair. The company has several focus developments including Marker Fifty-Five on the ICW and the Wild Dunes Community with dunes as high as 35 feet.

Cooke Realtors
#1 Causeway Dr., Ocean Isle Beach
• 579-3535, (800) 622-3224

This company, on the island since 1976, specializes in sales and construction on Ocean Isle Beach. It does a brisk business in new and resale condominiums as well as cottages and single-family homes. Windjammer Condominiums is a new complex of 1,000 square-foot units that start at $175,000.

Sand Dollar Realty
102 Causeway Dr., Ocean Isle Beach
• 579-7038, (800) 457-7263

In business since 1985, this real estate company sells properties on Ocean Isle Beach and along the coast of Brunswick County. It is an

agent for Seaside North and Branchwood Village, two manufactured home subdivisions, and Riverhills, a single-family, site-built development on the backwaters of the Shallotte River. Homes and sites at Riverhills are priced beginning around $95,000 for a 1,440 square-foot home.

Sloane Realty
16 Causeway Dr., Ocean Isle Beach
• 579-1144, (800) 237-4609

The first permanent family to live on Ocean Isle Beach owns this company. It represents Bent Tree Plantation, a waterway community, as well as homes and lots on the beach. Club Villas at Baytree and the Colony II at Oyster Bay Plantation are its exclusive residential golf course developments.

Century 21 Sunset Realty
502 N. Sunset Blvd., Sunset Beach
• 579-1000, (800) 451-2102
(Island Office) 401 S. Sunset Blvd.
• 579-5200

Founded in 1982, this large company handles residential and commercial properties on Sunset Beach, throughout the

INSIDERS' TIP

Most gated golf course communities welcome club members who don't live within the community and all of them invite guests to play for a fee.

A parade passes before Wilmington's historic performance center, Thalian Hall, in 1919.

South Brunswick Islands as well as North Myrtle Beach. It is licensed in both North Carolina and South Carolina. It is the exclusive marketing developer for Sunset Beach. Two properties it represents are Waterway Oaks, an upscale waterway community, and Ocean Ridge Plantation. Relocation services are available through Century 21 Relocation.

Simmons Realty
1021 Beach Dr., S.W., Sunset Beach
• 579-0192

This small real estate company has been working in sales on Sunset Beach since 1990, but broker Beth Simmons is a lifelong native of the area. The company offers general real estate services on the island and the adjacent mainland. It handles single-family homes, cottages and condominium units. There are three agents — or an agent for every mile of this 3-mile island.

Sunset Properties
419 S. Sunset Blvd., Sunset Beach
• 579-9900, (800) 446-0218

On the island since 1988, this company regularly handles 225 properties only on Sunset Beach. Single-family homes dominate this quiet residential island that attracts second-home investors, retirees and people who simply appreciate living away from it all.

ERA Callihan, Peal, Skelley and Assoc. Realty and Pinehurst Builders
10239 Beach Dr., S.W., Calabash
• 579-4097, (800) 833-6330

This company handles commercial and residential properties through nine offices. Its range is from Wilmington to Pawley's Island south of Myrtle Beach. Pinehurt Builders built approximately 80 percent of the homes in Carolina Shores, an exclusive retirement community in Calabash. It is a member of the ERA Relocation Service.

Topsail Island

Beach Properties of Topsail Island Inc.
P.O. Box 4140, Surf City • 328-0719, (800)753-2975

This is a relatively new business in name, but the broker, a permanent resident on the island, has been handling Topsail Island, Sneads Ferry and Holly Ridge properties since 1988. This firm is the marketing agent for Pleasant Cove, Portofino and Shea's Landing.

Cathy Medlin Real Estate
405 Roland Ave., Surf City • 328-2323, (800) 622-6886

Cathy Medlin has been selling properties on Topsail Island and the mainland in Onslow and Pender counties since 1979. She was one of the founders of the Topsail Island Board of Realtors in 1992. This small company sells beach, waterway and mainland homes and lots.

Topsail Realty
712 S. Anderson Blvd., Topsail Beach
• 328-5241, (800) 526-6432

Topsail Realty specializes in south Topsail Island's finer sales and rental properties. It is located in Topsail Beach at the south end of Topsail Island on N.C. Highway 50, 6.3 miles south of the stoplight in Surf City.

Jean Brown Real Estate
522-A&B New River Dr., Surf City
• 328-1640, (800) 745-4480

This small and personable company sells properties on Topsail Island including Topsail Beach, North Topsail and Surf City as well as mainland properties in Onslow and Pender counties. It also offers property management services on Topsail Island through its rental department.

Ward Realty
116 S. Topsail Dr., Surf City
• 328-3221,(800) 782-6216
101 N. Front St., Wilmington • 763-8222

This company was the original developer of Topsail Island in 1947. Channel Bend and Pirate's Cove are two of the 19 subdivisions this company has developed. The owner, Alva Hill Ward Jr., was the first President of the Topsail Island Board of Realtors as well as mayor of Surf City in 1954.

Retirement

North Carolina's southern coast is tremendously attractive to retirees from around the country and even the world because of its beautiful scenery, services, recreational opportunities, cultural resources, relatively low taxes, low crime and, perhaps most importantly, mild weather.

Throughout most of this century, especially during the latter half, many a winter-weary Northerner has gone to latitudinal extremes in search of respite from snow and ice. Snow and ice are rare in New Hanover, Pender and Brunswick counties, making a snow shovel about as useful in the region as a wool coat in the Caribbean. While many retirees settle in Florida, land of sunshine, some are viewing the year-round warmth as too much of a good thing. As a result, North Carolina is experiencing a rebound effect as retirees leave Florida and head here for more seasonal variety within reasonable temperature ranges.

Wilmington's temperature range is moderate due in large part to its maritime location. Afternoon sea breezes make the summer heat more comfortable. Although there can be some beastly hot days with high humidity, there is nothing to match Florida's excessively relentless summer heat. Afternoon temperatures in this area may reach 90 degrees F or more a third of the days in midsummer, but several years may pass without reaching the 100-degree mark. The average temperature in July is 79.8 degrees.

Most winters here are short and mild. Polar air masses heading for the Atlantic Ocean must pass over the Appalachian Mountains first, which takes the bite out of the bitter cold before the air masses reach North Carolina's coastal area. According to records kept since 1870, there is only one entire day each winter when the temperature fails to rise above freezing. The mean temperature in January, for example, is 47 degrees. Rainfall in the area is usually ample and well-distributed throughout the year, concentrated mostly in summer thunderstorms between June and August. Retirees who enjoy gardening will appreciate the fact that the growing season may be as long as 302 days for some flowers and vegetables. A year-round average temperature of 68.7 degrees makes this climate extremely pleasant.

In addition to agreeable weather patterns, the southern coast has much to offer its retired population. There is ample shopping, first-rate medical care, affordable housing opportunities, a full range of cultural activities, the benefits of a progressive university and a robust industry developing around service to older citizens.

The median age of the overall population was 36 in 1995 and it is projected to move to 40 in two decades, a statistic that suggests what most people here know instinctively. At this writing, New Hanover County/Wilmington is experiencing an increase of 10 percent per year in the population of citizens who are 60 and older. More than 16 percent of the residents of New Hanover County were in this age bracket in 1995 according to projections by the U.S. Department of Commerce and the North Carolina Office of State Planning. Frankly, these figures are probably conservative. Until a full census is done in 2000, the possibly much larger percentage of citizens who make up the growing senior population will not be known. But ponder this: According to state projections, there will be more than 26,000 people age 60 and older in New Hanover County alone in 1997-98. Almost 2,000 will be 85 and older. New Hanover, Pender, Brunswick and nearby Columbus counties combined will have nearly 60,000 people older than 60 by 1998.

Seniors are increasingly being attracted to North Carolina on the whole. North Carolina ranks fifth in the nation for migratory retirees, according to the North Carolina Division of Aging. Given the special attributes of coastal North Carolina, it would not be surprising to see this area rank higher than the overall state.

Where To Live

People from all walks of life and all socioeconomic circumstances will discover attractive options for living in this area. If you are fortunate enough to have good health and a comfortable financial situation, you have many neighborhoods from which to choose. You may not wish or need to move into a retirement community at this point in your life. In fact, there seems to be a trend, particularly in the area's gated communities, that suggests older people want to live in communities with a full range of ages and household configurations. For those who don't, there are attractive, reasonable options.

Living options range from exclusive, wall-enclosed, suburban neighborhoods with security guards and golf courses to lower-cost patio-home communities with built-in maintenance services. There's also the artsy, urban neighborhood in Wilmington's downtown historic district for senior adults who favor afternoon strolls to one of several coffee shops or evening walks to restaurants or theater. There are vast choices in terms of the view thanks to the coastal scenery and, although beach real estate is quite high near Wilmington, there are some extremely reasonable condominium developments along the Brunswick Beaches and Topsail Island. Whether you're buying or renting, visit with a local Realtor for information. (See our Real Estate chapter.)

Retirement Communities

Senior Adult Retirement Communities, neighborhoods with congregate housing intended specifically for older occupants, offer a variety of social and recreational amenities. These communities feature single homes or apartments centered around several services. Services may include meals in a central location, pools, transportation and activities. They may or may not feature healthcare services. You are advised to contact the chamber of commerce in the area you choose for relocation (see our Area Overviews chapter) and to contact the Cape Fear Council of Governments, Department of Aging, 1480 Harbour Drive, Wilmington, 395-4553. This organization is a rich resource through its Area Agency on Aging administrator. The agency oversees senior services in New Hanover, Pender, Brunswick and Columbus counties. A free *Community Resource Guide*, published by the agency, is available at its office on Harbour Drive.

Brightmore of Wilmington
2324 41st St., Wilmington • 350-1980

This brand-new facility welcomes active retirees who wish to combine "independence with a strong sense of community." A basic package includes a complete apartment with utilities, (except for phone service), 24-hour security services and medical-emergency call, housekeeping and flat linens, regularly scheduled transportation, daily choice of meals, an ice-cream parlor and recreational programs. Studio, one-bedroom, one-bedroom deluxe, two-bedroom and two-bedroom deluxe apartments are available. Monthly rates begin at $1,295 with payment of a onetime membership fee of $10,000 for a studio apartment under Plan A. Plan B offers the option of a monthly rate with no membership fee. Under Plan B, the studio apartment rate begins at $1,550. Prospective residents can get on the waiting list with a $500 fully refundable deposit. Due to Brightmore's affiliation with nearby Liberty Commons Assisted Living and Liberty Commons Nursing Center, home-care services may be contracted within one's own apartment.

Capeside Village
1111 The Cape Blvd., Wilmington
• 392-0051

This community at The Cape Resort and Golf Club has manufactured homes in a landscaped, golf course setting. Three-bedroom,

FYI

Unless otherwise noted, the area code for all phone numbers in this guide is 910.

Photo: Bill DiNome

Even in cold weather, the beach attracts a crowd.

two-bath homes begin at $84,900 including homesite. Close to shopping, entertainment and the beach, this community south of Wilmington is pleasantly secluded. Residents enjoy full lawn maintenance, in-ground utilities and irrigation systems. The ability to drive is important in this location. One resident of a home must be at least 55 years of age. Children younger than 18 may visit but are not allowed to be permanent residents.

Catherine Kennedy Home
207 S. Third St., Wilmington • 762-5322

This downtown Wilmington home is a non-denominational, nonprofit private home operated by a self-perpetuating board of directors. It is the oldest home for the aged in the United States, organized in 1845 by Catherine deRosset Kennedy and known then as The Ladies Benevolent Society. In 1963 space and facilities were included for men. In 1995 impressive renovations were made to the residential wings. Residents enjoy three meals a day, stimulating activities and comfortable private rooms or suites with private baths. While there is an infirmary, the Catherine Kennedy Home is not a nursing home. Residents who apply must be 62 years of age or older, ambulatory and in good health upon admission. Residents may retain their own personal assistants.

An attractive feature of this home is its location on a beautiful campus in historic downtown Wilmington. It is a pleasant stroll away from shopping, dining and entertainment. Additionally, all of the city bus lines converge just a few blocks away. There is no admission or entrance fee. There is a nonrefundable fee of $2,500 upon moving into the home, and a schedule of the varying fees (based on accommodations and services required) is available by calling or writing. Rates begin at $940 per month.

Coastal Plantation,
A Jensen's Residential Community
U.S. Hwy. 17 N., Hampstead • 270-3520

Just north of Wilmington, Coastal Plantation is a beautifully landscaped community of individual manufactured homes. Residents purchase the house and lease the land. These quality homes range in price from the mid- to high $80s for a two-bedroom, two-bath plan and mid- to high $90s for a three-bedroom home. The price includes quite a few amenities. Each home has a utility shed, peripheral plantings, a cement driveway, carport, all appliances, energy-efficient heating and cooling systems, a screened porch and more. This is a community for healthy individuals who are at least 55 years of age and appreciate independence within the context of a planned community. A clubhouse, swimming pool, regular potluck suppers and activity groups provide social opportunities.

Liberty Commons
2320 41st St., Wilmington • 392-6899

Assisted living in a home-style environment is the focus here. Each of the spacious and airy rooms is individually climate controlled and each has a private bathroom with shower, a large closet and residential-quality furniture. Residents who wish to create their own decor are welcome to do so. Every room is equipped with a bedside and bathroom emergency call-response system. Cable television and private telephones are optional. Liberty Commons has 85 beds in its assisted-living residence and 50 in its special-care center.

Monthly rates for assisted living are $2,115 for private and $1,415 for semiprivate rooms. Personal-care rates are $2,555 and $1,830, and special-care rates are $3,305 and $2,555. These rates include meals, housekeeping and linens, personal laundry, the administration of physician-directed medication and transportation. Residents may choose among optional services such as barber and beauty shops, physical and speech therapy, dining out, theater and shopping trips and more. Licensed Practical Nurses and assistants are on call 24 hours a day.

Lake Shore Commons
1402 Hospital Plaza Dr., Wilmington • 251-0067

This neighborhood is in a park setting on picturesque Greenfield Lake near downtown Wilmington. The lake is a tremendously interesting ecosystem of cypress trees, Spanish moss and assorted amphibians, birds and reptiles. Sidewalks surrounding the lake allow for interesting walks or jogs. Three meals a day in an elegant dining area, housekeeping, all utilities and no-charge personal laundry are some of the features of this community. A monthly fee includes apartment rental, use of a private dining room upon occasion and regular use of the main dining room, library, chapel, television lounge, transportation and scheduled activities. There is an on-site beauty/barber shop. No healthcare service is provided, but the complex has a personal-care wing staffed by Certified Nurse's Aides and supervised by a Registered Nurse. There is no buy-in fee and the only upfront cost is a fully refundable security deposit equal to one month's rent. Apartments include studio, one-bedroom and two-bedrooms, ranging from $1,050 to $1,950. Lake Shore Commons is laying plans to build a second facility on the 17th Street Extension in 1997-98.

Plantation Village
1200 Porter's Neck Rd., Wilmington • 686-7181, In state (800) 334-0240, Out of state (800) 334-0035

Plantation Village is a life-care retirement community on 50 acres within Porter's Neck Plantation. The campus has a library, bank facilities, an auditorium, a swimming pool, a woodworking shop, crafts room and many more amenities.

The complex has 162 private apartments and villas in place with more construction on additional duplexes with garages ongoing. While the entry fee ranges from $95,112 to $235,916 there is a 90 percent return of capital plan. Monthly service starts at $1,161 and tops off at $2,100 for an individual. Add an additional $620 for a second person. This full-service package includes everything.

Plantation Village is a unique retirement community in that it receives people in good health age 62 and older and is able to offer professional, long-term nursing care services from nearby Cornelia Nixon Davis Center as a part of the monthly service fee. Before nursing care is needed, residents have access to a wellness center on the campus, a 24-hour nurse on call and the visit of a doctor each week. For the monthly service fee, residents may also receive 240 hours of assisted-living

INSIDERS' TIP

The New Hanover County Senior Center, 2222 S. College Road, 452-6400, is a great place to take in a yoga class, art instruction and a multitude of other health- and arts-related endeavors.

services. Garden spaces are provided for those inclined to poke about in the dirt. Gardeners will appreciate the fact that this was once a working plantation where peanuts, rice and cotton were grown in abundance.

Nursing Homes

Retirement, once considered a late-in-life event, is falling closer toward the middle years now. While many people are able to situate themselves in later life in retirement communities, living basically independent lives, there are some people who require more extensive care.

As life lengthens in the population and retirees outgrow the services of their chosen retirement community, there is increasingly greater demand for all levels of nursing homes. Three types of homes in the region fall under the category of nursing home. These types vary in the different levels of care offered to residents.

• A Skilled Nursing Facility (SNF) provides 24-hour nursing services for a person who has serious healthcare needs but does not require the intense and expensive level of care provided in a hospital. Many of the facilities are federally certified, so they may participate in Medicare or Medicaid programs.

• An Intermediate Care Facility (ICF) provides less extensive care than an SNF; nursing and rehabilitation services are generally not provided on a 24-hour basis. This kind of facility specializes in providing housing and services for persons who can no longer live alone but need minimal medical supervision or help with personal or social care. Medicare or Medicaid programs are usually available.

• Board and Care Facilities provide shelter, supervision and care but do not offer medical or skilled nursing services. This kind of facility is not licensed to participate in Medicare or Medicaid programs.

A partial listing of area nursing homes follows, and we have identified the type of home as to SNF, ICF and other categories.

Cornelia Nixon Davis Health Care Center
1011 Porters Neck Rd., Wilmington • 686-7195
SNF, ICF

At Porter's Neck Plantation just north of Wilmington, this is a 199-bed center that accepts Medicaid and Medicare. This center, on the site of a former plantation, is highly regarded for the quality of its care and attractiveness of its facility. Renovations underway in 1997 will allow the facility to have an Alzheimers disease unit.

Hillhaven Rehabilitation and Convalescent Center
2006 S. 16th St., Wilmington • 763-6271
SNF, ICF

Across from the New Hanover Regional Medical Center and in the midst of physician offices, this center provides occupational and physical therapy services in addition to being a skilled and intermediate care nursing facility. Medicaid and Medicare, VA, private insurance and private pay are the categories of acceptable payment.

Mariner Health Care Center
820 Wellington Ave., Wilmington • 343-0425
SNF, ICF, Assisted Living, Sub Acute

This 150-bed healthcare facility provides long-term medical services with three levels of care: skilled, intermediate and retirement. This center accepts Medicaid, Medicare and private pay.

Autumn Care of Shallotte
237 Mulberry St., Shallotte • 754-8858
SNF, Home for the Aged

This is a 110-bed nursing facility that offers its residents a full range of services including individualized physician care and 24-hour licensed nursing care. It provides in-house podiatry and dental care, a physical,

Pull up a chair under a beautiful old oak and enjoy the sunset.

occupational and speech therapy program as well as dietary services. It accepts Medicare, Medicaid and V.A. payment.

Ocean Trail Convalescent Center
430 Fodale Ave., Southport • 457-9581
SNF, Home for the Aged

Located less than a mile from Southport's historic waterfront, this restful setting offers 24-hour care for up to 106 residents. This is an older facility, described by the staff as "quaint," but renovations are underway in 1997. It offers access to physicians at nearby Dosher Hospital as well as a full program of rehabilitation including speech, physical and psychiatric therapy. It accepts Medicare and Medicaid.

Adult Day Care

If a person is able to reside in a private home setting with family or friends, but needs some assistance and supervision during the day, there is adult day-care service available in the area.

Elderhaus Inc.
1950 Amphitheater Dr., Wilmington
• 343-8209

This agency provides day care for adults. This Intermediate Care facility is supervised by Registered Nurses and other health personnel. The program offers a stimulating environment for persons primarily 60 and older who need daily care. Persons with Alzheimers disease and dementia are cared for in a safe, pleasant setting by a full-time professional staff. Field trips, arts and crafts programs, educational opportunities, lunch and snacks are provided for participants.

Activities, Organizations

An abundance of organizations, associations, support groups and activities are specifically designed for the senior population. Opportunities for involvement in senior programs, including volunteer work, employment, education, health and enjoyment may be found by contacting the following organizations.

Katie B. Hines Senior Center
308 Cape Fear Blvd., Carolina Beach
• 458-6609

This Carolina Beach center provides a full program of activities for senior citizens. Regular exercise programs, bingo, shuffleboard, blood pressure checks and regular covered-dish suppers are just a few of the activities. Don't miss the Pizza Supper once a month or line dancing and other special activities. People 55 years of age and older are welcome, although the center doesn't turn anyone away if they don't meet this criteria.

New Hanover Senior Center
2222 S. College Rd., Wilmington
• 452-6400

This large center is incredibly busy, offering a long list of classes and programs for participants. On Wednesday, there is a free ballroom dance for people older than 50. Tap dance classes, aerobics, jazzaerobics and line dancing are some of the other programs available. The center hosts a variety of support groups and computer classes and offers free haircuts to women the first Friday of each month. Lunch is served Monday through Friday, and payment is on a sliding scale basis.

Retired Senior
Volunteer Program (RSVP)
2222 S. College Rd., Wilmington
• 452-6400

RSVP puts the talents of retired members of the community to work. Its motto is "Sharing the Experience of a Lifetime." This is the largest RSVP in North Carolina with more than 1,000 active volunteers working in local non-profit agencies.

Service Corps of
Retired Executives (SCORE)
152 N. Front St., Room 212, Main Post Office Bldg., Wilmington • 815-4576

Retired executives share their knowledge with new business owners in a mentoring relationship.

Senior AIDES Program
709 Market St., Wilmington • 251-5040

Offering job counseling and training for senior citizens, the Senior AIDES program places people 55 and older into employment situations in expectation that the jobs will become permanent.

Seniors Health Insurance
Information Program (SHIPP)
2222 S. College Rd., Wilmington
• 452-6400

Volunteers with this organization are trained by the North Carolina Department of Insurance to help people with Medicare problems, questions about Supplemental Insurance or long-term care issues.

Region O Senior Games
2222 S. College Rd., Wilmington
• 452-6400

Seniors compete in sports events including archery, golf, running, swimming and more. The local group competes in national events and is known to bring home quite a few awards.

Twin Travel and Cruises
5751 Oleander Dr., Ste. 10 • 799-5225

This company offers "LJ Tours" geared, but not limited, to people age 55 and older. This full-service travel agency creates attractive package tours to Myrtle Beach shows, the Spoleto Festival in Charleston and the Biltmore House in Asheville.

For nonsurgical medical services, the Cape Fear area has an ample number of immediate care centers spread across the region.

Healthcare

The Cape Fear area offers excellent healthcare facilities and services across the spectrum. For most of this century, residents generally went inland to more sophisticated medical facilities in search of state-of-the-art technology to treat serious illness. That trend has changed and even reversed itself as inlanders now come here for exceptional healthcare services.

Active area physicians, numbering more than 362 in Wilmington and New Hanover County, have access to some of the most technologically progressive facilities and equipment in the state by way of the two larger hospitals that serve the area.

Several small hospitals dot the southern coast. Care beyond the scope of their services is referred to Wilmington's larger hospitals, but these smaller facilities also offer excellent healthcare for a broad range of medical services. Vacationers along the Brunswick Beaches and Topsail Island may find these smaller hospitals more convenient for medical services.

Hospitals

Wilmington

Columbia Cape Fear
Memorial Hospital
5301 Wrightsville Ave., Wilmington
• 452-8384, (800) COLUMBIA
Columbia Cape Fear Memorial is an acute-care hospital of 142 beds. A private community hospital, Columbia Cape Fear was purchased in 1996 by Columbia/HCA, one of the country's largest hospital management companies. The hospital offers medical, surgical and ambulatory care, including 24-hour emergency services. Outpatient surgery, radiology, ultrasound, magnetic resonance imaging, laboratory facilities and a sleep disorder center are some of the hospital's expanded service areas. It also offers pain management services, neurology and orthopedic surgery.

Women's Services, a hallmark of patient care at Cape Fear, offers classes, seminars and other opportunities for women to learn about their health as well as the issues that may affect their families. The Birthing Center, the hospital's family-oriented labor, delivery and postpartum services unit, offers families a personalized birth in a homelike setting with the advantage of immediate access to state-of-the-art medical care and equipment.

Neuroscience is one of this hospital's many medical specialties. This field includes endovascular coil occlusion, the process in which a catheter is used to close off an aneurysm and prevent it from rupturing. Columbia Cape Fear is only the third hospital in North Carolina to have performed this procedure. The hospital offers a full range of neurodiagnostics, including an updated CT scanner with spiral capability. This equipment allows a technologist to scan an internal organ in a matter of seconds.

Among the hospital's regularly held health-related classes are those that focus on nutrition, cardiopulmonary resuscitation certification, exercise, smoking cessation and stress management.

The hospital offers a program called Senior Friends for people age 50 and older that stresses wellness. For a yearly membership fee of $15 for an individual or $25 for a couple living at the same address, seniors can attend monthly meetings for interesting programs, enjoy discounts on particular services, get discounts on meals in the cafeteria and have a private room at a semiprivate rate. Members are also entitled to national pharmacy discounts, discounted health screenings, travel opportunities and special promotions through area merchants.

Safe Sitter, a national program for young adults, provides a comprehensive course on safe, responsible child care and teaches its students rescue breathing and choking techniques, and helps them understand the fundamentals of babysitting.

Columbia Cape Fear Memorial Hospital is accredited by the Joint Commission on Accreditation of Healthcare Organizations, the world's largest provider of healthcare services.

New Hanover Regional Medical Center
2131 S. 17th St., Wilmington • 343-7000

New Hanover Regional Medical Center is a 628-bed hospital with five intensive care units, including neonatal intensive care. It is operated by trustees appointed by the New Hanover County Board of Commissioners, and offers high-quality care with an increasing emphasis on specialized care for more critical illnesses and conditions. The hospital is staffed by 2,850 employees, making it one of the largest employers in New Hanover County.

New Hanover Regional's Coastal Heart Center, which has become a magnet for patients with heart disease from New Hanover and surrounding counties, provides some of the best physicians, surgeons and support staff in the state of North Carolina. Services of particular importance to a community with a booming retirement population include cardiac catheterization, angioplasty, open-heart surgery, cardiac rehabilitation and a new cardiovascular laboratory for diagnostic testing outpatient services.

Cancer services include chemotherapy, radiation, surgical and medical treatments as well as participation in clinical trials. CanSurvive, a support group for those who are coping with cancer, was created to allow these individuals and their families to share their experiences. Construction began on new 30,000 square foot Coastal Cancer Center in late 1996, and this facility, adjacent to the main hospital building, should be open in 1998. It will consolidate all cancer services in one location, including radiation therapy.

Designated by the state as one of eight regional Trauma Centers, this hospital provides a mobile intensive care unit, VitaLink, that can transport the most seriously ill and injured patients from the region's community hospitals at any hour of the day or night. Equipped with life-sustaining systems and trained staff, the vehicle is also in constant communication with the hospital until the patient arrives. A paramedic and registered nurse are always on board.

New Hanover Regional BirthPlace specializes in obstetrical services, offering more than two dozen rooms that combine homelike decor with sophisticated facilities to allow a family-centered birthing experience. In Women's Health Specialties, a team of perinatologists care for women with high-risk pregnancies. The area's only Board-certified reproductive endocrinologist works with women who are having difficulty conceiving, and a gynecologic oncologist specializes in cancer care for women.

The Center for Successful Aging is an outpatient department staffed by a geriatrician, nurses, social workers, therapists and a pharmacist. The hospital also has an inpatient Geriatric Unit.

The Medical Mall at the intersection of 17th Street and Glen Meade Drive makes outpatient services such as MRI, X-rays, mammography and lab tests convenient.

The Coastal Rehabilitation Hospital, 343-7845, is situated on New Hanover Regional Medical Center's sprawling 70-acre campus. Patients include those with traumatic brain injury, spinal cord injury, orthopaedic conditions and stroke.

Another component of New Hanover Regional Medical Center is the Coastal Diabetes Center, 1201 S. 16th Street, 763-6111, an American Diabetes Association-approved facility specifically devoted to diabetes education and management.

A freestanding psychiatric hospital on the hospital campus, The Oaks, 343-7787, attracts patients from the entire region. The Oaks' staff of 125 provides specialized care for 62 adult and

FYI

Unless otherwise noted, the area code for all phone numbers in this guide is 910.

adolescent inpatients in a serene, landscaped setting. The Oaks' partial hospitalization program provides day therapy and the outpatient program provides counseling services. Psychiatric evaluations are available 24-hours a day.

New Hanover Home Health, 815-5310, provides professional services to individuals and their families as an alternative to inpatient care. Services include skilled nursing, home infusion, medical social service, pediatric care, physical and occupational therapy, nutritional counseling and speech/audiology therapies.

New Hanover Regional Medical Center has the only Pediatric Unit in a six-county region and a new unit, specifically designed for children, is under construction in 1997.

A new service is VitaLine, a 24-hour health-information line where callers can get confidential and prompt answers to health-related questions. Experienced registered nurses and other professionally trained staff can help determine your need to see a physician, provide physician referral information and suggest community health resources. The Automated

Health Information component allows callers the option to listen to health tapes. At the touch of a button, the caller may leave the taped information and speak directly to a nurse. This free service is available by calling 815-5188 or (888) 815-5188.

New Hanover Regional Medical Center is accredited by the Joint Commission on Accreditation of Healthcare Organizations.

Outside Wilmington

Columbia Brunswick Hospital
U.S. Hwy. 17, Supply • 755-8121

Columbia Brunswick Hospital, owned by Brunswick County and leased by Columbia/HCA, is in central Brunswick County at Supply near Long Beach and Ocean Isle. It is licensed for 60 beds. The hospital has a 24-hour physician-staffed emergency department, full medical and surgical services and an inpatient adolescent psychiatric care program. A chest pain emergency center is also in the hospital.

Included among its comprehensive medical services are general medicine and a broad range of specialties including obstetrics/gynecology, opthalmology, nuclear medicine, pain management, urology and pediatrics. New programs introduced by Columbia/HCA include Senior Friends, Safe Sitter and Alzheimer's Disease and Neurological Support Groups. The Columbia Brunswick Hospital offers a Physician Referral Service, 755-1400, and also operates the Brunswick Shores Children's Center within the facility. The hospital is accredited by the Joint Commission on Accreditation of Healthcare Organizations.

J. Arthur Dosher Memorial Hospital
924 N. Howe St., Southport • 457-5271 (Emergency extension: 351)

J. Arthur Dosher Memorial Hospital is a 40-bed, acute care hospital that offers extensive outpatient services. Established in 1930, this small public hospital serves the Smithville Township area, attracting patients from Oak Island, Southport, Boiling Springs Lake, Bolivia and Leland. A public, tax-based facility, J. Arthur Dosher Memorial Hospital is focused on its community, offering outreach programs in the schools and working with local citizen organizations to promote healthy lifestyles.

The hospital has a 24-hour, physician-staffed emergency room. There are 12 medical specialties, including diagnostic imaging, cardiopulmonary services, speech and physical therapy and comprehensive surgical services. Support groups sponsored by Dosher Memorial Hospital include diabetes, head injury, hospice, stroke and weight control.

The hospital provides a valuable free publication, *Safe Vacation Guide*, distributed to hotels, motels and condominiums in the area. It advises visitors about potential health hazards related to sunburn, dangerous aquatic life and rusty fish hooks. It also gives safety tips about avoiding alligators and checking the ICW at low tide for obstructions before

you go tearing along in a boat. It offers a healthcare reference manual that explains all services of the hospital as well as a physician guide according to specialty.

Pender Memorial Hospital
507 Fremont St., Burgaw • 259-5451

Pender Memorial Hospital is a general acute medical and skilled nursing facility with a bed capacity of 66. It offers inpatient and outpatient services including ambulatory/same day surgery, laparoscopy, laboratory, radiology, respiratory and physical therapy.

Immediate Care

For nonsurgical medical services, the Cape Fear area has an ample number of immediate care centers spread across the region. Vacationers or residents with relatively minor injuries, illnesses or conditions may prefer the convenience of visiting these centers over making an appointment to see a personal doctor. Illnesses and injuries beyond their capabilities are referred to area hospitals.

These are convenient places to get vaccinations for the flu and tetanus or to have a limited variety of tests or physicals for school, sports or insurance purposes. Most have their own labs and X-ray services, and all are staffed by qualified, licensed physicians and nurses. Be advised most of the centers operate on a first-come, first-served basis, so don't expect to be able to make an appointment. However, serious illnesses, injuries or conditions will receive first priority.

These medical service facilities offer emergency care but are not open 24 hours a day. In many cases, they are not open seven days a week. If you need attention and choose one of these centers, you're advised to phone ahead. Visitors to Topsail Island are within a one-hour drive to hospitals and clinics in Wilmington. For serious injuries and illnesses, the coastal region has ample EMT services that can be reached by calling 911.

INSIDERS' TIP

An enormous range of support groups are listed in the daily calendar listings of the "Lifestyles" section of the *Wilmington Star-News*.

A keen sense of fashion goes a long way on the beach.

Wilmington

Doctor's Immediate Care, 4606 Oleander Drive, central Wilmington, 452-0800

Doctor's Urgent Care Centre, 4815 Oleander Drive, central Wilmington, 452-1111

MEDAC Convenient Medical Care, 3710 Shipyard Boulevard, south side of Wilmington, 791-0075

MEDAC II Convenient Medical Care, 1442 Military Cutoff Road, Landfall area of Wilmington, 256-6088

Northside Medical Center, 502 N. Fourth Street, downtown Wilmington, 251-7715

Outside Wilmington

Express Care, U.S. 17, Shallotte, 579-0800

Urgent Care Center, North Brunswick, 117 H Village Road, Leland, 371-0404

Penslow Medical Center, 206 N. Dyson Street, intersection of U.S. 17 and N.C. 50, Holly Ridge, 329-7591

Home Healthcare

There is an increasing demand for in-home care in the region. The following are representative of the private businesses offering in-home nursing care. They offer nurses' aides, LPNs, RNs, companions and other assistance depending upon individual need.

Assisted Care, 4010 Oleander Drive, Suite 2, Wilmington, 395-9998

Comprehensive Home Health Care, 3311 Burnt Mill Road, Wilmington, 251-8111

Eldercare Convalescent Service, 5003 Randall Parkway, Wilmington, 395-5003

Lower Cape Fear Hospice, 810 Princess Street, Wilmington, 762-0200

PRN Nursing Service, 5116 Wrightsville Avenue, Wilmington, 395-6468

Well Care and Nursing Services Inc., 2424 S. 17th Street, Wilmington, 452-1555

Physician Groups

Hanover Medical Specialists
1515 Doctor's Cir., Wilmington • 763-5182

Hanover Medical Specialists offers services in cardiology, endocrinology/diabetes, gastroenterology, hermatology/oncology and pulmonary/allergy. This group began in 1974. Each specialty is housed in its own building, and there is a wide range of in-house testing for cardiology. This group has the only certified diabetic teaching nurse in the area.

Hanover Urological Associates
Glen Meade Rd., Wilmington • 763-6251
5305 Wrightsville Ave., Wilmington • 452-5254

The specialities here are pediatric and adult urology, cancer care, male infertility and impotence, laparoscopic surgery, prostate ultrasound, penile implants and vasectomy surgery.

Timothy G. Kelly Ophthalmology
1915 Tradd Ct., Wilmington • 762-0057

Diseases and surgery of the eye are the focus of this practice. Eye exams, glaucoma evaluation and management, in-office laser surgery, diabetic eye management, intraocular lens implantation and other professional services are provided by this Board Certified ophthalmologist. Evening appointment hours are available in addition to day hours. Dr. Samuel F. Boles, a new member of the practice, is also an opthamologist and is the only glaucoma specialist in Wilmington.

Lower Cape Fear Dermatology Clinic
3904 Oleander Dr., Wilmington • 452-0400

Dr. Marylou Courrege and Dr. John Ruppe concentrate on medical services in surgery of the skin, skin disease and skin cancer. They also offer cosmetic procedures, spider vein sclerosing and facial peels. The clinic sells

INSIDERS' TIP

The New Hanover-Pender County Medical Society, 2259 S. 17th Street in Wilmington, 251-8455, offers a physician referral service.

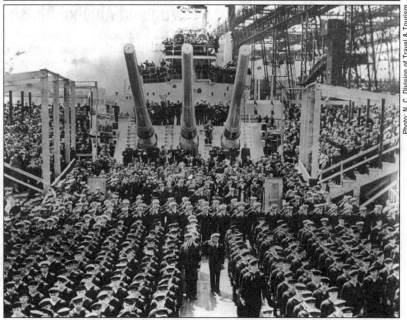

The USS *North Carolina* was commissioned on April 9, 1941, and is an important site for Memorial Day celebrations today.

skin products that are specifically geared to sun-damaged skin.

Surgical & Medical Eye Care
2310 Delaney Dr., Wilmington • 763-3664
This group of board-certified ophthalmologists does state-of-the-art laser surgery and cataract surgery. It also treats diseases of the eye and other eye-related procedures.

R. Henry Temple
2038 Oleander Dr., Wilmington • 251-2262
Temple's practice is unusual in that he practices gynecology but not obstetrics. Women past childbearing years or those not contemplating having children will appreciate the specialization. Dr. Henry Temple, former Chief of Staff at New Hanover Regional Medical Center, concentrates his practice on general gynecology and gynecological surgery.

University Professional Services
2131 S. 17th St., Wilmington • 762-8992
Operated in affiliation with the UNC School of Medicine at Chapel Hill and New Hanover Regional Medical Center Residency Programs, this facility offers internal medicine, obstetrics and gynecology, neonatology and surgery services.

Wilmington Ear, Nose and Throat Associates
2311 Delaney Ave., Wilmington • 762-8754
Specialties here are illness or conditions related to these areas of the body. The staff includes audiologists, a speech and language pathologist and medical doctors.

Wilmington Health Associates
1202 Medical Center Dr., Wilmington • 341-3300
This large group of physicians specializes in such areas as pulmonary medicine, cardiology, gynecology, obstetrics, gastroenterology, neurology, hematology/oncology, infectious diseases, dermatology and endocrinology. The physicians also offer general medical care and family practice.

Wilmington SurgCare
1801 S. 17th St., Wilmington • 763-4555

SurgCare is a Medicare-certified and state-licensed outpatient surgical center. It is a multispecialty, ambulatory surgical center.

Chiropractors

Friedman Chiropractic
1033-A S. Kerr Ave., Wilmington • 350-2664

Dr. David Friedman has a three-year doctorate degree in neurology and is a Board Qualified Chiropractic Neurologist. The author of a textbook, *Understanding the Nervous System*, he continues to do regular post-grad studies in neurology, nutrition, whiplash and other areas of chiropractic interest. His multifaceted approach to treating injuries and conditions offers a broad array of options to his patients. The practice is open six days a week. Evening hours may also be made by appointment.

Reese Family Chiropractic
2003 Carolina Beach Rd., Wilmington • 763-3611

This practice offers family healthcare through chiropractic from birth through geriatric years. Dr. Donald Reese has a weekly radio show on WAAV-AM, "Straightalk," that encourages individuals to call with questions about chiropractic care. The show airs Monday nights at 7 PM. The practice also presents free weekly healthcare classes on Tuesday nights. Call to make reservations.

Langas Chiropractic
501 Village Rd., Leland • 371-1900
Surf City, Topsail Island • 328-0520

Dr. Marc Langas offers a complete system for promoting health. He utilizes a "hands on, nonforceful procedure that allows for the removal of primary interferences, allowing structure and function to normalize." The practice addresses traumas, toxicities and neuroemotional work.

Drug and Alcohol Abuse

There are numerous organizations and agencies in the area to help people struggling with substance abuse. See our Volunteer Opportunities chapter for agencies that specialize in these problems or consult the phone book for counseling services. Under new laws, counselors are required to be licensed and certified by the State of North Carolina, so make it a point to inquire into this important credential.

A Center for Counseling, 306 Windemere Road, Wilmington, 392-5915

Alcoholics Anonymous, 3130 Wrightsville Avenue, Wilmington, 762-1230

Alpha Counseling and Development Center, 3415 Wrightsville Avenue, Wilmington, 791-5171

Southeastern Center for Mental Health, Developmental Disabilities and Substance Abuse, 2023 S. 17th Street, Wilmington, 251-6440

Wilmington Treatment Center, 2520 Troy Drive, Wilmington, 762-2727

Massage Therapy

The Cape Fear region has an abundance of practitioners of massage therapy for wellness, chronic pain, strain and injuries. Every therapist or practice offers particular methods that range through Swedish, deep tissue, myofascial release, neuromuscular, craniosacral therapy, trigger point, foot reflexology, polarity, shiatsu, acupressure, pre-natal and sports. The service averages around $40 per hour, but you can certainly find a therapist who charges less or more. Some massage therapists work in their homes, others in offices and a few will be happy to come to your own home.

Deborah Flora, CMT, Wilmington, 762-9073

Wilmington Center for Therapeutic Massage, The Cotton Exchange, 321 N. Front Street, Wilmington, 762-9484

Mary Ellen Bramble, CMT, The Cotton Exchange, 321 N. Front Street, Wilmington, 762-4893

Elizabeth Bryson, LMT, The Cotton Exchange, 321 N. Front Street, Wilmington, 343-0807

Teresa Jones, CMP, The Cotton Exchange, 321 N. Front Street, Wilmington, 343-2920

Sheila Mole, CMT, The Cotton Exchange, 321 N. Front Street, Wilmington, 762-9484

Laura Sullivan, CMT, The Cotton Exchange, 321 N. Front Street, Wilmington, 762-5272

Susan Whiteside, CMT, The Cotton Exchange, 321 N. Front Street, Wilmington, 762-7338

In 1996-97, 87.2 percent of the New Hanover County public school system's graduates planned to continue their education beyond high school.

Schools and Child Care

The southern North Carolina coast is served by three separate public school systems. New Hanover County has the largest system, as it encompasses the largest city on the state's entire coastline. Brunswick County Schools and Pender County Schools serve largely the rural populations to the southeast and northwest of New Hanover.

Additionally, the region offers a growing list of private schools, both secular and religion-based, that can meet a broad range of educational requirements

Students in New Hanover County should immediately be enrolled in a public or private school. To enroll a child in the public schools, the parent or guardian of a kindergartner must bring a birth certificate along with the child's Social Security card and immunization records to the school system office.

Children entering kindergarten must be 5 years old on or before October 16 of that year. Parents of students who have been previously enrolled in a different school should bring the student's last report card to the appropriate school. For information on schools and everything you need to know about how the public schools can serve your child, call the systems at the phone numbers listed at the beginning of their write-ups.

Public Schools

New Hanover County Schools
1802 S. 15th Street, Wilmington • 763-5431

The New Hanover County School System serves the city of Wilmington and the county, including the beach communities of Figure Eight Island, Wrightsville Beach, Carolina Beach, Kure Beach and Fort Fisher. In 1996-97, the system served 21,335 students from kindergarten through grade 12 in 30 schools. The 10th-largest public school system in the state, the mission of New Hanover County Schools is "to provide a high quality education that prepares all students to be productive and contributing citizens of a global society."

The system faces the familiar challenges encountered by most American school systems. Odds are the issues of education are pretty much the same here as where you live. There is a constant need for more funding and better facilities, and there's a continuing pursuit of educational excellence to serve the needs of children from diverse socioeconomic circumstances. The system addresses these concerns with a long-term plan called the Effective Schools Program. The system's stated goal is to be "one of the best school systems in the southeastern United States by the turn of the century." New Hanover earned an exceptional rating on accreditation standards applied by the Southern Association of Colleges and Schools.

North Carolina basic skills test scores for 1996 placed New Hanover County Schools at approximately the same range as state scores for Grade 4 writing, but well above the state average for Grade 7 writing. On the Iowa Achievement Test, students scored above the national average in all grades tested. Combined SAT scores averaged 1001, compared to the North Carolina average of 976. Although New Hanover's average is lower than the national average of 1031, it is important to consider that more students take the test in the South compared to other regions of the country. New Hanover County students taking the SAT accounted for 64 percent of seniors, compared to a national average of 41 percent.

In 1996-97, 87.2 percent of the system's graduates planned to continue their education beyond high school. More than $6.1 million in scholarships and financial aid was awarded to 1996 graduates. The system produced one National Merit Scholar and six National Merit Finalists in 1996. Twenty-three students were selected for enrollment in the North Carolina Governor's School, and four were selected to attend the North Carolina School of Science and Math. North Carolinas Scholars recipients, students recognized by the state for superior academic achievement, numbered 367.

The system has had the benefit of tremendous support from the business community and community volunteers. Volunteers in 1996 numbered more than 4,000. These individuals contributed in many different ways including tutoring, working to lower the dropout rate and offering opportunities for students to gain exposure to the corporate realm beyond the classroom. Volunteers contributed a whopping 169,153 documented hours of service to the system.

Much of the assistance from businesses comes through the Greater Wilmington Chamber of Commerce Education Support Foundation, a community education support organization that provides funding for mini-grants to supplement system-funded education each year. It sponsors "Best Foot Forward," a variety show put on by the schools at Thalian Hall each year in March. Proceeds from this lively event fund the mini-grant program. As of 1996, this event had generated $160,000 for grants, funding 114 projects. Other programs under the auspices of this foundation include Project Business, Cape Fear Careers, Community Resource File, ROCAME (Region O Council for the Advancement of Minorities in Engineering) and a Scholars Reception.

The 1996-97 budget for New Hanover County Schools was $126 million, with 63 percent coming from the state, 32 percent from

FYI

Unless otherwise noted, the area code for all phone numbers in this guide is 910.

local monies and 5 percent from the federal government. Per-pupil expenditure was $4,484. Of the total budget, 70 percent was used directly for instructional costs.

The system is organized as kindergarten through grade 5, grades 6 through 8 and grades 9 through 12, using the middle school concept instead of junior high schools. The school year runs from the end of August until the first part of June, though year-round schooling is now available at several elementary schools and one middle school as part of a pilot program. The program is voluntary for students and teachers. After considerable investigation, the Board of Education has found the advantages of year-round schooling include increased learning, a reduction in stress levels for both students and teachers, more time, greater opportunity for effective enrichment and remediation, and higher motivation.

While still in high school, students in New Hanover County schools may engage in advanced studies at the University of North Carolina at Wilmington or enroll in courses at Cape Fear Community College for part of the instructional day. In 1993, the Gregory School of Science, Mathematics and Technology opened its doors to allow students to experience a high-tech program of study that integrates science and mathematics throughout the elementary curriculum. This is the first magnet school in the system, and it has been enthusiastically received within the community. Other magnet schools are in the planning stages.

The system offers the Lakeside Alternative School for students with special needs, primarily those identified as at-risk, who may apply for admission. This school operates an extended-day program for students who also work.

There are four senior high schools in New Hanover County, and the middle schools that feed into these operate according to district lines that are under study in 1997 for change in 1998. This will allow the system to meet minority enrollment requirements and more effectively serve a rapidly growing community.

More than 288 courses are available to senior high school students including social studies, mathematics, computer science, En-

The Art of Discipline

CAPE FEAR ACADEMY

Member of NAIS, NCAIS, SAIS

Accredited by Southern Association of
Colleges and Schools

Contact: Director of Admissions

(910) 791-0287

FAX (910) 791-0290

Cape Fear Academy welcomes and admits students
without regard to race, color, national or ethnic origin,
or disability.

Whether it's hitting the right note on a tuba or the right key on a computer, mastering a skill requires discipline — self-discipline. At independent private schools, supportive teachers and a nurturing environment can help your child develop a sense of personal responsibility. We help turn hard work into accomplishment, because we believe that self-discipline leads to self-confidence—and to a successful future.

glish, foreign languages and the full range of sciences. Students can participate in Army, Navy and Air Force JROTC Honor units as well as a broad range of extracurricular activities and programs. There are many programs in vocational education, including marine sciences and oceanography. A cultural arts curriculum includes band, orchestra, chorus, drama, art and dance.

Middle schools offer a similar, though more limited, curriculum to that in the senior high schools. Elementary schools emphasize hands-on experience in all disciplines. Elementary school students participate in a curriculum based on the use of manipulatives to build a foundation that will support the learning of concepts in the middle grades and high school. A comprehensive program has been designed for exceptional children at all grade levels.

Basketball and football are big parts of the interscholastic athletic programs. What else would you expect from the sports-minded city that produced such athletes as Michael Jordan, Meadowlark Lemon and Roman Gabriel on its public school courts and fields? Volleyball, baseball, soccer, wrestling, golf, tennis and track are also offered.

Brunswick County School System
8360 River Rd. SE, Southport • 754-9282

The Brunswick County School System has a student population of approximately 10,000 and operates three high schools, three middle schools and six elementary schools. It offers an alternative high school, the Brunswick Learning Center, providing education for students who have left the regular program or have not had success in other programs.

In addition to the basic K-12 instructional program, Brunswick County Schools have a comprehensive program of instructional services for the exceptional child, vocational education, remediation and courses for the North Carolina Scholar.

The system's budget for the year is approximately $50 million with a per-pupil expenditure of $4,342. Average SAT scores for

Brunswick County in 1996 was 926. The professional staff to student ratio ranges from 12 to 16 students per teacher.

Pender County School System
925 Penderlea Hwy. • 259-2187

The Pender County School System has 11 accredited schools with an enrollment of nearly 5,700 students. There are five elementary schools, three middle schools, two high schools and one alternative school that serves students in grades 7 through 10. The system also offers one year-round school. It participates in the A+ Arts Program, a widely acclaimed program devised to integrate the arts into the academic experience.

The curriculum includes 20 major areas covered by more than 150 course selections. Students are afforded the opportunity to specialize in college preparatory, Tech Prep or any blend of courses to address individual needs. Both high schools operate on the block schedule, a system that compresses a full course into one semester by extending each class from 50 minutes to 90.

The Board of Education is beginning a campaign to construct and renovate school facilities and has recently identified $58 million in facility needs coming up between 1996 and 2006. The total budget for the system in 1996-97 was $30.6 million. The citizens of Pender County passed a $25 million school bond referendum in 1996, and an additional sum of $13 million from the state puts the facility upgrades well ahead of schedules. Per-pupil expenditure is approximately $5,000. SAT scores averaged 906 with 31 percent of seniors taking the test. The dropout rate for 1996 was 4.3 percent.

Private Schools

The Cape Fear region's private schools offer curricula and activities for children from preschool to high school. While tuition and expenses are the responsibility of the parent or guardian, most of these schools offer financial aid or easy-pay plans. In many cases, having more than one child in a particular school allows a discount on tuition for other children within the same family. All private schools aren't given here, but the following list suggests some alternatives to public education.

Cape Fear Academy
3900 S. College Rd., Wilmington
• 791-0287

Cape Fear Academy is the dominant secular private school in the region. Established in 1967, this coeducational day school is open to students interested in a traditional, college preparatory education. There are approximately 435 students in pre-kindergarten through grade 12. Pre-kindergarten and kindergarten students participate in half-day programs with after-school care available. The Lower School is comprised of pre-kindergarten through grade 5. Instruction by a professional faculty includes art, music, science, foreign language (Spanish), drama, computer science and physical education.

The middle and upper schools concentrate on college preparation in the classroom coupled with individual development through extracurricular activities. Students in grades 6 through 8 must satisfactorily complete courses in English, science, social studies, math, physical education, art, music, computer science and foreign language. At grade 9, students begin to fulfill graduation requirements. Challenging, Outward Bound-type ventures are part of the Middle and Upper school curricula. Ropes courses, rock-climbing and rappelling are among the activities that culminate with each student attending the North Carolina Outward Bound School for a week at the beginning of the senior year.

Community service is a key component of the Middle and Upper school programs as well. The Upper School student government organization has an entire branch devoted to community service. Group and individual activities are planned as students work to serve a minimum number of hours required for graduation. The school also has 7 acres of wetlands that have been developed into an outdoor science education area. Nature trails have been established, and teachers have participated in extensive training through the North Carolina Wildlife Commission.

As far as success rates for Cape Fear Academy go, 100 percent of the graduates attend four-year college programs, and approximately

85 percent of those students are accepted into their first-choice college or university. The average composite SAT score (all students are tested) is 1198, more than 200 points higher than North Carolina's average of 976.

Wilmington Christian Academy
1401 N. College Rd., Wilmington
• 791-4248

This is the largest private school in southeastern North Carolina. Founded in 1969 as a ministry of Grace Baptist Church, more than 580 students are enrolled in this academy, which serves kindergarten through 12th-grade students. The school is on a 40-acre campus at the eastern terminus of Interstate 40.

Wilmington Christian Academy's focus is on providing conservative Christian education. The school is committed to "offering our students an academically challenging course of study in an environment that is conducive to spiritual growth. Our goal is to produce students who will glorify God with their lives while successfully competing in today's world."

Academics, athletics and the fine arts are combined to give students a well-rounded educational experience. The academy's sequenced curriculum begins with phonics in kindergarten and progresses through physics in the high school.

The elementary curriculum strongly emphasizes the basic skills of reading and math, augmented by studies in English, spelling, science, history and health. Phonics-based reading instruction begins early and continues through the entire curriculum. Hands-on learning projects and practice drills are combined to enhance math instruction. The students are also trained in art, music, physical education and foreign language. Piano lessons are available during school hours. Each elementary classroom is equipped with a computer with a Pentium processor and CD-ROM capabilities for classroom instruction and tutoring.

The junior-senior high days consist of seven class periods covering five core academic subjects, one Bible class and one elective. Students in grades 9 through 12 follow one of three academic tracks: general, college preparatory or honors. The math curriculum progresses through calculus, while the science program culminates with physics. Mandatory computer training gives all graduates a working knowledge of word processing, spreadsheets and graphics. Most students graduate with 26 high school credits. Graduates gain acceptance into major Christian colleges and state universities across the country.

St. Mary Catholic School
217 S. Fourth St., Wilmington • 762-6517

St. Mary employs 14 full-time and 10 part-time teachers for approximately 300 students in grades 1 through 8. The school's mission is to "ensure learning for all our students within the framework of Catholic Christian values, to help our students grow in a manner consistent with their needs, interests and abilities, and to prepare them to live in a changing world as self-directing, caring, responsible citizens."

Grades 1 through 5 are structured, self-contained classes. Curriculum includes science, social studies, computers, Spanish, music, art, physical education, religion, reading, phonics in grades 1 and 2, creative writing and math. Grades 6 through 8 have departmental teachers who rotate to different classrooms. Classes include religion, science, social studies, math, language arts, literature, writing, computers, Spanish, music, art and physical education.

St. Mary School graduates are prepared to enroll in the honors courses offered by area high schools. The school's emphasis is on preparing students to be independent learners who maintain high academic achievements and standards throughout their high school and college years.

Special Education

Child Development Center, School for Developmentally Disabled
6743 Amsterdam Way, Wilmington
• 392-6417

The Child Development Center serves children with developmental disabilities from ages 2 through 7. The school is open weekdays from 8 AM until 5 PM, and the educational day is from 8 AM until 2 PM. The center can serve 52 children in a full-time educational setting. There are no fees for students from ages 3 to 7, as this center operates under the auspices of the public school system. Call for information on financial needs.

United Cerebral Palsy Developmental Center
500 Military Cutoff Rd., Wilmington
• 392-0080

Children from New Hanover and surrounding counties who have physical impairments can be referred by a parent, physician or community agency to this special education center. Known as "The Exceptional Preschool," the center serves children birth to 5 years old who have cerebral palsy or other physical de-

velopmental delays. The center also accepts children without disabilities because the administration believes it is beneficial to bring students with and without physical disabilities together in a quality preschool program. Educators and therapists facilitate learning through play and promote development in areas such as gross and fine motor skills, speech and language, and social-emotional, cognitive and independence skills. Although enrollment fluctuates, this center can accommodate up to 45 children.

Home Schooling

The State of North Carolina allows for schooling outside both public and private schools for children whose parents prefer to administer their education. Supervised under the auspices of the Division of Nonpublic Education, home schooling requires participation in standardized testing and immunization programs, and that the educational program is administered for nine months a year by a person with a high school diploma or equivalency certificate.

Wilmington Homeschool Organization provides information for parents interested in educating their children at home. A few questions around the community can produce a contact person reasonably quickly, but a call to the Division of Nonpublic Education in Raleigh, (919) 834-6243, is probably a surer way to find this information. The group is relatively informal at the moment since only about 100 students were being home-schooled in New Hanover County last year.

Child Care

Child care is an increasing concern and business opportunity in the area. Since the phone book is flooded with possibilities, including church-affiliated day-care centers, preschool development centers and after-school care, the choices can be somewhat bewildering for parents.

The Child Advocacy Commission, 1401 S. 39th Street, Wilmington, 791-1057, maintains a detailed data bank of child-care resources in the area. This organization does not make recommendations, but it offers information and referrals that allow parents to make informed choices. There is no charge for this service. The Child Advocacy Commission also works to develop cooperative efforts with governmental and other community service agencies to promote an awareness of children's issues. It sponsors community service activities, educational information and gives assistance to community agencies, civic groups and individuals. The commission offers on-site child-care training for providers and businesses.

There are approximately 50 day-care centers and services in the area as well as 92 day-care homes, although these numbers regularly fluctuate. The North Carolina Department of Human Resources regulates these businesses and establishes guidelines for enrollment capacity, as does the City of Wilmington. A small day-care home serves a maximum of five preschool children or up to eight children if at least three are school age, but there are various stipulations that may affect each situation. Check with the Child Advocacy Commission for information.

The Child Advocacy Commission provides helpful guidelines for deciding which center or service is right for you and your children. They offer detailed lists of things to look for when you go to investigate the suitability of a center such as staff qualifications, programs offered, amount of space, health and safety concerns, meals and fees. Parents can take

great comfort in knowing this kind of organization exists because, if their information packets are an indication, this organization takes a keen interest in the well-being of children. Ask for a general information packet that contains the important tips referred to above.

The following list of day-care centers is partial, and no recommendations are made. However, these centers have demonstrated consistent efforts in terms of longevity and quality of service.

Adventure World
4604 Longleaf Hills Dr., Wilmington
• 392-0868
1401 S. 16th St., Wilmington • 815-0017
In a relatively new location on S. 16th Street and another on Longleaf Hills, this Wilmington center has programs for children as young as 1 month and as old as 5 years. Focus is on child development and independent learning. Capacity is 200.

Carolina Preschool
6501 Carolina Beach Rd., Wilmington
• 392-1560
At Monkey Junction south of Wilmington, this 10-year-old center accepts children ranging in age from 6 weeks to 12 years. Child development and independent learning are the programs. The center offers field trips, summer day camp, computer classes and nutritious breakfast, lunch and snacks. Capacity is 40.

Children's House Academy
2618 Newkirk Ave., Wilmington • 799-7915

This child-care center, called Kindercare until 1995, accepts children ranging in age from 6 weeks to 10 years. It offers after-school programs, an extensive summer camp program including pool visits and regularly scheduled field trips throughout the year. It provides breakfast, lunch and snacks. Capacity is 120.

Classy Bears Learning Center
6620 Windmill Way, Wilmington
• 791-7872

Near Blair School on Market Street north of Wilmington, this center accepts children between ages 6 weeks and 11 years. This center also concentrates on child development and independent learning. Computer classes and gymnastics are offered. The Stretch and Grow program for 3-to-5-year-olds emphasizes physical fitness and health. Capacity is 179.

Creative World
4202 Wilshire Blvd., Wilmington
• 791-2080
2411 Flint Dr., Wilmington • 799-5195

This center is in New Hanover County near Wrightsboro, east of Wilmington on Flint Drive near New Hanover Regional Medical Center.

It accepts children from 2 months to 12 years of age. In addition to child development and independent learning, it also has an academic program, summer camp, field trips, gymnastics and even an on-site water slide. Capacity is 112 on Wilshire Boulevard and 245 on Flint Drive. Creative World has been in Wilmington for nearly a quarter of a century.

Early Childhood Learning Center
4102 Peachtree Ave., Wilmington
• 392-4637

In the Winter Park area since 1983, this center accepts children from 2 to 5 years of age in child development, independent learning and academic programs. Call to ask about extended-care hours and summer camp programs. Capacity is 88. The Early Childhood Learning Center is the only area school accredited by the National Academy of Early Childhood Programs.

Granny's Day Care Center
7010 Market St., Wilmington • 686-4405

Serving New Hanover County to the north and east of Wilmington, this center accepts children from 6 months to 5 years of age in a child development program. Field trips and dance are part of the fun. The center offers two nutritional snacks each day, and children

Photo: Brian and Mona Long

Academics aren't the only consideration among students choosing UNCW.

bring their own lunch. An expansion in late 1996 sets capacity at 80.

Headstart Program of New Hanover County
507 N. Sixth St., Wilmington • 762-1177

In downtown Wilmington, this center serves children who are 4 years old by October 16. This nonprofit child development and academic program also has an extensive food program, free to children from low-income families. Call to inquire about fees for additional programs. Capacity is 230.

Park Avenue School
1306 Floral Pkwy., Wilmington • 791-6217

Near Independence Mall off Oleander Drive, this center has preschool programs for children from 6 weeks to 4 years of age. It also houses a private elementary school for students from kindergarten through grade 5. The child-care component is based on child development, independent learning and academic development. Two snacks and lunch are provided, and there is an indoor swimming pool. Capacity is 200.

Shaw Speakes Child Development Center
718 S. Third St., Wilmington • 343-1441

This center is in downtown Wilmington right beside the Cape Fear Memorial Bridge. It accepts children from 2 weeks to 12 years of age. The nonprofit center bases its program on child development and independent learning. Capacity is 99.

South Brunswick High School's Aquaculture Program

The first words the instructor gives seem to be odd ones for a high school program: "Suit up and put your boots on."

When instructor Barry Bey gives that directive to the nine students in his Aquaculture 3 class at South Brunswick High School, he gets an immediate response. These students, juniors and seniors, bolt from their desks and scramble down the stairs to get to the day's assignment.

Close-up

Brunswick County Schools is a rural system with less than 9,000 students, but the Aquaculture program launched by Mr. Bey in 1987 has brought the system into North Carolina's educational spotlight. It is one of only 13 successful programs of its kind in the nation. The work of the instructor and students has been honored for six consecutive years with a "Best in Show" award in education at the New Hanover County Fair.

In Mr. Bey's classroom, students tend several large fish tanks filled with trout, brim, goldfish or whatever species of fish is required for a particular project. The walls are lined with aquariums that contain larger fish. Outside on the school grounds, a ditch is filled with netted areas containing various fish at several stages of development. Beyond the school campus, the class tends clam rafts in the intake canals at the nearby Brunswick Nuclear Plant.

"It's all experimental," says junior Royce Potter, a descendent of several generations of Brunswick County shrimpers. "In the case of the clams, we take small clams from South Carolina and see how we can make them thrive in the waters of the canal. We've had a 90 percent success rate so far and our knowledge, based on trial and error, is helping establish some guidelines."

Student Mike Mitchem was part of a project to stock tilapia at a golf course to eat algae and keep the pond healthier. Jason Reis and Jon Griffee came up with a plan to empty multiple aquariums faster than the standard and shared this knowledge with the school's

— continued on next page

Photo: South Brunswick High School

Students at South Brunswick High School take their study of aquaculture out into the field.

— continued from previous page

oceanography class. Edmund Randolph suited up on a very cold January day and wandered into the ditch to carefully release the young trout. The whole class participated in a project to transport and introduce catfish to a pond in Arbor Creek, a nearby residential development. The development paid for the fish, and the students had another opportunity to experience practical application of their classroom experience in the real world.

All of Mr. Bey's students seem completely engaged with the class and that, in itself, is a major accomplishment.

"This is an important area of research and my students appreciate that fact," he says. "They know this work will land them jobs one day, but they also understand they're on the cutting edge of something very valuable. Aquaculture is something we need to address on this planet and it's only going to grow in importance. It's a food source, a pet store source, a sports source. We need to learn to protect it in ways we never considered before because it's going to matter to all of us."

Mr. Bey's enthusiasm for his subject matter and his concern for helping his students find a meaningful, practical link between education and employment power the program that suffers from a lack of adequate funding. In search of grant money on a regular basis, Mr. Bey has faith it will eventually come.

"My students are helping to lay the groundwork for a technology that will have enormous impact in the future in terms of how we feed populations. This is the equivalent of agriculture, and it will have the same profound impact on the world. I think aquaculture isn't well understood at this point, so that makes grants a little harder to come by."

The NC Department of Agriculture reports that aquaculture is the fastest growing component of American agriculture. It provided nearly 12 percent of edible fish and shellfish production in 1990. By 1994, catfish production alone was valued at $439 million. North Carolina supplies about 10 percent of the fish market with 17 producers. As the oceans are overfished and pollutants come to have more impact on coastal waters, the significance of this young industry will become more apparent. Eventually, thanks to the persistence and vision of teachers like Mr. Bey, the economic value of aquaculture will catch the eye of state legislators, and funding will become more readily available.

In the meantime, South Brunswick High School's aquaculture students are preparing themselves for successful jobs. After learning the skills of tending to the young fish and clams, they can look forward to continuing education or immediate employment in fields that range from fisheries management to wildlife conservation and more. As they learn fish identification, water quality assessment, pond management and construction, disease identification treatment and more, they expand their career horizons.

Higher education in Aquaculture Technology is conveniently available to Mr. Bey's graduates at nearby Brunswick Community College where students can earn a two-year degree as an Associate in Applied Science. As part of the Tech Prep Track, high school students can go on to Brunswick Community College and then transfer for a bachelors degree at North Carolina State University in Raleigh or UNC-Wilmington in Aquaculture, Mariculture or Fisheries Biology.

Total Child Care Center
4304 Henson Dr., Wilmington • 799-3556

This center is in the Northchase neighborhood near Laney Senior High and Trask Middle schools at Wilmington's northeast corner by incoming Interstate 40. It accepts children from 6 weeks to 12 years of age. Computer classes, dance and gymnastics are offered. Child de-velopment and independent learning are the focus of the program. Two snacks and lunch are provided. Capacity is 127.

YWCA After School Program
2815 S. College Rd., Wilmington • 799-6820

The YWCA, a United Way agency, offers extensive after-school, school-out and sum-

Young students examine letters and artifacts aboard the Battleship *North Carolina*.

mer camp programs that serve children in kindergarten through 8th grade. The After School Program operates from 2:30 to 6 PM Monday through Friday and costs $37 a week, including transportation. The School Out Program, offered on teacher workdays and holidays, is a full-day schedule beginning as early at 6:30 AM and lasting until 6 PM.

Participation in these programs requires parent or guardian membership in the YWCA at a cost of $20 per year. Call about registration fees, financial assistance and program availability in other locations in the region. Gymnastics, dance and karate programs are available to participants in the After School Program for an additional fee.

Home Child Care

There is a robust cottage industry in child care in the area, evidenced by browsing through offers for child-care services in local newspapers and tabloids. According to the Child Advocacy Commission, the care providers list changes on an almost weekly basis, and a parent must be especially cautious in selecting home child care.

In-home care has some obvious advantages. If you have an infant, it's very nice to have a person come into your home. Live-in help or an in-home caregiver are the alternatives in this case. Word of mouth is an important way to learn about good nannies. Ask people with in-home child care about their experiences.

Since Wilmington is a vacation area, there are companies that specialize in both resort child-sitting services and regular sitting services for locals. The Sitter Network Inc., 256-9444, has sitters trained in child CPR, and it offers quality child care for vacationers and locals who need a break for short or extended times. It also offers nanny placement services and temporary sitting. Established in 1991, this agency has just become the area's AuPair in America representative, offering long-term child care through a respected international program. The central, national AuPair office in Salt Lake City may be reached at (801) 255-7722.

UNCW

CELEBRATING 50 YEARS OF EXCELLENCE

Tuesday • August 19, 1997
Convocation
(Trask Coliseum)

Friday-Saturday • October 17-18, 1997
Wilmington College Reunion
(Wise House)

Saturday • December 6, 1997
Fall Commencement
(Trask Coliseum)

Friday-Saturday • February 7-8, 1998
Homecoming
(Trask Coliseum)

Saturday • May 16, 1998
Spring Commencement
(Trask Coliseum)

For details on UNCW's Fiftieth Anniversary Celebration,
call University Advancement at 962.3616.

Higher Education and Research

Before Wilmington became the tourist mecca it is today, the Port City had always been a major commercial hub. Early centers for higher learning were accordingly of the vocational ilk, and it wasn't until the mid-20th century that institutions of broader education were established. The southern coast's present growing economy and desirable location are again attracting industry, creating the need for higher levels and greater specialization of learning as never before. Wilmington is now a true college town, being home not only to the University of North Carolina at Wilmington, a senior four-year institution with a master's-level graduate program, but also to the excellent vocational/technical schools Cape Fear Community College and Miller-Motte Business College. Institutions of higher learning nearest the greater Topsail Island area are Cape Fear Community College's Hampstead campus, Coastal Carolina Community College in Jacksonville and those in Wilmington, listed below. The South Brunswick area is served by Brunswick Community College.

Colleges

The University of North Carolina at Wilmington
601 S. College Rd., Wilmington • 962-3000

Celebrating its 50th anniversary this year, UNCW is successfully living up to its responsibilities as the only public university in southeastern North Carolina. In its most recent report, *U.S. News & World Report* ranked UNCW the fourth most efficient regional university in the south. The university's marine biology program, utilizing sites at estuaries and the ocean, was also ranked fifth best in the world by the Gourman Report (up from seventh a few years ago). The program's primary site is its 4-acre Center for Marine Science Research at Wrightsville Beach. The university's Cameron School of Business Administration is accredited by the American Assembly of Collegiate Schools of Business, a distinction earned by only 20 percent of the nation's business programs. UNCW is one of two sites nationwide to offer regular faculty training in hypermedia classroom instruction.

Thirty-nine undergraduate degree programs and fourteen graduate degree programs are offered within the university's four schools: the College of Arts and Sciences, the Cameron School of Business Administration, the Watson School of Education and the School of Nursing. Four-year undergraduate programs lead to the Bachelor of Arts and Bachelor of Science degrees. The many masters-degree programs now include the Master of Fine Arts in Creative Writing which boasts several authors of international renown on faculty. A cooperative program with North Carolina State University leads to a Ph.D. in marine science. There is also a variety of preprofessional programs and special programs in several areas including marine science research and continuing education. Through the Contract Extension Program, students may study freshman and sophomore level courses at three regional community colleges, including Brunswick Community College in Supply, and be eligible to apply for admission to UNCW as baccalaureate degree candidates.

The university originated as Wilmington College in 1947 and became a senior four-year college in 1969, expanding from three buildings in 1961 to the more than 70 that today occupy a 661-acre tract of land bordering S. College Road. UNCW is a fully-accredited, comprehensive level I university in the state's 16-campus University of North Carolina system.

Seventy percent of the nearly 500 instructional and research faculty members hold doctoral degrees. Class size averages less than 30 students, with a faculty-to-student ratio of 1-to-17. There are approximately 9,000 students currently enrolled.

The William Randall Library, 962-3760, contains more than 415,000 volumes, subscribes to more than 5,000 serial titles and employs state-of-the-art electronic informational resources. A 73-seat auditorium is equipped for various types of audiovisual use. The library is a partial depository for U.S. government publications and has a current inventory of 490,000 items in hardcopy and microtext. Randall Library is a full depository for North Carolina documents, which are readily available to all users, including nonstudents. Nonstudent memberships are available for $6 semiannually. The fee includes a parking permit, if needed.

The Center for Marine Science Research 7205 Wrightsville Avenue, 256-3721, is dedicated to fostering a multidisciplinary approach to basic marine research. Basic and applied research programs are available on undergraduate and graduate levels, making use of the center's 15 laboratories, video equipment/editing facilities, machine tool shop, aquatic specimens holding room and USDA-licensed animal facility. Additional lab space is available for research requiring constant flow-through seawater.

The center maintains nine research vessels ranging in size from 13 to 29 feet and highly specialized, state-of-the-art equipment that includes a robotic data-gathering vehicle. The center serves as host for the NOAA-sponsored National Undersea Research Center for the southeastern United States and houses headquarters for the North Carolina National Estuarine Research Reserve (NCNERR) in co-operation with the N.C. Division of Coastal Management. The NCNERR program manages four estuarine reserve sites as natural laboratories (see our Research Facilities section, below) and coordinates research and education activities.

Other instructional and research resources at UNCW include the 10-acre Bluethenthal Wildflower Preserve, the Upperman African-American Cultural Center, elaborate campus-wide computing services with Internet access, a new internship program with the nearby Screen Gems film studios, the Ev-Henwood Nature Preserve in nearby Town Creek, and the Division for Public Service and Extended Education. Continuing adult education is available through the Division for Public Service and Extended Education, comprising noncredit programs and courses in art, languages, investment and estate planning, scuba diving, photography, professional development, adult scholar enrichment, music and more. Programs may be custom-designed to fit particular needs.

Student life on campus is enhanced by a full battery of services and entertainment, food-service facilities, three student periodicals, a music-format radio station and student activities. Kenan Auditorium hosts theatrical, symphonic and instructional events year round. The university holds NCAA Division I membership and competes in the Colonial Athletic Association. The university fields 19 varsity teams, both men's and women's, including golf, basketball, tennis, soccer, swimming and diving. Both UNCW Ultimate Frisbee teams (men and women) are top-ranked nationally. Sports facilities include a 1,200-seat baseball stadium; tennis, volleyball, outdoor basketball courts; a track-and-field complex; an Olympic-size swimming pool with a diving well; and the 6,000-seat Trask Coliseum. Construction was begun in early 1997 on a new University Commons featuring three small lakes with fountains and a 200-seat sheltered amphitheater.

UNCW's school year is divided into four sessions consisting of the standard fall and spring semesters plus two summer sessions.

FYI

Unless otherwise noted, the area code for all phone numbers in this guide is 910.

For information on undergraduate admissions call 962-3243; for graduate studies call 962-3135. For information on Public Service Programs and Extended Education call 962-3193.

Cape Fear Community College
411 N. Front St., Wilmington • 251-5100

Concentrating on 35 one- and two-year technical and vocational programs, Cape Fear Community College exerts a major educational presence in the area and is among the state's most technologically advanced two-year institutions. There are now three campuses: the main campus overlooking the Cape Fear River in historic downtown Wilmington (between the Cotton Exchange and the Coastline Convention Center), which is currently undergoing expansion, and two Pender County satellite campuses, one in Burgaw, 259-4966, about 21 miles north of Wilmington, and the other in Hampstead, 270-3069, on U.S. 17. Two-year programs, some leading to associate degrees, include studies in the fields of business, chemical technology, microcomputing, criminal justice, college transfer, electrical and nautical engineering, hotel and restaurant management, nursing (RN) and paralegal technology. Among the one-year programs are administrative office technology, a renowned boat-building curriculum, dental assistance, industrial electricity and industrial mechanics, practical nursing, marine and diesel mechanics, and welding. Studies in basic law enforcement training, phlebotomy and real estate lead to certificates. CFCC maintains small and large sea vessels for its quality marine education curricula, and its library is open to the public at no charge. The college offers financial aid, courses in high-school equivalency (G.E.D.), adult literacy and human resources development. Many special programs and seminars are free or very reasonably priced. Day and evening classes are available at all campuses.

Miller-Motte Business College
606 S. College Rd., Wilmington
• 392-4660, (800) 868-6622

Miller-Motte is a well-respected 79-year-old collegiate alternative for students desiring employment-targeted training. The school is an accredited institution that maintains a strongly monitored job-placement service to assist their graduates in becoming employed — Miller-Motte's primary mission. With the help of a board of advisors made up of faculty, employed former students and regional employers, Miller-Motte's curricula are constantly updated to keep pace with changes in the regional job market. The school is well-known and trusted among employers in southeastern North Carolina.

Miller-Motte offers 15- and 18-month diploma programs in business management, accounting, administrative assistance, medical assistance and microcomputer specialties. Nine-month and 12-month certificate programs are available in word processing, general office accounting, general office technology and medical unit clerk studies. Financial assistance, student services and internships in some programs are available.

Mt. Olive College, Wilmington Center
1422 Commonwealth Dr., Wilmington
• 256-0255, (800) 300-7478

Founded in 1951 by the Freewill Baptist Church, Mt. Olive College is a private, four-year, liberal arts institution that operates two fully accredited distance learning centers designed to help nontraditional students complete their associates or baccalaureate degrees. Schedules are designed with students who must work full-time in mind. The distance learning centers are like mini-campuses, complete with their own registration offices, and have proven very successful. Enrollment at the Wilmington Center has tripled since its opening.

The Wilmington Center was opened in 1995 and offers two degree-completion programs, in criminal justice and in management and organizational development. Both programs confer bachelor of science degrees. The Wilmington Center preserves Mt. Olive's tradition of student-focused, supportive programming and teaching styles. Courses are discussion-oriented, emphasizing critical thinking and research papers more than tests. Classes meet at night and on weekends and are limited to 20 students who proceed through the curriculum together as a cohesive group, or "cohort." New cohorts are formed seven or eight times a year in a cycle of rolling admissions. Because of this frequency, admissions requests are typically answered quickly — within a couple of weeks or so. Most students attending Mt. Olive's Wilmington Center are in-state transfer students, and many are working to complete undergraduate requirements (such as the core liberal arts requirements) in preparation for career changes or further study. Tuition includes all books and fees.

Mt. Olive's Wilmington Center is at the intersection of Military Cutoff and Eastwood roads, between McDonald's and the First Union building.

Shaw University
The Wilmington CAPE
224 N. Front St., Wilmington • 763-9091

The Wilmington Center for Alternative Programs of Education (CAPE) is one of nine accredited satellite programs of Shaw University in Raleigh designed to offer a viable opportunity to the working adult who, because of per-

---

INSIDERS' TIP

When you're in need of a tutor for your child, call the Univeristy of North Carolina at Wilmington, 962-3000, and ask for the appropriate academic department office. They may be able to refer you to a graduate student who tutors.

sonal or job obligations, has been unable to attend other institutions of higher education. The Wilmington CAPE has been operating since 1986, offering night classes that lead to bachelor's degrees in psychology, sociology, criminal justice, religion and philosophy, public administration, business management and liberal studies. Transfer credits from two- and four-year institutions are accepted, and life experience can earn students up to 27 credit-hours. Classes tend to be small, and total enrollment is less than 200. Founded in 1865, Shaw University is affiliated with the Baptist church.

Brunswick Community College
**U.S. Hwy. 17 N., Supply • 754-6900,
(800) 754-1050**

With three locations — the main campus in Supply, a site in Southport and the Industrial Education Center in Leland — BCC serves more than 1,300 curriculum students and more than 3,000 others in continuing education courses. Established in 1979, the college offers one- and two-year certificate, diploma and associate's degree programs in 15 disciplines. These include aquaculture, administrative office technology, air conditioning, heating and refrigeration, various business studies, cosmetology, dental assisting, real estate, recreational grounds, nursing, medical records and welding. The College Transfer program leads to associate of arts and associate of science degrees and works in close partnership with the University of North Carolina at Wilmington to expedite transferals from Brunswick's two-year curricula to UNCW's four-year programs. BCC is committed to ensuring that course content, classroom instruction, textbooks, testing, grading procedures and academic support services meet university standards.

Through its New and Expanding Industry Program and its Small Business Center, BCC works closely with area businesses to tailor curricula to regional needs. The college also assists industry in seeking, evaluating, training and retraining employees according to changing standards. BCC will custom-design courses to fit various needs and typically conducts industrial courses at the job site to upgrade employees to associate degree levels. BCC is fully accredited and is widely known as a substantial educational value for the tuition dollar. The Supply campus is at the intersection of U.S. 17 Business and College Road, about 25 miles south of Wilmington.

Research Facilities

Not surprisingly, the major emphases of the research performed in the area are in the fields of oceanography, wetland and estuarine studies, marine biomedical and environmental physiology, and marine biotechnology and aquaculture.

Center for Marine Science Research

7205 Wrightsville Ave., Wrightsville Beach • 256-3721

The University of North Carolina at Wilmington is the primary local research organ with its Center for Marine Science Research. (See our description of UNCW above.) Additional research equipment at the center not mentioned in the description of the university includes a low-temperature aquarium room, an atomic absorption spectrophotometer and an extensive microscopy capability. The center serves as host for the NOAA-sponsored National Undersea Research Center (NURC) for the southeastern United States. NURC annually supports fisheries management, ocean-floor processes and other research projects from the Gulf of Maine to the Gulf of Mexico. This support is based upon competitive proposals.

North Carolina National Estuarine Research Reserve

UNCW Center for Marine Science Research, 7205 Wrightsville Ave., Wrightsville Beach • 256-3721

Masonboro Island and Zeke's Island are two of the four components of the NCNERR, the others being Rachel Carson Island near Beaufort and Currituck Banks in northeastern North Carolina. The National Estuarine Research Reserve system was created by Congress to preserve undisturbed estuarine systems for research into and education about the human impact on coastal habitats. The reserves are outdoor classrooms and laboratories for researchers, students, naturalists and hobbyists.

Masonboro Island is the last and largest undisturbed barrier island remaining on the southern North Carolina coast. It is also among the newest. Its 8 miles of thin beach and expansive marshes were separated from Pleasure Island in 1952 when Carolina Beach Inlet was cut through. A controversial move at the time, Masonboro's separation created one of the most productive estuarine systems along the coast. In plain English that partly means that endangered loggerhead turtles have a place to nest into the foreseeable future. This is also true for a multitude of bird species, mammals, lizards, shellfish and aquatic vertebrates. Masonboro is accessible only by boat. Fishing, picnicking, sunbathing, surfing, shelling and, for the time being at least, camping are permitted.

The **Zeke's Island** component of the reserve, immediately south of Federal Point in the Cape Fear River, actually consists of three islands — Zeke's, North Island, No-Name Island — and the Basin, the body of water enclosed by the breakwater known locally as the Rocks. Because the Basin has been relatively isolated from the river so long, it exhibits a salinity level nearly that of the ocean, presenting something of a huge ocean aquarium. Zeke's Island is similar to Masonboro in every way minus the ocean surf. Activities pursued on both islands are similar. Access to Zeke's Island is by boat and by walking across the Rocks, preferably at low tide, a potentially hazardous proposition. (For further information about these islands, see our chapters on Attractions; Camping; and Sports, Fitness and Parks.)

The North Carolina National Estuarine Research Reserve has limited its presence on Masonboro and Zeke's islands by allowing traditional activities to continue, including hunting within regulations, pending future conclusions that may result from monitoring.

Another preserve that has received its fair share of scientific scrutiny is **Permuda Island** (the name is an obvious corruption). This string bean of a spit bears substantial archaeological significance in that large tracts consist essentially of huge shell middens created by prehistoric inhabitants over a vast span of time. Such sites are rare in the ever-shifting, acidic soils of barrier islands. Despite decades of farming, the archaeological resources survived

---

INSIDERS' TIP

Adults can continue their education for credit or simply for the fun of it through UNCW's Division of Public Service and Extended Education, 962-3193.

fairly intact. The island passed into state ownership several years ago. Of further interest is the theory that Permuda Island represents an original barrier island later eclipsed by the growth of what today is called Topsail Island. A similar theory has been posited for North Island, mentioned above, and other privately-owned islands along the Pender County coast such as Hutaff and Lee islands. (The only other islands behind the barriers are dredge spoil mounds.) Permuda Island is not open to the public. It remains in a natural state and is managed by the North Carolina Department of Environment, Heath and Natural Resources/ NCNERR and the Department of Marine Fisheries.

To inquire about the Cape Fear components of the North Carolina National Estuarine Research Reserve and other coastal resource issues, call the Coastal Reserve Coordinator at UNCW's Center for Marine Science Research, 256-3721.

Division of Marine Fisheries
127 Cardinal Drive Extension, Wilmington
• 962-3900

Although this agency of the North Carolina Department of Environmental Health and Natural Resources maintains an office in Wilmington, all its research functions are conducted in Morehead City. The agency acts as steward for the protection of all coastal wetlands, waterways and the ocean within a 3-mile limit. UNCW's Center for Marine Science Research assists with research needed locally.

North Carolina State Horticultural Crops Research Station
Castle Hayne Rd., Castle Hayne
• 675-2314

Another field of research important to the region is horticulture, the primary local site for which is this research station. The station is one of 15 facilities in the state, nine of which are operated by the Department of Agriculture, the remainder by North Carolina State

University. The Castle Hayne facility is state-run. Its varied, ongoing research programs concentrate on crops of local economic importance, such as blueberries, strawberries, grapes, sweet corn, sweet potatoes and cabbage. Variety trials, breeding and herbicide tests are among the studies performed. The station works in limited association with the New Hanover County Extension Service arboretum, especially regarding soil studies, but primarily serves local horticulturists by making useful publications available to them.

LaQue Center for Corrosion Technology Inc.
702 Causeway Drive, Wrightsville Beach
• 256-2271

When driving along U.S. Highway 421 through Kure Beach, you may wonder what that large array of strange-looking racks on the oceanside of the road is all about. Another cluster stands across the road. Curiously, these are historical landmarks (in place since 1935) designated by the American Society of Materials Testing and used for atmospheric testing. They are the property of the LaQue Center for Corrosion Technology. The center (which pronounces its name "luh-KWEE") conducts tests upon any material subject to corrosion, particularly alloys and coatings such as window fixtures and paints, under various corrosive conditions, whether atmospheric, marine or artificial. Testing makes up about 98 percent of their lab work, but they also perform related research into corrosion technology. The LaQue Center sponsors seminars such as the ever-popular "Fundamentals of Corrosion and Its Control," which is offered four times a year at a local hotel. Through an internship program affiliated with UNCW and Cape Fear Community College, the center employs students as operating assistants for round-the-clock test monitoring. Open-house tours of the Wrightsville Beach facility are conducted periodically and may be arranged for groups on request.

INSIDERS' TIP

Recipes for locals' favorite desserts and dishes are available free at Great Harvest Bread, 4302 Market Street, 763-0003, in the North 17 Shopping Center.

The Fort Fisher Hermit

During the turmoil of the 1960s, people often came to the old man who lived alone on the salt marsh south of Fort Fisher to ask his opinions about those troubled times, which the man said were "a wave of mental illness sweeping the country."

The man was Robert Edward Harrell who, for 17 years until his death in June 1972, lived in a World War II-era concrete bunker not far from where the North Carolina Aquarium at Fort Fisher now stands. It's an inhospitable place, scorched and mosquito-ridden in summer, frozen and wind-scoured in winter. It's also beautiful, serene and teeming with wildlife. In the late 1950s it was desolate. The windowless bunker was stuffed with the hermit's ragtag accumulations of driftwood, Styrofoam surfboards, newspapers and tin cans. Steepled planks of wood sheltered the entrance. The 1929 Chevy in which he slept during his early years there was Fort Fisher's first dune buggy. The hermit's abode was everything to him, except when Hurricane Helene in 1958 drove him to hitchhike to Wilmington. "I like to be alone," he said, "but not that alone."

The hermit could talk a blue streak. Visitors were treated to endless conversation and were asked to sign his guest register. The hermit's frying pan, seeded always with small change, was in plain sight, and if people added to it or paid him for his photograph, he always gave something back. He generously shared his "millionaire's ration," made from any number of foods abundant on the tidal flats: crabs, oysters, fish, shrimp, turtles, raccoons and opossums. Sometimes he gave youngsters Civil War artifacts he had found.

— continued on next page

Photo: Fred Pickler

Robert Harrell fished with a seine net.

— continued from previous page

Robert Harrell was born on Ground Hog Day in 1893 near Gaffney, South Carolina. He eked out a living as a sidewalk tinker in Shelby, North Carolina, and as a linotype operator. He married and had four sons and a daughter who died young. When one of his sons committed suicide in the 1930s, his family moved north. Harrell stayed behind.

His first sojourn at Fort Fisher ended sometime prior to 1955 when his brother retrieved him from a Wilmington jail. The trouble had begun when Harrell went scurrying about, looking for something live to feed his pet jay bird. A local woman happened to inquire about his frantic behavior, and he asked, "Have you got anything that will wiggle?"

Photo: George Harrell

The earliest confirmed date of Harrell's permanent residence on the salt marsh is 1955, but he was fond of claiming that he "rode out Hazel" — Hurricane Hazel, that is — one year earlier. He subscribed to an unaccredited discipline called biopsychology and claimed to have come to Fort Fisher to write a book, *A Tyrant in Every Home*. He claimed to have finished a 500-page manuscript, but it has never been found. Some people speculate that Harrell came to get away from his troubles; he had been institutionalized in the past.

Robert Harrell lived for more than 17 years in the salt marshes of Fort Fisher.

At an age when most people think about collecting Social Security, Harrell began a new life with little more than the clothes on his back. He quickly became something of an attraction in Kure and Carolina beaches. He took to his celebrity well and recorded his visitors' signatures in old registers. One register survives, a 1949 calendar book containing about 2,500 signatures dated between November 1971 and June 1972, now part of the Cape Fear Museum's hermit collection.

Robert Harrell appealed to the hermit in everyone, that part of us that wants to be left alone, to live in harmony with nature, to escape our entanglements. But even he couldn't escape it all. Mystery surrounds his death and the investigation remains open to this day. Some of the hermit's artifacts are on display at the North Carolina Marine Resources Center at Fort Fisher. His final resting place, always strewn with flowers and seashells, is in the Federal Point Methodist Cemetery in Carolina Beach. His headstone bears the epitaph, "He Made People Think."

Examining and Improving the Quality of Life for Women

NEW HANOVER COMMISION *for* WOMEN

Our Mission...
Is to act as a resource for women and families to:

- Improve the status and quality of life for New Hanover Women.
- Encourage the development and utmost potential of women.
- Promote public awareness of women's needs, issues and achievements.
- Play a leadership role through coalitions with other women's and civic organizations.
- Serve as advocates for change concerning the status of women.
- Conduct research and assemble information to determine the status of women.
- Report and make positive recommendations regarding the status of women to the New Hanover County Commissioners, Wilmington City Council, the Wrightsville Beach Board of Aldermen and the Carolina and Kure Beach Town Councils.

Come join us...
The New Hanover Commission for Women meets on the third Wednesday of the month from 6pm to 8pm. Meetings are open to the public, call 458-0340 for location.

P.O. Box 15056 Wilmington, NC 28408

Volunteer Opportunities

When there is a need, Cape Fear people are there. While that's surely true of every community in the world to a degree, there is something particularly intense about the high level of commitment local people bring to volunteer projects. Part of this dedication to helping others may stem from the fact that even our largest city, Wilmington, is still a small town in its social structure. This intimate social environment makes it impossible to look the other way when someone is in need of help.

Part of the commitment comes from a mutual awareness that living at the edge of the sea creates a profound sense of unity, particularly during stressful times when hurricanes strike. In the aftermath of two hurricanes in 1996, million-dollar houses and mobile homes alike were damaged or destroyed — a testament to the democratic nature of monster storms. The whole community quickly rallied its resources and set to work to relieve both immediate needs and long-term ones. Area supermarkets shipped in truckloads of ice and water to distribute at no charge. The American Red Cross set up feeding stations. Chainsaw owners readily helped neighbors clear fallen trees from their roofs. People shared their homes with displaced friends.

Newcomers will quickly discover that involvement with good causes and organizations not only helps the community but also helps strangers become members of the family. People are known by their works, and those who involve themselves in doing good works will be welcomed into many social and business circles. Newcomers looking for employment would do well to involve themselves in philanthropic efforts because the volunteer arena offers a good and fast lesson on how the community functions.

The demand for volunteer time and talent is extremely high year-round. Regardless of your particular interests, you are likely to find plenty of places where you can donate your time and talents. It is, in fact, very easy to become overrun with requests for your help once you donate your efforts. Although tens of thousands of people volunteer annually — and this may be a conservative estimate — Wilmington lacks a central coordinating agency to match volunteers with tasks and organizations. This situation may change in 1997 if United Way is successful in receiving a grant to provide this needed service. The Information and Referral Service, 251-5020, housed with the Cape Fear Area United Way, can provide information about human service organizations throughout the region. The Community Services pages of the phone books contain a listing of all the human service agencies. There are limitations to both of these informational resources because many organizations that utilize volunteers aren't listed.

So the best advice on becoming involved is to select an interest and pick up the phone. The opportunities are overwhelming. The arts, the senior population, health services, nutrition, historic preservation, the environment, minority interests, business development, human relations, housing, schools and education, special festivals and more make up the volunteer possibilities in the region.

The following is a condensed listing of some of the organizations that would appreciate your involvement.

Human Services

American Red Cross, Cape Fear Chapter
1102 S. 16th St., Wilmington • 762-2683

Volunteer positions include blood services aides, registered nurses, disaster team members, service to military case workers, health and safety class instructors and office aides. This very active organization has a high community profile and is extremely responsive to people in need. During 1996's two hurricanes, the Red Cross sheltered more than 6,000 people, set up 15 feeding stations and raised more than $200,000 locally. The simple act of giving blood is an easy way to volunteer and this is a critical need since only 2 percent of the population donates blood. Give a pint and save a life.

Brunswick Family Assistance Agency
P.O. Box 333, Supply • 754-4766

Formerly named the Brunswick County Volunteer Information Center, this organization needs volunteers to help families in need of food, shelter, furniture and other necessities. It distributes nearly 500 Christmas baskets across Brunswick County and has a food pantry that distributes more than 22,195 pounds of food each year.

Brunswick County Literacy Council Inc.
104 Ocean Hwy. E., Supply • 754-7323, (800) 694-7323

This organization helps adults in Brunswick County learn to read by pairing them with interested volunteers. Volunteers are carefully screened, trained and matched with adult students. Volunteers are also needed in a variety of functions including publicity, office help and newsletter publication.

Cape Fear Area United Way
709 Market St., Wilmington • 251-5020

As with most United Way organizations, this is the funding body for a large number of community organizations. It has an Informa-tion and Referral Service associated with it that may direct interested volunteers to various human service organizations. It needs community volunteers to conduct and allocate an annual fund-raising program. In 1996 it raised a record-breaking $2,308,000 despite postponing the campaign after Hurricane Fran.

Cape Fear Literacy Council
608 Shipyard Blvd., Wilmington • 392-7323

As with the Brunswick County Literacy Council, this organization pairs volunteer tutors with adults who are learning to read. It also provides a computer literacy lab, training for parents and caregivers and a new readers support group. Additionally, it offers Babies and Books, a program provided through the prenatal clinic at New Hanover Regional Medical Center, to encourage expectant parents to begin reading to their children at birth. More than 300 tutors are needed on a yearly basis.

Columbia Cape Fear Memorial Hospital
5301 Wrightsville Ave., Wilmington • 452-8373

Senior Friends and Volunteer Services are housed together in one office, so expect the phone to be answered this way. See our chapters on Healthcare and Retirement for information about Senior Friends, a wellness program for people older than 50. Volunteers at Columbia Cape Fear are needed to work in the gift shop, at the general information desk, the surgical information desk, the outpatient rehabilitation center, central supply, purchasing, the pharmacy, imaging services, the patient representative program, the emergency center, the Lifeline program and as needs arise. The hospital's auxiliary has approximately 150 members.

Coastal Horizons Center
721 Market St., Third Floor, Wilmington • 343-0145
Crisis Line/Open House • (800) 672-2903
Rape Crisis Center • 392-7460

This private, nonprofit service agency serv-

The U.S. Coast Guard is a visible presence in the Wilmington area.

ing the tricounty area is for individuals who need assistance to help them recover from chemical dependency/substance abuse, sexual assault and other crisis situations. There is also an emergency care shelter for youths ages 8 through 18. Other programs include HIV/AIDS Outreach, pregnancy testing, criminal justice alternatives and food vouchers.

Domestic Violence Shelter and Services Inc.
P.O. Box 1555, Wilmington • 343-0703

Women and children who have suffered domestic violence are sheltered by this agency. Volunteers are needed to help with direct services, to work in the office, to provide transportation, to serve as children's advocates, to work in Vintage Values (the recycled clothing and goods shop), to serve as court advocates and to act as on-call workers in emergency situations. In 1996 more than 1,400 women and children were assisted by the shelter.

Good Shepherd House
511 Queen St., Wilmington • 251-9862, 763-5902

This day shelter for homeless people needs volunteers to work at the front desk greeting guests, answering the phone and distributing toiletry items for the shower. Volunteers are also needed to sort clothing, distribute fresh clothing, do laundry and drive the van to take

clients to work or on errands. People interested in working in the kitchen are needed to set up for lunch, serve meals and clean up.

Gay Rights of Wilmington (GROW)
341-11 S. College Rd. #182, Wilmington • 799-7111

This organization provides information regarding activities of particular interest to the gay and lesbian community. It is also involved in HIV-related services such as resources, transportation, information and referral, and patient advocacy. The switchboard number provides extension numbers for a variety of organizations and services.

Hope Harbor Home
P.O. Box 233, Supply • 754-5726, 24-Hour Crisis Line: 754-5856

At this domestic violence shelter in Brunswick County, volunteers are needed to serve as client advocates, work on the speakers bureau and help organize and implement fund-raising activities.

Hospice of the Lower Cape Fear
810 Princess St., Wilmington • 762-0200

This organization serves the needs of clients and their families when terminal illness occurs. Volunteers who will visit terminally ill clients, do office work and help with fund-raising events are needed. A new 12-bed residential center at 1406 Physicians Drive, Wilmington, will be completed in the summer of 1997. The Annual Festival of Trees is a major fund-raiser for Hospice.

New Hanover Regional Medical Center
2131 S. 17th St., Wilmington • 343-7704

While there are 70 set areas of volunteer involvement, opportunities are actually limitless. An average of 800 active volunteers work in the hospital each year in almost every sector of hospital activity. Direct patient service people, oncology volunteers, mailroom clerks, flower deliverers, transportation-providers for discharged patients, lobby receptionists, gift-shop clerks, clerical assistants and courtesy-van drivers are some of the volunteer positions available here. Volunteers may also be involved in helping care for newborns at the birthing center or, in the case of Kangaroo Kapers, helping children come to terms with a new baby in the house. People with ideas for new volunteer activities are encouraged to call.

Salvation Army
820 N. Second St., Wilmington • 762-7354

This organization provides shelter for the homeless and assistance for people in difficult circumstances. It needs volunteers in fund-raising activities and public relations efforts. Volunteers may serve on the Advisory Board, Ladies Auxiliary and in the shelter, which serves men, women and children. Volunteers may also work at the thrift store, on the Woodlot Project, Christmas fund raisers, the toy and food distribution center, the annual Coats for the Coatless drive and on disaster relief teams. The shelter provides emergency housing to more than 20,000 individuals each year and has a Soup Line serving meals seven days a week between 5:30 and 6 PM for the public. This food program serves nutritious meals to more than 60,000 people each year in Bladen, Brunswick, Columbus, Pender and New Hanover counties.

Southeastern Sickle Cell Association
508 Castle St., Wilmington • 343-0422

Volunteers provide support services as well as fund-raising activities and community education for this organization that concentrates its efforts on a disease that affects one in 400 African-Americans. Volunteers with public relations and promotions experience are needed to develop community awareness. Nurses are needed to do screenings.

St. James Shelter
25 S. Third St., Wilmington • 763-1628

This cold-weather homeless shelter in the basement of St. James Episcopal Church is a relatively new addition to Wilmington's humanitarian services for people without a place to sleep. Volunteers are needed to spend an occasional night welcoming guests and making sure the evening goes smoothly. It is open from 8:30 PM until 7:00 AM for women, men and children from November until March. Guests are referred by the Good Shepherd House.

Children

Public Schools

School systems offer a variety of volunteer opportunities that are essentially the same from system to system. Help in the classroom. Tutor. Serve as a mentor for at-risk students. Work in dropout prevention programs. Help minority students achieve success in engineering/science careers. Get involved with the PTA/PTO. If you want to volunteer your time to the public schools, contact the Community Schools/Public Information Office in each system: New Hanover County School System, 1802 S. 15th Street, Wilmington, 763-5431; Brunswick County School System, Central Office, Southport, 457-5241; Pender County School System, 925 Penderlea Highway, Burgaw, 259-2187.

Boy Scouts of America, Cape Fear Council
110 Long Street Dr., Wilmington
• 395-1100

This organization requires a tremendous number of volunteers to assist the many Boy Scouts in the Cape Fear area. Board and committee members are needed as well as a host of leaders, coaches and advisors. A new program, the Sports Club Program, is for inner-city boys from four housing developments that combines traditional Scout activities with a basketball league.

Brigade Boy's Club
2759 Vance St., Wilmington • 392-0747

This venerable organization, now a century old, needs volunteers who will serve as photographers, class instructors, arts and crafts teachers, coaches, tutors and group club leaders for both boys and girls. The club provides behavioral guidance and promotes the social, recreational, cultural, vocational, physical and mental health of youth.

Community Boys' Club
901 Nixon St., Wilmington • 762-1252

The Community Boys' Club primarily serves minority youth and it has produced some exceptional adults over the years. Basketball great Michael Jordan played here when he was a child. Meadowlark Lemon did too. The club relies upon volunteer involvement in fund-raising, implementing special programs and working as adult role models for youth.

Child Advocacy Commission
1401 S. 39th St., Wilmington • 791-1057

This organization works as an advocate for children in three main areas: child care resource and referral, the juvenile restitution program and Project First Stop, an educational/counseling program for first offenders younger than 16 and their parents. Volunteer assistance in many areas is needed, including a relatively new family nurturing program that helps Wilmington Housing Authority residents develop better parenting skills if their children, ages 4 through 12, are identified as at-risk for behavioral problems.

Girls Inc. of Wilmington
1502 Castle St., Wilmington • 763-6674

This organization that primarily serves minority girls needs tutors, group leaders and fund-raisers as well as volunteers in many other capacities. Girls Inc. is an after-school and summer program for girls ages 5 to 18 and offers programs in the areas of career and life planning, health and sexuality, leadership and community action, sports, cultural heritage and self reliance.

Girl Scout Council of Coastal Carolina
P.O. Box 328, Kure Beach • 458-5164

The Girl Scouts need volunteers in many positions. Troop leaders, consultants, organizers, trainers, product sales coordinators (we're talking cookies here) and communicators are needed to aid this organization that serves girls ages 5 to 17. This council serves girls in Brunswick, Columbus, New Hanover and Pender counties and offers leadership development for girls through fun and rewarding programs.

Family Services of the Lower Cape Fear
4014 Shipyard Blvd., Wilmington
• 392-7051

This organization offers family counseling, consumer credit counseling, Travelers Aid and the Big Buddy program for the lower Cape Fear. Volunteers are needed as office helpers, child sitters (while parents are in counseling sessions) and Big Buddies to be reliable, trusting friends to boys and girls in need of positive role models. The Big Buddy Program requires a minimum commitment of one year.

INSIDERS' TIP

Don't sightsee in the days immediately following landfall of a hurricane because fallen power lines, downed trees and loose limbs can pose greater safety hazards than the storm itself.

Wilmington Family YMCA
2710 Market St., Wilmington • 251-9622

If you're a real hands-on volunteer, this is certainly the organization for you. Be a youth sports volunteer, a nursery attendant, a Special Olympics volunteer or a person who helps with maintenance of this facility. There is a great aquatics program that offers different activities for individuals with a variety of disabilities, and volunteers who like to get in the water will enjoy this opportunity to help.

YWCA
2815 S. College Rd., Wilmington • 799-6820

Youth programs, clerical help and maintenance are just a few of the areas where the YWCA needs your volunteer assistance. If you would like to be a tutor at one of six locations throughout the Cape Fear area, this organization can use your help. The Y offers an extensive after-school program and a child-care center as well as programs addressing youth development, women's health issues, racial justice, employment training and counseling.

The Arts

Arts Council of the Lower Cape Fear
807 N. Fourth St., Wilmington • 762-4223

The Arts Council has a number of programs that need volunteer involvement. The annual Piney Woods Celebration of the Arts, a two-day cultural arts event held at Hugh MacRae Park, needs a host of volunteers to help with parking, admission, preparation, publicity and more. The Arts Council has a volunteer Board of Directors with administrative committees in the areas of advocacy, finance, fund-raising, membership and publications/information.

St. John's Museum of Art
114 Orange St., Wilmington • 763-0281

This extraordinarily fine museum of visual arts needs volunteers to work in many capacities. Things are always happening at this lively center, and volunteers are needed to serve as docents and in membership, publicity, fund-raising, the gift shop and much more. The

museum constantly has new projects underway such as a cookbook, art trips to other cities, film series, artist sales, exhibitions, educational programs and special events. If you love the visual arts, this is a wonderful place to offer your volunteer services.

See our Arts chapter for additional arts organizations that use volunteers.

Historic Preservation and Community Development

Downtown Area Revitalization Effort (DARE)
201 N. Front St., Wilmington • 763-7349

DARE concentrates on revitalization of the Central Business District in downtown Wilmington. Thirty-six volunteers, who represent a cross-section of the community, serve on the Board of Directors. Thirteen are designated by other organizations, seven are elected based upon their profession and 16 serve as at-large members. This body expedites quality development of the commercial district by offering a wide range of services and detailed information to potential downtown businesses.

Historic Wilmington Foundation
209 Dock St., Wilmington • 762-2511

Volunteers interested in preserving the architectural heritage of the region are invited to work in public relations, membership, the deRosset Committee (named for the Foundation's home that is under continual renovation), education, preservation action, urban properties and gardens. There is a yearly gala, the primary fund-raiser, that relies on a host of volunteers for logistics, publicity, entertainment, food and everything else required to throw a major, glittering party and auction.

Lower Cape Fear Historical Society
126 S. Third St., Wilmington • 762-0492

Volunteers are needed for publicity, fund-raising, membership drives and planning at this venerable organization that seeks to accurately preserve the history of the area. Volunteers also work as docents and archivists in the society's home, the Latimer House. The society sponsors the yearly Olde Wilmington by Candlelight Tour of Homes.

Wilmington Community Development Corp.
511 Cornelius Harnett Blvd., Wilmington • 762-7555

This organization nurtures business development through the Small Business Incubator and other programs aimed at economic development. A relatively new endeavor, this organization looks for volunteers interested in broadening the area tax base by helping launch new businesses by offering low-cost office space, financial advice, marketing advice and more.

Wilmington Harbor Enhancement Trust
P.O. Box 331, Wilmington • 251-9438

This organization exists to support the orderly development of property and recreational activities in and along the Cape Fear River and the Northeast Cape Fear River adjacent to the Wilmington city limits. Efforts of WHET focus on "development which is functional and attractive to all types of boating and river activities while considering the environmental, historic and natural beauty of the river." If you have an interest in working to protect the river, this small and new organization will welcome you.

U.S. Coast Guard Auxiliary
272 N. Front St., Wilmington • 343-4882

This organization relies upon volunteers to do recreational vessel inspection, tours of visiting Coast Guard vessels and activities related to boating safety.

Senior Citizens

Brunswick County Department of Older Adults
P.O. Box 249, Bolivia • 253-4746

This agency offers congregate and home-delivered meals, transportations, minor home repairs and other services to Brunswick County's senior population.

Elderhaus Inc.
1950 Amphitheater Dr., Wilmington • 251-0660

Program aides, activity assistants, meal servers and van assistants are needed for this agency that provides structured and stimulating day care for the elderly, including programs

Waterbirds like this heron are a common site in the area's marshes, lakes and waterways.

Photo: N. C. Travel & Tourism

Fort Fisher near Kure Beach is the site of the largest land-sea battle fought up until the time the fort fell in 1865.

for those with Alzheimer's Disease and dementia. Volunteer board members oversee the operation of this organization that serves seniors through fund-raising, public relations, education and more. Thanks to a successful capital campaign in 1996, Elderhaus is building a new center in 1997 to serve the area's increasing need for these services.

New Hanover County Department of Aging
2222 S. College Rd., Wilmington
• 452-6400

This governmental organization can point you in many directions if you wish to become involved in volunteer efforts that both serve and involve senior citizens. This agency was formed in 1983 to serve older adults by promoting visibility and representation, providing support services that encourage independent living and operating as the focal point of aging services in the community.

Retired Senior Volunteer Program
2011 Carolina Beach Rd., Wilmington
• 341-4555

RSVP taps the talents of retired people by sharing their experience with the needs of the community. Volunteers have special assignments matching their interests, skills and abilities in schools, libraries, hospitals, nursing homes and other places. Volunteers in this program are 60 and older.

Senior AIDES Program
709 Market St., Wilmington • 251-5040

This organization benefits from the assistance of volunteers in an advisory council capacity. People who volunteer to work for this program donate their time in public speaking, representing the agency at community fairs, preparing publicity materials, giving management and technical assistance and assisting in personnel placement

INSIDERS' TIP

If you see an oil spill on the water or waste being dumped in our most precious resource, call the Coast Guard at 343-4895 to report it.

of Senior AIDES through resume preparation, job interview skills, job search assistance and more.

Senior Citizen Services of Pender Inc.
312 W. Williams St., Burgaw • 259-9119

This Pender County organization provides services for the elderly, including transportation, in-home care, congregate meals and home-delivered meals. Volunteers are needed to deliver meals five days a week to homebound senior citizens, and to provide transportation to the center, doctor appointments, to pay bills and to the grocery store.

Arts, entertainment, local sports and essays/fiction make up *Encore Magazine*, a free weekly published each Tuesday since 1984.

Media

Wilmington's media scene has expanded moderately in the past few years with several new, successful entries in a very competitive market. It has also been remarkably stable in terms of long-term staying power for many of its newspapers, magazines and radio and television stations.

In the print medium, visitors will notice an abundance of tourist-oriented publications in street racks. While these aren't listed here, they're generally handy guides to the area's attractions. Some of them have been around for years, and others seem to drift in one day and out the next. Some of the newer ones aren't mentioned here because their staying power has not yet been demonstrated and, frankly, the research efforts and accuracy of some of the new arrivals are not the best. There's a robust business in publications on real estate, and these magazines or booklets, overwhelmingly reliable, can be found in racks on corners throughout the Cape Fear region.

Choices for radio listening are eclectic, ranging across talk, country music, beach music, urban contemporary, Top 40 and the diverse offerings of the city's own National Public Radio affiliate. Consensus is there could be more successful formats added to those successful stations already on the air, but surely time will change this situation to satisfy everyone.

Television is a somewhat limited medium unless one has cable or satellite services, in which case the whole spectrum of channels becomes available. Fox replaced CBS several years ago and, at this writing, it's difficult to get a clear picture of CBS transmission without cable. Public Television, broadcast from Jacksonville by way of Chapel Hill, has a strong signal.

The media listed below have settled into their own niches on what seems to be a permanent basis. In a volatile industry, these have proven themselves over time.

Newspapers

The Wilmington Star-News
1003 S. 17th St., Wilmington • 343-2000

The *Star-News*, offering two editions, is the only major daily paper in the region and dominates the print market along the southern coast of North Carolina. It is a New York Times-owned periodical that concentrates on the local scene as well as on national and international news. Established in 1867, it is the oldest daily newspaper in North Carolina. Wire services include the Associated Press, New York Times News Service, Knight-Ridder-Tribune News Service, Los Angeles Times-Washington Post New Service, Cox News Service and Bloomberg Business News. It covers New Hanover, Bladen, Brunswick, Columbus, Duplin and Pender counties, Jacksonville and Camp Lejeune. It is distributed throughout the Cape Fear region, and home delivery is available. Out-of-town subscribers can receive all editions or the Sunday *Star-News* only. Circulation is about 60,000 daily and nearly 70,000 on Sundays. StarLine, an audiotext service that makes information available 24 hours a day, can be reached by calling 762-1996.

The Challenger
514 Princess St., Wilmington • 762-1337, (800) 462-0738

The Challenger is a statewide, minority-focused publication based in Wilmington and Fayetteville. Published weekly on Wednesdays, it is a subscription-based periodical with limited newsstand distribution.

The Wilmington Journal
412 S. Seventh St., Wilmington • 762-5502

This weekly is the voice and mirror of the area's African-American community in New

Hanover, Brunswick, Pender, Onslow, Columbus, Jones and Craven counties. Each Thursday it is available at news racks throughout the city and by subscription. Circulation is about 8,600.

The Island Gazette
Pleasure Island Plaza B-4, Carolina Beach • 458-8156

If you're looking for real estate on Pleasure Island, the *Gazette* is probably your best first source. It is a weekly published on Wednesdays and is available at newsstands throughout Carolina Beach. Mail subscriptions are available. Its focus is on southern New Hanover County with emphasis on Pleasure Island and issues that affect it. Circulation is about 5,000.

The Topsail Voice
14888 U.S. Hwy. 17 N., Hampstead • 270-2944

This weekly, established in 1991, is published on Wednesdays and is the largest newspaper in the greater Topsail Island area. *The Voice* covers local politics, commerce and sports (often emphasizing fishing) throughout the region from Sneads Ferry south to Ogden. It includes classifieds and op-ed pages. With a circulation of about 5,000, *The Voice* is a fast-growing periodical available by subscription and at racks and news boxes throughout its coverage area and at a few locations in Wilmington.

The Brunswick Beacon
106 Cheers St., Shallotte • 754-6890

This weekly community newspaper, published on Thursdays, distinguishes itself by having won dozens of awards during the past decade for advertising and editorial content. It covers and distributes to all of Brunswick County, with particular emphasis on the southwestern portion of the coast. *The Beacon* is among the last of the small independents still

produced and printed entirely at one location. About 13,000 copies are circulated each week to subscribers, retail outlets and news racks, and departments include real estate and classified listings.

The Pender Post
210 E. Freemont St., Burgaw • 259-9111

This small but venerable independent community newspaper has a circulation of 5,000 and is available by subscription and in racks located throughout Pender and New Hanover counties. Published every Wednesday, it covers Pender County people and news.

The Pender Chronicle
110 Courthouse Ave., Burgaw • 259-2504

Owned by H.L. Oswald Corporation, an area publishing family, this community paper first went to press in 1897. Published every Wednesday, it's available by subscription and in racks throughout the Pender County area and beyond. It has a circulation of 5,725. Its focus is local community and church news.

The Wallace Enterprise
107 N. College St., Wallace • 285-2178

Although this paper is in Duplin County, Wallace has strong ties to the Wilmington area and is becoming something of a commuter route for people who may work in the city but want to live in a less fast-paced area. This is another H.L. Oswald Corporation newspaper that concentrates on community news for Wallace and Duplin County as well as nearby Pender County. It was first printed in 1922, and circulation is now 7,614. It is published every Monday evening and Thursday morning.

The State Port Pilot
105 S. Howe St., Southport • 457-4568

Covering the six towns in the Southport-Oak Island sphere, this weekly newspaper concentrates on community perspectives,

---

INSIDERS' TIP

Check out *Reel Carolina Magazine* to find out which stars are in town for filming.

At day's end, you'll have memories to savor.

carrying news on government, society and sports. With a circulation averaging more than 7,000, the *Pilot* includes a classifieds section and is available by subscription and at news racks throughout its coverage area every Wednesday.

Entertainment Magazines

Encore Magazine
255 N. Front St., Wilmington • 762-8899

Publisher Wade Wilson describes this as a "general what's happening" magazine for the Wilmington area. Arts, entertainment, local sports and essays/fiction make up this free weekly published each Tuesday since 1984. Certainly the most widely distributed free entertainment periodical in the region, *Encore's* many highlights include festival and holiday roundups, recipes, attractions, personal ads and Chuck Shepherd's syndicated "News of the Weird" column. Perhaps its most outstanding feature is a detailed calendar of weekly events. *Encore* is available at news racks prac-

tically everywhere in Wilmington, at many retail outlets elsewhere and by subscription. Circulation averages 18,000 year-round. *Encore* co-sponsors an annual fiction contest in cooperation with the Lower Cape Fear Historical Society. In addition to the magazine, *Encore* also publishes a "Guide to Boating and Fishing," available at marinas, and "Directions," a guide for students at UNCW. The "Guide to Cape Fear Leisure," available for perusal in hotel rooms around the area, is an annual *Encore* publication.

Reel Carolina Magazine
P.O. Box 1724, Wilmington • 392-5445

This monthly has a natural focus for the area's entertainment scene. It is a journal of film and video that keeps readers up to date on what's happening in the film industry in North and South Carolina. Production notes, a trades section, technical information, business profiles and interviews fill the pages. After three years of publication, circulation is at about 15,000. It is available by subscription and in racks across the Carolinas.

INSIDERS' TIP

Think Wilmington is lacking in foreign and art films? Cinematique, an expanding film series sponsored by WHQR-FM Public Radio, offers the best of both at Thalian Hall on a nearly regular basis.

The *John Taxis*, one of the oldest tugboats in the country, perches beside the parking lot at Chandler's Wharf.

Wilmington Magazine
201 N. Front St., Wilmington • 815-0600

Published every other month, this attractive and lively magazine established in 1993 addresses Greater Wilmington from historical, cultural, business and personality perspectives about the region's people and places. It is available by subscription, at newsstands and in bookstores and has a circulation of about 10,000. The managing editor is Wilmington's longtime mayor, Don Betz.

Wright Times
P.O. Box 496, Wrightsville Beach
• 256-0477

This little magazine, launched in 1995, covers news about Wrightsville Beach. It has an average circulation of 8,000 distributed for free at various sites around the beach and in Wilmington. Content makes this pub-lication tremendously appealing to locals and visitors alike, and it's a welcome addition to the area print scene. Gutsy, self-admitted "jarhead" publisher Grant Hoover doesn't mind taking punches at things that annoy him, and his brassy attitude is a breath of fresh air at moments. *Wright Times* includes features, town hall reports, a business section, a calendar of events and a police blotter.

Television Stations

WECT-TV 6, NBC
WWAY-TV 3, ABC
WSFX-26, FOX
WUNJ-TV 39, PBS

Cable television in Wilmington is provided by Time-Warner Cable of North Carolina, 763-4638.

Radio Stations

News, Talk, Sports
WAAV 980 AM and 94.1 FM
WBMS 1340 AM
WMFD 630 AM

Oldies and Beach Music
WCCA 106.3 FM
WKOO 98.7 FM

Adult Contemporary
WGNI 102.7 FM (and Top 40)

National Public Radio
WHQR 93.1 FM (classical, jazz, blues, news, National Public Radio and Public Radio International)

Country
WKIX 99.9 FM
WWQQ 101.3 FM

Urban Contemporary
WMNX 97.3 FM

Rock
WSFM 107 FM

Christian
WWIL 90.5 FM, 1490 AM

Big Band
WZXS 103.9 FM

Tourism is one of the most important industries to arise in the latter half of the 20th century in the southern coastal area.

Commerce and Industry

During most of the 20th century, the Greater Wilmington area has experienced what some business leaders have described as an immunity to national and state economic trends. There have been good and bad eras, but the general Wilmington economy has neither performed as well in prosperous times nor as badly in recessionary times as regions with similar demographics. Past economic immunity seems to have created a kind of unspectacular (but sometimes comforting) financial stability for the Cape Fear area.

This middle-of-the-road economic situation has made it hard for workers to get rich in traditional, professional employment because there is not tremendous opportunity to work for large corporations. Manufacturing accounts for about 15 percent of the jobs and a quarter of the economy, suggesting how cherished this kind of employment is to Wilmingtonians. Locals view the relatively few corporate professional employees with a degree of awe and speak with amazement of their high salaries and profuse benefits. By far, most people in the area work in smaller businesses for someone else or are engaged in some kind of enterprise of their own.

Statistics compiled by the University of North Carolina at Wilmington's Cameron School of Business indicate that the bulk of employment opportunities are in the services sector, a broad category that includes such diverse occupations as physicians, government workers, real estate brokers, educators and fast-food employees. An interesting statistic that stays fairly steady is New Hanover County's unemployment rate, generally riding just 6 percent for the past several years.

Geography seems to be the main factor that sets Wilmington apart from the overall North Carolina economy, and it is also driving some new trends that are positioning Wilmington to take advantage of a new and prosperous era at the end of the 20th century and beginning of the 21st. Its maritime environment creates opportunities for business based on what is naturally available — the sea, the river, the many beautiful views — instead of that which must be manufactured.

There have been, of course, significant times in history when Wilmington relied heavily on its natural resources in a manufacturing and agricultural way. Early settlers took advantage of the area's natural resources in the creation of their economy. In the 18th century, settlers used the area's lush pine forests to foster a lumber industry that continues today. The manufacture of lumber-related by-products, such as tar, turpentine and pitch, was the dominant business in the 19th century, but this sort of manufacturing has since fallen away. Rice was an early source of profitable income for the area; cotton was a primary source of commerce, too, and the downtown wharves were once the site of the largest cotton exporting operation in the world. After the War Between the States, the economy shifted away from cotton and rice plantations because the labor supply was no longer available.

Technology, by way of the railroads, provided jobs for 4,000 families in the first part of the 20th century and made Wilmington a major rail center. The Atlantic Coast Line, the evolution of the Wilmington and Weldon Railroad, was a technological marvel and the pride of the Wilmington economy at the time. Many an opulent downtown home was built on railroad dollars. The trains moved the area's products efficiently into the inland market, and there was popular speculation that the rails would move the economy into prosperity. Then, in 1955, the railroad announced the closing of the corporate office and sent a considerable segment of Wilmington's population south to Jacksonville, Florida in 1960. This was a severe economic loss that forced stunned Wilmingtonians to ponder their destiny. Not only were good-paying jobs lost with the railroad, but service businesses all over the area lost steady customers.

The Port

The North Carolina State Port Authority, seeking to cash in on the area's natural location as an international shipping port, established a deep-water terminal at Wilmington 50 years ago, a move that may represent the region's earliest foray into the realm of service. The loss of the railroad, however, was detrimental to the success of this facility for a long time. A lack of good roads was another problem that was not solved until 1991 when Interstate 40 connected Wilmington to the rest of the country's superhighway system. While the State Port endured land transportation obstacles, ships were getting bigger, and suddenly the turning basin in the Cape Fear wasn't deep enough. Thanks to aggressive lobbying, no doubt coupled with North Carolina's sudden awareness of Wilmington's appeal and potential, the state decided that the port is a positive economic force for all of North Carolina, and funding was allocated to deepen and maintain the ocean bar.

The Wilmington facility now receives more than 556 ships, loaded with diverse cargoes, each year. The main imports are metal products, general merchandise, tobacco and furniture. Leading exports are wood pulp, furniture products, general merchandise and food. The Port Authority has a chiller facility where perishables, such as Chilean fruit and vegetables, can be stored. In combination with the port at Morehead City and two inland facilities at Greensboro and Charlotte, more than 26,000 North Carolinians make their living through this increasingly vital industry that handles approximately 2.2 million tons of cargo a year. Trade ports that do significant business through the State Ports include Japan, Korea, Hong Kong, Taiwan, Germany, France, Belgium, the Netherlands, the United Kingdom and South Africa.

Tourism

Tourism is one of the most important industries to arise in the latter half of the 20th century in the southern coastal area. Since the scenery is a constant and people are drawn to the sea, this industry provides a strong economic center. Even in the midst of economic downturns in more prosperous Raleigh, Greensboro and Winston-Salem, people in those cities will still vacation at the beach. They may defer the mortgage, but they will not give up the opportunity to spend a week relaxing by the sea. The opening of Interstate 40, a fast, functional (though rather boring) corridor, threw wide the gate for all types of commerce and industry. No industry, perhaps, has witnessed such dramatic results from the laying of this precious asphalt as the tourism industry.

At this writing, more than 75,000 visitors a year drop by the Cape Fear Coast Convention and Visitors Bureau, 24 N. Third Street, 341-4030, in downtown Wilmington. On a typical summer weekend at Wrightsville Beach, more than 80,000 cars cross the bridge to the 5-mile-long island. Other area beaches have their share of traffic waits for summer vacationers to cross over their bridges. And summer is no longer the sole tourism season. Convention and Visitors Bureau officials recognize that Wilmington has moved from a three-month tourism season to an eight-month season that begins in March. Tourism efforts generated an estimated $220 million in 1995 alone and growth projections suggested an annual increase of 10 percent.

There are more than 7,000 beds in hotels, motels and inns in the Greater Wilmington Area, and these establishments are experiencing nearly full occupancy on a year-round basis. In the summer it is often difficult to find accommodations on short notice. Historic Downtown Wilmington alone has more than two dozen bed and breakfast inns. One also

Photo: Scott Taylor/Duke University Marine Laboratory

International shipping lanes terminate at the North Carolina State Port in Wilmington.

gets the sense someone sprinkled hotel/motel seeds around the Cape Fear region because they seem to be springing up from the soil overnight. The development of resort properties with recreational amenities is on the rise particularly in the waterway communities of Topsail Island to the north and the Brunswick Beaches to the south, although North Topsail Beach is currently undergoing extensive renovations in the wake of extensive hurricane damage.

Although the summer's storms put something of a temporary dent in tourism-related services in 1996, the people of the Cape Fear have encountered much tougher obstacles in the past and, so, bring their resilient spirit to the task. Consider this interesting statistic from the Convention and Visitors Bureau: 98 percent of the hotels and motels in Wilmington were open the day after Fran ripped across the area.

Tourism, of course, is much more than accommodations. Businesses that profit from the steady flow of visitors are also thriving. Convention facilities and all of the attendant services represent a growing segment of the economy. Visitors need a full range of services, and there are many entrepreneurs who are more than willing to provide them. Restaurants number in the hundreds and continue to proliferate at an astounding rate, with the best of them enjoying capacity dining on weekends.

Retail stores that serve tourist needs in beachwear, vacation items and souvenirs are readily available, but visitors also shop for gifts and groceries. Special tourist services such as horse and carriage rides in the historic district, entertainment, boat tours, sailing charter opportunities, a downtown Wilmington walking tour, educational tours in the historic district and many more enterprises continue to respond to high demand from visitors.

It is generally understood, at the close of the 20th century, that Wilmington's service-based economy is coming to be a positive factor. No single industry can determine the success or failure of the area's economy. It is the mixed bag of economic forces that creates a stable economic environment and is beginning to lead to a profoundly prosperous community.

Trade

Wholesale and retail trade, linked strongly to tourism dollars, account for about 30 percent of the local economy, compared with 22.5 percent in the state. Wilmington's retail businesses earned the city sixth place in retail sales among all North Carolina cities. Wilmington's retail sales are increasing at an annual rate of 7 to 8 percent, posting a gross total of nearly 2.4 billion dollars. The past two years have seen the opening of national and regional chains, such as Circuit City, The Gap, Barnes & Noble, and World Bazaar — stores Wilmingtonians never thought they would see. Belk-Beery, the city's premiere fashion department store, opened a second, though much smaller, store at Landfall Center in 1996. The city's retail corridor is pushing north with extremely heavy development in the vicinity of Wrightsville Beach. On every corner, there seems to be a new shopping center going up.

All of these businesses pivot on the area's natural scenic resources and on the tremendous appeal of Wilmington's beautiful architecture. Screen Gems Studio (formerly Carolco Studios), home to the prospering local film industry, opened here partly because of the scenery, period homes and varied location opportunities. The studio has eight sound stages and is a complete filming facility for motion picture, television and commercial productions. It has 100,000 square feet of soundstage space. Its three-block, four-story urban back lot has doubled for many of the world's major cities.

Film Industry

The film industry generated more than a half-billion dollars in 1993 and 1994 in the Wilmington area economy. In 1995, Wilmington captured the majority of North Carolina filmmaking with revenues totalling $240 million from 43 features and 25 television projects, and $18 million in commercials and other related services. These figures from the North Carolina Department of Commerce show an increase of $107.5 million over 1994. The film industry, according to the Wilmington Film Office, One Estell Lee Place, 763-0847, represents about 12 percent of the total area's economic base. At this writing, Wilmington does more film business than forty-five states. It is third in line only behind New York City and Los Angeles.

Stars seen during these two years have included Katherine Hepburn, Jeremy Irons, Julie Harris, Anthony Hopkins, Alec Baldwin and Kim Basinger. Big stars. In 1995 the movies filmed here included *Lolita*, *To Gillian on her 37th Birthday*, *Out of Carolina*, *Twilight Man*, *Gramps* and, of course, *Cannibal Vampire Schoolgirls from Outer Space*.

Apparently, Screen Gems' purchase of Carolco has widened the focus of the local studio to tap into a lucrative television commercial market. Under the guidance of Frank Capra, Screen Gems promises more activity in this sector of film. Past commercials made in Wilmington have included a memorable Maxwell House coffee spot that included the rugged good looks of Councilman Harper Peterson, as well as a McDonald's spot featuring area kids.

Senior Services

A major industry is beginning to arise around the retirement population. Again, this is a matter of geography and, of course, climate. The maritime location of the area makes the climate unusually mild for its latitude. There are four discernible seasons, an important factor for northern retirees who have grown weary of Florida's almost single season. An occasional snow and warm summers create a more interesting yearly cycle for retirees who yearn for diversity in the climate.

There are a wide range and consistently growing number of domiciliary care facilities in New Hanover, Brunswick and Pender counties. Nationally, North Carolina ranks fifth as a retirement destination for those people age sixty and older who are moving into the state, and they like to live in either the mountains or on the coast. Figures suggest this population will increase by 32 percent between 1995 and 2000. In response and expectation, planned retirement communities, senior services, recreational opportunities aimed at retirees, and other enterprises will represent a major component of the local economy. One of the benefits derived from the attraction of retirees from more prosperous economies in the north and west is that these people bring their nest eggs along with them and spend several decades buying goods and services, as well as contributing their skills and knowledge to area volunteer organizations.

Healthcare

Healthcare, both for the senior population and everyone else, is big business in the region. Three hundred physicians and five regional hospitals employ large numbers of medical personnel. There is a high availability of a skilled work force across the board in the area and the region's amenities seems to draw exceedingly qualified people in huge numbers. This is not particularly good news for people looking for work, but it is very appealing to businesses that can count on a large pool of talent at a reasonable cost. This situation may not long exist; by the dawning of the 21st century, Wilmington's increasing economic diversification is predicted to shift this picture in favor of employees.

Manufacturing

The largest manufacturing companies in the area include Corning Glass Works, (the Wilmington location is the largest manufacturer of optical fibers in the world); General Electric, which manufactures aircraft engine parts, nuclear fuel and components; Carolina Power & Light, the local energy company; E. I. Dupont de Nemours & Company, known widely as Dupont, which makes Dacron and polyester fibers; and International Paper Board, formerly Federal Paper, which manufactures paperboard from lumber in its Columbus County plant; and Hoechst Celanese, formerly named Cape Industries, which makes dimethyl terephthalate, ethylene glycol and terate resins.

On a lower tier in terms of number of employees, but still large companies, are Pharmaceutical Product Development, which provides clinical drug development services for pharmaceutical and biotechnology industries; Takeda Chemical Products USA, manufacturer of vitamins B1 and C; Exide Electronics, which manufactures uninterruptible power supply systems; Applied Analytical Industries, manufacturer of pharmaceutical products; Bedford Fair Industries, a women's apparel mail order company; Interroll Corporation, maker of conveyor components and motorized pulleys; Sturdy Corporation, which makes electronic and electromechanical control devices; and Occidental Chemical Corporation, manufacturer of sodium bichromate, chromic acid and sodium sulfate.

Smaller, strong companies such as American Crane Corporation, Block Industries, Corbett Package Company, Dorothy's Ruffled Originals, Louisiana Pacific Corporation, Wilmington Coca-Cola Bottling, Queensboro Steel, the *Wilmington Star-News* (the only local daily newspaper), Archer Daniels Midland, Wilmington Machinery, Holt Hosiery Mills Inc., Leslie-Locke Inc., Wright Corporation and Pender Packing Company employ thousands of Cape Fear people.

For a complete listing of area manufacturers, drop by the Wilmington Chamber of Commerce, One Estell Lee Place, 762-2611, where the Committee of 100 is housed. The Committee of 100, 763-8414, is a component of Wilmington Industrial Development Inc. and works to attract new business and industry to the area.

The University

The University of North Carolina at Wilmington is a significant factor in the local economy. Serving a student body of 9,077, the university is among the fastest-growing and most technologically advanced universities in the 16-campus UNC system. Organized into the College of Arts and Sciences (including a marine sciences program ranked seventh best in the world), the Cameron School of Business Administration, the Donald R. Watson School of Education, the School of Nursing and the Graduate School, the university offers bachelor's degrees in 38 areas of concentration, 10 pre-professional programs and 16 master's degree programs. The university's economic impact on the region is approximately $360 million, which accounts for 10 percent of the economic activity in New Hanover, Pender, Brunswick and Columbus counties.

The Future

At this point in history, it seems that Wilmington is poised perfectly in both time and space to take advantage of its natural resources, technological advances and entrepreneurial motivation in order to explore tre-mendous opportunities in the 21st century as the region expands its economic base. The Greater Wilmington Chamber of Commerce operates a Better Business Bureau that promotes and develops a favorable business climate in the community. The Better Business Bureau, 762-2611, is in the Chamber of Commerce office beside the Coast Line Center.

Office Space

Since the region has a high percentage of entrepreneurs, there is significant response to a demand for office space. Several office centers provide the individual or small company with turn-key services that include a central reception area, support staff services, use of office equipment and an opportunity to be in a professional setting. Utilities, excluding phone

Photo: Scott Taylor

The beach at Fort Fisher poses some underwater hazards to swimmers.

service, and janitorial services are included in the lease. **Landfall Executive Suites**, 1213 Culbreath Drive, Wilmington, 256-1900, adjacent to the residential neighborhood of Landfall and the Landfall Shopping Center, offers furnished office suites with long- or short-term leases near Wrightsville Beach. It is the largest center of its kind in Wilmington. Amenities include office supplies, a conference room and offices ranging from 130 to 300 square feet. Professional support services are available. It offers a corporate identity program to individuals or companies that are not housed on the site. **The Cotton Exchange**, 321 N. Front Street, Wilmington, 343-9896, has offices available for individuals or small companies in a center that overlooks the Cape Fear River in Historic Downtown Wilmington. It offers unfurnished offices with both long- and short-term leases as well as a corporate identity package that includes mailboxes, phone messages and receptionist answering services for businesses not physically located at the center. Professional support services are available.

A United Methodist Congregation

Helping

Overcoming

Praying

Encouraging

Come to a place where you can get a fresh start in life!

Where your family can grow together in love!

Where you can become a part of a caring community!

Kendall J. Guthrie, Pastor

Please Call 799-2440 for 10am worship location and directions

Worship

In the summer of 1996, one of Wilmington's historical landmarks was smashed to the ground by Hurricane Fran's 120 mph winds. The tallest of First Baptist Church's two steeples was wrenched from the building and scattered over Market Street. Locals were stunned into silence upon viewing thousands of smashed bricks and twisted copper. Reporters from around the world scrambled to cover the story in the morning after the storm had passed and First Baptist was a dramatic image to broadcast.

This 197-foot steeple, constructed during the Civil War, had withstood nearly a hundred years of coastal weather. This onetime lookout post for Union troops on the river held up to the blast of Hurricane Hazel in 1954. A constant feature of Wilmington's downtown skyline, nobody thought it would vanish. Then, in one violent night, it did.

Although the initial scene was one of devastation and immediate response was one of shock and grief, it didn't take more than a few days for Wilmingtonians to take the event in stride. The church members rallied, the community expressed its faith in the steeple's restoration, and people all over the world responded by sending checks to the church to pay for the repairs. The steeple will be replaced, and the summer's storm will become not only a story to tell but also a reminder of the value of faith. Material things can be broken, but a strong spirit is an enduring force.

Faith has been a significant factor in Wilmington's success as a community from the beginning. Stand on the corner of Market and Third streets in downtown Wilmington and notice the surprising number of churches and temples that dominate the immediate scene. These are only a few of the many spiritual centers in Wilmington, New Hanover, Brunswick and Pender counties.

As the architecturally important buildings that house many of them signify, worship is woven inextricably into the historical and social fabric of life in the Cape Fear area. Since the middle of the 18th century when the region was being solidly developed, religion has been a constant factor in Cape Fear region life.

Greater Wilmington has more than 200 churches and that number continues to grow. Much to the delight of the visitor who appreciates fine architecture and interesting history, as well as diverse worship opportunities, some of these churches and temples are among the most fascinating structures on the various historic tours.

Tour buses have recently been spotted stopping in front of some of Wilmington's fine examples of religious architecture. It's a bit of a shock to locals who regard their churches as spiritual homes and never counted on tourist appeal, but, just as fine European cathedrals draw their share of the tourist trade, so do American churches. And Wilmington is particularly rich in this resource.

St. James Episcopal on S. Third Street, for example, seems to have a steady stream of visitors wandering up the steps on weekdays to look at the remarkable architecture and hear colorful stories of Union occupation. Created by an act of the General Assembly in 1729, this parish covered all of New Hanover County. The cornerstone was laid in 1751. In 1781 the church was stripped and used as a blockhouse, a hospital and a riding school for the cavalry. During the Civil War, the church was made into a hospital by Union troops when its rector refused to offer prayers for President Lincoln. The church was designed by Thomas U. Walter, a Philadelphia architect best known for his cast-iron dome on the U.S. Capitol.

Saint Mary Catholic Church on S. Fifth Street in downtown Wilmington is another remarkable historical structure. Construction began on this Spanish Baroque-style building in 1908 and was completed in 1911. The brick and tile building is built on the plan of a Greek cross with a high dome over the crossing. Numerous historical writers have referred to it as a major architectural creation, partly because it is a stunning building, but largely because it was designed by Rafael Guastavino and his son of the same name. It was built without steel or wood beams or framing and without nails, according to Tony P. Wrenn in his book *Wilmington: An Architectural and Historical Portrait*. The building holds itself firmly together with a system of brick and tile that is both decorative and structural.

St. Stephen AME Church in downtown Wilmington was founded in 1865 by a black congregation that broke away from First Baptist Church. This is one of seven African-American congregations created after the freeing of slaves at the close of the Civil War. While the races had always attended church together prior to the war, it was on unequal terms. So, the races separated in their choice of worship sites and that situation has largely remained the same for more than a century, although there is a tremendous spirit of cooperation among the various congregations.

The Temple of Israel with its distinctive gold onion-shaped domes was home to the first Jewish congregation in North Carolina. Dr. Samuel Mendelsohn was rabbi for nearly a half-century. The building, characterized by Moorish Revival architecture, was once shared for two years with neighboring Methodists when the Methodist church was destroyed in 1886. The Christian and Jewish communities in Wilmington have historically enjoyed pleasant relations.

St. Nicholas Greek Orthodox Church is not in a particularly significant building, although it began in one. Originally housed in a portion of what is now St. John's Museum of Art in downtown Wilmington, this church relocated in the late 1970s to the building formerly occupied by Grace Baptist Church on S. College Road in the suburbs. Most of the families trace their origins to the Greek Isle of Icarus, and there is speculation that so many Greeks found their way to Wilmington because the landscape is reminiscent of their homeland.

St. Paul's Evangelical Lutheran Church on Market Street downtown came into being when Germans arrived in numbers in Wilmington in the early 1800s. North Carolina's Lutheran Synod took note of a growing German population and sent two pastors, Bernheim and Linn, to organize the church in 1858. The congregation began worship services in 1861, the same year as the advent of the Civil War. The Gothic-style building was temporarily occupied by Union troops during the war after the fall of Fort Fisher in January of 1865. The Bellamy Mansion down the block served as Union headquarters, and the enlisted troops camped in St. Paul's churchyard. Horses were stabled in the unfinished church, and wooden furnishings were used as firewood. Although the congregation was discouraged, they completed the building in 1869. The original building burned in 1894 but was promptly replaced. There have been several additions and renovations through the years.

First Presbyterian Church was organized as early as 1760. The Rev. Joseph R. Wilson was pastor of this church from 1874 until 1885. His son, Thomas Woodrow Wilson, grew up to become president of the United States. The building, a blending of Gothic, Renaissance and Tudor styles executed in stone, is the church's fourth home. The previous three burned down. The third sanctuary burned on December 31, 1925. Today's church is a fascinating union of several architectural forms that bear notice. Also, take a look at the steeple and notice the weathervane atop the steeple. It's a rooster.

A fascinating house of worship — or philosophy — is not far from Wilmington. The North Carolina Association of Buddhists has a temple in Bolivia, Brunswick County. It repre-

INSIDERS' TIP

Wilmington's Baha'i Center, at 15 N. Eighth Street, 762-7074, holds frequent workshops to contribute to community understanding.

sents an important addition to a listing of the region's religious and philosophical centers. The monastery has been building a Thai temple for nearly a decade and has relied on community donations to complete the work. It is an unusual sight in the Brunswick countryside to see this Far East temple rise from the coastal forests.

Naturally, these are just a few examples of the interesting historical and architectural features of some of Wilmington's houses of worship, but the essence of all of them is in the diverse faiths practiced within them.

As would be expected in a Southern city, Wilmington's dominant religious affiliation is Baptist, and nearly a quarter of the city's churches house some form of Baptist faith. Since the Baptists are a multifaceted denomination unto themselves, there are ample representations of Southern Baptist, Free Will, Missionary, Grace and Independent congregations.

The second-largest denomination is Presbyterian with 14 churches in New Hanover County; the United Methodists follow closely with 13 churches.

Other religions practiced in the Wilmington area include Judaism, African Methodist Episcopal, AME Zion, Mormon, Greek Orthodox, Russian Orthodox, Nation of Islam, Charismatic, Unity, Christian Science, Quaker, Moravian, Nondenominational, Lutheran, Unitarian, Baha'i, Eckankar, Episcopal, Roman Catholic, Unity, Metropolitan and Wesleyan.

As must be apparent from this partial listing, Wilmington's port city orientation allows for considerably more religious diversity than many Southern cities. You will find extremely conservative, middle-of-the-road and very liberal doctrines practiced within the various Wilmington houses of worship. Yet, there is a noticeably high level of tolerance of one religion for the other, and nothing in the area's history suggests so much as a twinge of discomfort with one denomination for another. There seems to be an understanding that an individual's particular religious inclinations are not only respected, but also encouraged.

The worshipping visitor can expect to be welcomed into churches throughout the area, and the would-be resident is virtually guaranteed a suitable spiritual home among the choices.

If you want to go to church or temple when you're on vacation, take note of this simple advice: People "dress" for Sunday worship in most cases, although there are certainly exceptions and you can check this out by calling ahead.

However, as one parishioner from St. James Episcopal remarked: "Oh, we don't mind how they're dressed as long as they come. In fact, when we see them in their vacation clothes, that lets us know they're from out of town and it gives us a chance to welcome them."

That sentiment is echoed in other congregations as well.

New residents with chosen denominations and affiliations must simply consult the phone book or *The Wilmington Star News* on a Saturday to select a church, temple, meeting house or zendo. The larger churches list service times and regular programs in the Yellow Pages.

The history of churches in the Cape Fear area is more than enough to fill several books. If you want to know more, drop by the North Carolina Room at the New Hanover County Public Library in downtown Wilmington.

Index of Advertisers

A & G Sportswear 150
Absolute Storm and Security 355
Alligator Pie 147
Alpha Mortgage X
Art Accents 210
Audubon Village 145
Bachman Realty 13
Basket Case 142
Battleship North Carolina 173
Big Daddy's 101
Blockade Runner .... Inside Back Cover
Brass Lantern 149
Break Time Billiards 119
Brierwood Realty 335
Brunswick Community College 403
Cape Fear Academy 387
Cape Fear Antique Center 155
Cape Fear Coffee & Tea Company 109
Cape Fear Community College 401
Cape Fear Coast Convention and Visitors'
    Bureau .... color insert
Carolina Beach/Kure Beach Chamber of
    Commerce 190
Carolina Temple Apartments 45
Catherine's Inn 49
Catherine Kennedy Home 366
Cellular One 363
Chamber Music Society of Wilmington 209
Chandler's Wharf Inn 51
Chase Mortgage 349
Children's House 391
Clockwise Clocks 137
Coast Line Inn 15
Coastal Condo-Let 71
Coldwell Banker Southport-Oak Island
    Realty 67
Columbia Cape Fear Memorial Hospital 377
Creative World 393
Cypress Island .... color insert
Curtis Kreuger, Photographer 217
Davies Realty 64
Down Island Traders 151
Easy Living 144
Eclectic Menage 153
Exercise Today 18
Fidler's Gallery 139
First Citizens Bank .... color insert
Forum 116
Fran Brittain Realty 36
Gardenia's 97
Golden Gallery 139
Great Harvest Bread Company 20
Greystone Inn 47
Hampton Inn Landfall Park 40
Harbour Town Associates 69, 357
Hiro Japanese Steak & Seafood 89
Hope United Methodist Church 432
Independence Mall .... color insert
Inn at St. Thomas Court 42
Island Appliance 27
Island Passage 142
James E. Moore Insurance ...... color insert
JJR, Builders (Jorge A. Vasquez, Builder)16
J. S. Anderson 150
Jimmy's Deli 19
Jubilee Amusement Park 177, 235
Just Looking 24
K 38 Baja Grill 21

K-O Realty 351
Katy's Great Eats 17
Landfall .... Inside Front Cover
Landfall Business Center Executive Suites.22
Learning Express 223
Leather Emporium .... color insert
Live Oaks Bed & Breakfast 48
Lumina Station 132
Makado Gallery 139
Malley's 86
Marina's Edge 95
Martha's Vineyard 135
McAllister & Solomon 146
McKenzie, Barbara 215
Moore Antiques 155
Murray Transfer 14
Murrow Furniture .... color insert, 159
New Hanover Regional Medical Center ......
.... color insert
New Hanover Commission for Women..407
Ocean 1 Realty 75
Oceanic Restaurant .... color insert
Old Wilmington Antiques 155
Oriental Palace 91
Outer Banks Hammocks 154
Peggy Brummitt Realty, Inc. 361
Perry's Emporium 152
Pilot House/Elijah's .... color insert
Pirate Fishing & Cruises 280
Pleasure Island Merchant's Association 10
Kure Beach Chamber of Commerce 190
Rogers Bay Family Campway 81
Romanelli's Restaurant .... color insert
Rucker Johns 167
Scott & Springfellow, Inc. 337
South Brunswick Islands Chamber of
    Commerce 33

Southern Exposure Photography Group.211
Stonebridge Realty .... color insert
Sunset Properties 74
Swensen's 92
Szechuan 132/130 93
Southport-Oak Island Chamber of
    Commerce 29
Subway 87
Teague's Gifts & Accessories 136
Temptations 141
Texas Steakhouse & Saloon 99
Theodosia's Bed & Breakfast 57
Tom's Drug Co. 136
Tomatoz 84
Townhouse Art & Frames 143
Tryon Palace 179
University of North Carolina Wilmington..398
University of North Carolina Wilmington-
    Campus Activities 202
Victoria's Interiors 20
WAAV Radio 25, 73, 127, 183, 359
Waterways Sailing School 254
Welcome Service of Wilmington 356
Western Sizzlin 94
Whitebridge .... color insert
Wilmington Academy of Music 213
Wilmington Christian Academy 389
Wilmington Concert Association 207
Wilmington Star News 162
Wilmington Symphony 205
Windrose 148
Winds Clarion 61
Worth House, The 46
Wrigley's Clocks 139
YMCA 302

Index

2001 248
219 South 5th 43
3 On 3 Memorial Basketball Tournament 304
3D Golf Vacations 341

A

A & A Rental Inc. 3
A & G Sportswear 141
A Center for Counseling 382
A Day at the Docks 192
A Proper Garden 136, 153
A-Plus 5
A-Plus Taxi Service 4
About Time Antiques 160
Accommodations 41
Acme Art 204
Ad Hoc Theatre Company 213
Adam and Hilliard Realty 353
Adult Day Care 372
Adventure World 391
Aerobics Hotline 308
Aerobics with Freddie J. King 310
Aeronautics 172, 311
Affordable Affluence Inc. 3
After Dark Limousine Service 3
Air Charters, Rentals, Leasing 6
Air Tours 172
Air Wilmington 172, 311
Airlie Gardens 164, 172
Airlie Moon 151
Airports 4
Alabama Theatre 246, 248
Alan Holden Realty 362
Alcoholics Anonymous 382
Alligator Adventure 246
Alligator Pie 136, 153
Alpha Counseling and Development Center 382
Alzheimer's and Neurological Support Groups 378
American Cancer Society Tournament 341
American Lung Association 320
American Lung Association Golf Privilege Card 341
American Pie 140, 206
American Red Cross,Cape Fear Chapter 410
Anasazi 138
Angel's Antiques and Auctions 160
Annual Events 191
Antique Emporium 160
Antique Mall, The 161
Antique Shopping 160
Antiques of Old Wilmington 160
Apple Annie's Bake Shop 241
Aquatic Safaris & Divers Emporium 264
Arbor Creek 351
Area Overviews 11
Ari Rang House 85
Art Accents 206
Art in the Park 194
Arts 203
Arts Council of the Lower Cape Fear
      19, 203, 204, 414
Ashton Farm Summer Day Camp 237
Assembly Building 163, 185

Assisted Care 380
Association of Carolina Shag Clubs 248
Athletic Zone 233, 304, 314, 316, 325
Atlantic Coast Line Railroad 171
Atlantic Marine 294
Atlantic Southeast Airlines 5
Atlantic Towers 54
Atlantic Vacations Resorts and Real Estate 73
Attic, The 247
Attractions 163
Audubon Village 144
Auld Stokley Antiques 161
AuPair in America 397
Aussie Island Surf Shop 150, 267, 306
Autumn Care of Shallotte 371
Autumn with Topsail Beach Arts & Entertainment
      Festival 196
Axis 118, 130
Azalea Coast Chorus of Sweet Adelines 208
Azalea Coast Smockers Guild 217
Azalea Festival 19
Azalea Festival Show 205
Azalea Plaza 143
Azalea Sale 193

B

B. Dalton Bookseller 141
Babbage's Software 234
Bachman Realty 353
Back Alley Lounge, The 126
Back Deck Grill 243
Back Porch Ice Cream Shoppe 242
Bald Head Creek 258
Bald Head Island 31, 351
Bald Head Island Annual Maritime Classic Road
      Race 321
Bald Head Island Club 104, 333
Bald Head Island Conservancy 31
Bald Head Island Ferry 8
Bald Head Island Fishing Rodeo 282
Bald Head Island Historic Tour and Lunch 179
Bald Head Island Information Center 72
Bald Head Island Marina 282, 297
Bald Head Island Real Estate 361
Baldwin-Copel andStudio of Dance 222
Ballet School of Wilmington 222
Barbary Coast 119
Barbee Branch Library 234
Barefoot Landing 246
Barefoot Princess Riverboat 246
Bark in the Park 197
Barnacle Bill's Fishing Pier 286
Barnes & Noble Booksellers 130, 146
Baseball and Little League 303
Basin, The 268
Basket Case, The 135
Baskin-Robbins 31 Flavors Ice Cream and Yogurt
      Store 241
Battleship North Carolina 164
Battleship North Carolina Memorial Day
      Observance 194
Battleship River Taxi 164, 166

Beach Access 269
Beach Club & Cafe 53
Beach Fun Rentals 260, 267, 282
Beach Harbour Resort 54
Beach Music Festival 195
Beach Properties of Topsail Island Inc. 364
Beaches 96
Beach's Best Pizzeria 113
Beacon House Inn Bed and Breakfast 54
Bear Mountain 135
Beau Rivage Plantation Golf & Country Club 333
Beaufort 250
Beaufort Grocery Co. 252
Beaufort Restoration Grounds 251
Bed & Breakfast at Mallard Bay 62
Belk-Beery Department Store 141, 149
Bellamy Mansion 165
Belvedere Plantation Golf & Country Club 337
Bendigo 163
Bert's Surf Shop 267
Bessie's 119
Better Business Bureau 430
Betty's Smokehouse Restaurant 113
Beverage Boutique 134
Bicycle Works 307
Big Daddy's Seafood Restaurant 102
Big Dawg Productions 213
Big Lake 265
Bike Paths 8
Bill Curry's Cycling and Fitness 307
Billiards 117
Bird Island 34
Birthday Parties 232
Black River 258
Blockade Runner Resort 176, 188
Blockade Runner Resort Hotel 51
Blue Heron Bar & Grill 335
Blue Point Marina 288
Blue Water Point Marina 288
Blue Water Point Marina Resort 298
Blue Yonder Flying Machines 311
Blues Society of the Lower Cape Fear 208
Bluff Island 31
Board of Education 237
Boat House Gifts 158
Boat Ramps 283
Boat Registration 257
Boater's World Discount Marine Center 262
Boathouse Marina 295
Boating 256
Boating laws 276
Bocci 85
Body Dimensions 309
Bogey's 127
Bogue Banks 250
Books-A-Million 143, 234
Boomer's Bikes & More 307
Bottom Time 264
Bowler's Choice 308
Bowling 117, 308
Boxing 308
Boxing & Fitness Center 233, 308
Boy Scouts of America, Cape Fear Council 413
Bradley Creek Boatominium 295
Bramble, Mary Ellen CMT 383
Branchwood Village 363
Brass Lantern, The 136
Brass Pelican, The 128
Breakfast Creek Bed & Breakfast 59
Breaktime Sports Bar, Billiards & Grill 85, 119
Breezeway Restaurant 114
Brick Landing Plantation 73, 335
Brick Yard 119
Bridge Tender Marina 282

Bridge Tender Marina and Restaurant 96, 295
Brierwood Golf Club 324, 335
Brigade Boys and Girls Club 237
Brigade Boys Club 413
Brightmore of Wilmington 368
Bristol Books 153
Broadway At The Beach 248
Brookgreen Gardens 246
Brown Real Estate 75, 365
Brunswick 11
Brunswick Beacon, The 420
Brunswick Community College 403
Brunswick County Airport 5
Brunswick County Bowling Center 308
Brunswick County Department of Older Adults 415
Brunswick County Library 234
Brunswick County Literacy Council Inc. 410
Brunswick County Parks and Recreation 304,
    309, 311, 325, 326, 341
Brunswick County School System 387, 412
Brunswick Family Assistance Agency 410
Brunswick Learning Center 387
Brunswick School of Dance 224
Brunswick Shores Children's Center 378
Brunswick Town 163
Brunswickland Realty 73
Bryant Real Estate 69
Bryson, Elizabeth LMT 383
Bud Light Chili Cookoff 198
Buddy's Crab & Oyster Bar 125
Bullard Realty 71, 359
Burgwin-Wright House 165
Bus Lines 3
Buses 3
Bushin-Kai Karate 318
Butterflies Castle Antiques 160
By-The-River Biathlon 306

C

Cabana De Mar Motel 54
Caffe Phoenix 85, 120
Calabash 34, 352
Calabash Golf Links 336
Calabash Nautical Gifts 158
Calabash Seafood Hut 112
Calder Court 164
Calhoun's Celtic Imports 138
Camellia Cottage 43
Camelot Campground 78
Cameron's Antiques & Collectibles 161
Camp Seaweed 238
Camp Tuscarora 238
Camping 77
Canady's Marina 294
Canady's Sports Center 77, 147, 257, 313
Candles Etc. 136
Candy Barrel 134, 241
Candy Express 241
Canoeing 258
CanSurvive 376
Canterbury Stable 311
Cape Fear Academy 315, 388
Cape Fear Academy Lacrosse Camp 315
Cape Fear Antiques Center 161
Cape Fear Area United Way 410
Cape Fear Astronomical Club 235
Cape Fear Boat Rentals 262
Cape Fear Camera Club 219
Cape Fear Chordsmen 208
Cape Fear Christmas House 137
Cape Fear Coast Convention & Visitors Bureau
    1, 164, 191, 228, 261, 426
Cape Fear Coast Visitor Information Bureau 279

Cape Fear Coffee & Tea 108
Cape Fear Community College 401
Cape Fear Contra Dancers 117
Cape Fear Council of Governments, Department of Aging 368
Cape Fear Cyclists Club 306
Cape Fear Filmmakers Accord 122
Cape Fear Filmmakers Accord 204, 219
Cape Fear Filmmakers Accord Haunted House 229
Cape Fear Flyers 320
Cape Fear Literacy Council 410
Cape Fear Model Railroad Club 171, 226
Cape Fear Museum 163, 165, 232, 237
Cape Fear Optimist Club 303
Cape Fear Outfitters 77, 151, 258, 259
Cape Fear River 11, 258
Cape Fear River Rowing Club 258
Cape Fear River Watch 299
Cape Fear Roller Hockey League 314
Cape Fear Rugby Club 320
Cape Fear Run 9, 305
Cape Fear Sevens Rugby Tournament 320
Cape Fear Shakespeare 215
Cape Fear Ski & Outing Club 303
Cape Fear Symphony Orchestra 210
Cape Fear Theatre Ballet 216
Cape Fear Youth Soccer Association 238, 322
Cape Resort and Golf Club, The 368
Cape, The 349
Capeside Village 368
Capt. Jim's Marina 184, 288
Capt. Maffitt Sightseeing Cruise 117, 166
Capt. Willie's Restaurant 112
Captain Dick's Marina 247
Capt'n Bill's Backyard Grill 325
Capt'n Pete's Seafood Market 288
Car Rentals 3
Cardinal Lanes 308
Carmike 7 Theaters 130
Carolco Pictures 122
Carolina Beach 26, 350
Carolina Beach Chamber of Commerce 34
Carolina Beach Municipal Docks 287
Carolina Beach Municipal Marina 296
Carolina Beach New Year's Eve Countdown Party 201
Carolina Beach Pier 284
Carolina Beach Realty 71
Carolina Beach State Park 79, 228, 283, 327
Carolina Beach State Park Marina 297
Carolina Beach Yacht Basin 282
Carolina Beach Family Campground 78
Carolina Beach Parks and Recreation 323
Carolina Heights 347
Carolina Inlet Marina 296
Carolina Kite Club 235, 317
Carolina Lake Park 328
Carolina Opry 247
Carolina Palace Theater 248
Carolina Place 22, 347
Carolina Preschool 391
Carolina Shores 352
Carolina Shores Golf & Country Club 336
Carolina Sport Fishing Charters 288
Carolina Temple Apartments 52
Carolina Trailways 3
Carolina Yacht Club 262
Carolina Yacht Yard 294
Carolina's Food & Drink 96
Carolina's PGA Seniors Pro-Am Golf Tournament 335
Carson Cards and Gifts 158
Cassatt, Mary 169
Castle Hayne Saddle Shop 312

Castle Stables 311
Caswell Beach 32, 352
Catherine Kennedy Home 369
Catherine's Inn 43
Cathy Medlin Real Estate 364
Causeway Cafe 240
CD Alley 138
Celebrate Wilmington! 197, 204
Center for Marine Science Research 400, 404
Center for Successful Aging 376
Century 21 Castle Realty 360
Century 21 Dorothy Essey and Associates Inc. 361
Century 21 Sunset Realty 363
Century 21, Sweyer & Associates 353
Century 21-Brock Mills 353
Cercle Theatre 248
Chadsworth Columns 137
Chadwick House 251
Chain Reaction Bicycling Center 307
Challenger, The 419
Chamber Music Society of Wilmington 117, 210
Chamber of Commerce 1
Champion Karate Center 319
Chandler's Wharf 135, 166
Chandler's Wharf Inn 43
Charles Tilghman Junior Tournament 249
Chart House, The 105
Charter Restaurant 250
Cheerwine College Tournament 335
Chestnut Street United Presbyterian Church 166
Child Advocacy Commission 390, 413
Child Care 385, 390
Child Development Center 390
Children's House Academy 392
Chiropractors 382
Chris's Restaurant 86
Christie's Gallery 206
Christmas 229
Christmas By-The-Sea Parade 200
"Christmas for Kids & Others" Concert 229
Christmas Lights at Calder Court 229
Chronicles of the Cape Fear River 11
Chuck E Cheese's Pizza 240
Cinema 4 130
Cinema 6 129
Cinematique of Wilmington 129
City Hall 170
City of Wilmington Summer Traditions Camp 239
City of Wilmington Public Swimming Pools 268
City Pier 285
City Transportation Planning Department 9
City Zoo, The 135
Clark-Teachey Realtors 354
Classy Bears Learning Center 392
Clawson's 1905 Restaurant 252
Clockwise Clocks 153
Club Astor 126
Coast Line Convention Center 44
Coast Line Inn 44
Coastal Cancer Center 376
Coastal Carolina Bike Trek 305
Coastal Condo-Let 71
Coastal Development and Realty 362
Coastal Diabetes Center 376
Coastal Fitness 310, 319
Coastal Golf Center and Carolina Custom Discount Golf 338
Coastal Golfaway 341
Coastal Heart Center 376
Coastal Horizons Center 410
Coastal Plantation, A Jensen's Residential Community 369
Coastal Rehabilitation Hospital 376
Coastal Sports Cards & Apparel 227

Cobb's Corner Lounge 126
Cockle Shell, The 158
Coldwell Banker Baker Properties 354
Coldwell Banker Sea Coast Realty 354, 361
Coldwell Banker Southport-Oak Island Realty 72
Coldwell Banker United Realty Group 360
College Road Cinemas 129
Colleges 399
Columbia Brunswick Hospital 377
Columbia Cape Fear Memorial Hospital 375, 410
Comedy Club, The 120
Comedy Zone 52, 125
Comfort Inn Wilmington 44
Commerce and Industry 425
Committee of 100 429
Community Arts Center 203, 204, 222
Community Boys' Club 413
Compass Rose Import Company 138
Comprehensive Home Health Care 380
Compton's on the Riverwalk 50
Connoisseurs' Wine & Art Auction 192
Cooke Realtors 363
Cooke's Inn Motel 59
Cool World Family Fun Center 225
Cornelia Nixon Davis Health Care Center 371
Cottage, The 102
Cotton Exchange 134, 431
Cottonpatch Farms 312
Country Vogue 144
Cove at Fort Fisher State Historic Site 328
Cove Surf Shop 267
Crabby Oddwaters Restaurant and Bar 110
Crafts 217
Creative World 392
Creek,The 127
Crescent Moon Inn 59
Crest Fitness Center 309
Crisis Line 410
Crook's By the River 86, 120
Crystal Pier 284
Cucalorus Film Festival 194
Curran House 44
Cypress Island 349, 354

D

Dairy Queen 242
Dallas Harris Real Estate Construction 354
Dance 216
Danceworks Studio for the Performing Arts 222
DARE 14
David Walker Day Festival and Concert 197
Davies Realty 71, 360
Davis Center 222
Daytrips 245
Deborah Jamieson and Associates Showroom/
        Gallery/In 206
Deck Family Entertainment Center 180, 268
Del's Restaurant 105
deRosset Committee 414
Dial-A-Sailor 19
Digh's Country Sports Gallery 286, 317
Dive Shops 264
Division of Marine Fisheries 405
Dixie Stampede 248
Dock House 251
Dockside Marina 295
Dockside Watersports 256, 257, 258, 262, 269
Docksider Gifts & Shells 160
Docksider Inn-Oceanfront 55
Doctor's Immediate Care 380
Doctor's Urgent Care Centre 380
Domestic Violence Shelter and Services Inc. 411
Down Island Traders 137

Downtown Area Revitalization Effort (DARE) 414
Doxey's Market & Cafe 97, 149, 326
Dragon Garden Chinese Cuisine 87
Dram Tree Park 283
Driftwood Motel 58
Driftwood Shell Shop 157
Driving Ranges 338
Duffer's Pub & Deli 110
Dunlea Realty 354
DuPont World Amateur Handicap
        Championship 249

E

E. F. Middleton Park 328
Early Childhood Learning Center 392
East Coast Discount Dive Center 265
East Coast Got-Em-On King Mackerel Classic 282
Easter Egg Hunt 232
Eastern Surfing Association 266
Easy Living 151
Easy Way Transport Service 4
Echo Farms 349
Echo Farms Golf & Country Club 332
Eckerd Drugs 141
Ecko Furniture 146
Eclectic Menage 140
Eddie Miles Theater 248
Eddie Romanelli's 87
Effective Schools Program 385
El Vaquero 240
Eldercare Convalescent Service 380
Elderhaus Inc. 372, 415
Elijah's 88
Elizabeth's Pizza 113, 240
Ella's of Calabash 112
Embellishments 153
Empie Park 326
Enchanted Toy Shop 230
Encore Magazine 421
Energizer Senior Tour Championship 249
Enterprise Rentals 3
Entropy Rentals & Charters 257, 264
Etrusca Ristorante 97
EUE/Screen Gems Studios 122
Ev-Henwood Preserve 329
Express Care 380

F

Fall Festival 197
Fall Native American Pow-wow 199
Family Fest 197
Family Kingdom Amusement Park 246
Family Services of the Lower Cape Fear 413
Fanboy Comics & Cards 225
Fantasy Harbour-Waccamaw 248
Far Side, The 120
Farms 228
Federal Point 178
Ferry Services 6
Festival By the Sea 198
Festival of Trees 199
Fidler's Gallery and Framing 206
Figure Eight Island 26, 349
Figure Eight Island Vacation Rentals 69
Figure Eight Realty 69, 354
Film 219
Finkelstein's Jewelry and Music Company 140
Finklestein's Music 223
First Baptist Church 166
First Presbyterian Church 167
Fisherman's Wife, The 150
Fishing 281

Fishing Licenses 281
Fishing Reports 284
Fishing Tournaments 282
Fit For Fun 233
Fitness Centers 308
Flo-Jo 263
Flora, Deborah CMT 382
Fly Fishing 286
Flying 310
Fontana Caffe 108
Football 311
Forest Hills 22, 348
Forever Fit Fitness Center 310, 319
Formal Limousine Service 3
Fort Caswell 180
Fort Fisher 26, 28, 163
Fort Fisher State Historic Site 178
Fort Fisher State Recreation Area 227, 319
Fort Fisher-Southport Ferry 178
Fort Johnson 181
Fourth of July Festival 195
Fourth of July Fireworks 195
Fox Fire Farm 311
Fran Brittain Realty 69
Franklin Square Gallery 182, 206
Freddie's Restaurant 102
Friedman Chiropractic 382
Friends of David Walker 215
Frisbee 324
Front Street Brewery 88
Front Street Grill 252
Front Street Inn 45
Fudge Company 242
Furniture Patch of Calabash 158

G

G. Flowers Realty 354
Galleries 206
Game Giant, The 225
Game Plan Video Game Exchange 225
Garden Hotline 174
Gardenias 98
Gardner Realty 71, 360
Gatlin Brothers Theatre 248
Gauntlet Golf Club, The 333
Gay Rights of Wilmington (GROW) 411
General Assembly 108
General Longstreet's Headquarters 119
Getting Around 1
Girl Scout Council of Coastal Carolina 413
Girls Inc. of Wilmington 413
Girls Incorporated Day Camp 237
Gold Rose Apparel, The 157
Golden Gallery 206
Golder Realty 357
Goldings Hobbies 226
Gold's Gym Fitness & Aerobics 308
Golf 331
Golf Bag, The 340
Golf, Myrtle Beach 249
Golf Tech 339
Golf Vacation Planner 249
Good Shepherd House 411
Goody Goody Omelet House 88
Goose Creek Bed & Breakfast 60
Granny's Day Care Center 392
Gray Gull Motel 59
Graystone Inn 45
Great Harvest Bread Company 147
Greater Topsail Area Chamber of Commerce 164
Greater Wilmington Antique Show and Sale 191
Greater Wilmington Chamber of Commerce 34
Greater Wilmington Tennis Association 323

Greek Festival 196
Green Swamp Game Land 312
Greenfield Lake 320
Greenfield Lake and Gardens 172, 227
Greenfield Park 326
Gregory School of Science, Mathematics and
    Technology 386
Greyhound 3
Griffith Gallery 206
Grouper Nancy'sFine Dining & Spirits 88
Grove, The 182
Gulfstream Realty 354

H

Halloween 229
Halloween Festival 199
Halloween History-Mystery Tour 198
Halloween Moonlight 5K Run 321
Hampstead Chamber of Commerce 34
Hampstead King Mackerel Tournament 282
Hampstead Village Pharmacy 282, 313
Handscapes Gallery 251
Hanover Center 141
Hanover Fishing Charter 263, 288
Hanover Medical Specialists 380
Hanover Stables 312
Hanover Urological Associates 380
Harbor Lite Bar & Grill 127
Harbor Village Marina 282
Harborside Seafood Restaurant and Grille 105, 128
Harbour Point and Pleasure Island Marina &
    Resort 296, 360
Harbour Town Associates Real Estate 355
Harbour Village Marina 293
Harbourside Lounge 58
Hard Rock Cafe 248
Haren 326
Harley-Davidson Charity Halloween Run 199
Harmony Belles 210
Harpoon Willie's Dock 251
Harris Teeter 141
Harvest Moon 88
Head Boats and Charters 287
Headstart Program of New Hanover County 393
Healthcare 375
Henrietta II 117, 168
Herring's Tackle 282
Herring's Tackle & Beach Shop 260
Hidden Beneath the Waves 178
Higher Educationand Research 399
Hilda Godwin's 140
Hillhaven Rehabilitation and Convalescent
    Center 371
Hilton, The 297
Hines Senior Center 372
Hiro Japanese Steak and Seafood House 89
Historic District Commission 14
Historic Downtown Wilmington Antique Dealers
    Association 160
Historic Preservation 414
Historic Wilmington Foundation 414
HobbyTown USA 149
Hobie Fleet 101 261
Hoge-Wood House Bed and Breakfast 46
Hoggard Lacrosse Club 315
Holden Beach 32, 352
Holden Beach Driving Range 339
Holden Beach Marina 288, 298
Holden Beach Pier 285
Holden Beach Pier Family Campground 80
Holden Beach Surf & Scuba 265, 267
Holden Beach True Value 282, 313
Holden Brothers Farm Market 228

Holden Realty 73
Holiday Flotilla 260
Holiday Inn 46
Holiday Inn SunSpree Resort Wrightsville Beach 52
Holland's Shelter Creek Campground and
    Restaurant 283
Holland's Shelter Creek Fish Camp 258, 282, 313
Holland'sShelter Creek Restaurant 114
Hollingsworth American Country 161
Holly Festival 199
Holly Shelter Game Land 312
Home Child Care 397
Home Healthcare 380
Home Schooling 390
Hook a Kid On Golf 341
Hope Harbor Home 411
Horse-drawn Carriage Tour 168
Horseback Riding 311
Hospice of the Lower Cape Fear 411
Hospitals 375
Hot Wax Surf Shop 267
Hotel Tarrymore 23
How Does Your Garden Grow? Show 191
Howard Johnson Plaza Hotel and Conference
    Center 46
Howard, Perry and Walston Better Homes and
    Gardens 69
Howard, Perry and Walston Realty Inc./Better
    Homes 355
Hugh MacRae Park 327
Hughes Marina 298
Hugh's Marina 282
Hungate's Arts-Crafts & Hobbies 226
Hunting 312
Hunting Licenses 313
Hurricane Fleet 117, 184, 247, 288
Hurricane Updates 41

I

Ice House, The 120
IMAX Discovery Theater, 248
Immediate Care Centers 374, 378
Incredible Pizza 113
Independence Mall 22, 141
Independence Mall Cinemas 129
India Mahal 89
Indian Trail Tree 182
Indigo Plantation 351
Inland Greens 332
Inlet Watch Yacht Club 296
Inn at St. Thomas Court, The 46
Instructor Certification Program of the
    Internation 315
Intracoastal Angler 287
Intracoastal Realty Corporation 69, 355
Island Appliance 157
Island Chandler Delicatessen 105
Island Gazette, The 420
Island Motel 60
Island of Lights Festival 200
Island Passage 138, 154, 258
Island Realty Vacations 73
Island Resort 58
Island Super Store 160
Island Tackle & Gifts 282, 313
Island Tackle & Hardware 157
Island Walking Club 321
ISO Aero 172
ISO Aero Service Inc. of Wilmington 311

J

J & C Sportscards & Collectibles 226

J. Arthur DosherMemorial Hospital 378
J. Council's 103
J.S. Anderson 150
J/G's Country Bar-B-Que 110
Jackson Pool 268
Jacobi Warehouse 138
Jake's Downtown 120
Java Lane 108
JCPenney 141
Jean Brown Real Estate 365
Jeanette Golder Realty 357
Jimmy's Deli New York Style Pizzeria 90
Joe Eakes Park 328
Johnnie Mercer's Pier 284
Johnson Marina 294
Johnson Marine Services 257
Jolly Roger Motel 62
Jolly Roger Pier 286
Jones' Seafood House 106
Jones, Teresa CMP 383
Jordan Discovery Gallery 22, 165
Jubilee Amusement Park 177
Jubilee Park 234
Julia, The 149
Julie's Bike Rentals 307
Julie's Rentals 260, 315
Jungle Rapids Family Fun Park 174, 232, 234
Jung's Tae Kwon Do Academy 319

K

K-O Realty 357
Katy's Great Eats 90, 121, 240
Kayaking 258
Kelly Ophthalmology 380
Kelly's Coffee Pub 109
Keziah Memorial Park 182
Kiddy Korner Kinder Kamp 238
Kids' Gym, The 233, 237
Kids' Night Out 234
Kidstuff 221
Kindermusik 223
King, Freddie J. 321
King Neptune 98
Kingoff's Jewelers 140
King's Motel 54
Kitchen Shoppe 134
Kite Flying 316
Kitty Hawk Air Services Inc 172
Kiwanis Loggerhead Golf Tournament 338, 341
Kmart 77, 145, 282, 313
Kona's Coffee Beanery 109
Kool Aid Golf Tournament 338, 341
Krazy Pizza & Subs 113
Kure Beach 26, 28
Kure Beach Pier 285
Kwanzaa 230

L

L Bookworm 236
Labor Day Arts & Crafts Beach Fest 196
Lacrosse 315
Laff Trax 52, 125
Lake Shore Commons 370
Lake Waccamaw State Park 81
Lakeside Alternative School 386
Landfall 23, 332, 348
Landfall Associates 357
Landfall Executive Suites 431
Landfall Shopping Center 149
Laney Real Estate 357
Langas Chiropractic 382
LaQue Center for Corrosion Technology Inc. 405

Largest Living Christmas Tree 201
Larry's Calabash Seafood Barn 112
LC's Taxi Service 4
Learning Express 236
Learning Express, The 148
Lebanon Chapel 172
Legends in Concert 248
Legion Stadium 327
Lejeune Grand Prix Series 321, 324
Leland District Park 328
Leland Library 234
Lenox China 246
Leprechaun Run 320
Lett's Taxi Service 3
Lewis Realty 75
Lewis Strawberry Nursery 228
Liberty Commons 370
Lighthouse Realty 71, 360
Limelight, The 121
Limousines 3
Linda's 157
Little Professor Book Center 158
Live Oaks Bed & Breakfast 47, 59
Living Christmas Tree 164
Lo-Di Farms 312
Local Call Surf Shop 267
Lockwood District Park 328
Lockwood Golf Links 334
Lois Jane's Riverview Inn 56
Long Bay Lady Anglers King Mackerel
    Tournament 282
Long Beach 32, 352
Long Beach Family Campground 80
Long Beach Horse-A-Thon 192
Long Beach Pier 285
Long Island Pizza 114
Lower Cape Fear Historical Society 414
Lower Cape Fear Hospice 380
Lower Cape Fear Dermatology Clinic 380
Lowe's 145
Lox Stock & Bagels 90
Lucky Fisherman 106
Lula's 121
Lumina 23
Lumina Daze 196
Lumina Station 153
Lynne's Hallmark Shop & Treasure Room 158

M

Maffitt, Capt. John Newland 166
Magic Mountain Water Slide 234
Makado Gallery 208
Malley's Restaurant & Pub 103
Manhattan Bagel 98
Mansion District 22, 347
MAP 136
Margaret Rudd & Associates Inc., Realtors 362
Marinas and the Intracoastal Waterway 293
Marina's Edge 104
Marine Corps Base 324
Marine Corps Base Camp Lejeune 268
Marine Expo 199
Mariner Health Care Center 371
Maritime Museum 182
Mark A. Sloan Memorial Cancer Benefit Golf
    Tournament 249
Marker Fifty-Five 363
Market Gourmet Gift Shop 159
Market Street 21
Marksmanship and Riflery 317
Marsh Creek 351
Marsh Harbor Golf Links 336
Marsh Harbour Marina 299

Martha's Vineyard 144
Martial Arts 318
Martial Arts Center 319
Martin Luther King Day March and
    Commemoration 191
Martin Luther King Jr. Center 222, 234
Masonboro Boatyard and Marina 295
Masonboro Island 26, 78, 186, 404
Mason's Marina 294
Massage Therapy 382
McAllister & Solomon Books 146
McClure Realty Inc. 74
McMillan Real Estate 74
MEDAC Convenient Medical Care 380
MEDAC II Convenient Medical Care 380
Media 419
Medical Mall 376
Medieval Festival 194
Medieval Times Dinner & Tournament 248
Medlin Real Estate 75, 364
Memorial Day Observance 194, 195
Memory Lane Comics 226
Mermaid, The 128
Metaphysic Expo 191
Mickey Ratz 121
Middle Island 31
Mike Chappell Park 328
Miller-Motte Business College 402
Miss Patti's Porch 158
Mobile Home Store & Hardware 313
Mole, Sheila CMT 383
Morehead City 250
Morse Cemetery 163
Motherwell 224
Motorboat Rentals 257
Movie Theaters 129
Mr. P.'s Bistro 106
MS Walk 321
Ms. Muffet's Yogurt Shop 242
Mt. Olive College, Wilmington Center 402
Murphy Pool 268
Murrow Furniture Galleries 146
Museum of Coastal Carolina 184
Museum of the Lower Cape Fear 22
Museums 204
Music 208
Music Loft, The 223
Myrtle Beach 245
Myrtle Beach Area Chamber of Commerce 34, 245
Myrtle Beach Factory Stores 246
Myrtle Beach Golf Holiday 249
Myrtle Beach Grand Prix 246
Myrtle Beach Pavilion Amusement Park 246
Myrtle Beach Speedway 246
Myrtle Grove Optimist Club 304
Myrtle Waves Water Park 246

N

N.C. Department of Motor Vehicles License Plates
    Office 257
N.C. Wildlife Resources Commission Boat
    Registration 257
Nancy Rassier Real Estate 358
National Beach Sweep 196
National Guard Armory 317
National Track Program. 320
National Youth Sport Program at UNCW 238
Native American Pow-wow 199
Neighborhoods 343
Nevada Bob's 339
New Bern 252
New Elements 208
New Elements Gallery 208

New Elements Motifs 208
New Hanover County 16
New Hanover County Extension Service
     Arboretum 174, 191
New Hanover County Fair 197
New Hanover County International Airport 14
New Hanover County Public Library 131, 228
New Hanover County School System 412
New Hanover County Schools 385
New Hanover County Department of Aging 416
New Hanover County Public Library Children's
     Room 236
New Hanover Home Health 377
New Hanover Regional BirthPlace 376
New Hanover Regional Medical Center 376, 412
New Hanover Senior Center 373
New Hanover Youth Baseball 303
New Hanover-Pender Medical Society Alliance 320
New Hanover International Airport 5
New Home Marketplace 357
New River Marina 282
Newspapers 419
Nightlife 117
No-Name Island 404
North Carolina Aquarium 28
North Carolina Aquarium at Fort Fisher 178, 221
North Carolina Aquarium at Pine Knoll Shores 250
North Carolina Azalea Festival 164, 193
North Carolina Coastal Boating Guide 257
North Carolina Department of
     Transportation 9, 305
North Carolina Fourth of July Festival 195
North Carolina Jazz Festival 192, 210
North Carolina Maritime Museum 251
North Carolina National Estuarine Research
     Reserve 187, 404
North Carolina Oyster Festival 198
North Carolina Oyster Festival Road Race 321
North Carolina Poetry Society 216
North Carolina Spot Festival 196
North Carolina State Horticultural Crops
     Research 405
North Carolina Symphony 117, 210
North Carolina Wildlife Resources
     Commission 281, 282, 312
North Carolina Writers' Network 216
North Carolina Aquarium at Fort Fisher 227
North Carolina's Central Coast 249
North Island 404
North Shore Country Club 338, 341
Northrop Mall 157
Northside Medical Center 380
Northside Park 327
Northwest District Park 328
Numero Uno 113
Nursing Homes 371
Nuss Strasse Cafe 90

O

Oak Island 32, 351
Oak Island Cab 4
Oak Island Golf & Country Club 334
Oak Island Senior Center Craft Shop 158
Oak Island Shag Club 128
Oak Island Tour of Homes 200
Oak IslandSchool of Dance & Art 224
Oak Winds Marina 294
Oakdale Cemetery 168
Oaks, The 376
Oarhouse Lounge, The 128
Ocean Aire Aviation 180, 311
Ocean City Fishing Pier 286
Ocean Crest Motel 58

Ocean Crest Pier 285
Ocean Isle 352
Ocean Isle Airstrip 5
Ocean Isle Beach 32
Ocean Isle Beach Golf Course 324
Ocean Isle Beach Rentals at The Winds Clarion
     Inn 260, 262, 267, 269
Ocean Isle Beach Water Slide 185, 234
Ocean Isle Inn 60
Ocean Isle Marina 256, 257, 288, 298
Ocean Isle Pier 285
Ocean Outfitters 265
Ocean Princess Inn 55
Ocean Ray 265
Ocean Rentals 307
Ocean Terrace Restaurant 51, 99
Ocean Trail Convalescent Center 372
Oceanic Restaurant, The 98
Oceanic, The 23
Oceanside Restaurant 114
Odell Williamson Auditorium 204
Odom Company 74
Off-Roading 319
Office Depot 143
Offshore Adventures 264
Oktoberfest Family 5K Fun Run 321
Ol' Nep's Lounge 125
Old Baldy Lighthouse 179
Old Brunswick Town State Historic Site 180
Old Smithville Burial Ground 182
Old Wilmington by Candlelight 200
Old Wilmington City Market 138
Olde Point 337
Olde Wilmington Toy Company 226
Oleander Drive 163
Oleander Urgent Care 380
Onslow County Parks and Recreation 304,323, 325
Opera House Theatre 215
Organizations 204
Oriental Palace 91
Original Calabash Restaurant, The 112
Orton Plantation 164
Orton Plantation Gardens 181
Osprey Charters 288
Outer Banks Hammocks 151
Outlet Park at Waccamaw 246
Overton's Discount Boating Supplies 262
Oyster Bay 335

P

P.T.'s Grille 92
Paleo Sun Cafe 91
Palliotti's Restaurant 63
Palomino Club, The 121
Paradise Cafe 104
Paradise Inn 54
Park Avenue School 393
Parks 326
Patio Playground 307
Patio Playground, The 185
Paula's Health Hut 147
Pawn USA 282, 313
Peachtree Stables 312
Pearl Golf Links, The 336
Pediatric Unit 377
Pelican Pointe Marina 298
Pelican Square Books & Ball Cards 158
Pender Chronicle, The 420
Pender County School System 388, 412
Pender Memorial Hospital 378
Pender Post, The 420
Pennington's Marine 262
Penslow Medical Center 380

Perfect Golf Practice Facility 338
Performance Halls 204
Performance Watercraft 255
Permuda Island 404
Perry's Emporium 141
Phar-mor 145
Philomena Moultries Boutique 158
Photography 219
Physician Groups 380
Physician Referral Service 378
Pier 1 Imports 143
Piers 284
Pilot House, The 91
Pine Valley 348
Piney Woods Celebration of the Arts 414
Piney Woods Cultural Heritage Festival 204
Piney Woods Festival 196
Pink Palace of Topsail 62
Pirate Fishing & Cruise Charters 288
Pizza Bistro 113
PK's 157
Plantation Village 370
Play It Again Sports 314
Playwrights Producing Company 216
Plaza East Shopping Center 151
Pleasure Island Spring Festival 194
Pleasure Island Surf Fishing Tournament 283
Poetry Readings 130
Poor Boy Shark Tournament 282
Pop Warner Football 311
Poplar Grove Christmas Celebration 201
Poplar Grove Herb Fair 193
Poplar Grove Historic Plantation 232
Poplar Grove Plantation 176
Poplar Grove Summer Fair 195
Port Charlie's 106
Port City Basketmakers 217
Port City Java 109, 121
Port City Properties 358
Port City Slickers 324
Port City Taxi Inc. 3
Porters Neck Plantation 349, 370
Porters Neck Plantation and Country Club 332
Ports of Call 9, 305
Preface v
Prestige Limousine Service 3
Pride! Productions 216
Private Schools 388
PRN Nursing Service 380
Pro Golf Discount 339
Pro Tee Practice Range 339
Pro-Fit 308
Project Bumblebee 35
Project First Stop 413
Provenance Antiques & Interiors 161
Prudential Carolinas Realty 358
PT Connection 309
Public Schools 385, 412
Pusser's Landing at Wally's 99
Putt-Putt Golf & Games 232

Q

Quarter of Chandler's Wharf, The 136
Quarter, The 153
Quilters by the Sea 217
Quilters By the Sea Quilt Show 192

R

R. Bryan Collections 153
Rachel Carson Estaurine Research Reserve 251
Rack 'M Pub and Billiards 121
Racquetball 320

Radio Stations 423
Rainbow Bike Rentals 307
Ramada Inn Conference Center 47
Randall Library 400
Rape Crisis Center 410
Rare Cargo 138
Rassier Real Estate 358
RE/MAXExtraordinary Properties 359
Real Estate 343
Real Estate Companies 353
Rebecca's Lingerie Ltd. 144
Recreation Departments 303
Red Carpet, Dorothy Essey & Associates Inc.,
      Realty 72
Red Dinette, The 147
Redix 154
Reel Carolina Magazine 421
Reese Family Chiropractic 382
Region O Senior Games 373
Reindeer Romp 320
Research Facilities 403
Restaurants 83
Retired Senior Volunteer Program 373, 416
Retirement 367
Rigby's Restaurant and Lounge 46
Ripley's Sea Aquarium 248
River Club, The 124
River Inn, The 48
River Pilot Cafe 105
River Road Park 284
River-to-Sea Bike Route 9
Riverfest 19, 197
Riverfront Park 327
Riverhills 363
Riverside Motel 58
Riverwalk 19, 168
Robert Ruark Chili Cookoff 192
Robert Ruark Festival 199
Robert Strange Park 327
Roberto's Pizzeria & Restaurant 110, 114
Robert's Market 25
Rock-ola Cafe 240
Rocking Chair Bookstore 251
Rockits Rhythm & Sports Grille 124
Rocky Point Shooters World 318
Rogers Bay Family Campway 80
Ronnie Milsap Theatre 248
Rosehill Inn Bed and Breakfast 48
Rose's 141, 313
Rourk Branch 234
Rucker John's Restaurant and More 92
Rudd & Associates Inc., Realtors 72, 362
Rugby 320
Running and Walking 320

S

S & S Water Sports 256, 267
Safe Sitter 376, 378
Safe Vacation Guide 378
Sailing 260
Saint Mary'sRoman Catholic Church 169
Saks Fifth Avenue 246
Salon Deja Vu 136
Salty's Pier 286
Salty's Surf Shop 267
Salvation Army 412
Sam's 145
Sand Dollar Realty 363
Sandfiddler Seafood Restaurant 107
Sanitary Fish Market 250
Santa Claus at Independence Mall 229
Saratoga Restaurant 115
Scentsational 136

School for Developmentally Disabled 390
School Room 237
Schools 385
Scott's Hill Marina 294
Scruggs & Morrison Realty 72, 362
Scuba Diving and Snorkeling 263
Scuba South Diving Company 265
Scuttlebutt 251
Sea Captain Motor Lodge 58
Sea Captain Restaurant 58, 107
Sea Horse Gallery, The 157
Sea Horse Riding Stables 312
Sea Lady Charters 263
Sea Mist Camping Resort 80
Sea Trail Golf Resort & Conference Center 336
Sea Turtle Program 31
Sea Vista Motel 63
Seahawk Chess Club 236
Seapath Yacht Club 294
Sears 141, 226
Seashore Weavers and Spinners 217
Seaside North 363
Seasoned Gourmet, The 149
Select-Internet Realty 359
Senior AIDES Program 373, 416
Senior Citizen Services of Pender Inc. 417
Senior Friends 375, 378
Seniors Health Insurance Information Program 373
Service Corps ofRetired Executives 373
Seven Seas Ice Cream 242
Seven Seas Inn 56
Shackleford Banks and Carrot Island Ferry
    Service 251
Shades Bar & Grill 53
Shallotte 35
Shallotte District Park 328
Shallotte Marine Supplies 257
Shannon's Services Inc. 73
Sharky's Pizza & Deli 111, 325
Shaw Speakes Child Development Center 393
Shaw UniversityThe Wilmington CAPE 402
Shell Island 23, 350
Shenanigans Beach Club Bar & Grill 129
Ship and Shore Communications Inc. 257
Shipp Pool 268
Ship's Store Windsurfing & Sailing
    Center 260, 262, 269
Shopping 133
Showtyme Skating Center 174, 314
Shuckers 128
Sickle Cell Open Tennis Tournament 323
Silver Cloud 137
Silver Dollar 104
Simmons Realty 364
Sir William's Pub 129
Sitter Network Inc. 397
Skate Barn, The 321
Skateboarding 321
Skating 314
Sloane Realty 74, 363
Smith Cemetery 163
Smithville District Park 328
Smudged Pot News Bar 109
Sneads Ferry King Mackerel Tournament 282
Sneads Ferry Public Library 235
Sneads Ferry Shrimp Festival 196
Snoopy's Magic On Ice 248
Snow's Cut Landing Marina 296
Snow's Cut Park 327
Soccer 322
Society for Masonboro Island Inc. 187
Society of Stranders 248
Softball 323
Something Special Florist and Gifts 149

Soundside 115
South Brunswick Islands Chamber of
    Commerce 34, 321
South Brunswick Isles King Mackerel
    Tournament 282
South Carolina Welcome Center 245
South Winds Motel 59
Southeastern Center for Mental Health,
    Development 382
Southeastern Sickle Cell Association 412
Southern Lights Festival 192
Southport 28
Southport 2000 Visitors' Center 164
Southport Christmas Home Tour and Flotilla 200
Southport Library 234
Southport Marina 283, 288
Southport Marina Inc. 298
Southport Scuba and Water Sport 265
Southport Trail 182
Southport-Fort Fisher Ferry 6
Southport-Oak Island Masters Putting
    Tournament 334
Southport/Oak Island Chamber of Commerce 34
Space Savers 143
Special Education 390
Spinnaker Surf & Sport 159, 267
Sports, Fitness and Parks 303
Spouter Inn 252
St. James Episcopal Church and Burial
    Ground 169
St. James Plantation 351
St. James Shelter 412
St. John's Art Academy 223
St. John's Museum of Art
    19, 169, 203, 204, 223, 414
St. Marks Episcopal Church 169
St. Mary Catholic School 389
St. Paul's Evangelical Lutheran Church 170
St. Philip's Episcopal Church 182
St. Philip's Parish 183
St. Regis Resort 62
Stadium Batting Cages 176
State Port Pilot 420
Steamers Restaurant & Lounge 128
Stede Bonnet 163, 182
Stewart Hardware 257, 282, 313
Stork's Nest, The 140
Stover's Martial Arts 319
Streets and Byways 2
Studebaker's 248
Stump Sound Rotary Golf Tournament 338, 341
Sugar Shack 111
Sullivan, Laura CMT 383
Summer Camps 237
Summer Fun Beach Days 180
Summer Sands Motel 53
Sun & Sea Taxi Cab 4
Sunset Beach 32, 352
Sunset Celebration at the Hilton 125
Sunset Pier 285
Sunset Properties 74, 364
Sunset Skating Center 175
Sunset Vacations 75
Sunset Watersports 256
Sure Catch Tackle Shop 282
Surf & Turf Triathlon 321
Surf 107-FM 267
Surf Cinemas 130
Surf City 36
Surf City Pier 286
Surf City Surf Shop 267
Surf Fishing 288
Surf Reports 267
Surf Shops 267

Surf Suites 53
Surf, Sun & Sand Celebration 195
Surfing 265
Surfrider Foundation 266
Surfside Motor Lodge 55
Surgical & Medical Eye Care 381
Sutton Lake Game Land 312
Sutton-Council Furniture 145
Suzuki Method Music Education 224
Suzuki Talent Education of Wilmington 211
Swan Point Marina 288
Swansboro 250
Swayne's Crafts & Things 157
Sweetwater Cafe 104
Sweetwater Surf Shop 154, 267
Swensen's 93, 242
Swimming 267
Szechuan 132 93

T

T.S. Brown Jewelers 134
Tackle Express Tackle Mart 282, 313
Tapestry Theatre Company 216
Tavernay's Jewelers 149
Taxis 3
Taylor House Inn Bed and Breakfast 49
Teagues 140
Tee Smith Custom Golf Clubs 339
Tee-Times Inc. 341
Television Stations 422
Temple of Israel 170
Temple, R. Henry 381
Temptations 141
Tennis 323
Tennis With Love Ltd. 323
Thai Peppers 107
Thalian Association 216, 223
Thalian Hall 19
Thalian Hall Center for the Performing Arts
    117, 170, 203, 205, 229
The Exceptional Preschool 390
The Scoop Ice Cream & Sandwich Shoppe 241
Theater 212
Theodosia's Bed and Breakfast 56
Tiara Park at The Cape 354
Tidal Creek Food Co-op 326
Tileston School 236
Time-Warner Cable 422
Tomatoz American Grille 93
Toms Drug Company 242
Toms Drug Store 140
Topsail Area Chamber of Commerce 341
Topsail Area Chamber of Commerce and Tourism 34
Topsail Area Spring Fling 194
Topsail Greens Golf and Country Club 337
Topsail Island 35, 352
Topsail Island Museum: Missiles and More 185
Topsail Island Trading Company 159
Topsail Island Vacation Rentals 75
Topsail Marina 282
Topsail Motel 63
Topsail Offshore Fishing Club King Mackerel
    Tournament 282
Topsail Realty 75, 365
Topsail Scenic Boat Tours 159
Topsail Scenic Boat Tours at Topsail Island
    Trading 185
Topsail Scenic Flights Inc. 186
Topsail Skating Rink 185
Topsail Turtle Project 36
Topsail Voice 420
Topsail Water Sports 256, 257, 260, 262, 267, 269
Total Child Care Center 395

Tote-Em-In Zoo 222
Town Creek District Park 328
Townhouse Art & Frame Center Inc. 148
Toy Jam 200
Toys R Us 226
Track and Field 324
Trails End Steak House 94
Transportation 3
Treasure Coast Taxi 4
Treasure Island Family Fun Park 186
Trek Headquarters Wilmington 306
Trends Home Furnishings 151
Triangle Rental 3
Trinity United Methodist Church 184
Tryon Palace 253
Tucker Bros. Realty 360
Turtle Island Ventures 159, 188, 259
Tuscarora Tack Shop 312
Twin Lakes Restaurant 111
Twin Lakes Seafood Restaurant 112
Twin Travel & Cruises 341, 373
Two Sisters Bookery 135
Two Wheeler Dealer 307

U

U.S. Coast Guard Auxiliary 256, 415
U.S. Open King Mackerel Tournament 18, 283
U.S. Power Squadrons 256
U.S. Trolls 227
Ultimate 324
UNCW Athletics Department 321
UNCW Summer Science by the Sea Day Camp 238
UNCW's Center for Marine Science Research 405
UNCW's University Children's Academy
    Camps 238
Unitarian Universalist Fellowship 326
United Beach Vacations 72
United Cerebral Palsy Developmental Center 390
University of North Carolina at Wilmington
    17, 203, 224, 238, 399
University Professional Services 381
University Theatre 216
Urgent Care Center 380
USAir 5
USTA Team Tennis Association 324

V

Valley Golf Center & Driving Range 338
Van Service 4
Verandas, The 49
Verrazano, Giovanni da 11
Vesta 163
Vic's Corn Popper 242
Villa Capriani Resort 63
Vinnie's Steak House & Tavern 101
Vintage Values 411
Visitors Information Center 1
VitaLine 377
VitaLink 376
Vito's Pizzeria 113
Volleyball 325
Volunteer Opportunities 409

W

WAAV 423
Waccamaw Pottery 246
Wacky Golf Cart Parade 195
Wal-Mart 77, 145, 282, 313
Walden's Gym 308
Walk-In Messiah 201
Walker Realty 72, 360

Wallace Enterprise, The 420
Ward Realty 75, 365
Water & Woods Hunting & Fishing 317
Water Street Restaurant & Sidewalk
     Cafe 94, 125, 131
Water Ways Sailing School 176, 261
Water-Skiing 265
Waterfront Park 184
Watersports 255
Wave Hog Saloon 125
WBMS 423
WCCA 423
WECT 422
Weekly and Long-term Cottage Rentals 65
Well Care and Nursing Services Inc. 380
Wes' Card Shop 227
West Marine 151
Western Sizzlin'Restaurant Steaks and More 95
WGNI 423
WhiteBridge 349
Whiteside, Susan CMT 383
Whiting & Company 151
WHQR 423
Wild Dunes Community 363
Wild Water and Wheels 246
Willis Richardson Players 216
Wilmington 11, 12
Wilmington Academy of Music 211, 224
Wilmington Adventure Walking Tour 170
Wilmington and Weldon Railroad 13
Wilmington Art Association 205
Wilmington Athletic Club 308
Wilmington Athletics 303
Wilmington Bike Map 9, 305
Wilmington Boys Choir 200, 211, 224
Wilmington Bus Terminal 3
Wilmington Center for Therapeutic Massage 382
Wilmington Chamber of Commerce 429
Wilmington Choral Society 212
Wilmington Christian Academy 389
Wilmington Community Development
     Corporation 415
Wilmington Concert Association 117, 212
Wilmington Concert Band 212
Wilmington Dance Academy 224
Wilmington Ear, Nose and Throat Associates 381
Wilmington Elks Lodge 224
Wilmington Family YMCA
     238, 304, 309, 319, 320, 322, 325, 326, 414
Wilmington Film Office 428
Wilmington Golf Association 341
Wilmington Golf Course 333
Wilmington Hammerheads 322
Wilmington Hammerheads Professional Soccer
     Club 238
Wilmington Harbor Enhancement Trust 415
Wilmington Health Associates 381
Wilmington Hilton 50
Wilmington Historic Foundation 14
Wilmington Homeschool Organization 390
Wilmington Journal, The 419
Wilmington Magazine 422
Wilmington Marine Center 297
Wilmington Marine Operator 256
Wilmington Parks and Recreation 304, 309, 322,
     323, 325
Wilmington Polo Club 349
Wilmington Railroad Museum 163, 171
Wilmington Roadrunners Club 320
Wilmington Seagulls Tennis Association 323
Wilmington Sharks 304
Wilmington Shuttle 4
Wilmington Star-News 419
Wilmington SurgCare 382

Wilmington Symphony Orchestra 117, 212
Wilmington Table Tennis Association 236
Wilmington Tennis Ladder 324
Wilmington Transit Authority 3
Wilmington Treatment Center 382
Wilmington Tri-Span Run 320
Wilmington Triathlon 324
Wilmington's Cape Fear Optimist Club 323
Windjammer Condominiums 363
Windjammer Restaurant & Lounge 107
Windrose Furniture Company 148
Winds Oceanfront Clarion Inn 60
Windsurfing 268
Wine House, The 51
Wing Chinese Restaurant 95
Wings 154
Winner Cruise Boats 117, 179
Winner Gulf Stream Fishing & Cruise Boats 288
Winter Holiday Fest 201
Winter Park Optimist Club 304
Wish You Were Here Greetings and Gifts 138
WKIX 423
WKOO 423
WMFD 423
WMNX 423
Wolber's Garden Deli 242
Wolber's Ice Cream 242
Women of Wilmington Chorale 212
Women's Health Specialties 376
Wonder Shop, The 145
Worship 433
Worth House, The 51
Wrestling 326
Wright Times 422
Wrightsville Beach 23, 350
Wrightsville Beach Holiday Flotilla 199
Wrightsville Beach King Mackerel Tournament 282
Wrightsville Beach Museum of History 177
Wrightsville Beach Ocean Racing Association 261
Wrightsville Beach Park 327
Wrightsville Beach Parks and
     Recreation 266, 268, 304, 324, 326
Wrightsville Beach Vacation Rentals 69
Wrightsville Beach Parks & Recreation 240, 325
Wrightsville Gallery, The 208
Wrightsville Marina 294
Write Place, The 134
Writing 216
WSFM 423
WSFX 422
WUNJ 422
WWAY 422
WWIL 423
WWQQ 423
WZXS 423

Y

Yacht Basin Provision Company 108
Yaupon Beach 32, 352
Yaupon Pier 285
Yellow Cab 3
YMCA 268, 304
Yoga 326
Yogurt Plus 242
YWCA 268, 414
YWCA After School Program 395
YWCA of Wilmington 240, 309, 319

Z

Zebulon Latimer House 171
Zeke's Island 404
Zeke's Island Coastal Preserve 313

Going Somewhere?

Insiders' Publishing Inc. presents 40 current and upcoming titles to popular destinations all over the country (including the titles below) — and we're planning on adding many more. To order a title, go to your local bookstore or call (800) 955-1860.

Atlanta, GA	Maine's Mid-Coast
Boca Raton and the Palm Beaches, FL	Minneapolis/St. Paul, MN
Boulder, CO, and Rocky Mountain National Park	Mississippi
	Myrtle Beach, SC
Bradenton/Sarasota, FL	North Carolina's Central Coast and New Bern
Branson, MO, and the Ozark Mountains	North Carolina's Mountains
Cape Cod, Martha's Vineyard and Nantucket, MA	Outer Banks of North Carolina
Charleston, SC	The Pocono Mountains
Cincinnati, OH	Relocation
Civil War Sites in the Eastern Theater	Richmond, VA
Denver, CO	Southwestern Utah
Florida Keys and Key West	Tampa/St. Petersburg, FL
Florida's Great Northwest	Virginia's Blue Ridge
Golf in the Carolinas	Virginia's Chesapeake Bay
Indianapolis, IN	Washington, D.C.
The Lake Superior Region	Wichita, KS
Lexington, KY	Williamsburg, VA
Louisville, KY	Wilmington, NC

THE INSIDERS'® GUIDE

Insiders' Publishing Inc. • P.O. Box 2057 • Manteo, NC 27954
Phone (919) 473-6100 • Fax (919) 473-5869 • INTERNET address: http://www.insiders.com